American Diplomacy and the End of the Cold War

An Insider's Account of U.S. Policy in Europe, 1989–1992

ROBERT L. HUTCHINGS

THE WOODROW WILSON CENTER PRESS
Washington, D.C.

THE JOHNS HOPKINS UNIVERSITY PRESS
Baltimore and London

Editorial offices:

The Woodrow Wilson Center Press

One Woodrow Wilson Plaza

1300 Pennsylvania Ave., NW

Washington, D.C. 20523

Telephone 202-691-4010

Order from:

The Johns Hopkins University Press

Hampden Station

Baltimore, Maryland 21211

Telephone 1-800-537-5487

Second printing, hardcover, 1998

Paperback edition, 1998

2 4 6 8 9 7 5 3 1

All photographs courtesy the Bush Presidential Library

Library of Congress Cataloging-in-Publication Data

Hutchings, Robert L., 1946–

American diplomacy and the end of the Cold War : an insider's

account of U.S. policy in Europe, 1982–1992 / Robert L. Hutchings.

p.   cm.

Includes bibliographical references and index.

ISBN 0-8018-5620-5 (cloth : alk. paper).—ISBN 0-8018-5621-3

(paper : alk. paper)

1. Europe—Foreign relations—United States.   2. United States—

Foreign relations—Europe.   3. Europe—Politics and

government—1989–   4. United States—Foreign relations—1981–1989.

5. United States—Foreign relations,—1989–1993.

I. Title.

D1065.U5H88   1997   96-48308

327.7304—dc21   CIP

For Kim

Contents

Preface

IN THE SPRING OF 1988, I gave a speech at the University of Virginia, where I had done my doctoral work a decade earlier. I argued five propositions: Soviet foreign policy had undergone an historic shift, Germany's role in Europe was changing fundamentally, the "European idea" was stronger than at any time since 1919, the United States was retreating from an active role in European affairs, and Eastern Europe would be the arena in which Europe's future would be decided, as it had been twice already in the century.[1] It was a forecast of impending major change in Europe and an appeal to American leadership.

Little did I suspect that just a year later I would be called on to play a role in these events as director for European affairs with the National Security Council. Still less could I have imagined how broadly these perspectives were shared at the senior levels of the incoming Bush administration, which set about acting on them with a decisiveness that belied my lament on declining U.S. leadership even while vindicating the other four propositions.

This is not to imply causality. I had no role in influencing the views of President George Bush, Secretary of State James Baker, or National Security Adviser Brent Scowcroft before Bush's inauguration as president in January 1989. As a nonpartisan professional, I was involved neither in the campaign nor with the transition team but rather was asked to join the NSC staff by virtue of my background in East European and German affairs.

I came to this field late, in my second year of graduate school, and almost by accident. A course in East European politics, taken mainly out of curiosity, piqued an interest that soon deepened. This field seemed where everything that mattered in international politics came together. It was where East met West, where liberal democracy confronted the communist experiment, where Karl Marx met John Stuart Mill. Moral questions were sharply defined; the human dramas were compelling. After graduate school I became deputy director of Radio Free Europe in Munich, diverted from an academic career by one of those opportunities too good to miss. For five years in the early 1980s I lived in divided Germany, among RFE's brilliant émigré communities, spending every working hour and many private ones totally absorbed in Central and Eastern European affairs. By the end of the 1980s, when Poland and Hungary stood on the threshold of revolutionary change, it was as if my whole career had been preparation for playing a role in Eastern Europe's liberation and Germany's unification.

So perhaps it was fate or destiny that brought me to the Bush White House in 1989. Or maybe it was just luck. It certainly was not political connections, because I had none. Indeed, it was emblematic of Bush's bipartisanship in foreign policy that in three and a half years at the White House, no one ever asked which political party I belonged to or for whom I voted in the 1988 election. I had reason to believe I would fit in with the Bush administration's general foreign policy orientation but was surprised—or rather, thrilled—to find how closely the thinking of Bush, Baker, Scowcroft, and others who mattered coincided with my own. More than once in doing the research for this book, I came across a Baker speech of which I had been unaware yet felt that I might have drafted it myself, so closely did it reflect my own views.

This book is part political memoir, part eyewitness account, and part scholarly analysis. I have gone over events and decisions twice, as it were—first as a participant or witness, second as a relatively detached scholar striving to understand and assess this period independent of my personal role in it. I have tried to combine the insider's unique perspective with the scholar's balanced judgment.

I was one of the dozen or so senior U.S. officials operating on the inside of policy making toward Europe and the Soviet Union at the end of the Cold War. Of course there were hundreds of officials involved in these policies and dozens more senior and influential than I. But only a handful of senior advisers around President Bush and Secretary Baker had a strategic vantage point and a direct role in formulating and implementing our broad strategies and policies toward Europe and the Soviet Union. On some issues—the diplomacy of German unification, for example—the "dozen or so" grew to perhaps twice that number as negotiations proceeded. On others, notably strategy toward Central and Eastern Europe after the revolutionary crowds had gone home and the first flush of enthusiasm had faded, the number dropped to fewer than a half dozen.

This book concentrates on aspects where I had personal, direct, and intense involvement: Central and Eastern Europe before, during, and after the revolutions of 1989, Germany during the period of unification and thereafter, and broad strategies toward Europe and the Soviet Union throughout the period. It also covers, but in less detail, aspects where my involvement was more peripheral: U.S.-Soviet relations, arms control, security policy, and trade relations.

This book thus encompasses the whole story of the end of the Cold War in Europe, but from a particular vantage point, one that was as good as any other and better than most for assessing the diplomacy of the period. It was arguably the *best* vantage point, if one believes, as I do, that the countries of Eastern Europe were the key to ending the Cold War and the key to the post–Cold War order in Europe. This is where the issues that had divided East and West for forty years came together; this was the arena of most intense activity during the period; this was where Soviet, West European, and American policies met and interacted.

This book's span of time coincides with my tenure with the National Security Council from early 1989 to mid-1992. It begins with the development of American strategy at the beginning of 1989, continues through the revolutionary developments of 1989–90 and the security issues arising therefrom, and concludes with the collapse of the Soviet Union at the end of 1991. Key events immediately thereafter, such as the deepening Yugoslav war, are dealt with selectively.

Roles and Perspectives

We NSC staffers liked to think of ourselves as advisers to presidents and secretaries of state, and so we were. We were expected to be the principal initiators of policy ideas, which were then approved, rejected, or amended at the political level. This was our main responsibility and the reason we took the job in the first place.

Yet the more prosaic tasks like note taking went with the territory, too. When the president met with foreign counterparts here or abroad, my role most often was to take notes. This was my admission ticket to hundreds of presidential meetings during the period. My policy role was played beforehand and afterwards. During the meetings themselves, I was rarely called on to offer an opinion. Like the model child of yesteryear, I was expected to be seen but not heard. Even more obscure was the role I played as note taker for presidential telephone calls, of which there were many under Bush. Typically, I would monitor and transcribe the calls from the White House Situation Room, with my telephone on receive only, so that I could be neither seen nor heard. (Occasionally, when the president made a call unexpectedly in the early morning or on weekends, it would be patched through to me at home so I could monitor from there. I had no capacity to mute the transmit side of my home phone, however, so foreign leaders were occasionally startled to hear the bark of my trusty German shepherd, Kazimierz—after King Kazimierz III, for you students of Polish history—in the background. He must have sounded like Millie, the Bush dog, on steroids.)

These prosaic functions were also important for the telling of this story. As note taking required only two or three brain cells, the rest were free to roam intellectually. I could observe and reflect, watching history unfold before my eyes. I imagine that I experienced more sheer joy and excitement in seeing history being made than did Bush, Baker, or Scowcroft, with their unending responsibilities.

Watching political leaders at close range is instructive. They are not like you and me. Their analytic capacities may not be as finely honed, but their political instincts and intuitive skills are much keener. They are trained to action, not reflection. They know how to size up situations, improvise, and make decisions under pressure. Their natural element is interaction with leaders who bear responsibilities comparable to their own. They understand the subtleties of political power in ways the rest of us could not possibly appreciate.

In discharging their daunting responsibilities, they look to their senior staff to provide the main ideas. They are used to relying on their staffs, but also distrusting them. Most of their best ideas have come from their staffs, but so have many harebrained or dangerous ones. They alone bear the responsibility to decide, usually on the basis of incomplete information; often they must do so under intense time pressure to act, with life-or-death consequences.

In writing this book I did not dwell on the internal debates within the administration. This was not due to squeamishness or timidity. In the relatively few instances of significant policy differences, I have analyzed the differing views in detail. Otherwise, I have employed the royal "we" to connote the broadly shared views among the senior foreign policy-makers in the Bush administration: the president and his national security adviser, the secretaries of state and defense, the chairman of the Joint Chiefs of Staff, and their most senior advisers. Thus "we in Washington," "we in the administration," or simply "we" stands as shorthand for the collective views of these senior officials. Where I have used "we" in some other sense, I have tried to make the distinction clear so as to avoid further ambiguity. It is not a perfect device, but it suits the purposes of this book. I was interested in the question "why" more than the question "how"—in policy rather than process. Besides, the Bush administration foreign policy team was about as collegial in style and like-minded on the major issues as one could imagine; a detailed accounting of the internal decision-making process would only divert attention from the larger story of how American diplomacy helped to end the Cold War.

The "we" should not be confused with "I." I claim no personal credit, except as part of a larger group of advisers to the president and his National Security Council. For the record, I was more right than most in seeing the coming collapse of East European communism, slower than many in recognizing the prospects for German unification, and somewhere in the middle of the pack in gauging Soviet intentions. Others lined up differently. No one was right on all the issues all the time. What mattered were the collective judgments that were translated into policy. Even where individuals erred in their forecasts, it was often for sound and valid reasons that helped shape effective policy. Besides, foreign policy decision making is not some sort of parlor game in which the grand prize is awarded to the most accurate forecaster. The proper measure of American policy was the extent to which our actions were consistent with the possibilities before us and our larger interests.

The temptation in a book of this sort to inflate one's own role is enormous, and I am conscious that I have not always resisted it. Thucydides set a standard that was hard to follow. Still, there were events for which I was the only witness, where my perspective was unique, or where a personal observation could lend verisimilitude. When in doubt about relating a personal event or perspective, I have tried to employ two criteria. Was the story essential for the larger one I am trying to tell? Was it necessary to tell it in my own voice?

The Perils of "Immediate History"

T. E. Lawrence, in the foreword to *Revolt in the Desert*, complained that his "interest in the subject . . . was exhausted long ago in the actual experience of it."[2] My feelings were rather the opposite. The period 1989–92 was so rich and complex that even those who lived with these events as they were happening and had a certain role in shaping them could not possibly absorb their totality. I could not be done with them until I had put them in such perspective as I could gain with the benefit of research and reflection.

The perils of writing "immediate history" are several. First is the matter of perspective: no one writing close on the heels of major events can possibly have the historical perspective that future generations will have. What is transitory is taken for permanent; what turns out to have been a trend of profound importance is missed altogether.

In the relatively few years since the collapse of the Soviet empire, already there have been several "paradigm shifts." A writer recounting the events of the preceding two years in Europe around the time of the Paris Summit of November 1990 would have been influenced by the then-prevailing euphoria over the seeming triumph of democracy. Six months later, the writer would have been less sanguine about democracy's prospects in the formerly communist countries but newly impressed by the military triumph of U.S.-led coalition forces in the Persian Gulf—and so might have seen the makings of a "new world order" in which the United Nations worked as its creators intended. A year after that, as Yugoslavia descended into the most egregious carnage Europe had seen since the defeat of Nazi Germany, any chronicler would have been affected by the deep sense of pessimism the international community felt because of its helplessness in the face of Europe's first post–Cold War crisis. The passage of a few years has lent a more balanced perspective, but no book written so soon after these epochal events can hope to capture their meaning in the broad sweep of history.

Second is the problem of sources. The great bulk of the official record of what transpired is still classified and inaccessible; no account based on memory, even supplemented by personal notes, interviews, and publicly available evidence, can substitute for the full documentary record. In that respect, the period 1989–92 was unusual in that some of the official documents are already in the public domain. The greatest number of these have come from the East German and Soviet archives, but some key U.S. documents, including presidential decisions on Soviet policy in 1989, have already been declassified.[3] Press accounts, interviews, and a burgeoning memoir literature also help fill out the historical record. Moreover, as modern diplomacy is conducted semipublicly, there is a vast and largely underutilized body of public documents on which this book relies. Every day, the White House and State Department issue reams of paper—press briefings, public statements, fact sheets, and the like. Most of it is forgettable, but among the trivial and routine are official statements that offer a reasonably good record of the thinking at the highest levels of government.[4]

I supplemented these sources with interviews with Soviet, German, French, British, and East European officials who had been involved in these events, but I deliberately avoided conducting extensive interviews with American officials. I occasionally sought information about a key event where I was not present or where memory failed, but I was wary of getting too close lest this book take on a corporate character as a kind of authorized account of Bush administration foreign policy. This is interpretive history, and I wanted to maintain a critical distance.

A third peril, specific to political memoirs like this one, is the temptation to engage in retrospective rationalization and self-justification. One is tempted to trumpet one's successes and disguise one's failures. As an honest and usually self-effacing sort of fellow, I had not expected this to be as great a problem as it turned out to be. Vanity is of course part of the explanation. So is the way one works through events as they are occurring, building up a set of rationalizations almost without knowing it. One does it in everyday life: the squabble with a coworker gets quickly rationalized, as one excuses or explains away one's own motives and behavior. For public officials, it is also a matter of conditioning: having been trained to defend government policies as part of the job, one instinctively continues doing so after leaving office. More than once in writing this book, I had to correct myself when I began to give the official explanation of an event or a policy as I had so often done as a member of the administration. I have tried to offset these tendencies by exposing my views to the no-holds-barred critiques of outside readers, documenting my assertions as thoroughly as was possible, and applying as much intellectual honesty as I could muster.

Although I could not hope to escape these perils entirely, the passage of time worked in my favor. The book took longer to write than I had expected, and this turned out to be a blessing (except for my long-suffering family). The historical perspective became somewhat clearer, significant new sources opened up to enrich the account, and my own role shifted more easily from participant to chronicler.

"Immediate history" has one great advantage over history produced at a greater distance from events. A biographer friend once complained that most biographies are written from the perspective of knowing how the life in question turned out in the end. The omniscient biographer thus tends towards condescension in treating the subject; to lend order, events that do not fit the biographer's pattern are discarded or minimized. Yet this is not how a life is actually lived. We confront issues and make choices not knowing how the next act of our personal drama will turn out. Confusion and occasional bewilderment come with the territory. So it is with history. Most historical writing suffers from what the French philosopher Henri Bergson called "illusions of retrospective determinism."[5] Knowing how the story turned out, the historian goes back in time and decides upon a certain structure, sifting out evidence that does not fit the pattern and marshalling all the political, economic, and social factors that drove history along its predetermined course. Yet this is not how history looks to those making it. They deal with confusion, contrary trends, and incomplete knowledge. The best of them may have foresight (in the sense of prudence, one of Bush's favorite terms), but they cannot have foreknowledge. They cannot turn the clock forward to see how their courses of action might influence future events.

Thus "immediate history," for all its demerits, can have the virtue of recapturing the moment and "humanizing" history, as it were, by restoring the sense that real choices were made by real people. This is the drama I have tried to capture in this book. It is how life is lived. It is how history happens.

Acknowledgments

AT THE WHITE HOUSE from 1989 to 1992 and the State Department in 1992 and 1993, I had the privilege of playing a role in the central drama of my generation. I was doubly privileged to have worked for two of the finest public servants our country has ever known—Brent Scowcroft and Larry Eagleburger—and to have served at one step removed under two others, George Bush and James Baker. Without the opportunity to serve under their leadership, there would be no book.

A Woodrow Wilson Center fellowship in 1993 and 1994 afforded me a full year of uninterrupted research and writing in as congenial a setting as one could imagine. It is a better book for the company I kept, particularly the long discussions over lunch in the fellow's dining room on the fourth floor of the Smithsonian Castle. I learned more from a Ghanaian philosopher, an Indian journalist, a historian of sixteenth-century England, and other scholars with whom I shared my fellowship year than from specialists in my own field.

Another year at the Woodrow Wilson Center filling in as director of its international studies program enabled me to finish the book only a year or so behind schedule. My thanks and affection go to all my colleagues there, particularly the Center's deputy director, my friend Sam Wells. I am grateful to the Woodrow Wilson Center Press, especially to Joe Brinley, director, and Robert Poarch, editor, for shepherding the manuscript through its final stages, and to my research assistants, led by Sabina Crisen, for their invaluable support and unfailing good humor along the way. Many colleagues were kind enough to read all or part of the manuscript: Jim Brown, David Gompert, Peter Mulrean, Jan Nowak,

Joe Rothschild, Brent Scowcroft, Paul Shoup, Gale Stokes, Steve Szabo, Ron Tiersky, and Greg Treverton should be specially mentioned.

My deepest thanks go to my family, which endured my chaotic schedule during my time at the White House and then had to live through this period a second time as I wrote this book. I am grateful to my mother, Ruth Hutchings, and my mother-in-law, Pauline Schwartz, for helping out on the home front during my frequent trips abroad. My son, Jonathan, to whom my last book was dedicated, was a constant inspiration and a daily reminder that what really matters is right here at home. Most of all, I am indebted to my wife, Kim, whose love and support are the wind beneath my wings. This book is for her, in more ways than one.

American Diplomacy and the End of the Cold War

Introduction

WITHIN A FEW MONTHS in late 1989, communist regimes fell in Poland, Hungary, East Germany, Czechoslovakia, Bulgaria, and Romania. Less than a year later, Germany was reunited. A year after that, the Soviet state collapsed, returning Russia to the preimperial boundaries of sixteenth century Muscovy. Thus the end of the Cold War was also the culmination of the processes of imperial dissolution that spanned the entire century. Never in modern history, not even during the French Revolution, had changes of such magnitude occurred except as a consequence of major war.

The swift and largely peaceful course of these revolutionary developments tended to lend them a false air of inevitability and obscure the enormity of the changes left in their wake. Epochal changes that few would have thought possible in 1989 were by 1992 too easily taken for granted, as was America's pivotal role during the period.

There was nothing inevitable about the dramatic course of events beginning in 1989. The Berlin Wall would not have fallen in November 1989 but for the successful challenge to communist rule in Poland earlier in the year. Even after the fall of the Berlin Wall, there were enormous obstacles—beginning with Soviet opposition—to the successful unification of Germany with no restrictions on its sovereignty. Nor was the disintegration of the Soviet Union the inevitable consequence of the conflicts that raged through that country for most of 1991. There were several possible outcomes to the crisis of Soviet communism, not just one.

U.S. policy obviously did not *cause* these developments. They were deeply rooted in history and driven by the heroic efforts of democratic opposition leaders in Central and Eastern Europe. Former Soviet presi-

I

dent Mikhail Gorbachev deserves credit, too, for legitimizing change in the Soviet empire and for refusing to resort to forcible suppression even as those changes went far beyond anything he had considered at the outset.

Yet American policy exerted a strong, sometimes decisive, influence on the peaceful end of Europe's postwar division and the collapse of the Soviet empire. As German foreign minister Hans-Dietrich Genscher said with regard to the unification of his country, "If America had so much as hesitated, we could have stood on our heads" and gotten nowhere.[1] Although policy was at times reactive—given the pace and scope of change, it could hardly have been otherwise—it was also informed, to a greater degree than has so far been credited, by a grand strategy for ending the Cold War and laying the foundations of a new order.

Strategy is a term often associated with military campaigns. *Grand* strategy, however, is chiefly related to diplomacy. It is a higher type of strategy that aims at integrating policies and power toward achieving national objectives short of war.[2] The term is apt for describing American diplomacy at the end of the Cold War.

During forty years of Cold War, the United States and its allies had mobilized as if for war and came more than once to the brink of armed conflict with the Soviet Union. History suggested that so deep-seated a confrontation between great powers could only end violently. As Paul Kennedy noted in *The Rise and Fall of the Great Powers*, "The triumph of any one Great Power . . . or the collapse of another, has usually been the consequence of lengthy fighting by its armed forces."[3] That the Cold War ended peacefully and on Western terms was an achievement without parallel in modern history.

This book examines the sources, assumptions, and conduct of American foreign policy with respect to the revolutionary developments that began in Central and Eastern Europe in 1989. It reconstructs the relevant environment that confronted policymakers here and in Europe and illustrates the choices available at key junctures; it describes assumptions and judgments made on the basis of inevitably incomplete knowledge and critically examines choices made and not made in the light of what we now know. The book also explores the interactions among the major powers, particularly the United States, the Soviet Union, Germany, Great Britain, and France, as well as the countries of Central and Eastern Europe.

A leitmotif that runs throughout the book is the tension between strategic goals and tactical necessity. Effective policy called for both strategic rigor and tactical flexibility in devising and implementing plans with clear objectives, subjecting those plans to constant reassessment, and revising them, often radically, as yesterday's bold initiative was overtaken by today's new reality. Every day brought with it new and unexpected problems that had to be overcome for strategic goals to be realized, yet the process of dealing with these problems risked undermining the main goals being pursued in the first place. For example, achieving the dual goal of uniting Germany and assuring that it remained a full member of NATO required Soviet acquiescence to German unification. Yet gaining Soviet assent involved the risk that Moscow would pressure Germany to relinquish its NATO membership as the price of unity.

Under such circumstances, the diplomat had to be both fox and hedgehog. The fox, in Isaiah Berlin's essay, "knows many things" and pursues "many ends, often unrelated and even contradictory," while the hedgehog "knows one big thing" and keeps his sights fixed on "a single central vision" and organizing principle.[4]

In 1989, that "one big thing" was that Eastern Europe, where the Cold War began, was also where it had to end. This judgment, which contradicted the then-conventional wisdom that the United States needed to "meet Gorbachev halfway" and reach an "understanding" on the future of Eastern Europe, formed the basis of an American grand strategy that served us well in navigating the challenges at the end of the Cold War. This organizing principle and its corollaries—self-determination in Eastern Europe, deep reductions in Soviet forces, and the internal transformation of the USSR itself—lent a singleness of purpose that helped steer policy through a period of profound, often chaotic, change.

American diplomacy achieved great successes in 1989 and 1990, as the objectives we had set for ourselves were met and far exceeded. Our policies were less successful thereafter, as the multiple challenges of German unification, the Gulf War of early 1991, and a disintegrating Soviet Union diffused our strategic vision and undercut efforts to build a "new world order." This should not be surprising. Policy at the beginning of the period, while skillfully executed, was the culmination of four decades of consistent foreign policy through Democratic and Republican administrations alike. The changes with which American policy had to deal were revolutionary, but they fit a familiar Cold War frame of reference. Those reference points exploded with the precipitous collapse of the Soviet empire in 1990 and 1991.

We and our Western allies were conscious of certain parallels with the Versailles conference of 1919, which, among its other deficiencies, vastly underestimated Russian power on the morrow of the October Revolution and hence erected a postwar settlement that was never rooted in the realities of power.[5] In 1991 as in 1919, Russia was weak enough to ignore but had enormous latent power that would have made its exclusion short-sighted in the extreme. Thus the post–Cold War order we sought to build was one in which Russia would not be isolated but rather welcomed into the interstate system.

Although the concept of a "new world order" deserved closer study than it received, it ultimately failed to persuade—not so much for any conceptual deficiencies as for the inherent difficulty of defining America's place and role in a new era whose contours were only beginning to make themselves apparent. Operationally, then, the "central vision" of American policy for the immediate post–Cold War period was, perhaps inevitably, a more limited and transitional one. It sprang from the conviction that the United States had to remain in Europe to balance Russian power, lend a general stability, and help organize a durable post–Cold War order in which former adversaries were brought into a new system of cooperative security.

This orientation toward a post–Cold War order was not without its flaws. In placing such a high premium on military power, and specifically American military power, it accorded less weight to the political, economic, and other attributes of power and influence in a world that would no longer be dominated by hostile bipolar competition. To build secure democracies on the ruins of communist rule, the prime requirement of a viable post–Cold War order in Europe, was a task for which the traditional instruments of security policy were largely irrelevant. Nor was the traditional focus on armed aggression by one state against another of much use in dealing with threats arising *within* states among parties to a civil war. Iraq's aggression against Kuwait in 1990 fit the first category; the Yugoslav crisis that erupted about the same time belonged to the second.

The failures of U.S. and other Western policies toward a disintegrating Yugoslavia underscored how far Europe was from a secure post–Cold War order. Coming so soon on the heels of the U.S.-led coalition to defeat Iraq in the Gulf War, the Yugoslav conflict also seemed to call for an undiminished level of American engagement in the post–Cold War world, thus opening up a gap between the leadership we asserted and that which we were actually ready to provide. Above all, it raised doubts about the nature of America's post–Cold War role, absent the threat that had lent focus and coherence to American policy for forty years.

Still, the hedgehog's focus on certain sound, if imperfect, principles helped steer policy through a period of chaotic change, in which the dangers were great of conceding larger strategic objectives in the interest of tactical expediency. In this regard, American steadiness of purpose was itself an important stabilizing factor in a period of profound disorientation for virtually all of Europe, to say nothing of the republics of the former Soviet Union.

I

American Grand Strategy

THE BUSH ADMINISTRATION entered office in January 1989 predisposed to major change—to "dream big dreams," as the president put it, and to think unconventionally.[1] Though not quite the hostile takeover of government that characterized the transition from President Jimmy Carter to President Ronald Reagan in 1980, the Reagan-to-Bush transition was abrupt. At the first NSC staff meeting, Reagan administration holdovers were politely told that their services were no longer required. An entirely new team came in, representing foreign policy approaches fundamentally at odds with those of the Reagan administration. At the White House and the State Department, where the transition was equally abrupt, these changes were soon reflected in major shifts in policy—quite different from the image of continuity that the public at large perceived. There was no such thing as a "Reagan-Bush" foreign policy. Before 1989 there was Reagan; afterwards there was Bush.

At the NSC, the abruptness of the transition was made vivid in a physical sense. Along one corridor in the offices of the European and Soviet directorate on the third floor of the Old Executive Office Building was a long row of file cabinets—all empty, their contents having been packed up and sent off to the Reagan library. This was standard White House procedure, but it was one that astonished foreign officials whose parliamentary systems favored stability and continuity. It meant that we were unburdened with the policies of the administration just departed, but also that we had to start from scratch in developing our approaches. As it turned out, the events and issues with which we were confronted were so revolutionary that the file of "business as usual" policy papers and analyses would have been of little use anyway. There was no drawer labeled "in case of German unification, open file and follow instructions," nor were there any policy papers on "what to do if the Soviet Union disintegrates." We were entering uncharted waters.

In Europe and the Soviet Union, revolutionary change was in the air. Yet the *annus mirabilis* of 1989 began quietly enough. For all the hopeful trends associated with Soviet president Mikhail Gorbachev, fundamental change remained potential, not yet actual. Soviet military power was undiminished, one-party rule was intact in the USSR, the countries of Eastern Europe were ruled by governments that owed their existence to Soviet power, and half a million Soviet troops were still stationed in the center of Europe.

Gorbachev's early policies of *glasnost* (openness) and *perestroika* (economic restructuring) after coming to power in the spring of 1985 were cautious and incremental; only as these policies failed to produce the desired results did he consider more radical measures. The new openness he espoused had paved the way for organized political opposition, including national independence movements, while the economic half-measures associated with *perestroika* only deepened the economic crisis and eroded Gorbachev's domestic standing. In the West, however, his star was still rising, and a steady stream of Soviet arms proposals—advanced under the rubric of "new thinking" in Soviet foreign policy[2]—had caused public expectations to race well ahead of the real changes in Soviet international conduct.

Yet change was surely coming, most rapidly and irresistibly in Eastern Europe, where prolonged economic crises had given rise to mounting social pressures. Communist rule in Poland and Hungary was under assault—spurred by organized opposition groups and supported by reform-minded figures within the ruling establishments. The winds of change blowing from Moscow served further to heighten pressure on the communist regimes of Eastern Europe for more sweeping measures. Just as Metternich, after the election of Pius IX, reportedly said that he had "bargained for everything except a liberal Pope,"[3] the East European communists were ill-equipped to handle the consequences of a reform-minded Soviet leader. The more dogmatic among them found it hard to rule with the same ruthlessness, and even those predisposed to reform were unable to stay ahead of public demands for more sweeping change.

It was also apparent that, just as Gorbachev's reforms in the USSR encouraged and legitimized the far more radical efforts in Poland and

Hungary, successful challenges to communist rule in Eastern Europe would eventually blow back on the Soviet Union, particularly among its restive nationalities. This was the assumption of American policy from the earliest days of the Cold War, dating to NSC (National Security Council report) 58/2 of December 1949, which considered Eastern Europe to be the "weakest link" of the Soviet empire.[4] Indeed, it is hard to imagine the Soviet enterprise unraveling in any other sequence than it ultimately did. Under conditions of relaxation of control from the imperial center, the empire broke apart first in Central and Eastern Europe, next among the Baltic states, then in Ukraine and other republics, and finally in Russia itself.

Although a myth has developed that the world was caught unprepared for the events of 1989, many of us, inside government and out, had concluded already that communist rule in Eastern Europe was in deep crisis and that the "end of an era" was at hand.[5] If Soviet suppression of the Hungarian Revolution of 1956 and the Prague Spring of 1968 had killed communist ideology and the belief that it could be reformed, the crushing of the Solidarity trade union movement in Poland in 1981 had made it clear that Soviet power, or the threat of its application, was the sole remaining prop for the communist regimes of Eastern Europe. By the end of the 1980s, Soviet policy under Gorbachev had called into question that last prop, even as the example of his domestic innovations was fueling pressures from below in Eastern Europe for sweeping change.[6]

The question was not whether revolutionary upheaval was coming, but whether it would lead to catastrophe or liberation, and the answer hinged on Soviet attitudes. Was the "Brezhnev Doctrine," whereby Moscow claimed the right to intervene to preserve communist rule in Eastern Europe, still in force? Was the Soviet Union prepared, "new thinking" notwithstanding, to use military force if that alone could rescue an East European client regime? What were the limits of Soviet tolerance in its eroding East European empire?

Those of us responsible for U.S. policy put the questions in active voice: What could we do to expand the scope of Soviet tolerance? How could the United States, together with its Western allies, facilitate self-liberation in Eastern Europe and the end of Europe's division?

Two Events   Two events crystalized thinking in the early months of the administration. The first was Gorbachev's December 1988 announcement, before the United Nations General Assembly, of a unilateral reduction of five hundred thousand Soviet forces, with nearly half coming from Eastern Europe and the western military districts of the USSR. The pledge signaled for the first time Soviet acceptance, born in part of the urgent need to reduce defense spending, of the principle that a viable new military equilibrium in Europe demanded much deeper reductions on the Eastern side than on the Western. Thus it not only heralded the prospect of reducing Soviet military power in the center of Europe but also suggested how this might be achieved.

This initiative, more than any other step taken or proposed under Gorbachev up to then, went to the root of the Cold War and Europe's division. One could imagine an essentially unreformed Soviet Union withdrawing from Afghanistan or negotiating deep mutual reductions in strategic arms, but not relaxing its grip on Eastern Europe. On this point, Gorbachev also declared that the "use or threat of force cannot be and should not be an instrument of foreign policy. . . . Freedom of choice is . . . a universal principle, and it should know no exceptions. . . . This applies to both the capitalist and the socialist systems."[7] This was not quite the categorical renunciation of the Brezhnev Doctrine one might have wanted, but it went well beyond any prior Soviet assurances and, more importantly, put the pledge against the use of force in the context of the changes under way in Poland and Hungary.

Soviet officials later criticized the United States for focusing on the arms reduction initiative in the UN speech but ignoring this "turning point in Gorbachev's new thinking."[8] The fact is that while we in the Bush administration paid considerable attention to the passage in question, we did attach greater significance to the prospect of real force reductions, which would give substance to declaratory policy. What we probably underestimated was the extent to which Gorbachev's rhetorical shift was meant, for internal Soviet consumption, to prepare the ideological ground for radical departures yet to come in Soviet foreign policy.

The second event was the April 1989 Polish Roundtable Agreement between Solidarity and the communist authorities, which called for free and authentic parliamentary elections, albeit with certain prior guarantees for the ruling Communist party. It was clear then that the Roundtable Agreement, if fully implemented, was the beginning of the end of communist rule in Poland. And if communism was finished in Poland, it was finished everywhere in Eastern Europe, including East Germany, which in turn meant that German unification had just leapt onto the international agenda.[9]

These, of course, were very large "ifs"; our appreciation of the potential for such sweeping change was by no means a prediction that it
would actually occur, much less that it could occur within the year. Indeed, the very logic of the proposition, which we assumed was evident
to Soviet leaders as well,[10] underscored how much was at stake in
Poland's tenuous agreement, as well as in the similarly hopeful process
then under way in Hungary.

For all the uncertainties ahead, we nonetheless perceived an unparalleled, and perhaps short-lived, opportunity to promote the self-
liberation of the countries of Eastern Europe and so begin the process of
ending Europe's long division. It was toward these goals that American
foreign policy had to be harnessed with a single-mindedness seldom
seen in peacetime.

Four Prerequisites   There were, however, four prior requirements,
without which American leadership would not have been up to the task.
Execution of these tasks inevitably caused a delay in the presentation of
the new administration's foreign policy approach, a lag for which President Bush took considerable criticism; it also comported with a deliberate decision to defuse public pressure for a quick American response to
Soviet peace initiatives and to develop instead a series of proposals that
would test the seriousness of Gorbachev's "new thinking."

The first task was to restore foreign policy bipartisanship and overcome the deep divisions in the Congress, particularly over Nicaragua
and the Iran-Contra scandal. President Bush made this one of his highest priorities, as symbolized by the bipartisan accord on Central America that Secretary of State James Baker negotiated with the congressional leadership in March 1989.[11] It is as remarkable as it was essential
that, aside from differences over the level of aid to Eastern Europe and
the agonizing vote over U.S. military engagement in the Persian Gulf,
virtually every foreign policy initiative during the turbulent period of
1989–92 was undertaken with broad bipartisan consensus.

The second was to restore executive branch coherence, following a
period in which government departments were pursuing what seemed to
be independent foreign policies, much to the confusion of allies and adversaries alike. Toward that end, President Bush ordered a series of
wide-ranging strategy reviews that helped establish agreement on major
objectives and bring coherence to policies that had been scattered and
uncoordinated. These were not insignificant achievements. Otherwise,

however, these protracted sessions served mainly to demonstrate to anyone who needed further proof that effective policy cannot be made by committee.

The third requirement was to restore cohesion and common purpose among our European allies, whose confidence in American leadership had been badly shaken by the oscillations in U.S. policy from "evil empire" to the Strategic Defense Initiative and the alarming proposals at the 1986 Reykjavik Summit, initiatives undertaken with little or no consultation with allies.[12] Europe's discontent, accentuated by antinuclear demonstrations and the impact of Soviet "peace initiatives," had opened a wide transatlantic divide and had revived the Gaullist (*cum* leftist) rallying cry for the "Europeanization of Europe." Secretary Baker's February 1989 trip to every NATO capital, whirlwind and substantively thin though it was, signaled U.S. commitment to closer consultation with allies, while President Bush's early assurance that American forces would remain in Europe "as long as they are wanted and needed" helped restore confidence in American staying power.

The fourth and related task was to shift the international agenda away from Gorbachev's "common European home" toward a new and radical agenda for ending the Cold War. This was no mere public relations competition nor petulant reaction to "Gorbymania." Fundamental issues were at stake. The "common home" was flawed not because it excluded the United States—this Gorbachev quickly corrected—but because it proposed to validate and stabilize a status quo that was inherently unacceptable and unstable. As both Gorbachev and his foreign minister, Eduard Shevardnadze, made clear at the time, their vision demanded Western "respect for differing social systems" and disavowal of any attempt to "undermine" the Warsaw Pact.[13] It was also dangerous, because the attraction of "helping" a less aggressive and more accommodating Soviet leadership had made Western publics, including our own, vulnerable to a vision that would have eased Europe's division superficially without addressing any of its root causes. Thus the concepts of "beyond containment" toward a "Europe whole and free" that Bush would later present had psychological purposes in addition to their substantive content.

European Perspectives

For all the euphoria associated with "Gorbymania" among European publics, especially in West Germany, in the early part of 1989, European governments were cautious and circumspect. Their chief concerns were with the corrosive effects of Soviet public diplomacy on domestic attitudes and ultimately on Western cohesion, particularly in the absence of a persuasive Western answer to Gorbachev's initiatives. With the partial exception of the Bonn government, West European leaders were not much swayed by the argument that the West needed to "help" Gorbachev. In one form or another, all sought instead a coordinated Western approach that would test Soviet intentions without exciting further expectations among their own publics for sweeping arms reductions.

Analytically, our major European partners saw events in the East much as we did, with the British the most skeptical and the Germans the most hopeful. Yet the Germans, too, were circumspect: Chancellor Helmut Kohl had said as late as 1988 that he did not expect German unification in his lifetime.[14] The policy implications they drew from these events were quite different, however. Where the Germans saw new opportunities in the East and were eager to exploit them, the British saw new dangers for the West and were at pains to offset them, while the French saw new opportunities for "overcoming Yalta" but doubted their capacity to contain a newly resurgent Germany.

"A Well-Stocked Hat Full of Well-Armed Rabbits" British perspectives were informed by a deep, enduring skepticism of the reformability of communist systems, whether in the Soviet Union or among the countries of Eastern Europe.[15] Prime Minister Margaret Thatcher turned this perspective into a paradox: these systems must change but cannot. They must change, given the manifest superiority of liberal democracy and the conspicuous failures of Soviet-type systems; yet they cannot do so from within, because the same rigidities that produced failure also engendered a reactionary immobilism in the ruling apparatus.[16] While believing these systems were doomed to collapse in the longer term, she had little sense of *how* this might occur—save, one assumes, through revolutionary upheaval—and was therefore more impressed than most with their staying power in the short term. Meanwhile, her focus was on ensuring the cohesion of the Western alliance during what was likely to be a prolonged and skillful Soviet "peace offensive"; her worry was that a lax and irresolute West, above all West Germany, would be seduced by high-sounding but empty Soviet peace initiatives.

As Thatcher's foreign secretary, Sir Geoffrey Howe, put it in a speech in January 1989, "We must not confuse hope or even expectation with reality. . . . The Soviet Union has a well-stocked hat full of well-armed rabbits and . . . will be able to go on surprising us by drawing rabbits from that hat for many years to come."[17] Similarly, in her banquet speech during Gorbachev's visit to London in April, Thatcher lectured the Soviet leader on the steps necessary to translate words into deeds, adding that "one thing we shall never do . . . is base our policies on wishful thinking rather than on reality."[18] Ironically, though, Thatcher's assertion that Gorbachev was "a man we can do business with" contributed to the very "Gorbymania" she feared.

As to Eastern Europe, British policy in the 1980s was not unlike our own, combining expanded economic and political contacts with a strong commitment to human rights, strictly linking Western assistance to internal political reforms. While Thatcher was later to argue, in the context of German unification, that the East European countries were "Britain's natural allies,"[19] British policy never had the push behind it to constitute a separate *ostpolitik* (eastern policy) capable of offsetting German influence in the region. Even well into 1989, the British were skeptical that fundamental change was imminent and more doubtful still that Moscow would allow any substantial relaxation of its grip on Eastern Europe. As Foreign Secretary Howe put it shortly after the Roundtable Agreement in Poland, the East Europeans "may be on a longer leash, but it is a leash all the same."[20] By July, one of his ministers acknowledged that "reforms in parts of Eastern Europe have moved further and faster than anyone could have imagined," but warned that "it would be a grave mistake to believe that Europe's postwar divisions can be swept away at once."[21]

British analysis coincided neatly with British interests, for the United Kingdom had less reason to want to disrupt the status quo than most of its continental partners. Its preoccupations were with managing a difficult process of adjustment with the European Community in ways that preserved British freedom of maneuver, while maintaining the integrity of the Western alliance and the "special relationship" with the United States. It is not quite right that the British "never developed a grand design for Europe," as one writer suggested.[22] The design, offering consistency if not imagination, was status quo in the West and "status quo plus" in the East, where the hope was that gradual political liberalization would lead to a more secure, though essentially conflictual, East-West relationship. Execution of this design hinged on U.S. leadership; hence Thatcher's impatience with the Bush administration's slowness to engage Gorbachev, which she felt was eroding Western resolve and common purpose. Her efforts to mediate between the two leaders were reminiscent of similar attempts by previous British prime ministers, from Harold Macmillan on, to serve as "honest broker" between Washington and Moscow. (The unstated premise of this postwar pattern was that the British were fit to lead the alliance but lacked the power; the Americans had the power but were wanting in leadership and needed periodic prods to exercise the role that came so naturally to a British prime minister.)

If Thatcher betrayed occasional impatience with the United States, her real antagonism was directed at the West Germans, whom she believed had "gone wobbly" on security and were caving in to public antinuclear pressures. The immediate issue of contention—Bonn's push for early negotiations to reduce short-range nuclear forces (SNF)[23]—was part of a larger worry that another "zero option" of elimination of this category of theater weapons would lead to the complete denuclearization of Europe. This would leave Western Europe hostage to Soviet conventional preponderance and undermine the bedrock of nuclear deterrence. Not incidentally, such a process also threatened to involve British and French nuclear forces and thus raised the most sensitive issues of membership in the "nuclear club." British adamancy against an SNF "zero option" fueled German fears of being singularly exposed—as in "the shorter the range, the deader the Germans." Britain's attitude contributed to a chaotic breakdown of alliance consensus in the spring of 1989, reaching a crescendo at the time of Thatcher's semipublic row with Chancellor Kohl at their meeting at Kohl's home in Deidesheim in late April.[24]

British thinking in early 1989, in short, saw few prospects for meaningful change in the East and many dangers for the cohesion of the West. The main task for British diplomacy was to prod the Americans into organizing a cogent, coordinated Western response to Gorbachev that would both test the seriousness of Soviet "new thinking" and rein in those, like the Germans, who might be tempted down the garden path of denuclearization.

"Germany's Hopes Are France's Fears"   France, where "Gorbymania" had never caught on in the same way as in Germany or Italy, in many ways shared British skepticism about the prospects for change in the East and certainly shared its concerns about further denuclearization.

Having launched early on a campaign of "disintoxication" to cleanse the French Left of delusions about Franco-Soviet friendship, President François Mitterrand had remained cool to Soviet blandishments even after Gorbachev chose Paris for his first official visit to a Western country. Additionally, he worried that further nuclear force reductions would diminish the significance of France's independent *force de frappe*. Meanwhile, a more fluid situation in Central Europe threatened to upset the vision of an EC-centered Europe under French and German coleadership. As one French analyst put it in late 1988: "De Gaulle's France of the mid-1960s was a revisionist power, intent on modifying the existing European security system. Today France is, at heart, a status-quo power, whereas Germany's deepest hope must be to transcend the division of Europe between East and West. . . . As long as Germany's hope remains France's fear, . . . the French-German nucleus of Europe will . . . remain central but inadequate."[25]

To consider France in 1989 a "status quo power" makes sense only in the context of two seemingly contradictory factors: undiminished French ambitions to "overcome Yalta" and the substantial evolution in French strategic thinking, particularly during the 1980s, toward fusing France's future with "Europe."[26] As President Mitterrand put it in a November 1988 interview, "Yalta is the symbol of the division of Europe into zones of power and influence between the Soviet Union and the United States. I cannot make do with it. My dream is of a reconciled and independent Europe."[27] Yet, in French thinking, this ambition had to be deferred until "European construction" was complete, and this was still a long way off. Thus, while remaining deeply dissatisfied with the status quo in this larger sense, France was even more hesitant than Great Britain to disturb it in the near term, lest rapid change in the East undermine EC integration before Germany had been safely tied up in a more federalized Europe.[28]

Eastern Europe had little place in this strategic vision, except as part of the distant goal of a Europe free of the superpowers. Indeed, so inert had France become in this region that one French analyst began a 1989 article with the question, "Does French policy toward Central and Eastern Europe still exist?"[29] French disregard for the region had been expressed most notoriously in Foreign Minister Michel Debré's characterization of the 1968 invasion of Czechoslovakia as a "traffic accident on the road to detente." Then there was Prime Minister Pierre Mauroy's defense of the French decision to conclude a natural gas deal with the

Soviet Union just after the imposition of martial law in Poland in late 1981: "Let us not add to the sufferings of the Polish people those of the French people lacking gas." Leaving aside the callousness of the remarks, they reflected a strategic judgment that France's interests did not lie in separate links to the smaller countries of Eastern Europe but rather in the multiple relationships among Moscow, Washington, Bonn, and Paris. As late as July 1989—after the opening of the Hungarian-Austrian border, after the Polish elections—former French president Valéry Giscard d'Estaing could still maintain that "our relations with Eastern Europe do not differ essentially from those we will continue to have with other parts of the world. Physical proximity does not lend them any special quality."[30]

This orientation was understandable enough before 1989, but it made less sense thereafter, particularly in that the oldest tenet of French diplomacy was the *alliance de revers,* making common cause with the neighbors and rivals of one's potential enemy.[31] If German power was the concern, would it not have made sense for France to cultivate relations with the countries to Germany's east, particularly Poland? We in Washington certainly would have welcomed a stronger French role in the region, as a counterweight to what risked becoming excessive German economic and political influence. Given France's historic ties to the region and its ability to play balance of power politics more cynically and skillfully than the United States, such a role would have been natural. Yet Mitterrand had declined to accept Kohl's 1988 suggestion that France and Germany develop a joint *ostpolitik,* and when he belatedly decided to engage in the region, he chose, unaccountably, to begin with Bulgaria, where nothing interesting was happening, rather than one of the "lands between" Germany and Russia.

This would not be the last time that some of us in the U.S. administration were frustrated at French unwillingness to act in what seemed to us France's own interests. That French aims were in some respects antithetical to America's was something we could understand and live with; that France would fail to develop a strategy consistent with its own manifest interests was harder to credit.[32]

Strategic myopia may be part of the answer, for it did seem that events in the East were fast overtaking France's EC-centered strategy, but it is evident that French leaders were aware that the stakes were high in Eastern Europe. In a March 1989 radio interview, Foreign Minister Roland Dumas was asked why France was not playing the active role that West Germany was in Central and Eastern Europe. His answer was a lament, suggesting strategic fatigue more than myopia: "I am personally sorry that France, which also enjoys certain historic advantages and a certain prestige in that region, has not been able, over the past few years, to do equally well out of that situation; which is why we have fallen behind. . . . We had fallen so far behind that anything we win back will be welcome."[33] Mitterrand, asked roughly the same question a few months before, replied with a none-too-subtle criticism of West German *ostpolitik*: "While we kept our distance for moral rather than political reasons, other countries were brushing aside considerations of that sort and establishing themselves in East European markets. I think that, although we were not wrong, we should be there too."[34]

Morality, one can say with confidence, was not the deciding factor in French policy. Inability to keep pace with German economic and political involvement, along with an exaggerated sense of inferiority in the face of resurgent German power, was perhaps more to the point. There was a strategic purpose buried in this *agitation immobile,*[35] however: it was the deliberate aim of decelerating the process of change in the East while accelerating integration in the EC. This approach had much to recommend it from the point of view of French interests, but it presumed vastly more influence than France actually had to retard history's course. It was a race against time, and France was losing.

"Let's Take Mr. Gorbachev at His Word"   The West Germans, meanwhile, were not to be restrained. Their attitudes had been expressed in Foreign Minister Genscher's controversial speech in Davos in 1987, entitled "Nehmen Wir Gorbatschows 'Neue Politik' beim Wort." It is interesting that the title—literally, "Let's Take Gorbachev's 'New Policy' at Its Word"—was rendered in the foreign ministry's official English translation as "Let's Put Mr. Gorbachev's 'New Policy' to the Test." The latter, tougher-sounding title was actually closer to the sense of the text, which did not imply that Gorbachev should be taken at face value but rather called on the West to take his policies seriously and challenge him to translate his words into concrete actions. This, of course, is what the United States was proposing by early 1989, albeit with a more demanding set of challenges. It was the more provocative "at his word" that took hold, however, and gave rise to fears that the Federal Republic had succumbed to "Gorbymania." (Much was made of opinion polls showing that only 24 percent of the West German public considered the So-

viet Union a military threat,[36] but polls in Italy, the United Kingdom, and even the United States yielded similar results.)

To understand German approaches in terms of an assessment of Gorbachev is to get the analytic cart before the strategic horse. Policy toward the Soviet Union was part of a larger German *ostpolitik*, which in turn was driven by *Deutschlandpolitik*, aimed at expanding ties with the "other" Germany. Facilitating the ultimate goal of German unity, or at least doing nothing to retard it, was the determining objective. *Ostpolitik*, as it had evolved, pursued "change through rapprochement": its logic was that reassuring Moscow would allow it to relax its grip on Eastern Europe, giving reformers there greater leeway to pursue gradual change. Regime-led reform, in turn, would produce greater stability and confidence, which would encourage Eastern Europe and Moscow alike to undertake further steps toward reform. The result of this "virtuous circle" of reassurance and reform would be an easing of the division of Europe, making possible eventual rapprochement between the two German states.

Thus, West German policy was not wedded to "stability," any more than France's was wedded to the status quo. The German aim, in best dialectical fashion, was stable change, born of the belief that positive change could occur only under conditions of stability. The gamble inherent in this approach, as one French scholar put it, was that it is not clear "whether this increased self-confidence [on the part of the East European regimes] is supposed to bring the elites to lower their guard and to promote an unwitting . . . structural change, thereby working against their own real interests, or whether [the goal is] real stabilization which would allow them to keep their domination but dispense with the more pathological measures born out of insecurity."[37] Further, as a matter of policy born of geographic proximity and of their own history, the Germans had always been suspicious of change generated spontaneously from below, preferring regime-managed reform from above. This was particularly true of the Social Democrats, who had made it a habit to snub Lech Wałęsa and other Solidarity leaders during visits to Poland,[38] and to a lesser extent of Foreign Minister Genscher's Free Democrats, who tended to cultivate regime exponents of "reform Communism."

Germans of this persuasion backed the wrong horse, as subsequent events would show. *Ostpolitik* did not encourage the East European regimes to liberalize; to the contrary, by offering a degree of legitimation and considerable economic assistance, it helped them stabilize their rule without reform.[39] As it turned out, it did not matter much, so quickly did the events of 1989 sweep away the so-called reformers in Eastern Europe. There was also a certain complementarity between Bonn's closer relations with the East European regimes and Washington's (and London's) more consistent support for democratic opposition groups. And of course both we and the West Germans recognized that reform had to be led from above as well as pushed from below; U.S. policy, too, had long pursued a dual track, engaging East European regimes as well as regime opponents.

Three elements of *ostpolitik* need underlining. First, there were significant, though sometimes overstated, differences of approach between Kohl and Genscher. Kohl and his CDU (Christian Democratic Union) were products of West Germany and the tradition of Konrad Adenauer; their approaches toward the East proceeded from a profoundly Western orientation and conviction. Genscher and the FDP (Free Democratic Party) had their roots in East as well as West Germany; the integrity of the Western alliance was, for them, not the goal but the instrumentality for achieving the larger ambition of overcoming the division of Germany and of Europe. But to state the differences in this fashion is to overstate them; they were differences more of degree and nuance. To be sure, there were some in the Bush administration (though fewer than in the Reagan administration) who shared Thatcher's view of "Genscherism."[40] By the same token, there were many who shared the general perception in the Federal Republic that Genscher had a much keener sense of the historic moment. The two views were not, of course, mutually exclusive.

In any case, to the extent that "Genscherism" affected U.S. policy, it was rarely in the sense of "demonizing" the foreign minister, as was sometimes alleged[41]; rather, it was simply that Kohl was seen as more reliable than Genscher when it came to the integrity of the Western alliance and that it was therefore in American interests to support and strengthen the chancellor's foreign policy role. This perspective, attributable more to the NSC than to the State Department, never interfered with the administration's ability to establish relations of trust with both Kohl and Genscher; indeed, it invited a natural division of labor between the White House and the State Department that served us well, particularly during the diplomacy of German unification.

Second, German strategy depended on reassurance, gradualism, and predictability: West German goals, as Kohl put it in early 1988, were "long-term stable cooperation with the Soviet Union" and its emergence as a "more predictable security partner."[42] In this conception, too much detente was as risky as too little, for rapid change could be seen as threatening to East European and Soviet leaders and risked converting the "virtuous cycle" into a "vicious cycle" of revolt and repression.[43] (This predisposition stood in marked contrast to the approach, favored in American conservative circles, of doing nothing to help or reassure the East European and Soviet regimes, but rather letting them be hoist by their own petards.)

Finally, although some on the West German Left had argued in the 1980s for the "divisibility" (*trennbarkeit*) of East-West detente, meaning that European detente should proceed despite the cooling of U.S.-Soviet relations, both Kohl and Genscher proceeded from the conviction that *Deutschlandpolitik* and *ostpolitik* could not be divorced from broader Western approaches toward the East. As Horst Teltschik, Kohl's national security adviser, put it in June 1989,

> The West German government knows . . . that its freedom of action with respect to the Soviet Union or the other Warsaw Pact countries basically depends on the superpowers' relationship to one another. The better and more constructive the relationship between the USA and the USSR, the greater the freedom the small and mid-size countries in Eastern and Western Europe to cultivate relations with the leading power of the other alliance and among each other.[44]

Hence German ambitions required bringing the Americans and their European partners around to a new, coordinated pattern of engagement. Kohl's meeting with Gorbachev in Moscow in October 1988 and Gorbachev's reciprocal visit to Bonn in June 1989 were designed to accomplish just that. The centerpiece was a German-Soviet joint declaration, which Kohl considered a "sensational" document for its affirmation of the "right of all peoples and states to self-determination" and its commitment to "overcoming the division of Europe."[45]

In Washington, anticipation of the Gorbachev visit and the joint declaration, together with Horst Teltschik's admonition that "we ought not to ask too much of Gorbachev,"[46] lent urgency to the articulation of our own approaches toward Gorbachev. Indeed, between German eagerness, British skepticism, and French ambivalence, there was ample room for an American approach that could weld a coordinated Western approach toward Gorbachev and test the limits of Soviet "new thinking."

The Strategy Reviews: A Few Words on Process

It was against this backdrop that President Bush had ordered a series of wide-ranging strategy reviews. Aimed at prodding the foreign policy bureaucracy toward new thinking, with a view toward the longer term, the reviews instead demonstrated the difficulty of trying to craft policy by committee. Their essence seemed to have been anticipated nearly seventy years before by the estimable F. M. Cornford, writing in a different context. His droll observations are worth quoting at some length:

> There is only one argument for doing something; the rest are arguments for doing nothing. . . . [All] important questions are so complicated, and the results of any course of action so difficult to foresee, that certainty, or even probability, is seldom, if ever, attainable. It follows at once that the only justifiable attitude of mind is suspense of judgment. . . . At this point the arguments for doing nothing come in; for it is a mere theorist's paradox that doing nothing has just as many consequences as doing something. . . .
>
> As soon as three or more alternatives are in the field, there is pretty sure to be a majority against any one of them, and nothing will be done. . . . [A] few bad reasons for not doing something neutralize all the good reasons for doing it.

Cornford then explains the "Principle of the Wedge," through which action is inhibited by adducing all manner of implied, potential, or unforeseeable consequences. (Today this is known as the "thin end of the wedge," meaning that a small opening can be made larger.) On the "Principle of Unripe Time" (as in "the time is not yet ripe"), he observes that time "has a trick of going rotten before it is ripe." Finally:

> The Principle of the Dangerous Precedent is that you should not now do an admittedly right action for fear you, or your equally timid successors, should not have the courage to do right in some future case, which, *ex hypothesi*, is essentially different, but superficially resembles the present one. Every public action which is not customary, either is wrong, or, if it is right, is a dangerous

precedent. It follows that nothing should ever be done for the first time.[47]

Translated into the world of Policy Coordinating Committees (PCCs)—renamed Interagency Working Groups, or IWGs, in the Clinton administration—the policy process looked something like this. Meetings would be chaired by the cognizant assistant secretary (or his or her principal deputy) of the lead agency—the Department of State for most political issues. The NSC staff representative, serving as executive secretary, typically joined the State chair in trying to move the meeting to action (on which they had usually agreed in advance). Representatives of other agencies assembled on either side of a long conference table. Around the periphery of the room were assorted and anonymous "strap-hangers," whose function, one presumed, was to report back to their superiors what epochal decisions had been reached—or perhaps just to enjoy a brief diversion from their daily routines.

When it came time for decision, most representatives, especially from the economic agencies, came armed with a mandate to defend at all costs their particular bureaucratic sacred cows. But otherwise they were unwilling to support any policy decision, in which they took no interest and voiced no opinion. No one from Treasury could speak for anyone else. The Department of State would be represented by as many as ten or fifteen separate offices or bureaus, each claiming primacy within the department on at least a part of the action. Representatives of OSD (Office of the Secretary of Defense) and JCS (Joint Chiefs of Staff) typically engaged amiably in the debate but then refused to commit (or "reserved") on any decision or even to disclose what course of action their superiors might wish to see adopted. The intelligence community's role was to demonstrate that any possible course of action was fraught with danger or otherwise doomed to fail, while advancing the seemingly inconsistent view that events in the outside world were driven by deep impersonal forces not susceptible to human intervention.

These patterns, though offered tongue-in-cheek, represented very real concerns. They applied at every level but were particularly destructive of policy making at assistant secretary level and below, where not even the most senior participants could speak authoritatively for their departments or agencies on large issues. The absence of a crisis or action-forcing event could be paralyzing even at cabinet level. This problem was sometimes overcome by recasting the issue in a way that eliminated the do-nothing option and isolated those known to prefer inaction. Of course, sheer numbers inhibited action, which is why interagency Policy Coordinating Committees rarely served as vehicles for decision. So much for policy making by committee. Thereafter, policy making was conducted mainly among National Security Council principals, deputies, and their immediate advisers.

This is as good a place as any to say a few words about the decision-making process in the Bush administration. Formally, there were three tiers. The first consisted of NSC principals. The president, the vice president, the secretary of state, and the secretary of defense were statutory members. The chairman of the Joint Chiefs and the director of Central Intelligence were statutory advisers, and the president's national security adviser managed the NSC system.[48] Second was the Deputies Committee (DC), chaired by the deputy national security adviser and attended by deputy or undersecretaries from the same agencies. Third were the many Policy Coordinating Committees.

Full NSC meetings were common during the first six months of the administration, when principals were settling in and basic lines of policy were being drawn, but relatively rare thereafter. DC meetings proved to be the better venue for decision: they were efficiently chaired (by Deputy National Security Adviser Bob Gates) and easier to convene, given the crowded schedules of NSC principals, yet still at sufficiently senior level for decisions to be reached on the spot. PCCs generally met either to consider issues below the threshold of principals or deputies or to prepare issues for referral to the Deputies Committee. There were also various ad hoc committees such as the European Strategy Steering Group, which were devoted more to strategic planning than operational decision making.

The "NSC system," however, was much broader than the sum of its formal meetings: it embraced the whole pattern of interaction among the key agencies at every level. For issues of the greatest import, often there was no substitute for face-to-face discussions among principals or deputies, but the vast majority of decisions were reached outside the formal structure of NSC meetings, through a sequence of vertical (i.e., within-agency) and horizontal (interagency) deliberations. The day began with a series of staff meetings held within agencies and a round of telephone calls among agencies at several levels; it ended, usually well into the night, with another round of telephone calls to reach final agreement on issues that had to be decided by "COB," or close of business. In between, for each staff officer, were several rounds of meetings in each agency, perhaps one or more interagency meetings, and many dozens of telephone conversations.

Important cables to the field were handled by a "crosshatch" system of interagency clearance, with the cognizant NSC staff officer the last to clear, often from secure telephone at home in the small hours of the morning. (Even cables on which there was no substantive disagreement took the whole day to wend their way through the State Department's maze of internal clearances by COB. The NSC's COB was a few hours later, when the cable had been processed by the State Department operations center and sent to the White House Situation Room for NSC clearance.) Speeches by administration officials, briefing material for their meetings with foreign counterparts, initiatives undertaken by U.S. officials abroad, and all the other elements that went into the making and execution of policy were likewise subject to interagency clearance. All these steps were part of the "NSC system" in this broader sense.

Typically, the making of major policy decisions would begin at senior staff level, on the initiative of one or more of a relatively small group of senior officials at the NSC staff, State, and the Pentagon (plus Treasury and other agencies, depending on the issue). They would develop a proposed course of action and then go separately to their respective superiors, who would approve, disapprove, or amend, consulting among themselves as they saw fit. For large issues, the process usually was accompanied by formal memoranda; more often, it was done face to face or by telephone. The process was interactive: initiatives from staff level did not spring from a void but rather from daily, informal contact with cabinet principals, whose views were in turn shaped by their key staff members.

The system worked well, owing to the insistence of the president and his national security adviser, Brent Scowcroft, on cabinet government and the disciplined, orderly presentation of issues for decision. That meant, among other things, that the views of all relevant agencies, and especially of cabinet officers, were to be fully and faithfully represented in any memorandum for the president's decision. (One early casualty on the NSC staff paid with his job for trying to advance his favored policy outcome by circumventing the known views of a key cabinet officer.) It was also a tight and compartmentalized system, based on strict "need to know" access, so that decision-making circles were kept as compact as possible. The main lines of policy were of course widely circulated, but sensitive issues like negotiations with So-viet leaders were tightly held.[49]

The system was not leak-proof, but there were relatively few in-stances in which information was leaked to the media inadvertently. Leaks were supposed to have a purpose. Secretary Baker was the undis-puted master of the art, and the discerning reader of dispatches from the State Department press corps may have noticed that an anonymous and voluble "senior administration official" seemed always to be at Baker's side. (It was, of course, usually Baker himself.) Relations with the media were closely guarded, not so much to manipulate or cast cer-tain officials in favorable light (though such efforts were not unknown) as to avoid ceding the agenda and obliging the administration to react to the notoriously transitory issues and preferences of the media.[50]

It was, at the same time, an almost unfailingly collegial and coopera-tive interagency process, owing mainly to the tone and example set by General Scowcroft, Secretary Baker, and Secretary of Defense Dick Cheney.[51] Their weekly breakfast meetings and regular telephone com-munication helped resolve interagency disagreements before they could fester. (Sometimes the weekly breakfasts were used for decision making, a practice that caused more than a little confusion, in that none of the three was in the habit of briefing his staff on the results of these ses-sions.) Rivalry there was among agencies, along with tough policy fights, but there was almost none of the backbiting and turf warfare that had characterized other administrations. If this sounds too good to have been true, suffice it to say the NSC system under President Bush and Brent Scowcroft worked the way it was supposed to work.

In relations between the NSC staff and the State Department, Secre-tary Baker's well-known pattern of relying on a small circle of close ad-visers made matters easier. In the ceremony held upon his appointment as ambassador to the Court of St. James (the United Kingdom), Ray Seitz disputed this characterization, however, saying that he never felt excluded from an "inner circle." "It was more like a trapezoid," he said, as an amused Baker looked on. Circle or trapezoid, the pattern as-sured maximum focus on the key strategic issues, so that bureaus, even if cut out from the decision process, could be harnessed to priority ob-jectives that fully commanded the secretary's attention. It gave a coher-ence and single-mindedness to policy, rather than allowing the agenda to be routinized by the constant flow of issues large and small that char-acterizes the normal work of a bureau.

Like any model, it had its flaws; like most, its virtues were also its liabilities. This one worked particularly well through 1989 and to the end of 1990, when a confined set of the most vital issues related to Europe and the Soviet Union demanded, and received, priority attention. It worked less well thereafter, when a wider range of important but unrelated issues—including Iraqi intentions in the Persian Gulf—needed, but failed, to penetrate the inner circle. The closeness and congeniality among the key cabinet officers and their deputies, including particularly Deputy Secretary of State Lawrence Eagleburger, also had the effect of narrowing the range of opinions and options that found their way into the policy debate. The antidote to this danger is a more vertical process, with assistant secretaries and other senior staff officers accorded greater, and more nearly equal, access to key decision makers, but this then risks routinizing policy and obscuring larger strategic goals.[52] No model is perfect. Whichever is chosen should be done with an awareness that the process affects the issues, and the issues affect the process.

To return to the strategy reviews: although their results came to be characterized, with some justification, as "status quo plus," they nonetheless served certain purposes. Most obviously, they signaled a break from the past, in that the president had given a strong mandate to engage in a thorough-going review of every aspect of policy, without deference to the policy preferences of the administrations in which he had served as vice president for eight years. These interagency meetings had a very different tone from those held just a few weeks earlier, even though many of the participants were the same.

The reviews also helped restore interagency coordination by ensuring that at some minimum level there was an understood baseline of agreed policy. They facilitated policy coherence by bringing together offices and agencies that were focusing more or less independently on different aspects of much larger issues and tieing these strands together in a general statement of policy. They also helped reestablish the proper role of the National Security Council staff in foreign policy making and coordination, rather than as independent executors of policy. The reviews exposed some of the existing but unarticulated fault lines of policy and helped clarify what needed resolution, whether by persuasion or command decision, before anything innovative could be expected. On occasion, they surfaced some interesting ideas that ultimately found their way into policy, even if not into the formal review documents. In this regard, NSC staff members could be retailers as well as producers of policy, lifting ideas from their agencies of origin, where they had no chance of prospering, and putting them into circulation at cabinet level in a context that might produce action.

The Debate over Grand Strategy

The reviews also brought to the surface several issues that had been held over from the Reagan administration, chief among them an understanding of Gorbachev's reforms in the Soviet Union, the implications of Soviet "new thinking," particularly for Eastern Europe, and the consequences of these trends for U.S. strategy. The policies that ensued departed sharply from those of the Reagan administration, particularly in rebuilding support for nuclear deterrence and radically revising Soviet policy away from a narrow focus on arms control, toward a much more ambitious political agenda. Indeed, the foreign policy shift under the Bush administration in 1989 was as stark in substance (though not in style or rhetoric) as the change from Carter to Reagan in 1981.

The strategy reviews, disappointing though their results were, informed the more serious and substantive debate at the highest levels of the administration in early 1989,[53] leading up to a comprehensive presentation of U.S. strategy in five major speeches delivered by President Bush in April and May. Indeed, the speeches were not only the vehicles for articulating policy but also the means through which major policy decisions were reached in the first place. When the president said it, it became policy; thus there was nothing like the draft of a presidential speech to focus the mind and force decision.[54] Before turning to the speeches themselves, it is worth exploring in some detail the debates from which they derived.

Arms Control and Dilemmas of Nuclear Deterrence   In light of the long-standing public fixation on nuclear arms reduction as the principal measure of U.S.-Soviet relations, it is perhaps surprising that arms control issues generated little controversy within the administration. Rather, this public perception *was* the issue: how to make the case for nuclear deterrence to an American public whose views had been conditioned by the nuclear freeze movement, the television docudrama "The Day After" and the specter of "nuclear winter," the INF (Intermediate Nuclear Force) Agreement, and President Reagan's proposal at Reykjavik for the elimination of all strategic nuclear weapons. These, to-

gether with the false promises of SDI (the Strategic Defense Initiative, or
"Star Wars"), contributed to the perception that these evil weapons
could be, if not eliminated or frozen in place, rendered harmless by a
protective antinuclear umbrella. In Europe, meanwhile, and especially
in West Germany, the INF Agreement had accentuated fears that the
continent had been made "safe" for war waged by short-range tactical
nuclear weapons.

It is probably true that some quarters of the Bush administration harbored an excessive enthusiasm for nuclear weapons (akin to Thatcher's,
although one or two more closely resembled Dr. Strangelove, the movie
character who "learned to love the bomb"). This zeal was born of the
mistaken, monocausal view that nuclear weapons, rather than a combination of many factors, had, in the oft-repeated mantra, "kept the peace
in Europe for 40 years." But the main effort was to restore public support for the principle of nuclear deterrence, including extended nuclear
deterrence. This meant, while negotiations on START (Strategic Arms
Reduction Treaty) proceeded, avoiding further denuclearization in Europe and maintaining the coupling of our nuclear deterrence to Europe's
defense.[55] Above all, it meant shifting the prevailing logic away from
nuclear arms control for its own sake and focusing on the massive conventional imbalance in Europe. If negotiators, through the conference
on Conventional Armed Forces in Europe (CFE), could equalize the
number of conventional weapons held by each side, then and only then
would it be possible to negotiate reductions on tactical nuclear
weapons. Finally, CFE was seen in political as much as military terms as
a vehicle for relaxing Soviet pressure on its Warsaw Pact allies and so
facilitating political liberalization in Eastern Europe.

As President Bush was to put it in his first foreign policy address,
"Arms are a symptom, not a source of tension. The true source of tension is the imposed and unnatural division of Europe."[56] It was a judgment that consciously echoed the views of then-political prisoner (and
future Czechoslovak president) Václav Havel: "The cause of the danger
of war is not weapons as such but political realities in a divided Europe.
. . . No lasting, genuine peace can be achieved simply by opposing this
or that weapons system, because such opposition deals only with consequences, not with causes."[57]

Dealing with a More United Europe   As to U.S. attitudes toward Western Europe, there had been little agreement and substantial ambivalence

about the process of European unity. Certainly, our European partners perceived U.S. hostility toward the ambitions of "1992," the European Community's target date for creating a single European market. They felt that the United States supported European unity as an abstract ideal but not as an imminent reality. They were not wrong. Strategically, there was substantial, though not universal, support for the proposition that a more united Europe was profoundly in American interests: we wanted a strong, more cohesive Europe as our main partner in world affairs, and we were prepared to lend our support and encouragement toward that end. In this sense, the Bush administration was genuinely supportive of European unity, and certainly more disposed than its recent predecessors. But these abstract judgments still begged the question of what *kind* of Europe. Most immediately, there was the danger that "1992" would lead to a closed, heavily subsidized EC internal market and a protectionist "Fortress Europe," at least during the early stages of creating a single market.

Over the longer term, economic and monetary union inevitably would give new impetus toward European political union, with ambiguous implications. If political union were achieved, we could expect a more cohesive, stronger European partner, but one that was also more exclusionary and potentially in competition with the Atlantic alliance. Already there were signs that Franco-German security cooperation was tending toward a European security and defense identity that would be independent of, rather than integral to, the transatlantic alliance. Having linked our own security to Europe's for forty years, we were adamant that the United States not be excluded from decisions on core issues of European and transatlantic security. NATO would then become the "alliance of last resort," involved via its European members at the eleventh hour in conflicts for which neither NATO nor the United States had assumed responsibility or leadership. Under such conditions, the American public could hardly be expected to support a continued U.S. military presence in Europe.

The greatest concern, however, was not that efforts toward political union would succeed but that they would fail, yet in the trying would accentuate the pattern whereby decisions were reached within closed EC councils. These decisions would then become immutable, as none of the twelve member countries would wish to reopen issues that had been resolved after much internal bloodletting. This would be the worst of several worlds. We were prepared to deal with twelve interlocutors or with just one, but we could see ourselves being left with no reliable European partner. None of the twelve individually could negotiate, because they were bound by (or chose to hide behind) collective decisions already reached. Nor could the EC as a collective be a partner. The EC presidency country, rotating among the twelve every six months; the "troika" of past, present, and future presidency countries; and the EC Commission all lacked the power to negotiate reliably on behalf of the twelve. (This was precisely the pattern we confronted in negotiations over the Uruguay Round of the General Agreement on Tariffs and Trade, or GATT, when we were obliged to deal with multiple EC representatives, none of whom could speak authoritatively for the others.)

It was nonetheless clear that closer European unity, in the political as well as the economic arena, was coming whether we liked it or not and that U.S. policy therefore had to come to grips with a more cohesive and assertive European Community. A more supportive U.S. stance and the development of more regular U.S.-EC consultations would enhance our ability to shape the Community's development in ways consistent with U.S. interests. There was a current of opinion, particularly in the State Department, that enthusiastically and optimistically supported European unity, but the majority view remained, perhaps inevitably, supportive in principle but skeptical in practice. (My own view was that a strong Atlantic alliance was essential for European unity and that a stronger and more united Europe was essential for the future of the alliance, but I found more support for the first half of the proposition than for the second.)

The strategy review devoted to U.S.–European Community relations[58] had advanced policy in one small step. We moved from the position that the United States "supported European unity *but*," meaning that our endorsement was contingent on resolution of major concerns we had over protectionist trade practices and the exclusionary process of EC political consultations. Instead we took the view that we "supported European unity *and*," meaning that we intended to defend energetically America's commercial interests and push the EC to open up its decision-making process so that meaningful U.S.-EC policy coordination could take place. That U.S. support was qualified remained implicit in this new formulation, but the rhetorical shift also implied that the onus was on the United States as well as the EC to see that things came out right.

West Germany was the key, and there was general agreement that a greatly strengthened, more substantive U.S.-German relationship would be essential to U.S. interests and to what was later referred to as a "more mature" U.S.-European relationship. (The U.S.-German dialogue at that time was surprisingly thin and formalistic, vastly different from the frank, highly substantive discussions we always had with the British.) While Prime Minister Thatcher, in her memoirs, overstated the strength of America's intention to abandon Britain in favor of Germany as its principal European partner, she correctly perceived an early shift of emphasis.[59] A closely held NSC memorandum to the president in March 1989 put it bluntly:

> Today the top priority for American foreign policy in Europe should be the fate of the Federal Republic of Germany. . . . Even if we make strides in overcoming the division of Europe through greater openness and pluralism, we cannot have a vision for Europe's future that does not include an approach to the "German question." Here we cannot promise immediate political reunification, but we should offer some promise of change.[60]

It was from these basic judgments that the notion of the United States and Germany as "partners in leadership" emerged and ultimately found its way into President Bush's speech in Mainz in May 1989 (discussed below). Although the term came to be seen, in a kind of sentimental light, as a bestowal of American approval, it arose in the more neutral context of our recognition of the Federal Republic's emergence as the dominant European power, particularly in relations with the East. It also expressed our hopes that the Federal Republic's economic and political weight could be harnessed to greater leadership and responsibility.

"Testing" Gorbachev's New Thinking   The most important issue with which the administration grappled in early 1989, of course, concerned policy toward the Soviet Union. There was, in the first place, a calculated decision to undertake what Soviet leaders came to deride as the *pauza*: the "pause" was deliberate, aimed not just at giving the administration time to chart a strategy for the longer term but also at altering the psychology of U.S.-Soviet relations. Instead of the tit-for-tat pattern whereby Western leaders were expected to react to every Soviet "peace initiative," no matter how specious and self-serving, with their own (equally specious and self-serving) counterproposals, we wanted a rela-

tionship built on seriously considered Western interests, carefully coordinated among the major allies. Rather than being stampeded into hastily concocted initiatives for the sake of waging a public relations campaign, there were strategic as well as tactical reasons to let relations cool for a while.[61]

Opinions within government largely mirrored informed thinking outside. At one extreme were the hard-liners who felt any Western gesture would only abet a skillful adversary and encourage what they saw as a neutralist drift in Europe, especially in West Germany. For them, the Reykjavik Summit had shown the dangers of trying to beat Gorbachev at public diplomacy: there was always the risk that this Soviet leader might say *da* instead of *nyet*. Related to this perspective was a more widely held view that Western pressure, which had forced the Soviet leadership to undertake internal reforms, should be maintained, not relaxed, so as to compel further internal liberalization. At the other end of the spectrum were those who felt that Gorbachev was approaching the limits of tolerance of his hard-line critics and that U.S. policy should aim at ensuring Gorbachev's political survival. In this view, tangible signs of Western reciprocation, of "meeting Gorbachev halfway," were necessary to give him the mandate to continue down the path of reform and "new thinking."

Among senior administration officials, one of the more skeptical views came from Deputy National Security Adviser Bob Gates, who predicted in an April 1 speech in Brussels a period of "prolonged turbulence" in the USSR. Secretary of Defense Dick Cheney went a step further in an April 29 CNN television interview, predicting that Gorbachev was likely to fail and be replaced by someone "far more hostile" to U.S. interests.[62] It should be noted that the latter was an ad-libbed response to a question posed by the interviewer; Cheney's response to a similar query at an April 4 press conference had been more circumspect.[63]

The negative fallout from these remarks, particularly in Europe, persuaded Secretary of State Baker to issue a corrective and offer a more comprehensive statement of U.S. policy than had emerged up to then. Speaking at the Center for Strategic and International Studies on May 4, he rejected the view of "some who say that we don't need to do much of anything because the trends are so favorable to us. Their counsel is to sit tight and simply await further concessions." Stressing that the United States wished *perestroika* to succeed but noting that its reality had been both "promising and problematic," Baker suggested, in conscious evocation of West German foreign minister Genscher's 1987 speech in Davos, taking Moscow "at its word" and "testing" Soviet new thinking to see if its promise would be "translated into enduring action."[64]

These differences within the administration, while real enough, should not be overplayed. Analytical judgments about what one or another senior official expected to happen were one thing; policy was another. (In his memoirs, Secretary Baker noted that he did not disagree with the substance of Cheney's analysis, only with the wisdom of airing it publicly.[65]) Scholars and analysts outside government exaggerated the significance of these differences precisely because they tended to judge policies by the extent to which they conformed to their analysis, whereas policymakers crafted policies not to advertise their analysis but to advance their policy objectives. It is an altogether different optic, which helps explain why the policy-making and scholarly communities often talk past each other.

Policy toward the Soviet Union in early 1989 was developed not on the basis of predictions, which would have been a risky business indeed, but on the basis of interests and objectives. To be sure, policy was informed—or circumscribed—by a range of alternatives deemed more or less plausible, but no one predictive line dominated. Indeed, believing that we were entering a period of profound and essentially unpredictable change, we felt it all the more important to be absolutely clear on first principles and main objectives. Nor were we about to assume responsibility for the fate of *perestroika*, much less of Gorbachev's political future. The fundamental choices would be made within the USSR itself: while we hoped to nudge the process in directions congenial to U.S. interests, we were under no illusions that we could make the Soviet Union's choices for it.[66]

A secret cable from Jack Matlock, U.S. ambassador to the Soviet Union, dated February 22, 1989, put it this way:

> We have an historic opportunity to test the degree the Soviet Union is willing to move into a new relationship with the rest of the world, and to strengthen those tendencies in the Soviet Union to "civilianize" the economy and "pluralize" the society. U.S. leverage, while certainly not unlimited, has never been greater. That leverage should be used not to "help" Gorbachev or the Soviet Union, but to promote U.S. interests.[67]

The idea of "testing" Gorbachev was a common denominator that appealed to all but the most extreme policy advocates here and in Europe. The skeptics saw this approach as a way of calling his bluff and silencing the Gorbachev enthusiasts among Western publics, while the optimists saw this as a way of bringing to fruition the benevolent intent of Gorbachev's policies. The dominant view in Washington, however, was that those policies had the *potential* to cause significant change, whose scope was still to be determined. Soviet "new thinking," according to this perspective, was still an empty vessel that awaited filling; U.S. and other Western policy could exert a significant, perhaps decisive, influence on what substance might eventually find its way into the vessel. As vice president, George Bush had embraced the idea from his very first meeting with Gorbachev in 1985: "The challenge is not to 'help' him but to put forward U.S. interests in a way that affects his policy the way we want."[68]

But what kind of "test," and how ambitious should it be? Horst Teltschik, Chancellor Kohl's national security adviser, cautioned that we "should not ask too much of Gorbachev." Within the U.S. administration, our view was that "we should not ask too little, either."[69]

The greatest mistake would have been to accept the existing Soviet agenda as the starting point for our own approaches, which would have vindicated the view that nuclear arms reductions were the essential yardstick of East-West relations.[70] This, indeed, was stated explicitly in a report issued in December 1988 by a panel of 31 distinguished American experts: "An American strategy for developing its relations with the Soviet Union must take the present state of the relationship as its point of departure. It must also be grounded in the political realities of the situation in the Soviet Union."[71] Much like Genscher's Davos speech, its "agenda for the future" stressed arms control, confidence-building measures, expanded economic relations, and scientific and technical cooperation. The best that can be said of such a menu is that it was one to which Moscow would have agreed readily.

Acceptance of putative "political realities" was also the premise of a Trilateral Commission report issued by Valéry Giscard d'Estaing, Yasuhiro Nakasone, and Henry Kissinger,[72] and of articles by several American academics.[73] Although stressing the need to redress the problem of the preponderance of Soviet conventional forces in Europe, these various proposals gave pride of place to nuclear arms control and were nearly silent on the *sources* of East-West conflict. They said next to nothing about Eastern Europe: the Trilateral Commission report, for example, concluding that "the Soviet Union is not yet willing to implement in Eastern Europe the principle of nonintervention," proposed nothing more than that the countries of Central and Eastern Europe be given a special category of "association" with the European Community.[74]

Administration policy, soon to be unveiled publicly in the second of the president's major speeches, was delineated authoritatively in National Security Directive 23, classified secret, on "United States Relations with the Soviet Union."[75] Drafted and debated in April and May, NSD 23 stressed that "we will not react to reforms and changes in the Soviet Union that have not yet taken place, nor will we respond to every Soviet initiative." While applauding changes in Soviet declaratory policy, it called for words to be translated into deeds:

> A new relationship with the international system cannot simply be declared by Moscow. Nor can it be granted by others. It must be earned through the demilitarization of Soviet foreign policy and reinforced by behavior consistent with the principles of world order to which the Soviet Union subscribed in 1945 but has repeatedly violated since. . . . The United States will challenge the Soviet Union step by step, issue by issue and institution by institution to behave in accordance with the higher standards that the Soviet leadership itself has enunciated. Moscow will find the United States a willing partner.

The document then delineated specific conditions that would lead to a new cooperative relationship, including "deployment of a force posture that is smaller and less threatening," internal democratization to "establish a firm Soviet domestic base for a more productive and cooperative relationship with the free nations of the world," and adherence to the principle of "self-determination for the countries of East-Central Europe" and renunciation of the Brezhnev Doctrine.

Eastern Europe: Self Determination or Yalta II? The future of Eastern Europe was a matter of first importance. The assumption behind the Trilateral Commission report, among others, was that the United States and the West must renounce Eastern Europe as a precondition for better relations with the Soviet Union—and avert another "traffic accident on the road to détente," as it were. One could make the case, as a tactical

matter, that addressing Eastern Europe's predicament had to await a period of warming and reassurance in Western relations with Moscow;
this, indeed, was among the long-standing premises of West German
ostpolitik. (*Wandel durch Annäherung*, or "change through rapprochement," was a tenet advanced from the early 1960s. It also implied that
one had to "accept the status quo in order to change it.") The best that
could be said of this view in early 1989 was that it was based on a
flawed assessment of trends already well advanced in Poland and Hungary, where revolutionary pressures were not about to await Western
convenience. But more was implied than tactics in at least some of these
proposals: they advanced, as a basis of Western grand strategy, acceptance and legitimation of a Soviet sphere of influence in Eastern Europe
as a necessary precondition for improved East-West relations.

It was in this context that the so-called Kissinger Plan for a U.S.-
Soviet "understanding" on Eastern Europe was mooted.[76] The issue actually arose from the more prosaic question of whether Eastern Europe
should be added to the U.S.-Soviet agenda, along with such hardy
perennials as strategic arms, regional conflicts, and human rights. Given
all that was happening and about to happen in Poland and Hungary,
there was little disagreement that we ought to begin talking seriously
with the Soviet leadership about American interests and perspectives in
this region. We also agreed that the prospects for hopeful change could
be enhanced by assuring Moscow that we had no intention of exploiting events in Eastern Europe for unilateral advantage. The Kissinger
Plan implied something else altogether: a Yalta-like agreement by the
superpowers over the heads of the East Europeans. This idea was never
on the agenda, nor ever given serious consideration by any senior administration official.[77]

The administration's position could not have been more different
from these attitudes. Eastern Europe was not some sort of shared
"problem" that had to be overcome before we could get on to the serious business of improving East-West relations; Eastern Europe was
what it was all about. Here was the perspective, which Cold War revi-
sionists can take on if they wish: The Cold War was not, in its essence, a
set of misunderstandings, mistakes, and miscalculations. It was the
product of Soviet conduct, above all Soviet domination of Eastern Europe and the forward deployment of more than half a million Soviet
troops in the heart of Europe. The Cold War began in, and because of,
Eastern Europe, and it was there that it had to end. Eastern Europe,

therefore, was the key "test" of whether Soviet "new thinking" would lead to a fundamental amelioration of the Cold War division of Europe.

"Eastern Europe" thus was shorthand for several related objectives: self-determination in this region, Soviet military withdrawal from the heart of Europe, a shift toward more cooperative Soviet international behavior, and above all an end to a worldview that demanded a ring of "satellite" states on key Soviet borders. Additionally, events in this region were closely tied to changes inside the Soviet Union: just as Gorbachev's policies had encouraged and legitimized reform in Eastern Europe, the far more radical changes envisioned in this region, if realized, would ultimately "blow back" on the Soviet Union itself. Policy toward Eastern Europe was therefore closely tied to how we wished to see the Soviet Union evolve.[78]

Eastern Europe had been at the center of President Bush's thinking well before his inauguration. Asked about his attitude toward Gorbachev during the election campaign, in his first television debate with Governor Michael Dukakis, Bush observed that "the interesting [question], one of the things that fascinates me about *perestroika* and *glasnost,* is what's going to happen in Eastern Europe."[79] After the inauguration, the "interesting question" became what he was going to do about it.[80]

The U.S. policy of "differentiation" had for many years meant "rewarding," mainly through trade concessions or political gestures, East European countries that either (a) distanced themselves from Soviet tutelage or (b) embarked on a path of internal liberalization. (It was George Bush himself, as vice president, who spelled out this hitherto classified policy in great and ill-advised detail in a 1983 speech in Vienna, much to the alarm of the reform-minded Hungarian leadership.[81]) With Mikhail Gorbachev in the Kremlin, the first half of the differentiation formula had become counterintuitive and counterproductive—were we to reward East European hard-liners for distancing themselves from Soviet new thinking? The focus then shifted to internal liberalization, with Poland and Hungary being the two cases in point in early 1989.

In the bureaucratic trenches of the administration, this spawned a furious internal battle, which seemed in retrospect like debating how many angels could dance on the head of a pin, but which was serious enough at the time. The question was whether the United States should offer economic incentives to support *political* liberalization absent any significant movement toward economic reform.[82] The economic agencies, mindful of the mountains of credits Poland squandered in the

1970s, argued strongly against this approach. They were joined by adherents to "the worse, the better" school, who felt that economic deterioration had compelled Polish and Hungarian leaders to enact reforms and that more misery would produce further reform. Against these views were those holding that a political opening would have to *precede* economic reform and that carefully conditioned U.S. assistance could facilitate first political, then economic liberalization. Those of us advocating this concept within the administration were joined by leaders of the democratic oppositions in Poland and Hungary, with whom we maintained close contact,[83] and, of greater political relevance, by President Bush and Secretary Baker. We were given a mandate to draw up a set of U.S. economic initiatives toward Poland and Hungary.

Far more important than any economic assistance package was the effect of American leadership. This was the point that the British historian and journalist Timothy Garton Ash, but few others, correctly perceived: "At this crucial juncture, the United States linked the development of its relationship with the Soviet Union to Soviet conduct in East-Central Europe."[84] Indeed, this may have been the single most important contribution the United States made to the events of 1989. Rather than seeking a strategic partnership with a reform-minded Soviet leadership, the United States, in effect, held its bilateral relationship with the Soviet Union, and East-West relations generally, hostage to the end of Soviet domination of the countries of Eastern Europe.

However obvious it may look in hindsight, this strategic judgment was by no means widely shared at the time. Nor was it without risks. Had Gorbachev been removed from power during the course of 1989, there would have been no shortage of second-guessing that U.S. intransigence had contributed to the downfall of the best Soviet leader that system was likely to produce. The administration, and above all the president himself, was acutely conscious of the risks, beginning with the danger that self-determination in Eastern Europe might be more than the market could bear in the Kremlin. Indeed, the very prudence with which the president pursued these aims caused many to miss just how ambitious the central vision was.

Five Speeches: American Grand Strategy "Beyond Containment"

American grand strategy for ending the Cold War was elaborated in five major speeches delivered by President Bush in April and May of 1989.[85]

They were developed as a package, each building on the other and culminating with a summation in the May 31 speech at Mainz, West Germany.

Eastern Europe The first, delivered in Hamtramck, Michigan, on April 17, elevated Eastern Europe to the top of the agenda: "The Cold War began in Eastern Europe, and if it is to end, it will end in this crucible of world conflict." In response to the Polish Roundtable Agreement, the president offered a set of economic assistance measures—including preferential trade treatment, investment promotion, and debt relief—designed to "recognize the reforms under way and to encourage reforms yet to come." Noting that "if Poland's experiment succeeds, other countries may follow," he pledged that further U.S. and other Western assistance would come "in concert with [political and economic] liberalization" and articulated a "vision of the European future":

> We dream of the day when Eastern European peoples will be free to choose their system of government and to vote . . . in regular, free, contested elections. We dream of the day when Eastern European countries will be free to choose their own peaceful course in the world, including closer ties with Western Europe. And we envision an Eastern Europe in which the Soviet Union has renounced military intervention as an instrument of its policy—on any pretext. We share an unwavering conviction that one day all the peoples of Europe will live in freedom.

Stressing that "these are not bilateral issues between the United States and the Soviet Union," the president put them in the context of the future of Europe and pledged also to make them the centerpiece of the following month's NATO Summit. The final message was directed to Moscow:

> As East and West now seek to reduce arms, it must not be forgotten that arms are a symptom, not a source, of tension. The true source of tension is the imposed and unnatural division of Europe. . . . The United States . . . has never accepted the legitimacy of Europe's division. We accept no spheres of influence that deny the sovereign rights of nations. . . .

The Soviet Union should understand . . . that a free, democratic Eastern Europe as we understand it would threaten no one and no country. Such an evolution would . . . imply and reinforce the further improvement of East-West relations in all its dimensions—arms reductions, political relations, trade—in ways that enhance the safety and well-being of all of Europe. There is no other way.

So much for "Yalta II"! Eastern Europe, ever history's object, was now its subject, and self-determination in this region was, for the United States and its allies, the principal requirement for improved East-West relations. (Yugoslavia, it should be noted, was a blind spot from the beginning. To the extent it entered into our strategic thinking, it was in the context of a general liberalization in the region. We saw the warning signs of impending disintegration but drew no lessons from them.[86])

The Soviet Union   The second speech, delivered at Texas A&M's commencement on May 12, called for moving "beyond containment" in U.S.-Soviet relations:

> Wise men—Truman and Eisenhower; Vandenburg and Rayburn; Marshall, Acheson and Kennan—crafted the strategy of containment. They believed that the Soviet Union, denied the easy course of expansion, would turn inward and address the contradictions of its inefficient, repressive, and inhumane system. And they were right. . . . Containment worked. . . .
>
> We are approaching the conclusion of an historic postwar struggle between two visions. . . . Our goal is bold, more ambitious than any of my predecessors could have thought possible. . . . It is time to move beyond containment. . . . We seek the integration of the Soviet Union into the community of nations.

This was a conceptually new idea. The containment strategy had assumed that the U.S.-Soviet relationship was essentially conflictual. So did the policy of détente, which sought to carve out areas of cooperation and ease tensions, but within what was still a basically conflictual relationship. If the notion of containing Soviet power no longer carried the same weight as in the early days of the Cold War, the other premise of containment remained—namely, that the nature of the Soviet system had to change for the relationship to change fundamentally. It was this fundamental systemic change, rather than a superficial amelioration of the tone or atmosphere of East-West relations, that "beyond containment" sought to effect.

Arguing (along the lines of his NSD 23) that "a new relationship cannot be simply declared by Moscow or bestowed by others," the president delineated five conditions that would determine whether the vision could be fulfilled. He called for deep reductions in Soviet forces to less threatening levels as well as Soviet support for self-determination in Central and Eastern Europe (and "specific abandonment of the Brezhnev Doctrine"). He also stipulated that positive Soviet efforts to resolve regional conflicts were required, along with cooperative efforts in addressing environmental and other global challenges. And he called for respect for political pluralism and human rights within the USSR itself.[87] (These were the "tests," although the word was not used. They were also the yardsticks against which we would gauge the U.S.-Soviet relationship during the coming turbulent months.) While acknowledging the "hopeful, indeed remarkable" changes that had already taken place and expressing a "sincere desire to see *perestroika* succeed," he also stressed that "the national security of America and our allies is not predicated on hope. It must be based on deeds. We look for enduring, ingrained, economic and political change."

It was a tough, demanding speech, considering that it was delivered against the backdrop of Gorbachev's enormous popularity in early 1989.[88] Instead of "meeting Gorbachev halfway," it called on him to come the rest of the way to meet us; instead of "helping Gorbachev" stabilize the status quo, it asked him to infuse "new thinking" with substantive content and address the entire range of issues that had divided East and West for forty years.[89]

The Future of Europe   The third speech, which the president delivered in the company of French president Mitterrand at Boston University's commencement on May 21, aimed at conveying America's unambiguous support for European unity and its readiness to develop a new pattern of cooperation with the European Community as it moved toward closer economic and political unity. It did so through a characteristic blend of Wilsonian liberalism and a form of realism that embraced the power factor in world affairs, but without its balance of power assumptions:

The postwar order that began in 1945 is transforming into something very different. Yet certain essentials remain because our Alliance with Western Europe is utterly unlike the cynical power alliances of the past. It is based on far more than the perception of a common enemy. It is a tie of culture and kinship and shared values. . . .

Now a new century holds the promise of a united Europe. . . . The United States has often declared it seeks a healing of old enmities, an integration of Europe. At the same time, there has been an historical ambivalence . . . [to which] has been added apprehension at the prospect of 1992. . . . [But] this Administration is of one mind. We believe a strong, united Europe means a strong America. . . . We are ready to develop, with the European Community and its member states, new mechanisms of consultation.

The speech also outlined what Secretary Baker would later elaborate as the "New Atlanticism," welcoming West European efforts toward closer defense cooperation both bilaterally, particularly between France and Germany, and through the Western European Union. At the same time, it cautioned against letting hopes of a more benign Soviet Union outrace real changes, or accepting at face value "Soviet new thinking that has not yet totally overcome the old." On East-West relations, it laid principal stress on conventional arms reductions, "on negotiating a less militarized Europe" and building "a real peace . . . not a peace of armed camps."

Hardly noticed in the United States, the speech was well received in Europe, among those who were looking for, and found, a signal of U.S. readiness to build a more balanced transatlantic partnership with a more united Europe. While the results of this overture would be mixed, it at least had the effect of stimulating new forms of U.S.-EC consultations and new efforts to encourage and accommodate a European defense and security identity within the Atlantic alliance.[90]

Arms Control   The fourth speech, given May 24 at the Coast Guard Academy's commencement, returned to the "beyond containment" theme in the context of the changing security landscape. It recapitulated the key elements of the unfolding strategy:

We are witnessing the end of an idea—the final chapter of the communist experiment. . . . But the eclipse of communism is only one-half of the story of our time. The other is the ascendancy of the democratic idea. . . . There is an opportunity before us to shape a new world.

What is it we want to see? It is a growing community of democracies anchoring international peace and security, and a dynamic free market system generating prosperity and progress on a global scale. . . .

As to the Soviet Union, "We want *perestroika* to succeed. And we want to see the policies of *glasnost* and *perestroika*—so far, a revolution imposed from top down—institutionalized within the Soviet Union. We want to see *perestroika* extended as well."

This was the least successful of the five speeches, partly because the main impending initiative—a new U.S. conventional arms reduction proposal—was being hotly debated within the administration and could only be hinted at in the speech.[91] The main thrust of the arms control portion of the address aimed at restoring public support for nuclear deterrence and refocusing the East-West arms control agenda on the Soviet Union's massive advantage in conventional forces in Europe, which "far exceeds the levels needed to defend the legitimate security interests of the USSR. . . . The USSR has said it is willing to abandon its age-old reliance on offensive strategy. It's time to begin."

The president's positive reference to the unilateral reductions Gorbachev promised at the UN presaged his CFE (Conventional Armed Forces in Europe) initiative, unveiled a week later at a NATO Summit in Brussels, for further mutual reductions in NATO and Warsaw Pact forces to a level 20 percent below current NATO totals.[92] The obvious strategic aim was to seize the opportunity for deep and asymmetrical force reductions implied in Gorbachev's proposal. More important, the initiative had the political objective of facilitating a Soviet retreat from Eastern Europe by demonstrating that Soviet reductions, whether made voluntarily or under the pressure of a deteriorating economy and demands from Eastern Europe, would be met by corresponding Western reductions down to common ceilings.

Ending the Cold War   The final speech, delivered May 31 in Mainz, West Germany, offered a summation of the various elements of the strategy for ending the Cold War. It began with the call for the United States and Germany to become "partners in leadership." (Our German friends were as flattered by this as they were nonplussed by the sentence that followed: "Of course, leadership has a constant companion—responsibility.") The president then laid out the vision of a "Europe whole and free," which he held out as "the new mission of NATO":

> The Cold War began with the division of Europe. It can only end when Europe is whole. Today, it is this very concept of a divided Europe that is under siege . . . not by armies, but by the spread of ideas. . . . A single powerful idea—democracy . . . is why the communist world, from Budapest to Beijing, is in ferment. Of course, for the leaders of the East, it is not just freedom for freedom's sake. But whatever their motivations, they are unleashing a force they will find difficult to channel or control. . . . Nowhere is this more apparent than in Eastern Europe, the birthplace of the Cold War.
>
> As President, I will continue to do all I can to help open the closed societies of the East. We seek self-determination for all of Germany and all of Eastern Europe. . . . When I visit Poland and Hungary this summer, I will deliver this message. . . . And I will take another message: the path of freedom leads to a larger home—a home where West meets East, a democratic home—the commonwealth of free nations.

The president then laid out a series of proposals. He suggested ways to strengthen and broaden the Helsinki process[93] to promote free elections and political pluralism in Eastern Europe. He proposed ways to bring down the Berlin Wall and promote new cooperation between the two halves of the city as well as extend Western assistance for environmental remediation in the East. He also sought to create "a less militarized Europe" through several arms initiatives, including the new U.S. proposal for deeper reductions in conventional forces. As to the Soviet leaders, "Our goal is not to undermine their legitimate security interests. Our goal is to convince them, step by step, that their definition of security is obsolete, that their deepest fears are unfounded." Finally:

> Growing political freedom in the East, a Berlin without barriers, a cleaner environment, a less militarized Europe—each is a noble goal, and taken together, they are the foundation of our larger vision: a Europe that is whole and free and at peace with itself.
>
> A few years ago, [this vision] would have been too revolutionary to consider. And yet today, we may well be on the verge of a

more ambitious agreement in Europe than anyone considered possible.

Competing Visions of the European Future   Leaving aside the rhetorical excesses and strained metaphors that come from overwritten presidential addresses, the kind of European future the United States was proposing contrasted starkly with the Soviet vision outlined by President Gorbachev in his speech to the Council of Europe in Strasbourg a few weeks later. According to Gorbachev: "I know that many in the West see the presence of two social systems as the major difficulty. But the difficulty actually lies elsewhere—in the widespread conviction (sometimes even a policy objective) according to which overcoming the division of Europe means 'overcoming socialism.' But this is a policy of confrontation, if not worse. No European unity will result from such approaches."

As one writer later observed, "Gorbachev did not say that there were many social systems in Europe. . . . He said that there were just two, East and West, 'socialist' and not. By implication, the common European home should be built around, and in spite of, this central difference."[94] This, indeed, went to the nub of the matter: a Europe "whole and free" or a Europe based on the permanence of the "two social systems"; an end to the division of Europe or an East-West accommodation based on Western acceptance of "political realities" in the East.

Bush's vision also contrasted with the dominant European perspective, articulated most clearly by West German foreign minister Hans-Dietrich Genscher. The difference between these two perspectives was made vividly clear in speeches given ten days apart in April 1989. Here is an excerpt from Bush's Hamtramck speech of April 17: "Victor Hugo said, 'An invasion of armies can be resisted, but not an idea whose time has come.' My friends, liberty is an idea whose time has come in Eastern Europe."

On April 27, speaking before the West German parliament, Genscher also cited Hugo, but without attribution:

Nothing is more powerful than an idea whose time has come. This is the idea of eliminating hostility from East-West relations. It is is the idea of demilitarizing East-West relations. It is the idea of de-ideologizing East-West relations. It is the idea of dialogue and co-operation . . . , of developing new peace structures. These are the topics for the forthcoming summit of the Western Alliance.[95]

"Liberty" or "new peace structures"? Freedom or "dialogue and cooperation"? Ending the Cold War or "de-ideologizing East-West relations"?

At the beginning of 1989, there had been three competing visions of Europe's future—Gorbachev's, Bush's, and Genscher's. By the time of the May 1989 NATO Summit to which Genscher referred, there was one. Gorbachev's had been overtaken by our much more ambitious vision, around which the Western alliance had rallied. Here is how the NATO Summit communiqué put it: "Now, more than ever our efforts to overcome the division of Europe must address its underlying political causes. . . . In keeping with our values, we place *primary* emphasis on basic freedoms for the people of Eastern Europe. . . . Our goal is a sustained effort geared to specific tasks which will help . . . promote democracy within Eastern countries and thus contribute to the establishment of a more stable peace in Europe."[96]

With that, the United States had reversed the logic of the international agenda and offered a Western vision of Europe's future that helped expose the limitations of Gorbachev's "common European home" even as it sought to extend the potential of Soviet "new thinking." More important, it had put in place a strategy for ending the Cold War division of Europe, within the context of our relations with the Soviet Union and what we hoped that state could become.

To recapitulate, American grand strategy involved a sequence of steps. The first was to alter the psychology of East-West relations away from an accommodation based on existing "political realities" toward a much more radical vision of Europe's future. The second was to restore the cohesion of the Western alliance—beginning with a resolution of the SNF dispute at the upcoming NATO Summit and articulation of a common Western strategy—and to begin building a new transatlantic partnership that encouraged and accommodated a stronger, more united Western Europe. The third was to place Eastern Europe at the top of the international agenda and to engage American leadership on behalf of political liberalization and independence. Then, as U.S.-Soviet relations had been put on hold while the first three steps were being carried out, the fourth was to challenge the Soviet leadership to respond to specific proposals. These proposals were consistent with the spirit and promise of Gorbachev's "new thinking" but went well beyond its practice to date; they would address the sources rather than the consequences of East-West conflict. The ultimate aim was to end the Cold War and the division of Europe through the peaceful, democratic transformation of its eastern half.

Little did we know how quickly this ambitious agenda would be achieved, then exceeded. Our most hopeful expectation in the early part of the year was that Poland and Hungary were headed toward a two- or three-year period of power-sharing between the Communist parties and democratic oppositions, during which time democratic change would advance in those countries and spread beyond. We got the pattern of change right and correctly judged the potential for communism's collapse throughout the region, but we certainly did not see it coming so fast. Astonishing event followed astonishing event—the successful June elections in Poland were followed by the opening of the Hungarian border and the installation of Tadeusz Mazowiecki as Poland's first noncommunist prime minister in four decades. Then swarms of East Germans occupied West German embassies in Prague and Budapest seeking to flee from East Germany to freedom. Only as we witnessed these breakthroughs and above all, the breach of the Berlin Wall on the night of November 9, did we dare hope that the scenario we had imagined earlier in the year might actually be accomplished so swiftly and peacefully.

2

The Revolutions of 1989

IT WAS LATE IN THE AFTERNOON of December 21 that Adrian Moruzi lost his fear. He had gathered with a few dozen others in the main square in Braşov, Romania, in sympathy protest for the demonstrators killed in Timişoara four days before. Securitate forces arrived and sprayed bullets over their heads. Moruzi and the other protestors dropped to the ground. But after thirty seconds or so, they began rising, one by one, to face their assailants. These were acts as much of desperation as of bravery: if they were to be gunned down on that square that day, so be it, but they would no longer be cowed. As it turned out, the security forces held their fire, having lost their nerve or perhaps their sense of duty for attacking their own countrymen gathered in peaceful protest against an unspeakably cruel regime. At that moment, something fundamental changed in Romania. Moruzi told me his story over dinner in Braşov in May of 1992, shortly after he had become the city's first democratically elected mayor.[1] Pockmarks from the bullets fired that December day were still visible on building facades.

Stories like Moruzi's must have unfolded ten thousand times in cities and towns across Eastern Europe in the fall of 1989, albeit without the brutality of the Romanian regime.[2] Other stories of 1989 were more prosaic: a blue-collar worker in another city recalled thinking, when student protestors across the street yelled at him to join them, that the curb on which he hesitated was the dividing line between onlooker and participant. He crossed his personal Rubicon, and the authorities were soon faced down by a swelling crowd of defiance.

These events, from the heroic to the mundane, marked the end of fear as an agent of political authority in communist Eastern Europe.

They also signaled the ruling elite's loss of confidence in its own right to rule, which also belongs to the dynamic of revolutionary change, as Alexis de Tocqueville showed more than a century ago in his study of the French Revolution. As de Tocqueville put it, in terms as relevant to 1989 as to 1789, this phenomenon helped explain "why it was that an uprising of the people could overwhelm so abruptly and decisively [a regime] that . . . had seemed inexpugnable even to the men who were about to destroy it."[3]

In the summer of 1989, free elections in Poland led to the installation of Eastern Europe's first noncommunist prime minister since the imposition of communist rule, and roundtable negotiations in Hungary reached agreement on a multiparty system and fully free parliamentary elections. In September and October, tens of thousands of East German refugees made their ways via Hungary and Czechoslovakia to West Germany. Spontaneous demonstrations spread throughout East Germany, leading to the opening of the Berlin Wall on the night of November 9. The next day, veteran Bulgarian party leader Todor Zhivkov was replaced by a new leadership that announced the end of one-party rule and soon opened negotiations with a new "Union of Democratic Forces." In late November, spiraling public demonstrations in Czechoslovakia obliged the regime to open negotiations with opposition forces led by Václav Havel. Also in late November, Romanian leader Nicolae Ceauşescu was unanimously reelected president amidst the usual official accolades; a month later, he was deposed, sentenced to death, and executed by firing squad. Finally, on December 29, Havel, who had been imprisoned earlier in the year for political activities, was unanimously elected president by parliamentary vote. As a White House press release of that day put it, "In a year of astonishing events, none is more astonishing that the election of this playwright–political prisoner as president of Czechoslovakia."[4]

That these events occurred so quickly and peacefully defies satisfactory explanation, even in retrospect. The very speed of change was part of the dynamic, as was the cross-border impact of successful challenges to communist authority.[5] There were obvious linkages, such as the impact on the GDR (German Democratic Republic) of the Hungarian decision to open its borders to East German refugees and the July 1989 visit by Polish opposition leaders to Prague for meetings with Czech dissidents. Another was the presence of Hungarian dissidents in Czechoslovakia to help commemorate the August anniversary of the 1968 Warsaw Pact invasion.[6] But there were also more subtle ones, as successful defiance in one country emboldened opposition forces elsewhere even as it discredited and demoralized their ruling parties.

Of course, Soviet action—or, rather, inaction—was the permissive cause. When it became evident, after the Polish elections and especially after the opening of the Berlin Wall, that Soviet power was no longer at the disposal of the East European regimes, there was nothing to retard the headlong surge to freedom. The discredited and enervated East European regimes, now thrown on their own resources to preserve their grip on power, proved no match for peaceful democratic revolutions led by organized opposition movements—or even disorganized ones, as in Bulgaria and Romania. The ruling parties lacked the credibility to retain power by embracing pseudodemocracy; as it turned out, they lacked the will, or perhaps the capacity, to muster the coercive power required to subdue virtually their entire populations.

The first half of the year called to mind the interplay between Hungarian and Polish reform movements in 1956; the second half evoked the 1848 "springtime of nations," as national independence movements spread from city to city with astonishing speed and unexpected success.[7] It was as if generations of history were compressed into a few months.

Indeed, the very swiftness of these changes tended to impart, after the fact, an air of irreversibility to the process and inevitability to the outcome, contributing to Bergson's "illusions of retrospective determinism."[8] It was an irresistible temptation for scholars and political pundits, having failed to anticipate these events, to go back to find the evidence they had missed and then, by way of atonement, to adduce a powerful body of evidence purporting to show how and why things had to come out as they did. To make order out of chaos, the formula was simple: draw a straight line backwards in time, then go back to some convenient date and follow the line forward, showing all the social, economic, political, and other forces that drove history ineluctably along its predestined course.

This is not how it looked at the time; this is not how it was. It was a period of great uncertainty and was so perceived by protagonists in West and East alike; the Hungarians and Poles in particular had bitter memories of failed revolutions, both ancient and recent. (Those who followed the Polish events of 1980–81 at close range remember well how firmly many believed, right up to the moment that martial law was declared and Solidarity outlawed, that the Solidarity-led social revolution could no longer be reversed.[9]) Within the Polish opposition in the spring of 1989, few believed that Solidarity would win the election, and fewer still thought that the Wojciech Jaruzelski regime would honor such an outcome.[10]

Evocations of 1848 or of the French Revolution (captured in banners proclaiming, "1789–1989") were meant to exhilarate, but they also served to remind how quickly repression can follow liberation. Indeed, had the Polish opposition not decided to support General Jaruzelski's election as president—ultimately secured by the margin of a single vote—the history of the next several months might have been one of retreat and repression rather than democratic triumph. As if to underscore the point, the first round of the Polish elections was held on the day of the massacre in Beijing's Tiananmen Square. Similarly, in Leipzig on October 9, had maestro Kurt Masur not persuaded local authorities to issue a joint appeal for nonviolence, the huge street demonstrations that day might have led, not to triumph, but to disaster.[11]

Even later in the year, no one could be sure how Moscow would react: it was one thing for Gorbachev to countenance, even encourage, greater liberalization and autonomy in Eastern Europe, quite another for the Soviet leadership to preside over the dissolution of an East European empire. This clearly was never Gorbachev's intent; his assumption was that replication in Eastern Europe of his own policies of *glasnost* and *perestroika,* together with the advent of new leaders who were reasonable facsimiles of himself, would produce, somehow, a revitalized socialism. As late as July, in his speech at Strasbourg, Gorbachev continued to express his belief in the viability of East European socialism. Soviet foreign minister Shevardnadze seems to have understood better the bankruptcy of communist rule in Eastern Europe. So, ironically, did Gorbachev's hard-line critics, who knew only too well that force, and the willingness to use it, undergirded their authority. To his credit, though, Gorbachev never signaled that he was prepared to restore order through repressive means; at every critical juncture, he not only acquiesced but actively encouraged the process of change he had unwittingly helped to unleash.

U.S. Policy

A successful democratic transformation in Central and Eastern Europe was the highest priority for U.S. foreign policymakers, yet these were events effectively beyond our ability to influence, except indirectly. In this sense, the U.S. role, like that of the Germans and the Western allies collectively, was marginal. Foreign policy, even for a superpower, is usually made in the context of broad historical forces that can at best be nudged in one direction or another. Yet policy so conducted can make a difference, sometimes a decisive one.

U.S. policy was instrumental in five respects. First, following Yogi Berra's dictum, we made no "wrong mistakes" that might have threatened the hopeful course of events and sparked a reaction. Second, we elevated Eastern Europe to the top of the international agenda and made self-determination in this region the prime test of Soviet "new thinking." Third, we were unambiguous on principles: our goals were democracy and independence, not "reform communism" and "Finlandization." Fourth, recognizing that reform had to be led from above as well as pushed from below, we provided incentives for the Polish and Hungarian communist leaders to move along the path of political liberalization. Fifth, we worked to persuade Soviet leaders that democratic change in Eastern Europe could be accomplished without undermining legitimate Soviet security interests—and helped them redefine what constituted "legitimate" interests.

After the Roundtable Agreement in Poland, our near-term aim was to lend support to the process of political opening and, more immediately, to facilitate the faithful implementation of the accords. The Hamtramck speech of April 1989 had set the basic strategic goals and offered several modest initiatives designed to encourage the Polish and Hungarian regimes along the path of political and economic liberalization. And the NATO Summit and Mainz speech of late May had articulated a coordinated Western approach toward the region.[12] There remained the task of dramatizing U.S. leadership.[13] What better way than for President Bush to visit both Poland and Hungary, and to use the announcement of the visit as leverage for continued reform movement in both countries?

There were signs of change elsewhere in the region, as well, in the spring of 1989. In Bulgaria, the independent trade union Podkrepa (Support) joined an informal "Club for the Support of *Perestroika* and *Glasnost*," the environmental group "Ecoglasnost," and other pro-democracy movements as the seeds of organized opposition. In Romania, six former Communist party leaders sent an open letter to Ceau-şescu accusing him of "discrediting socialism," and veteran human rights activist Doina Cornea sent several open letters charging him, more pointedly, with crimes against human dignity.[14] A small but defiant group of asylum-seekers marched in Leipzig, demanding exit visas to West Germany. In Prague, Václav Havel was released from prison, halfway through his eight-month sentence, following public and international calls for his release. Shortly thereafter, he issued a petition entitled "Several Sentences"[15] calling for democratic reforms and for the regime to open a dialogue; its original 1,800 signatories were soon joined by thousands more.

In the Soviet Union itself, voters swept aside several prominent Communist party leaders in favor of independent candidates, including Boris Yeltsin, the former Moscow party leader whom Gorbachev had fired in 1987, for the new Congress of People's Deputies. Indeed, these elections, the freest in the history of Soviet rule, gave further impetus for democratic change in Poland and Hungary. If relatively free elections could be held in the USSR, why not in Poland and Hungary? Yet the Poles and Hungarians were at the leading edge of reform, and it was their progress, more than events in the USSR, that was seen elsewhere in Eastern Europe as the real test of Soviet intentions.[16]

U.S.-Soviet Relations   Managing the U.S.-Soviet relationship through this period was the most important and complicated aspect of policy. By mid-1989 we were clearly dealing with a Soviet Union in retreat, and a Soviet leadership beset with internal as well as external challenges to its authority. Our task was to help secure Soviet acquiescence without humiliation, so that Moscow would have a stake and a place in the emerging order and see its legitimate security concerns addressed. These political and diplomatic efforts, including arms control initiatives that helped Gorbachev save face while also meeting Soviet security concerns, were widely and favorably reported. Less well understood among Western publics, particularly the American public, was the importance of the uses of power, including its personal and psychological dimensions.

Here, President Bush understood the requirements better than clever pundits or advisers. His approach toward his counterpart in the Kremlin ran roughly as follows.[17] Soviet leaders, including Gorbachev, understood power and the "correlation of forces," and they also drew conclusions when power—not only military power—was arrayed against them. They certainly understood in the fall of 1989 that they were playing a losing hand. Yet they also knew, and knew that we knew, that they had a trump card—more than half a million troops in the heart of Europe and a military capacity that could threaten Europe for many decades to come, no matter the evolution of political events. Gorbachev and Shevardnadze, and indeed others within the Soviet leadership, were intelligent and imaginative men. While their position was too weak to deploy a grand strategy in Europe, neither were they unwitting dupes as one communist regime after another fell in Eastern Europe. Once these events were well advanced in the fall of 1989, they knew perfectly well what the game was and were fully capable of playing a weak hand well, as indeed they did. They needed to be treated with the utmost seriousness and respect, as indeed they were.

Securing Soviet acquiescence to the loss of empire would require the mobilization of diplomatic, political, military, economic, and, not least, psychological power toward this end. At the same time, as leaders in retreat can react unpredictably, even irrationally, power must be exercised with subtlety and sensitivity. Finally, just as the tsar consolidated power in the Kremlin when threatened at one of its imperial borders, a Soviet leader facing losses abroad would be more likely to guard jealously his personal power at home.

This venture into psycho-history may help explain some of the more controversial aspects of President Bush's approach: his initial slowness to engage Gorbachev in serious dialogue (while mobilizing the requisite power) and his reluctance to confront Gorbachev directly over the crackdown in the Baltic states. It may also explain his sensitivity to Gorbachev's domestic standing even after the Soviet leader's star was clearly waning.[18]

Another case in point was the president's May 1989 CFE (Conventional Armed Forces in Europe) initiative. It was designed to help Gorbachev find a way toward a less militarized Europe consistent with Soviet security interests. But it also made it plain what the alternative was: a united NATO, fully prepared to maintain and continue modernizing its forces into the indefinite future, leaving Moscow to cope on its own with an eroding empire and bankrupt economy. Appealing to Moscow's better instincts and showing the way to a more cooperative future was important, but so too was backing this vision with power and creating a new reality that made a return to "old thinking" a less plausible option.

Engagement in Eastern Europe   These strands came together in President Bush's visit to Poland and Hungary in July 1989. With events in those countries already moving in hopeful directions, we wanted to facilitate further democratic change without inadvertently provoking a backlash. Another failed revolution could have set the clock back a decade in Eastern Europe and derailed Soviet reform for perhaps a generation; as we were in no position to assure success or come to the rescue if things went awry, it was important that American intentions not be misunderstood. Operationally, we wanted to lend strength to the dominant forces of moderation within the Polish and Hungarian oppositions, as well as to reform-minded regime figures, and give the fire-breathing fringes no grounds for action.[19] (Our engaging of communist leaders willing to support reform, or at least not oppose it, was born partly of the assumption that they would be participants in the process for some years to come.) At the same time, we wanted the fact of the visit, along with the symbolism and substance of key events, to make it clear that our agenda for democratic change went far beyond the modest concessions made so far by the ruling establishments.

In May, I went to both countries to advance the president's trip. This, technically, was the "pre-advance" trip, in which we made tentative arrangements for what the president would do, where he would go, and whom he would see. Later, once our tentative arrangements had been approved, the "advance" team would go for a longer stint to prepare the logistics of the visit in excruciating detail, eventually to be incorporated into the "event book" everyone would carry on the trip. I have the Polish event book before me as I write; a single day in Warsaw runs to nearly a hundred pages. The "pre-advance" was the substantive trip, designed to ensure that the visit furthered our policy objectives.

In Warsaw, we had lunch at Ambassador John Davis's residence with key Polish opposition leaders and "independents," using the opportunity to compare notes on strategy and tactics. I reminded Solidarity adviser Bronisław Geremek that when last we had met, in April 1988, he had explained the strategy behind Solidarity's readiness to enter into an "anticrisis pact" with the Jaruzelski government. Now, a year later, that opening had produced the Roundtable Agreement, but the same dilemmas remained for Solidarity. The regime wanted to co-opt and eventually discredit the opposition by making it coresponsible for the painful economic austerity measures to come while retaining for the Communist party the essential levers of political power. Solidarity, having been created a decade before on the premise that opposition to communist rule had to come from independent social organizations operating outside, and parallel to, the ruling establishment, was now prepared to gamble for a share of political power to help arrest the virtual collapse of the Polish economy. Solidarity was by no means certain that its strategy would prevail over a regime that still had powerful instruments of control at its disposal.

On the regime's intentions, the "Soviet factor," and all the other fundamentals, our analyses were almost identical with those of Solidarity strategists. We also agreed that a frontal assault by regime opponents was less likely to succeed than the careful course which Solidarity had undertaken in the Roundtable Agreement. Beyond that, Solidarity's strategy was not for us to decide; we only needed to know how the United States could be helpful. What was needed, we were told, was U.S. moral support and leadership, a coordinated approach by the West, further incentives for the Polish regime to fulfill its pledges, and an approach toward Moscow that was firm on principles while avoiding any hint of gloating or triumphalism.[20] This guidance coincided with our own thinking and, *mutatis mutandis,* with that of Hungarian opposition figures as well. In a May 1 paper, which I had with me on the trip, the dissident Hungarian philosopher János Kis echoed the thinking of his Polish counterparts. One paragraph in particular was pertinent:

> The *Ostpolitik* which consisted in cooperating with governments only is to be rejected. But, in cases where there is a significant chance for negotiated transition, the Cold War attitude which involved a complete rejection of serious talks with governments should also be abandoned. What Western governments ought to support is not one side against the other but the making of a social contract between the two. This, however, must not mean abandoning the opposition to the good will of the so-called reformist wing of the Communist party leadership. By recognizing the de facto pluralism of the political arena, Western governments could contribute to its consolidation and further development.[21]

Against this background, the U.S. delegation began official negotiations with our Polish counterparts.[22] Some events, they informed us, were *de rigueur*: an arrival ceremony, wreath-laying ceremony at the Tomb of the Unknown Soldier, a meeting with General Jaruzelski, and a state dinner. The Polish government also assumed, rightly, that President Bush would go to Gdańsk to see Solidarity leader Lech Wałęsa. Everything else was open. Indeed, we left all the Polish proposals open and refused to commit to any of them, even the "required" events, until we had secured Polish agreement to our main objectives, at that point unknown to them.

The first issue was the venue for a speech. We wanted President Bush to be the first foreign leader to address the first freely elected East European parliament since the onset of communist rule, and to use the announcement of this event to exert pressure on the Polish authorities to ensure that free and fair elections were held as promised. Understandably, our broaching of this idea evoked horrified looks on the faces of the Polish foreign ministry officials with whom we were dealing. They had no way of knowing whether the Polish government had any intention of allowing the elections to proceed as agreed, no way of knowing what the outcome would be, and no way of knowing whether the Polish authorities would honor the outcome if Solidarity won. They threw up a blizzard of objections and a host of alternative proposals. We remained adamant, making it clear that the trip itself might be in jeopardy unless we were assured that the president would speak to the Polish parliament. Ultimately they relented, but only after General Jaruzelski's personal intervention.

Our second main objective was to arrange the president's visit to Gdańsk and meeting with Wałęsa in ways that made it plain that our sympathies were with the democratic aspirations of the Polish people. First, we wanted a speech that would be emotional and symbolic, in contrast to the cooler and more analytical address to the Polish parliament. We wanted it out of doors, with huge crowds . . . in front of the Lenin Shipyard in Gdańsk. Here our own Secret Service showed greater concern than did the Polish authorities, but in the end they relented. What about the meeting with Wałęsa? We thought it would be a nice touch, after the stiff setting of a state dinner in Warsaw, for the President and Mrs. Bush to join the Wałęsas in their home for a private luncheon, accompanied only by interpreters. I do not know that President Bush ever heard how this was done; he might be amused to learn how we angled an invitation. Lech Wałęsa was out of the country, so we arranged to meet his wife, Danuta, together with a Solidarity adviser, at the Wałęsa home. Sitting around their small dining room table as assorted Wałęsa children walked in and out, we broached the idea of a small private luncheon, to which they were receptive. We suggested that Mrs. Wałęsa might want to send back with us a handwritten invitation to President and Mrs. Bush, which we thought would be literally an offer the president could not refuse. Mrs. Wałęsa agreed, worked out a text with her adviser, and the deal was done.

The last remaining issue, a logistical one with substantive implications, was what to do about General Jaruzelski. He, understandably, did not wish to be in Gdańsk for Solidarity's events. Neither would his sense of protocol allow him to have President Bush leave Poland without his being there to send him off. Nor, given Jaruzelski's pivotal role in overseeing a process of political liberalization, was it in our interests to snub him. Yet the president's schedule was too tight for him to fly back to Warsaw before going on to Budapest. Finally it was agreed that Jaruzelski would fly to Gdańsk after the luncheon and the speech, accompany the president to Westerplatte, site of the opening shots of World War II, and then see his plane off from Gdańsk. We were not thrilled with this second set of Gdańsk events that returned the spotlight to the Polish regime, but we were prepared to agree if all our other objectives, including the Polish parliament speech, were accepted.

These logistical issues may seem small, and indeed the other issues with which we dealt were smaller still, yet they had a substantive dimension as well. Even grand strategy is implemented in small steps.

In Budapest, where the political distance between the regime and its opponents was not so great, our task was much simpler. Our main interest was finding two sites for presidential speeches—one outdoors and emotional, another indoors but with a symbolically rich setting. Our first choice for the outdoor speech was Batthány Square, which memorialized Hungary's prime minister who was executed after the 1848 Revolution and which had become, in 1989 as in 1956, a symbol of protest and democratic defiance. This site the Secret Service ruled out for security reasons, the square being surrounded by close-in apartment buildings with countless windows. Ultimately, we settled on Kossuth Square just behind the Hungarian parliament building, with the president standing just under the statue of Lajos Kossuth, Hungary's great national hero of 1848.

The second speech venue came to us easily. We had already decided to take a look at Karl Marx University, whose reputation for espousing free market principles offered a nice philosophical juxtaposition. When we saw the reception hall with a huge bust of Marx, beneath which the president could speak about economic liberty, the choice was made. Otherwise, our main tasks were to see that the president met with the right balance of regime figures, which was a matter mainly for the Hungarian side to sort out, and representatives of the democratic opposition, which we accomplished via a large—and, as it turned out, not very successful—meeting with independent political leaders in the ambassador's residence.

One small vignette reinforced our general impression of impending major change. I was invited to a dinner in Budapest in honor of visiting Hungarian-Canadian industrialist George Sarlos (not to be confused with the Hungarian-American financier and philanthropist George Soros). Present as a speaker was Hungarian Communist party leader Károly Grósz. His remarks were bland enough; what was remarkable was the open criticism and condescension to which he was subjected by several Hungarians in the audience. Even in Hungary, this kind of treatment of a communist leader would have been hard to imagine a year earlier. If Hungary was indeed moving toward a multiparty system and free elections, I recall thinking, Grósz and his party are finished.

Poland and Hungary: Events Accelerate   By the time of the president's visit in early July, the Polish elections had returned a stunning victory for Solidarity candidates. In the freely contested elections for the new upper house, the Senate,[23] they won 99 of the 100 seats. In the lower (but more powerful) house, the Sejm, they won 160 of the 161 seats available to them, the remaining 65 percent having been reserved for the communist bloc.[24] No one inside Poland or out had expected such a landslide; indeed, many in the Polish opposition had thought it a blunder to agree to elections with only two months to prepare. Wałęsa himself had complained: "None of us wants these elections. They are the terrible, terrible price we have to pay to get our union back."[25] As the election results began to come in, the Warsaw Citizens' Committee of Solidarity watched, in stunned disbelief, from its informal headquarters in a place aptly called "Cafe Surprise."[26] Having succeeded beyond their wildest expectations in challenging communist rule in Poland, Solidarity now had to prepare for the unanticipated consequences of its success: assuming responsibility for the formation of the new Polish government. As Wałęsa put it, "I face the disaster of having had a good crop."[27] This was Wałęsa's usual overstatement, but it conveyed his sense of the unexpected challenges ahead.

In Hungary, meanwhile, there had been a similar acceleration. In May, portions of the Iron Curtain between Hungary and Austria were dismantled, symbolizing an open door to the West that would soon acquire even greater importance as the route of choice of thousands of East German asylum-seekers. In mid-June, government-opposition roundtable talks reached agreement on fully open parliamentary elections and other political reforms; at the same time, the long-awaited reburial of Imre Nagy, prime minister during the 1956 Revolution, touched off vast demonstrations in tribute. A week later, Károly Grósz, whose political future turned out to be even shorter than it appeared in May, was forced to share party leadership within a new presidium of four that included leading progressives Imre Pozsgay, Prime Minister Miklós Németh, and veteran economic reformer Rezsö Nyers.[28]

The timing of President Bush's visit thus turned out to be even more pivotal and delicate than we had imagined. The Hungarian government-opposition roundtable negotiations would be ongoing. In Poland, he would arrive in the midst of deliberations over the shape and composition of the new government. The position of his official host, General Jaruzelski, was now in doubt. The Roundtable Agreement had stipulated that the new president would be elected by the two houses of parliament, but Solidarity's sweeping victory called into question whether the power-sharing arrangement it had concluded with the communist regime could in fact be honored.[29]

Behind all this was the larger question of Soviet attitudes, which the president addressed in a *Washington Post* interview in early June.[30] His remarks, which combined insistence on the rights of the Poles and Hungarians to chart their own course with reassurance that the United States would not exploit these developments for unilateral advantage, evidently resonated well in Moscow. Georgi Shakhnazarov, Gorbachev's chief adviser on Eastern Europe, read the text carefully and told an American visitor that it was "extremely important and positive" and that, as far as he was concerned, "all of Bush's conditions can be fulfilled."[31]

Gorbachev's speech to the Council of Europe in Strasbourg,[32] delivered just a day before the president's departure from Washington for Poland, was another positive signal, and a seemingly conscious response to U.S. calls for a renunciation of the Brezhnev Doctrine. "Social and political orders in one or another country have changed in the past and may change in the future," Gorbachev said. "This is exclusively the affair of the peoples themselves. . . . Any interference in internal affairs and any attempts to restrict the sovereignty of states—either friend and allies or anyone else—are inadmissable." These remarks were studied closely in Washington. This was the most categorical statement yet that the Soviet Union would not intervene to save an allied regime. It was also the first time a Soviet leader had ever implied that a "socialist" country could choose "capitalism" and that—Marxist orthodoxy notwithstanding—history's wheel could turn the other way round.

In effect, Gorbachev had repudiated the Brezhnev Doctrine by which Moscow had claimed the right to intervene in a "fraternal" state if "socialism" were threatened. Indeed, two days later, at a Warsaw Pact meeting in Bucharest, Hungarian foreign minister Gyula Horn declared "the so-called Brezhnev Doctrine is over once and for all."[33]

Yet, here again, "illusions of retrospective determinism" come in. One can look back on this period and selectively assemble a powerful body of evidence putatively demonstrating that in public remarks as well as private deliberations, Soviet leaders had already reconciled themselves to the loss of empire and even to the prospect of eventual German unification. What was all the fuss about? But to reach these judgments is to neglect countervailing evidence that clouds the historical picture, and certainly clouded the picture that we were able to perceive at the time. Gorbachev's Strasbourg speech was not the only thing being said or written by Soviet officialdom at the time. Coverage by the official Soviet dailies *Pravda* and *Izvestia* of the events in Poland and Hungary was replete with ominous warnings of anti-Soviet and antisocialist activities,[34] code words reminiscent of Soviet commentaries during the Hungarian Revolution of 1956, the Prague Spring of 1968, and the rise of Solidarity in Poland in 1980–81. Which was the authentic, definitive Soviet position—Gorbachev's speech before a Western audience in Strasbourg or the line taken by the official Soviet press? The answer was probably both . . . and neither: Soviet attitudes were still in evolution and far from uniform.

From the point of view of U.S. policy, the most that could be safely assumed was that Moscow welcomed democratic changes in principle but remained wary about them in practice. It was against this backdrop of mixed Soviet signals that President Bush prepared to travel to Poland and Hungary. The goals of the trip were sketched out in a background briefing to the press by a "senior administration official"[35] on the eve of the president's departure:

> We seek to overcome the division of Europe and bring Eastern European countries into the commonwealth of free nations. . . . Con-

ceptually, this is a newly-vivid goal for American policymakers. In the past, the desire for an end to Europe's unnatural division seemed unapproachably distant. Recent events have now brought this ambitious objective into view. . . .

The historical symbolism of the President's trip to Poland and Hungary and the power of a simple restatement of what we stand for will, we think, tap a great well of popular sentiment in these two countries. . . . Memories, symbols, ideas all count in Eastern Europe to a very great degree. And that is why the very fact of the American President standing in these countries at this particular time and talking about their place in history and about freedom, about Western involvement in their future, is so important.[36]

The President's Trip to Poland and Hungary   With these objectives in mind, the president arrived in Warsaw on July 9 for a trip that would take him to Gdańsk, Budapest, Paris (for the G-7, or Group of Seven, Summit), and the Netherlands. In his speech to the newly elected Polish parliament, he sought to capture the essence of the moment, urging Poles "to forge a rare alloy of courage and restraint": "The future beckons with both hope and uncertainty. Poland and Hungary find themselves at a crossroads. Each has started down its own road to reform, without guarantee of easy success. . . . The way is hard. But the moment is right, both internally and internationally, for Poland to walk its own path. . . . Poland is where the Cold War began, and now the people of Poland can help bring the division of Europe to an end [and] redeem the principles of the Atlantic Charter."[37]

On East-West relations, his focus was on "greatly reduced levels of arms" and insistence that reductions in military forces must "take place in parallel with political change."[38] The president then cited Gorbachev: "Universal security rests on the recognition of the right of every nation to choose its own path of social development and on the renunciation of interference in the domestic affairs of other states. A nation may choose either capitalism or socialism. This is its sovereign right."[39] This was meant for multiple audiences: for Gorbachev, to turn his words back on him as the standards to which we meant to hold him; for the Polish regime, to convey that democratic change should have no arbitrary limits, nor any imposed by the putative bounds of Soviet tolerance; and for the Polish population at large, to encourage them to seize the moment.

Building on the "Hamtramck package" of economic assistance initiatives,[40] the president announced an additional set of measures and pledged to use U.S. leadership at the forthcoming G-7 Summit to galvanize coordinated Western assistance to Poland and Hungary. Of the new assistance measures, the most important was the capitalization of a new Polish-American Enterprise Fund, which would provide start-up loans and technical assistance to new Polish private business. Although we settled on the name literally on the eve of the president's departure, the Enterprise Fund concept was the product of much discussion and analysis. These efforts led us to the conclusion that Poland's newly emerging private economic sector, particularly small and medium-sized enterprises, would be the principal source of economic dynamism and growth during the initial transition toward a market economy. This was also the sector most likely to be neglected by the World Bank, as the loans involved would be too small for its usual programs, and the one where we could make the most difference.[41] Finally, as the fund would provide support directly to the emerging private sector, it was an approach that allowed us to help Poland's economy without having that assistance pass through its still-communist bureaucracy.[42]

The direct assistance measures were modest in the extreme, useful more as a symbol of American involvement than for their tangible economic benefits. They were meant to help lead Poland, including its communist leadership, along a path of reform that had not yet begun in the economic sphere. The administration (particularly the Treasury Department), recalling the gross misuse of Western credits in the 1970s by the regime of Edward Gierek, was perhaps overly concerned that our aid might be squandered or, worse, manipulated by the current regime to prop up its own rule. These were fair enough concerns at the time, but the paucity of the U.S. assistance package weakened the symbolic effect we hoped to achieve and, as will be seen, set the wrong example for our G-7 partners. We should have done more, and we certainly should have corrected our mistake later in the year, when political and economic reforms sweeping the region justified much greater financial assistance.

In his meetings with Jaruzelski, the president's aims were to establish a relationship of trust with the Polish leader, appeal to his patriotism,[43] and help persuade him to play a role in overseeing, or at least acquiescing in, a process of political liberalization. Bush argued that a political opening, based on acceptance of the results of the Polish elections, was the only way out of Poland's economic and political crisis. If Jaruzelski was prepared to support such an opening, he could count on U.S. help. The United States aimed to "assist in a process, an evolution," not enter into a contest with the Soviet Union over Poland. "We are not asking you to choose between East and West," the president told the visibly relieved Polish leader.[44]

Polish prime minister Mieczysław Rakowski, in his memoirs, summed up Bush's visit this way:

> It is quite certain that Bush did not choose the [timing of his visit] without consideration. He came to Poland in the middle of the process of shaping a new political balance, after the parliamentary election . . . and during ongoing negotiations on the presidency, government, etc. In my view he came with the idea of giving moral and political support to Jaruzelski, whom he described as "one of the leading political reformers in the countries of Eastern Europe." Undoubtedly that was a very deliberate statement.[45]

Rakowski's last sentence showed that he got the point. The statement was indeed deliberate. We did not believe Jaruzelski to be one of the leading reformers, but we wanted to turn Bush's assertion into reality by a combination of flattery and conditionality, to help Jaruzelski play the role we hoped he had the capacity to play.[46] Both Rakowski and General Czesław Kiszczak, the regime's chief negotiator during the Roundtable talks, later argued that Bush's visit was critical in persuading Jaruzelski to run for the presidency.[47]

The U.S. approach toward General Jaruzelski was based on the judgment, shared by most of the Solidarity leadership,[48] that his role (under the above conditions) was essential. He was needed to fulfill the commitments of the Roundtable accords and reassure Moscow that events in Poland, however unexpected or unwelcome they might be, were proceeding in an orderly and peaceful fashion. Like Solidarity's leaders, we believed that political liberalization in Poland had to be led, at least nominally, from above even as it was being pushed from below, and that this would be a multiyear process extending at least through the next scheduled elections in 1993. Indeed, Solidarity's assumed timetable was for a gradual transition to full democracy over a six-year period until Jaruzelski's term expired in 1995. Even after that point, they foresaw a Polish political system that retained strong elements of central control by the communist bureaucracy.[49]

The next day's visit to Gdańsk was designed to demonstrate America's solidarity with the aims and aspirations of Poland's democratic opposition, and to reinforce the theme of "courage and restraint" in navigating the difficult transition to democracy. The discussion over lunch was pure Wałęsa, as all of his meetings tended to be. He observed, rightly, that the direct U.S. assistance being offered was meager, though he underestimated (as he continued to do after becoming president of Poland a year and a half later) the importance to Poland's economy of the market-opening and investment-promotion measures being proposed. But the president's visit, as Wałęsa well knew, was not about economic measures but about the symbolic importance of American leadership and support at a critical juncture, dramatized by their joint appearance before a huge, emotional crowd in front of the Workers' Monument at the gates of the Lenin Shipyard.

In Budapest, as if in answer to Wałęsa's appeal for greater U.S. assistance, a homemade poster that was displayed when President Bush arrived at Kossuth Square read, in English: "Don't give money to the communists."[50] Well, we didn't give them much. The assistance measures the president announced were a scaled down version of the Polish package, along with the creation of a regional environmental center in Budapest and inauguration of a Peace Corps program in Hungary, the first ever in Eastern Europe.

Otherwise, the character of the Budapest visit was quite different from Warsaw and Gdańsk. Internally, the situation was in rapid flux but not nearly as delicate as in Poland. The Hungarian leadership, after the elevation of Pozsgay and Nyers to the party presidium, was vying with opposition figures to see which could control the reform process; the question was not whether reform would proceed, but on whose terms. And internationally, Hungary's room for maneuver was much greater than strategically pivotal Poland. Here, with echoes of 1956, was the interplay between Polish and Hungarian events: when Poland, with its geostrategic weight in Soviet thinking, got away with some new step toward political liberalization, the Hungarians saw this as a green light for themselves. And Hungary, precisely because it was strategically less critical, had more leeway than Poland to test the limits of the possible, in the process setting new standards to which the Poles could aspire.

The president's public remarks in Budapest were accordingly more aggressive, aimed at accelerating the process of change lest half-reforms by the party leadership overwhelm an opposition that was much less unified than Poland's. In his major speech at the Karl Marx University, the president applauded the beginning of limited Soviet troop with-drawals from Hungary, adding, "As those forces leave, let the Soviet leaders know they have everything to gain, and nothing to lose or fear, from peaceful change. . . . The United States believes in the acceleration of productive change, not in its delay. So this is our guiding principle: the United States will offer assistance not to prop up the status quo, but to propel reform."[51]

The official meetings likewise reflected the more nuanced relation-ships unfolding in Hungary's "negotiated revolution."[52] In a meeting with Nyers, Grósz, and Németh—as well as in a separate meeting with Pozsgay, the fourth member of the new party presidium—the president reassured them that "we are not going to complicate things for you. We know that the better we get along with the Soviets, the better it is for you." Repeating the line he had employed with Jaruzelski, he assured them the United States is not going to force you to "choose between East and West."[53]

That evening, the president met with ten leaders of the principal op-position parties and organizations, including the Hungarian Democratic Forum, the Alliance of Young Democrats, and the Free Democratic Party. Despite the perception in Hungary that the United States favored the Budapest intellectuals associated with the Free Democrats,[54] the president was at pains to distance himself from a partisan position in the Hungarian political debate.[55] Like Secretary Baker's subsequent (February 1990) meetings in Sofia and Bucharest with representatives of all the major opposition parties, the meeting was not very successful. The format encouraged participants to vie with one another for atten-tion and vent their partisan grievances, rather than present a cogent overall strategy on which all could agree. Still, the impression of the meetings, along with the tumultuous public response to this first ever visit by an American president, reinforced the sense that Hungary was moving rapidly toward multiparty democracy. The impression was con-veyed symbolically when the president was presented with a piece of the barbed wire that had been removed a few weeks earlier from the Hun-garian-Austrian border.

The impact of Bush's visit was electric. Among ordinary citizens in both countries, it helped replace public cynicism with a sense that meaningful democratic change might indeed be possible and worth struggling for. It is impossible to demonstrate the precise impact on Polish voters, but the anticipation of Bush's impending visit surely contributed to the stunning turnout in favor of Solidarity candidates. During the election campaign in Poland, a prominent Solidarity poster showed the American movie actor Gary Cooper, in a scene from *High Noon*, striding through town wearing, instead of his sheriff's star, a Solidarity badge. *That* was the image we were trying to project.

In both Poland and Hungary, Bush's visit almost certainly had the effect of advancing the political agenda well beyond what had been contemplated in the earlier negotiations between the regimes and opposition forces. Among the Western allies, the visits greatly strengthened the president's ability to command attention at the G-7 Summit and so elevate Eastern Europe to first place on the international agenda.

Concerted Western Action   The Paris Summit meeting of the Group of 7 was held to coincide with the commemoration of the two hundredth anniversary of the French Revolution, a fact that fit nicely with the aim of making democratic change in Eastern Europe the centerpiece of the meeting. The summit's first document was a "Declaration on Human Rights" adopted, in deference to our hosts, almost verbatim from the admirably concise French draft. (Never one to err on the side of deference, Prime Minister Thatcher took the occasion to remind her hosts, in a *Le Monde* interview on the eve of her departure from London, that "human rights did not begin with the French Revolution."[56])

Of course, G-7 summits were supposed to be about the state of the world economy,[57] but this one was dominated more than most by political events, above all change in the East and its implications for East-West relations. It was an occasion to compare notes on several recent encounters with leaders in the East. In addition to the president's just-completed trip to Poland and Hungary, Thatcher had recently hosted Jaruzelski in London, Mitterrand had visited Warsaw and hosted Gorbachev in Paris, and Kohl had just received Gorbachev for a state visit to the Federal Republic. During this visit the two leaders signed a broad joint declaration affirming, *inter alia*, "the rights of all peoples and states to self-determination."[58]

One divisive note in an otherwise shared G-7 perspective was the July 5 announcement that Chancellor Kohl was postponing once again his long-planned visit to Poland. The trip was hostage to an acrimonious conflict over the status of the German minority in Poland and the

German-Polish border,[59] punctuated by West German finance minister Theo Waigel's public hints of continuing German territorial claims against Poland.[60] Kohl's deference to his right-wing constituency on these issues, a pattern that was to continue through the early stages of German unification, did not help in demonstrating Western solidarity with the Polish cause. Kohl's electoral difficulties—there seemed always to be another Land election to which Bonn had to give priority—seemed an insufficient excuse to snub the Poles at this critical moment.

Nonetheless, there was general agreement on the president's proposal for developing "concerted Western action" in support of Polish and Hungarian reforms. The obvious motives behind our approach were to mobilize greater Western assistance, coordinate Western efforts so that they would be complementary rather than competitive, and ensure that assistance was conditional upon real movement toward political and economic reform. There was an equally important political objective, as well: we wanted to lift Western engagement of Eastern Europe out of the traditional zero-sum logic of East-West, especially U.S.-Soviet, relations. "These are not bilateral issues between the United States and the Soviet Union," the president had said in his Hamtramck speech in mid-April. The aim at Paris was to place U.S. engagement in Eastern Europe, which might have been seen in Moscow as an effort to destabilize, within a broader multilateral framework that would allay rather than excite Soviet fears.

Our initial suggestion, broached by the president in letters to his G-7 counterparts before departing from Washington, had been to establish a multinational conference under the aegis of the G-7 itself. As some had predicted they would, the French rejected any "institutionalization" of the G-7 process. With a stalemate developing during the plenary meeting devoted to the topic, Chancellor Kohl proposed, and President Bush and other leaders readily agreed, that the EC Commission be assigned the coordinating role.[61] So it was that the commission took the lead in organizing what came to be called the G-24, or Group of 24, industrialized democracies pledged to provide assistance to Poland and Hungary and ultimately to other countries of the region.

Another option would have been to assign the task to the OECD (Organization for Economic Cooperation and Development), which had much to recommend it from our perspective: it included all 24 of the countries that ultimately joined the assistance effort, and our membership would have given us greater influence over the coordinating process. The EC Commission, however, had better organizational capacity through its existing Brussels bureaucracy across most of the areas relevant to the tasks of economic transition. As association with, or eventual membership in, the EC was a common aspiration among democratic reformers in Eastern Europe, it also made sense for the Community to take the lead role in shaping the transition strategies of countries embarking on political and economic reform. Besides, the EC wanted to take the lead, and our larger European strategy looked to the Community's assuming a constructive leadership role in a more united Europe.

There was another compelling reason for allowing the EC to take the lead. As Willie Sutton put it when asked why he robbed banks, that was "where the money is." Our view from the beginning was that the West Europeans should assume the principal financial assistance burden; it seemed right that the recipients of Marshall Plan aid should take the lead in extending its benefits eastward, fulfilling the Marshall Plan's original pan-European vision.[62] Beyond these lofty considerations was the more prosaic fact that we were unwilling to come up with a significant U.S. financial commitment. Therein lay the principal weakness of our approach. No one questioned that Western Europe should bear the larger burden, but U.S. leadership was essential in helping define the scope of Western commitment. At Paris and even afterwards, when democratic change accelerated all across Eastern Europe, we made it clear that the United States was not prepared to consider assistance even approaching Marshall Plan dimensions. Absent such an American commitment, the European Community never rose to the challenge.

After Paris, the president made a one-day trip on July 17 to the Netherlands—which, like Hungary, had never before been visited by an American president. His speech at the Pieterskerk [St. Peter's Church] in Leiden, the home of Dutch freedom and the site from which many pilgrims departed for the New World, was the ideal venue for linking the Old World and the New and embedding Eastern Europe in this vision. It began with a strong reiteration, building on the Boston University speech two months earlier, of America's support for "a stronger Europe, a more united Europe" as "a natural evolution within our Alliance—the product of true partnership 40 years in the making." The president then turned to "the 'other Europe'—the Europe behind the Wall" and focused on extending the Atlantic idea eastward to embrace all of Europe. The speech summed up both strategic goals and tactical approaches:

Our hope is that the unnatural division of Europe will now come to an end—that the Europe behind the wall will join its neighbors to the West, prosperous and free. . . .

We will never compromise our principles. We will always speak out for freedom. But we understand as well how vital a carefully calibrated approach is in this time of dynamic change. . . . The Soviet Union has nothing—nothing—to fear from the reforms that are now unfolding in some of the nations of Eastern Europe. We support reform—in Eastern Europe and in the Soviet Union. . . . I want to see the Soviet Union chart a course that brings it into the community of nations.

We will play a constructive role in Eastern Europe . . . and in creating an international climate in which reform can succeed. And that is why America's relations with the Soviet Union are so important. Improved relations with the USSR reduce the pressure on the nations of Eastern Europe, especially those on the cutting edge of reform.

The new world we seek is a commonwealth of free nations working in concert—a world where more and more nations enter a widening circle of freedom. . . . Here in Leiden, where the pilgrims dreamed their new world, let us pledge our effort to create a new world in Europe, whole and free, a new world now within our reach.

Finally, citing Winston Churchill's 1946 speech at the same pulpit in the Pieterskerk, the president foreshadowed the belated vindication of Churchill's vision and its extension to all of Europe: "The great wheel has swung full circle. . . . Let freedom reign."[63]

With that, American grand strategy for ending the Cold War had been fully deployed, except for direct engagement with the Soviet Union at the highest level. With events in Eastern Europe moving faster than anyone had foreseen when the strategy was launched in April, a Bush-Gorbachev summit acquired new urgency. Accordingly, aboard Air Force One en route back to Washington, the president drafted an invitation to Gorbachev for an informal meeting to precede the formal summit planned for 1990.

Secretary Baker reiterated the invitation in a July 29 meeting with Soviet foreign minister Eduard Shevardnadze in Paris, using the occasion to discuss the revolutionary developments in Eastern Europe.[64] Though brief, it was an important meeting—not quite a meeting of the minds, but a convergence of thinking on several essentials. Shevardnadze's concern was not with the prospect of sweeping change per se; it was with the danger that the process could lead to a general "destabilization" that "could be catastrophic." His appeal to Baker, therefore, was that the United States act responsibly and not exploit the situation for unilateral advantage. Baker concurred. However, he added that the United States would continue to support democratic change in the region, which we believed did not endanger Soviet security, and that the use of force by the Soviet Union to suppress such changes would have the most severe consequences for U.S.-Soviet relations. Shevardnadze agreed that "it was up to these countries and their peoples to decide for themselves" and assured Baker, though not quite as categorically as we might have wished, that Moscow would not use force against them.[65]

Shortly thereafter, it was vacation time in Washington. The president was off to Kennebunkport, Secretary Baker went to Wyoming, and most of the rest of government scattered.

From Reform to Revolution

Meanwhile, events in Eastern Europe and the Soviet Union were accelerating rapidly. Movement among the Baltic states was particularly dramatic. On July 17, I met in my office with Vytautas Landsbergis, president of the independent Lithuanian popular front organization Sajudis. (Landsbergis was elected president of Lithuania in March 1990, so this, as it turned out, was the first of a series of meetings I had that year with opposition leaders who soon became presidents, prime ministers, or foreign ministers after the collapse of communist rule.) Sajudis, Landsbergis assured me, was unanimous in pressing for Lithuania's full independence and had no interest in some lesser form of autonomy or semi-independent status within the Soviet Union. The goal of Lithuanian independence was beyond question; the only debate was over tactics, and he put himself toward the moderate, gradualist end of the spectrum. His assessment, which I had no reason to disbelieve, was dramatic enough, but events on the ground in Lithuania were moving even faster. A month later, on the fiftieth anniversary of the Hitler-Stalin pact, the Lithuanian parliament declared the Soviet annexation of the Baltic states to be invalid, and Landsbergis issued a public call, in Sajudis's name, for a "free Lithuania."[66] The next day, more than a million people formed a "human chain" across Lithuania, Latvia, and Estonia condemning the Nazi-Soviet pact and demanding freedom and independence.[67] In Georgia, Armenia, Azerbaijan, and Ukraine, where proindependence groups staged a march through Kiev in early September, nationalist demands were also on the rise.

It was around this time that I wrote a memorandum for the president predicting that Czechoslovakia, where three thousand protesters defied the regime's prohibition to commemorate the August 21 anniversary of the 1968 invasion, could not resist the pressures for change much longer. It would be the next to go, and we should begin stepping up our engagement so as to be in a position to influence events as they unfolded. I recall writing that communist rule would be toppled within a year, then hedging my bet in the final draft to "within two years." It took about three months. And Bulgaria "went" even sooner: its veteran communist leader Todor Zhivkov was removed from power on November 10, the day after the night the Berlin Wall fell. (Thereafter my predictive capacities improved. When Alan "Punch" Green, our ambassador-designate to Romania, met with me in late October, shortly before leaving for Bucharest, I told him the Ceauşescu regime had no more than three months. Even then, I was too cautious by a month. The Ceauşescus were executed on Christmas Day.)

Poland Elects a Noncommunist Prime Minister   In Poland, meanwhile, a postelection crisis over Jaruzelski's election as president was resolved by the tactical decision of Solidarity leaders to secure the victory of the same general who had banned their union and thrown many of them into prison less than eight years before. It was a controversial decision within the opposition, achieved by the abstention of several Solidarity deputies and the deliberate invalidation of ballots by seven others. While the United States did not presume to offer specific advice on the issue, the president's public remarks in Warsaw and Gdańsk made it clear that we favored compromise ("a rare alloy of courage and restraint") and adherence by both sides to the terms of the Roundtable Agreement, including Jaruzelski's election as president.

In retrospect, this still seems to have been the right stance for the United States and, more to the point, for the Polish opposition, which bore primary responsibility, to have taken. At this early stage of the revolutions of 1989, Jaruzelski's defeat, and the loss by the communists of the defense and interior ministry portfolios, might have caused a reaction to begin crystallizing in Moscow. Even if these losses did not lead to anything so drastic as military intervention, they might well have prejudiced Soviet attitudes toward revolutionary events only beginning to unfold elsewhere, particularly East Germany. We will never know for sure. We know what Shevardnadze and his closest aides say they were thinking at the time,[68] but we cannot know what they might have *done*, much less what others in the Soviet ruling elite might have pressed on them.

Jaruzelski's election, by the margin of a single vote, cleared the way for negotiations over the composition of the new government. Having obliged on the question of the presidency, Solidarity was less inclined to do so on the composition of the government. If it was to assume coresponsibility for the fate of the Polish economy, Solidarity needed decisive influence over economic policy, including international economic policy. After nearly a month's tense negotiations, during which time two Jaruzelski nominees for prime minister were rejected, the regime and Solidarity ultimately settled on a broad coalition government headed by Catholic intellectual and veteran Solidarity adviser Tadeusz Mazowiecki. The Communist party retained the defense, interior, and transportation ministry portfolios but relinquished most others to Solidarity leaders or nonparty independents.[69] (In a last minute telephone call to Gorbachev by Mieczysław Rakowski, who had succeeded Jaruzelski as Polish Communist party leader, the Soviet leader refrained from involving himself in the composition of the new government aside from reaffirming his support for Jaruzelski.[70]) So it was that Eastern Europe's first noncommunist prime minister in more than four decades was confirmed by the Polish Sejm on August 24. As Wałęsa put it, what Solidarity had hoped to accomplish in four years, it had been obliged to do in four weeks.[71]

Of all the contributors to the peaceful revolutions of 1989 and the end of the Cold War, Tadeusz Mazowiecki ranks among the most important. It is hard to imagine Poland more responsibly led at this critical moment. Together with the key members of his government—Foreign Minister Krzysztof Skubiszewski, Finance Minister Leszek Balcerowicz, and Labor Minister Jacek Kuroń—and the heroic Bronisław Geremek, newly elected leader of the Solidarity group in the Sejm, Mazowiecki conveyed the right combination of resolve and conciliation. This is not to denigrate Wałęsa's indispensable role. Indeed, his decision to forego direct participation in the new government also contributed to its success, by removing himself as a potential lightning rod for hard-line opposition in Poland and, one presumes, Moscow as well. Besides, he was needed as an above-politics symbol of legitimation for the coalition government.

Mazowiecki's first speech to the Sejm was masterful: in direct, honest language that Poles had not heard from their government for a very long time, he outlined his main goals of restoring "a market-oriented economy," the "rule of law," and "freedom of conscience." Above all, while declaring that "we separate ourselves from the past with a thick line," Mazowiecki offered reassurance at home and abroad:

> The principle of struggle . . . must be replaced by the principle of partnership. . . . I want to be the prime minister of all Poles, regardless of their views and convictions, which must not be a criterion for dividing citizens into categories. . . . Poles themselves have to solve Polish problems. . . . The world is watching the transformations taking place [in Poland] with sympathy and hope. . . .
>
> Poland can fulfill an important role in the political, economic, and cultural life of Europe. . . . Europe is one, including the East as well as the West. . . . We desire to maintain good-neighborly, friendly relations with the Soviet Union. . . . We understand the significance of obligations resulting from the Warsaw Pact. To all its members, I state that the government that I will form will respect this treaty.[72]

Most of us dealing with these issues in the United States or in Europe had our epiphanies, our moments of realization that the end of Europe's division might actually be at hand—not just as an aspiration for the 1990s but as an imminent reality. For many it came with the opening of the Berlin Wall on November 9; others may have had premonitions already in early 1989 (although surely not as many as later claimed such prescience). Mine came with the election of Tadeusz Mazowiecki and the early steps taken by his government. The United States was working hard to persuade the Soviet Union that self-determination in Eastern Europe could be achieved in a manner consistent with legitimate Soviet security interests; now, in Poland, the Mazowiecki government was living proof of that contention, offering an early glimmer of what post–Cold War Europe might look like. (To be sure, even the most optimistic scenario for this transition was still being measured in years, not months.)

Polish Shock Therapy and the Stabilization Fund   The new government wasted little time in addressing its most immediate problem: the collapsing Polish economy. In late September, Finance Minister Leszek Balcerowicz visited Washington to present his economic restructuring plan to International Monetary Fund and administration officials.[73] American Embassy Warsaw had cabled an advance copy, which was quickly reviewed at the NSC, State, and Treasury. It was ambitious but conceptually sound, receiving high marks even from the most skeptical Treasury officials. Embedded in the plan, and crucial to its success, was a $700 million IMF loan and a $1 billion currency stabilization fund to be financed by additional Western contributions. (The fund was meant to provide a reserve in the event that the devaluation of the Polish *zloty* precipitated a run on the banks. The hope, which ultimately was fulfilled, was that the mere existence of this fund would be sufficient assurance and that it would not actually have to be drawn down.) When Balcerowicz met with General Scowcroft on September 26, he made it plain that Poland looked to the United States to take the lead in assembling the stabilization fund. The general, as was his wont, was sympathetic but noncommittal.

At staff level, we went to work to develop a plan. Our starting point was that the United States must take the lead, as the Poles asked us to do. To win West European and other backing, the United States had to make the first commitment. Although the Poles had not specified the form of the stabilization fund, we concluded it should be in the form of grants rather than loans or lines of credit, as the latter would only add to Poland's enormous debt burden. This, in turn, would require congressional approval, so we needed to decide what our fair share would be and what would be acceptable on Capitol Hill. In an informal meeting with the NSC legislative staff, I proposed that our contribution be $250 million, or one fourth of the total; others felt a $200 million proposal had a better chance of success. So it was decided, and we began lining up bureaucratic support for the proposal, which ultimately gained approval at a full NSC meeting the next month. We had also established a kind of precedent: from that point on, 20 percent became the informal benchmark for America's fair share of the Western commitment to East European assistance. (Over the next year, as more and more East European countries began to line up for scarce resources, particularly for major balance of payments support, we began to fall in arrears of our "fair share.")

On October 4, we announced our $200 million contribution, and President Bush then sent letters to his G-7 counterparts asking that they pledge the remaining 80 percent.[74] The Europeans moved equally rapidly. On October 24 the European Community announced a $300 million assistance program for Poland and Hungary; West Germany and France followed suit with bilateral programs. At a specially convened summit in Paris on November 18, the EC announced further assistance measures, including creation of a European Bank for Reconstruction and Development.[75]

At a G-24 meeting in Brussels on December 13 (the first such meeting at ministerial level), Secretary Baker noted we were "close to our target" for the stabilization fund, with G-7 pledges totalling around 90 percent of the required $1 billion, and successfully appealed to others to make up the difference. (Except for our contribution and Great Britain's $100 million grant, all the other contributions were in the form of loans and lines of credit, a pattern that was to continue through the G-24.[76]) With that, we had successfully assembled a $1 billion Stabilization Fund—just in time for the January 1, 1990, launching of Poland's ambitious economic restructuring program.

When he visited Washington in mid-November 1989 to receive the Presidential Medal of Freedom and give an historic address before a joint session of Congress, Lech Wałęsa expressed his thanks for U.S. support but called also for a Marshall Plan for Eastern Europe as "an investment in freedom, democracy, and peace." The appeal galvanized congressional action for a substantial increase in U.S. assistance but failed to produce any serious consideration of aid of Marshall Plan dimensions. In addition to trying to prod the United States and other Western countries to "let deeds follow words," Wałęsa also addressed himself to Soviet sensibilities. Echoing Mazowiecki's remarks of two months before, Wałęsa's tone was conciliatory:

> Is there any sensible man understanding the world around him who could now say that it would be better if the Poles kept quiet because what they are doing is jeopardizing world peace?. . . Could we not say that stability and peace face greater threats from countries . . . which do their best to preserve the old, disgraced ways of government contrary to the wishes of their societies?
>
> Things are different in Poland. And I must say that our task is viewed with understanding by our eastern neighbors and their

leader Mikhail Gorbachev. This understanding lays the foundation for new relations between Poland and the U.S.S.R., much better than before.[77]

The Walls Come Tumbling Down

By the time of Wałęsa's visit to Washington in mid-November, the changes he spoke of were becoming an avalanche that would soon engulf all of Eastern Europe. In the early fall, Poland and Hungary were well advanced down the path of democratic transformation, but elsewhere communist regimes were resisting any steps in that direction. By the end of the year, all were gone, swept away by revolutionary upheavals scarcely imaginable just a few months before. Particularly after the opening of the Berlin Wall on November 9–10, events proceeded with such bewildering speed that U.S. and other Western policies could not hope to keep pace. It was in the first half of the year that U.S. policies had helped create the international context in which peaceful democratic transformation in Eastern Europe could occur; by late fall, as one communist regime after another succumbed to popular demands for democratic change, we in Washington often found ourselves in the role of thrilled, not to say astonished, onlookers.[78]

Hungary Opens the Floodgates   In Hungary, reform communism was fast losing ground to multiparty democracy. Lajos Für, leader of the opposition Hungarian Democratic Forum (and later to become Hungarian defense minister), had assured me during a meeting in my office on August 31 that the regime was finished and that the Democratic Forum would win the elections scheduled for March 1990. In separate meetings a week before, Balint Magyar and József Szajer, leaders of the other main democratic opposition parties,[79] had taken a different view, accusing the Democratic Forum of striking a Faustian bargain with the reformist wing of the Communist party, led by Imre Pozsgay. Indeed, the alleged tacit agreement whereby Pozsgay would become president, with the indirect support of the Democratic Forum, quickly fell apart, as the other opposition parties mounted a successful referendum in September calling for the president to be elected by the forthcoming parliament, rather than by the public directly.[80]

The Hungarian roundtable agreement of mid-September attracted less attention than its Polish counterpart in March–April, partly because the free elections it scheduled were still half a year away. It also lacked the drama of the long-running Polish struggle for power between two sworn enemies. In Hungary the contest was more diversified and, well, polite. How could a revolution be so civilized? Yet the results of the Hungarian roundtable were revolutionary indeed, heralding a political opening even more far-reaching than Poland's: opposition political parties, already operating in complete freedom, were to compete in fully open parliamentary elections, with no prior assurances for the ruling party. Hungarians were acting as if their country were already a multiparty democracy. Meanwhile, the party and state leadership scrambled to keep up with rapidly escalating public expectations, abandoning orthodox Marxism from the party platform, changing its name to the Hungarian Socialist party, and proclaiming a new Republic of Hungary (dropping the word "socialist") in which "the values of bourgeois democracy and democratic socialism are equally recognized."[81] It may not have been too little, but it was certainly too late.[82]

Waging a losing battle inside the country, Hungarian leaders took to the road looking urgently for external legitimation. In a mid-September visit to Washington, Mátyás Szürös, speaker of the Hungarian parliament, gave an interview in which he referred to Hungarian neutrality as an imminent possibility.[83] His purpose for coming, however, was to assure the U.S. administration that the new emigration legislation, on which we had insisted as a precondition for extending permanent Most Favored Nation (MFN) trade status, was forthcoming. Armed with that assurance, the president sent the required congressional notification on September 19.[84]

Indeed, Hungarian emigration policy was shifting in ways that were shaking the entire region. In mid-August, nearly two hundred East German "vacationers" in Hungary occupied the West German embassy in Budapest seeking emigration visas, with many more making their ways out illegally via the porous Hungarian-Austrian frontier. In early September, following intense consultations with Bonn, Hungary formally annulled its travel agreement with the GDR and opened its borders to East German emigration.[85] By the end of September, another forty thousand East Germans had emigrated via Hungary, an opening for which Hungary was soon rewarded with U.S. permanent MFN status and a one billion Deutsche Mark credit from Bonn.[86]

Fall of the Berlin Wall Far from relieving the pressure within the GDR, the existence of this escape valve only increased it. Thousands of

East German emigration-seekers were soon massed in the West German embassy in Prague, with at least one and a half million more back in the GDR having formally applied to emigrate.[87] Within the GDR, opposition activists formed an umbrella movement called the "New Forum" to catalyze organized demands for democratic reform (and also to help defuse pressures for mass emigration by creating a mechanism for promoting internal change). Pressure was mounting outside the country as well: at the UN General Assembly in New York in late September, West German Foreign Minister Hans-Dietrich Genscher and Secretary Baker met separately with the Soviet, Czechoslovak, and Hungarian foreign ministers to urge them to try to effect a relaxation of GDR emigration policy. The Erich Honecker regime tried to resolve the impasse through a "dual track" approach. They permitted East German "squatters" in Prague to travel via GDR territory to West Germany (a decision which Genscher announced in an emotional balcony speech in Prague), then tried to slam the door on further such problems by reimposing exit visa requirements for travel even to Czechoslovakia.[88] These combined signs of regime vulnerability and intransigence were all that were needed to excite further public demands for free emigration and democratic change within East Germany.

It is tempting to say that the GDR's fate was sealed at that moment, as some Bonn politicians later claimed to have concluded by late September.[89] Yet here again, "illusions of retrospective determinism" (and perhaps hindsight embellishing memory) come into play. I was in Berlin from October 1 to 3 for an Aspen Institute conference on "Strategic Directions for the Federal Republic of Germany in the 1990s," attended by prominent American, French, British, and German scholars and officials. The papers and my handwritten notes of the sessions make for instructive rereading. Much of the discussion focused on prospects for deployment of the follow-on to the Lance missile (FOTL), the topic du jour of the transatlantic security debate. While East German instability was on people's minds, no one was yet talking of regime collapse or of German unification, except as a long-term possibility. The most daring held out the scenario of an all-German parliament within a five- to ten-year period, but they stopped short of predicting such sweeping change. Nor did my official discussions in East Berlin and then Bonn give a premonition that Germany would be united in exactly one year; the preoccupation was on Honecker's October 3 decision to slam the door on emigration, a move which seemed to herald further repression and spiraling instability in the GDR. (One notable exception was Ambassador

Vernon ["Dick"] Walters, who was already on record as predicting early unification, much to the consternation of official Washington.[90])

Nor did Gorbachev see unification coming when he visited East Berlin October 7 for the GDR's fortieth anniversary celebrations, despite his prophetic warning to East Germany party leader Erich Honecker that "life punishes those who come too late."[91] Of course, Gorbachev's widely quoted remark was itself part of the subsequent dynamic. He was no mere observer of the East German scene but a protagonist in the unfolding drama, and this comment, as well as his public pledge that "all walls . . . will fall,"[92] signaled unmistakably to the East German populace that Soviet power would not rescue the discredited GDR regime. Within days, demonstrations erupted in Leipzig, Dresden, Berlin, and other cities, with a bloodbath in Leipzig October 9 narrowly averted by the last-minute agreement among demonstration leaders and local authorities.[93] Neither Honecker's ouster on October 18 nor the frantic efforts of his successor, Egon Krenz, could stem the torrent. On November 9, through what Krenz would later call a "slight mistake,"[94] a vaguely worded politburo decision to liberalize procedures for emigration and "private trips abroad" was translated by harried border guards into free access through the Wall into West Berlin. Within days, the Berlin Wall was being physically as well as symbolically dismantled.

Bulgaria: From Coup d'État to Revolution   Just a few hours after the opening of the Berlin Wall, Bulgarian party leader Todor Zhivkov unexpectedly resigned in favor of Foreign Minister Petŭr Mladenov, thus ending a 35-year reign that was, as J. F. Brown pointed out, the longest in Bulgarian history—longer even than Tsar Simeon's 34-year reign in the late tenth and early eleventh centuries.[95] Although not fully apparent at the time, opposition to Zhivkov within the party leadership had been building for several years. Georgi Atanasov, Bulgaria's prime minister from 1986 to 1990, later told an interviewer that he and Mladenov spoke in July 1988 about making changes to the party central committee. By July 1989 they and others in the top leadership, including Andrei Lukanov and Defense Minister Dobri Dzhurov, were actively conspiring to bring Zhivkov down.[96]

The opportunity presented itself in October, when a CSCE (Conference on Security and Cooperation in Europe) environmental meeting in Sofia sparked public demonstrations by Ecoglasnost and other nascent opposition groups. While in the meeting hall, the Bulgarian regime was subjected to harsh Western criticism over its brutal repression of its ethnic Turkish minority. Indeed, in response to the mass expulsions of Bulgarian Turks in May 1989, we had recalled our ambassador and sent cables to West European capitals asking whether, or on what terms, Western countries should agree to attend the Sofia meeting. After further debate within the administration, the United States agreed to participate because the subject matter of the conference was both important and directly pertinent to Bulgaria's most significant opposition group, but we also insisted that Western representatives miss no opportunity to hammer the Bulgarian regime over its treatment of ethnic minorities.[97]

Otherwise the U.S. role in these events was nil. When word reached us at the White House of Zhivkov's resignation, my NSC colleague Condi (Condoleezza) Rice and I looked at each other in utter bemusement. We had been so totally preoccupied with Germany—this being the day after the night the Berlin Wall fell—that we had not even thought about Bulgaria for weeks and certainly had no premonition of impending change.

The direct Soviet role was likewise minimal. Atanasov revealed that the Soviet ambassador in Sofia had been informed on November 4 that Zhivkov would be replaced at the November 10 Central Committee plenum. For the next week, Moscow was silent as members of the Bulgarian party's Politburo, coming singly and in groups, went to Zhivkov and urged him to resign. Finally persuaded that he had support neither in Sofia nor in Moscow, Zhivkov relented and announced his resignation to the Central Committee on November 10.[98]

The new Bulgarian leadership, like the Hungarian before it, moved quickly to try to get into step with history. Petŭr Mladenov, the new party leader, promptly announced the end of one-party rule, called for free elections the following spring, and proclaimed full observance of civil liberties on the road to a democratic Bulgaria. It was, as Gale Stokes observed, an "amazing" performance "for a man who had been at the center of single-party Communist power for almost twenty years."[99] "Incredible" might have been a better word: the new leadership had stolen the march on the fledgling democratic opposition, coopting its agenda and embracing the vocabulary, but not the substance, of pluralistic democracy.

It was as good a strategy as any; all it lacked was authenticity and plausibility. There were, to be sure, many within the party leadership who understood that Bulgaria could no longer be governed in the old way and who were ready to embrace *glasnost* and *perestroika* on the road to a more humane, but still socialist, Bulgaria. It was harder to credit that the hearts of committed democrats had been beating within their breasts through long years of service to the Zhivkov regime, nor did their sudden conversion seem entirely believable.

The early, skillful steps by the new Bulgarian leadership did, however, galvanize the main opposition movements to concerted action through a new Union of Democratic Forces, formed December 10 under the chairmanship of dissident philosopher Zhelyu Zhelev. By year's end, a more cohesive party and a more united opposition were preparing for formal roundtable negotiations on Bulgaria's political future, particularly the terms of the forthcoming elections.

The "Velvet Revolution"   After the fall of the Wall, nearly everyone expected Czechoslovakia to be the next to experience a democratic breakthrough. Yet, there had been no movement toward reform from its dogmatic communist regime. In 1988, I was in Prague with a congressional delegation led by Senator John Glenn. When Glenn asked his regime interlocutor, the hard-liner Vasil Bil'ak, why Czechoslovakia did not emulate Soviet reforms, Bil'ak replied, "You Americans used to accuse us of being Soviet puppets, of slavishly following the Soviet model. Now you accuse of us not following the Soviet model closely enough!" It was a good line, but Bil'ak was still a thug.

The Czechoslovak regime nonetheless had been obliged to make some modest concessions to pressures for reform. In December 1987, Gustáv Husák, who had been installed as party leader after the 1968 Soviet invasion, was replaced by Miloš Jakeš; a year later Bil'ak was dropped from the party leadership. Jakeš was a long way from being a reformer, but he and his regime began to adopt the vocabulary of *glasnost* and *perestroika* (or *přestavba*, the Czech version of economic "restructuring"). None of these measures produced real reform, but they had the effect of further weakening the regime's authority. It would not reform, but neither could it continue the ruthless repression which alone could secure its continuation in power. The regime's hesitancy, in turn, prompted dissident and religious activists to begin probing the limits of the possible.

Yet even after the Zhivkov's ouster in Bulgaria, eerily little was happening in Czechoslovakia. On November 13, foreign correspondents contrasted the faint signs of protest in Prague with the vast demonstrations held the month before in Leipzig, only 160 miles away.[100] Jiří Dienstbier, one of the founders of the human rights group Charter 77 (and soon to become, improbably, his country's foreign minister), spoke plaintively to an interviewer a week after the breach of the Berlin Wall: "What surprised everybody was the quick unraveling of things in East Germany. . . . The next step? I hope it's Czechoslovakia. . . ."[101] By the time the interview was published on November 18, Dienstbier's hope was turning into reality.

On November 17, a small, officially sanctioned student demonstration grew spontaneously to an estimated thirty thousand protestors, several thousand of whom broke off from the authorized route and headed for Wenceslas Square, where they were stopped and brutally beaten by riot police. This, as Garton Ash put it in his vivid firsthand account from the revolution's chaotic command center in the Magic Lantern theater, was "the spark that set Czechoslovakia alight."[102] The next day, a gathering of opposition groups convened by Václav Havel formed a "Civic Forum" to serve as spokesman for the democratic aspirations of society at large; the day after, Slovak intellectuals led by the artist Ján Budaj and the prominent movie actor Milan Kňažko[103] met in a Bratislava art gallery to create a similarly inspired organization called "Public Against Violence." Armed with videotapes of the November 17 assault, student supporters went to factories and farms across the country to widen the base of support. An alliance of intellectuals and workers began to form, of the kind that had long existed in Poland but never in Czechoslovakia, not even during the Prague Spring.

On November 20, another demonstration took place on Wenceslas Square, this time gathering hundreds of thousands of ordinary citizens. As demonstrations continued, Havel was joined in Wenceslas Square for a dramatic joint appearance with Alexander Dubček, prime minister during the Prague Spring, providing a powerful symbol of historical continuity and (Dubček being Slovak) national solidarity.

The resignation of Jakeš and the rest of the party leadership on November 24 did nothing to slow the momentum of protest. When virtually the entire country joined in a two-hour general strike on November 27, just ten days after protests had begun, the tide had shifted decisively to the democratic opposition, who correspondingly escalated their demands to include a voice in the composition of a new coalition government. The proposal by new prime minister Ladislav Adamec for a sham "coalition" government with almost no opposition figures was rejected out of hand by Civic Forum. Adamec himself resigned almost as soon as he had been appointed, replaced by Marián Čalfa, an obscure Slovak communist who left the party in early 1990.

As with Bulgaria, the direct American role in these events was negligible. We did, however, exert indirect influence where it counted most—with the Soviet leaders. On December 1–3, during the most delicate phase of negotiations between Civic Forum and the communist regime, Presidents Bush and Gorbachev met off Malta for their first summit.[104] The success of the summit, covered extensively by Czechoslovak television, served to embolden opposition leaders and the populace at large, just as Gorbachev's subsequent meeting with Warsaw Pact leaders in Moscow served to persuade Czechoslovakia's communist regime that its time was up.[105]

The new Czechoslovak government, with noncommunists in the majority, was sworn in on December 10. At month's end, Dubček was named chairman of the Federal Assembly, which then elected Václav Havel president of Czechoslovakia. *Havel na Hrad!*—Havel to the Castle!—had gone from daring chant to improbable reality in a matter of a few thrilling weeks.

Romania: From Revolution to Coup d'État   Ever the maverick, Romania had so far resisted the changes sweeping the region. Indeed, because the Ceauşescu regime had made a career of distancing itself from Moscow, and of developing its own elaborate system of internal security rather than relying on Soviet power, it was less directly affected than others by Gorbachev's reforms. These same factors also made it a more brittle regime, incapable of ruling in any fashion other than the repression that had grown increasingly brutal as conditions in Romania worsened and public restiveness grew. Whether Ceauşescu and his wife and coruler, Elena, were oblivious to these conditions or all too aware of their political implications—one could adduce evidence on both sides of the ledger—hardly mattered toward the end. After the collapse of communist regimes elsewhere in the fall of 1989, all that was needed was an event to trigger a revolution to unseat the Warsaw Pact's last and most truly evil leader.

It began in Timişoara, with Romanians and Hungarians from this multiethnic community joining in protest against the expulsion of Hungarian reformed pastor László Tökés from his home and parish. Following several days of growing protests, army units arrived December 17 to crush the demonstration in a massacre that left nearly a hundred dead, though widely reported estimates at the time placed the number in the thousands.[106] Within days, as Brown put it, "the Timişoara rioting had become the Romanian Uprising."[107] As demonstrations erupted throughout the country and army units began to join the protestors, Ceauşescu cut short a visit to Iran and returned to Bucharest, making what proved to be his last public appearance before a huge crowd in Palace Square on December 21. And a bizarre one it was: television cameras captured Ceauşescu's bewilderment as ritual cheers from the combined "official" and spontaneous crowd below turned to shouts of derision, before Elena ushered him off the balcony and the television screens went blank in Romania. The next day, a group of former party officials, joined in the course of the afternoon by well-known dissidents, appeared on Romanian television as leaders of a self-proclaimed National Salvation Front, declaring itself the new provisional government and pledging to establish full democracy.

Here is how a White House statement of that day put it: "Today, December 22, 1989, a terrible burden appears to have been lifted from Romania: the burden of despotic dictatorial rule. . . . The United States salutes the decision by representatives of the Romanian Government to order a cessation of the brutal police repression and to bring a merciful end to the Ceauşescu dictatorship. . . . We hope the Romanian Government will now move quickly to respond to the demands of its people for democratic change."[108] The verb "appears" turned out to be well chosen, for the events of the next few days were confusing in the extreme.

With most of official Washington away for the holidays, an interagency working group had been formed to coordinate U.S. policy during the crisis, through daily teleconferences and frequent telephone calls.[109] We were not lacking for information: television coverage, along with a constant flow of cables from Embassy Bucharest and other posts (reporting reactions of key foreign governments) allowed us to follow these events, responding as necessary, literally as they unfolded. In this case as in others, the glut of information was itself one of the problems of crisis management: keeping up with the mountains of reporting, essential though it was, also threatened to intrude on the more pertinent business of producing sensible policy.

After December 22, our main aims were to throw U.S. support behind the provisional government, discredit as "outlaws" the remaining

Ceauşescu loyalists, and help end the bloodshed by underscoring the futility of further resistance by those forces. We also sought to ensure the widest possible support for those positions among foreign governments, including the Soviet. Given the uncertainties surrounding the Front and its intentions, as well as the ambiguous roles played by Securitate officials, we were at pains to link our support to the popular mandate for democratic change and the Front's expressed commitments to that end. Together with other Western countries, we also made it clear that we would extend economic assistance to the new government as and if it proceeded down the path of political and economic reform. Whatever our misgivings about the Front and its early, mysterious behavior, this course of action was clearly preferable to remaining neutral and waiting for the dust to settle.

One event bears explanation. On December 24 Secretary Baker was quoted as supporting a Soviet intervention in Romania on behalf of prodemocracy forces. It was an unfortunate comment, but one that was not quite as egregious as it seemed.[110] The context was this. The day before Baker made his remark, officials of the provisional government appealed to Moscow and the West for help, claiming they were running out of ammunition and feared being overwhelmed by the well-armed Ceauşescu loyalists. Responding to this appeal, French Foreign Minister Roland Dumas offered to send a brigade of volunteers and said he would welcome Soviet assistance as well, without specifying whether he meant sending fresh supplies of ammunition or rendering more direct "assistance." It was in response to a question about Dumas's position that Baker made his statement. The desire not to offend his French counterpart may be part of the explanation, but Baker evidently was swayed by the argument that Soviet intervention on the side of prodemocracy forces, in response to their specific appeal for help, would be preferable to seeing the revolution fail and the Ceauşescus returned to power. It was an argument that had a few adherents at staff level during those chaotic days, during which a successful counterrevolution by Ceauşescu loyalists seemed a real danger; however, the dominant view was that the United States could not legitimize Soviet intervention in Eastern Europe, no matter the circumstances. This position was made clear the next day in a White House "clarification" of the secretary's remarks, expressly opposing any Soviet intervention in Romania.[111]

The unfortunate irony of this episode was its juxtaposition with the ongoing U.S. intervention in Panama. After Moscow had politely declined the offer to intervene in Romania, the image seemed to be that of one superpower disdaining the role of forcible arbiter of its neighbors' disputes, while the other continued to reserve the right to do so. A Soviet foreign ministry official suggested bitterly that Moscow had ceded the "Brezhnev Doctrine" to the United States.[112]

By Christmas Day, the question was moot as far as Romania was concerned, as word of the capture, trial, and execution of the Ceauşescu pair reached the outside world. The episode nonetheless helps recapture the enormous confusion and uncertainty surrounding the Romanian Revolution and its aftermath. Was it a revolution or a palace coup? That spontaneous revolts broke out in several Romanian cities is indisputable. That prior contacts existed among disaffected or former officials of the Ceauşescu regime is likely but undocumented, nor do we know the scope of any organized or semiorganized coup-plotting among those who emerged as leaders of the National Salvation Front. These and many other mysteries of the events of December 1989 in Romania will have to be sorted out by future historians.

Available evidence and informed analysis to date suggest that this was a revolution followed immediately by (or coincident with) a coup d'état. Yet the role of the National Salvation Front remained controversial. Did it rescue the revolution by stepping in to fill a vacuum of power, or was the revolution "hijacked" and its democratic goals betrayed by the Front and its supporters?[113] From the perspective of U.S. policy, these were issues not to be judged a priori but rather demonstrated by the subsequent deeds of the NSF-led provisional government. We viewed its mandate, pending the free elections it had pledged, to derive from the democratic aspirations of the popular revolution (the "spirit of Timişoara") and its expressed commitment to democracy. Thus, from our perspective, the Romanian Revolution, like those that preceded it in the fall of 1989, was an authentic democratic revolution.

A Summing Up   The superficial similarities of the revolutions of 1989 were striking: spiraling mass demonstrations, creation of umbrella opposition movements with similar names (New Forum, Civic Forum, Democratic Forum) that even their organizers sometimes confused,[114] regime crackdowns followed by vacillation and then concessions, and formal roundtable negotiations leading to eventual regime capitulations. Yet the processes at work were much more differentiated than they first

appeared. Poland and Hungary followed expected paths, albeit with unexpected results, consistent with the long history of their experience
under communist rule. Yet if these were both "*refolutions*," to borrow
Garton Ash's term for a combination of reform from above and revolution from below, then the accents were different: more on reform in the
Hungarian case, more on revolution in the Polish. Bulgaria's evolution
came closest to what might have been expected for the region as a
whole: communist leaders jettisoning the hard-line leadership and seizing the mantle of democratic reform, using their considerable material
and organizational resources to divide and co-opt opposition groups.
That Romania would be the exception was predictable: it would have
been hard to imagine a regime in which power and position were linked
so personally to the ruling family, relinquishing power through peaceful
negotiation.

The two most surprising cases were the East German and the
Czechoslovak, for few would have predicted that such cynical and hardened party leaderships would have thrown in the towel so quickly. In
retrospect, one can perhaps see why this happened. When public demands exploded in the fall of 1989, there were three basic options for
the East European communist leaderships: capitulation, brutal repression, and temporizing negotiation. The third option, tried by the Polish,
Hungarian, and Bulgarian leaders (Romania again being a case apart),
was unavailable to the Czechoslovak and East German regimes. The
former lacked credibility because of its role as liquidator of the Prague
Spring reforms, while the latter could not embark on democratic reform
without calling into question the GDR's raison d'être as a separate German state. As an East German party official put it in an August 1989
interview, "What right to exist would a capitalist GDR have alongside a
capitalist Federal Republic?"[115]

For these regimes, therefore, there were but two options,[116] and both
regimes, it should be noted, pursued repression as the preferred course
of action before their ultimate capitulation. Even at the eleventh hour,
when force on a massive scale would have been required, a "Chinese solution" (referring to the June 1989 massacre in Tiananmen Square) was
actively considered. As has been seen, the Honecker regime in fact ordered such a crackdown on October 9;[117] similarly, as late as November
24, only hours before the entire party leadership resigned, the Czechoslovak defense minister's proposal for a massive military crackdown was
narrowly defeated by the party's central committee.[118]

The metaphors one grasps to describe these events—tumbling walls, avalanches, and sparks that ignited, to say nothing of falling dominos—point to the difficulties of analyzing any one of these revolutions in isolation from the others, or outside the larger international context. (It is for these reasons that the burgeoning literature on "regime change" falls wide of the mark in trying to explain the revolutions of 1989.[119]) The Velvet Revolution would not have happened—at least not in 1989—had not the Berlin Wall fallen, and that would not have occurred save for the prior, successful challenges to communist rule in Poland and Hungary. And none of these events would have transpired—not so soon nor so peacefully—had not there been a Soviet leadership that had undertaken a fundamental redefinition of Soviet security interests and which was further redefining those interests as wholly unexpected events transpired. Much of this redefining was attributable to Mikhail Gorbachev and Eduard Shevardnadze, and much of it was born of the necessity imposed by an eroding empire and a deteriorating economy.

Yet Soviet attitudes were shaped by the international context and by the efforts of the United States and its Western allies to rally firmly behind democratic change in Eastern Europe and to conduct themselves in ways that helped persuade Gorbachev and Shevardnadze that these changes could be accommodated on a radically new basis. Publicly and privately, President Bush and Secretary Baker must have said a hundred times that the changes unfolding in Eastern Europe "did not threaten legitimate Soviet security interests." It was hard to disentangle truth from tactics in this assertion: we believed the Soviet Union could find its security in ways other than a ring of client states around its borders, but there was no gainsaying the loss of Soviet power and influence that these events portended. It was obviously in our interests to push this line, just as the notion of a "Europe whole and free" served certain immediate interests, even though its ultimate meaning was obscure.

The scope and speed of change likewise made it difficult for Moscow to arrest the process, even if such had been its intent. As an NSC briefing paper put it just before President Bush's December 1–3 meeting with Gorbachev off the coast of Malta, "The Soviets had lost control of their policy toward Eastern Europe. They had not anticipated current developments [and] were now reacting to events day to day."[120] Indeed, by the time of this long-awaited meeting between the two leaders, Soviet attention and ours already had moved from democratic change in Eastern Europe to the prospect of a headlong rush toward German unification.

3

The Diplomacy of German Unification

AFTER THE ACHIEVEMENT of German unity in the fall of 1990, many Germans, beginning with Chancellor Kohl, were effusive in their gratitude for U.S. support, saying that unification could not have happened without us. For American officials who had worked so hard for German unity, those were nice words to hear. But they were not quite accurate. Unification could have occurred without us, all right, but it could only have been consummated as a result of a separate German-Soviet arrangement. If the United States had joined the French and British in opposing unification, what choice would the Germans have had but to strike whatever deal they could with Moscow, which held the key by virtue of its military occupation of East Germany? Who could have blamed the Germans, if they had been abandoned by their closest allies at the moment that their deepest national aspiration was at hand? And if Bonn had been left alone to deal with Moscow, what kind of terms would the Germans have been obliged to accept, with what infringements on German sovereignty, and with what implications for the future of European security?

U.S. support was essential, not so much for German unification itself, but for ensuring that the process came out right—with Germany enjoying full sovereignty from the moment of unification; with all of Europe, including the Soviet Union, accepting and supporting this outcome; and with the essential structures of European and transatlantic security intact and ready to adapt to radically changed circumstances. Although our West German counterparts never fully grasped this fact, the United States had as much at stake in the process of unification as they did. Our diplomacy during this period was harnessed to securing, not German, but American interests and to broader considerations of European stability and security. Happily, American and German interests, though not identical, converged to a large degree; indeed, U.S.-German relations during the period, while more complex and difficult than has been recorded to date, achieved a remarkable level of coordination in successful pursuit of our common goals.

An account of American diplomacy during the period should in no way detract from Bonn's masterful role in overseeing economic and political union between the two German states in less than a year, and in managing its delicate relationship with Moscow. These aspects of the story have been well told by key West German participants in the process.[1] Yet the successful conclusion of German unification also required close U.S.–West German cooperation, and there was nothing foreordained about the extraordinarily close coordination that was achieved in 1989 and 1990. Foreign Minister Hans-Dietrich Genscher later put it this way: "If America had so much as hesitated, we could have stood on our heads" and gotten nowhere.[2]

Nor was it foreordained that Moscow, whose role was of course crucial, would assent to unification and to Germany's remaining in the Atlantic alliance. Timothy Garton Ash was right in concluding that by mid-1990 Gorbachev "was weak enough to feel he had to concede German unification within the Western Alliance but still strong enough to push this through at home," but Garton Ash too quickly ascribed this state of affairs to the handiwork of "Lady Luck."[3] To be sure, the deterioration of the Soviet internal situation was the product of forces beyond U.S. influence. But it was "no accident" (as the Marxists used to say) that Gorbachev by mid-1990 was confronted with a solid international consensus in support of Germany's unification within the alliance and so was in a weaker position to try to oppose this outcome. This international solidarity was the product, in large measure, of strenuous American diplomatic efforts from the beginning, based on a dual strategy of isolation and reassurance. We also assigned a high priority to strengthening Gorbachev's position internally—not, as some pundits argued, out of nostalgic allegiance to a Soviet leader whose star was already waning, but because we felt that Gorbachev's continued foreign policy authority was essential to gaining Soviet acceptance of German unification within the alliance.

Alexander Moens, in his crisp analysis of American diplomacy during the period, identified four pivotal points in which it was decisive:

"First, it shielded Chancellor Kohl in early December 1989, when he jumped ahead of other world leaders on the unification issue. Second, it committed France, the UK and the USSR to the Two-Plus-Four negotiating framework in February 1990. Third, it forged a common Western position on German membership in NATO in late February. Fourth, it brokered a package of guarantees in May and June that led the USSR to accept the idea of a united Germany being in NATO."[4]

To these should be added one prior consideration that made our initial steps more surefooted than those of the British, French, Soviets, and indeed the Germans themselves: namely, that German unification was on our agenda long before the opening of the Berlin Wall on November 9, 1989. This prospect was embedded in our thinking by the time of President Bush's May 31 speech in Mainz, in which he advanced the idea of the United States and Germany as "partners in leadership." In his memoirs, Bush recounts a long discussion about German unification that he initiated with French President Mitterrand during a meeting in Kennebunkport on May 20.[5] While we, like the rest of the world, were caught by surprise by the speed of the process, we nonetheless had seen it coming, had considered our options in the context of a broader strategic review, and were better prepared than others to respond creatively to the tumultuous events beginning in the fall of 1989.

It was an extraordinarily complex period. In the spring and early summer of 1990, according to one count, President Bush and Chancellor Kohl met four times, Secretary Baker and Foreign Minister Shevardnadze ten times, Baker and Foreign Minister Genscher 11 times, and Genscher and Shevardnadze eight times in May and June alone.[6] Added to these were many NATO, European Community, and Conference on Security and Cooperation in Europe (CSCE) meetings, others associated with the Two Plus Four process, and countless telephone conversations and messages. Owing partly to the speed of events, it was a period in which pure diplomacy, unencumbered by the usual domestic political processes, played a central role more reminiscent of nineteenth- than twentieth-century international relations. Karl Kaiser was not overstating the case in calling this the "most intensive phase of bilateral and multilateral diplomacy in European history."[7]

The present chapter cannot do full justice to this rich diplomatic history, still less to the complex set of Two Plus Four negotiations so skillfully led on our side by Secretary Baker. It focuses instead on the most critical issues involved, chiefly but not exclusively from the American perspective. Its judgments do not depart radically from those already offered by West German participants in the process and by scholars with access to American and other policymakers,[8] but it depicts a much more complex set of relationships—between the United States and Germany, particularly—than has so far been described. With all due consideration of the gravity of the issues involved, the diplomacy of the period had the character of a complex, high stakes chess match—or, rather, if the metaphor will stretch this far, of multiple, interrelated chess matches in which moves on one board simultaneously affected the play on other boards.

Opening Moves

This was not the way it was supposed to happen. German unification was supposed to be a *consequence* of the end of the division of Europe, not one of its driving forces. This logic and sequence were embedded in West German *ostpolitik* from the time of Willy Brandt onward. Germans and non-Germans alike had thought that the *German question* would arise within the context of an already much transformed European scene, following a period in which the prospect of a reunited Germany could be debated, its future contours shaped, and the new reality gradually (perhaps grudgingly) accommodated.

Yet, as West German president Richard von Weizsäcker once put it, "A question does not seek to exist merely because no one has an answer for it."[9] When the question arose in the fall of 1989, a consequence of East Germany's peaceful, democratic revolution, it caught most of the world by surprise. This unpreparedness helps explain the confused and highly emotional reactions on the part of the French, British, Soviet, and other leaders, who sought first to dismiss the prospect altogether and then to defer it to some distant, more convenient date (preferably long after their terms in office had expired).[10] There is no doubt that initial American reactions were more measured and sensible than those of our French, British, and Soviet counterparts, and no amount of retrospective rationalization on their part can explain away the clumsiness of their early steps. (The French would have us believe that Mitterrand's early meeting with Gorbachev in Kiev was designed to help German unification along; Shevardnadze later said he saw it coming from the beginning and was only trying to secure the best possible terms; and so on.) Yet there was more method to their seeming madness than has so far been credited.

The chess metaphor is apt, for the policies of key leaders immediately following the opening of the Berlin Wall are better understood if one thinks of this period as the opening stage of a chess match, in which players are trying to establish a position in the middle of the board. These moves were not yet directed toward an ultimate strategy; rather, they were designed to establish a strong position against any possible countermoves. The players would then wait to see how the game developed before acting more boldly. Dropping the metaphor—and not a moment too soon!—the efforts of the key participants in this early period were to establish their influence over the process of German unification. The West Germans were as determined to establish their primacy as others were to make it known that German unification affected their interests as well and that they meant to defend those interests, even at the risk of giving offense.

Soviet Warnings   Helmut Kohl later termed his June 1989 heart-to-heart talk with Gorbachev in the chancellor's bungalow overlooking the Rhine "the decisive moment" in securing Gorbachev's acceptance of German unification. Moreover, he saw the German-Soviet joint declaration issued during that visit as a "sensational" document for its affirmation of the "right of peoples to self-determination."[11] These are extravagant judgments. They may capture the evolution of Gorbachev's thinking on Germany and especially his hopes for Soviet-German cooperation, but they go much too far in implying that the Soviet leader had by that time accepted German unification as an imminent reality.

When President von Weizsäcker raised the question of German unity during a visit to Moscow in mid-1987, Gorbachev went so far as to acknowledge that history would decide what would happen in a hundred years—an interval that von Weizsäcker was able to halve by gaining Gorbachev's agreement to the proposition, "or perhaps fifty."[12] By the time of his meeting with Kohl in Bonn two years later, events in Poland and Hungary had pushed the issue closer to the fore. But it was still sufficiently remote, or so it seemed, to permit Gorbachev to ruminate about future possibilities, comfortable in the belief that no action was required on his part to arrest the process. Foreign Minister Shevardnadze's *post facto* contention that he saw German unification as "inevitable" as early as 1986 belongs in the same category, as does a far-reaching presentation on "ending the division" (of Europe and of Germany) reportedly was made by Vyacheslav Dashitschev to an advisory council of the Soviet foreign ministry in November 1987. As Garton Ash put it,

> There is enough retrospective and circumstantial evidence to suggest that by 1987, in the context of a general questioning and rethinking of all the basic positions of Soviet foreign policy, even the question of eventually overcoming the division of Germany into two states was privately discussed at a high and even at the highest level in Moscow. But there is no evidence whatsoever that this was translated into operative policy. Quite the contrary. Dashitschev himself says that his speculative proposals were roundly repudiated by virtually the whole foreign policy apparatus of the Soviet party-state.[13]

As the spiral of events in the late summer and early fall of 1989 brought the German question into sharper relief, Soviet policy hardened considerably. In a speech to the UN General Assembly in late September, even as he was working with Secretary Baker and Foreign Minister Genscher to enable East German asylum-seekers to reach West Germany via Hungary and Czechoslovakia, Shevardnadze issued a blistering assault on "national selfishness" and warned against those who would "ignore the interests of other peoples": "Fascism, which started the war, is the extreme and ugliest form of nationalism and chauvinism. German Nazism marched under the banner of revanchism. Now that the forces are again becoming active and are seeking to revise and destroy the post-war realities in Europe, it is our duty to warn those who, willingly or unwillingly, encourage those forces."[14]

A few days after the opening of the Berlin Wall, Shevardnadze warned more pointedly about the "attempt of some circles in [West Germany] to place the question of the reunification of Germany on the agenda."[15] Gorbachev, in a speech of the same day, declared German unification "no issue of current policy."[16] Both warned visiting French foreign minister Roland Dumas that talk of German unification was causing "great anxiety" and also sent frantic messages to Western leaders calling for urgent Four Power consultations. Later on, as if reciting the mantra could make it so, the Soviet foreign ministry spokesman repeated the official attitude toward German unification: "It is not on the agenda."[17]

An "Anglo-French Axis"?   French, British, and other West European leaders were scarcely less determined to push the German question off the immediate agenda and into the indefinite future.[18] Just after the fall of the Berlin Wall, French president Mitterrand undertook a series of steps that belied his earlier protestation that he was "not afraid of unification"—convening an urgent EC summit in Paris, publicizing the fact of a long telephone conversation with Gorbachev about the German situation, and, without consulting Kohl, announcing an early visit to East Germany.[19] At the Paris Summit on November 18, Mitterrand and other EC leaders were at pains to relegate German unification to the distant and indefinite future. As Prime Minister Thatcher put it at the close of the session (as well as in a message to President Bush just before her departure for Paris), "The question of borders is not on the agenda. They should stay as they are."[20]

At the time, we in the U.S. administration knew very well of the antipathy of the British and French, to say nothing of the Soviets, toward unification and suspected they would seek to derail or at least postpone the process. The reality was worse than we knew. In her memoirs, Thatcher recounts having discussed her opposition to unification with Gorbachev in Moscow in September, and even earlier with Mitterrand.[21] At the EC Summit in Strasbourg in December, in two private talks with Mitterrand arranged at the latter's suggestion, the two leaders agreed on what she termed an "Anglo-French political axis" to "check the German juggernaut," later working out specific joint measures to try to slow down German unification.[22]

While Thatcher later laid the blame on Mitterrand for "the fact that little or nothing in practical terms came of these discussions,"[23] it was in fact the French who proved the more determined and effective in using their not inconsiderable influence to retard the process. They seized the diplomatic initiative within the EC, exploited the Polish border issue to disrupt the Two Plus Four process, and worked separately with Moscow and East Berlin to try to build a constituency against early unification before finally abandoning this rear guard effort in the spring of 1990. The British foreign office, meanwhile, never translated the prime minister's tough position into consistent policy. To the contrary, although British negotiators could be tough on key points, their drafting skills more often than not facilitated the Two Plus Four negotiations.

However emotional the response and clumsy the execution, both leaders successfully (perhaps only semiconsciously) conveyed another message: we may not be able to stop unification or even slow it appreciably, but we can certainly make life difficult unless our concerns are taken into account as participants in the process. It was a message that Bonn and Washington alike had to take seriously.

American Support for Unification   American support for unification was as swift and unequivocal as British and French reactions were grudging and, at best, ambivalent. The reasons, as has been seen, were several, and more complex than the seemingly automatic U.S. expression of support might have suggested. Not everyone in the U.S. administration shared former secretary of state Henry Kissinger's conviction that unification was "inevitable" as of mid-November 1989, or Ambassador (to the FRG) Vernon Walters's earlier prediction that unification would come quickly.[24] For one thing, the leaders of the East German revolution were at that moment declaring themselves in favor of a separate, democratic, and "socialist" GDR. While this "third road" seemed no more likely to succeed than previous efforts elsewhere in Eastern Europe toward "reform communism," we did not then know how quickly these figures and their political platform would be eclipsed by a headlong rush to unity. Nor had the full magnitude of the East German economic collapse yet made itself manifest. Our view, rather, was that the process of internal change in the GDR was "inexorable," as President Bush put it, and that unification was the likely, but not the inevitable, result.[25] Not even the boldest forecasters saw it coming within the year.

Thus, while surprised by the speed of events, we had nonetheless seen unification coming sooner than others, including the Germans themselves, and had thought through our position well in advance—even before the president's May 31 call in Mainz for the United States and Germany to become "partners in leadership."[26] We had seen this potential at the time of the Polish Roundtable Agreement in the spring of 1989,[27] worked to build a strong partnership with Bonn in anticipation of this prospect, and made clear our unequivocal support for German unification well before November 9. From the perspective of core interests, we did not have the British and French worry of strategic loss and indeed had much to gain from the prospect of a strong, democratic, and united Germany, whose security would no longer require such a massive investment of American resources.

Our support, therefore, was genuine, consistent with our principles, and based on careful consideration of our interests. Yet along with this positive endorsement was the consideration that the United States could not be seen as opposing German unification, or even showing hesitancy: if it were coming, as we believed likely, it would come whether we willed it or not. Moreover, active U.S. support would be required to ensure that it occurred in a manner consistent with European stability and our own interests. This meant, among other things, that we needed to forge the closest possible coordination with Bonn during the process of unification and lay the foundations for a strong German-American partnership thereafter. The German question, after all, was not only about unification but about how, or whether, Germany could fit into a secure and stable European order. Mindful of Kissinger's earlier judgment that Germany was "too big for Europe, too small for the world," we held the conviction that a strong U.S. link was needed both to balance the weight of a united Germany in Europe and to encourage this new entity to play an active and constructive global role.

Given the outspoken opposition of the British, French, and especially of the Soviets, it was imperative to move from rhetorical U.S. support to active U.S. leadership. Accordingly, we worked quickly to arrange a series of key meetings before and after President Bush's Malta Summit with Gorbachev, which had been announced at the end of October. These included meetings with Genscher in Washington on November 21, with Thatcher at Camp David on November 24, with the NATO allies at a summit in early December (just after Malta), and, finally, with Mitterrand at St. Martin in mid-December.

During Genscher's discussions with President Bush and Secretary Baker, both sides agreed that events in the GDR were pushing unification closer to the fore, perhaps at a faster pace than anyone had been expecting. They felt that there was a danger that the growing chorus of international opposition would prejudice the prospects for German unification before the process had even begun. Both sides also saw a need to lend some stability to the process, in order to avert a chaotic breakdown of order and possible violent backlash in the GDR, whether deliberate or unintended, that could set back the prospects for eventual unification.[28] As he had done with Kohl in two earlier telephone conversations, the president assured Genscher that the United States would lend its active support to unification. More specifically, he would use the forthcoming meetings with his British, French, and Soviet counterparts to avert early intrusion of the Four Powers in a process that should be a "matter for the Germans" to decide.[29]

Kohl's Gambit: "Ten Points"   A week later, Kohl made his own dramatic move to preempt Four Power involvement, as well as regain the initiative domestically, in a speech to the West German parliament outlining a ten-point, stage-by-stage process toward eventual German unification. It called for urgent humanitarian and other economic assistance to the GDR and the development of "confederative structures" between the two Germanies (after the holding of free elections in the GDR). The eventual goal would be the "reattainment of German state unity" within the context of European integration and the overcoming of the division of Europe.[30] The speech was an exercise in political brinkmanship, aimed at setting the terms and pace of German unification before British, French, and Soviet efforts to arrest the process had been fully formed.

The "ten point" speech was nearly as much of a surprise, though not quite the bombshell, in Washington as it was in London, Paris, and Moscow[31]—the key difference being that we shared Kohl's main objectives while the others did not. We could also understand Kohl's reasons, as he explained them in a telephone call to President Bush the next day, for keeping the speech secret even (or especially) from his own foreign minister. And while some of us at staff level saw it as a "clear breach" (to borrow Prime Minister Thatcher's characterization[32]) of the spirit of close coordination we thought had been agreed upon, we could not help but admit that Kohl had pulled off a tactical coup, which we might have tried ourselves had we been in his shoes.

I also figured, although no German official ever said so, that it was meant to send a signal not only to Paris, London, and Moscow, but also to Washington—virtually on the eve of the president's meeting with Gorbachev off Malta—that Bonn intended to assert primacy on the German question and not defer leadership on this issue to the Four Powers individually or collectively.[33] On that point, there was no disagreement in Washington. Nor did Kohl's speech, irritating though it was to have it sprung on us, prevent the establishment of the exceptionally close American–West German coordination that characterized the entire process of German unification. It did, however, underscore that points of tension, competition, and, on some issues, real political differences existed beneath the surface harmony of our bilateral cooperation.

The Evolution of American Strategy

Our immediate concern was that Kohl's brinkmanship might backfire and provoke a hardening of British and French attitudes or even an instinctive, potentially dangerous Soviet effort to prop up a failing East German regime. Accordingly, it was important for the United States to weigh in with a policy statement that renewed our support for unification while also offering some reassurance to Moscow and others that the process was not spinning out of control. (Was this the reaction Kohl hoped to provoke from his American friends? If so, his gambit worked to perfection.) This U.S. position, then, would be the basis for President Bush's discussions with Gorbachev at the Malta Summit and, at a NATO Summit in Brussels immediately thereafter, for gaining allied endorsement of a set of generally shared Western principles on unification.

The day after Kohl's speech, Secretary Baker previewed "four principles" on German unification that the president would advance in Malta and Brussels: (1) "self-determination should be pursued without prejudice to its outcome"; if there is to be unification, it should occur (2) "within the context of Germany's continuing alignment with NATO and an increasingly integrated European Community" and (3) as a "peaceful, gradual, . . . step-by-step process"; and (4) following the principles of the Helsinki Final Act (of the Conference on Security and Cooperation in Europe), the inviolability of existing borders should be respected.[34] Two of these four dealt specifically with what we considered crucial elements missing from Kohl's ten points: NATO membership and the border issue (meaning the permanence of the existing German-Polish border).[35] Thus, while offering strong American support to German unification in the face of sharply negative international reactions to the Kohl speech, the principles were designed to superimpose an American agenda over and above the points the chancellor had outlined. By stressing gradualism and a controlled process, the principles also aimed at building a firm Western consensus and assuaging British, French, and especially Soviet concerns about what seemed a runaway unification train.

Crisis Contingencies   Soviet attitudes, like ours and Bonn's, were also preoccupied with the mounting instability in the GDR and the danger of confrontation that might involve East German and Soviet military forces. These concerns reached a peak in early December, with renewed street demonstrations (prompted by revelations that Stasi [East German state security] files were being systematically purged) and confrontations, or near-confrontations, at East German and Soviet military installations. What appeared in the open press was but a fraction of the reports, most of them fragmentary and inconclusive, that we were receiving through official channels. That many of the incidents smacked of Stasi provocation—i.e., events either manufactured or greatly magnified to provide a pretext for a crackdown—only heightened our concern, particularly in light of evidence, such as that emerging from Gera on December 9, that some Stasi officials were inciting their units to armed resistance.[36]

Soviet intentions were difficult to gauge. Soviet military forces in the GDR were placed on higher alert status, ostensibly to protect Soviet military bases and nuclear weapons depots, and we were warned by Soviet officials that these units "would be obliged to use force" if the security situation got out of control.[37] While we judged these measures to be defensive, we could not exclude the possibility that they might be preparatory to a Soviet-led effort to impose martial law and restore communist rule.

Here a brief digression is in order, examining such evidence as has so far emerged. Well after this period, Shevardnadze spoke of pressures within the Soviet establishment for military intervention to rescue the East German regime. In an interview with *Literaturnaya Gazeta* in April 1991, four months after his resignation as foreign minister, Shevardnadze said that "we" (presumably himself and Gorbachev) "were urged fairly actively to apply force" in Eastern Europe in 1989. By whom? Shevardnadze does not say. We know that Romanian party leader Nicolae Ceaușescu was actively pushing for such steps as late as the December 1989 Warsaw Pact Summit, shortly before his own ouster and execution. We do not know whether Shevardnadze was referring to Ceaușescu or to unspecified figures within the Soviet establishment.

As to the GDR specifically, Shevardnadze said during the same interview that "our opponents" were urging that the Soviet Union "start the tank engines."[38] In defending his German policy in a June 1990 *Pravda* interview, he argued that the only alternative to a negotiated settlement would have been "to use our half-million troops in the GDR to block unification," implying but not saying directly that this option was being actively pushed.[39] Shevardnadze also mentioned this military option in his memoirs, but wrote that he learned of this pressure only after the fact and went on to assert categorically: "The question of our interference in the G.D.R. or anywhere else was not posed, nor will it be."[40]

Until further evidence becomes available, we cannot know how much weight or credence to attach to Shevardnadze's cryptic and somewhat contradictory statements on the subject. One reading would be that while there may have been pressures for military intervention, and perhaps specific planning (of which Shevardnadze learned only later) for military action in the GDR, these questions were never "posed" in the sense of being actively considered by the top Soviet leadership. Other interpretations are also possible. And of course Shevardnadze's *post facto* accounts cannot be accepted uncritically. He may have exaggerated these pressures as an exercise in *post facto* self-vindication, or he may have downplayed them, feeling it was too early for a full revelation. We do not know. As future historians sift through new evidence, it will be worth considering whether calls for military intervention, to the extent they in fact constituted a real danger at the time, might have acquired greater weight had the United States and its Western partners behaved differently in late 1989 and early 1990. The fact that the military option was not used does not mean that it *might* not have been under different circumstances. (Such are the "illusions of retrospective determinism.")

To return to the period at hand: not knowing how the story would come out as we were living through it (and indeed being protagonists in the unfolding drama), we in the U.S. administration were obliged to take seriously the danger of Soviet military action or, more plausibly, a ratcheting up of tensions that could lead to unintended but potentially uncontrollable confrontation in the GDR. During this period, I was involved in preparation of a contingency paper examining various crisis scenarios. It recommended U.S. actions in response to border incidents, uncontrolled emigration, confrontations at Soviet military installations, provocations there or along Berlin access routes, and attempts by East German or even Soviet authorities to impose military rule. Mercifully, the paper was consigned, unneeded, to the files (under the category, one might say, "in case of emergency, break glass and remove instructions").

Publicly, we revealed none of our concerns lest they create a climate that could make them self-fulfilling. Indeed, to dampen media speculation of an impending crisis that might prompt Soviet intervention, Secretary Baker cited, during a press briefing, the conclusions of a classified cable from the U.S. embassy in East Germany: despite the "disorder born of change, . . . demonstrations continue peacefully amidst rumors of potential violence."[41]

It was in the context of these concerns that we reluctantly acceded to urgent Soviet appeals for a meeting of the Four Power ambassadors, held in Berlin on December 10, as a means of reassuring Moscow that its voice would be heard and averting a situation in which it might take some unilateral step to assert its "rights and responsibilities" in and around Berlin. (The British and French had been nearly as eager as the Soviets to reaffirm Four Power prerogatives. As one French official said after the meeting, "The purpose was to remind the Germans who is in charge of Berlin."[42]) We had insisted, however, that the December 10 meeting have a restricted agenda[43] that did not include consideration of the German question itself, and we refused to agree to follow-up meetings.

The Malta Summit　　The Malta Summit of early December 1989 made no great breakthrough in Soviet attitudes toward unification, nor was one expected. President Bush's main aims, which he previewed by telephone with Chancellor Kohl just before leaving for Malta, were to reiterate our "four principles," without any expectation that Gorbachev would sign on to them at this early date. He wanted to lay primary stress on the rights of the German people to self-determination, which Gorbachev himself had affirmed in principle several months before.[44] From this it followed that the next essential step was for free and fair elections to be held in the GDR—the first ever in that state's history—so that its people could express their wishes in what would amount to a referendum on unification. Meanwhile, it would be inappropriate for the Four Powers to intrude or interfere in the process. (In addition to being consistent with logic and lofty principle, this sequence also comported with our strategy of deferring external involvement until the German "process" was well advanced.) Finally, the president sought to begin—only to begin—shifting Soviet thinking away from unification per se, which we insisted was a matter for the Germans to decide, toward consideration of the future security situation that might arise in the context of unification, which was indeed a legitimate subject of U.S.-Soviet and broader international dialogue.

For his part, Gorbachev stressed "the reality" of two German states as the "decision of history" and warned against "any artificial acceleration" of relations between the two Germanies, yet his reactions were not as categorically negative as we had expected. (In President Bush's briefing material for the meeting was a paper I had drafted as "Gorbachev's Talking Points on Germany"—i.e., the main arguments I judged that the Soviet leader would make in the meeting, designed to help the president anticipate the tenor of the discussion. As it turned out, Gorbachev's line was milder than my draft had anticipated.[45]) The great surprise was Gorbachev's unsolicited assertion that U.S. military forces should remain in Europe as a stabilizing factor. Apart from contradicting decades of Soviet declaratory policy,[46] this position revealed the extent to which Gorbachev already was considering the implications for Soviet security of a confederal, perhaps even a united, Germany. He seemed, in other words, already to be thinking of a continued, if reduced, American military presence as a useful counterweight to a newly powerful Germany.

The Malta Summit, as both leaders were later to confirm, was a turning point in U.S.-Soviet relations and in the relationship between Presidents Bush and Gorbachev in particular.[47] It was important mainly for the intangibles of U.S.-Soviet relations—building a degree of trust and understanding between the two leaders, including the shared confidence that each was prepared to take the other's security concerns into account. It also helped establish an agenda, even if not yet fully endorsed by the Soviet side, that would facilitate Gorbachev's finding his way through the seemingly intractable dilemmas for Soviet security and prestige posed by German unification.

Malta did not, however, overcome the enormous differences between the two positions on the core issues of German unification. (Indeed, the president had not pressed as hard as we on his staff would have liked, judging that it was too early to engage Gorbachev frontally on the German question. His political instincts were probably more sound than those of his impatient advisers.) Just three days later, Gorbachev told Mitterrand during their meeting in Kiev that if Germany were reunited "there would be a two-line announcement that a Marshal had taken over my position."[48] Then, briefing his Central Committee on the results of the Malta meeting, Gorbachev issued an assurance to the GDR and a veiled threat to Bonn: "We firmly declare that we will see to it that no harm comes to the GDR. It is our strategic ally and a member of the Warsaw Treaty. It is necessary to proceed from the post-war realities—the existence of the two sovereign German states, members of the United Nations. Departure from this threatens with destabilization in Europe."[49]

Of course, one needs to "deconstruct" these statements and conversation fragments, considering not only what was said but to whom, in what context, and for what political purpose. The first was given to and disclosed by a French president who, as Gorbachev subsequently revealed to Kohl and Genscher, urged the Soviet leader during the meeting to prevent unification[50]; the second, to a gathering of Communist party officials already alarmed by the imminent collapse of the Warsaw Pact. There were also different levels of meaning to consider, as in Gorbachev's following his seemingly ironclad assurance to the GDR with an escape clause—"*to proceed from* the post-war realities"—that seemed to hold the door open to an alteration of those realities. Still, there was no mistaking Moscow's rejection of unification as an issue for the immediate future. This message was underlined when Gorbachev and Shevardnadze, meeting with Genscher in Moscow during this same period, denounced Kohl's ten points as a *diktat* and an "attempt to annex the GDR."[51]

Gaining Allied Support for the "Four Principles"   Immediately after Malta, the NATO Summit in Brussels endorsed President Bush's "four principles." Symbolically, the president's private dinner with Kohl on the eve of the summit made it clear that the United States stood firmly behind unification. (As he recalls in his memoirs, the president's "gut feeling" was that Kohl would push for the earliest possible unification.[52])

The aim during the summit itself, as with Gorbachev at Malta, was to override opposition to unification per se by addressing related issues of concern, both procedural and substantive. Affirmation of a united Germany's continued membership in NATO and a more integrated European Community were of course key for Britain and France respectively, points the president underscored in his separate meetings with Thatcher and Mitterrand.

By advancing principles around which all of the alliance could rally, the president helped circumscribe the opportunities for unilateral actions by any one member—meaning not only France and Britain but also Germany and, for that matter, the United States. Yet this by no means eliminated French and British divisiveness, nor prevented Prime Minister Thatcher during the summit meeting from insisting that German unification would have to wait another ten to fifteen years. Instead, the principles provided a reference point of agreed allied policy through which we and the West Germans could begin isolating and neutralizing first British, then French objections.

As Margaret Thatcher put in her memoirs, the NATO Summit made it clear "there was nothing I could expect from the Americans as regards slowing down German reunification."[53] Precisely so. Neither the

British nor even the French would find it easy publicly to depart from the shared allied support for unification, which meant that the Soviet Union would find itself increasingly isolated should it continue down that path. The strategy, in other words, was to isolate those who would obstruct unification, while also assuring all concerned that the process would occur in an orderly way, within a broader European and transatlantic context.

As we had hoped, the NATO Summit evoked a positive Soviet response. In a December 19 speech at the European parliament,[54] Shevardnadze said the Soviet leadership was giving "careful and scrupulous study" to the NATO communique, which "differ[ed] greatly from previous documents of its type." We in Washington paid similarly scrupulous attention to the Shevardnadze speech, whose jarring mixture of truculence and conciliation, we now know, was the product of two competing drafts from within the Soviet establishment.[55] Our main focus, however, was on two related elements of the speech. First was the assertion that "we [in the USSR] . . . do not want to set ourselves at odds with the legitimate interests of the Germans," followed by a seeming openness to finding a solution "through the mutual agreement of all parties concerned." Second was a list of what Shevardnadze termed "seven questions" that would arise in the context of German unification, including recognition of existing borders, the future status of German armed forces and troops stationed on German soil, the place of a united Germany in Europe's "military-political structures," and (twice) the national security interests of other states. While these struck us more as "seven demands," they also amounted to an agenda—in places problematic, but as a whole reasonable—for finding the "mutual agreement" of which Shevardnadze spoke.

Like the British and French, the Soviets had gone a long way from the assertion that German unification was "not on the agenda" toward reluctant acceptance of this prospect, so long as it occurred within an orderly, step-by-step framework. At year's end, we in Washington and our counterparts in Bonn could take some satisfaction in having helped create an atmosphere more conducive, or at least less resolutely obstructionist, to unification.

"The Faster, the Better"   By this time, however, we in Washington already had abandoned the notion of a "gradual, step by step" process, as had the government in Bonn.[56] Secretary Baker's meetings with the new

GDR leadership in Potsdam December 13 and Chancellor Kohl's tumultuous reception in Dresden December 19 already indicated the impotence of the East German regime.[57] In early January, East German prime minister Hans Modrow's clumsy attempt to revive the hated Stasi and revelations of the full state of the East German economic collapse,[58] coupled with the rising emigration tide to an estimated two thousand daily, persuaded Bonn and Washington alike that the prospect of an orderly movement toward unity over a period of years was rapidly being overtaken by the virtual implosion of the East German state.

The German question, in short, was not only "on the agenda," it demanded a prompt answer, whether the world was ready with one or not. Chancellor Kohl's ten-point plan, which had caused such a furor in late November, now seemed tame indeed. From that point on, the assumptions from which we developed our strategy were that unification was inevitable and was coming very fast; that faster was better, given that the alternative of a separate, democratic GDR was now foreclosed, and that a more rapid pace of unification would offer fewer opportunities for obstruction and delay. Strong and agile U.S. leadership would be required for unification to be achieved successfully and in a manner consistent with European stability and our own security interests.

Legally, the four wartime Allies—the United States, Britain, France, and the Soviet Union—had residual rights and responsibilities that had to be disposed of before unification could be finalized. Politically, there was every danger that Soviet intransigence, coupled with misgivings or worse on the part of Britain, France, and others, could lead in any of a number of uncontrollable directions: an international peace conference amounting to open season for any country with a grievance, a protracted Four Power regime to oversee a semisovereign Germany, and/or a disorganized process that would leave Germany vulnerable to Soviet blackmail. It was not a process that the Germans could manage alone. Indeed, the United States had to be more attentive to German sovereignty than the Germans themselves, lest the pressures, especially from Moscow, induce them to accept a settlement that would prejudice the structure of European security for generations to come.

While few harbored "Rapallo fears" of a separate Soviet-German peace or worried that the Germans would be swayed by a repetition of the 1952 Stalin offer of a reunited but neutralized Germany, there was considerable concern that Moscow might press Germany to accept any of a number of lesser infringements on its sovereignty. The possibilities included, if not exclusion from NATO, then a ban of nuclear weapons on German soil, withdrawal of stationed forces, limits on the size of the German army, and acceptance of a special status for East German territory. If one or more of these conditions were seen by the Bonn leadership as the necessary price for German unification, its capacity to resist would be sorely tested, particularly if some of Germany's neighbors allowed their own anxieties to become tacit endorsement of Soviet demands. If the Germans were abandoned by their Western allies at the moment when unification was within reach, could they be blamed for cutting a separate deal with Moscow to achieve their goal? And if the choice were between unity and alliance, could any German leader's answer be in doubt? One key concern for American diplomacy was to ensure that the question was never posed in that fashion.

Our strategy was to recast the issue in Soviet calculations by lining up preponderant international support for a fully sovereign Germany. We would then direct Soviet attention away from the issues of unification and NATO membership, which we insisted were matters for the Germans to decide, toward broader considerations of what kind of Europe was emerging, with what kind of security structures and what kind of role for the United States and the Soviet Union. Process and sequence were crucial. It was important to resist early invocation of Four Power rights. Then, after the East German people had expressed their will through free elections, we would insist that the role of the Four Powers be strictly confined to the tasks of relinquishing all remaining rights and responsibilities and restoring full sovereignty to a united Germany.

Meanwhile, practical steps taken between the two Germanies toward unification would constitute a series of faits accomplis that Moscow could oppose only at great and increasing cost. (Here is where the speed of the process would work to our advantage.) We would also work to address and, where possible, anticipate legitimate Soviet security concerns: President Bush's proposal, in his State of the Union Address in late January, for further conventional force reductions down to 195,000 on each side, for example, was designed to show that as Soviet troops were being pushed out of Eastern Europe, including potentially the GDR, the United States would voluntarily draw down its own forces as well.

The strategy, in short, combined isolation and reassurance: we wanted to make it harder for the Soviet leaders to say *nyet,* while working to resolve their security concerns so they would find it easier to say *da.* As Soviet deputy foreign minister Yuli Kvitsinky later put it, "from day to day, we had lost one trump card after another."[59]

Beyond the immediate task of winning Soviet acquiescence, we were also looking to the larger question of a viable European order after unification had been achieved. It was imperative to avoid a Versailles-like settlement that left Europe divided once again between victors and vanquished. All parties, above all the Soviet Union, needed to accept the settlement and have a stake in the emerging order. Reconciling this longer term strategic objective with the tactical exigencies of the process of German unification was neither easy nor always successful, however. History probably will record that we achieved more success with the latter than the former. Let it also record that, aware of these larger responsibilities, we tried to do both.

The Bonn-Washington Nexus   The first task was to ensure the closest possible cooperation with Bonn. There is ample testimony from Kohl, Genscher, and many others to the extraordinary degree of coordination, at all levels, between Washington and Bonn throughout the period of German unification. And so there was. This was all the more remarkable given what was at stake: for Germans, the unification of their country; for Americans, the future U.S. role and presence in Europe; for both, the future structure of European security and of their relations with the Soviet Union. Our main objectives and interests were in close harmony, but they were not identical—nor could they be, given that one was a global power with global interests and responsibilities while the other was a continental power with more parochial interests. The U.S.–West German relationship during the period was thus more complex than the image of "seamless" cooperation to which Genscher later alluded.[60]

The interplay between Kohl's "ten points" and Bush's "four principles" already implied a process of mutual adjustment between Washington and Bonn. We would lend full support to unification, which entailed considerable latitude for Bonn's separate diplomacy toward that end. They in turn would line up unequivocally behind the future integrity of the Western security system. This meant that unification would not be pursued at the cost of Germany's continued membership in NATO. By early January, this process of adjustment was under way but not yet complete. The positions needed to be brought into even closer harmony if we were to achieve the level of coordination needed to see the unification process through to successful conclusion.

Such coordination was all the more important in that the diplomacy of German unification demanded a certain division of labor. In mobilizing Western consensus in support of unification, Bonn would need to play the major role in securing the support of France and the European Community, while Washington's role would be more important with Great Britain and within the Atlantic alliance. (That Bonn would take the lead in relations with the GDR and in managing the internal aspects of unification was of course understood from the beginning.) Only after developing a solid international consensus would the way be clear to begin securing Soviet concurrence. This, too, required a division of labor. Dealing with the many bilateral issues arising from the removal of Soviet forces from the then-GDR necessarily would be Bonn's responsibility. Here U.S.-German coordination was not always compatible with the requirement that there had to be an historic settling of differences between Bonn and Moscow, a process in which we could not be full participants. By the same token, there were many areas of Soviet concern that only the leader of the Western alliance could address; some would have to be addressed through U.S.-Soviet arms negotiations to which the FRG was not party.

Given these numerous opportunities for slippage, it was essential that there be solid agreement between ourselves and Bonn on principles and main goals. Accordingly, with Genscher already scheduled to meet with Secretary Baker in Washington, Deputy Secretary of State Lawrence Eagleburger and Deputy National Security Adviser Robert Gates traveled to Bonn on January 29 to consult with Kohl and also arrange for the chancellor to hold extended talks with the president at Camp David in late February.[61]

Meanwhile, the drive to unification was accelerating much as we had envisioned. On January 28, just before departing for a meeting with Gorbachev in Moscow, East German prime minister Modrow had been obliged by the government-opposition roundtable to advance the timetable for parliamentary elections, which had been scheduled for May, to March 18. In Bonn, Chancellor Kohl had quietly formed a "Unity Committee" within his cabinet to prepare the way for unification and avert an avalanche of East German emigration. As Kohl put it, "If the DM [Deutsche Mark] doesn't come to Leipzig, then the Leipzigers will come to the DM."[62]

Soviet Questions, German Answers   Soviet thinking was also adjusting to the new realities. While *Pravda* continued to rumble that "destabilization of the situation in the GDR is fraught with unpredictable consequences, . . . above all for the Germans themselves,"[63] Gorbachev was taking a more forthcoming posture, remarking to journalists just before Modrow's arrival that "no one ever cast doubt in principle on the unification of the Germans."[64] Gorbachev also declined to endorse Modrow's call for "treaty-based association" between the two Germanies as a step toward eventual confederation, suggesting that the Soviet leader realized that events already had passed that point.

In his extended public comments on the Modrow visit, Foreign Minister Shevardnadze expressed the evolving Soviet attitude. Leaving aside the occasional rhetorical bouquet thrown to hard-line elements in his own leadership (such as his rejection of "aggressive neo-Nazi actions in the FRG and the GDR"), Shevardnadze's presentation was substantively consistent. He supported "the eventual creation of a united, peace-loving and democratic Germany" but insisted that unification was not the affair of the Germans alone and that the process must be "gradual and pass through certain stages." He also repeated the "seven questions" from his December 19 speech to the European parliament, this time adding (though not specifically endorsing) Modrow's call for the two German states to declare "military neutrality."[65]

Of course, Shevardnadze's insistence on gradualism, at a time when he and Gorbachev must have realized that events were moving rapidly, may have been designed to increase Soviet leverage (as well as assuage his hard-line critics). The call for military neutrality, as if united Germany could be turned into a somewhat larger Switzerland, may have been influenced by similar considerations, as Gorbachev and Shevardnadze groped for some answer to the question of a united Germany's security position. If such was their aim, they did not have long to wait.

In a major speech at the Tutzing Academy on January 31, Foreign Minister Genscher asserted, without consulting any of his allies (or, for that matter, Chancellor Kohl), that "proposals for incorporating the part of Germany at present forming the GDR in NATO's military structures would block intra-German rapprochement." Nor was this all. Speaking not about the GDR but about Poland, Czechoslovakia, and Hungary, Genscher added: "What NATO must do is state unequivocally that whatever happens in the Warsaw Pact there will be no expansion of NATO territory eastward."[66] Preemptive capitulation as regards the GDR was one thing, arguably within the purview of the foreign minister–presumptive of a united Germany; preemptively sacrificing the future security of the new democracies of Central Europe on the altar of German unification, quite another.

Of course, Genscher may have advanced these positions purely for Soviet consumption, with no intention of binding NATO or himself to them, as a means of conditioning Moscow to Germany's continued membership in NATO. The speech nonetheless underscored the danger that, left to themselves, the Germans might pay—and make others pay—an unacceptable and unnecessary price to win Soviet acceptance of unification.

Forging a Western Consensus

By late January, the administration's aim of deferring Four Power involvement was in any case becoming harder to sustain. We had agreed reluctantly to the December 10 meeting of the Four Power ambassadors, as has been seen, but we had since rebuffed repeated Soviet demands for further meetings. Already there had been half a dozen such entreaties, including two separate messages from Shevardnadze in the space of ten days. A stream of other proposals recommended deferring settlement of the German question to the conclusion of a postwar peace treaty, placing it on the agenda of the ongoing, 35-nation Vienna talks on confidence building measures, and subjecting the question to an "all-European referendum" (in which the United States and Canada would also participate).[67]

The French and British, too, were increasingly insisting on Four Power involvement to slow down the process and, as Prime Minister Thatcher put it, ensure that Germany's "narrow nationalist goals" were subordinated to the broader interests of European security.[68] Indeed, Shevardnadze's January 10 message to Secretary Baker asserted that as a result of recent Soviet contacts with the United States, Great Britain, and France, "a consensus is emerging about the desirability of maintaining within the 'Big Four' an exchange of views on German affairs." As we had joined no such "consensus," it evidently was a Franco-British-Soviet one.[69]

Creation of the Two Plus Four   We on the NSC staff and at the State Department had already been thinking of the best strategy for bringing the other powers into the process. As we learned when the Genscher entourage arrived February 1, the West Germans had been thinking along the same lines and had reached similar conclusions. Months before, Genscher had told President Bush that in the 1940s and 1950s the Four Powers had met to decide Germany's future, while the Germans had been relegated to the *katzentisch,* or side table. He made it clear that the Germans did not want to be on the *katzentisch* again.[70] Nor did we want them there. For reasons of principle, we believed from the outset that the two Germanies should take the lead in deciding their future; as a matter of strategy, we did not like the political arithmetic of a Four Power process that was stacked three against one, with the United States the only defender of German unification.

From this emerged the concept of the Two Plus Four—the two German states plus the United States, Great Britain, France, and the Soviet Union—an idea we had already broached in outline form to British foreign secretary Douglas Hurd. Even there the mathematics were potentially unmanageable, so it was equally critical to delimit the scope of activities of the Two Plus Four process. Here, too, we and the West Germans were in full agreement. The internal aspects of unification—that is, whether and in what fashion Germans east and west chose to live together in one state—were strictly up to the Germans, pending only the forthcoming elections in which the people of the GDR would express their wishes. The Two Plus Four were to deal only with the external aspects of unification—and only those aspects required to return full sovereignty to a united Germany. Questions such as alliance membership, military forces, and future European security arrangements were beyond its purview. The role of the Four Powers was solely to discharge and then relinquish all residual rights and responsibilities in Berlin and Germany as a whole.

The question of timing was important as well. We did not want the Four Powers involved until the Germans had sorted out their future, and certainly not until formation of a new GDR government following the March 18 elections. Yet there was also a risk of leaving Soviet entreaties unanswered, particularly in light of Chancellor Kohl's planned visit to Moscow in mid-February. Hence the State Department in particular wanted to reach agreement on the Two Plus Four framework as soon as possible, so that Gorbachev and Kohl did not feel pressure (or see an opportunity) to turn their meeting into a "One Plus One" deal on Germany's future.

With Baker having reached agreement with Genscher on all these points, we then undertook the usual double-tracking with Chancellor

Kohl. (This was still only two days after Genscher's Tutzing speech, in which he spoke on the most sensitive issues of German foreign policy without so much as an advance warning to Kohl.) It was tedious always to have to reach agreement with Kohl and Genscher separately. However, the fact that there was virtually total agreement between the State Department and the White House (and constant coordination and communication between the two) meant that sometimes we could supply Bonn with the policy coordination it lacked. Knowledge being one of the currencies of power, it also gave us added leverage in dealing with Bonn, in that we occasionally knew more about where Kohl or Genscher stood on an issue than either of them knew of the other. To return to the point at hand, Kohl was in full agreement on the Two Plus Four formula, so the way was clear to work toward securing agreement among the other parties.

Secretary Baker then took to the road to sell the Two Plus Four idea. He secured the reluctant agreement of French foreign minister Dumas during a refueling stop at Shannon Airport[71] and then shopped (but did not yet sell) the idea to Gorbachev and Shevardnadze in Moscow before continuing on to Ottawa for a meeting of NATO and Warsaw Pact foreign ministers.[72]

Ottawa was a three-ring circus. Shevardnadze held five separate talks with Baker and three with Genscher, and also met individually with Hurd, Dumas, and Polish foreign minister Krzysztof Skubiszewski, all in a single day. In his memoirs, Shevardnadze also recalled that while he could see Two Plus Four turning into Five Against One—"and it was not hard to guess that the Soviet representative was the 'one' "—he was persuaded that this mechanism, coupled with assurances Moscow could gain bilaterally with Bonn and Washington, offered the best leverage available to secure Soviet interests.[73] Shevardnadze no doubt had a premonition of what actually transpired. Each Two Plus Four was preceded by a "One Plus Three" meeting to forge agreement among West Germany, Britain, France, and the United States.[74] These key gatherings, supplemented by Bonn's bilateral diplomacy with East Germany, turned out to be instrumental in forging a five-way consensus that Moscow found hard to resist. Nonetheless, the nonstop bilateral diplomacy at Ottawa—between and among Baker, Genscher, and Shevardnadze, particularly—led to unexpectedly swift agreement. The two Germanies and the Four Powers created what came to be known as the Two Plus Four mechanism "to discuss external aspects of the establishment of German unity, including the issues of security of the neighboring states."[75]

The Polish Border Issue Among these issues was the question of borders, with the Polish-German border being the case in point. This complicated issue can only be outlined here.[76] Chancellor Kohl, wanting to handle the issue in a way that did not alienate politically important constituencies (above all, the organizations of German expellees from the immediate postwar period), took the firm position that as a legal matter the issue could not be settled except by an all-German parliament, which did not yet exist. There seems little doubt that Kohl genuinely believed this to be the case under international law, but it was convenient to his political purposes as well.[77] The Poles, understandably worried that a new, postunification German parliament might take a very different line, demanded firm guarantees beforehand. There is nothing like having one's country wiped off the map of Europe for 125 years, as Poland was after the partitions of the late eighteenth century, to engender a certain suspicion of the assurances of benevolent intent from one's neighbors.

There was a further danger that concerned me and some at the State Department. We worried that Kohl's motivations may have included one that he could not say openly: namely, that he did not want to go down in history as the chancellor who gave up Germany's "eastern territories" once and for all. It was not that Kohl harbored aggressive intentions against Poland—far from it—but that he wanted to leave this issue open for resolution by future generations. That, we felt, would only encourage right-wing irredentist dreams in Germany and excite fear and anxiety in Poland. German-Polish relations could never be mended so long as this issue was left open. Once it was closed, Germans and Poles could leave this legacy behind them and begin building a new relationship. (This perspective was shared in some quarters at the State Department, but it was a minority view at the NSC, which tended to take Kohl's assurances at face value.)

The border issue pitted Kohl against nearly everyone else, including his foreign minister and the other five countries of the Two Plus Four. The immediate American concern, shared even by those who accepted unreservedly Kohl's repeated private assurances that the question would be unambiguously resolved at the time of unification, was that the border issue could seriously complicate the Two Plus Four process, with the

French and others championing the Polish cause as a means of slowing unification.[78]

Our many discussions with the Bonn government on this issue aimed at urging Kohl to find a way to resolve the issue quickly, and to Poland's satisfaction. This task was complicated by another compelling objective: to strengthen Chancellor Kohl's position internally so as to enhance his leadership role in the unification process. On issues of European security and particularly the question of NATO membership, as will be seen shortly, we wanted Kohl's voice, not Genscher's, to be decisive.[79] Having set about consciously to strengthen the chancellor's position, we were prepared to defer to his judgment on the tactical handling of the border issue so long as it did not begin poisoning the Two Plus Four negotiations.

President Bush had listed "inviolability of existing borders" as one of his "four principles" of November–December 1989 and reaffirmed them privately and publicly during his Camp David meeting with Kohl in late February 1990 (discussed below). The visit to Washington of Polish prime minister Tadeusz Mazowiecki in late March provided the occasion for the president's direct mediation between the Poles and the Germans. This Bush did directly with Mazowiecki in Oval Office meetings on March 21 and 22, as well as in telephone calls to Kohl before, during, and after Mazowiecki's visit.[80]

Ultimately an acceptable formula was found whereby the parliaments of the two German states issued simultaneous resolutions recognizing Poland's western border to be final (with the text of this passage agreed to beforehand by the Poles and Germans) and calling for a binding treaty between Poland and a united Germany. Within the Two Plus Four process, it was agreed that the Polish foreign minister would participate in the meeting where borders were discussed.[81] While the episode left a bitter aftertaste, especially for the Poles, it nonetheless led to a satisfactory legal resolution of the border issue, and it was managed in a way that solidified U.S.-German coordination on the increasingly complex set of issues related to unification.

Overcoming Opposition to Unification   This increasingly close U.S.-German cooperation was most crucial during the intense round of diplomatic negotiations in February 1990. Just before Kohl's arrival in Moscow on February 8 for his first meeting with Gorbachev since the opening of the Berlin Wall, the chancellor received two messages. One was from Secretary Baker, reviewing his just-concluded meetings with Gorbachev and Shevardnadze and the progress he had made toward gaining Soviet agreement to unification and the Two Plus Four formula. The second was a long and intimate letter from President Bush, which Kohl later termed "one of the most important documents in the history of U.S.-German relations."[82] It not only reaffirmed full U.S. support for German unification but detailed specific steps the United States was prepared to take to counter possible Soviet efforts to impede unification, restrict the sovereignty of a united Germany, or prejudice the future of the Atlantic alliance by seeking to limit Germany's role therein.[83] The immediate political objective of the letter, coupled with the February 7 announcement of Kohl's forthcoming trip to Washington, was to stiffen Kohl's resolve and strengthen his hand for his meetings with Gorbachev.

Indeed, the Kohl visit to Moscow achieved a breakthrough that complemented the Ottawa agreement on Two Plus Four. Immediately after his meeting with Gorbachev, Kohl announced their agreement "that the Germans themselves must resolve the question of the unity of the German nation and themselves decide in what kind of state system, in what time frame, at what speed, and under what conditions they wish to bring about this unity."[84]

This was all the assurance Kohl needed to move aggressively to build a pro-unification coalition of East German conservative parties,[85] called "Alliance for Germany," and help it score a resounding victory in the March 18 elections. At Kohl's urging, the new East German prime minister, Lothar de Maizière, had already committed himself and his party (CDU-East) to rapid unification via Article 23 of the "Basic Law" (the West German constitution). This meant in effect that the states (*länder*) of East Germany would simply vote themselves into the existing Federal Republic of Germany. The alternative route was via Article 146, which would have amounted to a merger of two separate states and the creation of a new legal entity, requiring a new constitution and renegotiation of existing treaties and other legal commitments. Although not, strictly speaking, our business, Article 23 was our preference as well, in that it created fewer new issues to be settled and meant that Germany's relationships with the EC, NATO, and other institutions need not be renegotiated. In subsequent interviews, Soviet officials noted that they, too, saw unification via Article 23 as tantamount to an "*anschluss*" (annexation) of the GDR, which they rightly feared would make NATO membership a virtual fait accompli.[86] Indeed, the point was quickly confirmed, as negotiations began immediately toward economic and social union, and then full political union, between the two Germanies.

Among their other consequences, the results of the East German elections prompted a sharp reversal in French thinking—away from the vain hope of slowing unification. Instead they formed a new strategy of using the relatively brief interval of maximum influence on Bonn to secure firm German commitment to accelerate the process of European integration. The West Germans, having asserted repeatedly that unification would not hinder but rather strengthen "European construction," were vulnerable to subtle French blackmail on this subject. Any hesitation on Bonn's part would be read, or at least portrayed, by its neighbors as confirmation of their worst fears about a united Germany's propensity to *alleingang* (going it alone). Hence, whatever private reservations Kohl or the *Bundesbank* (German federal bank) may have had, the chancellor acceded quickly to Mitterrand's proposal for a joint letter to their EC counterparts in mid-April, calling for an accelerated timetable for reaching EC economic and political union by 1993.[87]

Germany and NATO   The concern, then, was not with whether unification could be achieved—by early 1990 the momentum had become irresistible, as all the participants had come to acknowledge—but with what kind of Germany would emerge from the process, and with what the implications would be for the future of Europe and the transatlantic link. Even after German unification was well advanced, few experts outside government held out continued NATO membership by a fully sovereign Germany as a plausible outcome of the unification process or a realistic goal of American policy. Some in the United States and West Germany even argued that U.S. support for united Germany's NATO membership constituted an obstacle, perhaps a deliberate one, to unification. Voices on the West German Left argued that "a unified Germany and NATO membership are mutually exclusive."[88] Even the most respected commentators and analysts here and in Europe advanced various schemes for a united Germany that would be disarmed or demilitarized, temporarily or permanently bifurcated through dual membership in NATO and the Warsaw Pact, or consigned to some other form of semisovereignty.[89] One such commentator, saluting Gorbachev's statesmanship, lamented the lack of "parallel subtlety of understanding on the Western side" and called on the United States to abandon its support for Germany's NATO membership.[90]

Within the administration, we considered these outcomes unacceptable. In early February, I drafted a paper for internal consideration, listing some 17 different security outcomes for a united Germany, beginning with a fully sovereign Germany with its alliance relationships intact and ending with a demilitarized and neutralized Germany cut adrift from its NATO and EC partners.[91] In between were permutations and combinations regarding nuclear weapons, stationed forces, the size and status of the German military, and membership in various political or security institutions. One did not have to go far down the list before European security began to unravel. Most obviously, if German membership in NATO or the presence of U.S. forces were sacrificed on the altar of unification, the fundamental transatlantic security link would have been severed, leaving a post–Cold War jungle not unlike that described in Mearsheimer's widely read *Atlantic* article.[92] Whether NATO could or should be replaced at some future date was another matter; our concern was that the sole functioning European security institution not be jettisoned in the midst of rapid and unpredictable change. As a matter of principle as well as policy preference, we also refused to accept that a democratic, united Germany should be denied full sovereignty, including the right to choose its own alliance relationships.

The U.S. position, spelled out in countless public statements during the course of 1990 and closely coordinated with Bonn, was that a united Germany should be fully sovereign from the moment of unification, with no new discriminatory constraints on its sovereignty. Germany should also remain a full member of NATO, including its integrated military structure, and substantial U.S. forces should remain in the country. Our conviction was that there was no reason, 45 years after the war, for a united, democratic Germany to be singled out for special status. Of course, we had no way of knowing whether, or to what extent, these ambitious objectives could be realized. (As it turned out, what emerged from the Two Plus Four process was the second of 17 outcomes on our list, with German sovereignty limited only by the special security status accorded the territory of the former GDR. But this successful outcome seemed distant indeed in the early months of 1990.) What we did know was how much was at stake in the outcome; we knew, as well, that the United States had to remain absolutely clear about its main objectives and harness policy single-mindedly to those ends. Our task, then, was to secure Moscow's acquiescence to a state of affairs that successive Soviet leaders would have considered a reversal and betrayal of the USSR's great historic gain of World War II—the emasculation of German power.

Mixed Signals from Bonn   While trying to condition the Soviet leadership to this prospect, as President Bush did at Malta and Secretary Baker did in his February visit to Moscow, our main effort was to weld a united Western position behind Germany's NATO membership. The first requirement was to secure an unambiguous commitment from the West Germans, whose public statements to date had been muddy at best. These concerns were not pulled out of thin air. Devotees of original sources, we at the NSC staff made a practice of studying the texts of major speeches by foreign leaders. Having noted with more than passing interest that Chancellor Kohl's "ten point" speech omitted reference to NATO, we also focused on this summing up in Foreign Minister Genscher's Tutzing speech: "We want to place the process of German unification in the context of EC integration, of the CSCE process, the West-East partnership for stability, the construction of the common European house and the creation of a peaceful European order from the Atlantic to the Urals."[93]

To be sure, Genscher affirmed German membership in NATO—a more political, less military NATO—earlier in the speech, but the alliance did not figure in this key passage in his final paragraph. An oversight? Here was Genscher's almost identical formulation two months later, in a major address to the Western European Union: "We seek the process of German unification in the context of EC integration, the CSCE process, East-West partnership for stability, the construction of the common European house and the creation of a pan-European peaceful order."[94]

Tired speechwriters? Perhaps, but not too tired to insert a conspicuous addendum when Genscher presented the now-familiar formulation in a speech before a U.S. audience in early April: "We want German unity *as a member of NATO,* in the context of the integration of the European Community and in the CSCE process. We want it as a contribution to the development of a partnership between West and East based on stability, to the construction of the common European house, and to the establishment of the peaceful order spanning the whole of Europe."[95]

This kind of textual analysis can be carried too far, and perhaps we have carried it too far already. But words matter, as veteran politicians know well. They use major speeches to affirm priorities and signal intent, often indirectly. What is *not* said can be as important as what is. It was for these reasons that *our* words, and the words we urged visiting Western leaders to utter at every opportunity, laid stress on united Germany's remaining "a full member of NATO, including participation in its integrated military structure" (a phrase I must have written into draft remarks a hundred times during the spring of 1990). They were words meant for Moscow's attention, and also for the attention of certain German politicians who might be inclined to allow NATO membership to become a bargaining chip. They were words meant to rally the Western alliance in support of Germany's continued membership in NATO as a vital element of European stability and security.

Clearly, these differences were primarily about tactics. Genscher feared that raising the NATO issue at this early date might provoke a negative Soviet reaction and a premature hardening of the Soviet position. He thought that even his qualified references to NATO in the Tutzing speech put Germany on "thin ice."[96] Better to tread lightly on the issue until Moscow had been conditioned to react more favorably. Our concern was that this approach risked leaving the impression that Germany's future membership in NATO was subject to discussion and negotiation. It was an invitation for Soviet probing of German resolve.

While our concerns were mainly over tactics, we were also conscious that Genscher already had offered a unilateral and uncoordinated concession on the future status of GDR territory within the alliance. What other concessions might he be prepared to make? It is important to be precise here. The general view in Washington was that Genscher hoped and expected that united Germany would remain in NATO and that he was working with us toward that end. Yet many also saw Genscher as a Europeanist first and an Atlanticist second, a characterization that Genscher surely would not have disputed. Because NATO membership ranked lower on his list of priorities than on Kohl's or ours, he was more likely than the chancellor to concede on issues we considered vital to the future of European security.

Rallying International Support   We therefore attached great importance to Chancellor Kohl's joining President Bush in affirming these points publicly when the two met at Camp David on February 24 and 25. We at staff level wrote our standard formulation—"[Chancellor Kohl and I] share a common belief that a unified Germany should remain a full member of the North Atlantic Treaty Organization, including participation in its military structure"—into the draft statement President Bush would read after their meeting. We then ran it by Horst Teltschik, the chancellor's security adviser, who readily agreed to its inclusion. Later, Kohl expressed irritation at the implication that his fidelity to the alliance was in doubt, asserting that he had stressed the need for Germany to remain in NATO in a hundred speeches before the Camp David meeting.[97] Perhaps. But it is worth noting that it took the U.S. side to say so publicly at Camp David; Chancellor Kohl's statement at the same press conference referred only to "the security link between North America and Europe,"[98] an essentially meaningless formulation. And in their private talks at Camp David, Kohl had floated—and Bush rejected—the idea of a "French solution," whereby united Germany would remain in NATO's political alliance but not in its integrated military structures. Bush's reply was that "we can't let the Soviets clutch victory from the jaws of defeat."[99]

If Genscher's reticence on NATO membership was primarily tactical, that of the committed Atlanticist Helmut Kohl was almost entirely so. But too much was at stake to allow this ambiguity to persist. Besides, it was easier for the United States to speak forcefully and often on the issue than it was for West Germany, which was in the position of *demandeur* with respect to Moscow. And it was important that we do so, lest Western circumlocutions on this key issue lead Moscow to question Western resolve or exploit perceived differences. After Camp David, it was clear that there were no such differences to exploit between Bonn and Washington.

Indeed, by the time of his meeting with Mitterrand in Key Largo on April 19, President Bush could claim virtually Europe-wide agreement: "President Mitterrand and I both believe that a united Germany should remain a full member of NATO, as called for by Chancellor Kohl. All of our allies and several Eastern European countries share this view as well."[100] This two-line assertion represented the conclusion of strenuous U.S. diplomatic efforts throughout the spring of 1990.

Among the allies, France's position was of course the most problematic. On the one hand, the French favored a continuing U.S. military presence in Germany and wanted united Germany to be wrapped in a warm multilateral embrace; on the other, they were loath to accept the revitalization of NATO's role that was required to make either of those goals possible. The Key Largo meeting was therefore an occasion for blunt talk as well as compromise, with the U.S. side making it clear that a continued American presence in Europe demanded French acceptance of a continuing strong role for NATO. We made it plain that American troops would not stay in Europe as mercenaries if a more united EC cut the United States and NATO out of key decisions on issues of European security.[101] At the same time, Mitterrand was reassured that the United States did not oppose but in fact welcomed a stronger European security and defense identity, as a natural evolution in the EC's movement toward economic and political unity.

We also attached considerable importance to the positions of the new East European leaders and their influence within the still existing, if rapidly eroding, Warsaw Pact. The Poles and Hungarians were enthusiastic supporters of NATO, and German membership therein, from the outset. Czechoslovakia was more problematic. Its new president, Václav Havel, had carried from his days in opposition the conviction that both "military blocs," NATO and the Warsaw Pact alike, should disband and be replaced by a new "pan-European peace order," with the CSCE (Conference on Security and Cooperation in Europe) evolving into a new system of collective security. Given Havel's tremendous moral authority and his ability to influence thinking well beyond his own country, we considered it important to help him understand why the United States felt that while the CSCE should indeed take on new roles, it could not replace NATO as an agent of European security. Secretary Baker had made these points to Havel during a visit to Prague in early February—the same trip that took Baker to Moscow and on to Ottawa—and President Bush amplified them during Havel's official visit to Washington later that month.[102] Official Czechoslovak thinking shifted markedly as a result of these efforts and the surprisingly close personal affinity between Presidents Bush and Havel—one a man of the world and the other a man of the intellect.[103] By late spring, Havel had joined his Polish and Hungarian counterparts as an outspoken, if still hesitant, supporter of NATO; shortly thereafter he was clamoring for Czechoslovak membership in the organization.

The final East European recalcitrants were newly elected GDR prime minister Lothar de Maizière and Foreign Minister Markus Meckel. Their views were akin to Havel's initial position but much more troublesome, in that the East Germans had a seat at the Two Plus Four table. Even late in the Two Plus Four process, Meckel was advancing various uncoordinated initiatives for "pan-European security structures" and even for a Central European demilitarized zone encompassing Germany, Poland, and Czechoslovakia. Kohl and Genscher naturally took the lead in averting East German divisiveness in the Two Plus Four setting, resorting to arm-twisting when diplomatic persuasion failed. Ours was a supporting role: in addition to Secretary Baker's diplomacy with Meckel, President Bush hosted de Maizière on an official visit to Washington (the first and last such visit by a GDR leader) in early June. I recall beginning the president's briefing memorandum by noting that "Lothar de Maizière presides over a government whose chief function is to negotiate itself out of existence," but adding that he nonetheless pursued his role with a sense of great responsibility. Bush's personal diplomacy secured de Maizière's public support for "the continuing vital role of the alliance and of U.S. forces stationed in Europe as guarantors of stability and security."[104]

Securing Soviet Consent: "Seven Questions," "Nine Assurances"

By late spring, the essential work of developing a strong international consensus was complete. If there was to be a skunk at the Two Plus Four picnic, it would be Moscow alone, with all that implied for the future of German-Soviet relations and the future of Europe if a united and powerful Germany were cut adrift from its key alliance relationships. Already Moscow had come a long way toward the view that if unification was inevitable, NATO and the U.S. military presence were important instruments for containing a newly powerful Germany. Gorbachev and Shevardnadze increasingly came to understand that permanent neutrality was not really an option for a country of Germany's geostrategic weight. For them, the prospect of a reconstituted German general staff and German military doctrine, two logical consequences of a Germany cut adrift from its NATO allies, must have evoked vivid memories. (Certainly, we missed no opportunity to drive these points home.)

Moscow and the NATO Issue Yet the prospect of united Germany's remaining in NATO was more than the Soviet leadership was yet prepared to accept, not just for security reasons but also because of internal political resistance. As Shevardnadze told Baker in late March, unification is coming "too fast": "We don't want to see a neutral Germany. We want to see your troops remain. But we have a problem with NATO." The problem, he continued, was the short-term one of appearances and selling the idea domestically—"It would look like you had won and we had lost"—and the longer-term problems for Soviet security.[105] Subsequently, Shevardnadze argued that he and Gorbachev delayed giving consent to Germany's NATO membership in order to "bring Soviet public opinion around," exact Western concessions on NATO's transformation, and resolve other Soviet security concerns.[106] There is undoubtedly considerable truth in those assertions, though they have to be weighed against the element of retrospective rationalization in Shevardnadze's strained, and not altogether convincing, explanation of why "our starting position differed substantially from our finishing one."[107]

While signs of a softening of Soviet attitudes were evident as early as the Malta Summit and Secretary Baker's visit to Moscow in February, we in Washington also had to reckon with the prospect that Gorbachev and Shevardnadze, whatever their own predilections, might be unable to overcome opposition elsewhere in the Soviet establishment. Nor does the fact that both were probing for ways to deal with the NATO issue mean that their ultimate acceptance was a foregone conclusion. Certainly, the official statements issued at the time by Gorbachev and Shevardnadze showed little flexibility. In a March 6 interview with West German television, Gorbachev replied categorically to the question of united Germany's remaining in NATO: "We will not agree to that. That is absolutely excluded."[108] Shevardnadze repeated the point during a visit to Washington in early April: "What is unacceptable to us . . . is united Germany's remaining in NATO."[109]

At the first Two Plus Four ministerial meeting, held in Bonn on May 5, Shevardnadze's statements reflected the mounting pressures that he and Gorbachev faced, both externally and internally. The international community was as united in support of Germany's continued NATO membership as the Soviet establishment was adamantly against it. In a very tough speech, Shevardnadze reiterated the conditions first advanced in his "seven questions" address at the European parliament and proposed, more ominously, that "a decision on the internal and external aspects of German unity should not necessarily coincide in time." "Even after the creation of a single parliament and government in Germany," he continued, there would remain in force "over a certain number of years . . . certain measures related to decisions on external aspects of the settlement."[110] My copy of the speech has this apt marginal notation made at the time by one of my NSC colleagues: "Unity without Sovereignty!"

This, as we feared, was the new tactical approach: if Soviet security concerns were not addressed by the time of unification, then some form of Four Power supervision should be continued into the indefinite future. It was a recipe for protracted difficulties between a semisovereign Germany and a defeated, embittered Soviet Union. Europe had seen these ingredients in combination once before, had it not? They had contributed, in E. H. Carr's characterization of the period, to the "twenty years' crisis" between the two world wars.[111] It was precisely to avert a latter-day "twenty years' crisis" that we continued to insist that Germany should be fully sovereign from the moment of unification and that legitimate Soviet security concerns should be addressed before that time rather than be projected into an uncertain future.

At the Two Plus Four meeting, Secretary Baker stood fast against Shevardnadze's proposed "decoupling" of the internal and external aspects of German unity, a formula to which Genscher was ready to subscribe until being overruled by Kohl (after a quick Kohl-Bush telephone call). Once again delivering the result we needed, Baker gained agreement that the Two Plus Four process should be limited to external issues arising directly from unification, rather than becoming an open forum for discussion of all manner of extraneous security matters.[112] At the same time, as Shevardnadze later recalled approvingly, Baker stressed that "we must find a solution where there won't be any winners and losers, but where everybody wins."[113]

On the question of NATO membership, Shevardnadze reiterated the Soviet Union's "negative attitude" but also offered an opening: "Both we and you speak about the prospects of transforming the two blocs. [But] when will this happen, and will it happen at all? No guarantees in this regard have yet been developed." As important as his substantive positions were Shevardnadze's several allusions to the internal political pressures that gave rise to them. "Our political flexibility is severely limited," he asserted. "This is a fact of our real life . . . [that] neither the current nor any other Soviet leadership will be able to disregard. . . . The population of our country . . . is uncompromisingly against the idea of including a united Germany in NATO. . . . These are also the sentiments of our Supreme Soviet. We cannot ignore this."

Conflicts over Baltic Independence   In his private conversations with Secretary Baker in Bonn, Shevardnadze distanced himself further from the positions he had taken in the speech, explaining the pressures he and Gorbachev were under from their conservative critics on German policy and the gathering drive for independence among the Baltic states. Indeed, much of their discussion was on the economic embargo Moscow had imposed on Lithuania in response to the latter's recent declaration of independence. Baker sought and received Shevardnadze's assurance that force would not be used, but the secretary also made it clear that concluding a U.S.-Soviet trade agreement (to which the Soviet side attached great importance) by the time of the Washington Summit in late May would be "very difficult" unless there were serious negotiations toward Baltic independence.[114]

The soft U.S. line on the Baltics, for which the president took much criticism, needs to be understood against this backdrop. Our main effort was to press for private assurances that force would not be used against the Baltic states, in the belief that a peaceful process of change would create a new reality of de facto independence that Moscow ultimately would have to recognize. Our public posture, however, was deliberately restrained, in order to give Gorbachev and Shevardnadze the breathing space to find a peaceful, negotiated solution. The question we asked ourselves was not which approach would have been more satisfying rhetorically—a ringing call for "freeing the captive nations" would have made all of us feel better—but which was most likely to achieve the goal of independence for the Baltic states. In the end, the goal was achieved, albeit a year and a half after the Baltic states declared their independence. Even with the benefit of hindsight, it seems doubtful that a more strident (some would say, "more principled") approach would have achieved a quicker or more satisfactory result.

A more serious question is whether Washington and Bonn subordinated the aspirations of the Baltic peoples to German unification. This, certainly, was the view of Lithuanian prime minister Kazimiera Prunskiene during her meetings in early May with President Bush in Washington and Chancellor Kohl in Bonn. As Kohl related in a telephone call to the president after Prunskiene's visit, he took a "brutal" line, telling her that the Lithuanians had done "everything wrong" and risked upsetting all the positive developments in Europe—beginning, of course, with the prospect of German unification.[115] It is no small irony that Prime Minister Thatcher had admonished the Germans, about the same time and in similar terms, for insisting that "German reunification should take priority over everything else" and urged them to put a "longer view of Europe's needs before their more narrow, nationalist goals."[116]

The Germans, then, were probably guilty as charged of placing their unification above Baltic aspirations. So, to some extent, were we, though we tended to see Baltic and German aspirations as part of the same problem of imperial dissolution, both demanding sensitivity to Soviet security concerns and to the delicacy of the Soviet internal situation. As President Bush put it, "I don't want people to look back 20 or 40 years from now and say, 'That's where everything went off track. That's where progress stopped.'"[117]

U.S.-Soviet Relations at Endgame Here, then, was the context of U.S.-Soviet relations in late spring 1990. Following the February 27 Supreme Soviet vote granting sweeping new presidential powers, Gorbachev and Shevardnadze had unprecedented authority over foreign policy,[118] and both demonstrated openness toward a solution on German unification that would restore Germany's full sovereignty and affirm its continued membership in NATO. To deliver, they needed our help (and Bonn's) in strengthening their hands against conservative critics at home,[119] yet our ability (and willingness) to provide that help was prejudiced by the crackdown in the Baltic states. We therefore aimed to find a way through these cross-pressures in order to secure our objectives for German unification. Additionally, the restricted mandate of the Two Plus Four process (on which we had insisted from the outset) meant that it would be up to U.S. and West German bilateral diplomacy to address some of the many concerns Gorbachev and Shevardnadze had raised.

We had already been working to address legitimate Soviet security concerns. In his State of the Union Address in late January, President Bush had announced a new initiative on CFE (Conventional Armed Forces in Europe), calling for U.S. and Soviet force reductions down to a level of 195,000 each. As with the May 1989 initiative, this was designed to make it easier for Moscow to accept what was being forced on it anyway (by East European calls for Soviet troop withdrawals) and to show that even the prospect of the removal of Soviet forces in the GDR would be accompanied by reciprocal cuts on the American side. (The president was also careful to place a floor on U.S. reductions and to begin "delinking" U.S. and Soviet troop withdrawals, lest the principle of reciprocity be taken to mean that if all Soviet forces eventually left Europe then all U.S. forces should do so as well.)

In a major speech at Oklahoma State University on May 4, President Bush called for an early summit meeting of NATO leaders to undertake a wholesale review of the alliance's military and political missions, proposing also that CSCE be strengthened as a forum for helping to overcome the division of Europe. He also called for accelerated negotiations toward a CFE treaty, to be followed by U.S.-Soviet negotiations on short-range nuclear forces, and announced the unilateral cancellation of the follow-on to the Lance missile (FOTL) and of NATO's nuclear artillery modernization program.[120] These initiatives aimed at a substantially transformed Atlantic alliance—the "transformation of the blocs" that Shevardnadze had called for in Bonn.

During a visit to Moscow two weeks later, Secretary Baker listed these initiatives among what became known, almost biblically, as the "nine assurances" the United States and its Western allies were providing to address legitimate security concerns arising from German unification:

(1) agreements to limit the size of the German armed forces;

(2) commitment to negotiate on short-range nuclear weapons;

(3) reaffirmation of Germany's nonnuclear status;

(4) revisions of NATO strategy to make it less threatening;

(5) a pledge not to deploy NATO forces in the former GDR;

(6) a transitional period for Soviet forces in Germany;

(7) renunciation of any future German territorial claims;

(8) strengthening the CSCE and the Soviet role therein; and

(9) extensive German economic assistance to the USSR.[121]

Coordinating U.S. and West German Approaches As the "nine assurances" involved a combination of U.S., West German, and broader Western initiatives, it was important to establish the closest possible coordination between Bonn and Washington as both sides pursued their bilateral diplomacy with Moscow. Accordingly, a large West German delegation headed by Kohl and Genscher arrived in Washington on May 17 for a general stocktaking and coordination of initiatives toward Moscow as the Two Plus Four process entered its most critical stage. Several events were key: the just-concluded trip to Moscow by Kohl's foreign policy adviser, Horst Teltschik, in which he presented a variety of economic assistance measures; Baker's trip to Moscow; the forthcoming Bush-Gorbachev summit in Washington at the end of the month; and the subsequent NATO summit that the president had called for in his Oklahoma State speech.

The summary I wrote immediately after the meeting is worth ex-
cerpting at some length, in that it captures the sense of the moment and
the tenor of U.S.–West German relations:

> Atmosphere. Couldn't have been better. Kohl particularly, but
> all the Germans, were effusive in their gratitude for U.S. support.
> What a contrast to a year ago, when our mutual trust and confi-
> dence were slipping badly.
>
> Unification and Two Plus Four. Continuing broad agreement on
> the essentials:
> —Germany should remain a full member of NATO, including par-
>   ticipation in its integrated military structure.
> —NATO's security guarantee should apply to all the territory of
>   the united Germany. [Germans less explicit than we.]
> —U.S. military forces should remain stationed in the united Ger-
>   many and elsewhere in Europe. [Kohl was particularly strong
>   on this.]
> —The Two Plus Four talks should terminate Four Power rights
>   and responsibilities at the time of unification, with no new con-
>   straints on German sovereignty. [Germans seemed more solid on
>   this than we might have expected.]
> —Two Plus Four should not decide issues like German member-
>   ship in NATO, the status of stationed forces, or the size of the
>   Bundeswehr. [Germans agree in principle but not as explicit as
>   we.]
> [The Germans want to conclude Two Plus Four before the CSCE
> Summit. We also think that by pressing ahead toward a settle-
> ment, Moscow will find it harder to maintain a position in
> which the USSR alone wants to retain occupation rights after
> unification.]
>
> Soviet troops in the GDR. The Germans said they could accept
> Soviet forces remaining for a transitional period but only that.
> The President . . . worries that the longer Soviet troops remain,
> the more there will be a perception of "parallelism" with U.S.
> forces. . . .
>
> Timing of unification. Germans want to finish the job before
> the CSCE Summit. They expect to sign the treaty on economic and
> monetary union next week. Kohl expects a "big noise" when this
> is submitted to the Bundestag.

Helping the Soviet economy. Kohl painted a dark picture of the Soviet economy and was looking for ways we and the Germans could help Gorbachev. . . .

U.S.-Soviet Summit. . . . The Germans particularly wanted the President to present our position on unification and Two Plus Four. Kohl also thought it important that Gorbachev be treated— and be seen to be treated—as an equal. The President agreed. [Kohl is more concerned than we that we do all possible to keep Gorbachev in the saddle.]

NATO Summit. The President reviewed his proposal that the Summit launch a wide-ranging strategy review. . . . There wasn't much discussion, though the Germans fully support the idea. [Genscher made the point that the Soviets were mounting a campaign domestically to remove NATO's "demonic image."]

Despite this close convergence of views, one of our overriding concerns by this time was that Gorbachev or Shevardnadze might come to the Germans with their final offer or, in Washington parlance, their "bottom line." They would say, in effect, "We have said we can accept German unification. We can even accept your remaining in NATO. But you must understand the implications of these developments for our security. . . ." Then would follow the Soviet conditions, which might have included withdrawal of U.S. as well as Soviet forces, removal of all nuclear weapons from Germany, withdrawal of all stationed forces, total demilitarization of GDR territory, or some other mix of Soviet demands. (According to Kohl's security adviser Horst Teltschik in subsequent conversations, the "deal" was never proffered. If such an offer had been made, what would the German answer have been? Teltschik could not say, though he admitted that "some members of the government would have said that we have to accept it. Others would have resisted, but for how long?"[122]) While there was nothing we could do about it directly if Bonn were prepared to accept such a deal, recognition of this danger underscored the importance of our efforts. The United States needed to resolve Soviet security concerns lest Gorbachev and Shevardnadze look to the West Germans for answers.

The Washington Summit   The Bush-Gorbachev Summit thus emerged as the most important U.S.-Soviet meeting ever held.[123] It was a summit essentially unlike any that had gone before. The issues under discussion went to the root of Cold War conflict: the division of Germany and of Europe, significant reductions in the Soviet military threat to the West, and the transformation of the U.S.-Soviet relationship toward one of genuine cooperation. In this regard, the two presidents' long, informal discussions at Camp David the next to the last day of the summit turned out to be more important than any of the formal White House events or even the agreements that were signed. Yet Gorbachev's preoccupation was with his own deteriorating domestic situation. Boris Yeltsin, now a serious rival, had been elected the day before as parliamentary leader of the Russian republic, and Gorbachev was due to face a restive party congress in early July. For the U.S. side, therefore, the task was both to achieve a breakthrough on the key security issues—arms control as well as Germany—and to help Gorbachev answer his domestic critics. Nor could the two tasks be separated: if Gorbachev did not survive the party congress with his political power intact, whatever other breakthroughs we might have achieved could quickly be reversed. Gorbachev needed a successful summit, and we meant to give him one.

While there were differences within the administration as to how far we should go to give Gorbachev the help he felt he needed, there was general agreement, certainly as far as the president and Secretary Baker were concerned, that we should do what we could to build Gorbachev up for his forthcoming party congress. For Gorbachev and Shevardnadze, the most important result was the signing of a U.S.-Soviet trade agreement, a point to which both kept returning as a crucial symbolic vindication of their foreign policy line. Technically, our pursuit of a trade agreement hinged on Soviet emigration policy and passage of accompanying legislation then pending in the Supreme Soviet. Politically, the issues were Soviet intransigence on Baltic independence and ongoing economic sanctions against Lithuania, points we felt as strongly about as Congress did. Although the Soviet side was not yet in a position to resolve these issues to our satisfaction, the president sought and received Gorbachev's renewed commitment to resolve Baltic independence demands through peaceful dialogue. At Gorbachev's urging, the president reluctantly agreed not to make an explicit link between the trade agreement and Lithuania. Instead, he announced simply that he would sign the trade agreement but would not send it to Congress for approval until the Supreme Soviet passed its emigration law.[124] (Whether a different course would have hastened or hindered Baltic independence is debatable. The president's judgment, for which he knowingly took considerable criticism from the Baltic-American community and others, was that the course he chose to take was the one most likely to secure German unification *and* Baltic independence.)

More than a dozen other separate agreements were signed, including critical ones on nuclear testing, chemical weapons reductions, and especially strategic arms (affirming near-agreement on a START treaty). From the U.S. perspective, however, the most important was an agreement to accelerate negotiations toward a CFE treaty, so as to make sure that agreed military reductions kept pace with and reinforced the breakneck pace of political change. We did not want to approach the final stages of German unification with the question of future agreed force levels in Europe left undetermined, particularly in light of ongoing discussions between Bonn and Moscow on limiting the size of the future German armed forces. With so much in flux, a few fixed points of reference were needed. We therefore attached particular importance to the joint statement in which President Bush and President Gorbachev declared that they considered a CFE agreement "the indispensable foundation" of European security and "committed themselves to intensifying the pace of the negotiations in Vienna and to reaching rapid agreement on all outstanding issues."

On the question of Germany's NATO membership, Gorbachev returned to the idea of united Germany's being simultaneously a member of both NATO and the Warsaw Pact. Recalling President Bush's naval background, he offered the view that "if one anchor is good, two anchors are better." Yet it was clear that he was still casting about for a solution.[125] Ultimately, by shifting the logic of the discussion from outcome to process, the president gained Gorbachev's reluctant agreement that sovereign states should be accorded the right to choose their own alliance relationships. Thus, with Soviet consent, we were able to insert the following key passage into the president's public statement at the close of the summit: "President Gorbachev and I . . . are in full agreement that the matter of alliance membership is, in accordance with the Helsinki Final Act, a matter for the Germans to decide."[126] It was a major breakthrough.

Equally important, discussion of the issue was framed in the right way—not on NATO membership per se, but on the broader questions of what kind of Europe was emerging, with what kind of security structures and what kind of roles for the United States and the Soviet Union.

While this was precisely what we had been working for many months to achieve, it also placed the burden squarely on our shoulders to demonstrate that NATO was indeed transforming itself in ways that Moscow should find reassuring. It was a point that was reinforced a few days later at a CSCE foreign ministers' meeting in Copenhagen, where Shevardnadze told Baker privately that the Soviet Union could accept united Germany's membership in NATO if the "nine assurances" could be codified.[127]

Our first opportunity came immediately thereafter, at a meeting of NATO foreign ministers in Turnberry, Scotland, on June 7 and 8. In his speech on the first day of the meeting, Secretary Baker called on NATO "to accelerate the alliance's ongoing process of reassessment and renewal" and to "look beyond the narrower task of preventing war to the broader one of building the peace."[128] That evening, in one of those surreal experiences of this period in which all the old rules were changing, several of us were called away from dinner to draft a response to a communiqué just issued by Warsaw Pact foreign ministers (then meeting in Moscow), who had declared an end to hostility between the two alliances. Accordingly, the 16 delegations prepared a "Message from Turnberry" in which NATO "extend[ed] to the Soviet Union and to all other European countries the hand of friendship and cooperation." The main communiqué was pretty thin gruel, however.[129] It called on the alliance to "adapt . . . to the enormous changes now taking place" and endorsed the initiatives in President Bush's Oklahoma State speech. Owing partly to the reluctance of Prime Minister Thatcher (who, as host, opened the meeting) to countenance any weakening of nuclear deterrence policy, it offered nothing further of substance as regards the promised "wide-ranging strategic review."

It was therefore up to the United States to lead NATO in a substantially new direction and to articulate a new common vision by the time of the London Summit, now less than a month away. The pivotal importance of this summit was underscored at the second Two Plus Four foreign ministers' meeting, held in Berlin on June 22. Although less strident than in the first meeting, Shevardnadze's official position had not moved much. He called for a five-year transitional period during which the Four Powers would continue to oversee semisovereign Germany and would reciprocally reduce their forces stationed there down to no more than "token contingents." During this transition, Germany would remain simultaneously bound—doubly anchored, as it were—to NATO and the Warsaw Pact. Secretary Baker and British foreign secretary Hurd forcefully rejected these proposals, which Shevardnadze himself disavowed in his private discussions with Baker. Explaining that his presentation was a "Politburo document" that had been forced on him and Gorbachev, Shevardnadze made it plain that their ability to prevail depended on the outcome of the NATO Summit.[130]

The London Summit: A Transformed NATO   It is not often that policymakers—or historians, for that matter—can trace the lines of policy from conception through execution to demonstrable impact. The "London Declaration on a Transformed North Atlantic Alliance" was one such case. The NSC staff took the lead in drafting, coordinating (i.e., with the Departments of State and Defense), and gaining the president's approval for a bold, plain-language text, which was then passed via presidential message to allied leaders and revised on the basis of their comments. At the London Summit, allied leaders approved a final version, identical in most respects to our original text though somewhat diluted, which Secretary Baker sent in advance draft form to Shevardnadze while the Soviet party congress was in session. Aboard Air Force One en route back from London, the president also sent Gorbachev a message highlighting the ways the declaration addressed Soviet concerns. Thus when the declaration was released in London, Gorbachev and Shevardnadze were able to react promptly and positively before hard-line critics were able to weigh in. Both later stressed publicly as well as privately that the London Declaration was critical to their acceptance of German unity within the alliance and to their ability to override domestic political opposition.[131]

The declaration pointed to a transformed alliance in four main areas. First, it set as its new political mission the development of cooperation and partnership with former adversaries. The alliance pledged never to be the first to use force, proposed a nonaggression pact with members of the Warsaw Pact, and invited those governments to establish diplomatic liaison missions at NATO headquarters in Brussels. Second, it called for changing the character of conventional defense by moving away from the doctrine of "forward defense" and relying increasingly on more mobile, truly multinational forces. The summit also proposed follow-on conventional arms control negotiations (after the conclusion of a CFE treaty) to further limit offensive military forces in Europe. Third, it announced a new NATO nuclear strategy, modifying "flexible response" to reduce reliance on nuclear weapons and "making nuclear forces truly weapons of last resort." Fourth, it proposed strengthening the CSCE process by giving it a new mandate to promote democratic institutions, operational capacity in the area of conflict prevention, and, for the first time, institutional expression through a new secretariat and other bodies.[132]

Agreement on these proposals came through a combination of compromise and duress, both within our own government and among the allies. "Institutionalizing" the CSCE process was anathema to some in Washington who feared that the organization would eventually undermine NATO or felt that the CSCE, because of its diverse membership and rigid procedures, was inherently incapable of playing a real security role. The modification of "flexible response" was adopted over the strenuous objections of Prime Minister Thatcher, who insisted that the "last resort" formulation be preceded by the statement that there are "no circumstances in which nuclear retaliation to military action might be discounted."[133] The French, always the most problematic, opposed any expansion of NATO's role eastward and objected, with some justification, to launching the "new" NATO via the old pattern of having a "made in USA" draft thrust on them at the last moment. (We paid a price for our heavy-handedness, in the form of hardening French attitudes toward the alliance and what they saw as continued, unalterable American dominance of the organization. Yet this aggressive approach was perhaps the only one that could have produced the desired result at the London Summit, which had to go beyond the usual mush that comes from communiqués drafted by committee.)

When one rereads the London Declaration some years after the fact, the document seems much less dramatic than it was at the time.[134] It went about as far as allied leaders were prepared to go, but not far enough in preparing NATO for a radically different role in a Europe undergoing revolutionary change. Indeed, early in the drafting stage, we played around at staff level with proposing that NATO's name be changed—to "Euro-Atlantic Treaty Organization" or some such—to mark a symbolic break with the past and underscore the alliance's intent to transform itself fundamentally. Although this controversial idea never made it beyond the level of informal discussions, mainly at staff level, it was emblematic of our recognition, even at that early stage, that NATO's survival would require a far more wrenching adjustment than anything envisioned in the London Declaration.[135] Still, the declaration was bold enough to enable the alliance to stay a step ahead of the enormous changes then unfolding. And it was forthcoming enough to pass the immediate test, which was to satisfy Soviet concerns sufficiently to pave the way for agreement for a united Germany within the alliance. Together with the Washington Summit and the U.S.-Soviet trade agreement, the London Summit helped Gorbachev to emerge from his party congress with his political authority intact. Moreover, these measures provided the essential backdrop for the dramatic meeting in the Caucasus between Kohl and Gorbachev.

Two Plus Four Adds Up to One Germany

Since the first Two Plus Four ministerial (held in Bonn on May 5), the West Germans had been working virtually nonstop to address Soviet security concerns and extend emergency economic assistance. As this part of the story has been recounted by German officials who were directly involved, its key elements can be reviewed in telegraphic form here. In mid-May, following a visit to Moscow by the chancellor's security adviser, Horst Teltschik, Bonn offered to assume all East German economic obligations to the USSR and to extend the country a $3 billion credit as part of a package of agreements linked to German unity. Meanwhile, in four separate meetings with Shevardnadze in May and June, Genscher offered compensation for the costs of maintaining Soviet forces in Germany during a transitional period. He also sought to answer Soviet demands for limitations on the future level of the German armed forces, assurances on the military status of GDR territory, and renunciation by Germany of weapons of mass destruction. With these issues close to resolution, Chancellor Kohl traveled to the Soviet Union in mid-July for meetings with President Gorbachev in Moscow and then at Gorbachev's home near Stavropol in the Caucasus.

"V-E Day II": Agreement in the Caucasus   While expecting further progress during the visit, neither we nor the Germans dared hope that the result would be as stunning as it was. By the end of the visit on July 16, the two sides had reached agreement on all major issues. Germany would remain in NATO, with Four Power rights terminated at the time of unification. Soviet forces would remain for a transitional period of three to four years, during which time NATO structures would not be extended into GDR territory. United Germany would renounce produc-

tion or possession of nuclear, biological, and chemical weapons and would reduce its military forces to a level of 370,000.

Some journalists termed it "Stavrapallo," combining Stavropol and Rapallo (site of the signing of a separate peace treaty between Germany and the USSR in 1923) and implying that it was another bilateral deal struck over the heads of other powers. Given the intensity of the coordination between Bonn and Washington, this was hardly our view. At the NSC, not normally known for its party-like atmosphere, we celebrated over champagne (agreeing that German *sekt* would have been better). In private, we termed July 16, 1990, "V-E Day II," signifying the belated liberation of the continent, nearly two generations after the Allied victory in Europe in 1945.

From that point on, the terms of German unification were effectively set. The third Two Plus Four foreign ministers' meeting, held in Paris the day after the agreement in the Caucasus, reached agreement on the Polish-German border and on an outline of a final agreement on German unification. To be sure, there were a vast number of issues still to be resolved and substantive disagreements still to be overcome. At a "One Plus Three" political directors' meeting I attended in London in August, we listed some 25 separate issues, many of them complex and contentious, that needed to be resolved—in just over a month—in order for German unification to be finalized. Yet the main political battles had been won. The rest was anticlimax.

NATO's future role in East Germany was the last significant unresolved issue when the Two Plus Four political directors met in Moscow in early September to agree on a treaty text. That the GDR should have "special status" had been agreed on long since.[136] Yet the Soviet side insisted that, even after the withdrawal of their forces from GDR territory, non-German forces could neither be stationed nor "deployed" in that territory. So, for a time, did the Germans, tabling language that allied forces "shall not cross a line" into this territory except for access to Berlin.[137] Even after the Germans backed away from this formulation, important questions remained. Could NATO forces conduct maneuvers in eastern Germany? Could they discharge their treaty responsibilities in the event (however remote or unlikely it may have seemed at the time) of some future military threat to Germany? Would, in other words, Germany be partly in NATO and partly not?

Ultimately, these concerns were resolved by the device of an "Agreed Minute" to the treaty, stipulating that "any questions with respect to the application of the word 'deployed' . . . will be decided by the Government of the united Germany in a reasonable and responsible way."[138] It was a remarkable formulation and indeed may have constituted a unique case in international law, whereby the interpretation of an element of a multilateral treaty is left solely to the discretion of one signatory. Equally remarkable was that the Soviet side, in what can only have been an oversight by their negotiating team, agreed to this blanket formulation in the following article (Article 6): "The right of the united Germany to belong to alliances, with all the rights and responsibilities arising therefrom, shall not be affected by the present Treaty." As we read the two formulations, NATO's role in Germany was undiluted, and Germany would freely render a decision when questions arose. We could hardly ask for more than that. With that issue behind us, the way was clear for agreement.

"The Treaty on the Final Settlement with Respect to Germany" was signed by the Two Plus Four foreign ministers in Moscow on September 12.[139] German unification was formally consummated on October 3, welcomed by President Bush during his visit to the united Germany November 18, and blessed by the 34 members of the CSCE at the Paris Summit from November 19 to 21. What had seemed a remote aspiration scarcely a year before had become reality.

Final Reflections on the "Final Settlement"   The American role in helping secure German unification surely will be recorded as one of the most successful diplomatic endeavors in the history of American statecraft. Nearly all our main goals were achieved. Germany was united "in peace and freedom," enjoying full sovereignty from the moment of unification. It remained a full member of the North Atlantic alliance and an active proponent of a more united Europe. German unification was endorsed by all of Europe, including the Soviet Union, and, in the end, was genuinely welcomed by most. It was achieved within the context of an emergent democratic order in Europe and the transformation of its key institutions. The United States remained in Europe as a factor of stability, its continued political, economic, and military presence not only tolerated but actively encouraged. Our successes were attributable to a coherent strategy and to the single-mindedness with which we pursued our objectives, even when the chances of fulfilling them seemed remote. They were attributable also to President Bush's statesmanship and political judgment, Secretary Baker's skills as strategist and negotiator, and the close coordination between the National Security Council staff and the Department of State, as well as between Washington and Bonn.

Our broader objective of embedding German unification within a stable new European order proved more elusive. Given the revolutionary flux in the East and the imminent disintegration of the Soviet Union itself, this goal may well have been unattainable. Still, with the benefit of a few years' hindsight, some questions persist. First, was Prime Minister Thatcher really so wrong in protesting that the rush to unity was threatening the future of European security? Did the priority we attached to the unification process cause us to neglect other objectives that would have helped "synchronize" Germany's unification with Europe's? Second, did our cooperation with Bonn during this period establish, as we hoped it would, the United States and Germany as "partners in leadership"? Were we right in seeing the U.S.-German relationship at the center of a future European and transatlantic order, and did we succeed in laying the foundations of future partnership? Had we, finally, helped achieve German unity without answering the German question? It is obviously far too early to pass historical judgment on these issues, but a few preliminary thoughts can be ventured.

As to the speed of the process, our assumption (and Bonn's) that we needed to move rapidly, while we still had a Soviet leadership able and disposed to compromise, seemed less compelling after the breakup of the Soviet Union and the advent of Boris Yeltsin's government in Russia. Perhaps we did not need to work so feverishly to "get the hay in the barn before the storm comes," as Chancellor Kohl put it, or set German unification so far above other objectives, such as supporting the democratic transformation of Central and Eastern Europe. Yet we did not have the opportunity in 1990 to turn the clock forward to see what the next few years would hold in store. (Nor, of course, would there have been any guarantee that this putative "future" would have been the same had we not acted as we did.) Moreover, while a more measured, step-by-step pace of German unification might have been preferable for the sake of future stability, the virtual implosion of the GDR made this option elusive and perhaps unattainable. It is not clear that the East German state could have been propped up even if all concerned had sought to do so. Even if inter-German rapprochement had been pursued via the stages envisioned in Kohl's ten points, the reality would have been very rapid merger, whether labeled "confederation," "treaty-based association," or something else.

As to the future U.S.-German relationship, "partners in leadership" may have set an unrealistically high standard, which not even our close cooperation during unification could fulfill. Some in Washington presumed that German "gratitude" for U.S. support would translate into political capital. They were soon, and predictably, disappointed, notably by Germany's failure to act decisively in resolving U.S.-EC disputes over the Uruguay Round of the GATT (General Agreement on Tariffs and Trade).[140] We should not have expected gratitude for actions that were in our interests as well, nor should we have sought to build a new relationship on this transitory sentiment. Many of us also tended to extrapolate from the unification period an exaggerated convergence of U.S. and German interests and, by the same token, to underestimate the extent to which the "partners" concept collided with Germany's relations with its EC partners, especially France. Indeed, when German president von Weizsäcker later paid a state visit to the United States, President Bush sought to answer these concerns: "A united Germany, champion of a more united Europe, stands as our partner in leadership. . . . Strong German-American cooperation is fully compatible with development of a more united Europe, a goal that the United States has consistently supported over the years, just as unequivocally as we supported German unity."[141]

While "partners in leadership" led to extravagant expectations springing from our close cooperation in 1989 and 1990, its initial conception was not based on a sentimental or naive view of future U.S.-German relations. It proceeded from our anticipation of the emerging reality in pre- and postunification Europe and our recognition that U.S.-German relations would be key to realization of important U.S. interests in Europe and beyond. The relationship that came out of the unification period was a sound one, built on the foundation of successful cooperation toward shared goals. Yet just as that cooperation was the product of a complex and sometimes difficult process of mutual adjustment during unification, its extension into the new era could not simply be assumed.

The German question was never about unity alone but about fitting a powerful Germany into a stable and secure European order. In 1990, the question was not so much about Germany but about the European order into which it needed to fit. Germany's democracy and its European and Atlantic credentials were no longer in doubt, but the country's moment of unification occurred in the midst of profound turbulence that could only complicate its settling into a stable new role. Within the European Community, unification had been accompanied by renewed commitment on the part of Germany and its partners to economic and political union and to the realization of the Community's early vision of a broader unity that spanned the continent. The Atlantic alliance, again with Germany's strong support, had undertaken a process of renewal, also aimed at helping overcome Europe's division. Whether these efforts would succeed hinged on the progress of postcommunist transformation in the East and the gradual integration of these emerging (or aspiring) democracies into a broader democratic community.

The German question, in short, was still open, but this time it was not the fault of the Germans. Linked as always to the European question, it was in any case not amenable to final and definitive resolution. For this historical moment, the answer to the German question had to be found within a still-elusive post–Cold War European order.

4

Toward a Post–Cold War Order

WHEN PRESIDENTS and prime ministers from all of Europe and North America convened in Paris in November 1990, it was a moment of triumph for the principles and values that had animated Western policies for four decades and more. In the glowering presence of Soviet defense minister Dimitri Yazov, a symbol of an era now drawing to a merciful conclusion, the Paris Summit codified the decisive end of the Cold War and of Europe's long division. (When Hungarian Prime Minister József Antall delivered a speech calling for the dissolution of the Warsaw Pact, I happened to be sitting behind Antall and directly across the table from Yazov. The latter's look of now-impotent malevolence seemed as good a symbol as any of the passing of the old order.[1]) Its stunning achievements would have been hardly imaginable a year before: acknowledgement of German unification, conclusion of an agreement for deep military reductions, issuance of a joint declaration of friendship between members of NATO and the soon to be defunct Warsaw Pact, and publication of a "Charter of Paris" heralding a new era of European peace and comity.

Yet the triumphalism of the Paris Summit was already being overshadowed by the sober realities of the post–Cold War world: the Iraqi invasion of Kuwait in August 1990, the looming crisis in Yugoslavia, and the growing fragmentation of the Soviet Union. These were but the most egregious portents of a wider instability. There were fears of resurgent German power, of failed democratic experiments in Eastern Europe, of revived national conflicts and border disputes, all arising outside the confines of the known bipolar system, without the galvanizing element of a common threat.

The end of the Cold War, it seemed, was also the end of the "long peace" in which nuclear deterrence had inhibited conventional war as well.[2] And the institutions and policies of the bygone era were showing themselves inadequate for the one now upon us. As Macauley had written in a different context, "The revolution [eliminated] one class of evils, but had at the same time—such is the imperfection of all things human—engendered or aggravated another class of evils which required new remedies."[3] Among these were the tasks of transforming Western institutions to meet radically new challenges, building a new order in which the Soviet Union and the states of Eastern Europe would find a secure place, and dealing with new threats to European security arising from the ashes of communist rule.

Even more fundamental was the task of democratic consolidation in the East, without which no amount of "architectural" innovation or conflict resolution mechanisms among European institutions would have any prospect of success. Democratic development in Central and Eastern Europe, then, was preeminently a security issue. More than that, it was *the* preeminent security issue for post–Cold War Europe. It was a challenge for which Western policies and institutions were ill-prepared. Indeed, the daunting tasks of postcommunist transition served as a reminder that the end of the Cold War had reopened the *Eastern question* that had preoccupied Europe at Yalta, Versailles, and the Congress of Vienna.[4]

If averting another Versailles-like German settlement had been an urgent priority of the diplomacy of German unification, so too was preventing the emergence of a latter-day Weimar Republic, this time in the form of an embittered, defeated Soviet Union. We did not want Russia any more than Germany to be "singularized" or isolated in the emerging order. Thus, the strenuous efforts to address Soviet security concerns during 1990 had been aimed not only at facilitating German unification but also at creating conditions that would permit the Soviet Union to assume a strong and secure place in the international community. In form as well as substance, these measures sought to build a pattern of relations that would carry over to a post–Cold War world of concerted action among former adversaries. The losers had to have a stake in preserving the settlement, just as the winners needed to find ways of sustaining their cooperation into the new era. As one writer put it, "The diplomacy that preceded unification was reminiscent of concert diplomacy in the nineteenth century except that the big powers [were] no longer the sole arbiters of Europe's fate. The principle [was] the same: concerted policies are likely to protect the interests of each state better than unilateral action."[5]

The "New World Order"

Elements of this conception were to be found in the efforts to articulate and shape a "new world order." The concept, it must be admitted, failed to persuade, partly because the term betrayed an unfortunate American proclivity toward universalism and grandiosity. Then there was the "Holy Roman Empire" analogy of seeming to its critics to be none of the three—in this case, neither new in concept, worldwide in application, nor orderly in practice. Outside the European context, particularly in the Middle East, the term suffered from what was seen as an incongruity between principles and interests. Was it high principle that led us to oppose the Iraqi invasion of Kuwait, or was it oil? The obvious answer—that it was both, along with regional stability and weapons of mass destruction—never satisfied the domestic need for moral clarity, so the term took on the crusading rhetoric of a "Pax Americana" that was never intended. And it was held to the impossibly high standard that its principles should find universal adherence and the order it promised guarantee perpetual peace.

Although the concept later acquired ambitious theoretical and institutional trappings, the "new world order" proceeded from a simple idea. President Bush and General Scowcroft were fishing off the Bush compound in Kennebunkport, Maine, in August 1990, just after Secretary Baker and Foreign Minister Shevardnadze had issued a joint condemnation of the Iraqi invasion of Kuwait and shortly before Bush and Gorbachev were to meet in Helsinki to issue a similar joint statement. If the United States and the Soviet Union could find common cause in opposing aggression waged by a longstanding Soviet client state, Bush and Scowcroft thought, then perhaps there were opportunities to translate the successes in Europe into a framework of global cooperation in which the United States and its traditional allies were joined by the Soviet Union itself. This was the foundation of the concept: not an aggrandized United Nations or a U.S.-Soviet strategic partnership but rather the pragmatic notion that the Soviet Union might now become an active contributor to the resolution of global problems, particularly in cases of international aggression. This, indeed, had been embedded in Bush's thinking from the time of the Texas A&M speech in May 1989,[6] but the events of the intervening 16 months had made the aspiration newly vivid.

Conceptually, the "new world order" deserved closer study than it received. Its principles were drawn from the most basic American values and interests—democracy, free markets, the rule of law—which were also to be found in the United Nations Charter and the Helsinki Final Act.[7] It combined the realist's appreciation of the permanence of the power factor in world affairs with the liberal internationalist's recognition that democracies make better partners than dictatorships in building a secure order.[8] It offered a reasonable structure, with the Western allies at the core of an expanding democratic community, facilitating the gradual development of a modern version of the nineteenth-century concert system in which the major powers calibrated and coordinated their actions with due consideration for the interests of all.[9] It looked to a revitalized United Nations and other institutions, such as a strengthened CSCE, to legitimate and facilitate common action. It called on a secure, prosperous, and more united Europe, in which the new democracies of the East joined our traditional allies, to assume new responsibilities as our main partners in global leadership. In this sense, it was meant to be both a challenge to Europe and a point of reference for the American public in the post–Cold War world.

The "new world order" was articulated first in September 1990. Bush and Gorbachev had just met in Helsinki, where the two leaders issued a joint statement insisting that "Iraq's aggression must not be tolerated. No peaceful international order is possible if larger states can devour their smaller neighbors." Using this as his point of departure, the president invoked the prospect of a new world order in a September 11 address before a joint session of Congress:

> We stand today at a unique and extraordinary moment. The crisis in the Persian Gulf, grave as it is, also offers a rare opportunity to move toward a historic period of cooperation. Out of these troubled times . . . a new world order can emerge . . . , a world where the rule of law supplants the law of the jungle, a world in which nations recognize the shared responsibility for freedom and justice, a world where the strong respect the rights of the weak.
>
> This is the vision that I shared with President Gorbachev in Helsinki. He and other leaders from Europe, the Gulf, and around

the world understand that how we manage this crisis could shape the future for generations to come. The test we face is great—and so are its stakes. This is the first assault on the new world that we seek, the first test of our mettle.

America and the world must defend common vital interests. . . . Vital issues of principle are at stake. Saddam Hussein is literally trying to wipe a country off the face of the earth. . . . Vital economic interests are at stake as well. . . . An Iraq permitted to swallow Kuwait would have the economic and military power . . . to intimidate and coerce [neighboring countries] that control the lion's share of the world's remaining oil reserves. We cannot permit a resource so vital to be dominated by one so ruthless. . . . Iraq will not be permitted to annex Kuwait. That is not a threat; that is not a boast; that is just the way it is going to be.[10]

The concept fared best when extrapolated from the European context, as in the president's November 1990 Prague speech, which made explicit the goal of seeking to replicate on a global scale that which was already being approximated in Europe. The speech was meant to weave into a coherent whole several disparate strands: the realization of a Europe "whole and free," in the context of the president's visit to Czechoslovakia and then to united Germany en route to the Paris Summit as well as the threats to this new order posed by the Iraqi invasion of Kuwait and the gathering Yugoslav crisis. (As will be seen, we had wanted to make Yugoslavia a major theme at Paris, but found little support or interest in Europe for a topic that might put a damper on the festivities.[11]) The president's speech was at once a celebration, a challenge, and a warning:

Europe, east and west, stands at a threshold of a new era—an era of peace, prosperity, and security unparalleled in the long history of this continent. Today, Europe's long division is ending. . . . Working together, we can fulfill the promise of a Europe that reaches its democratic destiny—a Europe that is truly whole and free. . . .

Europe's celebration of freedom brings with it a new responsibility. Now that democracy has proven its power, Europe has both the opportunity and the challenge to join us in leadership—to work with us in common cause toward a new commonwealth of freedom . . . , a moral community united in its dedication to free ideals . . . , a world in which the use of force gives way to a shared respect for the rule of law. . . . That is why our response to the challenge in the Persian Gulf is critical. [It] is a warning to America as well as to Europe that we cannot turn inward, somehow isolate ourselves from global challenges. . . .

More and more, the Soviet Union is demonstrating its commitment to act as a constructive force for international stability. More and more, the United Nations is functioning as its creators intended—free from the ideological confrontation that frustrated collective action. . . . From this first crisis of the post–Cold War era comes an historic opportunity . . . to draw upon the great and growing strength of the commonwealth of freedom and forge for all nations a new world order far more stable and secure than any we have known.[12]

It was a complex set of ideas—too complicated for a twenty-minute speech. Perhaps the most difficult was the linkage between democracy and international relations. Those of us who were developing the idea of a "new world order" did not require or expect that all states be democratic, nor did we assume that a world of democracies was the answer to all the ills of humankind. Rather, the concept rested on the proposition that democratic principles observed *within* states could inform an order *among* states which could, over time, induce more states to adhere internally to these broader norms. As more countries embraced the principles, the international order would gain strength, which in turn would encourage yet more states to adapt domestically to principles they might otherwise flout. And so on, in a happy Wilsonian virtuous cycle.

This might seem implausibly idealistic coming from practical men like Bush, Baker, Cheney, and Scowcroft. But this progression approximated what had just happened in Europe, as the principles undergirding the Western democracies established, via CSCE and elsewhere, international norms to which the communist regimes of the East ultimately succumbed. As more states embraced democratic values, the international community was able to strengthen and elaborate a set of international principles based on human rights, democratic values, free market economies, and the rule of law. Expanded to the global scale, the "new world order" thus conceived did not require that every state be democratic but only that democratic norms increasingly inform an international order. (The logical extension of this in the Middle East would have had the Saudi monarchy ultimately yielding to pressures for democratic change or at least toward greater political participation for its citizens, but we could not very well say that—another reason that the concept seemed so cynical in application.)

The problems with the "new world order" were several. Most obviously, it was caught up in the euphoria of a unique moment of democratic ascendancy in the wake of the Cold War, in which it was all too easy to mistake the transitory for the permanent. It was hard to resist the Wilsonian temptation to believe that the principles themselves were so compelling that no one dared flout them. Those who did—like the Serbian leadership—were branded outlaws from this new order, as if that would move them to alter their behavior.[13] It was also a state-centered approach that may have been useful for addressing clear cases of military aggression like the Iraqi invasion of Kuwait, but which had no answer to conflicts springing from impoverishment, civil disorder, or ethnic nationalism. The concept was focused on international aggression, the predominant threat to the international order but by no means the only source of conflict. The Wilsonian panoply of policies—moral suasion, economic sanctions, and, as a last resort, military force in the name of collective security—were hard enough to invoke against sovereign states. They had little or no utility when directed against parties to a civil war.

In the final analysis, however, the deficiencies of the "new world order" were not so much conceptual as political: the term involved not just the articulation of a set of principles but a statement about American readiness to defend an "order" whose contours were only beginning to make themselves apparent and a set of interests that remained elusive. It demanded a domestic political constituency that had yet to be molded—a challenge that the administration never took seriously enough. Thus, when it came to assuming new burdens, the "new world order" conflicted with public expectations of a handsome post–Cold War "peace dividend" that would enable us to eschew foreign commitments and focus on pressing needs at home. Nor was the United States alone in groping for its role and purposes in the new era: our major partners and especially our former adversaries faced even greater uncertainties, which made calculations of a new order premature at best.

Competing Visions of the New Europe

Political leaders are animated as much by their visions of the future—
intellectual constructs about the desired or assumed future state of affairs—as by dispassionate analysis of present and likely future trends. In
short, visions matter, and they can be impervious to inconvenient realities. If the American administration was moved by thoughts of a new
transatlantic partnership as the foundation of an emergent global order,
politicians in Paris, Brussels, and elsewhere were equally bent on seizing
the moment to create a more united, post-Yalta Europe that ended the
continent's dependency on American power. Others wanted to scrap existing institutions and create out of whole cloth a new post–Cold War
European order. Indeed, although political commentators decried the
lack of "vision" on the part of statesmen on both sides of the Atlantic,
the problem was not a dearth of new ideas but a surfeit of competing,
unreconciled visions. At least four distinct conceptions, with overlapping adherents, were evident at the time of the Paris Summit.

First was the Atlanticist vision, advocated most forcefully by the
United States and Great Britain, of a permanent American political and
military presence in Europe and a seamless transatlantic security community, albeit with a new balance of U.S. and European roles to accommodate an increasingly assertive European Community. U.S. power, in
this conception, was required to balance continuing, if diminishing, Soviet military preponderance, serve as a counterweight to a newly powerful Germany, and lend a general stability. Its adherents saw the world as
still a dangerous place, in which the requirement for traditional military
security was reduced but still substantial. NATO, as the institutional expression of this vision, was required to continue performing its traditional functions as well as help fill the security vacuum developing in
the East as Soviet power receded and the Warsaw Pact collapsed.

Second was the Europeanist vision, championed by the French and
"Brussels" (meaning the burgeoning EC bureaucracy there, in Strasbourg, and elsewhere), of a more united, cohesive European Community,
moving resolutely to build economic and political union among the
twelve member countries even as it widened its scope to accept new
members. Advocates of this vision presumed and desired a continuing but
gradually diminishing American role during a transitional period until
"Europe" had developed the capacity to assume full responsibility for its
own security. Security, in this conception, was defined less as a traditional

military concern but rather in terms of economic interaction, common values, and shared history and tradition. As these were more relevant than NATO's military might to the problems of the eastern half of the continent, it was argued, the European Community had the responsibility to take the lead in ending the division of Europe and realize the initial vision of Jean Monnet and Robert Schuman of a fully united Europe.

Third was the "Vancouver-to-Vladivostok" vision of a pan-European, CSCE-based security community, advocated with differing motivations by the Russians, Czechoslovaks, and others. They foresaw the CSCE supplanting both NATO and the Warsaw Pact and developing new institutions and capacities for collective action. Cooperative security was their watchword. The CSCE, it was argued, was an inclusive institution embracing all of Europe and North America and hence was uniquely suited to bring together former Cold War adversaries. In the most ambitious conception, the CSCE was to become the institutional expression of a "pan-European peace order" that would impel Europe toward perpetual peace and harmony. Even the more limited conception of the CSCE as a forum for political consultation and an umbrella over existing institutions was burdened with the usual problems of collective security arrangements. The most demanding requirement was that states find common purpose and undertake joint action against threats, wherever they might arise, to the stability and integrity of the system—in this case a region encompassing Europe, Eurasia, and North America. "Indivisible security"—a concept that German politicians in particular liked to invoke—meant that every state's security was linked to the security of all others. It was an assumption likely to be proven false the first time it was tested.

Fourth was a "Europe of the States," a vision embraced openly only by Prime Minister Thatcher but shared privately or even unknowingly by many others, not least the French. It was, in fact, a neo-Gaullist conception, which gave primacy to preserving national sovereignty and thus favored bilateral relations and traditional diplomacy. (In her memoirs, Thatcher concluded with her familiar injunction "to shift the emphasis in Europe back toward the original Gaullist idea of a *Europe des Patries.*"[14]) Existing multilateral institutions like NATO, the EC, and the CSCE would continue to function and could even take on new responsibilities— but strictly in the service of their sovereign member states. Although conceptually the least ambitious of the four visions, it was as a practical matter nearly as demanding as the others, placing the major powers at the center of a latter-day concert system, whereby each would calibrate its policies and actions in service of the broader international order.

Few of the 34 delegations represented at Paris would have accepted this four-way division of their various aspirations for the future, and fewer still would have recognized how contradictory they were. Indeed, judging from the interminable speeches delivered by every head of state or government,[15] nearly everyone subscribed to the first three combined. The Germans in particular saw no difficulty in adhering equally to the first three—and, privately, to the fourth as well. German diplomats had a slogan, usually dialectical, to reconcile every contradiction and, as a political matter, to avoid taking sides on contentious issues at the moment of their national reunification.

Yet the differences among these visions were profound—and ultimately irreconcilable. There were differences of geography. "The French Europe," as a Danish writer put it, "is necessarily *Western* Europe," with Eastern Europe entering this picture not as an integral part but "as the *mission,* as the *task* for Western Europe."[16] The Atlanticist vision, by contrast, saw the western borders of "Europe" extending across the ocean and so was in theory, though not always in practice, more open to its eastward extension as well. If the United States described itself as a "European power," as we did, we could hardly quibble about the "Europeanness" of countries east of the old Cold War divide. In this, "Atlantic Europe" found an echo in Gorbachev's increasingly desperate plea for a "common European home" that would avert Soviet Russia's exclusion and marginalization. The new democracies of Central and Eastern Europe harbored similar fears but proffered different remedies: Europe's western boundary should stretch across the Atlantic to cement a Euro-Atlantic community, but "Europe" should stop at their eastern frontier. They would be in; Soviet Russia would be out. The notion of "Central Europe" also came to be used as a way of defining geographically who should be in and who out of the new Europe. The Bulgarians in particular resented the exclusivity of the Visegrád club (discussed below), which they saw as a device to ensure their marginalization.

There were different assumptions about the role of the state. For the French (and "Brussels"), the centralized state was to be replicated at the level of Europe, and intrusive, supranational institutions would wrest sovereignty from constituent states. The British, voicing what many others privately endorsed, insisted that sovereignty be retained by states, whose cooperation would be intergovernmental rather than supranational. Common policies would be the sum total of what member states agreed to undertake—nothing more, nothing less. The Germans, and to some extent their eastern neighbors, aspired to a "Europe where borders have lost their meaning"—which they saw as a consequence not of European federalism but of increasing economic, social, and cultural interaction beneath the level of formal political structures.[17] Although the French and German positions sometimes sounded alike when uttered in the argot of EC diplomacy (known irreverently as "Eurospeak"), the conceptual and practical differences between the two perspectives—between French supranationalism and German subnationalism—were vastly greater than either side saw fit to admit.

There were of course different institutional preferences. For the French, the European Community was at the center. For the United States and Britain, it was NATO. The Germans, as usual, wanted both; yet there were internal divisions between Kohl, who wanted both equally, and the foreign ministry, which gave priority to the EC. The Russians favored the CSCE, for the simple reason that they had a seat at the table. The Central and Eastern Europeans wanted to join both NATO and the EC—meaning that their support was genuine but qualified by the prospect of their admission—and, in the interim, placed a high premium on the CSCE for the same reason as the Russians. And there were differences among the Central Europeans: the Poles were the most ardent Atlanticists, because their historic concerns about German and Russian power could be met only through NATO, while the Hungarians, despite the genuine Atlanticism of their prime minister, focused more on the EC owing to their lesser concerns about Russia and Germany.

The coexistence of so many differing perspectives was an inevitable and in some ways a healthy consequence of the precipitous collapse of the old order. A degree of experimentation was necessary in the transitional period toward an uncertain future. Yet there was a danger that the simultaneous pursuit of multiple, competing visions would ensure the failure of all, in the process hollowing out existing institutions, weakening Western coherence and resolve, and disorienting the embryonic democracies to the east.

U.S. Strategy

With a "new world order" more an ambition than a goal that could be achieved in the near term, American diplomacy aimed instead to achieve a set of more practical and specific immediate objectives. Of necessity, they were built on points of convergence in the competing visions of Europe's future, and would become the basis of a coherent strategy that could gain broad, though not universal, adherence. U.S. approaches proceeded from the guiding principles that the United States had to remain in Europe to balance Russian power and provide stability so that a more united Western Europe could extend its zone of democratic stability eastward. Our presence was also needed to help organize a durable post–Cold War order in which former adversaries were brought into a new system of cooperative security. From these core principles several axioms followed.

First, NATO had to survive the demise of the threat it was formed to counter, for it remained the institutional link binding European and North American security and the only institution capable of providing for the collective defense. This, in turn, meant that U.S. forces had to remain in significant, though much reduced, numbers. Second, NATO's role in post–Cold War Europe called for its radical transformation—internally, toward a new balance of European and American roles and responsibilities; externally, by extending the Atlantic community eastward; and existentially, by adapting itself to the newly emerging security challenges in Europe. Third, the radical reduction of nuclear and conventional forces in Europe had to be accomplished in a way that did not introduce new instabilities and insecurities, so that Russian forces did not become, perversely, even more preponderant in a less militarized Europe and so that European military capacity and readiness were appropriate to new kinds of threats on the horizon. Fourth, the United States needed to embrace European unity, including the development of a common foreign and security policy, while also maintaining the indivisibility of transatlantic security—two competing tasks that proved easier to reconcile in principle than in practice. Fifth, the CSCE (Conference on Security and Cooperation in Europe) needed the institutional and operational capacity to play a stronger political role and assume new security responsibilities, particularly in the areas of conflict prevention and crisis management.

This orientation was largely transitional, aimed at creating a provisional new order for the challenges immediately ahead. It looked to proven institutions like NATO and the EC, rather than an aggrandized CSCE, to provide the essential leadership, relying on their ability to adapt to radically changed circumstances and indeed fulfill their original visions of a more united Europe.[18] We resisted efforts to leapfrog over this transitional stage, disband NATO along with the Warsaw Pact, and move immediately to create what the Czechs and others called a "pan-European peace order" in which the CSCE would be transformed, somehow, into a new system of collective security. If we saw more clearly than the Czechs how illusory such a new order was, and how reminiscent of the pious legalisms of the 1920s, however, they may have understood better the insufficiency of existing structures for the new requirements of European security.

Policy and Process   Policy was hammered out chiefly through a European strategy steering group, also known as the "Gates Group" after Deputy National Security Adviser Bob Gates, who chaired the sessions in the White House Situation Room. Created during German unification but extended to consider issues thereafter, the group met regularly at undersecretary level from the NSC, State, and Defense, including the Joint Chiefs of Staff. (International economic policy was handled by an interagency group chaired by the Treasury Department at undersecretary level.) It was essential to have a regular forum such as this, because cabinet principals were by this time preoccupied with events outside Europe. The president and General Scowcroft were consumed by the Gulf War, as of course were Secretary of Defense Dick Cheney and General Colin Powell. As the war wound down in the late spring of 1991, Secretary Baker devoted most of his energies to the Middle East peace process. And after the failed August coup against Gorbachev, all were focused on a rapidly disintegrating Soviet Union. European policy no longer commanded the undivided attention of NSC principals the way it did in 1989 and 1990, and policy became somewhat more disjointed— or, to be more precise, the follow-through on policy became less consistent and focused.

There were very few policy differences at the highest levels. Indeed, the "inside story" of foreign policy decision making in the Bush administration was not one of ferocious battles of the kind that had characterized most recent administrations, but of almost total agreement on the main lines of policy. Baker was the most sympathetic toward European aspirations—a disposition manifest in his more forthcoming attitudes toward the CSCE, the EC, and NATO's transformation—but within a generally shared strategic perspective. Bush, Baker, Scowcroft, Eagleburger, Treasury Secretary Nicholas Brady: all were men of similar age, experience, and outlook.[19] Cheney, Powell, and Gates, though younger, were men of like disposition. Among this group, with the partial exception of Baker, there was hardly a foreign policy difference of any moment. Firm internationalists, they believed in American leadership and the use of power, especially military power, in foreign policy. Theirs was a state-centered view of the world, in which military aggression conducted by one sovereign entity against another posed the chief challenge to global peace and security. Although they had shown great imagination and creativity in devising an American grand strategy for ending the Cold War, they did so from the familiar post–World War II frame of reference—and appropriately so. But it was a frame of reference less congenial to the brave new world we were about to enter.

The attributes that served U.S. policy so well in 1989 and 1990—the substance of policy as well as the collegial decision-making style—served us less well thereafter. Some of the virtues became liabilities: the commitment to American leadership of the free world, which had been indispensable to forging a Western consensus in 1989–90, carried over afterwards to a rigid insistence on an undiminished American role and made it harder to cede leadership gracefully to the Europeans. Instinctively, we clung to a role we were no longer ready to play.

And some of the preexisting biases that did us little harm in 1989–90 became serious liabilities in 1991–92. A somewhat antiquated suspicion of the European Community and exaggerated, although not altogether fanciful, fears of European protectionism complicated efforts to build up the U.S.-EC bond as part of a new transatlantic relationship. And the view the principals had of the EC remained ambivalent: was it European unity we feared, or European disunity?[20] The similarly outdated and ambivalent image of the CSCE—as a feckless debating club at best and, at worst, as a snare and a delusion or even a threat to NATO's primacy—obscured the organization's potential for bridging the two halves of Europe and taking the lead on "soft" security issues like conflict prevention and resolution. Baker, who took more interest in the CSCE, was able to overcome much of this resistance and put the United States in the lead on several key initiatives, but it was an uphill struggle that never enjoyed the full support of the administration. Finally, their collegiality evolved, by the midpoint of the administration, into a closed and self-contained decision-making circle, increasingly impervious to new and unconventional ideas at the very time that unconventional thinking was most needed.

These liabilities were replicated at senior staff level. Those of us who had been with the administration from the beginning had become more skillful implementors of policy by 1991, but our thinking was not as fresh and less open to ideas from outside.[21] We were running out of gas, and our batteries were low, but the journey was so compelling that we failed to notice.

The United States in Europe   The overriding focus on keeping the United States in Europe needs underlining. In terms of Isaiah Berlin's fox and hedgehog distinction,[22] this was the hedgehog's "one big thing"—our central vision and key organizing principle. It was the driving force behind the European strategy group and the main reason it had been created in the first place. No idea was more strongly and deeply held in the upper levels of the administration than the core conviction that the American presence was indispensable to European stability and therefore to vital American interests. This can be illustrated by passages from two speeches delivered a day apart in mid-May 1990 by Czechoslovak foreign minister Jiří Dienstbier and Secretary of State Baker. First, Dienstbier:

> We . . . hear the objection that NATO must be preserved at any price. We have nothing against NATO. It has successfully played its role and will continue to play it for a certain period of time. . . . Another objection against the replacement of the old bloc structures . . . is that it would mean the American departure from Europe. Well, for how long do we want the American people to pay for our freedom, for our inability to settle the conditions in Europe?[23]

Now, Baker:

> The visible reduction in the Soviet threat has led some to assume that our only reason for being in Europe over the last 40 years was to contain that threat. Beyond containment, in their view, lies the end of the American role. And so as the alleged "single cause" of America's involvement—fear of Soviet aggression—recedes, America's position in Europe should recede with it.
>
> This would be the most profound strategic mistake of the generation. We must leave not only the cold war behind but also the

conflicts that preceded the cold war. The reduction of the Soviet threat need not cause Europe to revert to an unsteady balance of power or a fresh outbreak of national rivalries and ethnic tensions.[24]

Dienstbier's was an argument not to be dismissed. Indeed, the great majority of Europeans and Americans alike would have seconded his sentiments unless their own political leaders could offer persuasive arguments to the contrary. President Bush and Secretary Baker were preoccupied with this concern. Privately as well as publicly, Bush came back to it again and again; he saw it as his chief foreign policy responsibility to hold back the inevitable pressures for disengagement, if not isolationism, by creating the conditions for an active and continuing American role.[25] Here is Bush speaking at Aspen in August 1990, just after the Iraqi invasion of Kuwait:

> The U.S. will keep a force in Europe as long as our allies want and need us there. . . . We will remain in Europe to deter any new dangers, to be a force for stability—and to reassure all of Europe, east and west, that the European balance will remain secure. . . .
>
> The brutal aggression launched last night against Kuwait illustrates my central thesis: Notwithstanding the alteration in the Soviet threat, the world remains a dangerous place with serious threats to important U.S. interests *wholly unrelated to the earlier patterns of the U.S.-Soviet relationship.*[26]

The case for continued American engagement had to reckon not only with the decline of the Soviet threat but also with the advent of a more united Western Europe, eager to assume responsibility for European stability and security. During the course of German unification, we had worked—so far with success—to delink the American military presence in Europe from Soviet troop withdrawals. Now we had also to delink the American presence from the process of European integration. The importance of the American role, we believed, transcended Europe's achievement of greater economic and political unity; it had to do with semipermanent factors of power and geography.

We knew where it should come out in the end: a permanent American presence that would facilitate European unity and so reduce the burden on ourselves, yielding a new transatlantic balance of roles and responsibilities. But getting there would require a careful balancing act. We wanted to encourage European unity, but not so effusively as to cause our own public to conclude our presence was superfluous. We wanted to reduce American preponderance via NATO in European affairs, but not so rapidly as to cause Europeans to believe we lacked staying power. There was a delicate balance between the short-term, tactical requirements of flexibility and the longer-term, strategic necessity of sticking to core principles: too much flexibility would jeopardize ultimate goals, and too much rigidity would prevent the experimentation needed to revamp the institutions and habits of forty years of transatlantic relations.

The American presence we had in mind had an economic as well as a security dimension and indeed was acquiring an increasingly economic logic and rationale. As the military dimensions of security receded, trade issues loomed larger—and now would be played out without the galvanizing element of the Soviet threat. It was, as Bush put it in a speech in the Netherlands just before the Maastricht Summit, "the danger that old Cold War allies will become new economic adversaries— cold warriors turned to trade warriors."[27]

Indeed, the Uruguay Round trade negotiations loomed at least as large as security matters in U.S.-European relations after 1990. The negotiations toward a new, more open worldwide trading regime involved all members of the General Agreement on Tariffs and Trade, or GATT. Once agricultural subsidies were identified as the key stumbling block, however, the talks centered on differences between the United States and the European Community. Having sought and received from Congress special one-year negotiating authority, Bush spent more time on the Uruguay Round in 1991 than on any other foreign policy issue save the Gulf War and Soviet policy. He feared—rightly, as it turned out— that the EC's unwillingness to reduce agricultural subsidies in the face of French (and other) protectionism would prevent a Uruguay Round agreement from being concluded and dash his hopes for the development of a more open world trade system. At a personal political level, it would be Bush who would pay the price in the 1992 presidential election for having bucked domestic protectionist sentiment and failing to deliver an agreement on account of EC intransigence.

Moreover, the negotiating style we encountered in the Uruguay Round talks confirmed everyone's worst fears about the post–Cold War EC. We negotiated bilaterally with Kohl, John Major, Mitterrand, and all the other EC heads of state or government, and we dealt in their "collective" capacities with the EC's designated negotiators, the commission, the presidency country (which changed every six months), and the "troika" of past, present, and future presidency countries. None could deliver or speak authoritatively for the Community as a whole; all invoked the EC's consensual decision-making rules to explain or excuse their inaction. The Germans, whose interests ran clearly in the direction of freer trade, were particularly disappointing. Kohl would expound at length about his commitment to free trade (which we had no reason to doubt) but did little to alter the EC position, choosing to treat this as a U.S.-French political problem that Washington was supposed to solve. Genscher did even less, choosing to forget that besides being foreign minister he was also vice chancellor and leader of the free-trading FDP (Free Democratic Party) and so had broader responsibilities for ensuring the success of GATT negotiations. On the substance of the negotiations, to be sure, there was plenty to criticize on both sides; Bush himself had plenty of frustrations with his own negotiating team. But whatever the complaints EC leaders had about substantive positions taken by the United States, they cannot have had the same frustrations as we with the way the negotiations were conducted.[28]

Thus these two realms—the economic/commercial and the political/security—interacted and overlapped after 1990. Conflict over the first-ever U.S.-EC declaration was a portent of difficulties ahead. Responding to overtures made by Bush as early as the Boston University speech of May 1989 and by Baker in his December 1989 Berlin speech, the Germans took the lead in proposing such a document so as to give U.S.-EC relations a more intense and regular character, cemented by common principles. They also sought to allay American misgivings as the Community worked toward economic and political unity. The two sides had worked out a text to be issued at the time of the Paris Summit, seeing this venue as a good one for affirming the "new European architecture." It was a nice, four-page document, mostly hortatory but with a few specific commitments inserted at our insistence over French objections.[29] Inauspiciously, however, U.S.-EC Uruguay Round negotiations hit an impasse over agricultural subsidies on the eve of the Paris Summit. Bush and Scowcroft were loath to sign a lofty agreement whose spirit, they felt, was being violated by unyielding European protectionism. It was only after eleventh-hour negotiations on the margins of the Paris Summit that the U.S.-EC declaration was issued—so quietly that it passed unnoticed. The White House did not even publish a copy or issue the customary press release, lest the embarrassing contradiction between word and deed be pointed out by the media.

All this of course reinforced preexisting biases within the Bush administration about the EC and helps explain the ambiguity of our approaches. On the one hand, we wanted a more united and capable Europe and knew in any case that American policy had to take into account the reality of a more ambitious EC. On the other, we did not like the kind of EC that seemed to be emerging and so adopted policies that seemed to oppose the Community at every crucial turn. It was not that American policy was duplicitous—that would be too easy an historical judgment—but rather that the two strands of thinking were equally strong and frequently in conflict. The concern, put in simplest terms, was that the United States would be shut out of the new Europe, both economically and politically, and that we would be dealing with a Europe that was protectionist, exclusivist, inward-looking, and difficult to deal with. State Department counselor Robert Zoellick, in a September 1990 speech, posed the question whether the new Europe would be "insular, itinerant, or international"—that is, internally preoccupied; globally engaged but wandering as an independent force; or, as we hoped, internationally engaged in a new partnership with the United States.[30]

The hope, as expressed in President Bush's Prague speech and elsewhere, was that the end of the Cold War would create the conditions not only for a continued transatlantic relationship but a stronger and more natural one. American military preponderance in European affairs was a requirement thrust upon both sides by the exigencies of the Soviet threat in the heart of Europe. The American presence had provided the shield that enabled Europe to build greater unity and prosperity, but it also stifled the full realization of Europe's aspirations. In this sense we in the administration—some of us at least—were sympathetic to the French complaint. Freed from this unnatural imbalance of roles and responsibilities, we saw new possibilities for U.S.-European relations. We looked to Europe—as well as to other allies, notably Japan—as our main partner in world affairs and in solving global problems that we had neither the desire nor the capacity to tackle alone.[31]

President Bush made the point during German president Richard von Weizsäcker's state visit in early 1992. The reference was to Germany but the sentiment applied equally to Europe as a whole:

Just as Germany has transcended and triumphed over its past, so has the German-American relationship shed the burdens that were history's legacy. A united Germany, champion of a more united Europe, now stands as our partner in leadership. Together, we have achieved our common goal of a Germany united in peace and freedom.

But our partnership did not end with that. To the contrary: now that we are free of the dangers and divisions of Europe's Cold War confrontation, the German-American partnership has really just begun.[32]

For "Germany," substitute "Europe"—meaning not just a Europe of the twelve EC member countries but a Europe widening to embrace the new democracies of the eastern part of the continent—and you have the essence of what we were trying to achieve in and through our transatlantic relations after 1990.

Strategy   From our core interests and objectives we developed a multipronged strategy. Conceptually, we tried to develop a new consensus around our basic aims, building on the major goals of the key players and shaping them into a workable structure of security. To reaffirm NATO's continuing role and lead its more radical transformation, we relied on the firmly Atlanticist British, Dutch, and others, as well as NATO's able secretary-general, former German defense minister Manfred Wörner. We embraced European unity, forging more intense and frequent contacts with the European Community, including commission president Jacques Delors, with whom President Bush met bilaterally on several occasions. And we championed a stronger CSCE, which we aimed to shape in ways that did not vitiate NATO but rather enhanced CSCE's role as a forum for political dialogue and agent of conflict resolution.

In his two Berlin speeches—December 1989 and June 1991—Secretary Baker developed the theme of "interlocking institutions" with flexible and complementary roles.[33] Warning in the first speech that "a Europe undivided may not necessarily be a Europe peaceful and prosperous," Baker proposed "a new architecture for a new era." The term was designed to appeal to West European political elites in the midst of their own "architectural" debate. Calling for a "fundamentally different approach to security," especially in nonmilitary dimensions, he proposed a set of new and complementary relationships among the key European and transatlantic institutions—NATO, the EC, the CSCE, the Council of Europe, and others. In particular he wanted to develop a much strengthened U.S.-EC relationship, "whether in treaty or some other form." The second Berlin speech updated and expanded on these ideas in the context of the challenge "to extend the trans-Atlantic Community to Central and Eastern Europe and to the Soviet Union":

> As we extend the Euro-Atlantic architecture to the east, we need to be creative about employing multiple methods and institutions. . . . CSCE will contribute by creating the political, economic, and security conditions that may defuse conflict. . . . [NATO] provides a foundation of stability within Europe as a whole. . . . The EC, the Council of Europe, and OECD are creating a network of political and economic support [that] both strengthens the new market democracies internally and signals any would-be threat that these nations are part of a larger community with a stake in their success.

Operationally, we worked mainly through NATO to keep the respective roles of key institutions in plausible harmony (to borrow Somerset Maugham's nice turn of phrase). As the communiqué of the June 1991 meeting of NATO foreign ministers rather awkwardly put it, "Our common security can best be safeguarded through the further development of a network of interlocking institutions and relationships, constituting a comprehensive architecture in which the Alliance, the process of European integration, and the CSCE are key elements."[34] In this effort, we had reasonably good success with NATO and the CSCE, much less with the EC.

The strategy was played out in our key bilateral relationships as well. Our conspicuous (if ambivalent) support for European unity also aimed at pushing a reluctant Britain toward "Europe," because British participation was critical for realization of the EC agenda. Additionally, we wanted Britain's global and Atlantic perspective to influence the outlook of an increasingly cohesive Europe: we needed a more Europeanized Britain because we wanted a more Anglicized Europe. Thatcher had more reservations about our approach than did John Major, who succeeded her as prime minister in the fall of 1990. We took a position on European unity at variance with the British government not because we valued Britain's role less but because we knew we would need its involvement even more as Europe moved toward closer economic and political unity. The Anglo-American "special relationship," in other words, was as important as ever but it would hinge less on a global partnership than on Britain's position in Europe. Our approach was only partly successful: British policies on key issues were almost always congenial to U.S. interests, but British influence remained limited by its reluctance to embrace European unity before and after the Maastricht Summit of late 1991.

With the French, we worked intensely in late 1990 and early 1991 to arrive at a formula that would permit creation of a European security and defense identity that did not undermine but rather strengthened NATO and might pave the way for France's drawing closer to the alliance, a prospect for which there was sympathy in some French quarters. In a post–Cold War world no longer dominated by superpower competition, we judged, NATO without France was probably doomed. To have a chance of bringing France fully back into NATO, we were banking on the close Franco-American cooperation that had developed in the Gulf War, as well as on President Bush's good personal relations with President Mitterrand. (Baker's relationship with French foreign minister Roland Dumas, to put it mildly, never warmed.) The aim was not a complete meeting of minds, which was out of the question, but a shared understanding, at the most basic level, that a continued U.S. role in Europe (via NATO) was essential and that it need not conflict with the goal of a more united Europe. The French connection, as it turned out, was the least successful dimension of our European strategy. Bush worked extremely hard at cultivating Mitterrand—and Delors as well—but could not overcome the deep-seated suspicions that Mitterrand and especially his foreign ministry continued to harbor.

Among the Western allies, Germany was key. France was a driving force in the EC but not in NATO; Great Britain was influential in NATO but much less so in the EC; Germany exercised substantial influence in both. And of all the major players, Germany had an agenda and set of interests that were closest to ours, particularly with respect to Western engagement of Central and Eastern Europe and the Soviet Union. Accordingly, we sought to forge the closest possible ties with the Federal Republic both before and after unification. Whenever possible, we gave tangible expression to being "partners in leadership" by issuing joint declarations, cosponsoring initiatives on the eve of important

NATO or CSCE meetings, and working to see that there was little or no daylight between U.S. and German positions on any of the major issues. Baker's relationship with Genscher was as strong as Bush's with Kohl, and these close ties were replicated easily and naturally at senior staff level. The relationship worked well, but it was frequently in conflict with the Franco-German partnership. It was easy to say to the Germans, as we often did, that we fully understood the importance of Franco-German cooperation and were not asking them to "choose between Washington and Paris," but there was no getting around this tension when it came down to cases like the Uruguay Round or development of a common European foreign and security policy. In both cases, what we wanted was precisely what France did not.

The Eastern Conundrum: A Europe "Whole and Free"?

"Central and Eastern Europe and the Soviet Union," Baker said with breathtaking understatement in his second Berlin speech of June 1991, "are the still incomplete pieces of our architecture." With Moscow, our aim of bringing our erstwhile adversary into new patterns of cooperation ran up against the inescapable realities of diminished Soviet influence and deepening internal strife that vitiated many a well-intended initiative. As to the new democracies of Central and Eastern Europe, the prospect of entering or reentering Western institutions was an indispensable point of orientation for societies in the midst of such wrenching change. This was also the essence of the integrationist strategy we had embraced in 1989, with the ultimate goal of overcoming the postwar division of Europe—not just as a formal or rhetorical matter but as one embedded in the economic, political, and social life of the continent.

Regional Cooperation   Between isolation and integration was the important intermediate stage of enhanced regional cooperation. This was a conscious aim of Western policy from the beginning, especially among the more advanced Central European countries. Western policymakers had the dual aim of encouraging cooperation to fill the void left by the discredited institutions of the past (the Warsaw Pact and Comecon[35]) and to ameliorate some of the conflicts that had plagued this region in the past. Secretary Baker had addressed this issue directly in a February 1990 speech in Prague:

In a region that has suffered so greatly from the distortion of national interest and from international isolation, I am encouraged by the first signs of coordination and possible new association among the newly democratic states . . . [and efforts] to build international civil society and overcome old animosities. . . . We welcome recent discussions [among] Hungary, Poland, and Czechoslovakia, including a possible free trade agreement. . . . The purpose of such closer ties should not be to isolate the countries in association from others. . . . The choice of whether to associate and in what form is, of course, entirely yours to make.[36]

The formulations on regional cooperation had been the subject of internal debate in the administration, as well as with our Western partners, that continued on the secretary's plane during the flight to Prague. Should we take a leaf out of the Marshall Plan and oblige the Central and East European governments to work out their own common strategies, with regional integration an explicit political goal? Should we make Western assistance conditional upon these steps toward regional integration? Would this be an important means of helping these countries transcend the national antagonisms that had torn this part of the world apart in the past? Could this cooperation be a stepping stone for their eventual integration into "Europe"—much as EFTA (the European Free Trade Area) had been, for some West European countries, a kind of preparatory stage for entry into the European Community? Or was such an approach inappropriate for countries at such different stages on the road to political and economic reform?

Did we risk slowing down Polish reforms by insisting that Poland synchronize its policies with Hungary and Czechoslovakia? Was it wise to promote regional integration when there were already-functioning Western institutions like NATO, the EC, and many others to which the Central and Eastern European countries could gradually adhere? These were the terms of our internal debate, which we had also broached, in almost precisely those words, in informal discussions with the British and Germans. Internal EC debates mirrored this transatlantic dialogue.

We and our West European partners settled on the middle ground reflected in Baker's speech. The postcommunist transformations would be hard enough without our imposing new requirements for access to Western assistance, particularly in light of the modest levels of aid being proposed. These countries were trying to escape the Warsaw Pact and Comecon and had no desire to create successor organizations. They had just rid themselves of one "Big Brother" in the form of the USSR and did not need another telling them how to live their lives. Emerging from nearly half a century of foreign domination, they needed some breathing space to establish and consolidate democratic rule before deciding what forms of external cooperation they might choose to undertake.

Our approach, rather, was to do all we could to encourage these new governments to adopt common strategies and cooperative regional arrangements and to offer inducements toward that end, short of making Western assistance conditional on an explicitly regional approach or the creation of new regional institutions. As a practical matter, the most important inducement was not aid but membership in Western institutions—particularly the EC and NATO but also the Council of Europe, the Organization for Economic Cooperation and Development (OECD), and others. Accordingly, we and our Western European partners agreed that Poland, Hungary, and Czechoslovakia, as the most advanced of the postcommunist states, should be treated as a group and encouraged to synchronize their policies and approaches toward affiliation and perhaps eventual membership in some or all of these institutions.

The new democratic leaders of the region were thinking along the same lines, and it was to their spontaneous cooperation that Baker referred in Prague. In an address to the Polish Sejm in late January, Czechoslovak president Václav Havel had called for Central European regional cooperation, warning that "to return to Europe individually . . . would certainly take much longer and be much more complicated than acting together."[37] A logical extension of the contacts among Polish, Czech, and Hungarian dissidents in the 1980s, regional cooperation thus conceived aimed at hastening their entry into "Europe" and ameliorating the national antagonisms that lay just beneath the surface. These sentiments, echoed by others in the region, led to an informal and largely symbolic "summit" in Bratislava in March 1990.

(A second, more ambitious summit was held in February 1991 at Visegrád, a castle on the Danube just north of Budapest, in conscious evocation of an earlier summit meeting of Polish, Czech, and Hungarian leaders on that site. [The year was 1335; the leaders were Kings Kazimierz III of Poland, John of Bohemia, and Charles Robert of Hungary. Their cooperation helped usher in one of the brightest periods in the history of east-central Europe.] The 1991 Visegrád Declaration, signed by Presidents Wałęsa of Poland, Havel of Czechoslovakia, and Árpád Göncz of Hungary, as well as Hungarian prime minister József Antall, proclaimed that the three countries were pursuing "essentially identical goals," affirmed "the rights of each nation to express its own identity," and advanced an extensive but vague common agenda.)

Our notion, and theirs, of the "Visegrád process" was never that it should be an end in itself or accompanied by elaborate institutions. Rather it should serve to coordinate their main foreign policy programs and facilitate joint action when it made sense, such as in promoting free trade and thus enlarging their respective markets. Although this cooperation was to founder after the split of Czechoslovakia in January 1993, it proved of great utility in strengthening their hands in negotiations with Moscow, particularly with regard to the withdrawal of Soviet forces, and coordinating approaches toward the West. Cooperation via other groupings like the "Pentagonale" and "Alpe-Adria," which included Austria and Italy,[38] also contributed to a web of overlapping and mutually reinforcing ties. Like the Visegrád process, we saw these ties not as substitutes for joining the European mainstream but stepping stones in that direction.

Integration into Western Institutions   In his Prague speech of February 1990, Secretary Baker also proposed a step-by-step process of integration into European and transatlantic institutions. The proposals were cautious, proceeding from the reality of the Warsaw Pact's continued existence and the presence of substantial Soviet forces still deployed in the region. On European security, Baker noted President Bush's recent CFE (Conventional Armed Forces in Europe) proposal for deeper force reductions, which "should minimize and deter the threat of any army of invasion and end the unjust presence of any army of occupation." NATO and the U.S. military presence should continue "for as long as our allies desire it," serving "to reassure the nations of Europe, large and small, that we will stand by them to resist invasion, intimidation, or coercion." Presaging initiatives that the president would unveil at NATO's July 1990 London Summit, Baker said that the alliance "must evolve to assume new missions" and "help address old and new European animosities and fears—outside and inside NATO." Then, in a line he was to repeat many times, he warned that "we must leave behind not only the Cold War but also the conflicts that preceded it."

In addition to NATO's new opening to the East,[39] Baker focused on the need to "integrate the new market democracies into the international economic system" via the international financial institutions, the OECD, and the newly created European Bank for Reconstruction and Development. He proposed that the latter be located in Prague as a sign of Europe's center of gravity shifting eastward. He also called on Western countries to open their markets to East European trade and facilitate those countries' access to high technology through a liberalized COCOM (Coordinating Committee for Multilateral Export Controls). Finally, Baker held out the prospect of a "special relationship with the EC, the nations of EFTA, or the United States" toward Central and Eastern Europe's gradual integration into European and transatlantic institutions. "No longer," he said, "should the circumstances of this continent subject you to characterization as 'the lands between.'"

Yet in their efforts to "return to Europe," the Central and Eastern Europeans were aiming at a moving target. Hungary and others considered applying for membership in the European Free Trade Area (EFTA),[40] only to find that EFTA countries were lining up to join the European Community. By the same token, Central European hopes of joining the EC were pushed off to the distant future as they were obliged to take their places behind the economically more advanced "EFTAns." Finally, as the Central Europeans shifted gears to focus on negotiating the "association agreements" the EC had promised in November 1990, they found a newly protectionist Community that resisted any opening in "sensitive" sectors like agriculture, textiles, and steel— where Central Europe could have been competitive immediately. The EC sought even to raise tariffs in areas where they had been generous in 1989 and 1990. It was only after the failed coup attempt in Moscow in August 1991 that the EC gave the process a new push, culminating in the signing of the "Europe agreements" with Poland, Czechoslovakia, and Hungary in December 1991.[41]

Indeed, Western approaches toward the East after 1990 took place against the backdrop of growing conflict verging on chaos in the Soviet Union that made coherent planning elusive. Soviet foreign minister Shevardnadze's abrupt resignation on December 20, 1990, coincided with tangible actions that seemed to bear out his warning of incipient "dictatorship."[42] The influx of hard-line military and KGB officers into the top leadership was evident in every aspect of Soviet policy: efforts to broker a separate peace with Saddam Hussein on the eve of Operation

Desert Storm, violations of the freshly signed CFE treaty, and a new truculence at home. Since mid-1990, Gorbachev had beat a steady retreat from democratization and opened a wide rift with radical reformers led by Boris Yeltsin, leader of the Russian Federation. Most ominous were military crackdowns against Baltic independence movements in the two "Bloody Sundays" of January 13, 1991, in Vilnius, Lithuania, and January 20 in Riga, Latvia. Nor did Gorbachev's rambling and implausible denial of personal responsibility help matters. As Soviet ambassador to the United States (and soon to be Shevardnadze's successor as foreign minister) Aleksandr Bessmertnykh confided to Deputy Secretary Eagleburger, "The situation is almost out of control."[43]

Although the immediate crisis abated, the situation continued to deteriorate as Gorbachev sought to carve out a middle ground between hard-liners and reformers, in the process alienating both and facilitating the coup attempt against him in August 1991. Thereafter, the ascendancy of Russian Federation president Boris Yeltsin and the collapse of the Soviet Communist party led to recognition of the independence of the Baltic states and, by year's end, the disintegration of the Soviet Union itself.

Gorbachev's early boast that he would deprive the West of a threat was taking on an existential meaning that he surely did not intend. The burden was therefore intense on Western governments, especially ours, to reach out to the newly independent states while also preserving the transatlantic security community without the threat it had been created to counter. At the same time, the Central and Eastern Europeans, at the front line of a Soviet Union that seemed on the brink of violent or at least chaotic disintegration, were clamoring for a more forthcoming Western response to their security concerns.

Not everyone in Central and Eastern Europe shared Lech Wałęsa's sense of "deadly danger" to Poland or took seriously Russian Federation foreign minister Andrei Kozyrev's warning that "if the forces of darkness prevail in the Soviet Union, Central Europe is next on their agenda,"[44] but all feared a set of lesser threats. Short of military aggression, which seemed unlikely given the chaotic state of the Soviet leadership, there were more plausible, indeed actual, dangers arising from curtailment of essential energy supplies, collapse of foreign trade generally, or waves of refugees fleeing economic and social disorder. Moscow was also adopting a tougher posture about the withdrawal of Soviet forces from Central Europe, dragging its feet on dissolving the military arm of the Warsaw Pact, and exerting pressure on the Central and Eastern Europeans to sign new bilateral treaties that would have given the Soviet Union a kind of *droit de regard* in the region.

The countries of Central Europe were indeed "the lands between," and not only in the geographic sense. Of the West but not in it, in the East but not of it, they still belonged to a security organization—the Warsaw Pact—that offered only insecurity. Yet with Soviet forces still on their territory, they could not yet aspire openly to the one organization—NATO—that could provide real security. Central and Eastern European leaders generally recognized that the answers to the threats they faced lay mainly in strengthening their own internal stability through a deepening of democracy and market-based economic systems. But they saw these imperatives as linked to their countries' external situation, for the collapse of the Soviet market and the growing chaos on their eastern borders had generated new economic and social instabilities in their own countries. What these countries sought from the West, at a minimum, was a perspective for the future—a strategic plan that assured them of their eventual, gradual integration into Western institutions as they consolidated democratic rule at home.

The Soviet Factor   The calls were urgent, reasonable, and consistent with U.S. interests in enlarging Western Europe's "zone of stability." Indeed, the ardently pro-American and pro-NATO Poles, Czechs, and Hungarians were essential to our larger vision of a new Euro-Atlantic community. Yet Western policies had also to consider the danger of strengthening hard-line sentiment in Moscow by what might have seemed a provocative acceleration of the integration of Moscow's erstwhile allies into Western security structures. In the often repeated phrase of the day, we did not want to "draw new lines in Europe" that left the Soviet Union on the other side, defeated, embittered, hostile.

The dilemma for Western policy was acute. In 1990 it had been fairly easy to adopt a gradualist approach toward opening Western institutions to association with the East, putting the Soviet Union and the Eastern European countries on roughly the same footing. Now there was greater urgency among Eastern Europeans to have their countries brought in more rapidly and integrally, and greater merit to their contention that their progress toward stable democratic rule warranted sharper differentiation from an unstable and more authoritarian Soviet Union. As to the latter, while not wishing to isolate or alienate Moscow, we and our Western partners were finding its leadership increasingly difficult to deal with constructively (in contrast to our extremely good bilateral relations with Poland, Czechoslovakia, and Hungary).

The Western Europeans took a similar position, sympathetic to the Eastern Europeans but preoccupied with Moscow as well as their own internal negotiations toward European union. The Germans were the most consistent advocates of an accelerated integration strategy, but they, too, attached first priority to relations with Moscow in the context of the protracted withdrawal of Soviet forces from eastern Germany. The French were at the other extreme, opposing any opening to the East that might upset their strategy of building European union and so containing Germany with a tight European embrace. Mitterrand's early proposal of a "European confederation" was rightly seen as a device to keep Central Europe out of the European mainstream, as was Delors's proposal for a "European Economic Space."[45]

U.S. and other Western approaches therefore had to balance Central and Eastern European insistence on inclusion against Soviet and then Russian fears of exclusion. In NATO, for example, we aimed to find a formula that would treat all former Warsaw Pact members equally as a formal matter but would in practice be highly differentiated in favor of the new democracies of Central and Eastern Europe. This was no mere diplomatic compromise but a sober calculation of the existing and potential distribution of power in Europe. In 1919, the Versailles conference had vastly underestimated Russian power on the morrow of the October Revolution and hence erected a postwar settlement that was never rooted in the realities of power.[46] Again in 1991, Russia was weak enough to ignore but with enormous latent power to have made its exclusion shortsighted in the extreme.

Such was the thinking at the highest levels of the administration, and it was a sound basis for long-term strategic engagement of a Russia in the midst of another "time of troubles." The problem was with the execution of this strategy in the short run. No amount of Western largesse could alter the plain facts that the Soviet empire was lost, its political and economic system in profound crisis, and, for the immediate future, its global role negligible. The burden on the U.S.-Soviet (and later the U.S.-Russian) relationship was particularly heavy. With arms control an issue largely of the bygone era and economic cooperation foundering because of Gorbachev's refusal to embrace internal reform, we had to grope for other ways to engage Moscow and embed a disintegrating Soviet Union in a cooperative international order. The efforts of the United States and its Western partners to facilitate Soviet and later Russian participation in the G-7, the IMF and World Bank, and the Middle East peace process made good strategic sense, albeit in a largely symbolic way. When it came to the transformation of European and transatlantic institutions, however, deference to Soviet/Russian sensibilities amounted to a self-imposed veto over steps needed to help secure the new democracies of the East and overcome the continent's division.

Although a minority in Washington pushed consistently for accelerated efforts to integrate the new democracies into Western institutions, we and our Western partners erred almost always on the side of Soviet sensibilities. This cautious approach was reasonable enough at the time, given how much was at stake in a successful Soviet transition. The hitch was that a go-slow approach could always be justified, no matter the course of events in Moscow. If reformers were ascendant, they needed our support to vindicate their approach. If hard-liners were pushing their way to the fore, we had to be careful not to provoke or embolden them. And if things were stable, why rock the boat?

The same administration that had judged wisely in 1989 that we could not make the Soviet peoples' choices for them or allow the Soviet agenda to dictate our own began to forget its own lessons, greatly exaggerating our ability to influence the Soviet internal dynamic and international role. As President Bush had said way back in his Texas A&M speech—was it really less than two years before?—"a new relationship cannot be simply declared by Moscow, or bestowed by others." At Mainz in May 1989, Bush sought to convince the Soviet leaders "that their definition of security is obsolete, that their deepest fears are unfounded." By 1991, reacting to the most atavistic forces in Moscow, we were discarding some of our core principles on U.S.-Soviet relations, in the process missing an opportunity to assist consolidating democratic rule in Eastern Europe, where we *could* make a difference. In our understandable preoccupation with Soviet Russia and the Western security system, we were neglecting the "lands between." In 1989 we had rightly judged that Eastern Europe was the key to ending the Cold War, but we failed to see that this region was also the key to the post–Cold War order in Europe.

President and Mrs. Bush with Solidarity leader Lech Wałęsa in front of the
Lenin Shipyard in Gdańsk, July 1989. Bush's electrifying visit helped Poland
awaken to the possibility of genuine independence and democracy.

White House departure ceremony for Czechoslovak president Havel, February
20, 1990. Havel is holding a portrait of Thomas Masaryk, Czechoslovakia's
first president, a gift from Bush.

President Havel and the new Czechoslovak government meet President Bush in the Cabinet Room, February 20, 1990.

The President and President Göncz of Hungary in the Oval Office, May 18, 1990. The genial, intelligent Göncz was one of Bush's favorites.

Presidents Bush and Gorbachev at the Washington Summit, May 31, 1990, about to begin negotiations that would pave the way to Soviet acceptance of German unification

West German and U.S. leaders get ready for the last phase of German unification, May 17, 1990, in the Cabinet Room. Chancellor Kohl, in the middle on the right, is flanked by Foreign Minister Genscher, to his right, and Defense Minister Stoltenberg; Bush, by Vice President Quayle and Deputy Secretary of State Eagleburger.

Bush cracking wise on the way into the Oval Office from the Rose Garden in June 1990, flanked by Scowcroft and Gates, with the author just behind.

The President and Polish Prime Minister Mazowiecki enjoy a light moment in Bush's suite at the Waldorf Astoria during the UN General Assembly, September 29, 1990. Polish Foreign Minister Skubiszewski, gazing upwards, does not seem to be amused.

French President Mitterrand prepares to open the Paris Summit of the CSCE (Conference on Security and Cooperation in Europe), November 1990, signaling the end of the Cold War. Baker and Bush are at left, next to Genscher and Kohl, with Gorbachev and Shevardnadze on the right.

Presidents Bush and Havel signing a U.S.-Czechoslovak declaration of principles in the Cabinet Room, October 22, 1991. Havel was signing on behalf of a country to disappear from the map of Europe just over a year later.

NATO leaders pose for their "class photo" at the November 1991 Rome Summit, where they approved NATO's "new strategic concept." Bush stunned his allied counterparts by demanding to know that if Europe intends to organize its security without the United States, "Tell me now!"

Presidents Bush and Gorbachev sign bilateral agreements—including, later in the day, the START treaty reducing strategic arms—at Gorbachev's *dacha* in Moscow, July 31, 1991, with Secretary Baker and Foreign Minister Bessmertnykh looking on. Three weeks later hard-liners staged a coup attempt against Gorbachev.

Presidents Bush and Yeltsin at Camp David in February 1992, where they issued a joint statement declaring "Russia and the United States do not regard themselves as potential adversaries."

5

The Challenges of
Postcommunist Transition

THE DAY AFTER THE BREACH of the Berlin Wall, Lech Wałęsa had a premonition that Poland would "pay the price" for this event because of German preoccupation with the challenges of unification.[1] Indeed, all the countries of Central and Eastern Europe paid a price because of Western preoccupation first with German unification, then with the Iraqi invasion of Kuwait in August 1990, and finally with the disintegration of the Soviet Union after the failed coup of August 1991. Eastern Europe continued to engage U.S. and other Western attention, but never with the priority and focus that it commanded in 1989 and 1990. The leadership that the United States provided in Eastern Europe during this early period would in any case have been hard to sustain, as the revolutionary drama gave way to the more prosaic challenges of structurally transforming these political, economic, and social systems.

In 1989 and through 1990, the United States and the European Community responded swiftly and appropriately, if not always generously, to the urgent needs of the new democracies of Central and Eastern Europe. The major Western and transatlantic institutions—NATO, the European Community, the Conference on Security and Cooperation in Europe, the Western European Union, and the Council of Europe—all moved quickly to help integrate the new democracies, as did the newly created Group of 24. By the end of 1990, all these countries had joined or rejoined the General Agreement on Tariffs and Trade (GATT), the International Monetary Fund, and the World Bank, and most were admitted as associate members of the Organization for Economic Cooperation and Development (OECD). A series of reciprocal market-opening measures implemented with the EC as well as the United States in early

1990 helped enable Hungary and especially Poland to register trade surpluses with the West in their first difficult year of economic transition.

It was at the beginning of 1991 that Wałęsa's premonition manifested itself, for the West's growing neglect coincided with a sharp deterioration within the region. A combination of factors were at work: the growing number of countries joining Poland and Hungary on the road to reform and competing for scarce Western resources; a sharp downturn in regional trade, owing to the disappearance of the East German market and virtual collapse of the Soviet market; and the severe (and uncompensated) impact of international sanctions against Iraq and later Yugoslavia. Most serious, as has been seen, was the growing fragmentation of the Soviet Union, which generated urgent calls from Central and Eastern Europe for integration into Western structures. Yet at the very time that a renewed Western commitment and an updated strategy were most urgently needed, the United States and Western Europe alike were elsewhere preoccupied, their strategic vision diffused and resources stretched by the costs of the Gulf War and the burgeoning assistance needs of the Soviet Union. Additionally, a Western recession, aggravated by the high cost of German unification, constricted Western markets and fueled new protectionist measures against East European products. Western markets that were opened to them in 1990 were slammed partially shut in 1991. This was hardly the economic and political chaos of the 1920s, but neither was it an international economic environment conducive to economic recovery and growth.

First Encounters

In early 1990 the countries of Central and Eastern Europe were poised uncertainly between the old order and the new. Elections had been held only in Poland, and even there the power-sharing stipulations of the Roundtable Agreement had assured communist control of the presidency, as well as the key defense and interior ministries, and 65 percent of the seats in the Sejm (the lower, and more important, of the two houses of the Polish parliament). Elsewhere, the revolutions of 1989 had produced stunning changes of power at the top, but these new leaders presided over political and economic systems that were essentially unaltered. This jarring duality was brought home on a trip by Secretary Baker to Prague, Sofia, and Bucharest from February 7 to 11, 1990, rendered here in a series of impressions and vignettes.

With Havel and Kafka in Prague   Accompanying Secretary Baker to Prague in early February 1990, just a few weeks after the "Velvet Revolution," was a surreal experience. Prague Castle, where I had been not so many months before with a congressional delegation led by Senator John Glenn for meetings with some of the worst of the East European communist leaders, was now occupied by the flower children around President Václav Havel. The world, it seemed, had been turned upside down. Or had it? This was, after all, Kafka's castle; his book of that title was written just around the corner.[2] Havel's aides recounted an event that occurred a few days before we arrived. Havel, it seemed, needed to communicate with President Gorbachev by telephone but was not sure how this could be done. As they were discussing the matter in a corridor, a hidden door opened from one of the walls and out came a security official with a telephone wired into the Warsaw Pact circuit. They had not known about the circuit, the hidden room, or the man behind the wall, who evidently had been waiting patiently for his services to be required by his new superiors. The story made one wonder how many other ghosts from the past were lurking behind the walls of postcommunist Eastern Europe.

There was something Kafkaesque, too, about the ubiquitous *Havel na Hrad!* (Havel to the Castle!) posters. I spotted one miniature in a working-class beer hall that I used to frequent during my student days in Prague in the late 1970s and had revisited a couple of times since. It was just above the cash register, in exactly the same spot that a picture of communist leader Gustáv Husák once hung. Surely this time the image was placed out of real conviction! (Havel would have appreciated the irony, for he had begun his celebrated essay "The Power of the Powerless" with the story of the conformist, and therefore culpable, greengrocer who dutifully displayed regime propaganda slogans in his shop window.) And surely the federal assembly had voted its conscience in electing Havel president without a single vote against. Of course, this was the same federal assembly (give or take a few changes pushed through during the Velvet Revolution) that shortly before would approve, also unanimously, anything sent to it by the communist regime, including vitriolic denunciations of that infamous "enemy of the people" Václav Havel, but never mind.

The meetings took place in a gilded chamber of Hradčany Castle. Havel, looking uncomfortable in a new suit and tie, spoke in long, complex monologues that his interpreter struggled heroically to follow. I recognized her from my last trip to Prague, when she was interpreting the rather simpler stock phrases of Vasil Bil'ak and other egregious exemplars of Czechoslovakia's communist leadership. Like the man behind the wall, her presence was a jarring link with a past whose legacy would persist for a long time to come. Chain-smoking and looking down at his hands, glancing up furtively every so often as if embarrassed to find others in the room with him, Havel spoke in a low monotone that obliterated the usual sing-song of Prague-style Czech. His main lines of thought, familiar from his many essays published abroad, bore interestingly but not always wisely on his unexpected new political responsibilities. He spoke eloquently about the moral and political devastation of his country. Introducing morality into Czechoslovak foreign policy was among his priorities, and he felt that his small country had a particular mission to help overcome Europe's division into two hostile blocs. He saw the Conference on Security and Cooperation in Europe (CSCE) as the foundation of a new "pan-European peace order" that would supplant the two military alliances.

Our concern was that Havel's ethical compass would prove an untrustworthy guide for the difficult world his country was entering. With exquisite politeness, Secretary Baker observed that we did not see the United States and the Soviet Union, NATO and the Warsaw Pact, as two sides of the same coin. Nor did we believe that the CSCE could replace the North Atlantic alliance as a reliable security organization. NATO, as a defensive alliance of democracies and the institutional link that bound the United States to European security, should be preserved as a factor of stability. This was no abstract matter. Baker was headed the next day for Moscow, where he hoped to begin persuading Gorbachev and Shevardnadze to accept continued membership in NATO by a united Germany.[3] Against this backdrop, we worried that Havel, in all innocence and with the best of intentions, could do considerable harm, including to his own country, by placing his hopes in, and lending his considerable moral authority to, an elusive and illusory peace order.

Secretary Baker's major speech, discussed below, was delivered at Charles University, in the same hall where my graduation ceremonies had been held from the university's Summer School of Slavonic Studies in 1977. Nowhere in view were the miserable party hacks who had taken over the university under the so-called normalization following the 1968 invasion; instead, Baker was introduced by Radim Palouš, who had been dismissed in 1977 for signing Charter 77 but was quickly installed after the Velvet Revolution as Charles University's new rector. Building on his December 1989 Berlin speech, which had been devoted to "the new Europe, the new Atlanticism," Baker focused his remarks on "how we might promote, perpetuate, and protect Europe's democratic revolutions."[4]

Czech-Slovak Dissonance   After Prague, Secretary Baker continued on to Moscow for discussions on German unification and our proposal for a Two Plus Four process, ultimately agreed to at the conclusion of the trip in Ottawa. (Indeed, for all the drama associated with the Velvet Revolution, the trip was dominated by German events: the usual careful background briefings to the traveling press on the secretary's plane dealt almost exclusively with Germany.) Inasmuch as my NSC colleague Condoleezza Rice was responsible for the Moscow leg of the journey, I remained behind in Prague—waiting for the Baker entourage to decide whether he would visit Bulgaria and Romania after Moscow. Romania was the stumbling block. Given our misgivings over the actions and intentions of the National Salvation Front since the December 1989 Revolution, there was a debate as to whether a visit by the secretary of state would advance democratic change. Or would it provide undeserved legitimation of a government that had yet to demonstrate its democratic bona fides? Ultimately the secretary decided to stay a full day in Sofia but stop only for a few hours in Bucharest, using the opportunity to press a democratic agenda on the ruling establishment and lend support to the fledgling opposition parties.[5]

With time on my hands, I arranged to visit Civic Forum headquarters in Prague and then travel to Bratislava, the Slovak capital, to give a talk at an academic institute and meet with officials of Public Against Violence (Civic Forum's Slovak counterpart) in their new headquarters. The energetic staff at Civic Forum—headquartered near the Magic Lantern theater, Havel's "command post" during the Velvet Revolution—offered the remarkable revelation that none of them had been to Slovakia since December, so preoccupied had they been with organizing at the grass roots in the Czech lands of Bohemia and Moravia. Yet Bratislava was only a three-hour drive, and two months was an eternity given the rapidity of political change in the country. It was an early indication that the long-suppressed differences between Czechs and Slovaks might resurface sooner rather than later; indeed, the symbolic solidarity between Havel, a Czech, and Alexander Dubček, a Slovak, that had helped spark the Velvet Revolution already seemed a dim memory.

These fears were borne out in Bratislava. The political and economic agendas of Civic Forum and Public Against Violence were already diverging, and resentment was building among Slovaks that they were being ignored and taken for granted by the Czechs. Their complicated relationship with the Czechs also translated into an unexpected wariness tinged with mistrust of American intentions. For one thing, Slovak perceptions of the United States for the most part had been filtered through the distant and suspect prism of Prague. In this respect, there was a certain similarity with East Germany, where attitudes were shaped via the Federal Republic and thus similarly distorted. It was not hostility but rather a philosophical distance and disconnectedness that contrasted sharply with the easy familiarity and instinctive pro-Americanism one encountered among the Poles, Czechs, and Hungarians.[6]

A brief tour of Bratislava revealed another surprise.[7] In the hills in which the former communist *nomenklatura* resided was one particularly imposing villa—still occupied by Vasil Bil'ak. The policy of conciliation espoused by Havel and others—of giving officials of the former communist regime a dignified exit—was going to be harder to apply in the case of a man like Bil'ak. He was among the anti-Dubček conspirators in 1968 and one of those who had requested the Soviet invasion.[8] Such questions presaged the difficult battle over the Lustration (*Lustrace*) law of bringing to light the crimes of the communist period. They also foretold the special difficulties Slovakia would have in ridding itself of the remnants of the old guard. Precisely because the latter days of communist rule had not been as repressive in Slovakia as in the Czech lands, the break with the past was less decisive, more ambiguous.

Bulgaria   Arriving in Sofia on February 9, a day ahead of the Baker entourage, I arranged through our embassy to visit the headquarters of the Union of Democratic Forces (UDF) and have separate meetings with several of its leaders, who would also meet with Secretary Baker. It was a pivotal time in Bulgaria. The Bulgarian Communist party, in an extraordinary congress a few days before, had changed its name to "Socialist," and a stormy roundtable meeting with the opposition had set a date for early national elections. The UDF, having finally secured office space from the still-communist Bulgarian government (which remained the country's sole landlord as well as its sole employer), had just moved in the week before to a dilapidated building with just one telephone and no copiers, fax machines, or computers. The dim lighting illuminated one or two bearded, Tolstoyesque figures. Despite its meager infrastructure, the UDF had managed to produce the first edition of the newspaper *Demokratsia* and was trying to weld a cohesive political movement out of a congeries of disparate personalities and agendas.

A meeting with several opposition leaders that afternoon in my hotel room was a preview of what Baker would encounter the next day. Sofia being one of those cities where everyone knows everyone else, these opposition leaders knew well what the regime was up to. They spoke with precision about the regime's strategy and what would have to be done to counter it. The regime had co-opted their agenda and called for early elections, confident that it could sufficiently restrict the opposition's ability to organize and publicize its campaign. They needed maximum international pressure to have a fighting chance in the elections, and they needed to hold together despite the disparity of their political orientations. It was a diverse group, held together in plausible harmony by the self-effacing and conciliatory UDF chairman Zhelyu Zhelev.[9] A former dissident philosopher, Zhelev had now become an unlikely but effective political leader, if only because his ego was smaller than those of other UDF leaders. The next time I saw him he was visiting the White House as president of Bulgaria, the first Bulgarian head of state or government ever to do so.

Baker arrived the next day, fresh from a small breakthrough with Gorbachev and Shevardnadze on the Two Plus Four concept.[10] It was the first visit to Bulgaria by an American secretary of state. The main official meeting was bizarre: it was around an enormous round table in a cavernous room, with the Bulgarian side represented by Petŭr Mladenov and Alexander Lilov, who had succeeded Todor Zhivkov as president and party leader respectively, and new prime minister Andrei Lukanov. Mladenov, who did most of the talking, was a nonentity; Lilov, an *apparatchik* who looked vaguely familiar. Lukanov was a smooth talker who knew how to strike the right themes with Western leaders. "Lukanov the *lukav*," meaning unprincipled and crafty, was how Bulgarian critics saw him. Baker saw him, rightly, as the one to do business with.

Baker was blunt. Although he must have been preoccupied with German affairs and the diplomatic challenge facing him in Ottawa the next day, the secretary had mastered his brief in consummate lawyerly fashion. He knew before the meeting began exactly what he wanted to achieve. He meant to push these officials a few steps further down the road of supporting democratic change by making it clear that the United States was not about to support sham democracy or reform communism. They could expect our help if and only if the new government took further, demonstrable steps toward political and economic liberalization; otherwise, we would cut them off from G-24 and IMF assistance. In what I came to learn was his standard operating procedure, Baker quickly cut through their thundering generalities to focus on the specific, tangible, and measurable. In Sofia (and, the next day, Bucharest), it was the parliamentary elections scheduled for early summer. He pressed them on electoral laws and procedures, campaign financing and organization, media access, and impartial election observers. The presentation was direct to the point of lecturing, even bullying.

This was the first time I had seen Baker at work in a confrontational setting, the meeting with Havel having been a love-fest. I was taking mental notes, from which I later drew when thrust into the unfamiliar role of dealing with ministers, prime ministers, and presidents on my own. Somehow, his bearing, courtesy, mastery of detail, and seriousness of purpose enabled him to say the most undiplomatic and demanding things without giving offense. Or perhaps it was that his manner did not allow his interlocutors to show offense. (One of Havel's chief advisers later remarked that when Bush or Baker entered the room it was as if the entire history and power of the United States entered with him.[11] Perhaps these Bulgarian officials were similarly awed.) Of course, he knew, and knew that they knew, that they were the ones who needed something and we were the ones who needed to have our concerns met. He was not going to waste his time or theirs with diplomatic niceties; he wanted to let them know precisely what we wanted to see happen. They got the message. What they would do with it remained to be seen.

The secretary's meeting with opposition figures was less successful. Like President Bush's meetings with opposition leaders in Budapest in July 1989, this was a setting that invited posturing. There was little of the strategic precision of the day before; instead, speakers seized the occasion to curry favor with the American secretary of state, generally at the expense of other opposition leaders. Zhelev sat in bemused silence, intervening only occasionally for the purpose of gently steering the conversation away from partisan backbiting. Baker did his best, shifting from the role of secretary of state to former manager of four presidential election campaigns, three of them successful. He spoke of building and maintaining electoral unity in order to topple the communists,[12] making it clear that while the United States would be formally neutral, our sympathies and support were for parties of the democratic opposition. It was a point Baker made emphatically in addressing a small but enthusiastic rally awaiting him at our hotel after the day's events.

Romania   If Prague had been surreal, Bucharest was eerie. Otopeni Airport, the presidential palace, and University Square were pockmarked with bullet holes. It was like a war zone, as indeed it had been just six weeks before. We traveled in what must have been the world's longest motorcade. For some reason, no vans or buses had been laid on for the Baker party and the traveling press, so the whole crowd went in cars, the motorcade snaking its way to meetings in three separate locations in three hours—with the new government headed by Prime Minister Petre Roman of the National Salvation Front, with NSF Chairman Ion Iliescu, and with key opposition and independent figures.

Since the December revolution, the self-proclaimed provisional government of the National Salvation Front had made a series of retreats from its initial agenda. Elections would be held as promised, but instead of acting as caretaker and then stepping aside, Iliescu, around whom a Ceauşescu-like personality cult was already forming, had announced that he would run for president. The Front, instead of playing a temporary function as facilitator of democratic elections, was hunkering down for a permanent role. The authors of the revolution, meanwhile, were growing increasingly disenchanted with a ruling team that looked too much like the one they thought they had just got rid of. Student activists declared Bucharest's University Square a "communist-free zone" and were soon to establish a tent city in permanent protest.

Baker's pitch was much the same as in Sofia, adjusted to reflect our greater concerns about the political evolution in Romania. His focus was again on elections, particularly on the widest possible participation of election observers. Because we feared that the elections would be neither free nor fair, we wanted to be sure to have unambiguous evidence with which to mobilize continued international pressure. The secretary must have repeated a dozen times that we looked to the new Romanian leadership to issue public invitations for the CSCE and other institutions to send election observer missions. This, too, was typical for Baker: the more skeptical he was of progress, the more specific his demands. Inviting election observers may not have been much, but at least it was tangible, verifiable, and directly related to our larger objectives. While assuring Iliescu and Roman of our continued willingness to provide emergency humanitarian assistance, the secretary made it clear that other forms of economic assistance would be conditioned on real progress toward market democracy, of which there was scant evidence so far. Restoration of most favored nation status, which they sought as a symbol of American approval, would be forthcoming only in response to significant progress.

With Iliescu I experienced a sense of déjà vu: his manner and physical appearance were similar to Alexander Lilov's. And now I placed whom Lilov had reminded me of: Károly Grósz, Hungarian party leader in 1988 and early 1989, who in turn bore a resemblance to Miloš Jakeš, Czechoslovakia's communist leader up until the Velvet Revolution. A year later, traveling with Baker in Tirana, I added Albanian communist leader Ramiz Alia to the list. Iliescu, Lilov, Grósz, Jakeš, Alia: all were gray men, short of stature, with bland visages and impenetrable eyes. They came across as clever but unimaginative. These were the archetypical second generation East European communist leaders: not as evil as their predecessors and not as ideological, either, they were careerists, survivors, opportunists. They personified the banality of East European communism after its revolutionary fire had burned out. Veterans of many a leadership reshuffle or policy "new course" during the communist era, they were thoroughly creatures of the party-state bureaucracy from which they were spawned. Iliescu, it should be noted, had been purged by Ceauşescu for allegedly harboring reformist sentiments and so may have possessed an independence of mind, perhaps even a degree of personal courage.

After the official encounters with the National Salvation Front, we repaired to the ambassador's residence for meetings with opposition leaders. The residence was once the home of Ana Pauker, a first generation Romanian communist purged in 1952 by Gheorghe Gheorghiu-Dej, Ceauşescu's predecessor, but not before she had added a grand indoor swimming pool to provide the "vanguard of the proletariat" respite from its revolutionary labors. After a private meeting with Reverend László Tökés, whose defiance touched off the December revolution, Baker met in another large roundtable setting with some thirty opposition leaders. This was even more a shambles than the meeting in Sofia. For all their well-founded criticism of the Front's antidemocratic behavior, they evinced no shred of strategy for combating it. Baker lectured them on the need to stay together and mount a common electoral strategy if they hoped to defeat the NSF, but his words were falling on deaf ears. We left Bucharest more pessimistic than we had arrived.

In Prague, "the man behind the wall" suggested that the communists and their vestiges would be hard to expunge. In Romania, they were still running the country. The "spirit of Timişoara"—the revolutionary impulse as well as the manifesto of democratic reform embodied in the Timişoara Declaration of December 1989—served as a reminder that "democracy, market, Europe" were the aspirations of the revolution's true authors, but these brief first encounters in postcommunist Central and Eastern Europe were portents of the enormity and complexity of the challenges ahead.

"Democracy, Market, Europe"

For most of its modern history, Eastern Europe had been a collection of weak, multiethnic, unprotected lands between two large and powerful neighbors—Germany and Russia. Allowing that the generalization would need qualification to hold universally, it nonetheless captures the essence of the East European problem, and the problem Eastern Europe posed for a wider stability. The dilemma was therefore threefold: economic and political weakness, a legacy of bitter national conflict, and, to put it mildly, an international system that did not make room for the smaller nations of Eastern Europe. These three together dashed the hopes of East Europeans after 1848, when virtually the entire region rose in revolt against Habsburg rule; again after 1919, when most of these nations gained or regained their independence; and of course after 1945, when the entire region fell under Soviet domination.

1990 was a long way from 1848, but the same threefold dilemma of weakness, conflict, and exclusion were still evident. The similarities of the revolutions of 1989 were often superficial—spiraling public demonstrations leading to the swift and, with the exception of Romania, peaceful capitulation of the existing regimes, and their replacement by leaders of anticommunist umbrella movements with virtually identical democratic agendas. They tended to mask the much more complex and differentiated processes at work. So, too, did the commonality of the first phase of political and economic transformation, which included preparing the legal and political ground for the first round of free elections and establishing the constitutional foundations for democratic rule. It also involved embarking, under the guidance of the International Monetary Fund, on programs of macroeconomic stabilization, whether of the "shock" or gradualist varieties. These early steps were necessarily led from above by the new democratically elected governments, with little public debate or involvement. Thereafter began the much more variegated, intensely political, structural transformations of the political and economic systems, each with its own logic born of specific national circumstances.[13] The revolutions had just begun.

From the Balkans to the Baltic, "democracy, market Europe!" was the rallying cry, with "Europe" meaning not only integration with a prosperous, secure West but also replication of Western Europe's postwar success in overcoming destructive nationalism. To be "European," for Eastern Europe's new leaders, was, as one writer put it, "to think beyond their frontiers, to transcend the provincial and destructive terms of traditional debates."[14] The task confronting the peoples of the region and their new leaders was unprecedented, for they were undertaking three simultaneous, overlapping revolutions in the political, economic, and social spheres.

In prior cases of transition from authoritarian rule, at least some elements of a market economy or liberal democracy were already in place—an existing market-based economic system, for example, or a stable ruling elite. Among the postcommunist countries, everything had to be changed in one way or another, and everything was related to everything else. New elections had to be held even while constitutions were being revised and wholesale economic restructuring undertaken. Society at large, meanwhile, had to acclimate itself to new responsibilities, for, as de Tocqueville said with regard to the French Revolution, "Political freedom had been so long extinct . . . that people had almost entirely forgotten what it meant and how it functioned."[15]

The postcommunist transitions inevitably would be messy, intensely political processes, unlikely to conform to prescriptions hatched in Western social science laboratories or advanced by visiting teams of "expert advisers." The very term "transition" was misleading, implying movement from one fixed point to another "post-transition" destination.

There were, of course, alternative models of transition from authoritarian rule. General Augusto Pinochet's Chile and General Chun Doo-Hwan's South Korea were two models commonly adduced and sometimes studied in the region. Yet for the countries of Central and Eastern Europe, the "Korean model" of capitalist development undertaken by a still-authoritarian government was not what was being espoused or pursued by the new governments and their populaces. Their aspiration was democracy *and* the market. The alternative, and the danger, was authoritarianism pure and simple, not some new "model" that combined political authoritarianism and economic liberalism. It was probably true that the "Korean model" was inherently flawed, containing the seeds of its own destruction, in that free market systems inevitably generate internal pressures toward an eventual loosening of authoritarian rule. (The Chilean, South Korean, and Taiwanese examples supported the point, as each government was obliged eventually to bow to pressures for greatly expanded economic and political participation, though such was not the initial intent of the ruling establishments.) This was certainly true for postcommunist Central and Eastern Europe, whose populaces were not likely to be satisfied with economic freedom alone (nor shoulder its attendant burdens) if their hard-won political liberties were denied.

In this sense, it was reassuring that "democracy, market, Europe" were inseparable aspirations for most of the new Central and Eastern European leaders and the standards to which they were held by their publics. Political, economic, and social change under these circumstances could not be separated or pursued sequentially. Suspending the economic transformation in order to consolidate democratic rule or suspending democracy to push through painful economic reforms were recipes for achieving neither.

The political, economic, and social spheres interacted in complex ways. The Polish sociologist Jadwiga Staniszkis cited a former Polish minister of industry as saying, "I represent interests that do not exist yet."[16] It was a provocative thought. The minister did not say the interests were not yet articulated; he said they did not even exist. Of course, something related to "industrial interests" could be identified, but they amounted to the bureaucratic, monopolistic interests of an as yet unreformed managerial class, not those of an economically vibrant industrial sector manifesting itself in ways conducive to market-based economic competition. To be real in this sense, industrial interests had to be backed by social and economic power; to be politically relevant, they had to be accompanied by a devolution of power and creation of new avenues of political participation. To take another example: Most of the countries of the region had political parties that could be called "liberal" in the European sense of the term. Yet how could a European-style liberal party exist without a politically active entrepreneurial class wielding real economic power? Without these social and economic roots, the embryonic "parties" were more political "clubs" organized around a set of personalities and political orientations, a consideration that may explain why the "liberals" in Central and Eastern Europe soon lost their initial popularity and support.

One paradox was that the new, democratically elected governments were obliged to create the conditions for their own demise. Replacing the intrusive role of the state in social, economic, and political life was among their most important tasks, yet it required an exceptional concentration of governmental authority to destroy the old command system and replace it with less intrusive, regulatory government. They had, in short, to amass power in order to dispose of its excesses. The economic monopoly of the state had to be broken for democracy to take root, just as democratic legitimacy (and a measure of governmental efficiency) were required for structural economic transformation.

Over the longer term, the key to secure democracy would be civil society. The building, or rebuilding, of democratic civil society required economic empowerment and democratic devolution, as well as the cultivation of all the institutions and habits that go into making democracy work from the bottom up.[17] This would entail the democratization of public policy: devolution of power to lower levels, rebalancing legislative and executive authority, and, above all, enhancing public participation in the policy process through the development of private voluntary organizations (PVOs), nongovernmental organizations (NGOs), and other intermediate institutions that were leveled under the Stalinist *gleichschaltung* four decades before. These measures were not just adjuncts of democratic and market development; they were integral to the overall process of postcommunist transition. Their successful accomplishment would demand an awareness, as one writer put it, "that civil society and the market are vital to democracy—that there can be no democracy without a civil society, and no civil society without a market."[18]

In the economic realm, there were certain necessary and irreducible steps—price liberalization, macroeconomic stabilization, foreign trade liberalization, currency reform, small-scale privatization, and private sector promotion—that all of these countries undertook, albeit with differing levels of conviction and commitment.[19] These were the essentials of "marketization," which was often but wrongly equated with "privatization." The key elements of a market-based economy could be introduced relatively quickly and successfully, even if large areas of the economy remained under state ownership. Over the longer term, it was essential—for democracy as well as a market economy—to reduce the state's economic monopoly; thus a rational plan for mass privatization needed to be part of a longer-term (say, decade-long) strategy of economic restructuring. (Here again was the paradox of the government's crucial role in managing the economic transformation in a way that reduced its own role in managing the economy.) Yet this was also the politically most difficult task, for it raised the specter of mass unemployment of workers in hitherto protected positions. The task for the new governments of the region was not to privatize overnight but rather to put in place a rational and politically tenable process of mass privatization. Subsidies had to be reduced in order to control inflation and free up scarce resources for critical investments, a measure of market discipline was needed so as to reduce inefficiency, and conditions had to be created that would attract urgently needed foreign investment. Even that limited agenda would prove hard to fulfill.

During the initial period of economic restructuring, while much of the state-owned sector remained unreformed and unprofitable, it would be the new private sector that generated economic growth and provided new jobs. It would be imperative to nurture this sector, so that fledgling small businesses could prosper and expand—first in the service sector and then into light manufactures and other productive sectors. Improved access to Western markets was essential both for private sector growth and the attraction of foreign investment. Creation of new capital markets was also crucial, requiring financial reform and bank privatization as well as the creation of private pension funds and other new sources of indigenous capital.

Even under the best of circumstances, these economic measures were sure to spawn social discontent and generate new inequalities, among the populations at large as well as regionally. The diamond-shaped socioeconomic structure associated with advanced industrial democracies, with small upper and lower classes and a large middle class bulge, would be years in the creation. Nor would opportunities for social mobility emerge quickly. Instead, these transitions were likely to produce pyramidal socioeconomic structures, with a vast and resentful underclass and a small but conspicuously wealthy group at the top. Lacking the social welfare benefits that the East Germans acquired as a result of unification with a prosperous Federal Republic, the rest of Central and Eastern Europe had little capacity to redress these burgeoning social and economic inequalities and the political dangers associated with them. Absent external underwriting of costly social safety net programs, the only available answers were to be found in economic growth and job creation, along with a streamlining of existing welfare systems. These would take time.

Meanwhile, the burden would fall on the new political leaders of the region, whose inexperience called to mind Edmund Burke's characterization of the leaders of the French Revolution: "Among them . . . I saw some of known rank; some of shining talents; but of practical experience in the state, not one man was to be found. The best were only men of theory."[20] The tasks in 1989 as in 1789 were immense for, as Burke elsewhere put it, "To make a government requires no great prudence. . . . To give freedom is still more easy. . . . But to form a free government; that is, to temper together these opposite elements of liberty and restraint in one consistent work, requires much thought. . . ."[21] These reflections were echoed in 1990 by the Polish historian Adam Michnik, who stressed that "the victory of freedom has not yet meant the triumph of democracy": "Democracy is something more than freedom. Democracy is freedom institutionalized, freedom submitted to the limits of the law, freedom functioning as an object of compromise between the major political forces on the scene."[22]

New democracies, as Samuel Huntington observed, face an inevitable dilemma: "lacking legitimacy they cannot become effective; lacking effectiveness they cannot develop legitimacy."[23] Throughout Central and Eastern Europe there were debates over measures to strengthen governmental authority via a powerful presidency or electoral laws that aimed at limiting the number of small parties, for example by requiring parties to gain more than 4 or 5 percent of the popular vote to qualify for seats in the parliament. With or without these special measures, governments throughout the region were obliged to retreat in one fashion or another from radical reform measures in the face of popular backlash. As a long-term proposition it may be true, as Huntington argued, that public disillusionment is not only inevitable but salutary, in that "the lowered expectations it produces are the foundation of democratic stability,"[24] but in the short term it would prove a source of *in*stability and indeed, in some instances, of protracted governmental crisis.

Ralf Dahrendorf put it succinctly. "The issue is how to establish the constitution of liberty and anchor it firmly. The heart of the problem lies in the incongruent time scales of the political, the economic, and the social reforms needed to this end."[25] Free elections and a democratic constitution could be effected in a matter of months, while structural economic transformation demanded a period of years, with the result that passage through the inevitable "valley of tears . . . will always take longer than the lifetime of the first parliament and . . . engender a degree of disillusionment which will threaten the new constitutional framework along with the economic reforms."[26] During the still longer process of building a civil society rooted in democracy, with much of the old managerial class still in place, these societies would remain vulnerable to what Václav Havel would later call the "post-communist nightmare" of authoritarian ultra-nationalism.[27]

Laying the Foundations

But to tell the story this way is to get too far ahead of events and the circumstances in which U.S. and other Western policy was actually made. At this time—that is, early 1990—General Jaruzelski was still president of Poland, Václav Havel sat atop an essentially unaltered political system, and "reform communists" or newly minted "democrats" of dubious authenticity ruled in Romania, Bulgaria, Hungary, and East Germany. Not counting the open but circumscribed June 1989 elections in Poland, free and fair democratic elections had yet to be held anywhere in the region. Stalin-era constitutions were still in place, as were the main institutions of the discredited but not yet dismantled communist party-state. In the economic sphere, only Poland (and, under different circumstances, Yugoslavia) had embarked on serious programs of market reform. It was probably too late for die-hard communists to turn the clock back, but neither could the clock be turned forward to reveal secure democracies throughout the region.

The essential task for Western policies was to consolidate the gains of the 1989 revolutions by facilitating the prompt withdrawal of Soviet troops and other elements of Soviet control and influence, promoting free and fair elections, and supporting the nascent democratic forces against the still formidable power of the ruling establishments. We could also provide emergency assistance where needed so as to avert a chaotic breakdown of order and assist with the transition from a rapidly collapsing system of central planning toward market-based economies. It was important, too, to establish an international consensus on the principles that should guide these unprecedented transitions and ensure that the governments of Central and Eastern Europe, as well as the Soviet leadership, endorsed them.

The traditionally cool U.S. attitude toward the Conference on Security and Cooperation in Europe (CSCE) was being revised rapidly, as the demise of East European communism pointed to a whole range of functions that an invigorated CSCE was well placed to perform. As early as his Mainz speech in May 1989, President Bush had called for adding free elections to the CSCE's mandate, an initiative later endorsed by the November 1990 Paris Summit. The CSCE at this point had no institutional character aside from the periodic conferences held under its purview, the most recent being the Vienna conference that concluded in January 1989. It needed to develop an institutional and operational capacity to fulfill what was now becoming its new mandate—the consolidation of democracy in Eastern Europe. Toward that end, the CSCE needed to agree on and establish a set of principles, building on but going far beyond the general precepts codified in the Final Act of the 1975 Helsinki conference.

A "Magna Carta of Free Enterprise"   The March–April 1990 Bonn conference on the economic dimensions of security—the so-called second basket of the 1975 Helsinki agreement of the CSCE—provided the right venue for reaching agreement on the principles of the transition from centrally planned toward market-based economic systems. The conference grew out of a 1987 West German proposal that the United States had reluctantly supported (at the Vienna review conference ending in January 1989) despite misgivings about offering economic concessions to unreformed Eastern economies.[28] This was the familiar West German preference for East-West contacts against the American (and British) insistence on conditionality. By early 1990, the circumstances were radically different, and we saw the Bonn conference as an ideal opportunity to affirm the principles that should guide the postcommunist economic transformations and on which the conditionality of Western assistance should be based. (While the Germans doubtless would argue that they were once again at the leading edge of history while the Americans only belatedly caught up, it was the circumstances more than U.S. attitudes that had changed.) We therefore attached a significance to this conference that may have surprised our European partners, long accustomed to American suspicions of the CSCE debating club. It was the beginning of a new U.S. look at the CSCE and its possibilities.

Accordingly, at the opening of the session, the U.S. delegation proposed ten principles that were ultimately accepted in the conference's concluding document. Affirming the link "between political pluralism and market economies," the principles included, with unusual specificity for a document of this kind, "fiscal and monetary policies that . . . enhance the ability of markets to function efficiently," "international and domestic policies aimed at expanding the free flow of trade," "free and competitive market economies where prices are based on supply and demand," and "protection of all types of property including private property." The declaration called special attention to the "particular importance of small and medium sized enterprises" and "the introduction of undistorted internal pricing." Finally, it called for "an efficient price mechanism and for progress toward convertibility," laying particular stress on "reform of the banking system, introducing a money market, reform of the investment laws, transformation of public enterprises, taxation, structural adjustment policy, [and] organization of a labor and capital market as well as a foreign exchange market."[29]

It was, as one commentator put it, a document that amounted to a "Magna Carta of Free Enterprise."[30] This was not an abstract exercise in declaration-drafting. Real choices lay ahead for postcommunist Eastern Europe as well as for the Soviet Union, with direct relevance for Western efforts to provide support and assistance. Poland's "shock therapy," which was to achieve remarkable if painful results in its first year, was being watched with a mixture of interest, skepticism, and disdain elsewhere in the region. The new leadership in Prague spoke of a "soft landing" on the way to a mixed economy, while Hungarian economists continued to debate a "third road" between capitalism and socialism. The Bulgarians and Romanians had not even begun to dismantle the old system of central planning.

While we did not intend at Bonn or elsewhere to dictate how the peoples of the East should organize their economic lives, we did consider it vitally important to reach agreement on the basic elements of market-based economic development and the terms on which these countries could expect Western help. Politically, we also wanted to support those forces in the East that genuinely wanted to build democracy and make it harder for the die-hards to legitimize their continued rule through some pseudodemocratic authoritarian rule.

The Bonn conference was followed in June 1990 by a conference in Copenhagen devoted to human rights, now called, in the argot of "Eurospeak," the "human dimension." As with the Bonn conference, we had expressed reservations about this series of meetings, particularly a planned 1991 meeting in Moscow. At Vienna, we and the British had bowed to the CSCE consensus on this issue but made it clear that our attendance hinged on significant improvements in the Soviet human rights record. (Little could we have known that the Moscow session ultimately would be held just after the failed hard-line coup attempt of August 1991 and the imminent collapse of the Soviet state, or that this would be the meeting that formally admitted into the CSCE the Baltic states of Lithuania, Latvia, and Estonia as sovereign, independent states.) Our attitude had shifted markedly by the time of the Copenhagen meeting, however.

Copenhagen began with the admission of Albania into the CSCE. This event, poignant to those of us who had followed Albania's self-imposed isolation on the Adriatic and listened to Radio Tirana's vitriolic English-language broadcasts, was accomplished in an odd fashion. Danish foreign minister Uffe Ellemann-Jensen, chairing the session, began by reading a letter from his Albanian counterpart formally petitioning to attend the conference as an observer. Ellemann-Jensen then said, "I assume there are no objections?" paused for a millisecond, and then moved on to the next item on his agenda. There was confused whispering among the delegations, with no one quite sure what had just transpired. At the first break, it became clear that Ellemann-Jensen, believing that Paragraph 54 of the Helsinki Final Act guaranteed observer status to all European states (plus the United States and Canada), had accepted the proposal without submitting it to a vote or even a debate.

Our concern, like that of many delegations, was with establishing a framework and set of procedures for Albania's eventual membership that would place an onus on that country to adhere to the democratic principles enshrined in the Helsinki Final Act and subsequent documents. In other words, we wanted to use the admission process for political purposes. We had in mind not just Albania but potential future applicants—not suspecting just how many there would be within the next two years!—for admission into a body that was now acquiring a much more ambitious character than anyone envisioned when the Final Act was signed. We insisted, for example, that applicants affirm their intention to abide by "Helsinki principles" and accept an initial observer mission to review the extent to which it met or deviated from those standards before membership was accorded. These procedures, later adopted at the Paris Summit of the CSCE in November 1990, proved useful indeed in dealing with the new states that emerged from the Soviet Union upon the latter's dissolution at the end of 1991.

Toward a CSCE "Constitution"   Secretary Baker's speech at the opening of the Copenhagen conference, one of his best, aimed at breathing new life into the CSCE, which he called "the conscience of the Continent," and signaling a new American approach toward it:

> We are present at the creation of a new age of Europe. It is a time of discussion of new architectures, councils, committees, confederations, and common houses. These are, no doubt, weighty matters. But all these deliberations of statesmen and diplomats, scholars and lawgivers, will amount to nothing if they forget a basic premise. This premise is that "all men are created equal, that they are endowed by their Creator with certain inalienable Rights, that among these are Life, Liberty, and the pursuit of Happiness." It is "to secure these rights [that] Governments are instituted among them, deriving their just powers from the consent of the governed." *That* is why we are here. . . .
>
> Three challenges lie before us. First, we must ensure that the freedoms so recently won are rooted in societies governed by the rule of law and the consent of the governed. Second, we must ensure that all peoples of Europe may know the prosperity that comes from economic liberty and competitive markets. And third, we must ensure that we are not drawn into either inadvertent conflict or a replay of the disputes that preceded the Cold War.[31]

Among the specific U.S. proposals Baker advanced for the next CSCE Summit (held in Paris in November 1990) were ones to endorse the Bonn Principles of Economic Cooperation, strengthen the CSCE's role in conflict resolution (with specifics to be worked out at a meeting to be held in Valletta, Malta, in January 1991), and expand CSCE political consultation through annual foreign ministers' meetings and biannual review conferences. He also called for the CSCE to develop, as a first step toward its "institutionalization," mechanisms for promoting and monitoring free elections and to adopt at Copenhagen a concluding document that set forth "the elements of democratic society operating under the rule of law."

Baker also had raised this issue in his February 1990 Prague speech, echoing President Bush's call (at the 1989 Paris Summit of the G-7) for adding free elections to the human rights obligations of all members of the Conference on Security and Cooperation in Europe. Anticipating the round of elections scheduled in virtually every East European country between March and June of 1990, Baker proposed that all CSCE member states join with the United States in sending observing delegations. Previewing the message he would carry with him to Sofia and Bucharest a few days later, Baker added that "we are troubled by indications that some of the governments in the region have engaged in practices that will obstruct truly free and fair elections. . . ." There may not have been much we could do directly to guarantee that the Bulgarian and Romanian elections would be freely conducted, but we did have the capacity to raise the international stakes on those regimes and provide further encouragement elsewhere.

The Copenhagen document, whose final shape owed much to the work of the American delegation led by Ambassador Max Kampelman, was even more remarkable than the Bonn document in its programmatic detail.[32] Its commitments on election procedures were precise: "The participating States [i.e., the 35 members of the CSCE] will hold free elections at reasonable intervals, as established by law; permit all seats in at least one chamber of the national legislature to be freely contested by popular vote; . . . ensure that votes are cast by secret ballot or by equivalent free voting procedures . . . ; provide that no legal or administrative obstacle stands in the way of unimpeded access to the media . . . ; [and] invite observers from any other CSCE participating States and any appropriate private institutions and organizations who may wish to do so to observe the course of their national election proceedings."

The document went on to affirm fundamental freedoms and the rule of law, including commitments to specific practices that would give practical and measurable content to rights too often observed in the breach:

A clear separation [should be created] between the State and political parties; in particular, political parties will not be merged with the State. . . .

No one may be deprived of his property except in the public interest and subject to the conditions provided for by law and consistent with international commitments and obligations. . . .

Everyone will have the right to freedom of expression, the right of association . . . [and] the right to freedom of thought, conscience and religion. . . . [States will] ensure that individuals are permitted to exercise the right of association, including the right to form, join and participate effectively in nongovernmental organizations . . . , including trade unions and human rights monitoring groups.

The imposition of a state of emergency must be proclaimed officially, publicly, and in accordance with the provisions laid down by law; . . . such measures will not discriminate on the grounds of race, colour, sex, language, religion, social origin, or belonging to a minority. . . .

The participating States will protect the ethnic, cultural, linguistic and religious identity of national minorities on their territory and create conditions for the promotion of that identity. . . . [They] clearly and unequivocally condemn totalitarianism, racial and ethnic hatred, anti-semitism, xenophobia and discrimination. . . .

As one commentator put it, "Concepts such as a 'pluralist democracy' and 'the rule of law' had not been previously mentioned in CSCE documents. . . . True, these are merely words, but no such words have been allowed into any CSCE document between 1975, when the Helsinki Final Act was signed, and June 1990, when the [Document of the Copenhagen Meeting] was adopted." This "landmark international charter," he continued, "in its political scope and significance, is unmatched by other international human rights instruments."[33] Munich's *Süddeutsche Zeitung* offered the headline, "The CSCE States Adopt a Constitution." Like the Bonn document before it, the Copenhagen declaration had direct practical significance—in affirming the main goals of postcommunist transformation, establishing the conditions of Western assistance, and informing a broadly shared assistance strategy.

Western Assistance Strategies

The aspirations to "democracy, market, Europe" formed the basis of Western assistance strategies, which included emergency aid for the immediate tasks of the transitions toward democratic rule and sustained technical and financial assistance for creating the foundations of market-based economic systems. Western leaders also undertook multilateral efforts to support the integration of these economies into the broader European and global economy. To coordinate these activities, as has been seen, G-7 leaders had created a new forum for "concerted Western action" that became the Group of 24 industrialized democracies (G-24) under the chairmanship of the Commission of the European Community.

The common assumption during the heady days of 1989 was that a three- to five-year burst of external assistance—balance of payments and structural adjustment support from the international financial institutions, bilateral technical assistance programs coordinated through the G-24, and facilitation of foreign trade and investment—would propel these countries toward integration into the global economy. This assumption proved much too optimistic, and Western assistance efforts had to adjust to the longer term challenges of postcommunist transformation.

The U.S. Assistance Program   Eastern Europe figured prominently in President Bush's State of the Union Address in late January 1990: "There are singular moments in history—dates that divide all that goes before from all the comes after. . . . The events of the year just ended [mark] the beginning of a new era in world affairs. . . . Today, with communism crumbling, our aim must be to ensure democracy's advance . . . to take the lead in forging . . . a great and growing commonwealth of free nations."[34]

The next day, in his presentation to Congress of the administration's foreign affairs budget request, including $300 million for the SEED (Support for East European Democracy) Act, Secretary Baker offered a cautionary note:

The old world of dogmatic dictatorships is on its way out. But the new world of secure, prosperous, and just democracies is not yet here. It will not arrive automatically. If we fail to support the principles that brought us this far, we could end up living in a future that resembles the past—the past of the Cold War and the conflicts that preceded it. Too many nations have won the war only to lose the peace. We cannot afford to let that happen now. The stakes are too high and can only get higher.[35]

And indeed Eastern Europe enjoyed priority attention for a time. At the end of 1989, the president had named Deputy Secretary of State

Lawrence Eagleburger as his coordinator for East European assistance, responsible not only for all programs administered under the SEED Act but for other assistance-related activities as well. It was a choice we on the NSC staff had pushed. Other options that we presented for the president's consideration were, in our view, clearly inferior. Letting the Agency for International Development (AID) run it was out of the question, as AID had no presence in the region and a developmental ethos ill-suited to the urgent needs of relatively advanced Central and Eastern European countries. Besides, at the senior levels of the administration there was a visceral aversion to AID that persisted even after the agency acquitted itself well and imaginatively in Central and Eastern Europe. Putting the NSC in charge was better, but Scowcroft felt (rightly) as a matter of principle that the NSC should not take on such a highly operational role.[36] Treasury lacked the strategic perspective that was needed, and a joint State-Treasury program (among the options offered) would only confuse lines of authority. State was the right agency to oversee the process, and the deputy secretary was the right level of seniority. This particular deputy secretary also knew the region well and exercised a degree of authority even beyond his rank.

At the same time, we wanted this to be a multiagency effort, so as to draw on the specific strengths of Treasury, Labor, the Environmental Protection Agency, Energy, and others, as well as to produce the widest possible backing within the administration. Given the active role being played in the region already by Labor Secretary Elizabeth Dole and other powerful cabinet officers, it was going to be multiagency regardless. (As it turned out, departments and agencies that could not be kept out of the action in 1989 and 1990 were by 1991 and 1992 invisible. Eastern Europe had become yesterday's news.) Under any arrangement, Treasury's role would be indispensable: it was, by long tradition, the lead agency with respect to policy on international debt, the international financial institutions (the IMF and World Bank), and other issues that bore directly on the postcommunist transitions. Accordingly, the president named Deputy Treasury Secretary John Robson, together with Council of Economic Affairs Chairman Michael Boskin, as Eagleburger's deputy coordinators. They were later joined by a third deputy, AID Administrator Ronald Roskens.

The day-to-day direction of the East European assistance program was devolved to Eagleburger's special adviser for East European assistance (a position I held in 1992 and 1993[37]), who chaired an interagency working group of State, NSC, Treasury, and AID (replicating, more or less, the coordinator and deputy coordinators) and an expanded group that included all of the 18 agencies engaged in the assistance effort. All assistance activities by any government agency—every trip to the region, each initiative or proposal, every dollar spent or promised—had to be coordinated with and approved by Eagleburger. The dynamics of the group evolved over time. Treasury's role diminished somewhat as the main lines of macroeconomic policy were established in the region; in contrast, AID's role expanded as assistance moved from the conceptual phase to implementation and monitoring. After the first year or so, the State/NSC/Treasury/AID working group became the venue of policy making, and AID became the lead implementing agency, all under the direction of the coordinator.[38]

The organization of U.S. assistance involving multiple agencies was a model of how to get things done. This was no interagency debating club; it was a operational body that made quick and authoritative decisions, whether at the level of the deputy secretary or his special adviser. It was the most efficient, streamlined, and collegial interagency effort anywhere in government. It was also a model of foreign assistance well suited for an era of budgetary stringency. It engaged the strengths of multiple agencies, including those charged with advancing U.S. commercial interests; embedded foreign assistance in a larger strategic design that was linked to domestic policy as well; and created innovative and cost-effective partnerships with the American private sector, business and nonprofit alike. It was, as well, woefully underfunded, though this liability made itself felt only later, as Poland and Hungary were joined by Czechoslovakia, Bulgaria, Romania, and others in competition for scarce resources.

In his February 1990 "From Revolution to Democracy" speech in Prague, Secretary Baker had laid out the main elements of the strategy, designed to "promote, perpetuate, and protect Europe's democratic revolutions." First was short-term emergency aid—food, medicine, disaster relief—of the kind we had already delivered in large quantities to Poland and Romania. This had logical priority, both to meet urgent immediate needs and to avert a chaotic breakdown of public order that would undermine economic and political reforms before they had really begun. Second were bilateral and multilateral (i.e., through the international financial institutions) efforts to facilitate debt restructuring and support macroeconomic stabilization programs so as to reduce hyperinflation and provide a stable economic environment conducive to growth and market development.

Third were various forms of technical and financial assistance. In the economic arena, our efforts focused on promotion of foreign investment, which would bring in capital, know-how, and new jobs, and on seed money and technical assistance for local private ventures so that a new and dynamic private sector could emerge. Later, as several countries embarked on programs of structural economic transformation, we also provided considerable assistance for the privatization of large-scale enterprises and banking systems. Finally, there was a wide variety of programs, albeit of modest scope, to help build the foundations of democratic rule through constitutional and electoral reform, assistance to nascent political parties, and others aimed at the reconstruction of civil society. (One specific program Baker announced in Prague was an International Media Fund to provide capital, equipment, and technical assistance to independent media, both print and electronic.)

In an address delivered in mid-February 1990, just ten days after Baker's Prague speech, Deputy Secretary Eagleburger spoke more operationally, in his new capacity as the president's coordinator for East European assistance:

> We can no longer think of Eastern Europe as a bloc. We must now think of each country in the region in its own light, with its unique history, aspirations, and potential. . . . Our efforts should be focused on projects where we can make a difference, not dispersed over so many programs that none in the end will have a substantial impact. . . .
>
> There have been calls . . . for a new Marshall Plan for Eastern Europe. . . . [But] we are not dealing with a situation similar to postwar Western Europe, where we had to help rebuild a region that was physically devastated but which still possessed the technical skills, public institutions, and market experience to recover quickly. In Eastern Europe, which is emerging from a 40-year time capsule and which lacks those skills and institutions, our strategy must be different. . . . Our primary goal, at least in the early stages, must be to provide the democratic institution-building skills and entrepreneurial know-how without which the privatization of the Eastern economies simply will not succeed.[39]

These tasks called for engagement of the American private sector and creation of a public-private partnership to use scarce public funds as a catalyst for much greater private engagement. President Bush focused on this aspect in his commencement address at the University of South Carolina in May 1990, in which he announced creation of a Citizens Democracy Corps as a "center and clearinghouse for American private sector assistance and volunteer activities in Eastern Europe."[40] Like the Enterprise Funds and the International Media Fund, the CDC had a private board of directors, announced but not formally appointed by the president, that made decisions with a minimum of governmental oversight, our idea being that eminent private Americans were better able than bureaucrats to take swift, effective action. The Enterprise Funds, with their mixed boards of Americans and citizens of the country in which they operated, proved particularly successful in providing loans and technical assistance to local businesses, serving also as catalysts for American investors. The Polish and Hungarian Funds, created after the president's July 1989 trip, were followed by Czechoslovak and Bulgarian Enterprise Funds in 1990 and 1991, respectively.[41]

Most other programs in the U.S. assistance effort were in the same spirit of public/private partnership—from the Peace Corps (whose Polish program soon became its largest) to the American Bar Association's Central and East European Legal Initiative (CEELI).[42] This program combined public funds with pro bono legal services provided by private American lawyers. In this way, we could use scarce public funds to leverage substantial assistance and also create self-sustaining programs that could continue even after Central and Eastern Europe no longer commanded priority attention. Indeed, by 1992 we faced the unanticipated problem that some of the Enterprise Funds actually turned a profit. Hence we had to amend their bylaws so that provision was made for disposing of their assets when the time came to close them down.

The U.S. program naturally evolved over its first three years. As I put it in congressional testimony in early 1993,

> In 1989 and 1990, we sought "targets of opportunity" and put a premium on getting programs up and running as quickly as possible. It was politically essential to do so—to show U.S. engagement at that critical moment. In 1990 and 1991, we put in place the "building blocks" of the program. These included the four Enterprise Funds, partnership programs in various sectors, and large

institutional contracts [in areas like privatization] that are administered regionally but deployed according to each country's specific needs. [In 1992] we developed more detailed country strategies—tightly argued, real-world statements of our priority
objectives and the programs we have or intend to advance those
objectives. . . .

In that thrilling fall of 1989, when our assistance program
began, no one knew what lay ahead. . . . We engaged as fast as we
could and learned as we went. We were willing to take risks because of the importance and urgency of the task at hand, and we
adapted the program to changing circumstances. Now 3 ½ years
later, we are wiser, perhaps, but no more able to predict what the
next few years will bring. These countries are still in the midst of
profound and essentially unpredictable change; the economic transitions are in some cases well advanced, but the revolutionary
transformation of these societies is only beginning.[43]

A program that was adequate to the requirements of 1989 and 1990
was by early 1991 eclipsed by the advent of new Eastern European
claimants for scarce resources and a much deteriorated international
economic environment. By March 1991, when Lech Wałęsa visited
Washington as Poland's new president,[44] the administration had together one further assistance package. In addition to a U.S.-brokered international agreement to reduce Poland's external debt burden by more
than half, there were three new initiatives aimed at the region as a
whole.

First was a Trade Enhancement Initiative (TEI), substantially opening
the U.S. market to Central and Eastern European exports, including politically sensitive ones like steel, textiles, and agricultural products. The
result of intense internal negotiations among USTR (Office of the U.S.
Trade Representative), the Commerce and Agriculture Departments,
and others, the TEI also expanded duty-free benefits under the U.S.
Generalized System of Preferences (GSP). Even allowing that the United
States was not going to be a major destination of most Central and
Eastern European exports, this was a major market-opening measure
that had the additional advantage of putting pressure on the Western
Europeans to follow suit: "The President is challenging the European
Community, Central and Eastern Europe's largest market, with the
largest potential for trade expansion, to redouble its efforts to open its

markets to Central and Eastern European countries and to open all sectors (including agriculture) for liberalization under the free trade area agreements now under negotiation with Poland, Hungary, and Czechoslovakia."[45]

Second was an American Business Initiative (ABI), a $45 million program carried out by the Agency for International Development (AID), the Department of Commerce, the Overseas Private Investment Corporation (OPIC), and the U.S. Trade and Development Program (TDP). Its purpose was to help the countries of the region promote U.S. trade and investment in key sectors: agriculture and agribusiness, energy, environment, telecommunications, and housing.[46] Although the ABI was to have uneven results in practice, owing partly to Commerce's slow implementation of its part of the package, some of its more successful programs helped Central and Eastern European countries take advantage of hundreds of million dollars in export and investment insurance programs administered by OPIC, the Export-Import Bank, and TDP. (When Polish prime minister Bielecki visited the White House in September 1991, President Bush announced a new housing loan guaranty program to promote the private housing sector in Poland and other countries of the region.[47])

Third was the president's decision to include in his budget a 50 percent increase in U.S. assistance to Central and Eastern Europe, from the $300 million authorized in 1989 to $470 million for the fiscal year beginning in October 1991. Originally intended for three countries in Central Europe, the SEED program was by 1991 stretched to cover more than a dozen from the Balkans to the Baltic, with a combined population of some 135 million. But Congress, which had trebled the president's 1989 request for Eastern Europe, was by this time in a different frame of mind and reduced the president's request to $400 million. Caught between a penny-pinching Republican minority and a Democratic majority flexing its muscles in anticipation of election year 1992, the president was not inclined to buck the political tide again.

Coordinating International Assistance   After its creation in July 1989, the G-24 sprang into action quickly, meeting in August, September, November, and again in December to garner financial pledges from member countries, organize the first shipments of food and other humanitarian aid to Poland, and begin developing an overall strategy of assistance. Given the enormity of the tasks ahead of the new democracies and the modesty of Western financial assistance pledged or contemplated, it was important to be clear about where and how Western support could make a difference. Aside from the example of Western economic and political success, the most important thing Western assistance could do was to encourage the Central and Eastern European governments to pursue policies that would promote continued democratic and free market development. In other words, the G-24 countries, individually and collectively, needed to provide economic incentives, technical assistance, and political suasion to help these new governments pursue the policies they should have been pursuing anyway. Beyond that, Western assistance could show the way and offer targeted assistance in key areas, but the chief burden would fall on these countries themselves, no matter the scope of outside aid.

"None of us should underestimate the difficulty of the work ahead," Baker had stressed in his February 1990 Prague speech. It was a warning that President Bush, Secretary Baker, and their Western European counterparts repeated at every occasion, but it always seemed to fall on deaf ears, so eager were the peoples of this region to believe that liberation would lead swiftly to prosperity.[48] While American and other Western leaders may have contributed to that impression by emphasizing that prosperity would eventually be theirs if they stayed the course of market reform, no one ever said the process would be easy or that it could be accomplished quickly.[49] For most in Central and Eastern Europe, West Germany's postwar "economic miracle" was their aspiration, their inspiration, their expectation. They failed to recall that the *wirtschaftswunder* was more than a decade in the making and was achieved under economic circumstances that were, relatively speaking, less difficult than Eastern Europe's economic, political, and social devastation after four decades of communist misrule.

The G-24 did well to affirm the conditions of Western assistance, a role that was particularly important in the early, chaotic period of postcommunist transition. On the American side, these proceeded from what Secretary Baker, in his Prague speech, called a "new democratic differentiation": "Because the circumstances of each nation differ considerably, it would be a mistake to apply a mechanistic assistance formula. . . . Any backsliding in the movement to create legitimate governments will isolate a nation from the support we can provide." In addition to the obvious practicality of offering support only to those countries in a position to make good use of it, this formula was meant as a warning to those resisting reform and a boost to the struggling democratic oppositions, particularly in Bulgaria and Romania. Through the PHARE (Poland/Hungary Aid for Restructuring of Economies) program, the European Community adopted essentially the same set of standards, linking its assistance to compliance with IMF-endorsed economic stabilization programs and continued movement toward democracy.[50]

There was broad agreement that the problems facing these countries were unlike those of traditional underdevelopment, but rather of severe, sometimes bizarre "mis-development." The Central European countries in particular had highly educated populations, skilled work forces, and existing, albeit decrepit, industrial bases, which meant that well-targeted external assistance often could achieve wonders by helping open up the inherent potential of these economies and societies. On the other hand, the legacy of some four decades of communist misrule meant that virtually every aspect of political, economic, and social life had to be reformed in one way or another.

Progress would be neither uniform nor orderly: some changes might be implemented from the top down, but most would proceed from the bottom up in the helter-skelter of daily efforts to make things work. These countries were in the midst of revolutionary flux, with the old system of central planning collapsing before anything could be created to replace it, and most were led by new and inexperienced leaders from the democratic opposition who faced extravagant popular expectations that the democratic revolutions would produce instant prosperity. In addition to direct financial support for macroeconomic stabilization programs, what was needed was the transfer of knowledge and the diversity of Western experience across the full range of political, economic, and social life.

Although a cumbersome and overly bureaucratic institution, the G-24 played an important role in coordinating overall approaches among the 24 participating countries, each with its own legal and bureaucratic structure and often a separate agenda. Its key achievement can be put this way: when the EC Commission's chair—Jacques Delors for ministerial-level meetings, Franz Andriessen for "senior officials" meetings—offered an introductory overview of the countries of the region and their assistance priorities, there was rarely a word of disagreement. It was not unusual for Andriessen's main points to be almost identical to those in the U.S. delegation's (and presumably other) briefing books. Achieving that level of consensus among so disparate a group was no mean feat. The commission also provided an important element of continuity and consistency as governments changed and attention was diverted elsewhere. We in Washington sometimes railed at the EC bureaucracy, but these particular "Eurocrats" became the close allies of all those in G-24 governments trying to keep priority attention focused on the ever-changing, ever-increasing needs of the Central and Eastern Europeans.

The G-24 also offered a forum for coordination with the international financial institutions and working out a certain division of labor. The IMF and the World Bank took the lead in macroeconomic stabilization and sectoral transformation.[51] Their standards, rigorously and indiscriminately applied at first, became more sensitive to the special circumstances surrounding the postcommunist transitions. The OECD proved particularly helpful in analyzing, in close consultation with the governments concerned, the structural changes required for market-based development.[52] Through its Center for Cooperation with Economies in Transition, established in 1990, and a "Partners in Transition" program, created in 1991 at U.S. initiative as a halfway house toward full membership, the OECD developed detailed sets of recommendations with candidate countries, beginning with Poland, Hungary, and Czechoslovakia. On the political side, the Council of Europe served, as it were, to translate CSCE principles into practical steps toward democratic governance and the rule of law; its "Demosthenes" program played a particularly useful role in helping bring the new democracies into conformity with wider European legal and human rights practices.[53] Other institutions, too numerous to name here, also fit into the general mosaic.

Among donor countries, a division of labor also developed, half by design and half spontaneously. The U.S. program focused on economic growth, private sector development, and civil society, whereas the EC's preference was for "social market" programs in public infrastructure, industrial restructuring, and social welfare. The difference between the two perspectives was more pragmatic than philosophical. The U.S. approach, favored also by the British, had nothing to do with "Reaganomics" or Thatcherism: It derived from the view that we should do what we could to help these countries produce wealth so that they could make their own choices. Since no one in the West was about to come up with the billions of dollars needed to underwrite social safety nets, finance major infrastructure projects, or clean up the environmental devastation, we wanted to help these countries develop as quickly as possible the financial wherewithal to address these problems themselves. This, we believed, was preferable to promulgating grandiose plans without providing any external resources toward their realization. Besides, it made sense for the United States to draw on its natural strength—a vibrant and diverse private sector—and leave most of the government-to-government programs to the European Community, to whose standards and norms the Central and Eastern Europeans needed to adapt anyway. (When the Office of Management and Budget and General Accounting Office lobbied to organize assistance programs, many of us bridled at the idea of transferring our own suffocating bureaucracy to our new friends in Central and Eastern Europe. Let the Western Europeans take on that task.)

Yet the G-24 never supplied the kind of strategic, operational coordination of assistance envisioned at its inception. Perhaps it never could have done so, given its close links to the EC bureaucracy and the jealously guarded national prerogatives of G-24 member countries, including the United States. The haphazard nature of Western approaches was acceptable during the initial phase of the postcommunist transitions, when Central and Eastern European governments were disorganized and when a degree of experimentation was inevitable. But the duplication of effort and competition among G-24 countries became increasingly costly as the Central European reform programs progressed. Over time, we in Washington developed close and surprisingly cordial cooperation with the EC Commission, as well as with the IMF, World Bank, and OECD, but there was little operational coordination, with the result that a great deal of duplication and competition persisted among donor countries.

The European Bank for Reconstruction and Development (EBRD) was a case in point. It was proposed in October 1989 by President Mitterrand without prior consultation and had more to do with French ambitions for wresting control away from the World Bank, which they saw as too much the creature of Washington, than with the needs of its nominal beneficiaries, the Central and Eastern Europeans. Despite skepticism on the part of the Dutch, Italians, British, and Germans, EC countries approved the proposal at the December 1989 EC Council meeting in Strasbourg, leaving the details for further negotiations.[54] From late 1989 into 1990, there was strenuous behind-the-scenes wran-

gling and horse-trading over the location and leadership of the bank.
We had proposed Prague, with Vienna our second choice, so as to situ-
ate the bank in the region of its intended activities, and we wanted it led
by a distinguished international financier already conversant in multilateral lending operations. We were outflanked from the beginning, however, and could do no more than help effect a compromise of sorts,
whereby the bank would be headquartered in London rather than Paris
under the presidency of Mitterrand's key foreign policy adviser, the
flamboyant Jacques Attali.[55]

More substantive were disputes over the question of Soviet membership in the EBRD, which France supported but we opposed on grounds
that Eastern Europe's needs would be eclipsed by the virtually unlimited
needs of an essentially unreformed Soviet economy. A related dispute
was whether the EBRD should lend chiefly to governments, as France
proposed, or to private businesses, which we favored on grounds that
these new firms were in greater need and likely to show greater promise
as generators of jobs and financial profit. Both issues came to compromise: the USSR would join but with strict limits on its borrowing rights
(so as not to deplete resources meant for Eastern Europe),[56] and lending
rules were established that permitted both public and private borrowing
but stipulated that at least 60 percent of loans must be to private business. After an excruciatingly slow start, the EBRD gradually acquired
expertise that helped shift its initially statist, highly politicized agenda
toward a more balanced one that had some relevance to the needs of
the countries it ostensibly had been created to assist.

Why No Marshall Plan?   The G-24's chief failure was the paucity of
aid offered by its members. By early 1992, the cumulative total of Western assistance to Central and Eastern Europe, according to the G-24
"scoreboard," was around $37.5 billion (30 million ECU),[57] a figure
which included lines of credit and "commitments" and so was vastly
greater that the amount actually received. Even allowing that the slowness of disbursements was often due to recipient countries' failure to
meet the minimum appropriate conditions attached to assistance, the
claimed total was wildly inflated. Nearly two-thirds was in the form of
loans or lines of credit (often at prevailing world market rates) that the
heavily indebted countries of Central and Eastern Europe could never
draw on. Of the remaining third, many of the grants were total commitments for programs that would be funded over the course of several

years, if at all. Yet everything was thrown into the hopper for the G-24's running scoreboard.

The U.S. share was 17 percent of the overall total but 32 percent of the total grant aid; Germany's was 20 percent of the overall and 22 percent of grants. The EC PHARE program and European Investment Bank contributed 12 percent and 10 percent respectively; all others were far behind.[58] The U.S. preference was for grant assistance, on grounds that it made little sense to offer loans at unfavorable rates to Central and Eastern European countries already laboring under huge debt burdens. This was a matter of principle but also of necessity, for U.S. credit reform (legislated in the wake of the savings and loan crisis of the late 1980s) required that every foreign loan have a budgetary offset pegged to the foreign country's creditworthiness. For most of Central and Eastern Europe, that meant up to fifty cents on the dollar. A $100 million loan, in other words, had to be backed by $50 million in the administration's already strained assistance budget. EC member countries had no such constraint; their governments could simply undertake a loan commitment without budgetary impact. These policy differences often led to acrimony in G-24 meetings in 1990 and into 1991, but by the end of that year the increasingly exposed Europeans joined the United States in showing caution before extending further loans.

Among the more onerous tasks the G-24 was obliged to perform was to solicit contributions for IMF-led stabilization programs. The typical pattern was for the IMF to come up with a funding level short of that actually needed and then to look to the G-24 to provide an additional amount of up to $1 billion. These were known in G-24 parlance as "gap-filling exercises," which produced heated exchanges between the United States and its Western partners. As has been seen, the United States led the effort to amass the $1 billion Polish stabilization fund, but we did so with $200 million in grant funding that we could not replicate thereafter. When it came time to support similar funds for Hungary and Czechoslovakia, we were able to offer only much smaller grants of $10 and $15 million respectively, leaving the EC to bear the lion's share of the burden. When Bulgaria and Romania joined the queve, neither we nor the EC met the IMF's targets, leaving those two countries to pursue macroeconomic stabilization programs that were seriously underfunded.[59]

By the beginning of 1991, the inadequacy of G-24 assistance levels had become all too apparent. Resources had not increased to meet the growing number of recipient countries, much less offset severe new external shocks to these nascent democracies. The virtual collapse of the East German and Soviet markets, together with the high cost of sanctions against Iraq and later Yugoslavia, contributed to a region-wide recession. In 1991, gross domestic product (GDP) declined by 8–10 percent in Poland, 10 percent in Czechoslovakia, 7–9 percent in Hungary, 9 percent in Romania, and a staggering 25 percent in Bulgaria.[60] During the winter of 1991–92, as will be seen, Albania came perilously close to extinction as a functioning society[61]—this at the very time that the Yugoslav civil war was threatening a wider Balkan conflagration.

This was the time for a new burst of Western assistance, supported by an entirely new Western strategy to deal with a situation in Central and Eastern Europe that had deteriorated markedly since Western leaders last gave the region serious attention in 1989–90. Yet no such effort was undertaken, as Western leaders were preoccupied with other concerns. Worse, existing resources increasingly were diverted to providing emergency aid to the Soviet Union in the form of subsidized Western food shipments that directly undercut Central and Eastern European exports. By 1991, G-24 meetings occasionally turned into name-calling affairs, with the EC criticizing the overall low levels of U.S. contributions and the United States reminding the Europeans that their claimed assistance levels were vastly inflated. The deeper truth was that neither we nor the European Community rose to the challenge of providing the levels of help needed for countries in the midst of profound economic transformation. Which side was the more culpable was hardly the relevant question.

We in Washington looked increasingly to our Western European partners to take the lead, and to some extent they did, but there was no replacing U.S. leadership when it came to setting and implementing a post–Cold War European and transatlantic agenda. The Marshall Plan offered little in the way of a model, except as a demonstration of the scope of American commitment. It was, as George Kennan, one of its principal architects, stressed, directed at the specific problems associated with postwar reconstruction in Western Europe,[62] almost none of which applied to the postcommunist states of Eastern Europe. The main problems they faced—creation of a new private sector and managerial class, mass privatization of thousands of state enterprises, and establishing the foundations of democratic civil societies—were not the work of a few years, no matter the scope of external assistance.

The inaptness of the Marshall Plan analogy and the unprecedented character of postcommunist transformation had the perverse effect of forestalling among Western governments a serious, ongoing review of the appropriate levels of Western assistance. (It also prejudiced subsequent debate over aid to Russia and the other states of the former Soviet Union, as Western governments settled on similarly insufficient levels of support.) While assistance on the scale of the Marshall Plan would not have yielded a commensurate increase in the probability of success in Central and Eastern Europe, nor appreciably reduced the social pain these populations had to endure, a strong case could have been made for a doubling or tripling of Western assistance as an investment in the stability of post–Cold War Europe.[63] Such an increase was not forthcoming nor even seriously debated here or in Europe.

There is no satisfactory explanation for Western failure to provide adequate resources for Eastern Europe. On the American side, a partial explanation was that the internal decision-making process continued to treat these issues as matters of foreign assistance rather than national security.[64] If the consolidation of democracy in Central and Eastern Europe was among our highest national security priorities, as it was, the expenditure of an additional $500 or $600 million toward that end should have been obvious and should not have required special pleading before cabinet officers. It was a modest sum relative to a defense budget running in the hundreds of *billions* of dollars.

As it turned out, the naming of a coordinator for East European assistance had the unintended effect of removing East European assistance issues from the ongoing, active agendas of cabinet officers. After Eagleburger's appointment, not a single meeting of the National Security Council (i.e., formal sessions chaired by the president), nor even of the NSC Deputies Committee, was devoted to East European assistance strategy. Of course, Eagleburger talked to Baker and Scowcroft, both of whom talked to the president, but that was not the same thing. Thus, instead of elevating Eastern Europe in the bureaucratic scheme of things, the coordinator's position had the effect of marginalizing the region from broader strategic considerations. A deputy secretary of state, especially one as effective and respected as Larry Eagleburger, is a powerful figure, but not powerful enough to single-handedly deliver cabinet officers. When it came to tough choices—garnering more money for assistance, bucking domestic lobbies in efforts to open U.S. markets to East European imports, and the like—Eagleburger was left without the ongoing support of Bush, Baker, and others. Perhaps the most telling fact is that Baker, in his memoirs running to 687 pages, does not refer once to the East European assistance program.[65]

There were at least three respects in which the Marshall Plan offered lessons that should have been applied in Central and Eastern Europe. First, responsibility for devising economic recovery programs should have rested more firmly with the peoples and governments concerned, just as it had in Western Europe under the Marshall Plan. Too much time, energy, and money were spent on issues like the launching of the EBRD, which had more to do with competing Western ambitions than with assisting countries in transition; too little attention was paid to supporting the first new democratic governments, which bore the full brunt of public disapproval. Second, encouragement of regional cooperation should have been a more explicit strategic goal of foreign assistance. While there was no need for strict conditionality to promote regional institutions, more could have been done to support and indeed insist upon cooperative efforts among Poles, Hungarians, Czechs, and Slovaks. Those in Prague or Budapest hoping to outrace their neighbors into the European Community should have been made to understand that membership in Western institutions entailed responsibilities that began with one's immediate neighborhood, and Western governments should have adopted a strategic design and backed it with financial inducements. Finally and most important was the strategic priority of the task: support for this region, like postwar Western Europe, was a matter not of foreign assistance but of European stability and security. It was a lesson that became vividly clear with the violent disintegration of Yugoslavia and the risks this posed for spreading instability.

6

The United States and Eastern Europe

IT WOULD BE HARD to exaggerate U.S. influence among the peoples of Central and Eastern Europe and their new political leaders in 1990 and 1991. They looked to us as the victor of the long Cold War against their chief oppressor, the champion of the ideals that had animated their own democratic revolutions, and, with our swift military triumph in the Gulf War in early 1991, the world's sole and unchallenged superpower. Wildly inflated though they often were, these perceptions gave us, during this early period, enormous influence over attitudes and policies in the region. At the same time, they gave rise to extravagant expectations of U.S. readiness to provide security for these embryonic democracies and provide levels of direct assistance that would propel them on the path to prosperity. Later on, as the drama of revolution gave way to what President Bush liked to call "the hard work of democracy" and our own attention wandered, U.S. influence correspondingly diminished, and the countries of Central and Eastern Europe gravitated naturally toward their immediate Western neighbors. But during this early period, U.S. influence was enormous—easily as great as that of the countries of Western Europe combined.

Yet the authority we commanded did not always translate into meaningful influence over the course of the postcommunist transitions. These hinged on fundamental changes well beyond the influence of the United States or even of the West collectively. It was all too easy to confuse the two: to mistake the influence we seemed to have with that which we were able to turn into tangible results. Our chief influence, naturally, was on the international context in which these democratic experiments played out. We were instrumental in securing the completion of Soviet military withdrawal and ending the vestiges of Moscow's imperial dominion, as well as in drawing these countries into a cooperative international system. U.S. leadership was instrumental in creating an international framework of assistance and laying the conceptual foundations for the postcommunist transitions in Central and Eastern Europe, as well as in pointing the way for the embryonic transitions farther east.

The United States also exerted substantial influence over the policies these new governments adopted—their foreign political orientations as well as their domestic reform programs—though our influence varied greatly by country. It was strongest in Poland, where we were consistently and actively engaged, much weaker in Hungary or Bulgaria, where high-level American interest was more episodic. Throughout the region, our main efforts were to engage the new leaders of the region on their most urgent security concerns, lending our support to those committed to building democracy and keeping the pressure on the recalcitrants, like the Romanians, to follow the same path.

The following surveys of U.S. bilateral relations with the countries of Central and Eastern Europe cannot do full justice to the extraordinarily rich and complex evolution of these countries in their first few years of postcommunist existence.[1] Inasmuch as they are told from the American perspective, this being a book about U.S. foreign policy, they may also tend to magnify the American role and hence should be seen against the backdrop of broader Western engagement in the region and the multiple dramas being played out in the Central and Eastern European countries themselves.

Poland: The Special Relationship

U.S. policy from the beginning had focused on Poland, owing to that country's geostrategic weight, the importance for the entire region of its trailblazing program of economic "shock therapy," and the friendly pressure exerted by the large and effective Polish-American community. The Balcerowicz plan of rapid "marketization" achieved swift results after its introduction on January 1, 1990: after prices were liberalized and the economy opened to foreign trade, empty shelves were soon filled with goods, albeit at prices beyond the reach of many Poles, and a vibrant new private sector began to spring up. Forecasts of severe winter food shortages had prompted a massive external assistance effort, but the fears proved largely groundless. For all the uncertainties ahead, the early results of the economic reforms were encouraging.

Prime Minister Mazowiecki in Washington   Although President Bush had exchanged long messages with Tadeusz Mazowiecki and had dispatched high-level investment missions to Poland, we and the Poles had agreed that an official visit to the United States by the prime minister should come only after the Polish reform program was launched. We thought we could do more to lend him support if he had already established his own program and agenda. Accordingly, the White House announced in late January that Mazowiecki would visit in mid-March 1990. Having successfully mobilized international support for the $1 billion Polish Stabilization Fund and (thanks to Senator Paul Simon and other leading Democrats in Congress) tripled our initial assistance package for Poland, our aims now were to throw our weight behind Mazowiecki and his reform program. We also intended to strengthen his hand in securing Poland's full independence and lay the groundwork for Poland's integration into the Western community of nations. Because there were no new assistance measures announced, the media, especially the resolutely superficial White House press corps, failed to grasp how important this visit was for Poland's transition to democracy and full independence.

In their meetings—following the usual formula of arrival ceremony, one-on-one meeting in the Oval Office, and expanded meeting in the Cabinet Room[2]—Mazowiecki detailed Poland's experiment in "shock therapy," which had progressed as well as could have been hoped in its first three months. He and Foreign Minister Krzysztof Skubiszewski then turned to their international agenda. They reiterated Poland's unambiguous support for German unification, arguing that a country that had been partitioned for 125 years could do no less than support the right of self-determination for its neighbor, even for a country that had destroyed Poland's independence more than once. Their concern, however, was with securing the finality, as a legal matter, of the German-Polish border as the two Germanies moved swiftly toward unity.[3] Their other concerns lay in the complex of issues related to the future of the Warsaw Pact, the withdrawal of Soviet troops from Poland, and, more fundamentally, measures that would enhance Poland's newly won, but still precarious, independence within a broader European and transatlantic community.

Privately and in his public remarks, the president echoed those themes and referred prominently to Poland's border:

America wants to help Poland succeed. We want to welcome Poland as a full partner in the community of free nations [and help it] achieve its full measure of democracy and independence. . . . At this time of great and turbulent change . . . the United States will remain a European power—a force for freedom, stability, and security. . . . We see a new Europe in which the security of all European states—and their fundamental right to exist secure within their present borders—is assured.[4]

Bush and Mazowiecki connected well personally.[5] In a follow-up meeting the next day arranged at Bush's invitation, Mazowiecki focused particularly on the question of Soviet troops and the more general difficulty he was having of persuading Soviet officials of Poland's independence. Bush asked if there was anything else that he could say or do that would be helpful. Mazowiecki said that a statement affirming Poland's positive role in building the future of Europe would be helpful. After the meeting, Bush repaired to a prescheduled press conference dealing mainly with Central America. Before any of us could get to him to remind him of Mazowiecki's request, Bush ad libbed a reference to their meeting, noting that "we discussed questions of European security and Poland's place in a new Europe. And I told the prime minister that we see an important role for a free, democratic and independent Poland as a factor for stability in Europe." Later in the press conference, asked about Soviet troops in Poland, the president stated, perhaps too plainly, that "there isn't any need for Soviet troops in Eastern Europe, and the sooner they get out of there, the better."[6] (We on the NSC staff cringed whenever Bush got asked the question, because he always went for the blunt rather than the diplomatic response.)

Breakdown of Solidarity   Back at home, Mazowiecki's honeymoon with the Polish people was short-lived. After his domestic popularity plummeted, it became fashionable, within Poland and outside, to blame Mazowiecki and Finance Minister Leszek Balcerowicz for failures of leadership. This was unfair. To be sure, they might have done better in explaining to the population what was coming and why, as Labor Minister Jacek Kuroń tried to do in his weekly television spots, and it may also be true that Mazowiecki was too much the aloof intellectual to play that role. But the Polish leadership was trying to rescue an economy that had been in steep decline for a decade and more. No amount of inspired leadership could have altered the fundamental facts that the needed economic reform measures would hit hardest the average Polish worker, Solidarity's main constituency, and that tangible benefits for the bulk of the Polish population would take years to be realized.

Nor were Polish attitudes to be changed overnight. Most Poles might have conceded the need for sweeping economic change, but they were uncertain what this might entail and impatient for quick results. It is hard to imagine any Polish leadership successfully undertaking essential reform measures, and the economic dislocation inevitably attending them, while also retaining popular support. Mazowiecki and Balcerowicz deserve great credit for doing the first while others were pandering to public grievances without advancing a credible alternative. Along with Foreign Minister Skubiszewski, they also built up tremendous support for the Polish cause among Western countries, above all the United States, as well as skillfully managing relations with Moscow.

Two figures loomed in the background in mid-1990: Lech Wałęsa, on the political sidelines for the first time in a decade, and President Wojciech Jaruzelski, an embarrassing reminder that Poland's once-radical political reforms had been eclipsed by democratic elections elsewhere in the region. Jaruzelski posed a problem for us as well, particularly after Wałęsa decided to break the Roundtable Agreement and challenge Jaruzelski in new presidential elections. During his July 1989 visit, President Bush had invited Jaruzelski to pay a reciprocal visit to the United States some time in 1990. A year later, the circumstances surrounding that invitation had been wholly overtaken by events. President Bush, who believed deeply that breaking commitments of this kind would be both unethical and a dangerous breach of the trust on which political leaders have to rely, would not hear of our suggestion at staff level that he renege on the invitation, so we resorted instead to having Embassy Warsaw make periodic queries to see whether Jaruzelski was still planning to come. The invitation was of course still in force, we stressed; we just wondered whether the visit was still on in light of the new circumstances. Ultimately, Jaruzelski decided not to run for president and, taking our repeated hints, to cancel the U.S. visit—two further signs of dignity, perhaps even patriotism, on the part of this man of ambiguous legacy.[7]

Wałęsa's motives in challenging Jaruzelski for the presidency ostensibly were to effect a political acceleration.[8] Feeling the brunt of worker discontent, he argued that the economic reform program, directed largely from on high, was stifling democratic development. Leaving aside matters of personal ambition, Wałęsa had hit on one of the dilemmas of the postcommunist transitions: whether to maintain political solidarity, meaning in effect a suspension of full democratic participation, in order to pursue essential but painful economic reform measures, or to give priority to democratic expression even knowing that this would result in an antireform backlash. Another dilemma was buried inside this one: whether to enhance the power and efficiency of the executive, through a strong presidency or electoral laws that erected barriers to small parties (e.g., by requiring that a party gain 4 or 5 percent of the votes cast to qualify for seats in parliament), or whether to strengthen political participation even if it meant a plethora of squabbling microparties. These were not, strictly speaking, dilemmas but rather questions of balancing competing objectives, and Poland experimented with various formulas in its early postcommunist transition. Indeed, Wałęsa himself jumped to the other side of the argument soon after becoming president, pushing for sweeping presidential powers in order to drive through further economic reforms.

Our view in Washington was that the Poles would be making a mistake to break ranks less than a year into their economic reforms, but the choice was Poland's to make, and we would support whatever was decided so long as it was done democratically. We were determined to keep ourselves out of Poland's internal affairs, despite pressures from some Polish quarters to discourage Wałęsa from challenging the new political set-up so early in Poland's postcommunist transition. Not for the last time, we focused instead on the broader issues of Poland's democratic and free market development. Given Wałęsa's highly ambivalent public statements on the economic reforms—sometimes he argued they were moving too slowly, other times he would say that "if we try to move to the market in one jump, we will break both our legs"[9]—we used our still considerable influence to stress how crucial it was for the Poles to stay the course of an economic reform program that was working. This was our consistent line through the terms in office of two Polish presidents and six prime ministers from 1990 to 1992. It was this steadiness of purpose and support, more than any specific policies or assistance measures, that was the greatest American contribution to the Polish cause during this turbulent period.

Wałęsa won the December 1990 presidential elections, disposing of Mazowiecki handily but needing a runoff ballot to beat back an unexpected challenge from a bizarre émigré businessman named Stanisław Tymiński.[10] Wałęsa's initial steps were reassuring, owing partly to behind the scenes advice, coordinated with the administration, from the Polish-American Congress.[11] He retained Balcerowicz as finance minister, though demoting him from his position as deputy prime minister. For the successor to Mazowiecki as prime minister, Wałęsa overrode parliamentary pressures in favor of former Solidary lawyer Jan Olszewski, a critic of "shock therapy," and pushed through as his personal choice Jan Krzysztof Bielecki, a respected proponent of market reform.[12] The prematurely gray Bielecki was to turn grayer still in the coming year.

Wałęsa's State Visit   We and the Poles set about promptly to arrange an early trip to Washington by Wałęsa in his new capacity, agreeing on a full protocol state visit in March 1991. High on their agenda was the signing of a bilateral treaty, which they saw as a counterweight to one they were negotiating with Moscow and an adjunct to the other such documents with which they were littering the European landscape. (Czechoslovakia's new leaders were even more fascinated than the Poles with these pieces of paper. The spectacle was reminscent of the "spirit of Locarno" in the 1920s, when Europeans east and west produced dozens of bilateral and multilateral treaties—none of which did anything to arrest or deter Hitler's aggression.) While open to such a document, we wanted it to be an informal political declaration rather than a formal treaty.[13] On that basis, we drafted a notional text and negotiated it with Wałęsa's representatives in the weeks leading up to the visit.[14]

The U.S.-Polish "Declaration of Principles" was a nice two-page document that recalled the past close association between the two countries and peoples, "which survived even during the long periods when Poland's independence and liberty were denied." Its thrust was toward the future, however, affirming the principles and policies that would guide U.S.-Polish relations in the years ahead. The Poles had wanted an ironclad security guarantee but settled for this more general formulation, which was as far as we were then prepared to go: "The United States attaches great importance to the consolidation of Poland's democracy and independence, which it considers integral to the new Europe, whole and free."

The declaration was prepared at Poland's request, but there were also elements we insisted on, including codification of Poland's, especially Wałęsa's, commitment to free market democracy: "Poland and the United States share the conviction that the development of a market economy in Poland is essential to its stability and security. . . . Poland's firm commitment to an economic reform program that enjoys the endorsement and support of the International Monetary Fund has made possible the mobilization of substantial new financial and other economic assistance from the international community."[15]

Although overshadowed by the liberation of Kuwait less than a month before and a wave of independence declarations by Soviet republics, Wałęsa's visit was an almost complete success. At staff level, we had been working feverishly to conclude several new initiatives to support Poland's economic transition and further cement Wałęsa's commitment to it. The first and most important measure was agreement on reduction of Poland's official debt burden by more than half. Although this had been under negotiation for many months among Poland's official creditors in the Paris Club, Wałęsa's visit gave the Treasury Department added impetus to finish the deal quickly—a task that was facilitated by a series of messages and telephone calls by President Bush to each of his G-7 counterparts. Under terms of the agreement, creditors were also permitted to reduce bilateral debt by as much as 70 percent—which we did, using the additional debt relief to finance a new environmental foundation in Poland.[16]

The other measures, covered in the preceding chapter, included a Trade Enhancement Initiative and American Business Initiative—aimed at promoting trade and investment and challenging the European Community to follow suit—and a 50 percent increase in U.S. assistance to Central and Eastern Europe. They were directed at the region as a whole and were meant to give new impetus to postcommunist reforms that had been severely complicated by external reversals, notably the international sanctions against Iraq and the collapse of trade with the Soviet Union and the now defunct East Germany. As President Bush put it in the arrival ceremony welcoming Wałęsa, "Today we rededicate ourselves to the success of free market democracy in Poland and throughout Central and Eastern Europe."[17]

Wałęsa was at his most gracious and statesmanlike. Whereas he had been known to criticize the West for its niggardliness, he used his arrival statement publicly to thank the United States and President Bush personally for their "political, economic and, above all, moral" leadership. In his toast at the state dinner that night, Wałęsa described Bush as "the most popular politician in Poland"—a tribute that was literally true according to recent public opinion polls there.[18] Wałęsa opened the official meetings by saying that Bush had anticipated and met all of the requests for help that he had planned to make. As his advisers said privately later on, the Poles were ecstatic about the visit, both for the tangible initiatives and for the symbolic boost it gave Wałęsa.

Wałęsa reaffirmed his commitment to an accelerated pace of economic reform and increased U.S. investment, but with typical ambivalence. In a meeting later in the day with American business leaders, arranged by the Department of Commerce, Wałęsa warned of wholesale instability in Poland if increased investment were not forthcoming. As an NSC colleague quipped, it was like the cover of a back issue of the American humor magazine *National Lampoon*, which showed a man holding a pistol to the head of a puppy with the caption "Buy this magazine or I will shoot this dog." Wałęsa's was precisely the wrong message to send to corporate leaders, who needed reassurance about Poland's stability and his own commitment to the market, not an invitation to invest their resources in a country on the edge of an abyss.[19]

Wałęsa also made clear his political agenda at home: a new constitution that secured strong presidential powers, a new electoral law that would exclude minor parties and so facilitate a stable governmental coalition, and new elections for the Polish parliament, whose current members were elected in June 1989 as a result of the Roundtable Agreement that guaranteed heavy communist representation. He was stymied on all counts in the spring of 1991. New elections would be held, but not until October and on the basis of the existing system; in addition, Wałęsa's growing chorus of critics in the Sejm (the lower, and more powerful, of the two houses of parliament) blocked his efforts to amass new presidential powers.

Political Fragmentation   As a frustrated Wałęsa hinted darkly at declaring emergency powers, one of his key advisers, Jarosław Kaczyński, visited Washington to test the American attitudes toward such a step.

When he called at the NSC on July 8, we were prepared for him, having been forewarned of his agenda by Embassy Warsaw. If the Polish president were to use his constitutional authority to exercise exceptional economic powers, we told him, there would be no objection from Washington, so long as this were done legally and democratically. But if this were done unconstitutionally, or had the effect of suspending democracy, neither the administration nor Congress would understand or support such measures. Under such circumstances, we would have to review the overall relationship and curtail most U.S. assistance. The message was blunt, and the trial balloon was never floated again. We never knew whether, or to what extent, Wałęsa was aware of this probe, but just in case Ambassador Thomas Simons delivered a similar message to him in Warsaw.

Whether the Polish economy was doing well or ill was open to debate as Poland prepared for parliamentary elections in October 1991. Statistics were often misleading. Trade liberalization and small-scale privatization had yielded full shelves and a burgeoning service sector, but wage restraints meant that most Poles could not avail themselves of these benefits. Poland registered a trade surplus in 1990, but much of this was accounted for by selling surplus goods at less than market value. On the other side of the ledger, unemployment was up, but a large share of it was made up of those actually employed in the new private sector but not declared (so that they could continue receiving unemployment payments and their employers could avoid paying taxes and benefits).

What was not debatable was that the majority of Poles felt, and probably were, worse off than they had been under communist rule, and they vented their anger at convenient targets like Balcerowicz, Bielecki, and the IMF. And of course when times are tough in this part of the world, conspiracy theories flourish. One of the prevalent ones was that a secret arrangement had been struck during the 1989 Roundtable Agreement to permit the exiting communists to acquire economic power and privilege under the new system. It was the fallacy of *post hoc, ergo propter hoc*—of an antecedent event being mistaken for a causal one. It was indisputable that a kind of "*nomenklatura* capitalism" had emerged, whereby former communist officials used their political connections (and, to be fair, their acumen as well) to acquire economic power, but it was simply preposterous to conclude that people of the stature of Wałęsa, Bronisław Geremek, and Adam Michnik had betrayed their country in the spring of 1989. Equally preposterous was a "Malta equals Yalta" conspiracy theory—also in vogue at the time—holding that the United States had reached some sort of understanding with Moscow allowing the latter to preserve a sphere of influence in Central and Eastern Europe. (Readers may refresh their memories of the unassailable evidence to the contrary in Chapters 1 and 2.)

The question of "decommunization" is more complex. What Solidarity leaders had done—with the full support of the United States and its Western partners—was to offer the communists a graceful, nonpunitive exit, on grounds that this conciliatory strategy was more likely than one based on vengeance to induce them to hand over power peacefully. It was the right strategy, for ethical as well as practical political reasons. Yet it made it possible for the most able among the former communists to acquire economic power and bide their time for another run at political power. How they would wield that power hinged on the depth and speed of democratic consolidation and perhaps on the redemptive power of the politics of conciliation—though one might not want to put too much faith in the latter.

The decommunization dilemma arose throughout Central and Eastern Europe in the early 1990s, with special bitterness in Poland, Czechoslovakia, and Bulgaria. With the benefit of a few years' hindsight, it is evident that advocates of conciliation, east and west, underestimated the danger that remnants of the old guard would pose for these fragile new democracies. Yet the alternatives proffered to this approach were even more dangerous: they came almost entirely from the radical Right and aimed at expunging communist influence through means that were vindictive, antidemocratic, and often unconstitutional.

In Poland, the issue was a powerful one that politicians of the Right played upon with considerable success in the October 1991 elections. The last vestiges of unity among the post-Solidarity political leaders were shattered: more than 60 parties fielded candidates, and 29 gained representation in the Sejm, leading to a government crisis that lasted nearly a year. In December 1991, protracted negotiations yielded a fragile center-right coalition headed by Prime Minister Jan Olszewski—the same Olszewski whose candidacy Wałęsa had successfully opposed at the end of 1990. The new cabinet reflected an antireformist, anticommunist, anti-Russian bias—the latter immediately evident in a newly aggressive Polish stance in negotiations over the withdrawal of Russian forces. Our counsel was to be firm on principle but flexible on tactics, giving the Russian leadership enough breathing space to find a solution. This was the approach we had adopted to good effect in winning Moscow's compliance with the CFE agreement.

It was a delicate moment for Poland, with the economic reform program under siege at the very time that the economy was poised for sustained growth. Again to show support and help Poland keep on the straight and narrow, we at staff level quickly went to work to arrange a visit by Olszewski, making it clear that we expected Poland's new prime minister to stay the course of political and economic reform. Indeed, when Olszewski visited in early April 1992[20]—the fourth Polish prime minister whom Bush had met in less than three years[21]—he was at pains to profess his commitment to continued reform. The White House press release captured the main lines of the discussion, including our specific push for Poland's IMF compliance and our efforts to increase American private investment in Poland:

> The President reaffirmed his strong support for the pioneering transformation to democracy and a free market in Poland, whose success is all the more important in light of the revolutionary changes farther east. . . .
>
> Prime Minister Olszewski outlined his government's economic policies and its commitment to working with the IMF on an agreed reform program . . . and welcomed the President's offer, made in a recent letter to President Wałęsa, to send a mission of U.S. business leaders to visit Poland with the aim of facilitating some of the many U.S. private investment projects now under negotiation.[22]

In the end it was not Russian policy or the economy but his own decommunization crusade that was Olszewski's downfall, as the Sejm forced his resignation in June 1992 in the wake of a series of scandals, including a crude and unsuccessful campaign to incriminate Wałęsa himself. After another month of negotiations, the Sejm approved a seven-party coalition headed by Prime Minister Hanna Suchocka, a little known but well respected lawyer who enjoyed support in Solidarity and church circles alike.

The President's Second Visit to Poland   At staff level, we had been working for months to see whether the president could add a stop in

Warsaw to his July 1992 trip to Munich for the G-7 Summit and to Helsinki for another CSCE summit. We even had an initiative up our sleeves. The Stabilization Fund the United States had helped create in the fall of 1989 had now run its course, and we proposed to convert our $200 million share to new uses and exert leverage on other contributors to make the remaining $800 million similarly available to Poland—and to make the entire amount contingent upon Poland's remaining in compliance with the IMF. The stakes were high, for the Paris Club debt reduction agreement, as well as hundreds of millions of dollars in World Bank loans, hinged on Poland's staying with an economic program that met IMF standards.

Despite significant election year pressures to curtail his European trip, the president agreed to pay a brief visit to Poland en route to the G-7 Summit in Munich. In the run-up to the visit, we worked with the Poles on a strategy for the Stabilization Fund, each side approaching the other G-7 members to join the United States in committing their shares to Poland's uses, with details to be worked out in Munich. There was also a highly significant symbolic event attached to the visit. The remains of the celebrated pianist, and independent Poland's first prime minister in 1919, Ignacy Paderewski, were returned to Poland fifty years after he had been interred in Arlington Cemetery to rest temporarily, in the words of President Roosevelt, "until Poland would be free."

Departing Washington on July 4, President Bush arrived the next morning in Warsaw—his third visit in five years and his second as president. His meetings with Wałęsa and Prime Minister–Designate Suchocka were important occasions to preview issues at the G-7 and CSCE Summits. But the real import of the visit was symbolic: the historic ceremony in which Presidents Bush and Wałęsa solemnly accompanied Paderewski's coffin to St. John's Cathedral and the tonic-like effect on an exhausted Poland of seeing the two men standing before a huge and exuberant crowd in Castle Square.[23] With his enormous personal popularity in Poland, Bush aimed at rallying Poland to the further challenges ahead:

> It was here in Poland that the Second World War began. It was here in Poland that the Cold War first cast its shadow. And it was here in Poland that the people at long last brought the Cold War to an end. . . . Today, Poland stands transformed. Your bold economic reforms have earned the world's admiration, and what is more, they are working. . . .

Reaching your dreams will be difficult, and I know that the sheer volume of new voices can sometimes be deafening, but from the clamor of new voices must come democracy, a common vision of the common good. Of course, in many places and for many people there is more pain than progress. But we must take care to separate cause from consequence. Poland's time of trial is not caused by private enterprise, but by the stubborn legacy of four decades of communist misrule. Make no mistake: the path you have chosen is the right path. . . .

America shares Poland's dream. America wants Poland to succeed, and we will stand at your side until success is guaranteed to everyone.[24]

The president announced that the United States would make its $200 million contribution to the Polish Stabilization Fund available to Poland for new uses and would call on his G-7 counterparts, during their summit meeting in Munich the next day, to follow the U.S. example, so that the entire $1 billion would remain committed to Poland. Although we did not advertise the fact, the initiative did not involve new financial help but rather was a recycled grant that we never expected back in the first place. It was like giving the sleeves from our vest, but the Poles did not seem to mind. Even those in the media who caught on to the gambit nonetheless understood that the importance lay in this further example of U.S. leadership on Poland's behalf. As the independent *Nowa Europa* put it, "Bush's support for Poland during the upcoming summit of the world's richest nations in Munich is worth more than a billion dollars. It is a statement of the consistency of American policy in Central and Eastern Europe."[25]

Czechoslovakia: The Velvet Annulment

In late February 1990, just two weeks after Secretary Baker's visit to Prague, President Bush received President Václav Havel and the new Czechoslovak government at the White House. The purpose was largely symbolic—to show U.S. engagement and lend support to Czechoslovakia and to Havel personally. Though celebrated in Western intellectual circles, Havel was in his own country either unknown or regarded as something of a curiosity, a Don Quixote tilting futilely at the windmills of communist Czechoslovakia after the post-1968 "normalization" and the general apathy it engendered. His name had become familiar during the Velvet Revolution, of course, but he remained an enigmatic figure. A meeting with the American president, therefore, was important in building up Havel's credibility and authority at home. Given the responsibilities that had fallen his way, he was going to need plenty of both.

It was symptomatic that the Czechs had failed to consider Slovak sensibilities in arranging the logistics for the visit. Only eight Slovaks were on the delegation of more than two hundred, and the only one appearing on their proposed lists for the White House meetings was Prime Minister Marián Čalfa, who only recently had left the Communist party and so lacked authenticity. It was only at my insistence that more Slovaks—still not enough—were added. These instincts were later confirmed: "Bush and a bunch of Czechs" is what Slovak viewers saw on Czechoslovak television, as one Slovak official told me. In his memoirs, another Slovak official bitterly recounted these events as the first of many examples of Slovaks being excluded from official delegations.[26]

The discussions, as with Baker, were at a fairly high level of generality. Havel spoke, as he did in his moving address to a joint session of Congress,[27] of the need to help Gorbachev effect economic reforms in the Soviet Union. Havel's appeal to Congress that "you can help us most of all by helping the Soviet Union" was particularly welcome in light of the task then before the administration of persuading Moscow to accept the demise of the Warsaw Pact and the unification of Germany. As to his own economy, the Czechoslovaks were divided as to how to proceed. Finance Minister Václav Klaus advocated sweeping market reforms, but Deputy Prime Minister Valtr Komárek abjured Polish-style "shock therapy" in favor of a gradual approach toward a mixed economy, and Havel himself spoke of a "soft landing" for the Czechoslovak economy. As if to dissociate themselves from their neighbors, they sought "trade, not aid" from Western countries. (It was a formulation they continued to favor even after their reforms were launched and their list of requests for assistance became very long indeed.[28])

At the departure ceremony after their meetings,[29] President Bush surprised Havel with a portrait of Tomáš Masaryk, Czechoslovakia's first president. The portrait had been offered to the president for the occasion by Fred Starr, president of Oberlin College. Behind it lay a nice story:

> This portrait was done at Prague Castle and kept by President Masaryk until his death, when he gave it to his successor at Charles University's Department of Philosophy, Jan Kozak. In

1939, at the time of the Nazi invasion, Professor Kozak had two hours to pack his belongings and to flee Czechoslovakia. Among the items he took with him was this portrait of his friend. Professor Kozak settled in Ohio at Oberlin College, and so did the portrait . . . until today. Now [in keeping with Kozak's bequest], with freedom returning to Czechoslovakia, so too should this portrait. . . ."[30]

At the president's invitation, Havel returned to the Oval Office the next day for an unscheduled, informal talk.[31] After hearing what was on Havel's mind—mainly his recounting of his address to Congress—Bush spoke for a long time on the U.S. role in Europe and why he saw NATO as the mechanism that would keep the United States engaged as a stabilizing force. It was a remarkable, even moving, performance from a man not noted for his eloquence, and it clearly made a powerful impression on Havel. The meeting cemented the personal chemistry between Bush and Havel, as did their emotional private talk in the Lincoln Bedroom in the White House, which they visited at Havel's request.[32]

The Bush Visit to Prague   By the time of President Bush's visit to Prague in November 1990, on the first anniversary of the Velvet Revolution, the international climate had altered radically. German unification was complete; agreement had been reached on the withdrawal of Soviet forces from Czechoslovakia and Hungary (though negotiations with the Poles were held up over transit procedures for Soviet forces scheduled to leave Germany). And all of Europe was preparing to revel in freedom's triumph and the Cold War's end at the Paris Summit of the CSCE, November 19–21. In the Persian Gulf, however, Iraqi forces had invaded and occupied Kuwait in August, and President Bush was mobilizing an international coalition to repel the Iraqis and restore Kuwait's sovereignty. The Prague visit—preceding a stop in Germany to celebrate unification with Chancellor Kohl en route to Paris—thus acquired a significance well beyond Central Europe.

There were several compelling reasons to visit Prague: to show the flag in the region, try to ameliorate the growing strains between Czechs and Slovaks, and lend support as the country prepared to launch a radical reform program. Czechoslovakia, victim of the Munich Agreement in 1938, was also the ideal venue to underscore why aggression far from home bore on Western freedoms as well. In his main address, the president made the connection explicitly, warning against seeing Kuwait's plight as "just a quarrel in a faraway country, between a people of whom we know nothing." It was Neville Chamberlain's dismissive line from 1938, which helped seal Czechoslovakia's fate at the hands of the Third Reich. Although delivered without attribution to avoid offending the British, it was of course instantly recognized by the president's audience in Czechoslovakia's federal assembly.[33]

The president's schedule reflected the delicacy of the internal balancing act among federal, Czech, and Slovak political leaders and institutions. Following an arrival ceremony at the airport and motorcade to Hradčany Castle, Bush met with (1) President Havel privately, (2) Havel and members of the federal government, (3) Prime Minister Čalfa, (4) Czech Republic premier Petr Pithart and parliamentary leaders, (5) Slovak Republic premier Vladimír Mečiar and National Council chairman František Mikloško, and, over lunch, (6) Havel and company again. It was a moveable feast, or perhaps the Mad Hatter's tea party, as we moved from one mirrored chamber to another. Even the hyperkinetic Bush was showing signs of fatigue, but his schedule was far from over. The president then paid a courtesy call on the aged František Cardinal Tomášek, met with federal assembly chairman Alexander Dubček, delivered his major speech at the federal assembly, and spoke before a tumultuous crowd that more than filled the enormous Wenceslas Square, where he pledged that "America will not fail you at this decisive moment."[34] It was a deeply moving event, made doubly so for the American delegation, especially those of us of a certain age, when a Czech folksinging group led hundreds of thousands singing, in English, the civil rights song "We Shall Overcome."

In his official meetings and public remarks, President Bush stressed the difficulty of the road ahead. He announced a package of economic assistance measures similar to those already in place in Poland and Hungary: an American enterprise fund, preferential trade treatment, technical assistance in various sectors, and substantial environmental assistance, to be delivered chiefly through the IMF and the World Bank. Privately, he also returned to issues of European security, assuring Havel that the United States did not accept a European future that left Czechoslovakia as a "buffer zone" or "no man's land" between a secure, prosperous West and a chaotic East. He stressed again the importance of NATO and the U.S. role before President Havel and Foreign Minister Dienstbier, whose early enthusiasm for a "pan-European peace order" had given way to a sober reappraisal of their country's real and prospective security situation. At the same time, Bush stressed that we did not see a military threat to Czechoslovakia's security; rather, we saw the main tasks as repairing the country's economy, consolidating democracy, and building a stable new relationship among Czechs, Slovaks, and other national groups in the region.

It was a more somber Havel than Bush had met in Washington six months before. In the spring, the Slovaks had led a bitter battle to change the country's name from Czechoslovak Republic to the infelicitous "Czech and Slovak Federative Republic," and the huge turnout in Bratislava during Pope John Paul II's visit lent further strength to those who embraced—and manipulated—the Slovak national cause. In the Czech lands and Slovakia alike, the June elections had surfaced a number of charges against former communists and collaborators, real or alleged. These revelations marked the beginning of an ugly debate over a *Lustrace* law to expose misdeeds of the communist era and the end of the spirit of tolerance Havel had espoused. Now Havel was embroiled in a Czech-Slovak conflict over a new constitution that threatened to erode the basis of the federal state. Indeed, he used his speech in Wenceslas Square to cite the *Federalist Papers* and urge his fellow citizens to follow the American example in overcoming a constitutional crisis and agree on a strong federal system.[35] The president had been urged to speak directly about the issue by a prominent American lawyer advising Havel on the constitution. Instead, Bush spoke more generally about the need to put the newly free country on a firm legal foundation, a point to which he also alluded in a radio address to the Slovak Republic.[36] (Less subtle was the advance team's distribution of copies of the Constitution and Bill of Rights to members of the federal assembly before Bush's speech.)

Czechs versus Slovaks: Lurching toward Divorce   Political differences were exacerbated by Slovak opposition to elements of the emerging, "made in Prague" economic reform plan. In September 1990, Finance Minister Klaus, having wrested control over economic policy,[37] won approval in the federal assembly for his "Scenario for Economic Reform,"[38] to be implemented beginning in January 1991. Its program of currency reform, price liberalization, and opening to foreign trade was as radical as Polish "shock therapy," albeit in a country whose economic crisis was not so deep as Poland's. In a way, the relative health of the Czechoslovak economy made the political task more difficult: the population at large felt little of the urgency their Polish counterparts did, at least at the beginning. And the parts of the economic system most in need of reform—including large and privileged defense plants concentrated in Slovakia—were the most resistant to change. At the same time, because Klaus had staked his career on the reform program, his subsequent dealings with the Slovaks undoubtedly were conditioned by the imperative of economic success in the Czech lands. This is not to imply that Klaus encouraged the division of his country for the sake of his reform plan but rather that the higher priority he attached to the latter made him less amenable to compromise with the Slovaks on matters he deemed economically essential.

The launching of Czechoslovakia's economic reform program in January 1991 coincided with the opening of debates over a new constitution and consideration of Havel's proposal for a referendum to determine whether Czechs and Slovaks wished to continue living in a common state. How had things come to this pass? As Havel put it in his "Summer Meditations" of 1991, "Most Czechs had no idea how strong was the longing of the Slovaks for autonomy and for their own constitutional expression." Acknowledging some of his own failures in that regard, Havel did profess to understand one thing: "the aversion the Slovaks feel to being governed from elsewhere." The judgment Havel rendered was perhaps harsh—and Slovaks doubtless found it typically Czech—but it does capture the Slovak mood in 1991 and 1992 and helps explain how easily it was exploited and manipulated by Slovakia's political leaders: "For many Slovaks, whether they are governed well or badly, with their participation or without it, with their interests in mind or without them, is less important than the bare fact that they are governed from somewhere else."[39]

Slovak economic fears, not without foundation, were the most easily manipulated. Although the macroeconomic stabilization plan succeeded in liberalizing prices, controlling inflation, and preparing for the transition to a market economy, there was no hiding its uneven impact on the two republics. Slovakia's less diversified economy, with many towns and regions dependent on a single large factory or defense complex, made it more vulnerable than the Czech lands to huge dislocations associated with economic reform. The inconvenient fact that Slovak politicians failed to mention was that many if not most of these factories were doomed for reasons unrelated to the reform program. If factories were producing goods for which there were no buyers, owing to the collapse of Soviet trade and the shrinking international arms market, whether the factory was "reformed" or "unreformed" was hardly the point. Yet the "made in Prague" reform program, together with Havel's early pledge to curtail arms sales on ethical grounds, made for handy scapegoats.

When Czechoslovak foreign minister Jiří Dienstbier visited the United States in mid-April 1990, his agenda was almost wholly economic, and almost wholly related to Slovak concerns. At the White House, he used a brief meeting with the president to talk about . . . cheese quotas. (Had he done his homework, he would have known that almost any other trade item would have had better prospects of success than cheese imports, which were regulated according to an elaborately worked out set of quotas affecting all importing countries.) With General Scowcroft, he also previewed what became known as the "Dienstbier Plan" for Western underwriting of a multibillion dollar payments system to revive trade and spur investment in the former Comecon area.[40] The plan never got off the ground, not only for want of money but for serious doubts here and elsewhere about its efficacy—particularly its reliance on dubious administrative measures rather than the market to shape trade relations in the region.

"Defense conversion" was next on Dienstbier's agenda, his plea being for U.S. assistance in converting Slovak defense industries to viable commercial use. His aim was mainly political—to demonstrate to Slovaks that the Prague leadership was trying to find answers for their economic problems. Though skeptical, we wanted to be helpful and so worked with our counterparts at the Pentagon to arrange for a defense conversion mission led by Deputy Secretary of Defense Donald Atwood. In retrospect, the mission was a mistake: it contributed to the illusion that "defense conversion" was a task susceptible to quick fixes and that solutions could be found through political or military channels rather than on the basis of commercial viability. It took us another year to get this issue back in the commercial domain where it belonged, and longer still before we could show even modest results. (As late as the fall of 1992, when I led an interagency assistance delegation to Bratislava, some Slovak ministers were still treating the issue as one that required only an act of political will on our part. Even later, NATO ambassadors were proposing a defense conversion "data bank," as if bureaucrats in Brussels could solve the problem.)

The political climate in Czechoslovakia continued to deteriorate. Civic Forum and Public Against Violence had both split—the latter abandoned by populist prime minister Vladimír Mečiar, who formed a new party called Movement for a Democratic Slovakia (HZDS). When Mečiar himself was forced to resign the prime ministership on charges springing from the *Lustrace* campaign, he set about systematically to foment and exploit Slovak national grievances. His party as well as the new Slovak National party demanded sweeping changes to the federal constitution; their aims ranged from loose confederation to outright independence, though the latter was rarely articulated openly.[41] Instead, Mečiar and others spoke of "autonomy," "confederation," or "international subjectivity," with the result that ordinary Slovaks, in supporting those who seemed most attuned to their grievances, never quite knew what agenda they were backing.

The U.S. Position By late summer 1991, we in Washington were viewing these developments with growing concern. Bush and Havel, who had communicated often at the time of the failed August coup against Gorbachev, would have a chance to discuss matters when Havel paid a state visit planned for October, but we at staff level felt the issue needed to be discussed with the Slovaks as well. So in mid-October, I hived off from an investment mission to Poland (led by Commerce Secretary Robert Mosbacher) to visit first Bratislava and then Prague, conveying U.S. attitudes and policies regarding the possible breakup of Czechoslovakia and, relatedly, to advance the notion of turning the "Visegrád Three" into the "Visegrád Four" (or at least "three and a half") so as to give Slovakia the status it seemed unable to find in federation with the Czechs.[42]

Having failed to prepare adequately for the disintegration of Yugoslavia,[43] we tried to apply sounder policy to the imminent collapse of the Czecho-Slovak federation. I therefore had drafted and gained interagency approval for a set of principles to guide our relations. Taking about a minute to recite, they boiled down to this: the United States, while not indifferent to the fate of Czechoslovakia and believing that the interests of its citizens would be best served in a common state, would accept any solution democratically and peacefully agreed to by the people of Czechoslovakia. Moreover, the United States would continue to base its relations and policies on enduring American interests in democracy, free markets, human rights, minority rights, and cooperative regional and international relations. Although those of us who cared deeply about this country considered taking a stronger position in support of the federation, it was clear for practical as well as ethical reasons that this decision was not ours to make or impose.[44] We judged it was better to focus on first principles than preferred specific outcomes, and to do what we could to promote minority rights and regional cooperation among the Visegrád Three—or Four.

I conveyed the U.S. position in a series of meetings on October 13 and 14 with Slovak politicians across the spectrum,[45] culminating in a private luncheon with former (and future) Slovak prime minister Vladimír Mečiar.[46] They considered it a reasonable position and felt that the Visegrád process was an important means of averting Slovakia's marginalization, particularly if the federation were to be dissolved. The ease with which many of these politicians lapsed into theories of conspiracy and betrayal, moreover, strengthened my conviction that the U.S. line was the right one. (Indeed, in early 1993, as the first senior American official to visit independent Slovakia, I was the first beneficiary of this policy. Our relations, although strained because of certain antidemocratic practices of the Mečiar government, nonetheless proceeded from a reasonably sound foundation, unburdened by a futile effort to try to hold together a doomed Czechoslovak state. Instead, I was able to return, credibly and authoritatively, to the same agenda we had advanced in 1991.[47])

Over lunch, Mečiar treated me to a disquisition on "international subjectivity" and criticized Havel for turning the Czech-Slovak debate into one of federation or separation, arguing that there were several intermediate possibilities. Brushing aside my suggestion that the European Community's notion of "subsidiarity" would give the smaller nations of Europe room for autonomy and self-expression, Mečiar countered that a confederal relationship with the Czechs was required lest the Slovaks, as he put it, become "lost in a European sea." One option that he advanced was a Slovak declaration of independence followed immediately by a new, confederal association with the Czechs. The idea was that Slovakia's moment of independence—literally a moment, in this conception—would enable the two sides to renegotiate their relationship on the basis of equality. The Czechs, of course, were having none of this.

The next day in Prague, I met with Foreign Minister Dienstbier to convey the same message to him and brief him on my conversations in Bratislava. Dienstbier was by this time resigned to the inevitability of a split, noting that most Czechs—starting with himself?—had put up with enough and were saying the Slovaks could "go to hell." I ventured that the United States did not want to meddle, but we were prepared to help where we could—by promoting the "Visegrád Four" notion or helping the Slovaks realize their "international subjectivity" through cultural exchanges and the like, adding impertinently that we in Washington could not detect anything resembling a strategy for addressing Czech-Slovak problems but rather a series of ad hoc initiatives that only made matters worse.

Havel's State Visit   While in Prague, I devoted half a day to previewing President Havel's impending visit to Washington with Havel's foreign policy adviser, Saša Vondra, and press spokesman Michael Žantovsky.[48] We finished negotiating a U.S.-Czechoslovak "declaration of principles," modeled on the U.S.-Polish declaration of a few months before, for the signature of the two presidents. Although their preference was for a treaty-like document rather than the informal statement we insisted on, it was a negotiation among friends that was wrapped up in less than an hour.

Havel's state visit, in late October 1991, was overshadowed by the drama in the Soviet Union following the failed August coup. Unlike Havel's first visit just eighteen months before, this one passed almost unnoticed beyond official circles. Central Europe's moment of world prominence had passed; its problems now seemed prosaic, if not ugly. And Havel's country, which he had hoped would contribute to a broader democratic stability, had become, as he lamented, a source of instability because of its imminent disintegration. In the expanded meeting in the Cabinet Room, Havel began by noting that his ministers around the table were mostly the same as when he had first visited in February 1990, but now they represented different parties and would be vying for office in the elections scheduled for June 1992. Finance Minister Václav Klaus, who distributed sample privatization vouchers in explaining his program of mass privatization of Czechoslovakia's state-owned enterprises, was leader of the Civic Democratic party, while Dienstbier led the Civic Movement, another offshoot of Civic Forum.

Security, or rather insecurity, was on Havel's mind. Although the withdrawal of Soviet forces from Czechoslovakia had been completed in May 1991, the failed anti-Gorbachev coup in the Soviet Union raised the prospect of new dangers arising in the East, not so much from naked aggression as from the spillover of a chaotic breakdown of order. Havel welcomed NATO's recent creation of a North Atlantic Cooperation Council[49] to bring in members of the now defunct Warsaw Pact but made it clear that Czechoslovakia's aim was eventual full membership in the alliance. In his public remarks as well as privately, Havel attached great importance to the joint declaration that the two presidents signed just before their meeting. Although not a binding document, it expressed the two countries' shared perspective on key elements of European security:

> The United States . . . considers [Czechoslovakia's] security and independence integral to the new Europe, whole and free. . . . Czechoslovakia and the United States will help to build a new system of cooperative security in Europe . . . which will complement NATO and its indispensable role. . . . The United States and the Czech and Slovak Federal Republic reaffirm the importance of cooperative regional ties [among] the states and peoples of Central Europe [which] will help them overcome historic national antagonisms and will advance their integration into Europe.[50]

It was perhaps a fitting irony that the declaration was not even issued in Czech but rather in English and Slovak only. This was the inadvertent consequence of my suggestion, in Prague, that the document be issued in English, Czech, and Slovak so as to assuage Slovakia's sense of exclusion and reflect its desire for "international subjectivity." Not wanting to set a precedent that might mean every future international agreement would have to be issued in both Czech and Slovak, Havel's advisers decided instead to issue it in Slovak only. So it was that my Czech friends negotiated a declaration on behalf of a state soon to disappear, in a language not their own. Kafka lives!

The Velvet Divorce   Over the next year, negotiations over a new constitutional arrangement were stalemated. The Slovaks insisted on a loose confederal system, which the Czechs rejected as tantamount to full separation, and neither side could agree to the country-wide referendum Havel proposed. When Havel met with visiting Secretary of Defense Dick Cheney in mid-December 1991, he was optimistic that the coming June 1992 elections would create the basis for a "new state" that nonetheless would preserve the federation. Slovak minister of inter national relations Pavol Demeš, an able young scholar who stood throughout as a voice of reason and moderation, similarly offered Cheney his personal view that the Czecho-Slovak state would survive. Foreign Minister Dienstbier, however, would venture only that Czechoslovakia would be "no Yugoslavia" and expressed concern, which we shared, that a split of the federation would jeopardize the status of the six hundred thousand Hungarians in Slovakia and further complicate Hungarian-Slovak relations. And in side discussions with me, Havel's key advisers, Vondra and Žantovsky, offered scenarios that supported Dienstbier's fatalism more than their president's optimism.[51]

The June 1992 elections brought coalition governments headed by Klaus in the Czech lands and Mečiar in Slovakia. Despite Klaus's protestation that he had no mandate to negotiate the dissolution of the country, he and Mečiar began doing precisely that. Public opinion polls in both republics continued to show a majority opposed separation, but Mečiar's campaign for a loose confederation (tantamount to destruction of the federal state) and the Czech backlash thereto created a momentum that neither Havel nor anyone else could arrest. Three years after the Velvet Revolution, the Czechoslovak federation was headed, now ineluctably, toward a "velvet divorce" that was, to many Slovaks, more an annulment of a union that never quite took. To stretch the metaphor perhaps to excess, those who had helped create the marriage—the United States and Great Britain—could only watch wistfully as it dissolved. It was destroyed in the first instance by two headstrong personalities of limited vision, but the differences between Czechs and Slovaks were far deeper and perhaps, for this moment in history, irreconcilable. Once the Slovaks made the first moves toward independence, Czech attitudes underwent a sea change, and sentiment in favor of the federal state was soon overtaken by biases just below the surface that association with Slovakia was dragging Czech culture and civilization eastward and backward. By the end, Czechs were more adamant than Slovaks that the federal state was finished.

When Havel met Bush briefly during the July 1992 CSCE Summit in Helsinki, he explained that the federation was lost and that he would soon resign as president in keeping with his pledge not to preside over the dissolution of the federal state—adding, however, that he would be available to serve as president of an independent Czech Republic. Observing this denouement to Havel's presidency and his country, it struck me as an uncharacteristically careless interpretation of his pledge from a man for whom words mattered so deeply. I was thinking in particular of Havel's essay "A Word about Words," which concluded with this: "[This] is not just a linguistic task. Responsibility for and toward words is a task which is intrinsically ethical."[52] Havel, no doubt, was thinking of the moral obligation to which he referred in his eloquent address to a joint session of Congress in February 1990: "Intellectuals cannot go on forever avoiding their share of responsibility for the world and hiding their distaste for politics under an alleged need to be independent."[53]

Hungary: From Euphoria to Disillusionment

U.S.-Hungarian relations after 1990 had little of the intensity or urgency that characterized our interaction with Poland and Czechoslovakia. It was not that Hungary was neglected entirely. Certainly, there was no shortage of American visitors, official and private. Indeed, so many American officials were finding excuses to visit Budapest and imposing on already harried Hungarian officials that Deputy Secretary Eagleburger's office had to issue an edict that sharply curtailed such visits, and blocked any that smacked of tourism dressed in official garb. But policy issues related to Hungary alone—that is, discounting region-wide policy initiatives—rarely commanded cabinet-level attention after 1989.

Hungary's political system was stable, perhaps too stable, after the March 1990 election of a coalition government headed by Prime Minister József Antall. Its gradualist economic reform—so gradual as to be sometimes imperceptible—did not occasion the political battles that characterized those farther north, though the social backlash was just as great. Hungary in 1990 had seeming advantages over its neighbors: an economy that was already semireformed and able to compete in Western markets and a geostrategic position that made it less buffeted by turmoil in the Soviet Union. In addition, the peaceful, negotiated revolution of 1989 had produced a stable governing coalition with a respectable opposition. Yet these assets were also liabilities, permitting the Hungarians to defer painful austerity measures, for which the population at large saw little justification, and contributing to a political style that made democracy mainly a matter for Budapest politicians.[54] Hungary also suffered from the success of its own propaganda, as Western governments tended to take at face value the claim of Hungarian politicians that their country was well ahead of the pack among the emerging democracies of the region. And again the matter of geopolitics: Hungary did not command quite the same sustained engagement as Czechoslovakia or especially Poland, the "lands between" Germany and Russia.

Nor did the Hungarians look so much to us for help. Antall was a committed Atlanticist, but his first priority was Europe and, within Europe, Germany. Although heavily indebted, the Hungarians (wisely) chose to repay rather than reschedule their debts so as to maintain a favorable international credit rating and so did not look to us for special help. Our dialogue on economic matters, though lively, was conducted largely at working level. At the highest levels, U.S.-Hungarian relations focused more on international issues: Hungary's integration into the Western community, the plight of Hungarian minorities in Romania and Slovakia, and, after conflict erupted in Yugoslavia, Hungary's exposed position as a front-line state with compatriots across the border in Serbian Vojvodina.

None of this is to denigrate Hungary's key role in setting a standard for the region as a whole, through its bold foreign policy initiatives as well as its economic and political reforms. Its elections of March 1990 were a model of democratic propriety that set a standard for the entire region. Given that these were the first fully free and open elections in postcommunist Central Europe, it is a tribute to the authors of Hungary's "negotiated revolution" that we felt no need to dispatch a Presidential Mission to observe the elections (as we did for those in Romania and Bulgaria), relying instead on observer teams arranged through CSCE and the American party institutes (the National Democratic Institute and the International Republican Institute).

First Encounters in Washington The president's May 18 meeting with newly elected Hungarian president Árpád Göncz was mainly ceremonial, in keeping with Göncz's limited authority under the Hungarian constitution; the event was meant to demonstrate symbolically U.S. support and commitment to Hungary's new leaders.[55] The genial, intelligent Göncz was not shy about speaking his mind, though, and he and Bush got on well, engaging in a long discussion about the Soviet Union and the conflict then raging between Moscow and Lithuania. Indeed, Bush was sufficiently impressed to pencil in a reference to his meeting with Göncz in his commencement address at the University of Texas the next day.[56] (The next meeting between the two, a year later at the White House, was equally successful, as an unusually animated President Bush began immediately to probe Göncz's thinking on everything from GATT to Gorbachev.[57])

Budapest continued to set the pace in foreign policy among the Central Europeans. Having reached agreement with Moscow for the removal of Soviet forces from Hungary by June 1991, the Antall government began preparing for Hungary's withdrawal from the Warsaw Pact. Hungary's new foreign minister, Géza Jeszensky, had earlier said that Hungary would remain a member of the pact "as long as necessary, but not one day longer," and at a Warsaw Pact meeting in Moscow in June 1990 gave notice that Hungary planned to withdraw by 1991.[58] As an alternative, Antall floated the idea of an "East-Central European Union,"[59] modeled on the Western European Union, to complement such emerging regional groupings as the Visegrád troika and the "Alpe-Adria," a loose association of substate regions of northern Italy, Bavaria, Austria, Hungary, Slovenia, and Croatia. Antall, it should be added, was too much the realist to place much stock in such arrangements. They were designed to camouflage his real aim of extricating Hungary from Moscow's grip and preparing the way for its integration into the European and transatlantic mainstream as quickly as possible. Hungarian neutrality, another idea that was sometimes mooted, was but a way station on the road west.

Antall's official visit to Washington in October 1990, a few days after German unification and less than a month before the CSCE Summit in Paris, similarly had a foreign policy focus. Indeed, in their several meetings and numerous telephone conversations, Antall and Bush hardly talked about Hungary. Their topics were the Soviet Union, European security, the Atlantic alliance, Yugoslavia, or whatever was hottest on the international agenda. Most of their discussion during this visit was about Iraq, about which Antall was as knowledgeable as he was hawkish. Although the two men never developed the personal chemistry that Bush had with Havel and Mazowiecki, the president came to value Antall's thoughtful, if long-winded, views. (In preparing talking points for the president's telephone conversations with Antall, I began to think that "Hello" and "Good-bye" were all that Bush needed for a half-hour call. Antall would take care of the rest.)

On this first visit to the White House, Antall wanted, and received, further U.S. assistance and increased support from the IMF and World Bank, but his main political objective was to gain American public recognition of Hungary's sovereignty and independence. This, too, he received. As Bush put it, with some overstatement, in his remarks during the arrival ceremony, "Hungary is no longer an emerging democracy; Hungary is a democracy. The government you head is a sovereign, pluralistic, democratic European state. . . . Hungary has taken its natural place as a valued member of the commonwealth of free nations."[60]

The president delineated several economic initiatives, including $47.5 million in credits for food grains to compensate for the effects of Hungary's severe drought that year. Recognizing the high economic price Hungary and others in the region were paying for their resolute support of UN sanctions against Iraq, he also announced that the United States would "ask the IMF to increase its lending to the countries of the region by as much as $5 billion and urge the World Bank to accelerate its assistance in the energy field, drawing on the $9 billion now committed." These pledges did not involve new U.S. resources, as the Hungarians knew well, but the commitment of American leadership in the "IFIs" (international financial institutions) was welcome. Antall—like Göncz and Jeszensky—an historian, delivered a thoughtful brief speech at the same ceremony, including this reference to warm the heart of an NSC adviser: "You, Mr. President, have spoken about all those matters that I could have also mentioned here when presenting my requests. . . . I think this is an indication of the fact that we have come here as friends. . . . And we are being received by friends who can perhaps read our minds."

"Gradualism" and Its Consequences　The confidence Hungary projected seemed vindicated for a time. Shortly after his return to Budapest, Antall was able to enlist the support of the socialist opposition in parliament to defuse a taxi drivers' strike that seemed destined to spread to other sectors and threaten the government's survival. A privatization law was passed, well ahead of any other country in the region; price liberalization and market regulatory measures were efficiently implemented; and foreign direct investment increased impressively. Despite ongoing conflicts over the respective powers of the president and prime minister, constitutional reforms implemented already in 1989 put Hungarian civic life on a more secure foundation than elsewhere. In recognition of these steps, in November 1990 Hungary became the first East European country to join the Council of Europe.

Yet the Hungarians succumbed to the temptation of deferring the toughest decisions. Because the modest reforms of the János Kádár era had introduced a degree of market rationality into pricing, Polish-style "shock therapy" was not required to bring the macroeconomic system into balance. New economic measures would be introduced in "separate bundles," Antall promised, warning that more radical changes could lead to a catastrophe.[61] To avert a social backlash, the government declined to cut the huge subsidies provided to state enterprises or to move forward with a mass privatization program. Antall's government based its program on recommendations of a prestigious Blue Ribbon Commission report of April 1990, but in erring on the side of caution failed to heed one of its cardinal warnings: "Deciding on a quantum leap is also a matter of political efficiency. Slowness can cause the early consensus supporting the government's program to collapse before implementation is completed and results become evident, because interest groups have time to mobilize and drag down the program."[62]

Once the opportunity for early, decisive action had been lost, a kind of paralysis set in. Antall's coalition was strong enough to resist pressures for more rapid change coming from the opposition Free Democrats and especially FIDESz (Alliance of Young Democrats), which were in any case too busy vying with one another to advance a unified alternative.[63] But the coalition was itself internally divided and increasingly preoccupied with issues of Hungarian nationalism, both on domestic policies and on matters affecting Hungarian minorities abroad.

Nationalism on the Rise   When Antall met with the president at the White House in early October 1991, his focus was almost entirely on Yugoslavia, where Serbian forces were launching brutal assaults on Croatian towns and villages in the aftermath of the Slovenian and Croatian declarations of independence. Antall got to the nub of the matter, as he had in two or three recent telephone calls to Bush: Serbia had to be confronted with the credible threat of force, and only a U.S.-led NATO effort could do the job, as the European Community was not up to it. This was wise counsel, but U.S. policy had become more inert than Antall knew since Secretary Baker's ill-fated visit to Belgrade in June.[64] The Hungarians looked to us for more leadership than we were prepared to provide; instead they got vacillation from the West Europeans, as they had feared. Antall's greatest concerns were the threat to the Hungarian minority in Vojvodina, across the border in Serbia, the influx of refugees into Hungarian territory, and the mounting domestic pressures on his government to galvanize stronger international engagement.[65]

Visiting Budapest in mid-December 1991 as part of a developing bilateral security dialogue with each of the Central European countries, Secretary Cheney heard these concerns in graphic detail in separate meetings with Antall, Foreign Minister Géza Jeszensky, International Economic Relations Minister Béla Kádár, and especially from our Hungarian host, Defense Minister Lajos Für. Whereas the security concerns Cheney had heard from his Polish and Czechoslovak counterparts were abstract and potential, arising from fears of resurgent Russian power, Hungarian concerns were actual. Serbian aircraft had violated Hungarian air space a few months before, and the Hungarians were without the minimum requirements of territorial self-defense. The mainstay of its air force was aged MiG-21s, which had been introduced in the USSR in the late 1950s and provided to Hungary a decade later, and half of them had to be cannibalized just to keep the others operational. Hungary lacked even detection and early warning capacities, the entire Warsaw Pact air defense system having been withdrawn to Moscow along with Soviet forces.

The domestic repercussions of the Yugoslav war within Hungary were strong indeed—particularly on top of continuing tensions with Romania and Slovakia over treatment of their Hungarian minorities. Another cause of tension was the long-standing dispute over Slovak plans to complete the Gabčikovo-Nagymaros dam along the Danube (despite the well documented evidence that it would cause environmental damage). Antall had proclaimed himself early on to be prime minister not only of the ten million Hungarians within Hungary's borders but also, in a spiritual sense, of the five million living outside.[66] And Antall was a force for moderation within his Democratic Forum: Jeszensky and Für spoke pointedly and often about their government's responsibility for the fate of Hungarians abroad. To be sure, they denied harboring current territorial claims, but their public comments tended to reflect popular nostalgia for "Greater Hungary."

The Yugoslav tragedy had the effect of pushing the Hungarian political climate further in the "national" direction. Antall, having earlier maneuvered to secure the removal of the outspoken nationalist József Torgyán from the leadership of the Independent Smallholders party, in coalition with the Democratic Forum, also faced a growing, and increasingly assertive, nationalist faction within the Forum itself. This erupted in August 1992, when Forum vice chairman István Csurka published a neofascist, anti-Semitic diatribe—and did so in the Forum's weekly *Magyar Forum*.[67] Although Antall later secured Csurka's removal as he had Torgyán's, he could not entirely remove the sources from which these views sprang. The familiar urban-rural split in Hungarian political culture—between the Western-oriented Budapest intellectuals and neo-Populists with roots in the countryside and a romantic attachment to Hungarian village life—was reasserting itself. Among the latter grouping, anti-Semitism was the familiar surrogate for attacking the patriotism of political opponents.

Economic and Political Malaise In economic policy, these political trends manifested themselves in several ways. Proponents of a Hungarian "third road"—between capitalism and socialism, with special measures to protect traditional rural life—were joined by those, mainly on the Left, who wanted to shield the working class and state bureaucracy from the painful effects of the market. Privatization was slowed and skewed by these twin forces, with the nationalists warning of a foreign takeover and remnants of the old managerial class trying to preserve their privileged economic position. Thus while small-scale privatization proceeded apace, privatization of large state-owned enterprises, as well as the banking sector, hardly began. Hungary's considerable head start in attracting foreign direct investment also slowed, with many prospective investors complaining that deals would be concluded, only to be reversed by a nationalist backlash in the parliament and held in abeyance by the State Property Agency. Large-scale privatization everywhere in Central and Eastern Europe was an intensely political affair, but in Hungary this was true to a marked degree. It was almost all politics, and foreign investors and private Hungarians alike complained that transactions were conducted behind closed doors on the basis of political favoritism or outright kickbacks.

Prime Minister Antall's rapidly failing health deprived the government of the coherent leadership it needed as the domestic situation deteriorated. His flagging energy was devoted almost entirely to foreign policy and fending off nationalist challenges within the coalition. The failures of his government to tackle the state sector made it harder to constrain subsidies, balance the budget (while also meeting onerous debt repayment schedules), and promote greater efficiency and profitability. Hungary's gross domestic product declined by nearly one-fifth between 1989 and 1992,[68] and sharply increased prices, even for basic foodstuffs, undermined living standards for most of the population and dissipated what little support remained for further reform. To be sure, much had been achieved in three short years in laying the foundations of a market economy, but the reality for most Hungarians was continuing economic decline with no visible prospect of improvement.

U.S.-Hungarian relations underwent a similar decline, as public sentiments ranged from disappointment (at failures, real or imagined, of American leadership) to outright anti-Americanism (among those who felt American business was exploiting Hungarian economic weakness for unilateral advantage). More important than whether we were liked was whether we could have done more to advance Hungary's democratic transition, and with it our own interests. The inadequacy of our overall assistance budget meant that our direct aid could do little more than facilitate change at the margins. Even granted those limitations, this was not an easy country to help: its hesitancy to embrace large-scale privatization and financial sector reform led us to deploy our scarce resources to Poland and Czechoslovakia, where reforms were being pursued with more determination and where our help could be effectively used.[69] Still, U.S. assistance to Hungary was never as large or successful as in Poland, owing partly to our failure to join other G-24 countries in providing significant balance of payments support in 1990 and 1991. That is when Hungary, like most of the rest of the region, was being hard hit by the loss of key foreign markets and the severe (and uncompensated) impact of economic sanctions against Iraq and Yugoslavia. Equally damaging was the failure of the United States and its Western partners to engage meaningfully in the Yugoslav conflict, whose spillover lent strength to ultranationalist forces and diminished the Western community as a magnet and point of reference. Thus, Hungary's transition to free market democracy, which had seemed so promising in early 1990, seemed to have stalled by 1992, with much of the populace disenchanted with their new political leadership and feeling that their lives had been better under the communists.[70]

Romania: "Diplomacy of the Absurd"

Although Romanians, particularly officials of the ruling National Salvation Front (NSF), accused the United States of neglect during their difficult transition after the December 1989 revolution, in fact we devoted a great deal of attention to Romania. We also delivered more assistance, mainly humanitarian aid, to this country than to any other in the region save Poland. The outpouring of American private assistance, together with more than $100 million in government aid, during the winter of 1989–90, was testimony to America's desire to help Romania overcome the immediate legacies of Ceauşescu's misrule and begin developing the foundations of liberal democracy.

The problem was not lack of attention so much as the sharply differing judgments we and the NSF leadership drew from postrevolutionary developments in Romania.[71] Our relations with the Front, to borrow the subtitle from a book about U.S.-Romanian relations at the end of the Ceauşescu era, was another episode in "diplomacy of the absurd."[72] Oddly, some leaders of democratic opposition parties, loosely allied under the Civic Alliance and later the Democratic Convention, also argued that we failed to give them sufficient support. This contention is best consigned to the file of theories of conspiracy and betrayal, and to the tendency—not unique to Romania, but particularly acute there—to blame others for one's own failings. If anything, the United States erred on the side of partisanship in favor of democratic opposition parties, both by rendering electoral assistance and by withholding support from the ruling NSF. Indeed, it was precisely those opposition leaders from the Civic Alliance who constantly urged us to withhold MFN status and other assistance so as to keep the pressure on the Front. They can hardly blame us for the consequences of their own political strategy. Scapegoating, like charity, ought to begin at home.

Of all the postcommunist countries of Central and Eastern Europe, Romania worried us the most. (Nor were we alone among Western countries: as late as 1993, the Council of Europe continued to deny admission to Romania for failing to meet its democratic standards.[73]) In the run-up to the May 1990 elections, the NSF had backtracked from its early promises and was using its grip on power to skew the electoral campaign in its own favor. During his February visit, Baker had gained Iliescu's agreement to welcome election observers, and we used the intervening time to mobilize as much outside involvement as we could. We also provided quick financial and technical assistance to the many independent newspapers and radios springing up around the country. In addition to the international observer teams already in the country, we (i.e., NSC staff and State) proposed, and the president agreed, to name a presidential mission to monitor the elections. This, we hoped, would ratchet up the pressure on the NSF and help document electoral abuses if, as we feared, they occurred. As it turned out, the presidential mission—whose composition, unfortunately, was left to the office of presidential personnel and selected on domestic rather than foreign policy grounds—gave a much more generous report than did any other observer team, including those representing European socialist and social democratic parties.[74] Consequently, in commenting officially on the fairness of the elections, we downplayed the presidential mission's statement. Instead, like our West European partners, we stressed the consensus judgment of the many other observer teams: while the elections were, with some notable exceptions, technically free and fair, the electoral campaign preceding them had been characterized by a pattern of media manipulation and local intimidation.[75]

The NSF won the May 1990 elections handily, and no doubt would have done so even if the electoral campaign had been fully free and fair. Iliescu retained the presidency with a landslide 85 percent, and with the Front's two-thirds of the seats in the new parliament, Petre Roman was easily elected prime minister. The most prominent opposition leaders, Radu Câmpeanu of the Liberal party and Ion Raţiu of the Peasant party, had both spent decades in emigration. Although decent and civilized men, their programs and personae were too dated to have much resonance beyond Bucharest intellectual circles. (Both visited Washington in early 1990, and I recall a conversation with Câmpeanu in which he outlined an agricultural policy derived straight from the Liberal party's program of the 1920s.)

Our concerns about the direction of Romanian politics were amply confirmed a month later, when some ten thousand miners from the Jiu Valley, pressed into service by the Front itself, swept through Bucharest's University Square, bludgeoning student protestors and ransacking the Liberal and Peasant parties' headquarters nearby. Clearly, the miners did not need much encouragement, and their rampage was probably a mixture of spontaneity and governmental instigation. Whether President Iliescu ordered, incited, or merely condoned the miners' assault was unclear, but his complicity was evident from his own public statements and actions.[76] The White House and State Department issued sharp rebukes, and our ambassador in Bucharest was recalled to Washington for consultations.

One vignette will serve to illustrate the tenor of U.S.-Romanian relations at the time. On June 20 and 21, veteran Romanian human rights activist Doina Cornea, together with Petre Bacanu, editor of the independent newspaper *România liberă*, visited Washington for meetings at the NSC and State Department. They had just come from Western Europe and Canada, conveying the message that the West should withhold assistance until the National Salvation Front demonstrated its commitment to democracy and human rights. Back in Bucharest, several parliamentarians demanded that the two be stripped of their Romanian citizenship if they persisted with this line in Washington, and the Romanian government suggested that these two not be received by U.S. officials. Not much liking the idea that Romanian officials could blackmail their own citizens and presume to tell the United States government whom it should see and not see, we worked at staff level on a ministrategy to counter this provocation. The idea was to ratchet up their official meetings in Washington and call public attention to them, so that any subsequent harassment of these two would constitute a slap at the United States as well. Deputy National Security Adviser Bob Gates readily agreed to meet Cornea and Bacanu in his office in the West Wing of the White House, as did Deputy Secretary Eagleburger at the State Department. We then drafted a couple of paragraphs of State Department press guidance, stressing that these high-level White House and State Department meetings demonstrated the importance the United States attached to such meetings with Romanians defending basic human rights. As press guidance of this sort goes into the daily briefing book but is used only in response to a query from the press, I called a journalist friend and made sure the question got asked. Once this was in the public domain, Cornea and Bacanu had no trouble in ensuring that it was widely quoted in Romania, providing them a measure of insurance against harassment upon their return.

On July 4, at a meeting of G-24 foreign ministers in Brussels, Secretary Baker restated U.S. insistence on "democratic differentiation," a policy first enunciated in his Prague speech in February 1990. He argued that Bulgaria, despite our continuing concerns, had met the basic conditions set by the G-24 and should be admitted conditionally into the G-24 process, joining Poland, Hungary, and Czechoslovakia. As to Romania, he minced no words:

> Romania has not yet met the conditions required for G-24 support. The Iliescu regime's complicity with the miners' violent repression of demonstrators and the arrest of the political opposition raised serious questions about its commitment to democratic reform and basic human rights. We look forward to the day when

we can include Romania in the G-24 process. However, we will require demonstrable progress on both political and economic reform and respect for human rights before that day can come.[77]

At staff level, we set about to specify what "demonstrable progress" we had in mind. Beginning with two Policy Coordinating Committee meetings (PCCs) on June 26 and 27, we worked out what came to be known as the "benchmark cable" (to Bucharest) delineating four main areas of concern—free and fair elections, democratic control over the Securitate, independent media, and equal treatment of minorities. We also described, with as much specificity as we could muster, the steps that would be required before we could consider any forward movement in our bilateral relations.[78] It was important to put this in writing, in a document that the Romanians could retain and to which we could refer as the standard to which they would be held. As the United States had adopted the toughest position toward Romania of all the G-24 countries, we also sent the cable to West European capitals so that their governments would know the bases of our position and understand what we expected to see before we were prepared to relent. Otherwise, it was entirely foreseeable that six months later we would be told by the French and others that the situation in Romania had "improved." This cable gave us a standard against which to measure "improvement."

This approach helped us exercise pressure but did not yield much in the way of tangible results. The hated Securitate was reorganized and partially purged (under the new Romanian Intelligence Service, or SRI) but not disbanded, and rumors persisted of direct links between Iliescu and a Securitate-type force within the SRI. The status of the Hungarian minority improved substantially, but anti-Hungarian incidents and invective flourished, some with the implicit or explicit endorsement of Prime Minister Roman and other leading government officials.[79] Independent newspapers operated in relative freedom, but the government used its control of newsprint and distribution to repress those it found troublesome, going so far as to propose (and then withdraw under pressure) a highly restrictive press law in the fall of 1990. Television remained largely under government control.

Romania was nonetheless moving haltingly toward political and economic liberalization, and U.S.-Romanian relations began to thaw in early 1991. There was an explosion of new political parties. Five leading democratic opposition parties, including the Hungarian Democratic Union of Romania, coalesced in November 1990 under the Civic Alliance. Yet extremist parties also flourished: on the far Right, the quasi-fascist party of Romanian National Unity, part of the much larger movement *Vatră Românească* (Romanian Cradle), gained strength and organization, including reputed links to the ruling NSF. On economic policy, Roman announced a bold, if hastily prepared, reform plan that enabled him to sign a "letter of understanding" with the International Monetary Fund in April 1991, paving the way for IMF loans and credits, entry into the G-24 process, and an eagerly sought meeting with Secretary Baker in Washington.[80] The meeting with Baker was also meant to reward Romania for its considerable help, during its period as a member of the UN Security Council in 1990 and 1991, in securing a succession of UN resolutions against Iraq after the latter's invasion of Kuwait. Seeking to capitalize on Baker's largesse, the Romanians mounted a diplomatic offensive for U.S. restoration of Romania's MFN status and the symbolic blessing they believed it would confer.[81]

Just as Washington's attitudes were softening, relations took another nosedive when Jiu Valley miners returned to Bucharest in September 1991. They were widely believed to have been brought in by Iliescu, this time to give a pretext for securing the resignation of Prime Minister Roman, whose competition with Iliescu for leadership of the Front had become increasingly open and bitter. Indeed, the many Romanian officials who visited Washington to lobby the NSC and the State Department for restoration of MFN status had been urging us to throw our support behind Iliescu, who was said to be striving to build democratic rule over the constant obstructions of Roman. If the visitors' loyalties were on the other side, then they urged us to support the genuinely democratic but misunderstood Roman against the unreconstructed Iliescu. (On one occasion, an American businessman returning from Bucharest sought me out to deliver a personal message from Iliescu for President Bush, the brunt of which was to discredit Roman and seek to forge a Bush-Iliescu understanding. It was not explained why Iliescu chose a private American to deliver the message rather than the many official channels available to him.) Endlessly conspiratorial, these visitors could not be persuaded that we had neither the time nor the inclination to involve ourselves in their internal machinations.

Opposition leaders like Nicolae Manolescu, leader of the Civic Alliance party, were nearly unanimous in arguing against restoration of MFN.[82] As the thoughtful and straightforward Manolescu commanded considerable respect in Washington, we made it clear after this second miners' rampage that MFN would not be considered until after the holding of the long-promised local and parliamentary elections. Although only 18 months had passed since the May 1990 elections, Romanians and outsiders alike felt that new elections were needed—as they had been in most of the rest of the region—to extend a new mandate and build legitimacy in a country still undergoing revolutionary transformation.

When local elections in February 1992 produced a democratic breakthrough, with parties of the Civic Alliance winning Bucharest and other major cities, we in the administration decided on a two-stage process toward restoring MFN. We would sign a bilateral trade agreement as a first step, thus recognizing the progress made already, but would defer granting MFN itself until after free and fair country-wide elections were held so as to retain some leverage over their conduct. Even those of us who had advocated a firm position—withholding support until the concerns detailed in our "benchmark cable" had been met—largely had come to the view that our use of the MFN issue had run its course and that we could extract no further policy benefits from it.[83] MFN had always been a blunt instrument, useful for extracting one concession but not able to be so finely calibrated as to extract several as an ongoing element of policy. With Romania, this was the most hopeful period since the June 1990 miners' rampage, and we wanted to marshal what influence we retained for the one purpose of ensuring that these parliamentary elections would be held as promised and that they would be freely and fairly conducted.

Armed with this mandate and responding to a long-standing invitation from Romanian foreign minister Adrian Nastase, I traveled to Bucharest in early April 1992 to detail the further steps that would be required for the United States to restore MFN. The message, worked out through interagency meetings and approved at cabinet level, was generally positive. The United States was encouraged by the February local elections and, as Romania prepared for new parliamentary and presidential elections, was prepared to take further steps to advance the bilateral relationship, including restoration of MFN. The question of whether MFN would be withheld until after the nationwide elections was still unresolved within our own government, so this had to be left vague. On the other main electoral issue—whether parliamentary and presidential elections should be held together or sequentially—we took no position.

Together with Ambassador John Davis,[84] we made these points, expanding on the political and economic steps we hoped to see, in a series of meetings with Foreign Minister Nastase, new prime minister Teodor Stolojan, and President Iliescu. Over dinner, we spoke at greater length with leaders of the principal opposition parties, including Petre Roman, who had broken with Iliescu to form a new party, and Ion Rațiu, who had come to play a moderating and civilizing influence on Romanian politics since abandoning his hopes for the presidency.

With Nastase, we stressed the importance of passage of two pending pieces of legislation, one governing (and liberalizing) radio and television broacasting and another providing for domestic election observers. Nastase agreed, noting that he had gotten assurances on the latter issue from Iliescu the previous day. But Nastase's preoccupation was Moldova, where he was flying, literally within the hour, for a quadripartite meeting of Soviet, Ukrainian, Romanian, and Moldovan foreign ministers. Their agenda was to discuss the crisis provoked by Soviet intervention in the Transdniester region, a military action ordered by Moscow ostensibly to protect ethnic Russians there but more broadly to counter the separatist movement in this predominantly Romanian republic. The U.S. position, as conveyed in a State Department statement a few days earlier, was on Romania's side in the dispute, but we advised the Romanians to show flexibility until the Soviet leadership could sort out its policy.

Prime Minister Stolojan, easily the most impressive of these Romanian leaders, was an able and self-effacing technocrat serving as caretaker until the coming parliamentary elections. Under next to impossible circumstances, he had kept inflation under control, made progress on macroeconomic policy, and, by dint of his own quiet authority, strengthened public confidence and external support for Romania's economic reform. He had also taken a courageous public stance against anti-Semitism and national chauvinism, at a time when neofascist journals like *România mare* (Great Romania) and ultranationalist political leaders like Cluj's new major Gheorghe Funar were commanding considerable support. Stolojan agreed on the need for new elections to break the current political impasse, but the irony was that new elections meant the end of his caretaker government and the loss to Romania of its most competent political leader.

The meeting with Iliescu was arranged unexpectedly at his request. It was emblematic of the importance Romania attached to U.S. support that the president of the republic would seek out a visiting NSC staffer for a private meeting. There were just four others—two Iliescu aides, an interpreter, and the deputy chief of mission of the U.S. embassy[85]— in a cavernous room in the gloomy presidential palace, which seemed nearly deserted in contrast to the hubbub of activity that always prevailed at the White House. Iliescu was at his most statesmanlike, confining his criticism to the dry observation that the United States had extended MFN status to Romania under Ceauşescu's despotic rule but was withholding it now under conditions that, however imperfect, were by any standards an improvement.[86] I acknowledged that the standards had changed but said that our current policy of "democratic differentiation" had been articulated clearly by Secretary Baker and was being consistently applied. Others had met and exceeded the standards; Romania had not, though we were confident that with free and fair elections Romania would qualify for MFN and a full range of U.S. assistance.

As it turned out, these meetings were but a dress rehearsal for a visit a month later (May 1992) by a large U.S. delegation headed by Deputy Secretary Eagleburger.[87] Eagleburger's foreign policy priority was to press for Romanian compliance with international sanctions against Serbia, on which he got correct but vague assurances. On internal Romanian matters, he delivered the same message that I had carried, obviously with much greater authority and import. Eagleburger pressed particularly hard for the holding of early parliamentary elections.

The elections were eventually held in September and October 1992, yielding another victory for Iliescu and the Front, which formed a coalition dominated by Iliescu's "Democratic National Salvation Front." Even before that, the administration proceeded, over the objections of those who wanted to wait until after the elections, to recommend the restoration of Romania's MFN status, only to have that recommendation overwhelmingly defeated in Congress in September 1992.[88] Nearly three years after the December Revolution, U.S.-Romanian relations, like the Romanian political scene itself, were characterized by the same ambiguities and suspicions that had plagued them throughout.

Bulgaria: Island of Stability?

U.S.-Bulgarian relations were in some respects a victim of bad timing. When we were engaged and ready to help, the political and economic standoff in Bulgaria made it difficult for us to do more than offer indirect support from outside. By the time the opposition had seized the reins of power in late 1991, our own crowded agenda and badly stretched assistance funds prevented us from rendering the kind of support Bulgaria needed. And the Bulgarians, beginning with the ardently pro-American President Zhelyu Zhelev, looked to us for a degree of political intimacy that we were not prepared to provide.

Yet, as a tactical matter, our timing was exquisite. Partly by design and partly through sheer luck, U.S. policy was a step ahead of the major political turning points in Bulgaria's rocky road toward democracy in 1989 and 1990. Already in 1989, U.S. and other support for Bulgaria's "Ecoglasnost" protestors during the CSCE environmental conference in Sofia strengthened the nascent domestic opposition that led to the peaceful revolution a month later. The pattern continued in 1990, as U.S. initiatives anticipated by precisely one month each subsequent breakthrough. The March roundtable agreement that created the framework for new elections was signed a month after Baker's visit to Sofia. UDF (Union of Democratic Forces) chairman Zhelev ascended to the presidency a month after Baker led the call for Bulgaria's admission into the G-24. Finally a broad-based coalition replaced the Socialist government in November–December, a month after Zhelev visited Washington and signed a comprehensive U.S.-Bulgarian trade agreement.

It would be too much to suggest that U.S. policy caused these events, but neither were they purely coincidental. Our reading from the beginning was that democratic progress in Bulgaria would have to be pushed from below, with public (and we hoped peaceful) protests obliging the regime to make concessions it otherwise would have withheld. Given the enormous influence of U.S. policy during this period of Cold War triumph, we needed to provide incentives for further progress, rewarding the regime for each step in the right direction, however ambiguous its purpose, and emboldening the opposition to continue pressing its case. In this sense, our approach resembled the ones we had taken toward Poland and Hungary in early 1989 and, as will be seen, toward Albania in 1991.

Following up on Secretary Baker's strong push for election observers, made during his February 1990 visit to Sofia, we assembled a presidential mission to reinforce the many international delegations already in the country and provided technical assistance to the newly created Bulgarian Association for Fair Elections.[89] The results of the elections, which were won by the Socialists (the renamed Communist party) with a near majority, were not so egregiously distorted as those of the Romanian elections held the month before, but were sufficiently flawed as to prompt significant criticism. The presidential mission expressed its "deep concern about significant inequities," including the "overwhelming imbalance of resources and widespread intimidation" but noted that "the major political parties have agreed to accept the election results and take their places in the new Assembly."[90] The White House and State Department took the same line, as did most West European governments, giving a qualified vote of confidence to Bulgaria's progress toward multiparty democracy. At the G-24 ministerial in Brussels two weeks after the Bulgarian elections, Secretary Baker had made this support tangible but conditional: "We have expressed our deep concern about the fairness of the recent elections. Nevertheless, pending formation of the new Bulgarian Government, and assuming continued democratization, we believe that progress toward reform has been sufficient for Bulgaria to be eligible for G-24 assistance."[91]

We did not have long to wait for our assumption to be vindicated. Two days later, Mladenov resigned the presidency, his position having become untenable because of public airing of an aside caught by television cameras during a December 1989 demonstration in Sofia: "The best thing to do is to bring in the tanks." After two weeks of contentious debate, spurred from the streets by a semipermanent encampment of protestors called the "City of Truth," the grand national assembly elected as president of Bulgaria the former dissident philosopher and political prisoner, now UDF chairman, Zhelyu Zhelev.[92]

President Zhelev's visit to Washington in late September for the annual World Bank/IMF meeting offered an opportunity to take another step in our bilateral relations and strengthen Zhelev's position at home. Bulgarian politics were still poised between the old order and the new, with Zhelev facing a Socialist-dominated parliament and government headed by Andrei Lukanov. Nonetheless, we decided to accelerate negotiations toward an ambitious bilateral trade agreement that extended MFN treatment and made Bulgaria eligible for Export-Import Bank, OPIC, and GSP (Generalized System of Preferences) benefits.[93] We finalized the package at a September 17 PCC (Policy Coordinating Committee), just in time for President Bush to announce the initiative in an Oval Office meeting with Zhelev on September 29. Zhelev was impressive in his laconic way, assuring Bush that Bulgaria was becoming an "island of stability" in a turbulent Balkan sea and wanted to be a close and reliable partner for the United States in the region.[94] It was an historic meeting—the first visit to the White House by a Bulgarian president—but one that was overshadowed by a cavalcade of other events.

It is worth digressing for a paragraph to enumerate the events of the week of Zhelev's visit, as they illustrate the enormity of President Bush's agenda during the period. After addressing the World Bank/IMF annual meeting and holding a signing ceremony for the transmittal to the Senate of the treaty on German unification, the president departed for New York, where he addressed the World Summit for Children (attended by more than seventy presidents and prime ministers, the largest summit meeting ever held). Later he spoke before thirty-five foreign ministers at a CSCE ministerial (the first ever on U.S. soil), addressed the UN General Assembly, and held no fewer than 27 separate bilateral meetings with foreign leaders in his suite at the Waldorf Astoria.[95] He ended his New York stay to return to Washington for an historic (and, as it turned out, politically disastrous) "budget summit" in which he and congressional leaders agreed on "revenue enhancement" (read: tax increase) measures. Upon returning to Washington, he hosted a Rose Garden reception on October 3 to celebrate German unity and taped a televised message to the German people. Small wonder that Bulgaria got neglected in the shuffle.

The Zhelev meeting, though brief, served the purpose of lending tangible U.S. support to the democratic process in Bulgaria. Once again the push came from below. Nationwide strikes in November and December forced the resignation of Lukanov's government, ushering in a broad coalition government headed by the political independent Dimitur Popov and committed to a new constitution (ultimately issued in July 1991) and new elections in 1991. Meanwhile, the new government, with the UDF controlling the key economic ministries, began the belated reform of an economy in deep crisis. The political struggles of the previous year had precluded creating any coherent governmental program, even as the economy was being hard hit by the collapse of the Soviet market, which had accounted for 60 percent of Bulgaria's foreign trade, and the impact of sanctions against Iraq. The new reforms achieved early successes, bringing inflation down from an estimated 300 percent annually to below 5 percent per month and gaining some control over the runaway state budget. With U.S. support, the IMF announced in mid-March a $500 million loan package, Paris Club official creditors declared a two-year moratorium on debt repayments, and the World Bank began preparing an additional $250 million loan.[96] We also assembled a package of bilateral U.S. assistance measures, concluding in April the trade agreement that was initialed during Zhelev's visit and, in July, launching a $50 million Bulgarian-American Enterprise Fund.[97] It was a respectable package within the constraints of our overall assistance budget, but it was paltry indeed compared to the magnitude of Bulgaria's problems.

The UDF in Power　The UDF, managing just enough cohesion to hang together for the September 1991 elections, won a narrow victory over the Socialists, many of whom were only too glad to let someone else take responsibility for the economic shambles. The new prime minister, Filip Dimitrov, was committed to deep economic reform but faced a still strong and obstructionist Socialist opposition. Nor was his own government and parliamentary majority cohesive. Dimitrov himself betrayed a radical anticommunism that set him apart from much of the UDF, including Zhelev.[98] In response to President Bush's congratulatory message, Dimitrov had written back to ask for the president's help in locating and liquidating communist-owned assets in the United States. Although mystified by the request, we replied through diplomatic channels—i.e., not using the president's imprimatur—that we were ready to provide appropriate assistance but could not involve ourselves in a partisan political struggle. Here again was the problem of how to deal with the decommunization issue. Had the matter been broached by more responsible political forces, we might have been more supportive; the fact that it smacked of a witch-hunt made it harder to do so.

With the new government showing signs of bogging down before it had a chance to address Bulgaria's huge economic problems, we at staff level wanted to dispatch a senior American delegation to show the flag and deliver friendly but pointed messages to the new government. But with the Soviet Union in a state of advanced disintegration and a virtual civil war raging in Iraq, no one of cabinet rank could undertake such a trip. (An oft-postponed trip by Eagleburger and his deputy assistance coordinators ultimately took place the following May.) Accordingly, one of Eagleburger's advisers and I took on the assignment, hiving off from meetings in Brussels and Berlin for a whirlwind 24-hour stay in Sofia, November 13–14, for meetings with the prime minister and all the major political leaders save President Zhelev, who was out of the country visiting NATO headquarters.[99]

In addition to conveying U.S. support and delineating what the new government could expect of us, our main efforts were to solidify political support behind continued economic and political reform.[100] In the manner of a Dutch uncle—having learned my lessons from Baker perhaps too well—I explained that we had seen a recurrent pattern in post-communist Central and Eastern Europe: no sooner had leaders of the democratic opposition defeated the communists than they began drawing long knives against one another. A degree of this was inevitable and indeed healthy for democratic development, but given the parlous state of the Bulgarian economy and the fragility of its democratic institutions, Bulgarians across the political spectrum needed to find ways to keep their divisions from paralyzing further economic and political reform.

With leaders of the powerful trade union Podkrepa, we stressed the larger responsibility they had for supporting the essential elements of economic reform even as they discharged their responsibilities to Bulgarian workers.[101] Among the latter, it was important that Podkrepa continue to include members of the large ethnic Turkish minority (roughly 10 percent of Bulgaria's population of 10 million) in its leadership and rank-and-file, lest they feel their only avenue of political action was via the Turkish-based Movement for Rights and Freedom (MRF). It was a point we reiterated in meetings with MRF and UDF leaders, adding that it was crucial that the MRF continue to be primarily a democratic party, allied with other democratic forces in the country, and only secondarily a Turkish party.[102] On the delicate issue of the constitutional prohibition of ethnically based parties, the United States stood firmly behind freedom of association, so we were uneasy with this provision. Yet we felt that the UDF, the MRF, and others had so far managed to interpret it in a reasonable way, as the MRF was represented in parliament where it had a substantial say in governmental decisions even though its members did not hold cabinet positions.

The Bulgarian Socialist party (BSP), whose leaders we met separately, was cynically exploiting anti-Turkish sentiment and positioning itself, incredibly, as the defender of Bulgarian national interests.[103] Our message, delivered mainly to George Pirinski, who subsequently became Bulgarian foreign minister under the Socialist government, was blunt: the United

States was prepared to develop cordial and constructive relations with the BSP, as it had with West European socialist and social democratic parties, but would have nothing to do with a party embracing chauvinistic and antidemocratic principles, as the BSP showed signs of doing. The aim was not to sway the hard core of the BSP, which was hardly likely to be impressed by this peroration from visiting American officials, but to influence, for the record, the internal debate then raging within the BSP over the party's future orientation.

Prime Minister Dimitrov was even more low-key than his president—the only Bulgarian, I later joked to Bulgaria's ambassador in Washington, who could make Zhelev look charismatic by contrast. In a separate meeting, we urged him to develop a public relations strategy to explain to the population at large what steps were being taken to transform the economy and why, and to set benchmarks that would allow the government to claim credit for each achievement. The conferring of MFN status and creation of the Bulgarian-American Enterprise Fund, for example, were tangible benefits for which he and his government could take credit. Dimitrov outlined his economic plan and the huge political obstacles in front of him. He seemed to have the economics right, but not the politics.

These had been evident the night before in what the embassy reporting cable termed "the Balkanization of a dinner." Dimitrov was all but drowned out by the sharp exchanges among four other key political leaders[104] in a debate focused mainly on Yugoslavia and Macedonia (and well lubricated with strong Bulgarian wine). The Bulgarians were unanimous in criticizing EC efforts to mediate between Serbia and Croatia, and the more nationalistic among them argued that the West was proceeding from the flawed results of Yalta and Versailles. Since no state frontier in Central and Eastern Europe predated Versailles, I observed, reopening these border issues was a recipe for endless conflict. They took the point and affirmed that Bulgaria had no territorial claims, but their disillusionment with Western policies was profound—and, as subsequent events proved, well-founded. They also solemnly vowed that Bulgaria would follow the international consensus on the question of Macedonia, a pledge that they promptly broke when Bulgaria became the first to recognize Macedonian independence. As for the internal scene, the atmospherics of the dinner made it plain that Bulgaria's new political power brokers were not about to set aside their differences and rally behind their young new prime minister.

Back in Washington, we began working on an early visit by Dimitrov, setting the stage in a mid-January meeting at the NSC with new Bulgarian foreign minister Stoyan Ganev. Despite his preoccupation with the conflict in Yugoslavia, which rendered strategic planning elusive, Ganev laid out an intelligent strategy of creating a base of strong bilateral relations with Bulgaria's neighbors and a gradual framework for multilateral Balkan cooperation. Apart from its precipitous recognition of Macedonia, a step that only hardened Greek intransigence, Bulgaria had pursued an exemplary foreign policy and had developed particularly good relations with neighboring Turkey.

Dimitrov's visit in mid-March focused more on Bulgaria's political and economic reforms. His Oval Office meeting with President Bush was not particularly successful, in that he missed an opportunity to drive home a short list of priorities for which he sought American support. Instead, he rambled, making the cardinal mistake of not knowing before a meeting began what specifically he hoped to achieve from it. The administration nonetheless did what it could to make the visit a success. As Deputy Secretary Eagleburger put it in addressing a Trade and Economic Conference held during the visit,

> When Americans think of the revolutionary changes in Europe over the past several years, they tend to remember the fall of the Berlin Wall and the heroic struggles of Lech Wałęsa in Poland and Václav Havel in Czechoslovakia. What until now they perhaps have not sufficiently appreciated is the fact that the Bulgarian revolution has traveled the furthest distance of any throughout the region; it has struggled against the greatest odds; and against all odds it has remained peaceful and democratic.

Eagleburger went on to warn that "destructive hatreds lie not far from the surface," adding that "the enemies of democracy within Bulgaria may try to exploit those emotions to thwart economic change which threatens their interests." This, of course, was a message aimed mainly at the Bulgarian Socialist party. Next came a message for the government: "We would like to see Bulgaria accelerate the pace of economic reforms. . . . Clinging to the remnants of the old system, . . . however comforting they may seem, is a recipe for permanent economic decline."[105]

These warnings, as we feared, fell on deaf ears. Zhelev won the January 1992 presidential elections, but by the time of Eagleburger's visit in May 1992, political infighting within the UDF-led government was well advanced. So, too, was the growing influence of organized crime, a danger delineated over dinner by a Bulgarian deputy prime minister.[106] Criminal elements, with patrons in government and among the security services, were putting down deep roots under the conditions of freewheeling entrepreneurship and lax regulation. After a spate of government crises over the summer, Dimitrov's government fell in October, just a year after gaining power, largely as a result of a showdown needlessly provoked by the prime minister himself. The successor "government of experts" headed by independent economist Lyuben Berov was destined to be a transitional one, giving the newly revived Socialists the opportunity they had sought to prepare for a return to power.[107]

Albania: Of Bunkers and Tree Stumps

Three images stand out. First was the tumultuous welcome Secretary Baker had received on his visit to Tirana in June 1991. Hundreds of thousands were massed in Skanderbeg Square, more than Tirana's entire population. They came by train, by bus, and on foot to see the American secretary of state and this tangible symbol of American presence and support. Security broke down entirely. The motorcade crept through masses of well-wishers pressing against the cars. They held up banners and placards, one reading "Baker-Messiah!"—an excess for which not even Baker's press secretary Margaret Tutwiler could have been responsible.

Second were the bunkers, tens of thousands of them, radiating in some fifty concentric circles from Tirana, defending that city from . . . what? They had been built, not in wartime, but in the 1960s and 1970s to protect Albania against, variously, the Soviets, the Americans, the British. They stood in mute testimony to Albania's compulsive isolation, longtime communist leader Enver Hoxha's paranoid delusions, and above all to the lengths to which his regime was prepared (or obliged) to go to justify the exigencies of a war economy and siege mentality.

Third were the tree stumps. With Baker in 1991, the motorcade had traveled the 15 kilometers from the vast civilian-military airport to the city square on a crude two-lane road bordered most of the way by trees spaced at close intervals. A year later, traversing the same route with

Deputy Secretary Eagleburger, we passed 15 kilometers of tree stumps, every one of those trees having been cut down for fuel during the intervening winter.

Diplomatic Relations   The United States restored diplomatic relations with Albania on March 15, 1991, two weeks before the country's first free elections and a month after prodemocracy demonstrators had toppled Hoxha's massive statue in Skanderbeg Square. There had been a debate within the administration as to the proper timing, with some arguing that diplomatic recognition before the elections would enable the Labor party (the renamed Communist party) of Ramiz Alia to take credit and others worrying that further delay on the issue would put us too much in the middle of Albania's elections. Besides, if Labor won, we would be hoist by the petard of a too clever strategy: as we could hardly withhold recognition indefinitely, we would eventually be obliged to bestow it on a new Labor government, thus conferring a symbolic blessing we did not intend. We therefore decided to hedge our bets, exchanging diplomatic recognition in a State Department ceremony with Foreign Minister Muhamet Kapplani but sharing the credit with Sali Berisha, presidential candidate of the opposition Democratic party, whom we had invited to Washington on a private visit. So ended a 53-year hiatus in U.S.-Albanian diplomatic relations.

If we had faced unrealistic expectations of U.S. support on the part of many new Central and Eastern European leaders, with the Albanians the case was extreme. In a meeting with Berisha and party vice chairman Gramoz Pashko at the State Department, we at staff level tried in vain to dampen their conviction that a Democratic party victory in Albania would propel that country to U.S.-bankrolled prosperity. Indeed, upon their return to Tirana, Pashko declared publicly that there would be a U.S. "blank check" if the Democratic party won the election. They were, nonetheless, an impressive pair, with Berisha's charisma complemented by Pashko's more analytical turn of mind. American eagerness to satisfy at least some of their extravagant expectations led to excesses of our own: our charge d'affaires in Tirana had to be reminded that appearing on the same platform with Berisha during his campaign stops was a step too far.

Following a pattern similar to those of Romania and Bulgaria a year before, Albania's first free elections, held on March 31, were won by the

Labor party (the renamed Communist party) with two-thirds of the vote. Labor dominated the countryside, where its campaign of intimidation was conducted largely outside the purview of foreign election observers. Ramiz Alia, who had led the cautious policy of opening Albania to the outside world and of internal liberalization, was elected president despite the indignity of losing his Tirana constituency. Berisha's Democratic party was strong in the cities and towns, however, and, like the UDF in Bulgaria a year before, it controlled the streets. "Controlled" is not quite the word for the mass demonstrations, verging on civil war, that followed the March elections, but the political agenda was being set by the masses of Democratic party followers in defiance of regime repression. Amidst social and economic chaos, tens of thousands of Albanian "boat people" floated to Italy, with a similar number fleeing across the border to Greece.[108] It was an alarming exodus for so small a country.

The Baker Visit   It was against this backdrop that Baker made his triumphal visit in late June. The aim, as in his visits to Sofia and Bucharest in February 1990, was to lend support to a peaceful, step-by-step process of democratization. He did this by extending American moral backing to the democratic opposition and providing inducements for the political leadership of Ramiz Alia and the multiparty government headed by Prime Minister Ylli Buffi (with Gramoz Pashko of the Democratic party as deputy prime minister). In his speeches, Baker noted that he was visiting at the invitation of Berisha, who was at his side throughout. Speaking to the newly elected assembly, he pledged U.S. humanitarian and economic assistance but also sounded a warning to Alia and the hated Sigurimi (security services) still at his disposal:

> Just as there is no turning back on the road to a new Albania, there is no place along that road for violence, no place for intimidation, no place for the use of force. . . . Let us see an end to all fear in Albania. This is a new Albania, and you are members of a new Europe. You have joined the nations that have pledged to uphold the standards of CSCE—standards that govern a state's behavior toward other nations and toward its own people. You have made a solemn compact with Europe and with yourselves. Do not forsake it.

He concluded with a long agenda for Albania's future:

> freeing all political prisoners . . . , full respect for religious and minority rights . . . , the opening of the media to genuine pluralism . . . , eliminating repressive security organs and bringing legitimate police functions under democratic controls . . . , depoliticizing and developing civilian control over the military . . . , freeing the factories, farms, and mines from political controls and mismanagement . . . , instituting a fair and open judicial process . . . , pursuing democratization at every level of government and society . . . , [and] holding free and fair elections at both the national and local level—elections that include a fair campaign as well as equal allocation of state resources, and fair media access to all parties. For these are the challenges of your new freedom, and the elements of lasting legitimacy.[109]

At Skanderbeg Square, overflowing with an estimated four hundred thousand joyous Albanians,[110] Baker gave an address that began "Free citizens of Albania. . . ." In contrast to his lecture to the parliament, Baker was emotional and personal:

> I have not come here today to instruct you on the virtues of freedom or democracy. You know how inhuman are the ways of totalitarianism. You know how difficult is the yoke of tyranny. And you know how it is to be cut off from the wider world. . . .
>
> I want you all to know we understand how hard you have toiled and we are anguished by the pain you have endured. . . . As I stand with you in this square at this historic time, I want for a moment to remember those of your countrymen who endured Albania's long winter but did not live to see the spring. Your long march to freedom owes a great debt to their suffering and their courage. . . .
>
> You will not be alone as you travel freedom's road. . . . For I have come to bring you a message from another free people—the American people. . . . You are with us, and we are with you.[111]

None of us—not even Baker, veteran of many a political rally—had ever experienced anything like it.[112] President Bush's speeches in Gdańsk in July 1989 and Prague in November 1990 were as emotional, but they did not equal Tirana for sheer exuberance. Even the most cynical journalists (if that is not a redundancy) among us were moved by the wild enthusiasm for the United States—and this after 45 years of the most relentless anti-American propaganda on earth. (German foreign minister Hans-Dietrich Genscher, who visited Tirana shortly before Baker, received a warm reception, but nothing like this.) Some of us on the trip later encountered dozens of Albanians who, never having traveled abroad or taken formal English language training, had taught themselves nearly flawless English from VOA and BBC broadcasts.[113] Hoxha's elaborate propaganda machinery—accessible to outsiders via Radio Tirana's vitriolic short-wave broadcasts—had backfired exquisitely. Because they assumed that the domestic media absolutely lied, Albanians tended to believe the polar opposite, with the result that official anti-Americanism helped foster a wildly exaggerated pro-Americanism.

Baker's meeting with President Alia conjured up images from his meeting eighteen months before with Iliescu in Romania. The rough physical resemblance of the two leaders has already been mentioned. Similar, too, were the reception rooms: while those in Albania's presidential "palace" were much more modest than their counterparts in Bucharest, they had the same eerily inhuman character. There was not a single work of art or piece of furniture to connect the inhabitants with the human experience. Albert Camus had described interiors that evoked feelings such as these. How communist leaders led their daily lives and even how they furnished their official quarters—from the Wandlitz compound in East Berlin to Brezhnev's dachas and the third-worldly meeting rooms in Tirana—were not just eerie but terrifying, symbolic of the fundamental inhumanity of these regimes and part and parcel of the violence they so casually perpetrated on their countrymen.

Alia, in retrospect, might seem to have been at his historic vanishing point, rendered irrelevant by the tide of emotion on the streets. Yet as the clashes of a few months before had demonstrated, the Sigurimi retained the capacity to wreak considerable vengeance in one last spasm of violence. Secretary Baker reiterated much of what he had said publicly, combining pledges of U.S. assistance with warnings against further resort to violence. Knowing that Alia's political strategy placed high priority on creating an opening to the West, beginning with the country's admission into the CSCE process, Baker laid particular stress on CSCE principles. At U.S. insistence, Albania's acceptance of a CSCE observer mission had been made a precondition for its membership. Our approach, and that of the observer mission, was facilitated by the specific provisions that had been endorsed at CSCE's Bonn and Copenhagen conferences a year before. As will be seen,[114] this general approach—of linking our bilateral relations to CSCE's specific provisions regarding political pluralism and free market economies—proved even more critical in managing our relations with the newly independent states of the former Soviet Union. Invoking CSCE principles was no guarantee that they would be observed, of course, but they gave us an opportunity to press an agenda of internal reform as a condition of American diplomatic recognition, political support, and economic assistance.

The Baker visit gave a boost to Albania's prodemocracy forces and to Berisha personally. (The ubiquitous Berisha had insinuated himself into Baker's motorcade, in the car just behind mine, and I watched as Berisha, waving and giving the victory sign, turned the event into a campaign swing past hundreds of thousands of newly enfranchised Albanian voters.) The visit may also have deterred remnants of the communist regime from resorting to major violence, but it did not avert a precipitous breakdown of order.

Back from the Brink   As disorder turned to chaos in Albania in the fall of 1991, the Democratic party pulled out of the government in October and negotiated a caretaker government pending new elections. Berisha visited Washington on November 5 and was received by Secretary Baker, who took the occasion to announce new humanitarian and other assistance programs aimed first at averting a humanitarian and social catastrophe in Albania and second at strengthening Berisha's hand. Baker had ordered these new programs literally on the plane returning from Tirana, along with the instruction that he would tolerate no delay in implementation. More importantly, he had intervened personally to throw U.S. weight fully behind Albania's immediate entry into the G-24, IMF, and World Bank, so that substantially greater assistance would be available than our limited bilateral efforts. Among the latter, our programs focused particularly on emergency food and medical assistance and on providing inputs (including such prosaic essentials as fertilizers and cotton) to jump-start the collapsed agricultural and textile sectors on which the Albanian economy depended.

These measures, together with similar efforts undertaken by the European Community and American private donors, did not prevent the catastrophic Albanian winter of 1991–92, but they did avert even greater human suffering and set the stage for a spectacular recovery of the agricultural and textile sectors the following year. They may also have helped the Democratic party to pull off a landslide 66 percent victory in the elections of March 22, 1992. The ever ebullient Berisha was elected president by the new parliament the next month, in time to receive Deputy Secretary Eagleburger and his large entourage for a brief visit in May 1992.[115]

Thousands of tree stumps on the drive from the airport were testimony to the enormity of Albania's challenge, yet the country had survived a test that nearly destroyed it as a functioning society. Its embryonic democracy was alive, the economy was flickering back to life, and the alarming depopulation of the country had abated. Perhaps national survival was the essential point.

A final image: Eagleburger and Berisha sipping coffee on a balcony of Skanderbeg's castle near Kruje, an hour's drive from Tirana, as the two looked down from the Albanian highlands and discussed the country's future. As it must have seemed to Skanderbeg, Albania's national hero, after he turned back the Turks from this castle in the mid-fifteenth century,[116] the miracle was that the Albanians still had a future to discuss.

A Summing Up

In mid-1992, two and a half years after the glorious revolutions of 1989, most of Central and Eastern Europe was mired in recession, with rising unemployment and social tensions threatening the political consensus behind these painful transitions. Yet there were spectacular successes as well: a dynamic new private sector in Poland, an upsurge in Western investment in Czechoslovakia, and an impressive expansion of Hungary's trade with new partners in the West. Free elections had been held and the results honored, and constitutional government was in place. In the Balkans, progress was more halting and uneven, owing partly to the spillover of the conflict in the former Yugoslavia; yet Bulgaria, Albania, and Romania largely maintained their commitment to democracy under difficult circumstances.[117]

Conditions varied substantially by country, but certain general patterns could be identified after 1989. The broad-based democratic coalitions of that year held together long enough to oust the communists, win the first free elections, and form the first governments. (In the

Balkans, the democratic parties generally lost the first elections but then pushed their way into government on the strength of public demonstrations.) Then they splintered, giving way to a proliferation of parties with no roots, organized around prominent personalities whose aversion to compromise made it hard to form stable ruling coalitions (the old us/them mentality being hard to shake). The introduction of the market produced successes that would prepare the way for a wider prosperity, but its initial impact was to generate new inequalities, with a small but conspicuously wealthy group at the top and a large and resentful underclass. Public impatience had fueled pressures for a retreat from painful austerity measures, further divided the erstwhile democratic coalitions, and created fertile ground for demagogues and would-be authoritarians. Civil society, the ultimate guarantor of secure democracy, was developing, but slowly, through the gradual strengthening of independent media, judicial systems, nongovernmental organizations, and all the other institutions and habits that go into making democracy work from the bottom up.

The most obvious generalization of the first two to three years of postcommunist experience was that building a stable democracy would take longer and be both harder and more complex than was assumed during the heady days of 1989 and early 1990. Yet the growing pessimism that had set in by 1991 was also misplaced, a reaction against the earlier inflated expectations of a swift transition to democracy and prosperity. Just as Wagner's music is said to be better than it sounds, the embryonic democracies of Central and Eastern Europe were more promising than outward appearances might have suggested. Gale Stokes offered an historian's perspective:

> Totalitarian states hide their weaknesses and present a surface of unity, efficiency, and strength. Pluralist societies hide their strengths and present a surface of disarray, confusion, and weakness. . . . The East Europeans have brought all of their problems to the surface at once, and they are severe. There is no hope that the new regimes will solve them all right away or even ever. But at least they are now available for solution. Each country in its own way will solve something here, something there, and when it does, the new arrangements will enter into a structural strength of that society, creating a new political culture and a new style of economic behavior.[118]

For all the disarray and disillusionment attending these transitions, the countries and societies of the region largely stayed the course of economic and political reform. The Poles and Czechs, who had kept moving steadily forward despite nearly continuous political upheaval, were well advanced toward secure democracy. So were the Hungarians and Slovaks, though their respective nationalistic preoccupations had diverted them from what should have been their main goals. In the Balkans, the embryonic forces of democracy faced powerful and relatively cohesive remnants of the communist old guard, economies in deep recession, and political cultures that retained strong authoritarian elements. Yet these were now pluralistic societies, vastly more open, humane, and free than they had been in 1989. Great uncertainties and questions surrounded the future of these newly liberated countries. For perhaps the first time in their modern histories, however, the answers were to be found within rather than imposed from outside.

U.S. policy was instrumental in helping these countries navigate the first difficult months of postcommunist transition and in creating an international environment conducive to their peaceful extrication from Soviet domination and their gradual integration into a larger democratic community. Our influence varied substantially by country. With Poland it was substantial throughout, sometimes to decisive effect. In Czechoslovakia, we helped shape the early foreign policy thinking of the new leadership and later exerted useful, if limited, influence over the dissolution of the federation. Our influence on Hungary was less significant, owing partly to neglect and partly to the higher priority it assigned to Germany and the EC. With Romania, our role was important in the negative sense of establishing firm rules of conditionality, but in the process we failed to engage this country around any positive agenda. Bulgaria looked to us for a level of support and intimacy that we failed to provide, even as a reformist government faced a severe economic recession and a powerful postcommunist opposition. With Albania, by contrast, our influence was timely and decisive in galvanizing international support at the moment of greatest danger to the country's survival.

The chief failure of American policy was its growing neglect of these countries after the enormous commitment of American leadership we made in 1989 and 1990. The new version of Europe's age-old Eastern question could be simply put. Would the forces of fragmentation on the loose in the East overwhelm the confidence, cohesion, and ultimately the institutions binding the Western democracies? Or would the Western community be able to extend its zone of democratic prosperity eastward, vindicating the vision of a united, free, and democratic Europe and creating a wider transatlantic community?

7

Europe in Search of Security

THERE WAS WISDOM in George Kennan's admonition, in early 1990, to observe a three-year moratorium on changes to European security structures.[1] Yet there was no stopping the disintegration of the Warsaw Pact, notwithstanding a brief Soviet effort to keep it alive as a forum for political dialogue, and Western leaders were under pressure from the East as well as their own publics to transform Western institutions to accommodate radically new realities. The luxury did not exist of creating a new strategic design in cloistered contemplation, free of the political exigencies of a world still in the midst of profound flux toward unknown ends.

These challenges would soon be put to the test. After the November 1990 Paris Summit of the Conference on Security and Cooperation in Europe, three other crucial meetings loomed. A NATO summit to be held in Rome in November 1991 was to present the alliance's "new strategic concept" and complete the vision of a "transformed alliance" heralded at the July 1990 London Summit. The following month, in December 1991, the EC was to meet in Maastricht, the Netherlands, to complete the "single European market" and point the way to European economic and political union. And in July 1992, a CSCE summit in Helsinki was to fulfill the Paris mandate to give the CSCE operational and institutional capacity for overcoming Europe's division and dealing with new threats to European security.

Dutch foreign minister Hans van den Broek, during the period of the Dutch presidency of the EC in late 1991, called Maastricht "a race against history."[2] Indeed it was. Not only were the key European and transatlantic institutions challenged to keep a step ahead of the pro-

271

found forces of change unleashed by the end of the Cold War; they were also racing against one another to try to shape the post–Cold War order in Europe. Secretary Baker had touched on this point in his December 1989 Berlin speech: "As Europe moves toward its goal of a common internal market, and as its institutions for political and security cooperation evolve, . . . we want our transatlantic cooperation to keep pace."[3] Thus the three summits, and the competing visions underlying them, lent focus, urgency, and occasional acrimony to European and transatlantic diplomacy through 1991 and into 1992.

The European security debate after the Paris Summit was couched in language more akin to engineering and the construction industry than the art of diplomacy: reinforcing structures, variable geometry, multiple speeds, bridges, linkages, and pillars. Sorting out the respective roles of key institutions—NATO, the EC, and the CSCE—was essential, but this debate tended to preempt more fundamental challenges. Chief among these was to preserve the institutions binding the Western democracies as the new era dawned and to bring former adversaries into the European and transatlantic community. Capacities for dealing with new threats to European stability and security also needed to be developed. As President Bush put it at NATO's November 1991 Rome Summit,

> We are not here as engineers but as trustees of democracy. . . . We must provide answers to four defining questions:
>
> First, in this uncertain world, how can we be sure that every ally can be safe from any threat of any sort?
>
> Second, how should we answer the calls of Europe's new democracies to join us?
>
> Third, how should we respond to the disintegration of Soviet power?
>
> And lastly, how should we relate to each other as Europe travels toward union?[4]

While American and European diplomats debated these questions, real threats to European stability and security were erupting. Like the violent disintegration of Yugoslavia, they were threats of a more ambiguous and intractable character, for which traditional military responses were insufficient. Originating not in outright military aggression mounted by one state against another, they sprang instead from social and economic upheavals and ancient ethnic animosities. Thus there emerged a wide gap between the furious but abstract debate over security policy on the one hand and the passivity and confusion of Western responses to actual threats that were erupting in the wake of the Cold War.

The "New European Architecture"

Well-publicized U.S.-French differences captured part of the transatlantic debate, which was by no means confined to two countries alone. Animated by the vision of an EC-centered Europe, rather than uneasy reliance on Anglo-Saxon power in its losing effort to retain preeminence over a resurgent Germany, France aimed to accelerate European integration while it still had political leverage over newly united Germany. This meant deferring consideration of new EC members lest they "dilute" the Community before the movement toward economic and political union had become irreversible. The "European construction" required a security organization to complement the Community's political and economic institutions. But French efforts to reinvigorate the Western European Union (WEU) or create a "Eurocorps" became locked in "zero-sum" competition with NATO. The French believed, with some justification, that the Americans wanted to preserve a NATO-centric European security order while (so they believed) gradually disengaging from an active role in European security. Hence efforts to transform NATO and develop new approaches toward the East were always viewed with suspicion in Paris, just as we were wary of French-led efforts to set up what appeared to be free-standing European security institutions in competition with NATO.

The debates that ensued were increasingly theological, with the British closer to our position and the Germans trying to straddle the middle but hazy about their own priorities—and increasingly divorced from the real world of post–Cold War Europe. The fact was that everyone was reducing military forces at a rapid clip, making it essential to rationalize and combine efforts to meet multiple new threats to European stability rather than set up competing centers of decision making. U.S., French, and British joint action in the Gulf War demonstrated that such cooperation could work in practice, yet we found it hard to replicate this in the loaded debate over the new "European architecture." For our part, it must be said, we found it easier to support the European defense identity in principle than deal with the reality of diminished American authority. Indeed, the Gulf War example cut both ways: it demonstrated the ability of the Western allies to cooperate in the first post–Cold War crisis, but it also made vivid European dependence on American power and reinforced the determination of our European partners to develop a capacity for joint action independent of the United States.

France and NATO   The pressure was particularly felt in Paris, prompting a reappraisal in some French quarters of France's relationship to NATO and the United States after German unification and the collapse of the Warsaw Pact. In the French defense ministry and at the Elysée (the presidential palace) in particular, there was a current of thinking that favored drawing closer to NATO lest France be marginalized in post–Cold War Europe.[5] These sentiments were reciprocated on our side: France's withdrawal from the military side of the alliance, which we had learned to live with after 1966, now acquired new significance in a Europe where the political and economic dimensions of security were ascendant. We needed France in NATO and indeed wondered whether the alliance could survive absent French participation.

Even before the Paris Summit, we had made overtures to the French, chiefly through Mitterrand security adviser Admiral Jacques Lanxade and his American counterparts, General Scowcroft and the NSC senior staff, about France's rejoining the military side of the alliance. At Paris, Scowcroft and Lanxade happened to share a taxi and used the long ride to discuss in some detail the prospects for France's drawing closer to the alliance. In a series of secret meetings thereafter, we explored what changes would need to be made for this to be possible. These were serious discussions but also exploratory, not yet involving Mitterrand directly and kept far away from the foreign ministry at the Quai d'Orsay, where hostility toward the idea was a given. When Lanxade and French defense minister Pierre Joxe visited Washington in early February 1991, they explained that the minimum requirement on the French side would be NATO's fundamental transformation and in particular the reform of its integrated military command. The existing structure, they felt, guaranteed an unacceptable level of American domination and in any case had lost much of its military rationale with the precipitous withdrawal of Soviet forces from Europe. The proposition seemed, in the new security environment, reasonable and interesting. General Scowcroft promised the United States would give it serious consideration.

What might have been an historic reformation of the alliance did not materialize.[6] Discussions broke down on both sides. On ours, the uniformed military, supported by Secretary Cheney, were adamantly opposed to a fundamental change to command arrangements that had served the alliance for forty years. It was, many of us felt, a shortsighted position: NATO's hallowed integrated command would not be of much use if the alliance failed to make the political transformation needed for its survival. But the Pentagon was not to be moved from the view that "if it ain't broke, don't fix it." On the French side, meanwhile, Lanxade could not overcome opposition from the foreign ministry nor bring Mitterrand around. This became evident at the Bush-Mitterrand meeting in Martinique in mid-March 1991, when the French president slammed the door on the idea, arguing that Europe had to develop the capacity to defend itself because American disengagement was only a matter of time.[7]

This was a prophecy that threatened to become self-fulfilling: If the Europeans, anticipating our eventual withdrawal, took steps to develop a security organization that excluded us, the case for our staying would indeed be harder to sustain. If the American public felt that Europeans preferred to organize for their own defense, they would be only too happy to oblige by withdrawing U.S. forces, whose role and mission absent a direct Soviet threat was in any case less compelling. Besides, Mitterrand's argument that Europe had to prepare for the inevitable American disengagement was only part of the story. If his many calls for "overcoming Yalta" were to be taken seriously, he was at least equally moved by the desire to extricate Europe from what he saw as American domination. The French were not aiming at the destruction of NATO, which they neither desired nor thought likely, but rather at keeping it from retaining the dominant role it had played during the Cold War. French behavior during this period therefore needs to be understood partly as a reaction to U.S.-led efforts to infuse the alliance with new missions and to strike a new strategic partnership with Germany.

Transatlantic Discord   Failure to find a way to bring France back into the NATO fold meant that even more was at stake in ensuring that the EC's efforts to build a European security identity did not undermine NATO. Already transatlantic conflicts were erupting over several European proposals issued in the context of an EC Intergovernmental Conference (IGC) launched in Rome in December 1990 with the mandate to produce a draft treaty on European political union in time for consideration at the Maastricht Summit a year later.[8] The phoenix-like Western European Union was convened at foreign-minister level a few days before the Rome IGC to see what role that body might play in the new security environment.

There was a frantic and ill-considered series of European diplomatic initiatives in late 1990 and early 1991. First, Kohl and Mitterrand circulated a letter to their EC and Western European Union (WEU) counterparts the first week of December proposing the European Community's eventual absorption of the WEU, which would become the EC's security and defense arm. Italian foreign minister Gianni de Michelis likewise called for an early "merger" of the two institutions, also without saying how this new entity would relate to the Atlantic alliance. WEU secretary general Willem (Wim) van Eekelen volunteered that the WEU might serve as a "temporary bridge" between the EC and NATO.[9]

EC Commission president Jacques Delors went further, proposing that the WEU's mutual defense commitment be inserted into the EC's political union treaty, without explaining how this new commitment would relate to the existing NATO Article 5 mutual defense guarantee. As Delors put it in summarizing the commission's draft treaty, "What we are proposing is a single [security] Community as a logical extension of the ambitions of European union." Asserting that there was broad agreement within the Community that "a common defence policy must be built on . . . the Western European Union," Delors called for the WEU to become "a melting-pot for a European defence embedded in the Community." What that meant, exactly, we did not know, but it seemed to have no connection to NATO or the United States. Delors concluded by acknowledging that "there is no point in concealing the fact that these plans, even in outline, have caused concern across the Atlantic."[10]

Mindful of Josef Joffe's characterization of the WEU as "the sleeping beauty of European security—often kissed but never awakened,"[11] we in Washington nonetheless saw considerable danger in these initiatives, which in effect would have created a separate, competing European security community. Moreover, France insisted on the narrowest possible definition of NATO's role, whereby Article 5 would apply only to full-scale aggression against a member state and not to any lesser or more ambiguous threats to European stability and security.

The French had long opposed NATO's assuming "out of area" responsibilities, but now they interpreted this to apply not only to the Middle East or North Africa but also to Central and Eastern Europe. If NATO had no role in this region, in our view, it had no role at all except as an insurance policy against a latent Soviet threat. NATO would be marginalized as an agent of European security.

From our perspective in Washington, however, we could see the United States becoming involved at the eleventh hour in such "out of area" European conflicts over which we had no influence because they had been handled in Europe-only channels. NATO would become the "alliance of last resort" rather than the mechanism for joint political and military action on the part of all members of the North Atlantic community.

The U.S. reaction was swift and sharp. A February 22 démarche to all allied capitals—dubbed the "Bartholomew message" because it happened to be signed out in the absence of both Baker and Eagleburger by Under Secretary of State Reginald Bartholomew in his capacity as acting secretary—warned against creating a European caucus in NATO and, worse, a separate European security organization in competition with NATO. The message provoked angry rebuttals from many quarters in Europe. It was criticized even by some who supported our posture as being too blunt and unyielding—needlessly so, given the extreme unlikelihood that the Europeans would actually create an independent defense identity. Better, they argued, to take a relaxed attitude while the Europeans experimented and to weigh in only later, as intentions clarified. Perhaps. But fundamental issues were at stake, and the drift in Europe was, we felt, toward a formula that ultimately would destroy NATO and undermine the basis for an enduring American presence, whereas there were any number of approaches that could have created a European defense capacity that actually strengthened the alliance.

Nor were we alone in our views. Indeed, our démarche was aimed precisely at influencing the debate among and within EC governments before positions hardened irretrievably. The British, supported by the Dutch and others, accepted the need for closer European coordination in foreign and security policies via the WEU but wanted the latter firmly tied to NATO.[12] British foreign secretary Douglas Hurd, speaking in Berlin in early December (en route from the WEU meeting in London to Rome for the Intergovernmental conference), came down hard and helpfully in favor of a "single collective structure based on multinational units comprising both American and European forces," proposing also that the WEU be transferred to Brussels so as to "build bridges to the [EC] Twelve as well as becoming truly the European pillar within the Atlantic Alliance."[13]

There were divisions within European capitals as well, particularly where coalition governments were in power. In Bonn, the defense ministry and the chancellery were closer to our view than was the foreign ministry, but the latter's influence had become much stronger after the resignation in late 1990 of the redoubtable Horst Teltschik as Kohl's foreign policy adviser.[14] In Rome, the Christian Democratic prime minister Giulio Andreotti and his security adviser, Umberto Vattani, were likewise closer to our position than his Socialist foreign minister, the flamboyant Gianni de Michelis.[15]

With the issues now exposed, the transatlantic debate in late spring and early summer 1991 focused on reconciling the competing perspectives. With the British and Dutch, along with NATO secretary general Manfred Wörner and WEU secretary general Wim van Eekelen, we worked out a "dual hatting" proposal, whereby European forces could be assigned either to WEU or to NATO command depending on the circumstances. The WEU, following Hurd's proposal, would be relocated from London to Brussels, so that NATO ambassadors could simultaneously be ambassadors to the WEU. Colocating NATO, the WEU, and the EC would also help coordination among organizations whose membership was overlapping but not identical. (The Danes and Greeks were in the EC and NATO but not the WEU, the Irish were in the EC but not NATO or the WEU, and the Turks, like us, were in NATO but not the EC or the WEU.) The formula was not hard to come by and had, from our perspective, much to recommend it, allowing for a European defense capacity that was simultaneously the EC's security arm and NATO's "European pillar." By the same token, it was anathema for the French, who felt that colocation could only mean the WEU's subordination to NATO, so the idea simply withered away. The critical point for us, however, was not who wore which hat but that there be one overarching transatlantic security organization—the Atlantic alliance—and not two competing ones. That was precisely the arrangement France did not want.

Germany in the Middle   The Germans were anxious to close the rift between Washington and Paris before the Rome and Maastricht Sum mits, but they had so far been wandering between the two positions without expressing their own. In a January 30 speech before the Bundestag, for example, Kohl had come down squarely on both sides of the issue: "In the field of security policy we aim to strengthen the European pillar of the Atlantic Alliance, which has proved its worth. President Mitterrand and I have suggested that the intergovernmental conference on political union consider how [the WEU] might be strengthened and ultimately incorporated in the European union."[16]

Although we could understand that leaders of the newly united Germany needed to show themselves to be both good Atlanticists and good Europeanists, this studied German ambiguity was weakening our case among other NATO members, notably Spain and Italy. We therefore had to secure a clearer expression of German support, being careful as a tactical matter to assure the Germans that we were not asking them to "choose between Washington and Paris" but merely to take a stand on an issue that should have been as important to them as it was to us. In early May, shortly before two crucial NATO meetings, Genscher and Kohl visited Washington on separate trips, and we at the NSC and State began working on draft statements that might be issued in the context of each.[17] The Germans were receptive. In a joint statement issued after their meeting, Genscher and Secretary Baker proposed a set of new measures to open the alliance to the new democracies of the east and strengthen CSCE institutions (discussed below). They then turned to the "European security identity and defense role":

> In their meeting today, Secretary Baker affirmed that the United States is ready to support arrangements the European Allies decide are needed for the expression of a common European foreign, security, and defense policy. Minister Genscher affirmed that . . . a European security identity should be reflected in the development of a European pillar within the Atlantic Alliance. They both agreed that to ensure this development will strengthen the integrity and effectiveness of the Atlantic Alliance, NATO should be the principal venue for consultation and the forum for agreement on all policies bearing on the security and defense commitment of its members under the North Atlantic Treaty.[18]

Inclusion of this last essential principle, which had become dogma for us, facilitated its adoption by the alliance as a whole in communiqués following the May 29 Defense Planning Committee (defense ministers and military commanders) meeting and the June 6–7 North Atlantic Council (foreign ministers) meeting. The latter statement also called for "appropriate links and consultation" among NATO, the WEU, and the EC.[19] The French, who participated in the NAC but not the DPC, were isolated but unaltered in their position, despite Secretary Cheney's talks with Mitterrand in Paris en route to Brussels for the DPC meeting.[20]

Ten days after Genscher, Kohl arrived on his first visit since unification. Although the president made little headway with him on the EC's position on the GATT round, there was progress on the European security identity. In a speech in Washington just after his meeting with Bush, the chancellor took on the issue, beginning on a disingenuous note but finishing well:

Deliberations with respect to a common European foreign policy—and in the long term a common defense policy as well—are being closely followed in Washington and, here and there, they evoke criticism—not all of which I understand. Let me make two things unequivocally clear:

My government does not want to see the long-standing Atlantic Alliance in any way weakened, still less replaced by a European structure.

My government is adamantly opposed to any suggestion that responsibility in some areas be divided. That would run counter to the principle of the indivisibility of our collective security and would only lead to the dissolution of the transatlantic security link.[21]

The issue was by no means closed, however, for the prevailing draft of the EC's political union treaty continued to use the preferred French position, with some concessions to the British.[22] Indeed, scarcely a month after his meeting with Bush, Kohl met with Mitterrand and the two vowed to reconcile their differences over the common foreign and security policy.[23] The French had been playing diplomatic hardball with the Germans for some time—particularly in the context of negotiations over a formula that would permit the continued presence of French forces in the Federal Republic. In a fit of pique just before unification, the French had hastily, and unwisely, declared that their forces in Germany would be withdrawn. It was one of several French diplomatic fumbles during Mitterrand's prolonged disorientation after the fall of the Berlin Wall. They were now having second thoughts, and the Germans were eager to oblige them so as to ground united Germany securely among its EC and NATO partners.

From this aim there developed the idea of a "European corps." The political objective was one we fully endorsed, for our own continued presence in Germany would be greatly facilitated if other countries also remained, but we saw considerable room for mischief in an October 1991 proposal by Mitterrand and Kohl for a Franco-German corps that would be open to other European forces as well in a new "Eurocorps." What would be the command arrangements of such a corps? we asked. Would it be in NATO or outside? We got no answers.[24] The Germans would tell us not to worry, that the Eurocorps was a means of bringing the French closer to NATO, but its evolution so far suggested that the French, via the Eurocorps idea, were taking Germany farther away.

The Rome Summit   In his address to NATO's summit in Rome in early November, the president took these issues head-on:

> The alliance is not an American enterprise nor a vehicle of American power. We never sought preponderance, and we certainly do not seek to keep it. Nor do we claim a monopoly on ideas for the alliance. If we did, none of us would be sitting here today, for the idea of the Washington treaty [establishing NATO] was Europe's. . . .
>
> The United States has been, is, and will remain an unhesitating proponent of the aim and process of European integration. This strong American support extends to the prospect of a political union—as well as the goal of a defense identity. . . .
>
> Even the attainment of European union, however, will not diminish the need for NATO. . . . We support the development of the WEU because it can complement the alliance and strengthen the European role in it. . . . But we do not see the WEU as a European alternative to the alliance.[25]

Behind closed doors, Bush was more blunt: "If Western Europe intends to create a security organization outside the Alliance, tell me now!" As his stunned counterparts shifted nervously in their seats, Bush explained that he would stake his presidency, if necessary, on the continued American commitment to European security via NATO, but he could not do so if America's closest allies were prepared to undermine and divide the alliance at the moment of its crowning success.

The Rome communiqué adopted compromise language that resulted from tough bargaining with the French. We got our formulation on NATO's role as "the essential forum for consultation among its members and the venue for agreement on policies bearing on the security and defence commitments of Allies under the Washington Treaty," papering over the huge differences in interpretation of what those commitments entailed. And the French got some of their favored formulations, including this labored sentence ending with a Delphic phrase that all sides could interpret as they wished: "We welcome the perspective of a reinforcement of the role of the WEU, both as the defence component of the process of European integration and as a means of strengthening the European pillar of the Alliance, bearing in mind the different nature of its relations with the Alliance and with the European Political Union."[26]

Neither Rome nor Maastricht settled these fundamental questions bearing on the future of the Western security community. Nor was the disposition of the still-emergent "Eurocorps" settled until the Germans—principally General Klaus Naumann, head of the armed services—finally noticed that the existing blueprint called for German integration with French forces into an entire corps operating outside NATO structures. It was in early 1992 that General Naumann, Admiral Lanxade, and the American SACEUR (Supreme Allied Commander, Europe), General John Shalikashvili, met quietly to work out the arrangement that should have been adopted at the outset: German forces assigned to NATO could be seconded to a Franco-German or European corps operating outside the alliance for purposes other than Article 5 security commitments. And the decision for such deployment should be made within the alliance. The issue was settled, more or less, of which forces were committed to which organization, and when. But this begged the question for which no one had an answer: for what purposes would these forces be used?

Even at the time, these debates seemed overwrought. With the benefit of hindsight, they appear shockingly detached from the real issues of security confronting Europe after 1990. Our own NATO-centered approach was right in principle but mistaken in practice. It would have been sound and sustainable if we were prepared to undertake the kind of fundamental restructuring of the alliance that some in Paris were urging on us. But we could not have it both ways—preserving a level of American dominance that was anathema to the French (as well as the Spanish and Belgians) while also insisting that any European effort be made within the alliance framework. The French position was the mirror image of ours. They wanted a European security capacity but systematically undermined efforts to transform NATO in ways that might have made their ambition feasible.

Both the French and American conceptions, and indeed those of the Germans as well, were, in any case, fast being overtaken by growing fragmentation in the East. The French were more transparent: the notion of a "European confederation" was rightly seen as a device to consign the East Europeans to an outer circle of European security, while they constructed what amounted to "Fortress Western Europe." Our approach, while conceptually more sound, proved too timid in practice. In particular, the rhetoric of NATO's lead role in European security was belied by the institution's passivity with regard to the unfolding war in the former Yugoslavia. Our acute ambivalence with regard to taking direct action in security threats to the East caused us to retreat, in fact if not in principle, to the mentality of "Fortress Transatlantica." Preserving NATO took precedence over adapting it or answering the hard question of how we proposed to use it. The notions of "Fortress Western Europe" or "Fortress Transatlantica," however attractive they might have seemed to war-weary Western publics, were built on the same false premise that the Western community could be preserved and even strengthened in the new era without addressing the main problems that threatened it.

Integrating the East

In his eloquent opening address to the November 1990 CSCE conference, French president François Mitterrand set the tone: "The Paris Conference, I hope, will be an anti-Congress of Vienna, since round this table we have neither victors nor vanquished, but 34 countries equal in dignity."[27] They were noble sentiments, echoed with evident sincerity by most Western leaders in their interventions at Paris. Yet their Eastern counterparts shared an unease tinged by distrust. Their misgivings were captured best by Polish prime minister Tadeusz Mazowiecki in his address:

We must all face the question [of] whether the borderline of the old Yalta-based division of Europe is not for a long time going to mark a civilizational division. Our common future may be darkened by the sinister clouds of the resurging conflicts of bygone days, unless the split into a rich and poor Europe, an 'A' class and a 'B' class Europe, is overcome. . . . This is the key to the unity of Europe as a whole; it is a fundamental issue . . . for which [a] determined and consistent solution cannot be delayed indefinitely.[28]

With the Warsaw Pact fast disintegrating, the countries of Central and Eastern Europe, and indeed the Soviet Union as well, looked to the CSCE as the sole institution where they sat on equal footing with the rest of Europe and North America. By design or simply for want of other institutional alternatives, they offered proposals to expand CSCE's scope and mandate to turn it, over time, into the preeminent political and security organization bridging the two halves of Europe.

Institutionalizing the CSCE   The Paris Summit itself had been a Soviet idea, coming from President Gorbachev's initiative in Rome in late 1989, just before his summit meeting with President Bush off Malta. Shortly thereafter, Polish prime minister Mazowiecki had proposed creation through CSCE of a "permanent council of European cooperation."[29] At Paris, Gorbachev came back to the idea, calling for an "All-European Security Council."[30] Still more ambitious was the proposal of Czechoslovak foreign minister Dienstbier, which envisioned, as a first step, creation of a "European Security Commission" among CSCE member states that would serve as a bridge between NATO and the Warsaw Pact. The second stage, in Dienstbier's conception, would be "establishment, on a treaty basis, of an Organization of European States, including the United States and Canada," leading, in the third and final stage, to a "confederated Europe of free and independent states."[31]

This, surely, was a bridge too far. We and most other CSCE members rejected such ambitious designs and aimed instead toward an evolutionary development of the CSCE in ways that would complement existing institutions like NATO and the EC. And we did not want to burden the CSCE with the false promise of collective security, with which Europe and America had recent and bitter experience through the League of Nations. (It will come as no surprise that the interpretation one found in the Bush administration was that the league's failure was only incidentally related to the U.S. refusal to join; it had much more to do with inherent and irremediable flaws in collective security systems of this sort.)

Based on initiatives advanced by NATO at its summit in London in July 1990, the Paris Summit had taken the first steps toward institutionalizing the CSCE as a forum for political dialogue between the two halves of Europe. They included creating a Council of [Foreign] Ministers, which would meet at least annually; a Committee of Senior Officials to convene regularly in the interim; and a parliamentary assembly, which, like the Council of Ministers, would meet at least once a year. To these were added a small permanent staff, located in a new secretariat in Prague, to provide administrative support and disseminate information to member governments, an office for free elections in Warsaw, and a conflict prevention center in Vienna.

Yet to list the new bodies in this fashion is to exaggerate their importance at this early stage. They did not yet exist and were in any case quite modest in conception. Some, like the parliamentary assembly, were still the subject of heated debate within CSCE, and between Congress and the administration in our own country. (We at the NSC staff had championed the Council of Europe's parliamentary assembly as the model for the new assembly but were obliged to beat a hasty and humble retreat after several irate members of Congress made plain their preference for the known venue of the North Atlantic Assembly.)

This modest approach may have been a sensible one for institutions so new, but the pressure was great and expectations high to turn the CSCE overnight into an institution that could bear a large share of the weight of overcoming four decades of division. Having rejected the more extravagant proposals for the CSCE's expansion, we and most other members nonetheless shared the view that the CSCE urgently needed to take on new tasks and functions. Developing regular forums for political dialogue was the first task: having met but intermittently in the past, in formal, highly stylized East-West encounters, the CSCE now needed to become the premier venue for serious discussion among all the states of Europe and North America.

The CSCE's role as a forum for political dialogue should not be undervalued, even allowing for the seemingly innate capacity of Europeans—but not Americans!—to sit endlessly in plenary session, listening to mind-numbing, content-free orations. Yet for the new democracies of Central and Eastern Europe, this was the *only* forum in which they could discuss the issues that concerned them most, and do so as equals around the table with all the countries of Europe and North America. There was plenty to talk about. In particular, there was a strong push to erect new mechanisms for conflict prevention and crisis resolution in the midst of the gathering storm in Yugoslavia. The first meeting of the Council of Ministers, set for June in Berlin, was to report progress on creation of these new institutions and mechanisms, which were to be finalized by the time of the next summit, scheduled for the summer of 1992 in Helsinki.

Events in the East quickly outpaced these evolutionary efforts through the CSCE. Soviet foreign minister Shevardnadze's resignation in December 1990, Gorbachev's cultivation of hard-line military and KGB officers, the crackdown against Baltic independence movements, and disputes over Soviet troop withdrawals all served to heighten security concerns in Central and Eastern Europe. Polish president Lech Wałęsa, as has been seen, warned of "deadly danger" to Poland emanating from what Lithuania's foreign minister called the "mad generals" in Moscow.[32] Another ominous note was sounded when, the day after the second "Bloody Sunday" in the Baltic states, Polish, Czechoslovak, and Hungarian foreign ministers were consulting in Budapest and calling for the early dissolution of the Warsaw Pact's military apparatus. In Moscow, *Pravda* warned about their efforts to set themselves "against the Soviet Union . . . as if the *troika* wanted to determine common approaches . . . without the participation of the remaining members of the Warsaw Pact."[33] Undeterred, the "troika" met at summit level in Visegrád, Hungary, on February 15, agreeing to strengthen political and military cooperation among the "Visegrád group," as it increasingly came to be called.

Although the immediate crisis passed with the resumption of talks on Baltic independence and Gorbachev's agreement to disband the Warsaw Pact's military arm,[34] continuing conflict in Moscow and among the republics leading up to the August 1991 coup attempt against Gorbachev kept Central European security concerns at a high pitch throughout 1991. Czechoslovak president Václav Havel, who had placed so much hope in the CSCE as the centerpiece of a pan-European peace order, now looked for more substantial and immediate security assurances, on grounds that "we cannot dream of the future only." In Brussels in late March for visits to NATO and the European parliament, Havel warned against leaving the region in a security "no man's land" or "zone of instability," and called for early membership in the EC and closer association with NATO.[35] Polish foreign minister Skubiszewski spoke in similar terms:

> Europe should be treated as a homogeneous security area. This is the approach of the Paris Charter of a New Europe, adopted by the CSCE Summit of 1990. In particular, central Europe cannot become a gray, buffer, or neutral zone from the point of view of security. . . . The North Atlantic Alliance is integral to European security and thus cannot remain indifferent to a threat to international security in any part of the Continent. . . . It is necessary to seek a certain fusion of the CSCE system with NATO.[36]

Even as the CSCE was struggling to implement the Paris Summit initiatives through regular meetings of the new Committee of Senior Officials, the pressure was shifting to the EC, WEU, and NATO as the institutions to draw the new democracies into a larger zone of security and stability. The EC's launching of two intergovernmental conferences in December 1990—one on economic and monetary union, the other on political union—had made it plain that its internal transformation took precedence over the prospect of new members. The "deepeners," led by France, were ascendant over the "wideners." Nonetheless, the EC Commission had been authorized to negotiate association agreements—formally called the "Europe Agreements"—with Czechoslovakia, Hungary, and Poland. Ultimately signed in December 1991, the agreements provided for political consultations as well as significant market-opening measures (except in sensitive areas like agriculture).[37]

As to the Western European Union, Secretary General van Eekelen visited Warsaw to explore "ways in which the security needs of these countries might be addressed by the WEU."[38] But neither these initiatives nor the EC's Maastricht Treaty opened the door to full membership or provided a timetable toward that end. The French in particular were at pains to push prospective membership off into the indefinite future, notably in Mitterrand's dismissive remark in June 1991 that the new democracies might have to wait "decades" to join the EC because of the dilapidated state of their economies.[39]

NATO's Opening to the East   Meanwhile, NATO's first steps toward reaching out to the East had about run their course. These measures, adopted at NATO's July 1990 summit in London, included invitations to Warsaw Pact member governments to establish regular diplomatic liaison missions at NATO headquarters. NATO extended invitations to Gorbachev and the Central and Eastern European leaders to address the North Atlantic Council and intensified military-to-military contacts, including visits by NATO military commanders to Eastern capitals. NATO's opening also legitimized and provided a framework for various steps taken bilaterally, including Secretary Cheney's visits to Poland, Hungary, and Czechoslovakia in the course of 1991, which capped extensive military contacts at lower levels. Similar visits were made by his allied counterparts. A number of nonbinding bilateral agreements also were concluded, such as the U.S.-Polish declaration of March 1991 and the French-Polish friendship treaty of April 1991, and bilateral military-to-military programs were becoming more regular and extensive.

With the hardening of Soviet policies in early 1991, we in Washington began developing initiatives to strengthen and formalize the NATO liaison relationships. Inasmuch as the French were working hard to block even the modest measures agreed to at London, it was clear that we would need German cosponsorship of any new measures to develop NATO's outreach to the East. Then, working bilaterally with other key allies, particularly the British, Italians, and Dutch, we could build a NATO consensus and so isolate the French when it came time for a decision.

To pave the way for the NATO foreign ministers' meeting scheduled for June in Copenhagen, Secretary Baker and Foreign Minister Genscher proposed a long list of initiatives to strengthen the CSCE process and expand NATO's links with the East.[40] Although watered down by the French, most of the initiatives were endorsed by the Copenhagen meeting. The ministers expanded the liaison function through political visits and military exchanges at all levels, a strengthened security dialogue, and participation by Soviet and Eastern European officials in certain NATO activities. One such activity was cooperation in "airspace management," a handy euphemism that enabled us to address Central and Eastern European calls for assistance in air defense without unduly alarming the Soviet military.

The Copenhagen communiqué also established a new principle for the alliance, anticipating NATO's "new strategic concept" being readied for the Rome Summit in November: "Our own security is inseparably linked to that of all other states in Europe. The consolidation and preservation throughout the continent of democratic societies and their freedom from any form of coercion and intimidation are therefore of direct and material concern to us."[41]

The Rome Summit took place against the backdrop of epic events in the Soviet Union: the failed hard-line coup against Gorbachev, the ascendancy of Russian president Boris Yeltsin, and the collapse of the Soviet Communist party. Recognition of the independence of the Baltic states was accompanied by the growing disintegration of the Soviet state. NATO's promised "new strategic concept" acquired new urgency, to put it mildly.

In September, President Bush had already announced a series of dramatic, unilateral arms reduction measures and challenged Moscow to reciprocate. These measures included elimination of all U.S. ground-launched short-range nuclear weapons, artillery shells, and short-range ballistic missile warheads as well as removal of all tactical nuclear weapons from U.S. surface ships and attack submarines. The president also announced a standing down from alert status of all U.S. strategic bombers and intercontinental ballistic missiles and termination of several nuclear weapons programs.[42] Gorbachev did indeed respond in kind, but by this time he was presiding over a state on the brink of extinction.

The burden was therefore intense on NATO to demonstrate its relevance in a world without the threat it had been created to counter. At the same time, the Central and Eastern Europeans, at the front line of a Soviet Union that seemed on the brink of violent or at least chaotic disintegration, were clamoring for a more forthcoming NATO response to their security concerns.

During the period of the Soviet coup, Western leaders instinctively extended such reassurances as they could to Eastern Europe. The day of the coup attempt, when its outcome was still in doubt, President Bush spoke by telephone with Wałęsa, Havel, and Antall, noting in a press conference the next day that he had assured them "that the democratic processes in their countries cannot be reversed."[43] Western European leaders did likewise, pledging also to accelerate negotiations on EC association agreements. NATO placed the three leaders' concerns high on the agenda of an emergency foreign ministers' meeting in Brussels in late August, with Secretary Baker calling on the alliance to consider "further concrete ways in which we can bolster the processes of economic and political reform in Central and Eastern Europe."[44]

With NATO's initiatives once again wholly overtaken by events in the East, we began working with the Germans, British, and others on a more radical approach toward opening the alliance to the new democracies of the East. Foreign Minister Genscher's planned visit to Washington in early October, on the first anniversary of German unification, provided an ideal opportunity for another joint statement, this one aimed at influencing NATO's Rome Summit. A visit to the White House by Chancellor Kohl two weeks earlier had been an even better occasion, for which we at the NSC had prepared a draft statement; however, the president, preoccupied with the Middle East in the aftermath of Operation Desert Storm, returned the draft two or three times for shortening before finally electing not to use it at all.[45] We therefore looked to the Genscher visit to carry the message.

The objective was to bring the new democracies of Central and Eastern Europe, particularly the Visegrád group, closer to the alliance, while also providing a forum for more regular interaction with the Soviet Union. Instead of irregular visits and exchanges, we had in mind an entirely new institution that would bring NATO allies and former Warsaw Pact adversaries together in a forum for political consultation and defense cooperation. Trying to square the circle between Soviet sensibilities and Central and Eastern European nervousness, we devised a formula that would treat all former Warsaw Pact members equally as a formal matter but would in practice be highly differentiated in favor of the new democracies.

Creation of the North Atlantic Cooperation Council   Toward that end, Secretary Baker and Foreign Minister Genscher issued a joint statement after their October 2 meeting in Washington, calling for the upcoming summits of NATO, the EC, and the CSCE and the "fundamental transformations" they heralded to be "complementary and interdependent." As to NATO, new initiatives called for direct participation by the Central and Eastern European countries and the Soviet Union in meetings of NATO's Political and Economic Committees and establishment of NATO information offices in Eastern capitals. More important, they also called for creation of a new "North Atlantic Cooperation Council" to bring the countries of Central and Eastern Europe, as well as Baltic states and the Soviet Union, together with NATO in regular consultations at ambassadorial or foreign minister level.[46] The initiative was welcomed within hours in a joint statement issued by the "Visegrád" foreign ministers of Poland, Czechoslovakia, and Hungary.[47]

Creation of the North Atlantic Cooperation Council, or NACC, at the Rome Summit marked a reasonably successful conclusion to a year's intense effort to transform the alliance in ways relevant to the new security situation in the eastern part of the continent. As Bush had put it shortly after the failed August coup, "The world has changed at a fantastic pace, with each day writing a fresh page of history before yesterday's ink has even dried."[48] Banal, perhaps, but it conveyed something of the difficulty of keeping NATO's transformation more or less in step with history.

Although the NACC served some immediate objectives, it fit uneasily into the alphabet soup of existing European and transatlantic institutions. In particular, it seemed to vitiate efforts to strengthen the role of the CSCE. If the NACC, bringing together the most powerful countries of Europe and North America, was to meet regularly at foreign minister level to discuss matters of European security, what role did that leave for the CSCE? The French disliked the NACC from the outset, seeing it as an American effort to undermine the CSCE process by usurping its mandate under a new institution susceptible to American control. Relatedly, the inclusion of NATO and former Warsaw Pact members in the NACC meant exclusion of European neutrals and the nonaligned, notably Finland and Austria. Where did they fit in? If they were invited to participate, as eventually they were, did not this accentuate the NACC's duplication of the CSCE's membership and mission?

The NACC's most serious deficiency was that it fell between two stools: in trying to balance Central and Eastern European insistence on inclusion in Western security organizations against Soviet fears of exclusion, it wound up meeting neither objective and satisfying no one. The Soviet Union, and later Russia, did not see it as an institution worthy of a great power, even an enfeebled great power. The Central and Eastern Europeans felt that participating alongside the Russians in a NATO-related institution could only mean their own marginalization and indeed defeated their purpose in associating with NATO in the first place. They would join—what choice did they have?—but with their security concerns unanswered.

The fatal blow to the NACC came at its second meeting, held in March 1992, shortly after the disintegration of the Soviet Union. The first question to be answered in arranging the meeting was whom to invite among the newly independent states of the former Soviet Union. The Baltic states, whose independence we had recognized some months before, were already in. But what other countries should participate? All of them? Russia only? Russia and Ukraine? The nuclear states— Russia, Ukraine, Belarus, and Kazakhstan? A minority of us in Washington favored the latter solution, but we were quickly overruled by the senior levels of the administration as well as by nearly all the allies, who insisted that all the states of the former Soviet Union be invited and indeed encouraged to join the NACC.

The same issue arose in the CSCE and was handled in the same way, but with different implications. As an inclusive institution based on shared principles, the CSCE was an appropriate instrument for bringing the newly independent states into a larger community of values. There we had a positive interest in their association, which we rightly urged on them and then utilized to leverage their adherence to CSCE principles. In early 1992, as will be seen, Secretary Baker did just that, traveling to each of the newly independent states, armed with a long list of CSCE principles that he linked to the establishment of U.S. diplomatic relations. As an operational matter, the advent of so many new members made CSCE decision making even more cumbersome and tedious than it had been before, but these liabilities did not vitiate the organization's purpose.

The NACC, by contrast, was meant to be a security organization; the hasty and indiscriminate invitation to new members thousands of miles beyond the traditional NATO area only served to muddle the nascent institution's purpose. The argument in favor of this course—that the successor states to the Soviet Union should not be discriminated against—was hard to refute as a matter of principle, but as a matter of policy it preempted whatever role the NACC might have played in helping overcome the division of Europe. Secretary Baker, in his intervention at the NACC ministerial meeting, gamely put it this way: "Today we welcome the new states of the former Soviet Union into the NACC. Their presence expands our horizons."[49] In truth, our horizons were expanded to the NACC's vanishing point. At the first expanded meeting of the NACC,[50] the manifest lack of interest in NATO issues on the part of the newly independent states of Central Asia, and the consequent neglect of a focused agenda relevant to countries like Poland and Ukraine, made it plain that the NACC was already irrelevant. And if the NACC was irrelevant, what of NATO itself?

New Threats to Security

At the Rome Summit, NATO approved the alliance's "New Strategic Concept." As the summit communiqué explained it,

> We no longer face the old threat of a massive attack. However, prudence requires us to maintain an overall strategic balance and to remain ready to meet any potential risks to our security which may arise from instability or tension. . . . Our new strategic concept . . . allows us, within the radically changed situation in Europe, to realise in full our broad approach to stability and security encompassing political, economic, social and environmental aspects, along with the indispensable defence dimension. . . .
>
> Our military forces will adjust to their new tasks, becoming smaller and more flexible. Thus, our conventional forces will be substantially reduced as will, in many cases, their readiness. They will also be given increased mobility to enable them to react to a wide range of contingencies, and will be organized for flexible build-up, when necessary, for crisis management as well as defence. Multinational formations will play a greater role within the integrated military structure. Nuclear forces committed to NATO will be greatly reduced. . . .[51]

The summit also reaffirmed NATO's four new "core functions" that had been agreed on at the Copenhagen meeting of foreign ministers in June 1991. The second, third, and fourth of the four core functions were the familiar ones of dialogue, deterrence and defense, and preserving the strategic balance. What was new was the first: "to provide one of the indispensable foundations for a stable security environment in Europe, based on the growth of democratic institutions and commitment to the peaceful resolution of disputes, in which no country would be able to intimidate or coerce any European nation or to impose hegemony through the threat or use of force."

General Colin Powell, chairman of the Joint Chiefs of Staff, put it more succinctly: "NATO's original purpose—providing security for the West—is still very relevant. NATO's new, added purpose is to help build stability in the east and, in turn, stability in all of Europe."[52]

This was, of course, the right orientation for NATO in the new era—indeed the only one for it to adopt if the alliance were to be relevant to the new threats to European security. The creation of a NATO rapid re-action force was an appropriate adaptation of the alliance to new challenges, as were similar efforts taken by the Western Europeans via the WEU and the new "Eurocorps." But "instability," "tension," and "uncertainty" were elusive enemies, for which NATO was not well suited. Taken together with the solemn reaffirmation that "the Alliance is the essential forum for consultation among its members and the venue for agreement on policies bearing on the security and defence commitments of Allies under the Washington Treaty," the Rome Summit had assigned NATO a potentially open-ended set of responsibilities for exorcising the demons unleashed with the end of Cold War rigidities.

CSCE's Role in Conflict Resolution　It was in this context that the alliance, following the lead of the Baker-Genscher joint statements, looked to a strengthened CSCE as "the organ for consultation and cooperation among all participating States, capable of effective action in line with its new and increased responsibilities . . . for effective crisis management and peaceful settlement of disputes." The Rome declaration called on the forthcoming Helsinki Summit to strengthen the roles of the Committee of Senior Officials, Conflict Prevention Center, and Office of Free Elections, as well as to establish organizational and operational links among the CSCE, NATO, the EC, and other institutions. It further proposed that CSCE decision-making rules, which required unanimous consent, be amended to what came to be known as "consensus minus one," whereby action could be taken against a state in "cases of clear, gross, and uncorrected violations of relevant CSCE commitments, if necessary in the absence of the consent of the state concerned."

Since the Paris Summit, the CSCE had been grappling with two separate dimensions of these problems: the rights of national minorities and mechanisms for the peaceful settlement of disputes. The first effort aimed at developing a set of principles and procedures that would help prevent or contain ethnic conflict before it erupted into violent confrontation; the second sought to develop a full array of conflict resolution mechanisms from arbitration and mediation through sanctions, peacekeeping, and potential peacemaking (i.e., imposing and enforcing a peace between two combatants).

Minority rights had been one of the most contentious issues at CSCE's Copenhagen conference of June 1990, which made little headway and so devolved discussion to a separate meeting of experts, convened in Geneva in July 1991. This meeting, too, reflected sharp divisions and essentially irreconcilable positions. There were definitional and conceptual problems. Which "minorities" are covered—national, religious, territorial? Do minorities have rights as individuals, derived from citizenship in states adhering to international human rights conventions, or do they have collective rights derived from their belonging to an identifiable group? Relatedly, should states be obliged simply to ensure equal rights and equal protection under the law on a nondiscriminatory basis, or should they take active measures to promote those rights, extending preferential treatment to disadvantaged minority groups?

Hungary wanted extensive, internationally supervised rights accorded to the millions of Hungarians living outside its borders; Romania opposed such measures as infringements on its sovereignty. A Hungarian draft proposal, for example, listed some twenty separate rights of national minorities, including the "right to an appropriate form of self-government," and would have enjoined participating states to "guarantee the protection as well as *the possibility for the effective exercise* of the rights of national minorities."[53] At Geneva, the head of the Hungarian delegation added that "special measures, including legal guarantees, should be adopted to ensure genuine equality and compensate for [minorities'] disadvantages."[54] Few countries were prepared to go that far, but most wanted to go beyond the language of existing international documents in recognizing group as well as individual rights.

As a statement of common principles, the Geneva conference report was a great success, by far the most extensive delineation of minority rights ever produced in an international document. As an operational document, however, it failed to establish specific commitments that could be invoked by the international community in cases of violations of the rights of national minorities or disputes arising therefrom.[55] The 11-page document began with the existing United Nations formulation of "rights of persons belonging to national minorities," but added that "peace, justice, stability and democracy require that the ethnic, cultural, linguistic and religious identity of national minorities be protected, and conditions for the promotion of that identity be created." The conference thus acknowledged the collective rights of minority groups while giving precedence to individual rights.

The document also distinguished between cultural rights, which were given extensive and precise treatment, and political rights, which were treated much more gingerly. Thus the report presented a long list of the rights of national minorities, including development of their ethnic, cultural, linguistic, and religious identities free from involuntary assimilation. It also specified the freedom to use one's mother tongue, establish institutions and associations, participate in public affairs, and engage in contacts across national frontiers. The report provided examples of specific political arrangements such as local and autonomous administration, commissions of mixed nationalities, and special provisions for minority representation in parliamentary bodies. But these were in no way binding on the signatory states and indeed were prefaced by the disclaimer that "the diversity and varying constitutional systems among them . . . make no single approach necessarily generally applicable."

Similar, but more damaging, limitations beset efforts to devise new mechanisms for conflict resolution, which was the mandate of an experts meeting held in Valletta, Malta, in January and February 1991. The meeting report, like that from Geneva, was long on principles and short on commitments.[56] It presented a reasonable set of measures for the peaceful settlement of disputes (known in CSCE jargon as the PSD), expanding the roles of the CSCE's Committee of Senior Officials and Conflict Prevention Center and establishing links with existing bodies like the International Court of Justice and Permanent Court of Arbitration. It also created a new facility, darkly termed "the mechanism," that specified a series of measures that could be invoked, including a list of mediators from CSCE members whose services could be drawn upon.

Yet none of these steps could be made binding on recalcitrant states. Under the heading "strengthening of commitments," each particular was prefaced by a qualifying phrase like "endeavor to," "to the extent possible," and, six times in a list of eleven measures, "consider" doing this or that. The entire document, moreover, was limited by an exceptions clause inserted at the end (Section XII) that prohibits use or continuation of "the mechanism" if any party considers that the dispute "raises issues concerning its territorial integrity, or national defence, title to sovereignty over land territory, or competing claims with regard to the jurisdiction over other areas."

Valletta's results were exasperating to those of us back in Washington who had been working to find ways and means to resolve the growing crisis in Yugoslavia. Every delegation at Valletta, including ours, made certain that nothing was agreed to that might potentially be invoked against its own country. The United States even shared responsibility for the meeting's failure to specify a CSCE lead institution for "the mechanism," so even the meager provisions agreed to remained inoperative. For reasons known only to the State Department's hardy band of experts, who had been steeped in the arcana of the CSCE process during the Cold War period but were not ready temperamentally to adapt the organization for new purposes, the U.S. delegation was instructed to oppose the EC's preferred institution, the Conflict Prevention Center. Other delegations were similarly staffed with CSCE hands of the old school—the "CSCE Jesuits," as I called them—which made innovation elusive.

It was a particularly egregious lack of diplomatic consistency, for, as the following chapter reveals, we had been littering Europe with cables urging concerted action to avert an impending crisis in Yugoslavia—yet we had failed to empower our own delegation at Valletta to make the CSCE an effective instrument toward that end. The reason for our inattention was that at the same time, in February 1991, the United States was preparing half a million coalition troops for the air and ground assault against Iraqi forces in Operation Desert Storm. Under the circumstances, one could hardly expect Secretary Baker—the only top administration official who paid attention to CSCE matters—to focus on the goings-on in Valletta.

By the time of the CSCE ministerial in Berlin in June, the senior levels of the administration were reengaged, having prepared the way with initiatives contained in the Baker-Genscher statement of the month before. This German-American coordination was especially useful, for Genscher, as foreign minister of the host country, was in the chair at Berlin and ran the proceedings with an efficiency not seen before in the CSCE. Like the Germans, we wanted to use Berlin, the first meeting of the Council of Ministers since the body had been approved at the Paris Summit, to strengthen the CSCE's conflict prevention capacities, with the Yugoslav crisis the case in point. Indeed, as will be seen, the main import of the Berlin meeting was the behind-the-scenes negotiations on Yugoslavia, to which Baker was flying immediately after the meeting.

Baker quickly overrode his experts and supported the EC in designating the Conflict Prevention Center as the lead institution for the peaceful settlement of disputes mechanism. With Baker and Genscher taking turns bluntly pointing out that history would not treat kindly ministers who failed to adopt measures relevant to the crisis in Yugoslavia, the Berlin meeting created a mechanism for calling emergency meetings on the demand of at least 12 countries, a number that could be easily come by if needed but sufficiently high to prevent frivolous or purely partisan convocations.[57] It was a small achievement, to be sure, but the fact that no such procedure existed before was illustrative of how urgently we were scrambling to give the CSCE even the rudiments of an operational capacity. Indeed, this new mechanism was used twice within two weeks, as we and others called for emergency meetings of the Conflict Prevention Center and Committee of Senior Officials to deal with the outbreak of violence in Yugoslavia. Finally, the Berlin conference endorsed mechanisms providing, in theory at least, an unprecedented level of intrusiveness in the internal affairs of a member state whose actions were seen as jeopardizing security and stability.

Under pressure from the unfolding crisis in Yugoslavia, the next CSCE meeting—the long-scheduled Moscow human rights conference, the last of a triad that began in Paris in 1989 and continued in Copenhagen in 1990—took further steps in this direction. Meeting in September and October 1991, the Moscow conference, in addition to admitting the three Baltic states as CSCE members, approved a "human dimension mechanism" to monitor human and minority rights commitments.[58] It authorized a progression of steps, beginning with a request by any CSCE member state for a human rights observer mission to be sent to any other state to investigate possible abuses and continuing with procedures incrementally more intrusive and mandatory. Under the mandatory procedure, one state seconded by nine others could direct that human rights observers be sent to any other state, immediately and without right of refusal. For the CSCE, since its inception in 1975 governed by the principle of voluntary consent, the adoption of mandatory procedures was revolutionary indeed. Even more so was Foreign Minister Genscher's call for the CSCE to employ collective sanctions against a member state in serious violation of CSCE principles, without that state's consent.

The Helsinki Summit of the CSCE   By the time of the Helsinki Summit of July 1992, culminating three and a half months of negotiations at Helsinki, CSCE had indeed acquired the institutional capacity for imposing sanctions, as well as for peacekeeping.[59] It had established itself as a regional organization under Chapter VIII of the UN Charter and forged institutional linkages with the EC, NATO, the WEU, the NACC, the Council of Europe, and other organizations, as well as with nonmembers like Japan. Its organizational structure was tightened through such measures as the formation of a "troika" of past, present, and future host country foreign ministers. It had created a CSCE "Forum for Security Cooperation" to deal with all European arms control issues, along with various fora devoted to economic development, migration problems, and the like.

New procedures had been elaborated to prevent any one state or group of states from preventing action by the others. Indeed, so extensive were the provisions under the human dimension mechanism (HDM) and peaceful settlement of disputes (PSD) mechanism, that the State Department's European bureau prepared a large spreadsheet, in small type, to keep track of the various mechanisms and modalities now available. The Helsinki Summit created the position of high commissioner on national minorities, as the CSCE's highest permanent official, whose mandate was early warning, conflict management, and crisis prevention. CSCE also had created a full array of mechanisms for dealing with conflict: early warning, political consultation and suasion, fact-finding and observer missions, mediation and arbitration, sanctions, and peacekeeping operations, including the capacity to call on NATO, the NACC, or the WEU to mount peacekeeping operations under the CSCE's mandate.

NATO's peacekeeping role had been the most contentious issue in the run-up to Helsinki. The French, clinging to their position that NATO's responsibilities should be strictly limited to Article 5 security commitments involving direct attack against an allied state, had opposed any role whatever in "out of area" peacekeeping. They sought instead to invest the CSCE alone with that mandate, leaving NATO and the NACC on the sidelines. Nearly every other CSCE member disagreed, seeing no point in creating a separate CSCE peacekeeping capacity when such capacities already existed elsewhere. Neither we nor any other state wished NATO to arrogate unto itself sole responsibility in this area: we not only accepted but actively supported a flexible approach that would allow the CSCE to call on any of several institutions or ad hoc coalitions of states, depending on the circumstances. At the opening of the Helsinki review conference in March, a large majority of states favored this approach; by the July Summit ending the session, France was outnumbered 51 to 1. Finally persuaded of the futility of opposing a NATO role that Russia, the Vatican, and every other European state welcomed, the French relented on the last day. In this instance at least, the "new European architecture" made good sense.

Although the CSCE's role in the Yugoslav conflict was much criticized, the deficiencies of international action were not institutional or architectural; they had to do with the more pertinent question of how national governments proposed to deal with the new threats to European security. Two problems were paramount and did not lend themselves to easy solution. The first was the problem of dealing with conflicts arising within rather than between states. Neither institutions nor their member states found it easy to engage with sufficient resolve in the internal affairs of another state until the problem had in fact moved from conflict prevention to crisis management. At that point the problem of mobilizing force against local conflicts arose.

Germany was constrained for historical and constitutional reasons from engaging directly in such military operations. The French and British had recent memories of the postcolonial conflicts in which they had been embroiled, and our own country had long been allergic to messy military entanglements. It was President Wilson who said, in trying to reassure the American public about the League of Nations, "If you want to put out a fire in Utah, you do not send to Oklahoma for the fire engine. If you want to put out a fire in the Balkans, . . . you do not send to the United States for troops."[60]

The CSCE could serve to filter out conflicts in which we had no desire to involve ourselves and refer those in which we did have a stake to NATO or the UN, where we could consider joining a multinational force, or the WEU, where we could perhaps take on a support role. But such modalities could not answer the questions of which conflicts involved important U.S. interests and whether we and other CSCE states were prepared to act decisively when such interests clearly were at stake, as in Bosnia.

8

The Return of History

JUST AS THE SECOND WORLD WAR was a continuation of the conflicts that had produced the First, the end of the Cold War summoned forth issues that had arisen at the beginning of the century from the breakup of the multiethnic Turkish, Austrian, German, and Russian empires. The disintegration of the first two was complete; on their ruins came a set of weak new states, some of them, notably Yugoslavia, the artificial constructs of the peacemakers at Versailles. The third great empire, the German, had its brutal revival under the Third Reich but ended with Germany defeated and divided.

Only the fourth empire, the Russian, survived. It was a close call. For much of 1919, the Red Army controlled little more than the territory of sixteenth-century Muscovite Russia.[1] Ukraine was not conquered until late 1920. The Caucasus, Central Asia, and eastern Russia were not subdued for two years more. So fractious and artificial was the new Soviet empire that only totalitarian dictatorship could hold it together. Yet survive it did, not only withstanding the German onslaught in World War II but emerging from the war with its territory enhanced by the annexation of the Baltic states and Bessarabia. The survival of such a state for nearly seventy years, and its acquisition of military power second only to the United States, was enough to impress even the staunchest adversaries with its staying power.

Yet the nature of totalitarian rule made it hard to detect the deep crisis in the empire of Soviet Russia. Causes had no effects: social and economic pressures that should have had profound consequences for the Soviet system produced none, at least none that could be discerned. Recurrent agricultural crises led not to agrarian movements and land reform but to a perpetuation of the agricultural system that had brought about the crises in the first place. The failures of central economic planning caused barely a ripple in the regime's economic strategy. Conflicts arising from the dispersed nationalities of this multiethnic empire were resolved with ruthless dispatch. "Kremlinologists" were reduced to investigating political struggles among the handful of top party leaders, as if those were the true manifestations of seventy years of history of a transcontinental power.

Inasmuch as the Turkish, Austro-Hungarian, and German empires broke apart with extreme violence, it had been assumed throughout the Cold War that the Soviet empire could only end violently.[2] It was an expectation reinforced by the history of another strange artifact of the century's first war—Yugoslavia. The semivoluntary "Kingdom of the Serbs, Croats, and Slovenes" proclaimed at the end of World War I had become a decade later a Serb-dominated dictatorship beset with separatist pressures, principally from the Croats. Under the conditions of German occupation, these national conflicts boiled over into a civil war that claimed over a million lives between 1941 and 1945. The unity imposed under communist rule initially followed the Soviet "model," but recurrent nationalist challenges led to a series of concessions to republican autonomy. By the time of Marshal Josip Tito's death in 1980, Yugoslavia was neither centralized enough for effective leadership in Belgrade nor decentralized enough for genuine federalism to take hold. And the galvanizing element of a Soviet threat was fast disappearing.

It should not have been surprising that the most artificial and tenuous of the states arising out of imperial breakup at the time of the First World War—Yugoslavia and the Soviet Union—were the first casualties of the post–Cold War era. They were anachronisms, lacking a raison d'être other than the authoritarian rule that had held them together for most of the century. So, to a lesser degree, was Czecho-Slovakia, another artifical construct of Versailles and the third early casualty of the new era.

Yet the disintegration of these states did catch the outside world by surprise. Of course, we could see the evidence of disintegration as events unfolded, but our frame of reference did not allow for a full appreciation of what these trends portended. We were intellectually prepared for the liberation of the countries of Central and Eastern Europe, including the Baltic states, as we were for German unification. The swiftness and scope of change may have been unexpected, but not the events themselves, for they fit our Cold War frame of reference. But the disintegration of the Soviet Union and Yugoslavia belonged to an entirely different logic, whose antecedents were to be found not in the period of Cold War but in the era of imperial dissolution at the beginning of the century.[3]

The end of the Cold War was not the "end of history" and the final triumph of liberal democracy, as Francis Fukuyama had argued in his controversial essay.[4] It was, rather, the *return* of history in the sense that the lifting of authoritarian control had opened the way for the interplay of competing forces through which history became possible. More than one observer reached for the metaphor of the deep freeze. It was apt. The warming of East-West relations had thawed out historical problems that had been frozen not only during the Cold War but, in the Soviet and Yugoslav cases, for most of the century.[5]

Well before the revolutions of 1989, Eastern European dissidents warned that powerful social pressures were waiting "under the ice" and that the seemingly powerless dissident movement would become the "icebreaker with a kamikaze crew."[6] These brilliantly jarring metaphors would prove all too prophetic with regard to the coming self-destruction of Yugoslavia.

The Yugoslav Tragedy

The bloody disintegration of Yugoslavia, and the helplessness of the international community in the face of it, revealed how far post–Cold War Europe was from a secure and peaceful new order. The failures of Western policy proceeded in part from the fact that this was the first major challenge to the emerging order and, in particular, the first test in this new era of the ill-defined concept of "self-determination" arising in a multiethnic state. If anything positive came of the conspicuous failure of efforts to hold together a fragmenting Yugoslav federation, it was that we applied these bitter lessons in our approach toward the (relatively uncomplicated) split of Czechoslovakia and, with greater success than has so far been credited, to the much more critical challenge of dealing with a disintegrating Soviet Union.

Yugoslavia was a portent of the post–Cold War era in another sense. At the heart of the problem for Western governments lay the judgment, reached early on in Washington and most European capitals, that Yugoslavia no longer mattered much because it was no longer likely to be an arena of East-West conflict. As Warren Zimmermann, the last U.S. ambassador to Yugoslavia, noted in his memoirs: "[Deputy Secretary of State] Eagleburger and I agreed that in my introductory calls in [in early 1989] in Belgrade and the republican capitals, I would deliver a new message: Yugoslavia no longer enjoyed the geopolitical importance that the United States had given it during the Cold War."[7]

From this flawed premise—a case of applying yesterday's strategic logic to tomorrow's problems—flawed policies ensued. As the conflict deepened, policy was caught between lofty principle and uncertain resolve. As it threatened to spread, Western policy awakened to the fact that this region did indeed matter, but for an entirely different set of reasons than had been assumed and internalized during the long years of Cold War in Europe.

Democracy versus Unity   The error was not that the administration failed to see it coming.[8] Well before 1989, it was clear that Yugoslavia was in deep crisis,[9] owing to the collapse of central authority (under the system of collective leadership Marshal Tito left behind) and to a Serbian campaign to overturn what a notorious 1986 memorandum of the Serbian Academy of Sciences argued was an anti-Serb conspiracy in federal Yugoslavia. It is probably true, as Zimmermann argued, that Serbian leader Slobodan Milošević was motivated by considerations of political power and not by ideology, but he quickly seized nationalist demagoguery as the vehicle to election as Serbian president in 1987 and to his consolidation of power thereafter.[10] As other republics, especially Slovenia, distanced themselves from Serbian-dominated federal institutions, the political agenda in Serbia turned increasingly toward creation of a "greater Serbia" inspired by its medieval kingdom and embracing Montenegro, most of Bosnia-Herzegovina, and perhaps Macedonia as well.[11]

Yet in the cavalcade of events in the fall of 1989, one passed almost unnoticed: the mid-October visit to Washington by Yugoslav prime minister Ante Marković, for meetings with President Bush and officials of the International Monetary Fund. In retrospect, we and our European partners should have paid more attention to Marković's efforts to forge a new Yugoslav consensus on economic and political reform. As it turned out, his visit was like the sound of one hand clapping: he got a polite hearing and words of encouragement, but no tangible economic or political support. After the U.S.-led "Friends of Yugoslavia" economic assistance effort in the early 1980s and the futile attempts to support the on-again, off-again economic reform program of Marković's predecessor, Branko Mikulić, we were wary of committing ourselves to another effort to support a Yugoslav leader who had yet to demonstrate his authority among the country's disparate republics.

Was Marković Yugoslavia's last hope, or was he already marginal to the real political struggle over the future of the federation? If the former was true, then we should have lent him all possible support. If the latter, we should have concluded that Yugoslavia was already doomed and begun preparing for its dissolution. Yet in the early fall of 1989, preoccupied as we were with the dramatic events taking place in Central Europe, we failed to translate our worry over Yugoslavia into meaningful policy.

By the spring and early summer of 1990, as the rest of Central and Eastern Europe was moving rapidly toward democratic rule, we were viewing events in Yugoslavia with growing alarm. Prime minister Marković's program of economic "shock therapy," launched in January 1990, produced encouraging initial results, but these were already being overshadowed by the steady disintegration of the federation. That same month the Yugoslav Communist party (the LCY, or League of Communists of Yugoslavia) adjourned in acrimony from its party congress, never to reconvene. Marković's hopes for Yugoslav-wide democratic elections were preempted by a series of elections in individual republics, beginning with Slovenia and Croatia in April and May.

With Yugoslav federal institutions crumbling, the political dynamic shifted to the republics. The question became whether the process of democratization within republics could produce leaders who would use their newly acquired legitimacy to negotiate among themselves a democratic arrangement for the Yugoslav state, reconstituted along looser federal or confederal lines. Indeed, had the democratic tide washed more evenly over the Yugoslav republics, such an arrangement might have been feasible—and consistent with Marković's economic and political reforms. As it was, embryonic democratic forces in Serbia were no match for the nationalistic hatreds unleashed and manipulated by Serbian president Slobodan Milošević. The newly elected presidents of Slovenia and Croatia, Milan Kučan and Franjo Tudjman, moved quickly to distance their republics from an increasingly repressive Serbia and the federal institutions it dominated. By July Slovenia had severed political and economic ties with the federal government, declaring itself a

sovereign republic whose laws took precedence over those of the federation. Croatia, meanwhile, had effectively disenfranchised its large Serbian minority by launching a propaganda barrage—particularly in areas
like Krajina, where Serbs held a local majority—and proclaiming the republic "the national state of the Croatian nation."[12]

By this time, it was evident that Yugoslavia was in the advanced
stages of disintegration. It was also clear that a breakup would be contested and violent. This, indeed, was the essence of a national intelligence estimate prepared during this period and leaked to the *New York
Times* upon its release in November 1990.[13] No one in the policy community disagreed with the main thrust of these judgments—only with
the smug finality with which they were rendered. Yet the estimate had
little impact, for it was so unrelievedly deterministic that it suggested no
possible avenue for American policy that might avert or at least contain
the violence attending Yugoslavia's seemingly inevitable disintegration.
Even when the intelligence community gets it right, as it did in this case,
it can get it wrong by being too detached from the exigencies of policy
making.[14]

The failures were not of analysis but of policy. Partly it was that the
crisis we saw coming was too catastrophic to accept. Senior staff are always prone to the hubris of believing they can change history's course
by dint of their own exertions and the farsightedness of their ideas.
These extravagances were accentuated in the Yugoslav case, for the crisis unfolded at the very moment of the democratic liberation of Central
and Eastern Europe. With democracy ascendant everywhere, it was
hard to credit what our dispassionate analysis told us: that the peoples
of Yugoslavia would choose this moment once again to reach for the
long knives.

When the foreign policy archives of this period are opened, the unfolding of Western approaches toward Yugoslavia in 1990 and the first
half of 1991 will present an exquisitely well-documented case study.
Thereafter, as the senior levels of government considered what to do as
Yugoslavia descended into civil war, the story became more opaque,
and much of the informal decision-making process was not recorded in
the official records. But in this initial period, nearly the full story was
laid out in a series of diplomatic exchanges between Washington and
every European capital, all carried via State Department cables. If the
future historian wants to know the official position of Norway, Romania, or the Vatican at the moment of Yugoslavia's breakup—as well as

the British, French, German, and Soviet positions—it will be laid out with a thoroughness and transparency rarely available in the annals of modern diplomacy.

In late summer 1990, we sent lengthy cables to every European capital, explaining, along the lines of the national intelligence estimate then being prepared (but issued a couple of months later), that our government believed that events were propelling Yugoslavia toward disintegration, that the disintegration would be bloody, and that this course of events no longer could be averted by the protagonists themselves. Strenuous, concerted engagement by the international community, the cable continued, would be required if catastrophe were to be averted. The cables did not propose a specific set of policies, but focused on such critical elements as a common international position on recognition of breakaway states and on the use of force to suppress independence movements. They also raised the issue of internationally supervised guarantees for national minorities—particularly the Serbian minority in Croatia. As this was preeminently a matter of European stability, we looked to Europe to take the lead in mobilizing the international community. The Yugoslavia crisis, the cables concluded, should be the subject of urgent consultations in NATO and at the CSCE Summit in Paris in November.

The replies that trickled in over the next few weeks were shockingly irresponsible. Only the Austrians and Hungarians, as I recall, fully endorsed our views. The Germans and British said that they shared some of our concerns but that we were overreacting and that it was certainly premature to consider the steps we proposed. The French likewise accused us of "overdramatizing" the situation, rejected NATO consultations, and warned that if we tried to raise this at the Paris Summit, they would consider it a "summit-breaker"—meaning that its inclusion was for them, as hosts, out of the question. More reasonably, several respondents argued that the international community should await the results of the remaining republic-level elections and particularly the Serbian elections in December 1990. With the senior levels of the U.S. administration preoccupied with Iraq and unwilling to press matters on Yugoslavia, we reluctantly agreed to wait. It was a mistake.

Absent a Western consensus, the State Department issued a statement on October 19 that carried a formulation we would repeat many times over the next year: "The US firmly supports unity, democratic change, respect for human rights, and market reform in Yugoslavia. We believe that democracy is the only enduring basis for a united, prosperous and voluntary Yugoslav union. . . . We would strongly oppose any use of force that would block democratic change in Yugoslavia."

By the beginning of 1991, the Yugoslav crisis had deepened. Serbia had become more truculent with the reelection of Slobodan Milošević as president. Slovenia, in its December 23 referendum, had voted overwhelmingly for independence, agreeing only to defer actual implementation for six months. With the clock ticking, we sent another round of cables to European capitals in January 1991. The replies from European capitals this time were more receptive, though the French and others who had argued in September that international involvement was premature now said it was too late!

The international community had missed a critical six-month period during which it might have organized for coordinated engagement of the Yugoslavs. As it turned out, it was only after the Serbian walkout from the Yugoslav presidential council in March—blocking the looser federal structure agreed to by the other republics and prompting Croatia to follow Slovenia in declaring its independence[15]—that the Europeans belatedly took up the challenge. A common strategy of sorts was hammered out then between the United States and the European Community.

The decision to keep NATO in the background was another mistake. It made some sense at the time, in that the EC had more immediate leverage over the Yugoslav protagonists—via a $4 billion economic aid package and the prospect of eventual association or even membership. But it was the wrong institution to exert credible pressure on the combatants once armed conflict erupted. Only NATO could do that, and NATO could do it only if the United States were prepared to lead. We were not. The upper levels of the administration overruled recommendations at staff level that NATO take the lead under CSCE mandate. Worse, the Department of Defense and the Joint Chiefs were at pains to exclude the military option a priori and, fresh from the military triumph in the Gulf, their opinions carried even more weight in administration councils than usual. In early June, for example, NATO's SACEUR (Supreme Allied Commander, Europe), General John Galvin, was quoted in a Belgrade daily as saying that "NATO [would] not intervene in Yugoslavia" because it was "not within NATO's defense zone."[16]

The European Community, newly committed to building political union, was eager to demonstrate its capacity for concerted action in foreign policy; Washington, having just led the international coalition to defeat Iraq in the Gulf War and still tied down with its messy aftermath, was eager to let the Europeans take the lead this time. In June, the EC dispatched commission president Jacques Delors and Prime Minister Jacques Santer of Luxembourg (in its capacity as EC presidency country on six-month rotation) to Belgrade. Shortly thereafter, Luxembourg's foreign minister Jacques Poos, speaking for the "troika" of EC foreign ministers, declared (in a line reminiscent of Neville Chamberlain's "peace in our time"), "This is the hour of Europe. It is not the hour of the Americans."[17]

U.S.-EC coordination worked well for a time. Secretary Baker and his EC counterparts conferred intensely on the margins of a CSCE foreign ministers' meeting in Berlin in late June, building support for the Community's taking the lead on behalf of the CSCE. The declaration issued at the end of the meeting "expressed friendly concern and support for the democratic development, unity, and territorial integrity of Yugoslavia" and called for continued dialogue among all parties "without recourse to the use of force and in conformity with legal and constitutional procedures."[18] It was a limp statement that came down too hard on the side of unity, but it was the best we could do, given that CSCE resolutions required unanimous consent. Yugoslav foreign minister Budimir Lončar agreed to this much only after intense lobbying in Berlin by Baker and EC foreign ministers, who also agreed that the secretary should convey their common position directly to Yugoslav leaders.

The Baker Visit to Belgrade Armed with a CSCE mandate of sorts and having coordinated with his EC counterparts, Baker flew from Berlin to Belgrade to make a last-ditch try at bringing Yugoslavia's leaders back from the brink. The visit—which I, among others, had recommended—was a mistake. Baker himself had misgivings, which were amply confirmed in Belgrade. For one thing, it came too late by several months at least. Positions among republics were all but fixed: Slovenia was already determined to declare its independence, and Croatia, not wishing to be left behind in a Serb-dominated Yugoslavia, was sure to follow. For another, in trying to avert disaster and embracing various formulae (advanced by federal prime minister Marković, Macedonian president Kiro Gligorov, and Bosnian president Alija Izetbegović) for a "new, democratic unity" with substantially greater autonomy for republics, we put ourselves in a position of equidistance between the

Slovenes and the Serbs. Worse, by warning equally against unilateral declarations of independence and the use of force to hold the federation together, we seemed to be sanctioning the latter if the Slovenes and Croats resorted to the former.

Baker tried heroically. In a 12-hour marathon he met first with Marković and Lončar, then with Kosovar Albanian leader Ibrahim Rugova,[19] throughout the afternoon and early evening with each of the six republic presidents, and finished with another meeting with Marković and Lončar over dinner. Zimmermann and I alternated as note-takers.[20] Baker's message was that the United States would support any future arrangement among the peoples of Yugoslavia that was reached consensually and peacefully; we would oppose any unilateral secession as well as the use of force or incitement to violence.[21] "If you force the United States to choose between unity and democracy," he said, "we will always choose democracy."[22] Tactically, he pressed hard to effect a mini-compromise, whereby the Serbs and Montenegrins would unblock the federal presidency (thus preserving an interrepublic negotiating forum, however weak) and the Slovenes would declare their independence but take no precipitous steps to implement it (thus preserving a possibility, however slim, for continued dialogue and negotiation).

Baker was disciplined, focused, persistent, and blunt—all to no effect.[23] His interlocutors were not to be moved. Milošević was a consummate dissembler and ruthless leader who might have been impressed by real military power but not by diplomatic overtures. Tudjman was a romantic lost in dreams of a glorious Croatian past that never was. Kučan, the Slovenian president, was a seemingly decent man who nonetheless was prepared to leave the Bosnians and Croatians to a bloody inferno that he knew his country would escape. Montenegrin president Momir Bulatović was a young rogue whose vote to block the rotation of the federal presidency gave him a role in history disproportionate to his meager attributes. Among the republic leaders, the only reasonable ones were Gligorov and Izetbegović, who had little to gain and much to lose by Yugoslavia's disintegration. But like Marković and Lončar, they were by this point marginal to the drama unfolding among the Serbians, Croatians, and Slovenians.

Baker summed up his meetings in a statement to the press based on a text that his staff and I had hastily drafted. Although noting that his interlocutors had expressed support for his appeals for dialogue and nonuse of force, he was pessimistic:

We came to Yugoslavia because of our concern about . . . the dangers of a disintegration of this country [which] could have some very tragic consequences. . . . The 34 other countries of the CSCE . . . have all expressed, along with us, our collective concern. . . . I have conveyed these very serious concerns about the future of this country in the meetings I have been privileged to have. In all candor, ladies and gentlemen, what I heard today has not allayed my concerns. Nor, I suspect, will it allay the concerns of others when we give them a readout of these meetings.

In all of these meetings, I stressed the importance of respecting human and minority rights, of continuing the process of democratization, and of continuing a dialogue to create a new basis for unity. In particular, I emphasized the need to move ahead on the constitutional rotation of the federal presidency, as well as the need to avoid unilateral acts that could preempt the negotiating process. . . .

We will be consulting with the European Community and other interested members of the international community. Based on these discussions today, I am very hopeful that notwithstanding all of the difficulties, there is some prospect for continued dialogue. . . . But in the end. . . , it is really going to be up to the people of Yugoslavia whether or not these problems are overcome.

In response to a question from the press, Baker asserted that the United States would not recognize Slovenia's forthcoming declaration of independence "because we want to see this problem resolved through negotiation and dialogue and not through preemptive unilateral actions." He then amplified what we meant by Yugoslav "unity" in the new circumstances: "a new basis for the unity of Yugoslavia" based on "the devolution of additional authority, responsibility, and sovereignty to the republics of Yugoslavia."[24]

Because Baker was silent on the question of possible military or other reprisals in the event of violent suppression of independence movements in Yugoslavia, the visit was later interpreted to have given Milošević and the Yugoslav national army (JNA) a "green light" to resort to force. This contention needs careful analysis. It is true that if Baker did not signal a green light, he did not flash a red one either. Had we concluded beforehand that trying to restrain the Slovenians and Croatians was at this point futile, we would have been better advised to devote all our energies to warning the Serbs and the Yugoslav military against the use of force, leaving open the possibility of Western military reprisals if they failed to heed the warning. Yet the question ultimately was whether we were prepared to *use* force, not whether we were prepared to threaten to do so—and certainly not what Baker said or failed to say in Belgrade. There would be endless opportunities for testing American resolve, so a mere bluff would not have deterred the aggression that followed. One therefore should not exaggerate the impact of the Baker visit on the main protagonists: the conflict would have unfolded pretty much as it did had Baker not gone. At best, the visit was worth the try, even though it failed. At worst, it was simply irrelevant.

The real impact of the visit was on U.S. policy, because the intractability of the conflict and the bloody-mindedness of republic leaders led Secretary Baker and others to wash their hands of whole mess. "We got no dog in this fight" was thenceforth the watchword of American policy.

Spreading Violence   Events moved rapidly thereafter. Within days of Baker's visit, Slovenia and Croatia declared their independence, the former seizing control of customs posts in one of the escalating steps Baker had urged them to forego. When Yugoslav army units moved in and armed conflict began, Slovenia declared a "state of war" and appealed for international assistance. Within a week, the EC troika had mounted three separate missions to Yugoslavia, two at foreign minister level, and the CSCE convened twice to condemn the use of force. Brandishing the threat of economic sanctions, the EC brokered the July 5 Brioni Agreement providing for the withdrawal to barracks of the Yugoslav army and the disarming of the Slovenian militia.[25] But the skirmish in Slovenia, which Milošević was never interested in fighting for anyway, was just the prelude to the real battles over Croatia and Bosnia-Herzegovina.

The Croatian leaders, surprised by Slovenia's successful defiance (which they had conspicuously failed to support), hastily moved to implement their own independence declaration—prompting Serb-dominated Krajina to declare its independence from Croatia. That move in turn led the largely Croatian city of Kijevo within Krajina to repudiate the latter's authority and declare *its* allegiance to Croatia. "Self-determination" at work! Serb-Croat clashes erupted and intensified in July and August. Cease-fires were repeatedly broken. JNA forces moved en masse from Serbia into Croatia in preparation for full-scale war. Like Milošević , the army had been prepared to see Slovenia go, but Croatia was another matter entirely. As Zimmermann put it in his memoirs: "The fighting in Croatia began with the illusion of evenhandedness. The Yugoslav army would step in to separate the Serbian and Croatian combatants. During the summer of 1991, however, it soon became clear that the JNA, while claiming neutrality, was in fact turning territory over to Serbs. The war in Croatia had become a war of aggression."[26]

While technically a civil conflict, the Yugoslav war had in fact become a "war of aggression," in that Milošević and the JNA were acting not to preserve but to dismember the federal state—not to restore order and protect the citizenry but to seize territory and expel non-Serbs in an effort to create an ethnically homogeneous "Greater Serbia." For its part, the EC condemned the "illegal" use of force, threatened further sanctions, and invoked an "arbitration procedure" (which later became the Badinter Commission). They then convened a peace conference, under the chairmanship of former British foreign secretary Lord Carrington, that took place in the Hague on September 7.[27] With these efforts showing no signs of success the action moved to New York, as the UN Security Council, having deferred so far to the EC, finally met in late September. Secretary Baker, in his address at the UN, condemned "outright military intervention against Croatia":

> The apparent objective of the Serbian leadership and the Yugoslav military working in tandem is to create a "small Yugoslavia" or "greater Serbia" which would exclude Slovenia and a rump Croatia. It would be based on the kind of repression which Serbian authorities have exercised in Kosovo for several years. This entity would also be based on the use of force—well underway in Croatia, and beginning to take shape in Bosnia-Herzegovina—to establish control over territories outside Serbia. The aggression within Serbia, therefore, represents a direct threat to international peace and security.[28]

Despite the tough rhetoric, U.S. policy was by this time inert. To be sure, the UN secretary-general's designation of former secretary of state Cyrus Vance as his personal envoy gave an American dimension to the EC-led mediation efforts, but this was the limit of our involvement. Even as Serbian aggression turned into the indiscriminate shelling of

civilian populations in the Croatian cities of Dubrovnik and Vukovar—
in the latter case, with the aim of forcibly expelling its entire population—the only U.S. policy option given serious consideration was to
continue our perfunctory support for the Vance-Carrington peace plan.

Any proposal for military action to halt the slaughter ran up against
the presumed lessons of Vietnam and the Persian Gulf War: unless the
mission was clear, commitment strong, and victory sure, as in Operation
Desert Storm against Iraq, any U.S. military engagement was depicted as
leading to a Vietnam-type quagmire. The superficially attractive idea of
a reversal of Desert Storm roles, with the United States providing airlift
and logistical support to a predominantly European effort, was rightly
rejected at the upper levels of the administration as militarily ineffectual.
But so, too, were more limited proposals, notably the use of combined
U.S., European, and other naval power (whether under NATO, WEU, or
some other command) to halt the shelling of Dubrovnik. Nor were they
prepared to use air power to interdict the long tank convoys rolling
along the highway from Serbia to support the leveling of Vukovar and
other cities. These limited missions, justifiable on grounds that shelling
civilian populations is a war crime, would not have demanded an open-
ended commitment to defend Croatia or defeat Serbia. Yet such proposals were rejected precisely because their advocates could not demonstrate a strategy guaranteeing ultimate victory.

This "in for a penny, in for a pound" philosophy was to haunt U.S.
policy thenceforth. Any initiative that surfaced from staff level was dismissed out of hand at the highest levels of the State Department and especially the Pentagon as being pointless unless we were prepared to see
the project through to its potential worst-case conclusion. Unless we
were prepared to commit hundreds of thousands of U.S. ground forces,
the argument ran, we should take no military action whatever.[29] And
since such a military commitment was ruled out a priori, no initiative
whatever was given serious consideration. Those of us advocating military options did so all too timidly, cognizant of the fact that the burden
was entirely on us to demonstrate their efficacy over the known opposition of NSC principals.

Thus the United States offered no alternative to the German-led campaign to recognize Slovenia and Croatia in order to "internationalize"
the conflict and better support them. We and most of the European
Community opposed the idea on grounds that it would ensure the
spread of the war to Bosnia-Herzegovina without addressing any of the

root causes of the conflict in Croatia. To "internationalize" the conflict would have made sense only if the Germans or others had developed an international strategy to deal with it. They had none, invoking instead the "right of self-determination"—as if that solved anything. Absent a credible military alternative that the United States was willing to propose and then support, however, we had no answer to the German argument that recognition was preferable to passivity in the face of brutal aggression.

On December 20, 1991, three days after the EC decided to move toward recognizing Slovenia and Croatia, Bosnia-Herzegovina declared its independence and requested international recognition. Bowing to EC insistence, the Izetbegović government held a referendum on the question in late February 1992, with 64 percent voting in favor but with most Serbs boycotting and moving instead to create a "Serbian Republic of Bosnia-Herzegovina." The United States supported Bosnia's call for recognition, which we linked to our recognition of the other two breakaway republics. Like the German position on Slovenia and Croatia, we invoked high principle but offered no strategic plan. How, we asked, could the international community deny recognition to Bosnia-Herzegovina, which had followed all the rules? Also like the Germans, we had no strategy to accompany the "internationalization" of the conflict—only the vague belief, or vain hope, that this course was preferable to denying recognition and consigning Bosnia-Herzegovina to the tender mercies of Milošević in a rump Yugoslavia.[30]

Sometime in March, Bosnian foreign minister Haris Silajdžić visited Washington, as he had in early January, urgently asking of the U.S. government two things: diplomatic recognition and protection against the inevitable attack on his new state by the well-armed Bosnian Serbs. My meeting with him in my office in the Old Executive Office Building was the most painful of my career. We were prepared to offer recognition but nothing more, though I knew he was right in saying that the attack on his country would commence within days. How, he asked, could we and the Europeans recognize a country and then permit it to be destroyed at the moment of its birth? How indeed?

Recognition of Bosnia-Herzegovina by the United States and most European countries came in early April. The only "protection" we could muster was modest indeed: a token contingent of the UN Protection Force (UNPROFOR) then arriving in Croatia was diverted to Mostar, and its headquarters was established in Sarajevo. Neither measure did anything to prevent the systematic and brutal dismemberment of Bosnia.

Serbian attacks began almost immediately. The systematic removal of Bosnian Muslims from towns and villages—so-called ethnic cleansing, in the grotesque term of Bosnian Serb leaders like Radovan Karadžić— was accomplished through brutal and inhuman means not seen in Europe since the defeat of the Third Reich. In May and June, we began receiving reports of Serbian atrocities—death camps, torture, and gang rape—that came to public light in a series of well-documented press reports in early August.[31] After a few weeks of hesitation owing to lack of independent verification, the administration confirmed the reports and called for an international tribunal to investigate war crimes.[32] As evidence continued to mount in the fall of 1992, Eagleburger—by then secretary of state[33]—issued a detailed accounting in December 1992 and named those, including Milošević and Karadžić, who bore responsibility as war criminals.[34]

The London Conference   The August 1992 London conference on Yugoslavia was perhaps the last chance to restore Western resolve before Bosnia-Herzegovina was destroyed irreparably. The Vance-Carrington effort was going nowhere, and the parties to the Yugoslav war were unmoved by Western inducements. This was the time to shift from negotiation to pressure and to pass responsibility from the EC to NATO, acting under CSCE mandate. As the *New York Times* put it in an editorial on the second day of the conference: "The U.S. and Europe have a number of military options short of limitless ground war. They can lift the arms embargo on Bosnia. They can use air power to silence the Serbs' big guns that still pound Sarajevo and other cities, and to attack military installations, arm-making plants, and air bases in Serbia."[35]

Instead, the London conference offered lofty rhetoric and uncertain resolve. The principles solemnly advanced were the right ones, but they could be upheld only through concerted international action. Inasmuch as the Serbian and Croatian leaders were continuing to wage war in defiance of international condemnation, effective international engagement would entail a readiness to use military force to punish and deter. But no such action plan was advanced. Participating states, represented by foreign ministers, almost universally proclaimed that they would "never recognize territory seized by force" and reaffirmed the "territorial integrity of Bosnia-Herzegovina," but without any hint of how the ongoing dismemberment of that country, and the genocide waged against its Muslim inhabitants, might be arrested.

The proceedings were as bizarre as they were tragic. Karadžić roamed the halls chatting amiably with members of various delegations even as he and Milošević (also in attendance) were being linked with "ethnic cleansing" and "crimes against humanity" in speeches by Eagleburger, German foreign minister Klaus Kinkel, and others.[36] Next door to our delegation's offices was the room assigned to the delegation of the rump Serbian-Montenegrin "Yugoslavia" and its new premier, a Serbian-born California businessman named Milan Panić. One of their advisers was a former U.S. ambassador to Yugoslavia, who had to pass the suite of the American delegation—headed by Eagleburger, another former ambassador to Yugoslavia—on his way to his adopted delegation.

This dual role of Karadžić—potential peacemaker or archvillain?—was emblematic of the growing tension between the international community's twin goals of mediation and enforcement. The former effort called for neutrality and impartiality, the latter, for sanctions and other punitive measures in a conflict that had passed from civil war to a war of aggression. The incompatibility of these two orientations was manifest at every level. An arms embargo imposed against all the parties had the effect of rewarding the well-armed Serbian aggressors and punishing their victims, the Bosnian Muslims. UNPROFOR, whose rules of engagement precluded entering the conflict as a protagonist, wound up abetting aggression by trying to uphold successive cease-fire lines, each determined by the aggressor. International mediators, insisting that they would not reward aggression, wound up doing just that by using these new territorial lines as the basis for the next round of negotiations, which they would supervise with strict impartiality. Humanitarian relief convoys carrying food and medicine had to pay tribute to Bosnian Serb forces controlling the supply route; forcing their way through would only have meant the closure of the corridor the next day and the complete cutoff of supplies to the besieged enclaves they were trying to assist. Operations mounted by the UN high commissioner for refugees (UNHCR) fell into the same pernicious logic of indirectly abetting "ethnic cleansing" by helping relocate Bosnian Muslims driven out their homes and villages by Serb forces.

None of this is to denigrate the heroic work done by UN bodies and nongovernmental relief organizations, nor is it to suggest that there are easy answers to these dilemmas. It was Western governments, including our own, that left these incompatibilities wholly unresolved. The international community could not produce a peace and would not confront aggression, yet it could not bring itself to admit either of those realities. In trying to pursue both mediation and enforcement, we adopted a set of policies so riddled with contradictions that both objectives were doomed to fail.

Who Lost Yugoslavia?   The European Community? NATO? The UN? CSCE? The United States? Some in Washington pointed the finger at the West Europeans, who pointed theirs back at us. The question, of course, presumes that Yugoslavia was someone else's to lose.

Ambassador Warren Zimmermann, in his valedictory cable—a stylistic masterpiece entitled "Who Shot Cock Robin?"—laid the blame at the atavistic forces of ethnic nationalism unleashed by the collapse of central authority and manipulated by unscrupulous politicians led by Slobodan Milošević. Many on both sides of the Atlantic took that view a step further: the conflict, however tragic, was born of age-old Balkan conflicts beyond American influence and remote to our interests. This contention was analytically dubious as well as conveniently exculpatory of American policy.

Hindsight is rarely 20/20, and some critics of American policy during the period surely exaggerated our ability to influence events for good or ill.[37] Indeed, hindsight could lead to judgments worse than those that were reached because these retrospective conclusions were based on an awareness of outcomes that seemed—but may not have been—the inevitable consequences of policies actually pursued. Like second-guessers after a football game, critics too easily assumed that the loss was a result of the coach's bad decisions. And of course second-guessers never see the consequences of their recommendations. They simply assume that their alternatives, had they been adopted, would have won the game. As the Yugoslav crisis deepened, everyone inside and especially outside government seemed to know what should have been done *before*, but no one seemed to know what to do *next*.

With those caveats in mind, there were three junctures in 1989–91 where a different approach might have made a difference. First was at the beginning: had we thrown our weight fully behind Marković and lent him all possible support, including substantial economic assistance, Yugoslavs might have rallied around a new blueprint for a democratic federal state. It would have been a slim chance, so far advanced were the forces of disintegration, but it would have been worth taking. Indeed, this was the approach the European Community adopted in early 1991, but by that time it was too late.

Second was the period from late 1990 to mid-1991, when Slovenia and Croatia were preparing their independence declarations. Had we focused not on formulae for preserving the federal state but on the modalities of its dissolution *and* backed this approach with massive international engagement, we might have helped avert the armed conflict that erupted almost immediately thereafter. This Western strategy should have been developed even earlier—by the summer of 1990[38]— and deployed immediately after Slovenia's December 1990 independence referendum, when Western leverage was highest. In fact, we and the EC did advance principles and conditions for recognition, including all the right ones—steps toward independence should be taken legally, constitutionally, peacefully, and consensually, with clear guarantees for the rights of national minorities. But we did so too late and too timidly. Indeed, to enforce these principles would have required highly intrusive international involvement, including tens of thousands of UN or CSCE peacekeeping forces (this even before a single shot had been fired in anger). It also would have required international supervision of conflicted areas like Serb-dominated Krajina. And the international community would have had to provide substantial economic assistance to cushion the disruptions, assist fledgling governments, and provide inducements to follow Western strictures. As a practical matter, it is always difficult for democracies to galvanize public support for engagement on that scale before conflict has broken out—by which time it may be too late. "Conflict prevention" is easier said than done.

The third juncture was in the fall of 1991, when Serb-sponsored JNA forces were shelling civilian populations in Vukovar, Osijek, Dubrovnik, and other Croatian cities. Tanks and other heavy weapons were being deployed in long convoys from Serbia into Croatia. Whatever the character of the conflict before that time, it had now become a war of Serbian aggression. Instead of allowing Germany to bring the EC to endorse the ill-advised recognition of Slovenia and Croatia, we had a chance to lead the international community in an altogether different direction by gaining consensus around a policy of threatening and, if need be, carrying out military reprisals specifically targeted at Yugoslav naval units and tank convoys. Whatever its merits, the military option certainly had better chances at this juncture, before JNA forces were already redeployed and dispersed.

Would any of these courses of action have made a difference? It is of course impossible to demonstrate a counterfactual, but it seems clear that each of them offered better chances of success than the policies actually pursued. The second and third, however, carried with them substantial American responsibilities against doubtful prospects. At any given point after hostilities began, it was always easier to "kick the can down the road" and defer tough decisions for a few weeks—by which time the options had gotten even worse. The administration's Balkan task force, which had been meeting via teleconference nearly daily since the conflict began, soon fell into a routine. As no one who mattered was prepared to support a serious policy initiative, the task force produced instead recommendations for the next 24 hours that amounted to little more than diplomatic busywork. Worse, participants began succumbing to the temptation of serving up what they believed their masters wanted to hear: that the hollow strategies we and our European partners were concocting might actually achieve their stated objectives.[39]

These considerations bring us back to the cardinal error of U.S. and other Western policies: We never decided whether important U.S. interests were at stake. We never decided whether Yugoslavia mattered enough to invest considerable American leadership and, if need be, to place substantial numbers of American men and women in harm's way to halt or at least contain the conflict.[40] Absent such clarity of purpose, any course of action—including the three alternatives outlined above— was doomed to fail. As my NSC colleague David Gompert put it in his incisive critique of Western policies: "Western leaders did not see—or if they saw, did not translate into public support and purposeful policies— that the crisis, in Bosnia especially, was setting the worst possible precedents for the new era. They did not appreciate the importance of defeating this case of fiendish nationalism before it had metastasized elsewhere in the former communist world."[41]

For all the policy failures in Yugoslavia, Western leaders remained largely faithful to core principles. (It was later in the conflict that Western leaders began succumbing to the perverse "tribal logic" then prevailing in the Balkans—that the only solution lay in segregating ethnic nations and building high walls between them, with UN "blue helmets" patrolling the perimeters.) It was critically important not to confuse the difficulty of enforcing basic democratic principles with the continuing validity of the principles themselves. In Yugoslavia, several of these principles came together in applying the slippery concept of "national self-determination," for which a brief digression is in order.

"Self-Determination" in Yugoslavia and the Soviet Union

Small wonder that President Wilson, reflecting at the end of the First World War on the chaos engendered by the principle of self-determination he had so uncritically embraced, soon had misgivings: "You do not know and can not appreciate the anxieties that I have experienced as the result of these many millions of peoples having their hopes raised by what I have said."[42] His secretary of state, Robert Lansing, anticipated these consequences even as Wilson was championing self-determination at the Paris Peace Conference of 1919: "The phrase is simply loaded with dynamite. It will raise hopes that can never be realized. It will, I fear, cost thousands of lives. . . . What a calamity that the phrase was ever uttered! What misery it will cause!"[43]

We in government at the end of the Cold War had reason to echo those sentiments. Although Wilson's name is the most closely identified with the quintessentially American concept of "national self-determination," it was a principle the United States had invoked regularly, and carelessly, since. For most of the post–World War II period, the United Nations had applied the concept exclusively to cases of decolonization, i.e., the pursuit of independence by European colonies, chiefly in Africa and Asia.

During the Cold War, the United States also used the term with reference to the Baltic states and other countries of Central and Eastern Europe, but with a different meaning. When successive U.S. administrations said "self-determination," they really meant "independence" or "liberation" from Soviet domination of countries in Central and Eastern Europe whose existence we already recognized. But these terms, like "captive nations" and "rollback," sounded too provocative and retrograde, so we invoked the more high-sounding principle of self-determination—imbuing it with a status that we would have reason to regret. For understandable tactical reasons, we allowed ourselves to be identified as champions of a principle of dubious legality or practicability.

What was meant by "self-determination"? In the spring and summer of 1991, we asked the State Department's Office of Legal Affairs to research the matter thoroughly. International law is ambiguous. To begin with, there is no agreement on who is the "self" in self-determination. Article 1, Section 2, of the United Nations Charter affirms the principle of "self-determination of peoples." But what is a people? Is it a nation, a state, a constituent republic of a federal state, or communities of people however constituted? In a multinational, federal state, who has the right to self-determination—the totality of the federation, the federal units, or the nationalities dispersed among these units? International law does not say.[44]

Nor is it clear what is meant by "determination," except that the term seems to refer to a process rather than an outcome—a right to seek but not necessarily to achieve a desired state of affairs such as statehood. It certainly does not imply the right of state independence. United Nations and CSCE documents affirmed the sanctity of existing borders but also allowed for the possibility of border changes so long as they were accomplished peacefully and consensually. The tension between sovereignty and self-determination is left unresolved. What if border changes are neither peaceful nor consensual? What if independence declarations are contested? International law is silent.

The Political Declaration of the G-7 (Group of 7) Summit in London in July 1991 offered this cumbersome interpretation of these principles with regard to Yugoslavia:

> We will do whatever we can, with others in the international community, to encourage and support the process of dialogue and negotiation in accordance with the principles enshrined in the Helsinki Final Act and the Paris Charter for a new Europe, in particular respect for human rights, including rights of minorities and the right of peoples to self-determination in conformity with the Charter of the United Nations and with the relevant norms of international law, including those relating to territorial integrity of states.[45]

The criteria for statehood are more straightforward, though still subject to interpretation. To qualify for recognition, states must possess a defined territory, a permanent population, a government capable of speaking and acting for its citizens, and the capacity to enter into relations with other states.[46] With respect to the disintegration of Yugoslavia and the Soviet Union, both the United States and the European

Community added a set of more demanding criteria derived from the UN Charter and various CSCE documents.

On September 4, 1991, the U.S. administration issued a set of principles that would guide its policy toward recognition of new states emerging from Yugoslavia, the Soviet Union, and elsewhere. The would-be states, we said, must

> — support internationally accepted principles, including democratic values and practices and the principles of the Helsinki Final Act;
> — respect existing borders, both internal and external, with change through peaceful and consensual means consistent with the principles of the Conference on Security and Cooperation in Europe (CSCE);
> — support the rule of law and democratic processes;
> — safeguard human rights, including minority rights; and
> — respect international law and obligations, especially the provisions of the Helsinki Final Act and the Charter of Paris.[47]

The EC's guidelines, issued three months later and amplified through the work of the Badinter Commission, were nearly identical:

> — respect for the provisions of the Charter of the United Nations and the commitments subscribed to in the Final Act of Helsinki and in the Charter of Paris, especially with regard to the rule of law, democracy, and human rights;
> — guarantees for the rights of ethnic and national groups and minorities in accordance with . . . the CSCE;
> — respect for the inviolability of all frontiers, which can only be changed by peaceful means and by common agreement;
> — acceptance of all relevant commitments with regard to disarmament and nuclear non-proliferation as well as to security and regional stability;
> — commitment to settle by agreement, including where appropriate by recourse to arbitration, all questions concerning state succession and regional disputes.[48]

As a practical matter, the United States, while invoking essentially the same principles, made a sharper distinction than did the EC between recognition and the establishment of diplomatic relations. The former, in our view, was a legal act and therefore subject to the narrower criteria for statehood, while the latter was a political act to which we attached much more stringent considerations.

These stipulations presented one further conceptual difficulty that arose in both Yugoslavia and the Soviet Union: namely, that the "self" invoking self-determination was not always the same "self" that sought recognition. As one writer put it, "The 'self' entitled to claim the right of self-determination [under the UN system] was limited to territorial entities under colonial rule or international trusteeship, and no other 'self' was recognized as a potentially legitimate claimant."[49] When Croatia declared its independence, this was done by and on behalf of Croatians within that republic, yet this territory was under the jurisdiction of the Republic of Croatia as a whole, and the vehicle for seeking recognition was the government of that republic. Thus, in Croatia, Bosnia, Ukraine, and elsewhere, the international community was obliged to deal with claimants that spoke for only part of the "peoples" within their borders.

Where self-determination and sovereignty collided, the relevant political pressure almost always came in support of the former. Americans tend to be Wilsonian. Our revolutionary origins and successive waves of immigrants fleeing oppression brought us down on the side of "the little guy." With the media and political commentators, this disposition was even stronger. It was easier to construct a morality play around David than Goliath.

In international law, the principles of self-determination and sovereignty are parallel to the concepts of change and stability. On that score as well, Americans tended instinctively to favor change and view the existing international order with disdain; Europeans, however, for reasons of geography and history, were more apt to equate change with a chaotic breakdown of order. The analytical predisposition of Americans also tended to see change as the natural order, or disorder, of things. To support the status quo was to be out of step with the hoofbeat of history.

It was against this backdrop, and with violent conflict in Yugoslavia unfolding before our eyes, that we addressed the potentially much graver prospect of a disintegrating Soviet Union. It was easy for Western publics, especially our own, to overlook how much mischief could be caused by abandoning the principle of sovereignty. The power of sovereign states may well have been dwindling at the end of the Cold War, but states nonetheless were the units of such international order as we had. They controlled the armies and the weapons—in the Soviet case, nuclear weapons capable of rendering the planet uninhabitable. There was nothing like the prospect of human annihilation to focus the mind. Such were some of the considerations that made the Bush administration less eager than its critics to revel in the prospect of a dismembered Soviet Union.

The End of the Soviet Union

After the crackdown against the Baltic states in mid-January 1991, the CIA's *National Intelligence Daily* offered a prescient summary: "Gorbachev has started a conflict without a visible program and with scant prospect of long-term success. He will not easily escape the predicament for which he is largely responsible, and he may become its principal casualty."[50] At about the same time, Polish president Lech Wałęsa reminded a *Figaro* interviewer that he "was the first political person to say that there existed only one solution for the Soviet Union—to dissolve itself."[51]

From Crisis to Crisis   For the rest of the year, Gorbachev beat one retreat after another, none gaining him the upper hand, each inviting further challenges to his authority. One week after the "Bloody Sunday" in Riga, Latvia, Gorbachev dispatched his new foreign minister (and former ambassador to the United States) Aleksandr Bessmertnykh to Washington to assure Bush and Baker that the use of force was "not presidential policy" and would not be repeated.[52] On the strength of this assurance and in deference to Gorbachev's plea for understanding, Bush, in his State of the Union Address the next day, withheld direct criticism of Gorbachev. But he noted that he had been given "representations" which, "if fulfilled, would result in the withdrawal of some Soviet forces, a reopening of dialogue with the republics, and a move away from violence."[53]

From the beginning, Gorbachev would have been better advised to have conceded Baltic independence, concentrating his energy and political capital on measures to hold together the rest of the union. The man who had leapt over history up until 1990 was now constantly trying to catch up to it—always too late and too timidly to shape it. Even allowing for the enormous pressure under which he was laboring, his handling of the crisis only served to embolden hard-line critics and strengthen secessionist movements elsewhere—without doing more than momentarily slowing drives for independence in the Baltic states.

The narrow public endorsement of a March 17 referendum on preserving the Soviet Union did nothing to arrest the growing disintegration of central authority. Six republics—Moldova, Armenia, Georgia, and the three Baltic states—boycotted the referendum and pressed ahead with preparations for full independence. They did so with the blessings of Boris Yeltsin, soon to be elected president of the Russian federation,[54] who had interposed himself as champion of the republics in their several struggles with the center. In late March he demonstrated his own independence by holding a huge rally near the Kremlin in defiance of police and interior ministry forces.

Once again obliged to retreat, Gorbachev met at his country house (dacha) on April 23 with leaders of the nine republics that had not boycotted the March 17 referendum to hammer out the terms of a new union treaty. The "Dacha Agreement," also known as the Nine Plus One, devolved substantially greater authority to the republics and also provided more workable modalities for secession. It was a formula that might have facilitated creation of a voluntary union, or reunion, among these republics, but it came so late that attitudes among the main protagonists were already hardened.

In trying to steer down the middle of the road, Gorbachev was being hit by traffic coming from both directions. Against the intransigence of hard-line opponents on center-republic relations and economic reform, Gorbachev could muster nothing more than belated half-measures—which only emboldened republic leaders to go their own ways. Yet the concessions they were able to wring from him further antagonized a growing hard-line faction of disaffected party, military, and KGB officials. Thus even as republic leaders, led by Yeltsin, were pulling the country apart from the periphery, hard-liners were conspiring to bring Gorbachev down and restore authoritarian control.

A secret CIA analysis of "The Soviet Cauldron" issued April 25 warned of the growing likelihood of a coup attempt but also judged that "the long-term prospects of such an enterprise are poor, and even short-term success is far from assured."[55] By late June, the agency's clandestine service had specific reports of an imminent attempt to strip Gorbachev of his presidential authority via a "constitutional coup d'état." President Bush sent a letter to Gorbachev warning him that a coup attempt would be mounted against him on June 21.[56] Secretary Baker, alerted to the threat while attending a CSCE ministerial in Berlin (just before his trip to Belgrade), conveyed the same message to Foreign Minister Bessmertnykh, also in attendance at Berlin.[57]

Such was the situation in the Soviet Union as two important summits loomed in mid- and late July. London was to be the site of a G-7 summit, to which Gorbachev had managed to get himself invited and where he was sure to lobby for substantial economic aid. The long-delayed Bush-Gorbachev Summit would take place in Moscow, where the two leaders were expected to sign a START agreement codifying further deep reductions in strategic nuclear weapons. They also hoped to resolve outstanding issues arising from Soviet backtracking from key provisions of the CFE (Conventional Armed Forces in Europe) treaty. The two summits framed the issues before U.S. policy: economic and political engagement of a Soviet Union in the midst of profound turmoil, and the conclusion of key agreements with the embattled leader of that country to "lock in" Soviet reductions in nuclear and conventional forces.

The relevant options for U.S. policy—and those pressed on us from various quarters—were basically threefold. First, we could begin distancing ourselves from Gorbachev and cultivate Yeltsin and other republic leaders, with the conscious aim of encouraging the dismemberment, full or partial, of the Soviet Union. This was the course urged on us by Yeltsin and the Baltic states, as well as independence-minded leaders in other republics, and it had support in some quarters of the administration, chiefly in the Pentagon. (The CIA and many outside pundits also favored this course but not necessarily the political objective; they merely wanted U.S. policy to conform to what they saw as the emerging reality.) Second, we could lend as much support as possible to Gorbachev in order to avert a hard-line coup and potentially a descent into civil war. This is of course what Gorbachev wanted from us, and it was supported by Chancellor Kohl and most of our other European allies, who feared above all a chaotic breakdown of order in the Soviet Union. Third, we could support Gorbachev conditionally, using our leverage to push him further down the path of economic and political reform. This was the premise of a "Grand Bargain" proposal advanced by two Harvard academics and former policymakers, in which the United States would assemble a three-year international assistance package of $15–20 billion a year in return for deep and sustained reform of the Soviet economy.[58]

Each of these courses of action had its liabilities. The first, by further weakening Gorbachev, would have undercut efforts to secure nuclear and conventional arms reductions and would have put us squarely in the middle of delicate and dangerous relations between republics and a diminished central authority in Moscow. The second presented the difficulty that there was precious little to "support," except rhetorically, so we risked backing a losing horse. Similarly, the third option presumed that there was a power or combination of powers in the Soviet Union that could deliver on its part of the bargain. There was not. It was not just that Gorbachev lacked the will to reform; he had by this time made pacts with so many devils that he lacked the political capacity to do so.

As it turned out, we tried a bit of option one by "diversifying" our relations with Soviet, republic, and local leaders and a bit of option three by advancing a modest set of economic assistance measures aimed at spurring reform, but we essentially came down on the side of the second option of supporting Gorbachev. However weakened, he was still the "linchpin" between the center and the republics and was the "communications node between the extremes," as one of my NSC colleagues put it.[59] Without him, it was hard to see what institutions or processes could facilitate negotiations among the rival centers of power. But the most important considerations derived from American interests: inasmuch as we lacked the capacity to determine the future of Soviet reforms or relations between the center and the republics, we acted to take care of issues that manifestly were in our interests—particularly in controlling and reducing Soviet nuclear and conventional forces.

Our Western allies felt much as we did. Chancellor Kohl was the most eager to provide economic assistance, owing chiefly to his urgent desire to secure the timely removal of Soviet forces from eastern Germany, but even he was loath to throw good money after bad. Accordingly, the G-7 Summit in London in mid-July was long on good wishes but, in the absence of any Soviet economic reform plan, short on new assistance measures. The G-7 leaders agreed to support the Soviet Union's "special associate status" in the International Monetary Fund, but even that fell short of Gorbachev's plea for full membership.[60] The main achievement at London, from our perspective, was resolution of the last issues on the START treaty,[61] clearing the way for its signature by Presidents Bush and Gorbachev at the Moscow Summit two weeks later. In the weeks leading up to London, President Bush had used his leverage with Gorbachev toward that end, withholding agreement to attend the Moscow Summit until the Soviet side had agreed to the terms of the CFE and START treaties. This was the bargain we pursued—not as grand as the other, but it had the virtues of being achievable and directly related to our vital interests.

The Moscow Summit at the end of July contrasted sharply with the Washington Summit of May–June 1990. In 1990, Gorbachev was embattled but still in charge, his role essential to the conclusion of German unification, the CFE treaty, and other key issues. A year later, there was no disguising his loss of power at home and abroad. Thus the Moscow Summit was anticlimactic, quite irrelevant to the real issues facing the Soviet state. Apart from the START treaty, the only achievement to which Gorbachev could point was President Bush's decision to send to Congress the U.S.-Soviet trade agreement, but this was merely the consummation of a document the two leaders had signed in Washington (and which Bush had held in abeyance pending passage of Soviet emigration legislation).[62]

The major event of the summit came not in Moscow but in Kiev. The reason for the president's stop there was to show understanding for the aspirations of Ukrainians and others; the purpose of the president's speech to the Ukrainian parliament was to promote the ongoing negotiations between Gorbachev and republic leaders toward the new union treaty. Neither objective was achieved. His address backfired because it persuaded his audience of American hostility toward Ukrainian self-determination. Quickly dubbed the "Chicken Kiev" speech,[63] it conveyed a useful distinction between liberty and state independence—the former being an aspiration that the United States unreservedly supported; the latter, a more complex matter to which peoples did not have an automatic right. Had the speech been given in Zagreb or Ljubljana, it might have served as a corrective to the indiscriminate invocation of the "rights of self-determination." As it was, Bush's condemnation of "local despotism" and "suicidal nationalism" was taken, understandably, as gratuitously offensive to the Ukrainian people and their leaders.

From Coup d'État to Coup de Grâce As the CIA's analysis had warned, the prospective conclusion of the new union treaty prompted the anti-Gorbachev coup-plotters to make their move. On August 18, just a few days before Gorbachev and nine republic presidents were to begin signing the treaty, a self-proclaimed "State Emergency Committee" seized Gorbachev, imposed a "temporary" state of emergency, and named Vice President Gennady Yanayev president in Gorbachev's stead.[64]

Among the limited options at our disposal, President Bush chose the right ones. Alone among Western leaders, he observed from the outset that "coups can fail."[65] Far from being the offhand intuitive remark it seemed, this judgment was the product of careful, ongoing analysis beginning with the CIA's April 25 report on "The Soviet Cauldron." While some of his counterparts, notably French president Mitterrand, were busily accommodating themselves to the new situation, Bush ensured that the outside world would rally behind a policy of nonrecognition that stressed the illegitimacy of the coup and its leaders.[66] (Had the coup succeeded, the United States eventually would have found ways to deal with the new leadership, but the president was not about to capitulate preemptively.) At the height of the crisis, Secretary Baker travelled to Brussels for an emergency NATO ministerial to hammer out an allied consensus on responding to developments in the Soviet Union.[67] As events unfolded, Bush's strong support for Boris Yeltsin, even while maintaining solidarity with Gorbachev, compensated for whatever slights he may have inflicted on the Russian leader before. Thus when the coup failed, the United States was well positioned to deal with Gorbachev and Yeltsin alike.

In the immediate aftermath of the coup, it was plain to all save Gorbachev that de facto political leadership had passed to Yeltsin.[68] In his first television appearance, Gorbachev called for the "renewal" of the Communist party; within a week he was forced to step down as its leader and acquiesce to Yeltsin's demand that party activities be banned altogether. Ukraine, Belarus, and five other republics promptly declared their independence. The Baltic states sought and received international recognition by most European states and, after a brief delay to spare Gorbachev needless humiliation, the United States as well. As Bush put it, "When history is written, nobody will remember that we took 48 hours longer than Iceland." Unfortunately, the line was so provocative that it would be cited in every contemporary account, including this one, assuring that "history" would indeed remember, at least for a while.[69]

American policy from that point on focused on the prospect of a radically altered and perhaps dismembered Soviet Union. Our concerns were with the modalities for negotiating the future relations among the republics and with the issues arising therefrom, chiefly the disposition of nuclear weapons in Russia, Ukraine, Belarus, and Kazakhstan, the four republics on whose territories nuclear weapons were deployed. An internal State Department memorandum of late August concluded that "the Center and its institutions continue to exist . . . largely at the indulgence of the republics," which "will try to sweep the Center aside and find a new vehicle through which to work out their relations" unless Gorbachev, implausibly, seized from Boris Yeltsin the agenda of radical reform.[70]

As Gorbachev's authority continued to diminish over the next few weeks, so did prospects for renegotiation of the union treaty. By late October, it was evident that, as a State Department policy paper put it, "The Soviet Union as we know it no longer exists. What matters now is how the breakup of the Soviet Union proceeds from this point onward. Our aim should be to make the crash as peaceful as possible."[71]

The differences within the administration by this time were not so much about the likelihood of disintegration nor even its desirability, but about the proper course of U.S. policy. For Secretary Cheney and the uniformed military, the possibility of the dissolution of the Soviet Union presented an opportunity that U.S. policy should exploit. We could do this by lending our support to independence movements among the republics and according prompt recognition to republics declaring their independence.[72] The president, Secretary Baker, and others were not so sure. The disintegration of our Cold War adversary was arguably in American interests, but it depended . . . on what kind of new states emerged from this process, and what kind of hands were on the nuclear trigger. As has been argued, we lacked the capacity either to save or destroy the Soviet state, so our better course was to tend to our own business, trying where we could to ensure a peaceful, negotiated outcome and working to ensure the responsible disposition of nuclear weapons.

We had said that "the Soviet Union *as we know it* no longer exists"; that formulation left room for the renegotiation among key republics, with Gorbachev nominally in the center, of the terms of a radically restructured Soviet Union. It was a possibility that we, as a matter of policy, neither promoted nor excluded; we simply kept it among the universe of possible outcomes as we engaged key leaders. President Bush's view was that if we were not certain of the outcome—and we were not—we should take a step back from the process and try to manage those aspects that bore immediately on American interests.

In early September, Secretary Baker had announced five principles that would guide our approaches toward the republics: self-determination consistent with democratic principles, respect for existing borders, support for democracy and the rule of law, human rights and the rights of national minorities, and respect for international law and obligations.[73] The other main line of policy was to press Gorbachev and key republic leaders on nuclear weapons issues: compliance with the START treaty, control over nuclear weapons, and adherence to the nuclear nonproliferation treaty. In late September, as has been seen, the president announced several unilateral initiatives on nuclear arms and proposed immediate discussions with the Soviet Union on nuclear command and control and warhead security.[74] Baker then pushed this agenda along with the "five principles" in a series of visits to every Soviet republic beginning with a long-scheduled CSCE human rights conference in Moscow in September.[75] Negotiations on nuclear issues were particularly arduous, stretching throughout 1991 and into 1992.[76]

It was a confluence of forces—some deeply rooted, others accidental—that brought about the disintegration of the Soviet state. If the Soviet Union were to survive as a voluntary association of republics and peoples, its very essence needed to be transformed. Such an outcome might have been possible had it not been for the rivalry between Gorbachev and Yeltsin *and* the structures of the institutions they led. Had there been a weak, mainly ceremonial Soviet presidency, as there was for most of the USSR's history, Yeltsin might have seen his way clear to retaining a much looser union with himself as first among equals. Or, had Gorbachev moved some months earlier, rather than in the immediate aftermath of the August 1991 coup, to resign the Communist party leadership and so separate the power of the party from the power of the presidency, Yeltsin might simply have challenged him for that position and felt no need to detach Russia from the union. So much for "what ifs." Suffice it to say that there were several plausible outcomes to the political struggle of the fall of 1991, not just one.

As it was, the irreconcilability of the issues at play between Gorbachev and Yeltsin made it impossible to transform the center in ways that might have induced key republics to remain. On December 1, Ukrainians voted overwhelmingly for independence. A week later, Yeltsin, newly elected Ukrainian president Leonid Kravchuk, and Belarusian president Stanislav Suskevich met in Minsk, Belarus, to declare that the Soviet Union had ceased to exist and to announce a new "Commonwealth of Independent States." Secretary Baker promptly undertook another trip to Moscow for meetings with Yeltsin and Gorbachev, traveling also to Ukraine, Belarus, and Kyrgyzstan, pressing the "five principles"—for which he sought and received specific commitments.[77]

On December 25, 1991, Mikhail Gorbachev formally declared the end of the Soviet Union. President Bush simultaneously announced immediate U.S. recognition of the independence of the 12 new states and the immediate establishment of diplomatic relations with six: Russia, Ukraine, Belarus, Kazakhstan, Armenia, and Kyrgyzstan. In keeping with the distinction we made between recognition, a legal act, and diplomatic relations, a political one that was subject to more stringent conditions, the president withheld the establishment of diplomatic relations with the remaining new states "until they have made commitments to responsible security policies and democratic principles, as have the other states we recognize today."[78] In February 1992, following Secretary Baker's visit to the remaining new states—except Georgia, then engulfed in civil turmoil—the United States established diplomatic relations with Moldova, Azerbaijan, Tajikistan, Turkmenistan, and Uzbekistan.[79] Finally, with Eduard Shevardnadze's assumption of the interim presidency of Georgia and Secretary Baker's visit there in May, we established relations with the last of the newly independent states.[80]

Yet in our zeal to be helpful to the struggling new states, we got off on the wrong foot. In an otherwise well-conceived speech at Princeton University in December 1991, Secretary Baker noted that "the opportunities are historic: We have the chance to anchor Russia, Ukraine, and other republics firmly in the Euro-Atlantic community and democratic commonwealth of nations. We have the chance to bring democracy to lands that have little knowledge of it. . . ."[81] The trouble was that neither "we" the United States nor "we" the Western community had any such chance. That chance belonged to the Russian people, and it was our responsibility to see that the opportunity was extended to them—but not to imply that democracy and integration into the Western community were gifts we could bestow. What may have begun as a careless rhetorical flourish soon became embedded in policy, setting the United States on a course toward objectives that were well beyond our capacity to deliver.

At a huge "coordinating conference" arranged in Washington in January 1992, President Bush made the sounder observation that "ultimate success or failure rests squarely with the efforts and wisdom of the peoples of Russia and the Ukraine and the Caucasus and Central Asia."[82] But the fact that the conference took place conveyed the impression that the United States and its Western partners bore the chief responsibility. Because the objectives were so extravagant, participating countries, beginning with the United States, wildly inflated their projected levels of assistance and disguised the conditions under which their assistance would be offered. When the levels of assistance actually extended fell far short of what seemed to have been promised, Russians increasingly believed that they had been misled by a Western community bent on weakening, not assisting, their country.

The administration moved quickly to engage the leaders of the newly independent states. Russian president Boris Yeltsin visited Washington and Camp David in early February. In early April, the president submitted to Congress the "Freedom Support Act" for assistance totalling $24 billion, a wildly misleading figure that mixed together old and new, U.S. and non-U.S., bilateral and multilateral, loans and grants, all in an understandable but ill-advised effort to impress.[83] Ukrainian president Leonid Kravchuk and Kazakhstan's president Nursultan Nazarbayev visited Washington in May, each signing with President Bush a declaration on bilateral relations.[84] Yeltsin followed in June with a full state visit, during which he and President Bush issued a "Charter for American-Russian Partnership and Friendship" and no fewer than 31 other agreements and joint statements.[85] Several of these were key, particularly those concerning weapons of mass destruction, but for sheer dramatic effect none matched the opening of the "Camp David Declaration" issued by Presidents Bush and Yeltsin during the latter's February 1992 visit: "Russia and the United States do not regard each other as potential adversaries."[86]

American Policy Revisited   The peaceful disintegration of the Soviet state was among the most remarkable developments in modern history. How much credit should go to American diplomacy? Our "five principles," after all, were essentially the same ones we had advanced to no avail with leaders of the Yugoslav republics. Did our approaches toward a disintegrating Soviet Union make a difference?

In the first place, our approaches were undertaken with the right frame of mind: in his meetings with leaders of every new state of the former Soviet Union, Secretary Baker presented the principles on which we and the rest of the CSCE community insisted. He also made it clear that our future relations would be based on these principles, and placed the onus on republic leaders to adhere to them. We had helped to estab lish a framework through which the international community could deal with independence declarations by Soviet republics, based on a shared set of principles and procedures. And the principles were the right ones, even though we could not compel compliance among the Soviet republics any more than we could in Yugoslavia. We pressed them with greater urgency, and with a stronger international consensus, in the Soviet case, but in the end it was the behavior of the protagonists themselves rather than outside pressure that made the difference. If our influence over the process of German unification was decisive, and our early engagement in Eastern Europe instrumental in paving the way for the revolutions of 1989, our influence, though important, was considerably less over the process of Soviet dissolution.

The most common critique was that the Bush administration held on too long to Gorbachev and "the center" and failed to engage leaders like Yeltsin and others among the republics. This assertion needs to be "deconstructed." It is true that the upper levels of the administration exaggerated the strength and staying power of the apparatus of the Soviet state—such is the tendency of leaders accustomed to dealing with other world leaders. Relatedly, our contacts with and understanding of the Soviet Union were Moscow-centric. One could count on one hand the number of experts within government on the non-Russian republics. It is also true that President Bush, having developed a relationship of trust with Gorbachev, went the extra mile to avoid embarrassing his Soviet counterpart.[87] It is true, finally, that the administration erred on the side of caution in dealing with independence movements among the republics.

Analytically, then, pundits outside government and some analysts within may have been closer to the mark than the senior levels of the Bush administration in divining the coming breakup of the Soviet state. Yet "illusions of retrospective determinism" come into play once more. The disintegration of the Soviet Union was not inevitable: had it not been for the power struggle between Gorbachev and Yeltsin, which was only distantly related to center-periphery relations, the Soviet Union might well have held together. The Baltic states would have left regardless, perhaps joined by Georgia, Moldova, and Armenia, but the "Slavic core" of Russia, Ukraine, Belarus, and Kazakhstan could well have renegotiated the terms of their union—as indeed they were doing in the spring and again in the fall of 1991.

More importantly, because the Soviet Union's disintegration occurred in a peaceful and orderly way, it was easy after the fact to come to the judgment that the United States should have acted more boldly in support of independence movements among the republics. Yet an aggressive American policy might well have precipitated reckless actions among the republics and galvanized a much more determined hard-line backlash in Moscow. It was what we refrained from doing, as much as what we did, that mattered.

It has already been mentioned here that scholars and pundits like to see policy conform to their analysis, whereas policymakers develop policies to advance their objectives. Those who argued loudest for a different American approach may have had it right analytically, but their policy prescriptions were unpersuasive. What, exactly, should the United States have done differently, and to what end? It was said we should have cultivated influential republic leaders, as well as the reformist mayors of Leningrad, Moscow, and other cities. But why, precisely? To "establish contact"? This was too woolly a prescription for serious policymakers. To "build up influence"? This was the working-level perspective of the State Department, which saw the world as a bank account into which the United States must make regular deposits—in order to increase its influence—but never make a withdrawal. U.S. interests did not require that we ingratiate ourselves with the up and comers among the republics. We might have done more, but our neglect cost us nothing.

Even the Kiev speech, which virtually everyone later agreed was a mistake, probably did little harm. Would history have turned out differently had Bush given a different speech? A safer, middle-of-the-road speech would have been better than the one Bush actually delivered, but events would have transpired pretty much the same. There is no evidence that it influenced the coup plotters one way or another. Arguably, however, had he delivered a fire-breathing call for Ukrainian independence, this might have energized hard-line opponents of Gorbachev and created a stronger constituency behind the August coup attempt. If he had to err, better to err on the side of caution before seeming to advocate the dissolution of a state bristling with nuclear weapons.

A stronger case was that the United States should have engaged the republics in order to influence the likely, even if not inevitable, dissolution of the Soviet state. This, as was argued above, was an option we should have pursued with regard to Yugoslavia. Yet interposing ourselves between the center and the republics would have been a risky strategy, more likely to backfire by provoking republics into precipitous action. It was arguably justifiable in the Yugoslav context, where we had reason to believe that the breakup would be contested and violent, but it was fraught with dangers in the Soviet case, where negotiations were proceeding well enough without us. The physician's counsel was good for diplomats as well: first, do no harm.

The harshest criticism was reserved for the administration's policy toward the Baltic states. The basic tone was set in the spring of 1990, when President Bush said that he did not want history to judge that this was where "everything went off track" and "progress stopped."[88] Instead of openly challenging Gorbachev on this issue, we worked behind the scenes to gain his assurance that force would not be used against the Baltic states and pushed him toward dialogue and negotiation. We held key Soviet desiderata—like a bilateral trade agreement—hostage to Soviet compliance with these stipulations. We took essentially the same position a year later, after the "Bloody Sundays" in Riga and Vilnius.

One can question the premises of this approach but not its results: the objectives, as we had framed them, were realized fully and with less bloodshed than we feared. The independence of the Baltic states was an aim from which we never wavered, but it was one that we balanced against other key objectives. Even had Baltic independence been the sole objective of American policy during the period, it is not clear that another course of action would have been more successful or succeeded more rapidly. Baltic leaders felt otherwise, however.

At the Helsinki Summit of July 1992, the president met with the three Baltic delegations. It was my last day on the job, as I would take up my new assignment under Deputy Secretary Eagleburger immediately upon returning to Washington. In the course of a discussion about difficulties with Moscow over the withdrawal of Russian troops, Tamas Meri, Estonia's former foreign minister and future president, noted offhandedly that he hoped the United States would not make the same mistakes with Yeltsin that it had made with Gorbachev. Before the president could reply, another of the Baltic leaders tactfully tried to change the subject; Bush, however, despite being preoccupied with his coming election struggle, was having none of it. "Wait! I want to finish this!" Asked what he meant, Meri opined that when the West showed understanding or tried to accommodate Russian concerns, this only lent strength to the hard-liners, whereas a tough posture would demonstrate resolve and so isolate hard-line opponents. As I was taking notes of the conversation, I was thinking that this was a preposterous bit of cheek given all the Bush administration had been through with Moscow over the past three years: the strategic and tactical planning, the measured use of power as an instrument of policy, the carefully calibrated approaches that combined firmness on principles with flexibility on tactics, and, not least, the successes. The liberation of Eastern Europe (including Estonia!), the unification of Germany, and the collapse of Soviet communism, all achieved peacefully and on Western terms: did Meri think all of this occurred by accident? Bush was as hot as I had ever seen him. He reviewed our approaches briefly but forcefully, coming as close as I had ever seen him to immodesty: "We like to think we know a thing or two about dealing with Russian leaders." Indeed.

Conclusion: Beyond the Cold War

"AFTER A LONG WAR, it is impossible to make a quick peace."[1] Harold Nicolson's judgment on the 1919 Versailles conference ending World War I is worth recalling in the aftermath of a far longer war. Indeed, the Cold War had gone on so long that it was easy to forget what it was all about in the first place—the stability of Europe, rather than the Soviet threat. With Soviet acquisition of nuclear weapons capable of destroying us and our allies, the Cold War and the Soviet threat became virtually synonymous. Our interests were seen almost wholly in terms of countering this threat, which helps explain our diminished sense of strategic purpose as that threat receded. Yet what animated American policy in the immediate postwar period was defense of interests that had not diminished with the disappearance of the threat.

From the Truman Doctrine to the Marshall Plan and the formation of the Atlantic alliance, our postwar strategy was to shield Western Europe so that it could recover economically, build democracy, and overcome its national rivalries. In the process it would become a more cohesive bulwark against further Soviet expansion and a magnet that would ultimately draw the countries of Central and Eastern Europe into its field. The Cold War was also a struggle over Germany and with the irreconcilable differences of the *German question*. While the resulting division of Germany was a de facto solution that survived for more than a generation, U.S. policy aimed from the beginning to overcome the postwar division of Germany and of Europe.[2]

These combined strategies were brilliantly successful but not yet complete, nor could their achievements in Western Europe be taken for granted. The great unresolved problem for European stability lay in the

East. It was, in the first instance, much the same *Eastern question* that preoccupied the peacemakers at Yalta and Potsdam, Versailles, and indeed the Congress of Vienna in 1815: how to deal with the breakup of the multiethnic empires in Europe's eastern reaches.[3] As before, it remained linked to the German question, which seemed finally to have been answered in 1990 with the achievement of unity "in peace and freedom" but which could be reopened if democratic stability remained elusive among Germany's eastern neighbors. Already the war in the former Yugoslavia had exposed deep fissures in the European Community and undermined its confidence in continued movement toward European unity. And of course there was the still larger Eastern question posed by Russia, Ukraine, and the other newly independent states of the former Soviet Union. The daunting challenges they faced served to dramatize how far we remained from a secure new order.

Much like 1919 and 1945, the mood at the end of the Cold War was the triumphalist expectation that the values that had won the war would now produce the peace. As before, triumphalism gave way to disillusionment and disorientation, both here and in Europe, as these sanguine expectations inevitably were shattered.

"Why this sudden restlessness, this confusion?" asked the Greek poet Cavafy, writing early in this century about the Roman senate before the fall of the Roman empire. His answer bore also on the challenge of finding America's place and role in the post–Cold War world, absent the threat that had lent focus and purpose to U.S. policy for four decades:

> Because night has fallen and the barbarians have not come.
> And some who have just returned from the border say
> there are no barbarians any longer.
>
> And now, what's going to happen to us without barbarians?
> They were, those people, a kind of solution.[4]

American Diplomacy at the End of the Cold War

American diplomacy in the period 1989–92 had exercised decisive leadership though the end of the Cold War, dealt reasonably well with the challenges immediately in its wake, and laid the foundations, incomplete though they were, of a viable post–Cold War order. The objectives which we had set for ourselves in early 1989—self-determination in

Eastern Europe, reduction of Soviet forces to less threatening levels, Soviet cooperation in solving regional disputes, and the liberalization of the USSR itself—had been met and far exceeded. Our successes in this period were attributable to the early recognition of an historic chance for ending the Cold War, the forging of a grand strategy appropriate to the challenge, the skill and coherence of the Bush administration's foreign policy, and the single-mindedness with which we grasped what we knew could be a fleeting opportunity.

Lady Luck played a role as well, for we were dealing at the end of the Cold War with a Soviet leadership still strong enough to override hard-line opponents domestically but too weak to offer effective resistance to the precipitous loss of empire. Still, Americans could take pride in the fact that at a critical moment, their government was on the right side of history and successfully pursued policies that were consistent with our principles and our interests. Lest these judgments seem unduly self-congratulatory, it should be added that the policies we pursued were not the work of a single administration but rather the extension of four decades of American leadership under Republican and Democratic presidents alike.

Our policies for the transitional period of the post–Cold War order were less successful. NATO was intact but slow to adapt itself to radically new circumstances. A new balance of American and European responsibilities was beginning to emerge, but transatlantic relations were beset by sharply divergent conceptions of the future "architecture" of European security. Among the postcommunist countries, progress toward democracy was well advanced in Central Europe but much more problematic farther East, and the integration of former adversaries into a stable new order remained a distant vision. The deepening conflict in the former Yugoslavia seemed to herald not a "new world order" but old world disorder.

Partly it was a failure of foresight. John Lewis Gaddis recalled the awkward silence that ensued when he inquired, at a meeting of foreign policy experts convened in Washington in early 1985, whether it might be useful to consider the possibility that the Cold War could end some day and to begin thinking about what kind of order might replace it.[5] By 1989, such thinking was indeed taking place, but the very suddenness of the revolutionary upheavals that began that year meant there was little opportunity to engage in a thorough assessment of the post–Cold War order and the American role in it.

Perhaps it was just as well. Prior examples of this kind of planning for a postwar peace were not particularly auspicious. The "Inquiry" launched by President Woodrow Wilson in the midst of World War I did little to inform a postwar order; its underestimation of the force of nationalism was as naive as Wilson's belief that he could tame the beast through the principle of self-determination.[6] Similarly, the "Advisory Committee for Post-War Planning," created by President Franklin Roosevelt in 1939, exerted little influence until it was transformed into a much more limited and operational body toward the end of the war.[7]

In both cases, planning suffered from the inherent difficulties, vastly greater than the participants realized, of divining the real power relationships that would emerge once the conflict was over and postwar reconstruction complete. Their recommendations, to the extent they penetrated the consciousness of the political leaders they served, tended to reinforce the belief that a properly designed new status quo could be sustained by reconstituting the wartime coalition as the defender of the postwar order. Both committees also ran up against the danger of trying to affirm in advance the precepts and attendant responsibilities that would bind the country in the postwar order. Roosevelt understood this better than Wilson and indeed may have learned the lesson too well. His assumption of renewed isolationist sentiment after the war led him to eschew considerations of a postwar political settlement in favor of a United Nations organization that would cement continued American engagement via a perpetuation of the wartime coalition. (At the end of the Cold War, as has been seen, the Bush administration looked to NATO in much the same way—as an institutional means of ensuring America's continued postwar engagement.)

During the two world wars, visions of the future peace also animated thinking outside of government, from democratic idealists to world federalists to balance of power realists. All three conceptions found adherents at the end of the Cold War; their ranks waxed and waned with each shift in the still emergent post–Cold War world. The democratic revolutions of 1989 and the triumphalism of the November 1990 Paris Summit led commentators to see an expanding "zone of peace" among ascendant liberal democracies.[8] By 1991, with democracy's outlook looking less bright in the postcommunist world but with the fresh success of the international coalition in the Persian Gulf, the focus had shifted to a revitalized United Nations and regional security organizations as the foundations of a new world order.[9] The messy aftermath of the Gulf War, together with the bloodletting in the former Yugoslavia, in turn, gave fresh impetus to balance of power realism and the hitherto forgotten virtues of spheres of influence. While some stuck to their conceptual guns throughout, the weight of political commentary during the period tracked exquisitely with these phases, sometimes with the same commentator shifting from one to another.[10]

The loss of focus at the end of the Cold War was accentuated by the manner in which it ended—not with military victory, demobilization, and celebration but with the unexpected capitulation of the other side without a shot being fired. We had mobilized as if for war and were mercifully spared the conflict that many saw as inevitable. The grand struggle had ended not with a bang but a whimper.

Americans of an earlier generation knew when V-E Day and V-J Day were; there were dates on the calendar marking victory in Europe and victory over Japan in 1945. But the Cold War ended on no certain date; it lacked finality. The exhilaration Americans felt at the fall of the Berlin Wall was real but somehow distant and abstract; it was detached from our own intense role in the city's history since 1945. The end of the Cold War thus evoked among the American public little sense of purpose fulfilled—and even less of responsibility for the tasks of postwar construction.

Instead of celebrating a stunning victory that vindicated our principles and filled us with new confidence for the tasks ahead, Americans seemed to feel that we had prevailed in a war of attrition but had exhausted ourselves in the process. It was as if we and the Russians were two punch-drunk boxers, equally spent after 15 rounds. The fact that one was still standing seemed almost beside the point.[11]

President Bush tried to counter this perspective in what turned out to be his last State of the Union Address in January 1992. But his assertion that "the Cold War didn't 'end'—it was won"[12] was misinterpreted as an attempt to gain personal credit during a presidential election year rather than a serious effort to get Americans to think positively about the role their country had played and needed to play in the future. Against the danger of post–Cold War disengagement, it was meant to be a call to continued American leadership. It was not a message Americans were ready to hear. The key to our future, they seemed to be saying in the 1992 election, lay within—in the regeneration of the domestic economy and the pursuit of a long agenda of pressing domestic problems deferred during the long years of the Cold War. It was a public mood that helped propel Bill Clinton to the presidency, but it also conditioned his administration to eschew foreign policy leadership in favor of an almost exclusively domestic agenda.

In short, the scope and rapidity of change after 1989, and the loss of a galvanizing threat, caused our ship of state to slip its strategic moorings. We were adrift, searching for the lodestar that would help us find our bearings.

In Search of the National Interest

In 1994 and 1995, the Council on Foreign Relations undertook a 15-month study, culminating in a two-day conference among some thirty foreign policy experts from around the country, to identify vital American interests after the Cold War.[13] The results were literally all over the map. Only one of the 12 "vital interests" on the final list enjoyed unanimous support: the physical defense of U.S. territory. Everything else was contested. As remarkable were items that did not make the final cut, notably the stability of Europe and the incorporation of Russia and China into a cooperative international order. The results of this commendable effort, in short, only confirmed the sense of strategic confusion that afflicted post–Cold War American foreign policy.[14]

Four decades of Cold War seemed to have robbed us of the capacity to think in terms of a foreign policy based on a set of core American interests that commanded broad public support. The Cold War tended to conflate principles and interests. Both, the American people overwhelmingly believed for nearly two generations, were threatened by a hostile adversary, against which the use of American power enjoyed broad domestic consensus. So the essential elements of foreign policy—principles, interests, threat, and power—all seemed to coincide in a balance that evoked relatively little opposition, but also little discriminating public debate, during the long years of Cold War.

The post–Cold War world looked much different. Of these four elements of policy, the threat had receded dramatically, and the currency of power had shifted markedly toward its nonmilitary dimensions. But our principles had not changed, or so one hoped, and our interests, to paraphrase Lord Palmerston, should have been more or less permanent. It was to these first principles and core interests that we needed to turn to find our way in the post–Cold War world.

Instead of carefully considering our interests, balancing them against our capacity and determination, and developing a strategy for advancing those interests, there was a tendency to conjure up new threats or to find a new catch-all for America's international role. Presidents Bush and Clinton both tried to define the new threats to American security and well-being as "uncertainty" and "instability." But those were elusive enemies, and a threat-based foreign policy in an era of multiple but lesser dangers was too diffuse and open-ended. So were approaches that tried to define America's role in terms of a single guiding principle, such as "democratic enlargement" or the "new world order."

The evolution of the "new world order" idea was instructive. Among its other deficiencies, as has been seen, the term suffered from what was seen as an incongruity between principles and interests. Was it high principle that led us to oppose the Iraqi invasion of Kuwait, or was it oil? The obvious answer—that it was both—never satisfied the domestic need for moral clarity, so the term began to migrate, each new formulation a bit more grand than the last. By the end, the Gulf War had become the moral equivalent of a holy war, and Saddam Hussein had been demonized as the spiritual heir of Adolf Hitler. When applied to the UN and to Europe—and imbued with the Wilsonian euphoria of the triumph of democratic principles—the term took on the crusading rhetoric of a "Pax Americana" that was never intended.

The concept of "national interests" was always difficult for Americans, for reasons of history, political culture, and the simple geographic fact of having two large oceans separating us from any potentially hostile power.[15] Considerations of national interest seemed to fly in the face of American exceptionalism—the belief that our country was not like any other. We had a moral mission, if not to save the world, at least to redeem it by our example. Thus, this "national interest" seemed to belong to an age of cynical balance of power politics that was inconsistent with our values and principles. For some, it conjured up images of gunboat diplomacy and a reckless disregard for the rights of others; the pursuit of narrow and transitory self-interest, it was argued, redounded ultimately to our own detriment.

Yet setting up interests against principles was a false dichotomy: promotion of core values and principles was part and parcel of our interests. We needed to uphold basic norms of international conduct for our own well-being, and we needed to support fundamental human rights—if only because the world was more dangerous when leaders of potentially hostile powers were not accountable to their own people. But principles alone were an insufficient guide in a world where the number of problems needing solution vastly exceeded the resources we had at our disposal for addressing them. They led either to an open-ended set of responsibilities that Americans in the end would be unwilling to shoulder or to the arrogance of believing we could and should impose our grand design on the rest of the world.

An interest-based foreign policy, by contrast, should bear some relation to capability—a consideration that would help set priorities and impose limits on our ambitions. Far from being immoral or illiberal, such a foreign policy would recapture a spirit of tolerance, respect for the legitimate interests of others, and a certain caution against intruding into other people's business unless it impinged on our own.

Lessons for the Post–Cold War Era

From the beginning of the Bush administration, we pursued an interest-based strategy. We resisted the pressures to "meet Gorbachev halfway"—to reciprocate Soviet peace initiatives and strike a strategic bargain with Gorbachev and so strengthen his staying power in Moscow. Embracing the Soviet agenda of half-measures or helping Moscow prop up a crumbling empire was not what we had in mind. We deliberately put U.S.-Soviet relations on a slow track, so as to build down public expectations of reciprocal U.S. steps on Soviet terms. We also undertook a systematic review of our interests that led to a grand strategy for ending the Cold War. We advanced our own agenda of deep reductions in Soviet conventional forces in Europe, Soviet acceptance of peaceful democratic change in Eastern Europe, and Soviet cooperation in solving regional conflicts. It was a remedy that went to the causes rather than just the symptoms of the Cold War division.

American foreign policy at the end of the Cold War—the largely successful approaches that guided American policy through the Eastern European revolutions of 1989, the unification of Germany, and the disintegration of the Soviet Union—offered lessons for the immediate future. Yet these lessons were not always grasped, even by those who crafted the policies in the first place.

At least five straightforward lessons could be drawn from this period. The first was that a secure, stable, and prosperous Europe was vital to our own security and well-being. That seemingly obvious proposition needed restating in light of tendencies among the American public to turn inward and among the political elites to become enraptured by our growing commercial interests along the Pacific rim. But Europe went to the core of our political, military, and economic security (to say nothing of our national identity) in ways that Asia did not. We had fought two hot wars and one cold one already; our presence in Europe had become so pervasive that it risked being taken for granted. As a practical matter, there were any number of challenges around the world that bore on important American interests, yet we had neither the capacity nor the desire to solve them alone. Where to turn for help? Naturally, to those countries that shared our values and our interests and with whom we had developed habits and patterns of cooperation—notably Europe and Japan.

If the stability of Europe was a vital American interest, what endangered that stability after the end of the Cold War? The answer was less obvious than in 1947, when most of Europe lay in ruins, with communist parties in Italy, France, Greece, and elsewhere exploiting economic and social unrest. At the end of the Cold War, the issue seemed to have become a contest between the forces of integration and of disintegration. Would Western Europe be able to extend its zone of democracy, security, and prosperity eastward, or would the forces of fragmentation on the loose in the East undermine the self-confidence, cohesion, and ultimately the institutions binding the Western democracies?

Thus a second lesson was that Eastern Europe, the key to ending the Cold War, was also the key to the post–Cold War order in Europe. In 1989, we elevated Eastern Europe to first place on the international agenda and, in effect, held U.S.-Soviet relations hostage to Moscow's acceptance of peaceful democratic change in this region. This was arguably the most important single thing the United States did in helping bring about the end of the Cold War. Of course, the United States did not cause the revolutions of 1989: those sprang from deep historic, economic, and political roots. But we did help create an international environment conducive to their success.

The success of the postcommunist transitions in Central and Eastern Europe—particularly the lands between Germany and Russia—should have been the highest priority for the new security order in Europe. Yet after the first flush of enthusiasm in 1989 and 1990, the United States and its Western partners devoted little attention and few resources to this task. As a matter of security rather than of foreign aid, what was

needed was more assistance for countries attempting to make these unprecedented transitions, as well as greater market access and a more
rapid integration into Western institutions. The bleak alternative was
being played out before our eyes in the former Yugoslavia, and the
Western response, timid though it was, proved much more costly than
the total of our foreign assistance to Central and Eastern Europe.

A third lesson was that the German question was still open, and
American leadership was still required to ensure it was answered in a
way consistent with our interests. In 1989 we saw, earlier and more
clearly than the Germans themselves, that the German question was on
the international agenda and that U.S. leadership was required to ensure
that it was answered in ways consistent with European security. Thus
our seemingly instinctive support for German unification—at a time
when Britain, France, and of course the Soviet Union were bitterly opposed—was actually the product of a careful consideration of U.S. interests. This thinking was embedded in American policy during President Bush's visit to Germany in May 1989, long before the fall of the
Berlin Wall.

We did not cause German unification any more than we did the revolutions of 1989. Unification was coming whether we willed it or not.
But if we had joined the British, French, and Russians in opposing German unification—or if we had merely remained passive—the Germans
would have had no choice but to cut the best deal they could with
Moscow. So we were looking not only to the process of German unification but to the future structure of European security and to Germany's role in a more united Europe.

The German question was never about unity alone but about
whether a powerful Germany could be accommodated within a secure
and stable European order. That question was still open, though this
time it was not the fault of the Germans. For forty years, Germans
across the political spectrum knew that their deepest national aspiration—the unity of their country—could be achieved only in cooperation
with their Western partners. That situation changed objectively after the
achievement of German unity. On some issues it became evident that
German interests were better secured by going it alone—as indeed Germany threatened to do in order to drag the European Community into
premature recognition of Croatia and Slovenia in the fall of 1991.

In the aftermath of unification, the Germans bent over backwards to
prove themselves good Europeans and Atlanticists, more often than not

subordinating or adjusting their particular interests to the larger interests of the cohesion of the European Union and the Atlantic alliance. But for how long? Just as American diplomacy in 1989 and 1990 worked to ensure that the Germans were never asked to choose between unity and alliance, the task afterwards was to ensure that Germans did not have to choose between alliance and their fundamental interests.

If, as Henry Kissinger once said, Germany was too big for Europe, too small for the world, the U.S. role was indispensable in both respects. We stood as a friendly counterweight to German power in Europe, and as a partner in other parts of the world that could help Germany play a global role commensurate with its economic and political weight. An integral part of this effort was to ensure that Germany play this new role in concert with its European partners, which in turn required a more united Europe, capable of assuming larger responsibilities.

Thus a fourth lesson was that European unity was even more important to us in the post–Cold War era and, somewhat paradoxically, could not be achieved without American leadership. Despite our constant assurances in 1989–91, Europeans believed we were ambivalent about a more united Europe, supporting it in principle but often opposing it when it came to specific steps being considered. They were right. The ambivalence derived from consideration of our interests, which made some conceptions of European unity congenial and others less so. The interests we pursued were the right ones: we wanted a Europe that strengthened rather than weakened the Atlantic alliance, and we wanted to see the Europeans develop a greater capacity for common action, especially in the East. In practice, however, we continued to cling instinctively to a dominant role that we were no longer ready to play and so found it difficult to cede leadership gracefully to the Europeans. And of course the Europeans did not make it easy, for American policy was obliged to deal with a highly ambitious conception of a federal Europe, driven by the French and "Brussels," that masked deep misgivings among the Europeans themselves. Moreover, the European Community's attempts to exert leadership in Yugoslavia—which we were only too ready to endorse—demonstrated how far the EC was from developing a serious capacity for concerted action in foreign policy.

It was also evident that our own ability to stay engaged in Europe required a more united, cohesive, and capable European Community. But what kind of unity? The United States could not be agnostic on so vital a question. For one thing, it was futile to support a vision of Europe that could not be fulfilled. We needed to recognize, as most Europeans privately did, that the grandiose objectives enshrined at the 1991 Maastricht Summit of European political, economic, and monetary union could not be achieved any time soon, and that continuing to pay lip service to these goals only distracted Europe and the United States from more urgent business. The main danger to the future of Europe lay in the postcommunist East, and that should be Europe's priority. The Community's reaching out to the new democracies via the "association agreements" was a step in the right direction, but much more weight needed to be attached to full accession by these countries according to clear criteria and timetables for membership. Debates within the European Union, as it was ambitiously and misleadingly called after Maastricht, between "deepening" (among existing members) and "widening" (to include new ones) proved a distraction from the more urgent practical tasks in the East.

The Atlantic alliance's debate over whether to accept new Central European members was likewise diverted, in NATO's case because the issue came to be seen as an act of hostility toward Russia. It was one thing to take seriously Russian fears of exclusion, quite another to give credence to the argument of Russian politicians that NATO constituted a threat to Russian security. One way of escaping this impasse was to return to the simple concept of alliance, which could be *for* as well as against something. Originally formed to counter a hostile Soviet Union, NATO was being turned to new purposes: pooling scarce military resources, integrating national military structures, strengthening shared values and interests, and enhancing the capacity to act on behalf of those interests, as in Bosnia. The North Atlantic Treaty had 14 articles; only one of them—Article 5—entailed mutual defense commitments. Article 1 involved the peaceful settlement of disputes, Article 2 concerned strengthening free institutions, Article 4 provided for political consultation. Article 10 nicely captured the logic of enlargement: "The parties may, by unanimous agreement, invite any other European State in a position to further the principles of this Treaty and to contribute to the security of the North Atlantic area to accede to this Treaty."[16]

Turning finally to Russia, a fifth lesson was that "a new relationship cannot simply be declared by Moscow, or bestowed by others." So said President Bush in his May 1989 commencement address at Texas A&M.[17] It was wise counsel then, and it was wise counsel even after the breakup of the Soviet Union. In 1989, rather than "meeting Gorbachev halfway," we instead challenged him to come the rest of the way to meet us. To begin with, we refused to allow ourselves to be held accountable for the fate of Soviet reforms, much less Gorbachev's personal fate. These were events well beyond our influence, except at the margins. The peoples of the Soviet Union had great, wrenching choices ahead of them. We could hope to nudge them toward policies congenial to our interests, but we were under no illusions that we could make the Soviet peoples' choices for them. Our focus was on Soviet international behavior, where our influence was much greater and which was a more legitimate focus for our policy anyway. Bush and Secretary of State Baker got considerable credit for their diplomatic and arms control initiatives that avoided humiliating a Soviet leadership in the midst of imperial breakup, but what was not as well understood was their sophisticated use of power—not only military power—toward those ends. As German unification proceeded, we mobilized an international consensus that made it harder for Soviet leaders to say *nyet*, even as our other initiatives made it easier for them to say *da*.

Yet by the end, the Bush administration had forgotten some of its own lessons, vastly exaggerating our ability to influence the Russian internal dynamic and embarking on a self-defeating strategy that had us intruding too deeply in Russia's domestic affairs. Worse, in our zeal to avert Russia's exclusion from the emerging international order, we allowed the Russian agenda to dictate our own and put ourselves in the position of trying to compensate Russia for lost influence. In the process, we inadvertently lent strength to the extremist forces we meant to oppose. We seemed to be legitimizing and accommodating ultra-nationalist demands that sprang from an obsolete definition of security based on spheres of influence and territorial control.

The Clinton administration accentuated these mistakes by elevating Russia's internal transformation to first place in our global agenda. As if to underscore the strategic confusion, a January 1996 essay in *Time* magazine criticized the Clinton administration's Russia policy as "outdated." But the essay nonetheless concluded that "the proper goal of American policy toward its former cold-war rival remains in 1996 what it was in '93: a peaceful, democratic, prosperous Russia fully integrated into the international community."[18] It was a widely shared view in and out of government, but it was misguided. The happy state of affairs it described was the proper goal of *Russian* policy, not American. Clearly, a democratic, peaceful, and cooperative Russia would be in America's interest and indeed in everyone's interest, but that outcome was so far beyond our capacity to deliver as to constitute mere wishful thinking or, worse, dangerous arrogance. When the United States intruded directly into the Russian political process in support of "reformers," we were more likely to generate anti-American sentiment than we were to advance the cause of reform.

In an article a few years earlier, John Gaddis had defined our objectives more modestly: "rehabilitate defeated adversaries and invite them into the international state system."[19] There was a world of difference between this formulation and the one just cited from *Time*. It was right to help "rehabilitate" the Russian economic and political system so that the Russian people could have the chance to decide on a democratic future. Whether they seized that chance, however, was beyond our capacity to decide. As regards Russia's involvement in the international system, "invite" was a better verb than "integrate." "Integrate" suggested that it was within America's capacity and indeed our responsibility to bring Russia in; "invite" was more in keeping with our real capabilities and also kept the onus where it belonged—on the Russians themselves. It also would have freed us from the task of trying to tell the Russians what their interests were and enabled us to focus on our own instead.

Countering the emergence of a hostile power capable of threatening the United States and its allies certainly belonged on a short list of American vital interests. So did controlling and reducing weapons of mass destruction. Both dangers arose in the Russian case, and they argued for a long-term, sustainable strategy—one that did not rest so heavily on the dubious proposition that we could influence Russian behavior by dint of our own good intentions. There was also the old-fashioned way of influencing a state's behavior by altering the international context in which that state operates. In this sense, it was worth considering the remainder of the passage cited above from Bush's Texas A&M speech of May 1989:

> The national security of America and our allies is not predicated on hope. It must be based on deeds. We look for enduring, ingrained economic and political change. . . . As we seek peace, we must also remain strong. The purpose of our military might is not to pressure a weak Soviet economy, or to seek military superiority. It is to deter war. It is to defend ourselves and our allies, and to do something more—to convince the Soviet Union that there can be

no reward in pursuing expansionism—to convince the Soviet Union that reward lies in the pursuit of peace.

Substitute "Russia" for "Soviet Union," and this was a set of principles that would serve us well for the post-Soviet era. Of course, the stress on military power was dated, but the uses of power more generally—meaning the economic, political, moral, and psychological aspects as well as the military—were not. Lest this seem unduly confrontational, it was worth recalling that we did not hesitate to play power politics with our friends, notably Japan, yet we tended to shrink from doing so with Russia. In the end, this would prove a more sound and durable basis for American policy, just as the advent in 1995 of a more tough-minded Russian foreign policy promised to yield, paradoxically, a relationship more solidly grounded in Russian national interests—and ours.

Perhaps the most compelling argument for an interest-based foreign policy derived from the evolution of U.S. policy toward a disintegrating Yugoslavia. At the heart of the problem for Western governments, as has been seen, was the judgment, reached early on in Washington and most European capitals, that Yugoslavia no longer mattered much because it was no longer likely to be an arena of East-West conflict. Even as Yugoslavia descended into the most brutal conflict Europe had seen since World War II, the Bush administration could not decide whether important U.S. interests were at stake. Did Yugoslavia matter enough to invest considerable American leadership and, if need be, commit American military forces to peacekeeping or peacemaking efforts? It was argued that the American public, eager for a post–Cold War "peace dividend," was unprepared to support such action, yet the case was never made in terms the public could understand and weigh. We even began to lose faith in our principles, succumbing to the perverse Balkan "wisdom" that peace could be built on the foundation of ethnic nationalism.

In 1993, the Clinton administration assumed office full of criticism for the failures of its predecessor but was similarly unprepared to make a case for American leadership. It was only after Croatia's military breakthrough in the fall of 1995 that the administration began to make its case for the dispatch of U.S. military forces as part of a NATO-led UN mission to Bosnia.

Finally, four years after the outbreak of hostilities in the former Yugoslavia, a serious debate had been joined over American policy—and it was a debate framed in the right way. What was at stake in Bosnia was the stability of the Balkans, and potentially of Europe as a whole. Also of grave concern was the precedent that might be set for authoritarian ultranationalism elsewhere in Eastern Europe and the former Soviet Union. The conflict was thus at the intersection of the Cold War division between East and West, and the manner of its resolution bore on our vital interests across two continents. Honorable men and women could and did come down on different sides of the debate over the proper role of the United States in this conflict, but it was a debate that finally could be conducted on the sound bases of American national interests and fundamental principles. Regaining the capacity to think about our international involvement in that way may have been the beginning of wisdom in the post–Cold War world.

For all the challenges ahead, the circumstances for American policy at the end of the Cold War were much more auspicious than in 1945 or 1919. There was no large external threat on the horizon. There was a functioning, if sluggish, global economy. A prosperous, democratic, and integrated Western Europe was a magnet and point of reference for the emerging East European democracies. The main European and transatlantic institutions were intact. Above all, the United States had not retreated across the ocean, as it had after World War I.

Just as the Cold War order and the strategy of containment took the better part of a decade to put in place, creation of a post–Cold War order was not to be the work of a few months or years. Yet long years of Cold War, and the success of strategies for ending it, had demonstrated a few simple truths: that the indivisibility of transatlantic security needed to be preserved into the indefinite future, that Europe's future depended on the fate of democratic transformation in its eastern half, and that American leadership would be as essential in the new era as it had been in the last.

Chronology

freest in Soviet history, voters reject several prominent communist leaders in favor of Boris Yeltsin and other independents.

April 5: Polish roundtable talks end with agreement on political reform; free parliamentary elections scheduled for June.

April 6: Radio Budapest announces that a partial withdrawal of Soviet troops from Hungary would begin on April 25.

April 9: Soviet troops break up a Georgian nationalist demonstration in Tbilisi.

April 17: The independent Solidarity trade union is restored to legal status.

Soviet Union announces that withdrawal of ten thousand troops and a thousand tanks from the GDR will begin on May 11.

May 2: Part of the Iron Curtain between Hungary and Austria is dismantled.

May 8–9: Hungarian Socialist Worker Party relieves former general secretary János Kádár of posts as party president and Central Committee member.

May 19–20: Thousands of ethnic Turks stage protests in Bulgaria.

May 25: Gorbachev is elected head of state.

May 30–31: NATO Summit in Brussels endorses President Bush's CFE (Conventional Armed Forces in Europe) proposal for deep mutual reductions by 1990; Bush meets with Chancellor Kohl in Mainz, delivers a programmatic speech on ending the division of Europe.

June 2–7: Bulgaria expels hundreds of ethnic Turks.

June 4: The first round of Polish elections is held.

Peaceful demonstrators are massacred in Beijing's Tiananmen Square.

June 6: Solidarity wins 99 of 100 seats in the new Polish senate and 160 of 161 available seats in the Sejm.

June 13–15: President Gorbachev visits West Germany.

Government-opposition roundtable talks convene in Hungary.

June 16: Former prime minister Imre Nagy is reburied, with vast demonstration in tribute at Budapest's Heroes' Square.

July 6: Hungarian supreme court legally rehabilitates Nagy.

Gorbachev addresses Council of Europe in Strasbourg.

July 7–8: Warsaw Pact Summit, in Bucharest, affirms the right of member states to choose own domestic policies without interference.

July 9–12: President Bush visits Poland and Hungary, announces economic assistance measures.

Soviet miners begin strike.

July 15: In Paris, G-7 leaders issue declaration supporting economic and political freedom in Eastern Europe and call for an international conference to coordinate aid.

July 17: European Community foreign ministers meet in Brussels to discuss a coordinated aid program for Poland and Hungary.

July 19: General Wojciech Jaruzelski is elected president of Poland by the margin of a single vote.

Aug. 3: East Germans occupy West German mission in East Berlin and West German embassy in Budapest, seeking emigration visas.

Aug. 21: Large mass demonstration is held in central Prague on the anniversary of the 1968 Warsaw Pact Invasion.

Aug. 22–23: Lithuanian parliament declares the 1940 annexation of the Baltic states illegal; human chain across the Baltic republics marks the fiftieth anniversary of Hitler-Stalin pact.

Aug. 24: Tadeusz Mazowiecki becomes Poland's first noncommunist prime minister in forty years.

Aug. 25: Hungarian prime minister Németh visits West Germany.

Sept. 21–22: Prime Minister Shevardnadze and Secretary of State Baker meet in Wyoming.

Sept. 25: In the biggest spontaneous demonstration in the GDR, thousands march in Leipzig, calling for political reforms.

Sept. 29: Polish finance minister Balcerowicz presents economic "shock therapy" plan.

Oct. 5: More than seven thousand East German refugees are transported to West Germany.

Gorbachev attends the GDR's fortieth anniversary celebrations.

Oct. 7–9: Demonstrations erupt in East Berlin, Dresden, and other cities.

Oct. 10: Hungarian Socialist Workers party changes its name to Hungarian Socialist party.

Oct. 16: One hundred thousand East German protesters march through Leipzig.

CSCE conference opens in Sofia amidst demonstrations by Bulgarian "Ecoglasnost."

Oct. 18: Erich Honecker is replaced by Egon Krenz as East German Communist party leader.

Oct. 23: Three hundred thousand march in Leipzig and other cities.

A new Hungarian republic is proclaimed.

Oct. 24: West Germany announces aid package for Poland.

EC pledges $300 million to assist Poland and Hungary.

Oct. 25: France announces aid plan for Poland.

Oct. 26–27: At Warsaw Pact meeting in Warsaw, new Polish foreign minister Skubiszewski pledges to maintain friendly ties with the Warsaw Pact allies "on the principle of equal rights."

Oct. 30: Three hundred thousand march in Leipzig; protest spreads to other cities.

Nov. 3: Demonstrations break out in Bulgaria.

Nov. 4: One million demonstrate in East Berlin.

Nov. 7–8: Entire East German council of ministers and Politburo resign, with Krenz continuing as party leader.

Nov. 9–14: Kohl visits Poland (interrupted for trip to Berlin).

Nov. 9: The Berlin Wall is opened.

Nov. 11: Bulgarian Communist party leader Todor Zhivkov is replaced by Petŭr Mladenov.

Demonstration in Prague is suppressed by police.

Nov. 11–12: Foreign ministers of Hungary, Austria, Italy, and Yugoslavia meet in Budapest and pledge regional cooperation.

Nov. 13: Two hundred thousand protesters in Leipzig demand free elections and an end to one-party rule. Hans Modrow is appointed prime minister of the GDR.

Nov. 15: Lech Wałęsa speaks to joint session of U.S. Congress.

Nov. 16: Hungary applies to become the first East European member of the Council of Europe.

Nov. 18: EC leaders meet in Paris to discuss Eastern Europe.

Nov. 19–23: Spiraling demonstrations in Prague and Bratislava call for democracy. Václav Havel meets with prime minister Adamec. Alexander Dubček makes his first public speech in 21 years.

Nov. 23–27: Mazowiecki makes official visit to the Soviet Union.

Nov. 24–25: Miloš Jakeš resigns as Czechoslovak Communist party leader. Hundreds of thousands rally in Prague to listen to Havel and Dubček.

Nov. 27: Workers stage two-hour general strike throughout Czechoslovakia. Two hundred thousand East Germans demonstrate in Leipzig.

Nov. 28: Kohl announces a ten-point plan for German unification.

Dec. 2–3: Presidents Bush and Gorbachev meet at Malta.

Dec. 3: East German Politburo, including Krenz, resigns.

Dec. 4: NATO Summit in Brussels supports the goal of German unification as a "gradual, step-by-step process."

Dec. 4–5: Hundreds of thousands of demonstrators rally in Prague.

New Czechoslovak cabinet is formed; the majority is noncommunist.

Dec. 6: Krenz resigns as chairman of the National Defense Council.

Mitterrand meets Gorbachev in Kiev.

Dec. 7: In Bulgaria, independent organizations join to form the Union of Democratic Forces (UDF), with chairman Zhelyu Zhelev.

Czechoslovak prime minister Adamec resigns. First Deputy prime minister Čalfa named to form new government.

Dec. 8–9: EC Summit in Strasbourg supports German unification so long as it is embedded in European integration.

Dec. 10: Prodemocracy demonstrators in Sofia, organized by the Union of Democratic Forces, call for roundtable talks.

Dec. 16–17: Police and demonstrators clash in Timişoara, Romania, after police tried to evict pastor László Tökés from his home.

Dec. 18–20: Clashes continue in Timişoara, extend to other cities.

Yugoslav prime minister Ante Marković unveils economic and political reform package.

Lithuanian communists declare independence from the Soviet party leadership.

Dec. 20–21: Mitterrand pays state visit to GDR.

Dec. 22: State of emergency is declared in Romania. National Salvation Front declares itself the new government while clashes erupt between armed NSF supporters and Ceauşescu loyalists.

Dec. 25: Nicolae and Elena Ceauşescu, having been tried by a military tribunal and sentenced to death, are executed by firing squad.

Dec. 26: NSF appoints Ion Iliescu its president.

Dec. 29: Václav Havel is elected president of Czechoslovakia.

1990

Jan. 11: Gorbachev visits Lithuania in an effort to halt the proindependence movement.

Jan. 15: Gorbachev dispatches troops to Azerbaijan after anti-Armenian riots.

Jan. 31: In his State of the Union Address, President Bush proposes deeper conventional force reductions down in Europe to 195,000 on each side.

Feb. 10: Chancellor Kohl meets President Gorbachev in Moscow.

Feb. 12–17: Ethnic riots erupt in Tajikistan.

Feb. 13: American, Soviet, British, French, and German foreign ministers agree on Two Plus Four talks during meeting in Ottawa.

Feb 24–25: Kohl and Bush meet at Camp David.

Feb. 25: Demonstrations throughout USSR signal growing opposition to Gorbachev on both the Right and the Left.

March 11: Lithuania declares independence; Gorbachev denounces the move as "illegitimate and invalid."

March 13: The Soviet Congress of People's Deputies repeals the Communist party's monopoly on political power.

March 18: In East German elections, voters back the prounification party allied with Kohl's Christian Democratic Union.

March 25: József Antall and his Hungarian Democratic Forum win plurality in the Hungarian elections.

March 30: Estonia proclaims its independence.

April 9: Havel, Wałęsa, and Antall meet in Bratislava to discuss trilateral cooperation.

April 13: Gorbachev threatens an embargo of Lithuania.

April 28: EC Summit in Dublin prepares the integration of East Germany into the European Community.

May 4: The Latvian parliament declares independence and is branded illegal by Gorbachev.

May 5: First Two Plus Four meeting is held in Bonn.

May 18: Treaty on Economic, Monetary, and Social Union between the two German states is signed.

May 20: National Salvation Front led by Ion Iliescu wins elections in Romania.

May 29: Yeltsin is elected leader of the Russian parliament.

May 30–June 2: Bush-Gorbachev Summit is held in Washington and Camp David; arms control and trade agreements signed; Gorbachev concedes it is "up to the German people" to decide on NATO membership.

June 10–17: The Bulgarian Communist party wins over prodemocracy parties in national elections.

June 12: Russia declares its sovereignty.

June 14–15: Student protests in Bucharest are violently suppressed.

June 22: Second Two Plus Four meeting is held in East Berlin.

June 25–26: EC Summit in Dublin supports German unification.

July 1: Economies of the two German states are unified.

July 2–15: Twenty-eighth Soviet party congress is held in Moscow; Yeltsin resigns from the Communist party.

July 5–6: NATO Summit issues "London Declaration on a Transformed North Atlantic Alliance," invites Gorbachev and East European leaders to visit NATO headquarters and establish liaison missions.

July 9–11: G-7 Summit is held in Houston.

July 16: Gorbachev and Kohl, meeting in the Caucasus, agree that the united Germany will belong to NATO.

Ukraine declares its sovereignty.

July 17: Bulgarian roundtable discussions begin with UDF.

Third Two Plus Four meeting is held in Paris.

Aug. 2: Iraq invades Kuwait.

Following demonstrations, Zhelev is elected Bulgarian president.

Aug. 3: Árpád Göncz is elected president of Hungary.

Sept. 9: Bush meets with Gorbachev in Helsinki to discuss Iraq.

Sept. 12: Treaty on German unification is signed at fourth and final Two Plus Four meeting, in Moscow.

Oct. 3: East and West Germany unite.

Oct. 27–28: In Rome, EC decides that transition to second stage of economic and monetary union will take place on January 1, 1994.

Nov. 9: USSR and Germany sign treaty of friendship and cooperation.

Nov. 19–21: At CSCE Summit in Paris, European and North American leaders sign "Charter of Paris"; CFE agreement, NATO–Warsaw Pact nonaggression pact, and U.S.-EC declaration are also signed.

Nov. 23: Gorbachev proposes new union treaty that will loosen ties between the central Soviet government and the 15 republics.

Nov. 27: UN Resolution 678 authorizes use of force against Iraq.

Dec. 9: Lech Wałęsa is elected president of Poland.

Slobodan Milošević is reelected president of Serbia.

Dec. 11: Albania abandons one-party rule.

Dec. 20: Shevardnadze resigns, warning of a hard-line dictatorship.

Dec. 20–21: EC begins negotiations with Czechoslovakia, Hungary, and Poland on new association agreements.

1991

Jan. 1: Jan Krzysztof Bielecki is named prime minister of Poland.

Jan. 2: Soviet troops seize buildings in Vilnius.

Jan. 13: Fifteen are killed in a "Bloody Sunday" in Lithuania.

Jan. 16: Military action against Iraq begins.

Jan. 20: Four demonstrators are killed in a "Bloody Sunday" in Latvia.

Feb. 15: Wałęsa, Havel, and Antall sign "Visegrád Declaration" on regional cooperation among Poland, Czechoslovakia, and Hungary.

Feb. 20: Slovenian and Croatian parliaments propose the dissolution of the Yugoslav confederation into separate sovereign states.

Feb. 25: Military structures of Warsaw Pact are dissolved.

Feb. 27: Kuwait is liberated.

March 15: The United States recognizes Albania after 53-year hiatus.

March 17: Soviet citizens vote in favor of the union treaty, but six republics boycott.

March 31: In Albania's first free elections, the (ex-Communist) Labor party wins two-thirds of the vote.

April 9: The Georgian parliament unanimously declares independence.

April 15: European Bank for Reconstruction and Development opens.

April 23: Gorbachev, Yeltsin, and the presidents of eight other republics sign treaty of union.

May 29: Croatia declares its sovereignty.

June 4: Coalition government is formed in Albania.

June 12: Yeltsin is elected to the newly created Russian presidency.

In Prague, Mitterrand proposes European confederation.

June 25: Croatia and Slovenia declare independence.

June 27: The Yugoslav army intervenes in Slovenia.

July 6: Civic Alliance party is formed in Romania.

July 15–17: G-7 Summit in London announces six-point assistance plan for the USSR.

July 30–31: Moscow Summit is held between Presidents Bush and Gorbachev; START (Strategic Arms Reduction Treaty) is signed.

Aug. 18–19: Hard-liners stage coup attempt against Gorbachev. Boris Yeltsin calls for general strike and civil disobedience.

Aug. 24: Gorbachev, following failed coup attempt, resigns as head of the Communist party.

Ukrainian and Byelorussian parliaments declare independence.

Aug. 26–Sept. 5: Vukovar, Okucani, Danuvar, Dubrovnik, and other Croatian cities are shelled.

Aug. 29: The Soviet parliament bans Communist party activities.

Sept. 2: The United States recognizes the independence of the Baltic states.

Sept. 27: President Bush announces a series of unilateral arms control measures and calls on Soviet Union to reciprocate.

Oct. 15: UDF and ethnic Turkish Movement for Rights and Freedom (MRF) win Bulgarian elections.

Oct. 16: Bosnia-Herzegovina declares independence.

Oct. 27: Polish elections produce fragmented parliament, leading to protracted government crisis.

Nov. 7–8: NATO Summit in Rome adopts "new strategic concept" and invites countries of the former Warsaw Pact to join a new "North Atlantic Cooperation Council."

Dec. 1: Ukrainians vote for independence.

Dec. 8: Yeltsin and the leaders of Ukraine and Belarus declare the formation of a "Commonwealth of Independent States."

Dec. 11–12: EC Maastricht Summit convenes and treaty is signed.

Dec. 16: EC's "Europe" agreements with Poland, Hungary, and Czechoslovakia are signed.

Dec. 17: EC agrees to recognize Croatia and Slovenia as independent states by January 15, 1992.

Dec. 24: Germany recognizes Croatia and Slovenia.

Dec. 25: Gorbachev resigns. The USSR ceases to exist.

Notes

Preface

1. The scenario was not quite right: I did not foresee German unification but rather much closer ties between two independent German states, which would increasingly act together out of their shared interests. The speech itself was never published, but I developed elements of the argument in an essay written later in the year and published as "Soviet Dilemmas in Eastern Europe," in Richard F. Staar, ed., *U.S.–East European Relations in the 1990s* (New York: Crane Russak, 1989), pp. 15–34, esp. 30–31.

2. T. E. Lawrence, *Revolt in the Desert* (London: The Folio Society, 1986), p. 13. [An abridgement of Lawrence's *Seven Pillars of Wisdom, Revolt in the Desert* was first published by Jonathan Cape, London, 1927.]

3. Many of these documents will be printed and analyzed in a forthcoming (1997) issue of the Woodrow Wilson Center's Cold War International History Project *Bulletin*.

4. Before and after important events, it is common for senior officials to give background briefings to the press; Secretary Baker was the unrivaled master of the art. Of course they are incomplete and are sometimes used to give the administration's particular "spin" on events, but the overriding motivation is to inform. Sometimes political leaders need to maintain absolute secrecy on operational plans; much more often they want to keep the press informed, lest their initiatives fall on deaf ears. They want the media to understand the intent behind a major speech or foreign policy initiative; they would rather have their policies criticized on their merits (or demerits) than have them misinterpreted or ignored altogether.

5. Cited in Timothy Garton Ash, *In Europe's Name: Germany and the Divided Continent* (New York: Random House, 1993), p. 44.

Introduction

1. Elizabeth Pond, *Beyond the Wall: Germany's Road to Unification* (Washington, D.C.: The Brookings Institution, 1993), p. 186.

2. See, e.g., the three definitions presented in Chas. W. Freeman, Jr., *The Diplomat's Dictionary* (Washington, D.C.: National Defense University Press, 1994), pp. 364–65.

3. Paul Kennedy, *The Rise and Fall of the Great Powers* (New York: Random House, 1987), p. xv.

4. Isaiah Berlin, "The Hedgehog and the Fox," in Isaiah Berlin, *Russian Thinkers*, ed. Henry Hardy and Aileen Kelly (New York: Viking Press, 1978), p. 22.

5. On this point, see Keohane and Nye in their introduction to Robert O. Keohane, Joseph S. Nye, and Stanley Hoffmann, eds., *After the Cold War: International Institutions and State Strategies in Europe, 1989–1991* (Cambridge, Ma.: Harvard University Press, 1993), p. 16.

Chapter 1

1. Bush's admonition came even before the inauguration, along with tentative planning by his transition team. See James A. Baker, III, with Thomas M. DeFrank, *The Politics of Diplomacy: Revolution, War and Peace, 1989–92* (New York: G. P. Putnam's Sons, 1995), p. 40.

2. See, e.g., Mikhail Gorbachev, *Perestroika: New Thinking for Our Country and the World* (New York: Harper & Row, Publishers, 1987).

3. As cited in J. F. Brown, *Surge to Freedom: The End of Communist Rule in Eastern Europe* (Durham, N.C.: Duke University Press, 1991) p. 4.

4. "Report to the President by the National Security Council (NSC 58/2): United States Policy Toward the Soviet Satellite States in Eastern Europe," December 8, 1949, in *The Foreign Relations of the United States, 1949*, Vol. 5 (Washington, D.C.: U.S. Government Printing Office, 1976), pp. 42–54.

5. In an article written in the fall of 1988 and published in 1989, I concluded that "the advent of the Gorbachev leadership . . . heralded the end of an era in Eastern Europe. . . . Eastern Europe is entering a period of flux more profound than at any time since the immediate post-Stalin period. The Gorbachev era may not be so explosive, but it is likely to introduce changes more fundamental and lasting." (Robert L. Hutchings, "Soviet Dilemmas in Eastern Europe," in Richard F. Staar, ed., *U.S.–East European Relations in the 1990s* [New York: Crane Russak, 1989], pp. 16 and 30.) See also Lincoln Gordon et al., eds., *Eroding Empire: Western Relations with Eastern Europe* (Washington, D.C.: Brookings Institution, 1987) and William E. Griffith, ed., *Central and Eastern Europe: The Opening Curtain?* (Boulder, Co.: Westview Press, 1989).

6. For background, see Robert L. Hutchings, *Soviet–East European Relations: Consolidation and Conflict* (Madison: University of Wisconsin Press, 1983; rev. paperback ed., 1987).

7. *Current Digest of the Soviet Press*, January 4, 1989, p. 3.

8. Anatoli Chernyayev, speaking at a Princeton University conference devoted to "A Retrospective on the End of the Cold War," Session III, February 26, 1993.

9. In an interview with Don Oberdorfer in early May, William Hyland offered the same judgment: "If there is some kind of new order in Hungary, Poland and perhaps Czechoslovakia, with less of a Soviet presence, a substantial reduction of troops and liberalization inside the countries with multiparty elections and so on, then the question is whether that can be applied to East Germany. And if it is, aren't you just a step away from the unification of Germany?" (Don Oberdorfer, *The Turn: From the Cold War to a New Era* [New York: Simon and Schuster, 1991], p. 346.)

It was the same logic back in 1980–81 that caused East German party leader Erich Honecker to conclude that if Solidarity prevailed in Poland, East Germany was finished.

10. Indeed it was, though we had no way of knowing it at the time. According to Sergei Tarasenko, Shevardnadze had concluded after considering the results and implications of the Polish elections in June 1989 that Eastern Europe would probably "go." Cited by Timothy Garton Ash, *In Europe's Name: Germany and the Divided Continent* (New York: Random House, 1993), p. 124.

11. Baker, *Politics of Diplomacy*, pp. 47–60. See also Jay Winik, "The Quest for Bipartisanship: A New Beginning for a New World Order," *The Washington Quarterly* (Autumn 1991): 123 ff.

12. Prime Minister Thatcher described her concerns over SDI's possible impact on nuclear deterrence and the "earthquake" caused by President Reagan's proposal at Reykjavik for the complete elimination of U.S. and Soviet strategic nuclear weapons. See Margaret Thatcher, *The Downing Street Years* (New York: HarperCollins, 1993), pp. 462–73.

13. See, e.g., Gorbachev's July 1989 speech in Strasbourg, discussed at the end of this chapter.

14. Angela Stent, "The One Germany," *Foreign Policy* No. 81 (Winter 1990/91): 60.

15. Edwina Moreton, "The View from London," in Gordon et al., ed., *Eroding Empire*, p. 246.

16. Thatcher, *Downing Street Years*, pp. 452–53.

17. "Alliances in a Changing World: How to Manage the Thaw," speech given at the Wehrkunde conference in Munich, January 28, 1989, Verbatim Service VS010/89, London Press Service. See also Howe's similar remarks in speeches given at the close of the CSCE human rights meeting in Vienna, January 17 (VS005/89) and the opening of the Conventional Forces in Europe Conference, also in Vienna, March 6 (VS023/89).

18. Speech at a dinner given for President Gorbachev at No. 10 Downing Street, April 6, 1989, Verbatim Service VS031/89, London Press Service release of April 7.

19. Thatcher, *Downing Street Years*, p. 770. See also the discussion of her 1984 visit to Hungary, pp. 455–58, and her 1988 trip to Poland, pp. 777–82.

20. "Europe's Role in NATO's Fifth Decade," speech at the Royal United Services Institute, London, April 11, 1989, Verbatim Service VS033/89, London Press Service.

21. "Change in Eastern Europe and the Response of the West," speech given by the Honorable William Waldegrave, minister of state for foreign and commonwealth affairs, at the Great Britain/East Europe Center, London, July 6, 1989, Verbatim Service VS067/89, London Press Service.

22. Moreton, "The View from London," p. 246.

23. Sometimes termed, in the arms control acronym of the day, Short-Range Intermediate Nuclear Forces, or SRINF.

24. Thatcher, *Downing Street Years*, p. 786. Margaret Thatcher termed the meeting "acrimonious . . . behind [its] stage-managed friendliness" and, with an instinct for the jugular, characterized the chancellor as "deeply uncomfortable, as any politician will be whose instincts and principles push him one way while his short-term political interests push him the other" (p. 747).

25. Dominique Moïsi, "The French Foreign Policy: The Challenge of Adaptation," *Foreign Affairs* Vol. 67 (Fall 1988): 157–58.

26. Steven Philip Kramer, "The French Question," *The Washington Quarterly*, Autumn 1991, pp. 83–96; and Samuel F. Wells, Jr., "Mitterrand's International Policies," *The Washington Quarterly*, Summer 1988, pp. 59–75.

27. *Libération*, November 23, 1988.

28. Ronald Tiersky, "France in the New Europe," *Foreign Affairs* Vol. 71, No. 2 (Spring 1992): 131–46.

29. Dominique Moïsi, "French Policy Toward Central and Eastern Europe," in William E. Griffith, ed., *Central and Eastern Europe: The Opening Curtain?* (Boulder, Co.: Westview Press, 1989), pp. 353–65.

30. Valéry Giscard d'Estaing, "The Two Europes, East and West," Speech to the Royal Institute of International Affairs, London, July 1989, *International Affairs* Vol. 65, No. 4 (Autumn 1989): 657.

31. Pierre Hassner, "The View from Paris," in Gordon, ed., *Eroding Empire*, pp. 191–3; and Moïsi, "French Policy Toward Central and Eastern Europe," p. 354–5.

32. Thatcher evidently harbored similar sentiments. See *Downing Street Years*, pp. 796–98.

33. Interview with Radio France *Internationale*, March 26, 1989, *Service de Presse et d'Information, Ambassade de France a Londres* (Sp.St/LON/36/89), April 3, 1989.

34. *Libération*, November 23, 1988.

35. For a discussion of de Tocqueville's characterization of *agitation immobile* as a recurrent theme in French policy, see Hassner, "The View from Paris," p. 231.

36. *Economist*, May 27, 1989, p. 47, citing a 1988 West German poll.

37. Pierre Hassner, "Western European Perceptions of the USSR," *Daedalus* (Winter 1979), p. 145.

38. The stance of the SPD toward Solidarity was egregious from the beginning. Snubbing Wałęsa showed more timidity than was asked of the SPD, even by General Jaruzelski.

39. These conclusions are argued persuasively in Garton Ash, *In Europe's Name*, esp. pp. 362–71. As he notes, West German policy had the unintended effect of making these regimes more brittle by helping them avoid internal reform, but there is no evidence of such a fiendishly clever intent in the considerable documentary record of *Ostpolitik*.

For their part, the East European regimes, beginning in the early 1970s, pursued a strategy of using Western trade and credits as a means of avoiding domestic reform and its attendant risks. See Hutchings, *Soviet–East European Relations*, pp. 10–11 and 192–205.

40. One colleague who harbored such concerns traced them to a speech he had heard Genscher deliver, in which the foreign minister had spoken for an hour about the FRG's past and present without once mentioning the United States or the Atlantic alliance.

41. There were a few in the Bush administration who harbored the worst suspicions of Genscher, but there was nothing like the broad anti-Genscher sentiment of the Reagan administration.

42. Speech at the 25th International *Wehrkunde* conference, February 6, 1988, as cited in Günter Müchler and Klaus Hofmann, *Helmut Kohl, Chancellor of German Unity: A Biography* (Bonn: Press and Information Office of the Federal Government, 1992), pp. 144–45.

43. Joffe, "The View from Bonn," pp. 151–53.

44. Horst Teltschik, "Gorbachev's Reform Policy and the Outlook for East-West Relations," *Aussenpolitik* Vol. 40, No. 3 (June 1989): 210.

45. Müchler and Hofmann *Helmut Kohl: Chancellor of German Unity*, p. 167; and Teltschik, "Gorbachev's Reform Policy," p. 212.

46. Teltschik, "Gorbachev's Reform Policy," p. 203.

47. F. M. Cornford, *Microcosmographia Academica* (Chicago: University of Chicago Press, 1945; first published in Great Britain by Bowes and Bowes, Cambridge, 1922), pp. 19–24. Another of his observations (p. 8), too impolitic to place in the main text of the present volume, also evokes the strategy reviews: "A caucus is like a mousetrap; when you are outside, you want to get in; and, when you are inside, the mere sight of the other mice makes you want to get out."

48. This was the "full NSC," in which other cabinet members participated depending on the issues under consideration. The "Principals Committee" was the same group without the president.

49. As an example, when I traveled as part of Secretary Baker's delegation, he usually invited me to attend his meetings with European counterparts—those being my NSC responsibility—but almost never with Soviet interlocutors.

50. The White House press corps was particularly prone to gossipmongering and trivialization, partly because they dealt with the whole range of domestic and foreign issues and partly because their stories almost always focused on personalities. Unless a speech or other policy initiative was backgrounded in advance, it was a given that its substance would be missed. The State Department press corps was much better.

51. See also Baker, *Politics of Diplomacy*, pp. 21–27.

52. Indeed, the Clinton administration opted initially for this model, particularly at the State Department, but soon found that they had paid a price in policy coherence.

53. The NSC staff's role in this period was particularly strong, owing not only to the president's activist foreign policy leadership but to the more prosaic fact that NSC staff members, unlike most of our counterparts at State and Defense, did not require Senate confirmation and hence were in place much earlier. Owing to the defeat of the Tower nomination, the Defense Department was at a special disadvantage: Secretary Cheney was not nominated until March, and many of his senior staff were not confirmed or even nominated until much later.

54. This was one of the all-too-rare periods when the NSC staff seized control of the drafting, coordinating (i.e., among other agencies as well as among White House offices), and revising of speeches. As the White House speech-writing staff had responsibility for all presidential speeches, foreign and domestic, the more common pattern on foreign policy addresses was a dog fight between NSC staff, which had responsibility for substance, and the speechwriters, who had responsibility for presentation. It was a muddy distinction that virtually guaranteed conflict and sometimes led to the chaotic situation of two versions of the same speech, one produced by the NSC and the other by the speechwriters, wending their way to the president at the same time. (At the State Department, by contrast, foreign policymakers, usually in the policy planning staff, wrote the speeches.)

55. In early 1989, as will be seen in Chapter 3, the main issue of contention in the "coupling" debate concerned FOTL, the Follow-on to the Lance missile.

56. Speech delivered at Hamtramck, Michigan, April 17, 1989, excerpted below in the present chapter.

57. Václav Havel, "An Anatomy of Reticence," in *Václav Havel, or Living in Truth*, trans. Jan Vladislav (London: Faber and Faber, 1986), p. 186.

58. The overall review was directed by Assistant Secretary of State (for European and Canadian Affairs) Rozanne Ridgway; the working group on U.S.-EC relations was chaired by Felix Block, whose laconic performance was perhaps explained by the fact that he was then under investigation on espionage charges and left the department shortly thereafter.

59. Thatcher, *Downing Street Years*, esp. pp. 768–69 and 813–14.

60. Memorandum from Brent Scowcroft to President Bush entitled "The NATO Summit," March 20, 1989, as cited in Philip Zelikow and Condoleezza Rice, *Germany Unified and Europe Transformed: A Study in Statecraft* (Cambridge: Harvard University Press, 1995), p. 28.

61. Cf. Michael R. Beschloss and Strobe Talbott, *At the Highest Levels* (Boston: Little, Brown and Co., 1993), pp. 7–71 *passim*, who offer persuasive evidence that the *pauza* was a deliberate, conscious policy decision, yet continue to imply that failure to engage Gorbachev was somehow a product of dithering.

Jack Matlock, U.S. ambassador to the Soviet Union at the time, makes a similar assertion in his memoirs but offers no argument to support his chapter title, "Washington Fumbles," except for vague and unpersuasive calls for economic engagement. (Jack F. Matlock, Jr., *Autopsy on an Empire: The American Ambassador's Account of the Collapse of the Soviet Union* [New York: Random House, 1995], pp. 177–200.) It was an oddly defensive complaint, particularly in that Matlock's main recommendations, as will be seen below, were endorsed in the president's policy of "testing" Gorbachev.

62. One prominent Kremlinologist predicted over the course of several years that Gorbachev would be out of office "within six months." Eventually he was proved right.

63. *American Foreign Policy Current Documents 1989*, ed. Nancy L. Golden and Sherrill Brown Wells (Washington, D.C.: U.S. Department of State, 1990), pp. 354–56.

64. "Address by Secretary of State Baker before the Center for Strategic and International Studies, May 4, 1989," Department of State *Bulletin*, July 1989, pp. 36–39.

65. Baker, *Politics of Diplomacy*, p. 70.

66. These points were also made in Baker's CSIS speech, esp. pp. 38–9.

67. This long cable, entitled "U.S.-Soviet Relations: Policy Opportunities," was declassified and made available by the National Security Archive, Washington, D.C., along with two other Matlock cables dated February 3 and 13, as a briefing book for a conference on "Cold War Endgame," Princeton University, March 29–30, 1996. See also Matlock's account in *Autopsy on an Empire*, pp. 186–90.

68. Beschloss and Talbott, *At the Highest Levels*, p. 8.

69. Michael Mandelbaum was asking exactly the same question at this time. See his prescient "Ending the Cold War," *Foreign Affairs* Vol. 68 (Spring 1989), p. 19.

70. It is interesting that Gorbachev's principal adviser, Anatoli Chernyayev, subsequently criticized Gorbachev on precisely these grounds, for seeing U.S.-Soviet arms negotiations as the essence of East-West relations.

71. "U.S.-Soviet Relations: An Agenda for the Future," A Report to the Forty-first President of the United States, Foreign Policy Institute, School of Advanced International Studies, The Johns Hopkins University, Washington, D.C., December 1988, p. 4.

72. Valéry Giscard d'Estaing, Yasuhiro Nakasone, and Henry A. Kissinger, *East–West Relations: A Report to the Trilateral Commission* (New York: Trilateral Commission, 1989). An adapted version of the report was also published in *Foreign Affairs* Vol. 68 (Summer 1989): 1–21.

73. Mandelbaum's "Ending the Cold War" is a notable exception, which holds up better than any of its contemporaries in the light of all that transpired since its publication in spring 1989. His diagnosis that "the core of the Cold War in Europe is Soviet domination of Eastern Europe," as well as his prescription of self-determination in that region, were precisely those being reached in the upper levels of the Bush administration at the

time. So was his judgment that "the division of Germany will be the last part of the cold war in Europe to be liquidated." We were both wrong on that point.

74. Giscard d'Estaing et al., *East–West Relations*, pp. 7 and 13.

75. National Security Directive 23 (SECRET), "United States Relations with the Soviet Union," The White House, September 22, 1989; declassifed November 1, 1995. Released under the Freedom of Information Act, copy courtesy of National Security Archive, Washington, D.C. (Although not signed until September, the document was drafted and approved in substance in the spring of 1989.)

76. The "plan," together with Secretary Baker's rejection of any U.S.-Soviet "arrangement" for Eastern Europe, is described in Thomas L. Friedman, "Baker, Outlining World View, Assesses Plan for Soviet Bloc," *New York Times*, March 27, 1989.

77. Although Baker flirted with Kissinger's idea of engaging the Soviets directly on Eastern Europe, the idea of cutting a deal with Moscow was never considered. See the accounts in Baker, *Politics of Diplomacy*, p. 40, and Matlock, *Autopsy on an Empire*, p. 190–92.

78. This was among the conclusions of the president's February 12, 1989, meeting with Soviet experts in Kennebunkport, as described in Beschloss and Talbott, *At the Highest Levels*, pp. 22–3.

79. Oberdorfer, *The Turn*, p. 330.

80. In his memoirs, written with Brent Scowcroft, President Bush notes that Eastern Europe figured prominently in their daily strategy sessions during January 1989. Scowcroft, in the same memoirs, called the emerging policy toward Eastern Europe one of "gentle rollback." (Forthcoming from Alfred A. Knopf, Inc.; draft manuscript shared with the author in July 1996.)

81. On Hungarian reactions to the speech, see Thatcher, *Downing Street Years*, p. 455.

82. Beschloss and Talbott, *At the Highest Levels*, pp. 53–4.

83. Through Ambassador John Davis and others in Embassy Warsaw, our contacts with Solidarity were particularly close. My own contacts during the period included meetings in Warsaw with, among others, Bronisław Geremek, the courageous and brilliant adviser to Solidarity, in early 1988, at the time of the so-called anti-crisis pact that led to the roundtable talks, and again in May 1989, when Polish strategists were worrying about how to translate the Roundtable Agreement into an action plan.

84. Ash, *In Europe's Name*, p. 123.

85. The speeches were compiled in *Beyond Containment: Selected Speeches of President George Bush on Europe and East-West Relations, April 17–June 2, 1989* (Washington, United States Information Agency, 1989). See also *American Foreign Policy Current Documents 1989*.

86. See Chapter 3 below for a thorough review of the administration's failed policies toward Yugoslavia.

87. This was a more ambitious version of the approach advocated by Graham Allison in "Testing Gorbachev," *Foreign Affairs* Vol. 67, No. 4 (Fall 1988): 19–32.

88. The only specific offers on the U.S. side were to explore once again Eisenhower's "Open Skies" proposal for aerial overflights and a pledge to work toward extending most favored nation trade status if Soviet emigration laws were codified and implemented in accordance with international standards. Although the American media predictably focused

on the "initiatives," or lack thereof, these were peripheral to what was meant to be a conceptual speech articulating U.S. policy for the longer term.

89. This is precisely how Shevardnadze saw the speech: "Are the Americans willing to do *nothing* to help us? Are *we* the ones who have to make all the moves? We take these huge steps and all we hear from Washington is, '*More! More! You must do more!*' " Cited in Beschloss and Talbott, *At the Highest Levels,* p. 60.

90. These often contentious aspects of U.S.-European relations after 1989 are covered in Chapters 4 and 7.

91. For details of the debate, see Beschloss and Talbott, *At the Highest Levels,* pp. 74–80.

92. See Chapter 3.

93. This refers to the Conference on Security and Cooperation in Europe (CSCE) and the process begun at the 1975 Helsinki Summit of 35 European and North American leaders.

94. Garton Ash, *In Europe's Name,* p. 3. Garton Ash, again getting the point that others missed, also draws the contrast between the Gorbachev and Bush speeches.

95. Speech to the West German Bundestag, embassy of the Federal Republic of Germany, London, April 27, 1989, as cited in Lawrence Freedman, ed., *Europe Transformed: Documents on the End of the Cold War* (New York: St. Martin's Press, 1990), p. 281.

96. "Declaration of the Heads of State and Government Participating in the Meeting of the North Atlantic Council in Brussels (29th–30th May 1989)," NATO Press Service, May 30, 1989, pp. 6–8. Emphasis added.

Chapter 2

1. In November 1987, brutal repression ensued in Braşov after several thousand workers marched to the center of the city and sacked the local party headquarters. Moruzi, a naturally ebullient man, recounted how he went into an almost clinical depression during these years, as hopeful events transpiring elsewhere in the region contrasted starkly with the deepening repression in his own country.

2. Poland and Hungary were exceptions, in that fear had long since lost much of its grip. Yet even in those countries, there was fear of losing one's job, of being denied travel opportunities, and of having one's children denied entrance into university.

3. Alexis de Tocqueville, *The Old Regime and the French Revolution,* trans. Stuart Gilbert (Garden City, N.Y.: Doubleday & Doubleday, Inc., 1955), p. 204.

4. Statement by the Press Secretary, White House Press Office, December 29, 1989.

5. J. F. Brown, *Surge to Freedom: The End of Communist Rule in Eastern Europe* (Durham, N.C. and London: Duke University Press, 1991), pp. 1–5.

6. Ronald D. Asmus, J. F. Brown, and Keith Crane, *Soviet Foreign Policy and the Revolutions of 1989 in Eastern Europe* (Santa Monica, Ca.: The RAND Corporation, 1991), pp. 134–36.

7. Michael Howard, "The Springtime of Nations," *Foreign Affairs* Vol. 69, No. 1 (Winter 1989–90): 17–32.

8. Garton Ash, *In Europe's Name,* p. 44.

9. I was Deputy Director of Radio Free Europe at the time, and remember vividly being called to the office in the early morning hours of December 13, 1981, where I lis

tened in stunned disbelief to General Jaruzelski's 6:00 a.m. speech explaining that Solidarity had been outlawed and its leaders imprisoned.

10. Timothy Garton Ash, "The Empire in Decay," *New York Review of Books* Vol. 35, No. 14 (September 29, 1988): 53–60, and the other two articles (in Nos. 15 and 16, October 13 and 27, 1988) in his three-part series on Eastern Europe. See also David K. Shipler, "Letter from Budapest," *New Yorker,* November 20, 1989, pp. 74–99.

11. Timothy Garton Ash makes this point in *The Magic Lantern: The Revolutions of '89 Witnessed in Warsaw, Budapest, Berlin and Prague* (New York: Random House, 1990), p. 68.

12. See Chapter 1.

13. Michael Beschloss and Strobe Talbott, *At the Highest Levels: The Inside Story of the End of the Cold War* (New York: Little, Brown and Company, 1993), pp. 80–81, quote Chief of Staff John Sununu as saying the "game plan" was to "whip Western Europe into line, then turn everyone's attention to Eastern Europe." It might have been stated more elegantly, but that was the general idea.

14. Gale Stokes, *The Walls Came Tumbling Down* (New York: Oxford University Press, 1993), pp. 146 and 162; Brown, *Surge to Freedom,* pp. 191 and 211.

15. The text is reprinted in Bernard Wheaton and Zdeněk Kavan, *The Velvet Revolution: Czechoslovakia, 1988–91* (Boulder, Co.: Westview Press, 1992), pp. 196–97.

16. Western observers made more of the demonstration effect of Soviet reforms. For most East Europeans, what was happening in the USSR was remote; it might or might not have any significance for them. Poland and Hungary were different: their progress, meaning their ability to implement democratic change without reprisal from Moscow or their own regimes, was seen as much more directly relevant to Czechoslovakia, Bulgaria, Romania, and the GDR.

17. For an interesting assessment of President Bush's approach (drawn partly from George Bush with Victor Gold, *Looking Forward* [New York: Doubleday, 1987]), see Joseph G. Whelan, *Soviet Diplomacy and Negotiating Behavior, 1988–90,* U.S. Congress, Committee on Foreign Affairs, Vol. III (Washington, D.C.: U.S. Government Printing Office, 1991), pp. 149–211.

18. These aspects of power evoked—to this staffer, at least—passages from Thucydides. Bush as Pericles?!

19. Among these were the Confederation for an Independent Poland (KPN, in its Polish acronym) and "Fighting Solidarity," which was calling for a violent showdown with the communist regime.

20. Beschloss and Talbott, *At the Highest Levels,* p. 85.

21. János Kis, "The Challenge of Democracy in Eastern Europe," paper presented at a conference on democratic revolution organized by the National Endowment for Democracy, Washington, D.C., May 1, 1989.

22. The leader of the Polish team was Vice Foreign Minister Jan Majewski, with whom I was to have subsequent (not altogether pleasant) experience negotiating the first ever U.S.-Polish "Declaration of Principles," signed by Presidents Bush and Wałęsa during the latter's March 1991 state visit to the United States.

23. The Roundtable accords provided for the restoration of the senate, an institution which had existed from 1919 to 1939 and was abolished by the postwar government after a fraudulent referendum in 1946. See Abraham Brumberg, "Poland: The Demise of Communism," *Foreign Affairs* Vol. 69, No. 1 (Winter 1989/90), pp. 79–80.

24. I.e., the Polish United Workers party and its "satellite" or "bloc" parties, the United Peasants party and the Democratic party.

25. Lawrence Weschler, "A Grand Experiment," *New Yorker,* November 13, 1989, p. 65.

26. Garton Ash, *The Magic Lantern,* p. 29. As Garton Ash notes, pp. 29–32, the elections embraced three related but separate surprises: the Communists lost, Solidarity won, and the Communists acknowledged that Solidarity won.

27. Cited in Stokes, *The Walls Came Tumbling Down,* p. 127.

28. Nyers, architect of Hungary's New Economic Mechanism launched in 1968, went on to succeed Grósz as party leader in October 1989.

29. In addition to the near sweep by Solidarity candidates, the traditional "bloc" parties (nominally independent but in fact aligned with the communists), the Democratic party and the United Peasants party, were evincing a new-found independence and refusing to support Jaruzelski's presidential nomination.

30. Oberdorfer, *The Turn,* pp. 351–2.

31. Beschloss and Talbott, *At the Highest Levels,* pp. 81–2.

32. *The Current Digest of the Soviet Press* Vol. XLI, No. 27, (1989), p. 6.

33. Hungarian television, July 9, 1989, as cited in Vladimir V. Kusin, "Mikhail Gorbachev's Evolving Attitude to Eastern Europe," *Radio Free Europe Research,* RAD Background Report/128, July 20, 1989, p. 4.

34. In the runup to the Polish elections, for example, *Izvestia* warned that "the election campaigns for the Sejm and senate have taken on the undertones planned by the secret orchestrators of anti-socialism and anti-Sovietism. It is no accident that the disturbances have broken out precisely at a time of favorable prospects for change in Poland and for Polish-Soviet relations." (*Izvestia,* May 21, 1989, *Current Digest of the Soviet Press,* Vol. XLI, No. 20 [1989], p. 20.) *Pravda,* commenting on the reburial of Imre Nagy in Hungary, likewise warned of "anti-Soviet attacks" and quoted FIDESz leader Viktor Orbán as calling for "smashing the communist dictatorship." (*Pravda,* June 17, 1989, *Current Digest of the Soviet Press,* Vol. XLI, No. 24 [1989], p. 27.) See also Garton Ash, *The Magic Lantern,* p. 41, on how Solidarity strategists in Poland viewed the mixed signals emanating from Moscow.

35. This was the usual formulation for "on background" briefings to the press when the speaker did not wish to be named. In this case, the "senior administration official" was Ambassador Robert Blackwill, NSC senior director for Soviet and European affairs.

36. "Background Briefing by Senior Administration Official," Office of the Press Secretary, The White House, July 7, 1989.

37. "Remarks by the President at Joint Session of Parliament, The Sejm, Warsaw," Office of the Press Secretary, The White House, July 10, 1989. The reference to redeeming the Atlantic Charter was of course particularly poignant to the Poles, for it was precisely those principles, they believed, that were sacrificed at Yalta.

38. This congruity was soon to acquire significance in the opposite sense, as we sought to launch arms control initiatives that would enable military reductions to keep pace with the breakneck speed of political change.

39. Mikhail Gorbachev, *Perestroika: New Thinking for Our Country and the World* (New York: Harper & Row, Publishers, 1987), p. 143. I recall looking long and hard for that quote on the eve of the president's departure. It would have been even better to have used a line from Gorbachev's Council of Europe speech, delivered just two days before the president spoke in Warsaw.

40. These included preferential trade access through the generalized system of preferences, authorization for OPIC (Overseas Private Investment Corporation) operations in Poland, support for World Bank loans, debt-for-equity swaps, and generous Paris Club rescheduling of Polish official debts.

41. As will be seen in Chapter 5, the Enterprise Funds, for which the Council of Economic Advisers deserves the most credit, turned out to be the most successful of all U.S. assistance efforts.

42. We had in mind the example of former Polish party leader Edward Gierek's exploitation of Western loans and credits for political ends.

43. This is not to say we had reached definitive judgment on the longstanding debate as to whether Jaruzelski was "Polish patriot or Soviet stooge," but it was in our interests, and Poland's, to accentuate the former aspect. It was a matter not of analysis, but of policy.

44. Oberdorfer, *The Turn,* pp. 359–60; and Beschloss and Talbott, *At the Highest Levels,* p. 89.

45. Mieczysław F. Rakowski, *Jak to sie stalo?* [How did it happen?] (Warsaw: Polska Oficyna Wydawnicza "BGW," 1991), p. 238.

46. Rakowski got the point; Beschloss and Talbott (*At the Highest Levels,* pp. 87–89), did not. They asserted, wrongly, that President Bush was trying to "prop up" Jaruzelski and favored "familiar processes and gradual, orderly change, even at the sacrifice of democratic ideals."

47. Rakowski, *Jak to sie Stalo?,* p. 240; and Witold Beres and Jerzy Skoczyslas, *General Kiszczaks Mowi . . . Prawie Wszystko* [General Kiszczak tells us . . . almost everything] (Warsaw: Polska Oficyna Wydawnicza "BGW," 1991), p. 272.

48. Garton Ash, *The Magic Lantern,* pp. 37–9; and Stokes, *The Walls Came Tumbling Down,* pp. 127–28.

49. Garton Ash, *The Magic Lantern,* pp. 36–7.

50. *Népszabadság* and *Magyar Hirlap,* July 12, 1989, as cited in *Radio Free Europe Research,* Hungarian Situation Report/13, August 18, 1989, p. 19.

51. "Remarks by the President at the Karl Marx University of Economics," Office of the Press Secretary, The White House (Budapest), July 12, 1989.

52. The apt term comes from László Bruszt, "Hungary's Negotiated Revolution," *Social Research* 57 (1990): 365–87.

53. Beschloss and Talbott, *At the Highest Levels,* p. 90.

54. A year later, having developed close relations with the government of Prime Minister Antall, leader of the Hungarian Democratic Forum, we were perceived as having thrown our support behind the center-right. It was hard to persuade the highly partisan Hungarian political elite that the United States really did not much care whether it was the center-right, center-left or some other configuration that governed Hungary, so long as the country was moving toward democracy and free markets.

55. Some of the particulars of the meeting were reported by Reuters, AP, and UPI, July 12, 1989.

56. Thatcher, *Downing Street Years,* p. 753.

57. The long Economic Declaration was confined mainly to broad general commitments, including a long section on environmental issues, and hortatory language such as calling for "further substantial progress in the Uruguay Round [of the General Agreement on Tariffs and Trade] in order to complete it by the end of 1990." The summit documents

were reprinted in the Department of State *Bulletin,* Vol. 89, No. 2150 (September 1989), pp. 1–3 and 13–17.

58. Horst Teltschik, "Gorbachev's Reform Policy and the Outlook for East-West Relations," *Aussenpolitik* III/89 (June 1989): 201–14; and Günter Müchler and Klaus Hofmann, *Helmut Kohl: Chancellor of German Unity* (Bonn: Press and Information Office of the Federal Government, 1992), pp. 158–61 and 167–71.

59. Horst Teltschik, "The Federal Republic and Poland—A Difficult Partnership in the Heart of Europe," *Aussenpolitik* I/90 (January 1990): 3–14; and Müchler and Hofmann, *Helmut Kohl,* pp. 162 and 172–80. See also *Keesing's* Record of World Events, News Digest, July 1989, p. 36830.

60. *New York Times,* July 7, 1989, I, 3:3.

61. This agreement was affirmed in the summit's "Declaration on East-West Relations," in which the G-7 countries pledged "to work along with other interested countries and multilateral institutions to concert support for the process of reform underway in Hungary and Poland" and called for a "meeting with all interested countries . . . in the next few weeks." Seconding the concept of "testing" Soviet intentions, the declaration also called "upon the Soviet Government to translate its new policies and pronouncements into further concrete action at home and abroad."

62. Poland, Czechoslovakia, and other countries had been invited to participate in the Marshall Plan but were denied that possibility by Stalin.

63. "Remarks by the President to the Residents of Leiden," The Pieterskerk, Leiden, The Netherlands, July 17, 1989, White House press release of that day.

64. James A. Baker, III, with Thomas M. DeFrank, *The Politics of Diplomacy: Revolution, War and Peace, 1989–92* (New York: G. P. Putnam's Sons, 1995), pp. 135–42.

65. *Ibid.,* pp. 140–1. These points of agreement were further cemented during Baker's three-day meeting with Shevardnadze at Jackson Hole, Wyoming, September 21–24, 1989. See Baker's account in *ibid.,* pp. 144–52.

66. *New York Times,* August 22, 1989.

67. Oberdorfer, *The Turn,* p. 399.

68. Garton Ash, *In Europe's Name,* p. 124, cites Sergei Tarasenko as saying that Shevardnadze had concluded after the Polish elections that Eastern Europe would probably "go."

69. Garton Ash, *The Magic Lantern,* pp. 39–45. (The transportation ministry was critical to Moscow because of the transit routes between the USSR and East Germany.)

70. This was not quite the specific intervention by Gorbachev that was widely reported at the time. See Stokes, *The Walls Came Tumbling Down,* pp. 129–30.

71. *Deutsche Presse Agentur,* August 28, 1989, as cited in Brown, *Surge to Freedom,* p. 57.

72. Associated Press, August 27, 1989, as reprinted in Gale Stokes, *From Stalinism to Pluralism: A Documentary History of Eastern Europe since 1945* (New York: Oxford University Press, 1991), pp. 240–42.

73. The plan, involving radical measures to halt hyperinflation, stabilize the Polish *zloty,* decontrol prices, and create the foundations of a market economy, was drawn from the reform strategy of Harvard economist Jeff Sachs, as outlined in Jeffrey Sachs and David Lipton, "Poland's Economic Reform," *Foreign Affairs* Vol. 69, No. 3 (Summer 1990): 47–66. For a more detailed description, see David Lipton and Jeffrey Sachs, "Creating a Market Economy in Eastern Europe: The Case of Poland," *Brookings Papers on Economic Activity,* 1990:1.

74. Statement by the Press Secretary, The White House, October 4, 1989. The statement, which began, "The world has watched with wonder . . ." included an invitation to both Mazowiecki and Jaruzelski to pay separate visits to the United States "at times convenient to each of them." Mazowiecki came on a state visit in March 1990; a Jaruzelski visit was postponed several times before being canceled altogether.

75. On the EC's assistance program, including the controversy over the European Bank, see Chapter 5.

76. There was a political dimension to this as well. Most of our West European partners could extend loans and lines of credit by executive decision, while we, because of credit reform, had to have a budgetary offset requiring congressional approval for every loan. These offsets ran to 50 percent and more of the loan amount for countries with credit ratings as low as the East Europeans' then were.

77. *New York Times,* November 15, 1989, A22.

78. As is described in Chapter 8, the rush of events caused us to neglect one that would soon come back to haunt us: a mid-October visit to Washington by Yugoslav prime minister Ante Marković, desperately seeking economic and political support.

79. These were SzDSz (Free Democratic party) and FIDESz (Confederation of Young Democrats), respectively.

80. Für was the MDF's initial presidential candidate in October but ultimately made way for the Free Democrats' Árpád Göncz, elected as a result of a compromise with the MDF.

81. *New York Times,* October 19, 1989, I, 3:5; and Ash, *The Magic Lantern,* pp. 58–9.

82. By the time Imre Pozsgay met with General Scowcroft in Washington November 2, it was clear that the reform wing of the newly renamed Hungarian Socialist party had been eclipsed, along with Pozsgay's presidential ambitions.
On December 15, I met with József Antall and Géza Jeszenszky, who were already looking beyond the scheduled March elections toward their new responsibilities as leaders of a democratic Hungary. Antall's firm Atlanticism, despite his reputation of being a Germanophile, was already firmly entrenched in his thinking in December 1989. (When I next met with them in the course of 1990, I observed that they had gone from being obscure Hungarian opposition figures to prime minister and foreign minister, respectively, while I was still in the same job.)

83. *Washington Post,* September 19, 1989. Here again was the interplay between Hungarian and Polish events: had a Polish official spoken openly about neutrality, this might well have provoked a reaction in Moscow, yet a Hungarian official's doing so strengthened the hand of the new Mazowiecki government in its evolving relationship with Jaruzelski's presidency.

84. Szürös met with General Scowcroft at the White House on the 19th. Following the required notification period, the United States formally extended permanent MFN status to Hungary in a White House ceremony on October 4.

85. The sequence of events was as follows. Hungarian prime minister Németh and foreign minister Horn visited West German Foreign Minister Genscher in Bonn on August 25. Horn flew to East Berlin September 1 to suspend the bilateral travel agreement. On September 10, in Budapest, Horn announced that Hungary's borders were open to any GDR citizens wishing to leave for West Germany via Austria.

86. *New York Times,* September 15, 1989, I, 10:1; and Elizabeth Pond, *Beyond the Wall: Germany's Road to Unification* (Washington, D.C.: The Brookings Institution, 1993), p. 96.

87. *New York Times,* August 14, 1989, I, 3:1.

88. Pond, *Beyond the Wall,* pp. 97–98. Honecker's decision to oblige asylum-seekers to return to the GDR before proceeding to West Germany only fueled popular discontent.

89. E.g., Elizabeth Pond's interview with Genscher, as cited in *Beyond the Wall,* p. 98.

90. "Walters: German Unity Soon: U.S. Ambassador Envisions an Early Reunification," screamed the front page of the *International Herald Tribune,* The Hague, Monday, September 4, 1989. The same story quoted East German foreign minister Oskar Fischer as warning that anyone who tries to redraw the map of Europe "plays with fire."

91. Garton Ash, *In Europe's Name,* p. 594, explains that Gorbachev's remark, delivered behind closed doors in a meeting with the East German party leadership, was somewhat differently phrased and did not explicitly refer to the situation in the GDR. Yet it was the shorthand version that stuck and had the political impact.

92. Speech at the GDR fortieth anniversary celebration, as cited in Michael J. Sodaro, *Moscow, Germany, and the West* (Ithaca, N.Y.: Cornell University Press, 1990), p. 377.

93. Pond, *Beyond the Wall,* pp. 112–20.

94. Sodaro, *Moscow, Germany, and the West,* p. 379.

95. Brown, *Surge to Freedom,* p. 181.

96. Stokes, *The Walls Came Tumbling Down,* pp. 147–48, and Professor Stokes's transcript of the interview, which he generously made available to me.

97. A similar debate within the administration took place at this time over U.S. participation in a CSCE human rights conference scheduled for Moscow in 1991. The outcome of the debate was provisional agreement to participate, subject to ongoing review of the Soviet human rights record. By the time of the conference, which we did attend, our reservations had long since been overtaken by events.

98. Stokes, *The Walls Came Tumbling Down,* pp. 147–48.

99. *Ibid.,* p. 148.

100. On November 13, the *New York Times* reported from Prague on the small turnout of ten thousand for a demonstration in Wenceslas Square; a week later, it was recounting a massive gathering of two hundred thousand in the same square. See Bernard Gwertzman and Michael T. Kaufman, eds., *The Collapse of Communism* (New York: Times Books, 1990), pp. 200–201 and 229–32.

101. *New York Times,* November 18, 1989, I, 6:1.

102. Garton Ash, *The Magic Lantern,* p. 80.

103. Kňažko, who later became Slovakia's foreign minister, bore a striking resemblance to the American actor Glenn Ford in the latter's younger days. A charismatic figure with a sense of irony more common in Czechs than Slovaks, he would be my chief interlocutor in Slovakia when I directed the U.S. assistance program in 1992 and 1993.

104. For details of the summit, see below in the present chapter and in Chapter 3.

105. Garton Ash, *The Magic Lantern,* p. 122.

106. Nestor Ratesh, *Romania: The Entangled Revolution* (New York: Praeger Publishers, 1991), p. 78.

107. Brown, *Surge to Freedom,* p. 219.

108. White House press release, December 22, 1989.

109. I well recall spending nearly all of Christmas Day on the secure phone at home, at one point calling (via pager) Bob Gates out of a movie theater with his family.

110. The most extravagant interpretations went so far as to link Baker's remark to a U.S.-Soviet conspiracy to unseat Ceauşescu and install the NSF. (See, e.g., Andrei Codrescu, *The Hole in the Flag* [New York: William Morrow and Co., Inc., 1991], pp. 205–6.) The reality was more prosaic. We had no prior knowledge of the Romanian Revolution or of any coup-in-the-making, nor were we in any way colluding with Moscow before, during, or after these events. Our contacts with Moscow as the revolution unfolded were much like our contacts with Bonn, London, Paris, and other capitals, with whom we compared notes and tried to ensure coordinated international support on behalf of prodemocracy forces. With Moscow as with others, there was a broadly shared desire to see Ceauşescu loyalists defeated, the bloodshed ended, and the democratic "spirit of Timişoara" vindicated, as well as agreement that the outside world should lend its qualified support to the NSF-led provisional government.

111. *New York Times,* December 24 and 25, 1989; Statement by the press secretary, the White House, December 25, 1989.

112. Beschloss and Talbott, *At the Highest Levels,* pp. 170–1. In his memoirs, President Bush recounts that Gorbachev told him during their meeting off Malta that "some are saying the Brezhnev Doctrine is being replaced by the Bush Doctrine." (Forthcoming from Alfred A. Knopf, Inc.)

113. For thorough accounts of these events, see Ratesh, *Romania: The Entangled Revolution,* esp. pp. 80–119; Martyn Rady, *Romania in Turmoil* (London: I. B. Taurus & Co., Ltd., 1992); and Matei Calinescu and Vladimir Tismaneanu, "The 1989 Revolution and Romania's Future," *Problems of Communism* (January–April 1990), pp. 42–59. For an exposition of the "hijack" theory, see Trond Gilberg, "Romania: Will History Repeat Itself?" *Current History* (December 1990), pp. 409–12.

114. Garton Ash, *The Magic Lantern,* p. 97, recounts that one of the drafters of a Civic Forum declaration in late November inadvertently wrote "Democratic Forum," before saying, "Oh, sorry, I was thinking of Hungary."

115. Radio GDR II interview with Otto Reinhold, rector of the party's Academy of Social Sciences, August 19, 1989, as cited in Brown, *Surge to Freedom,* p. 125,

116. A third, not very plausible option for the GDR would have been to strike a deal with Bonn, presumably to avert a chaotic breakdown of order.

117. That there was serious consideration, in Moscow as well as East Berlin, of a military crackdown long after October 9 is likely but so far undocumented.

118. From the "Report of the Commission of Enquiry on the Events Surrounding November 17," published in October 1990, as cited in Wheaton and Kavan, *The Velvet Revolution,* p. 72.

119. See, e.g., Samuel Huntington, *The Third Wave* (Oklahoma City: University of Oklahoma Press, 1991); Terry Lynn Karl and Philippe C. Schmitter, "Modes of Transition in Latin America, Southern and Eastern Europe," *International Social Science Journal* Vol. 128 (May 1991): 273–84; and Juan J. Linz, "Transitions to Democracy," *The Washington Quarterly,* Summer 1990, pp. 143–64.

120. Memorandum from Brent Scowcroft (drafted by Condoleezza Rice) to President Bush entitled "The Soviets and the German Question," November 29, 1989, cited in Philip Zelikow and Condoleezza Rice, *Germany Unified and Europe Transformed: A Study in Statecraft* (Cambridge: Harvard University Press, 1995), p. 125.

Chapter 3

1. On the diplomacy of German unification from key advisers to Chancellor Kohl and Foreign Minister Genscher respectively, see Horst Teltschik, *329 Tage: Innenansichten der Einigung* (Berlin: Siedler Verlag, 1991); and Frank Elbe and Richard Kiessler, *Ein Runder Tisch mit Scharfen Ecken* (Baden-Baden: Nomos Verlags Gesellschaft, 1993). The internal aspects are authoritatively covered by then West German interior minister Wolfgang Schäuble, *Der Vertrag: Wie Ich Über die Deutsche Einheit Verhandelte* (Stuttgart: Deutsche Verlags-Anstalt, 1991).

2. Elizabeth Pond, *Beyond the Wall: Germany's Road to Unification* (Washington, D.C.: The Brookings Institution, 1993), p. 186.

3. Timothy Garton Ash, *In Europe's Name: Germany and the Divided Continent* (New York: Random House, 1993), p. 363.

4. Alexander Moens, "American Diplomacy and German Unification," *Survival*, Vol. XXXIII, No. 6 (November/December 1991), p. 531. (The Two Plus Four talks, as is explained below in the present chapter, involved the two German states and the four World War II Allies—the United States, the Soviet Union, France, and Britain.)

5. Forthcoming (with Brent Scowcroft) from Alfred A. Knopf, Inc.; draft manuscript shared with the author in July 1996.

6. Moens, "American Diplomacy," p. 538.

7. Karl Kaiser, "German Unification," *Foreign Affairs*, Vol. 70, No. 1 (1991), p. 179.

8. In addition to Teltschik and Elbe, see Pond, *Beyond the Wall*; Stephen F. Szabo, *The Diplomacy of German Unification* (New York: St. Martin's Press, 1992); James A. Baker, III, with Thomas M. DeFrank, *The Politics of Diplomacy: Revolution, War and Peace, 1989–92* (New York: G. P. Putnam's Sons, 1995); and Philip Zelikow and Condoleezza Rice, *Germany Unified and Europe Transformed: A Study in Statecraft* (Cambridge: Harvard University Press, 1995).
Baker's memoirs and the book by my NSC colleagues Zelikow and Rice both came out after this chapter was written (during my 1993–94 fellowship year at the Wilson Center). Neither caused me to revise my text. The sole exception is a passage dealing with the Polish-German border issue: I had forgotten the extent of Bush's personal mediation, even though I was notetaker for all the relevant conversations, and so changed the account thanks to Zelikow and Rice. Otherwise, I have not changed a word of the text but rather have confined the relatively few points of difference to the notes.

9. Richard von Weizsäcker, "Only Cooperation Can Create Peace," *Die Zeit*, September 30, 1983.

10. These hopes were supported by a British foreign office analysis of the German question prepared in late October 1989, as cited in Zelikow and Rice, *Germany Unified*, p. 97.

11. "Joint Declaration of the Federal Republic of Germany and the Soviet Union, June 13, 1989," Embassy of the Federal Republic of Germany, Washington, D.C., June 13, 1989, in Lawrence Freedman, ed., *Europe Transformed: Documents on the End of the Cold War* (New York: St. Martin's Press, 1990), pp. 317–21.

12. Garton Ash, *In Europe's Name*, p. 108.

13. *Ibid.*, p. 109.

14. Cited in Freedman, ed., *Europe Transformed*, p. 340. (On the diplomatic activity at the U.N., see Chapter 2.)

15. *Pravda*, November 15, 1989.

16. Cited in Teltschik, *329 Tage*, p. 37.

17. *Washington Post*, November 30, 1989, p. A53.

18. That French official thinking was unprepared for unification, both analytically and emotionally, was demonstrated by the sharply negative reaction to an article written in late September 1989 by the French scholar Dominique Moïsi, in which he anticipated rapid movement toward German unity and warned of "the futility of any attempt to prolong an unwarranted division." (*International Herald Tribune*, September 25, 1989.)

19. *New York Times*, November 15, 1989.

20. *Washington Post*, November 20, 1989; Margaret Thatcher, *The Downing Street Years* (New York: HarperCollins Publishers, 1993), pp. 792–3.

21. Thatcher, *Downing Street Years*, p. 792.

22. *Ibid.*, pp. 796–97. Mitterrand, according to British officials, felt even more strongly that urgent joint actions were needed: "Mitterrand told Mrs. Thatcher that this was the worst crisis in fifty years, and in times of great crisis Britain and France have been together. He seemed to want to revive the *entente cordiale.*" (Cited in John Newhouse, "The Diplomatic Round," *New Yorker*, August 27, 1990, p. 81.)

23. *Ibid.*, p. 798.

24. *New York Times*, November 16, 1989; *International Herald Tribune*, September 4, 1989.

25. In early September 1989, President Bush also predicted, in an interview with David Frost, that the Berlin Wall would come down during his presidency. (*New York Times*, September 6, 1989; *Public Papers of the Presidents of the United States: George Bush, 1989* [Washington, D.C.: U.S. Government Printing Office, 1990], p. 1593.)

26. Baker, *Politics of Diplomacy*, p. 159, describes his very specific discussion of the prospects for German unification in a conversation with President Bush over lunch at the White House on May 17, 1989.

27. See, e.g., the March 20 NSC memorandum for the president that stressed that "our vision for Europe's future" must include "an approach to the 'German Question,'" as cited in Chapter 1. (Zelikow and Rice, *Germany Unified*, p. 28.)

28. Two days before the fall of the Berlin Wall, National Security Adviser Brent Scowcroft alluded to "reversals that could throw the entire development back by decades." (Remarks made on November 7, 1989, as cited in *Die Welt*, July 11, 1990.) Similarly, the *International Herald Tribune* of December 1, 1989, cited unnamed U.S. officials as worrying that "something very violent and very ugly" could derail the process of democratic change in the GDR.

29. These views were contained in my memoranda to Scowcroft (conveying the recommendations of an interagency working group) of November 11 and 20, as cited in Zelikow and Rice, *Germany Unified*, pp. 112–13, 404–32, and 405–35. See also Szabo, *Diplomacy*, p. 41.

30. "Speech by Chancellor Kohl to the Bundestag on Intra-German Relations," November 28, 1989, in Freedman, ed., *Europe Transformed*, pp. 372–76.

31. In Moscow, Foreign Ministry Spokesman Gennadi Gerasimov issued a terse statement: "Realities have to be respected. One is that Europe is divided into two military alliances, NATO and the Warsaw Pact. The second is that frontiers stand as confirmed in Helsinki and the third is that there are two Germanies." (*International Herald Tribune*, November 30, 1989.)

The British and French were incensed that they had not been apprised of the speech in advance. (When a French embassy officer asked me whether the U.S. government had been so apprised, I said that of course our German friends had given us an advance copy but told us, whatever we did, not to share it with the French. After letting him dangle for a while, I owned up to the fact that we had not been informed, either.)

32. Thatcher, *Downing Street Years*, p. 795.

33. Indeed, there were those in Washington, particularly at the Pentagon, who were perhaps overly eager to assert American rights as one of the Four Powers—not out of opposition to German unification but from the instinctive desire to exert control over what seemed a runaway process.

34. "Statement by Secretary of State Baker, November 29, 1989," in *American Foreign Policy: Current Documents, 1989*, ed. Nancy L. Golden and Sherrill Brown Wells (Washington, D.C.: Department of State, 1990), pp. 346–7.

35. Oddly, neither Baker in his memoirs nor Zelikow and Rice in *Germany Unified* explained or even noted the secretary's direct contradiction of Kohl on these two crucial elements. It is an important point, because it places the "quid pro quo" (active American support for unification in return for West German backing on NATO) to which Zelikow and Rice refer at the beginning, not in late January, as they assert (p. 173).

36. Pond, *Beyond the Wall*, p. 147.

37. *Washington Post*, December 8, 1989.

38. *Literaturnaya Gazeta* (Moscow), No. 14, April 10, 1991 (trans. in Foreign Broadcast Information Service/Soviet Union, April 12, 1991, p. 32).

39. *Pravda*, June 26, 1990, trans. in *Current Digest of the Soviet Press*, Vol. XLII, No. 33 (1990), pp. 19–20.

40. Eduard Shevardnadze, *The Future Belongs to Freedom*, trans. Catherine A. Fitzpatrick (New York: The Free Press, 1991) pp. 134 and 146.

41. *Washington Post*, December 8, 1989, pp. A21–22.

42. *International Herald Tribune*, December 12, 1989.

43. Although we consented to hearing Soviet concerns, the agenda was limited to review of the 1987 U.S. "Berlin Initiative" aimed at improving communications and contacts in and around Berlin. The meeting was also coordinated in advance with the West Germans through the "Bonn Group" (the FRG, United States, Britain and France).

44. This was the recommended approach I forwarded to General Scowcroft in my November 20 memorandum on "Handling the German Question at Malta and Beyond," as cited in Zelikow and Rice, *Germany Unified*, pp. 113 and 405 n. 35.

45. See also Zelikow and Rice, *Germany Unified*, p. 131.

46. Whether Moscow, even at the height of the Cold War, really wanted U.S. forces out of Europe is another matter. It seems more likely that Soviet aims were to see NATO weakened and divided but not so divided as to prompt the Europeans, especially the Germans, to mobilize seriously for their own defense.

47. In his memoirs, President Bush gives a detailed account of the Malta meetings in the strengthening of his personal relationship with Gorbachev. (Forthcoming from Alfred A. Knopf, Inc.; draft manuscript shared with the author in July 1996.)

48. Teltschik, *329 Tage*, p. 109. It was a one-liner that the French ostentatiously publicized.

49. "General Secretary Mikhail Gorbachev's Speech to the Central Committee, 9 December 1989," in Freedman, ed., *Europe Transformed*, p. 385. In a subsequent message to Kohl, Gorbachev made the threat more explicit. (Garton Ash, *In Europe's Name*, p 596.)

50. Teltschik, *329 Tage*, p. 109; Newhouse, p. 81. Gorbachev also told the Germans of a similar British overture, presumably the one made by Thatcher during her September 1989 visit to Moscow.

51. Teltschik, *329 Tage*, p. 69; *"Die Siegermachter warnen Bonn," Der Spiegel*, December 11, 1989, p. 17.

52. Forthcoming from Alfred A. Knopf, Inc.; draft manuscript shared with the author in July 1996.

53. Thatcher, *Downing Street Years*, pp. 795–96.

54. *Pravda* and *Izvestia*, December 20, 1989, *Current Digest of the Soviet Press* Vol. XLI, No. 51 (1989), pp. 9–12.

55. Interview by the American scholar Dan Hamilton with Soviet foreign ministry official Sergei Tarasenko, from Hamilton's manuscript on German unification and cited with his permission. The interview describes the contest between the Americanists around Shevardnadze and the "Berlin Wall" of Soviet foreign ministry Germanists.

56. Zelikow and Rice, *Germany Unified* (pp. 154–55, 159–60, 415 n. 9, and 417 n. 17), cite two memoranda that I drafted and forwarded to Scowcroft through Robert Blackwill, NSC senior director for Soviet and European affairs. The first, in mid- to late December, called for a slowing down of the process lest Moscow take precipitous steps to try to derail it altogether. The second, dated January 19, 1990, reflected our change of view toward "the faster, the better." Though I could be wrong, I recall the change of heart coming in a meeting with Blackwill in his office some time toward the end of the Christmas holidays—i.e., the end of December. The memo may have been the first formal written record of a new line we had already conveyed orally to Scowcroft. The substantive point was that the progression in our thinking corresponded precisely to the progression of thought in Bonn.

57. Although Baker's visit to Potsdam had been opposed by some within the administration as conferring an unintended legitimacy to the Modrow government, its aim was not to imply U.S. preference for a "two-state" solution but to secure Modrow's public commitment to setting a date for new elections and to avert precipitous regime collapse in the meantime. Some, nonetheless, considered the visit an exercise in "grandstanding" that could have the effect, even if unintended, of weakening U.S. support for unification. See Baker's account in *Politics of Diplomacy*, pp. 174–76, in which he describes his conviction at that point that "there will be de facto economic unification between the GDR and FRG in any event." See also Pond, *Beyond the Wall*, p. 169, and Szabo, *Diplomacy*, p. 44.

58. See, e.g., *Neues Deutschland*, January 11, 1990. Meanwhile, the resignation of the East German communist leadership on December 3 had left the party "headless and almost irrelevant," in the words of an American embassy cable. (Cited in the *Washington Post*, December 8, 1989, p. A21.)

59. Julij A. Kwizinskij [in German transliteration], *Vor dem Sturm: Erinnerungen eines Diplomaten*, trans. Hilde and Helmut Ettinger (Berlin: Siedler Verlag, 1993), p. 39.

60. Cited in Pond, *Beyond the Wall*, pp. 185–86.

61. Teltschik, *329 Tage*, p. 117.

62. Cited in Pond, *Beyond the Wall*, p. 172.

63. *Pravda*, January 31, 1990, *Current Digest of the Soviet Press* Vol. XLII, No. 5 (1990), p. 22. *Pravda* went on to express Soviet "concern over aggressive neofascist actions in the GDR and attempts by external right-wing radical forces to stir up and fan neo-Nazi sentiment" and condemned "the interference in the GDR's affairs by circles that are fomenting tension."

64. ADN wire service, February 1, 1990, as cited in Pond, *Beyond the Wall*, p. 171. Two days after Modrow's visit, Gorbachev received Gregor Gysi, head of the renamed communist party ("Socialist Unity Party of Germany—Party of Democratic Socialism"), and acknowledged that "in the context of the European process and in the building of a common home in Europe, the question of German national unity can also be resolved." (*Pravda*, February 3, 1990, in *Current Digest of the Soviet Press*, Vol XLII, No. 5 (1990), p. 23.)

65. *Pravda*, February 3, 1990, *Current Digest of the Soviet Press*, Vol. XLII, No. 5, pp. 23–4.

66. "German Unity within the European Framework," Speech by Foreign Minister Hans-Dietrich Genscher at a conference at the Tutzing Protestant Academy, January 31, 1990, *Statements and Speeches* Vol. XIII, No. 2, February 6, 1990, German Information Center. Teltschik, *329 Tage*, pp. 123 and 151, notes Kohl's extreme displeasure at having had no advance notice of the "Genscher Plan."

67. These Soviet proposals came mainly from Shevardnadze's December 19 speech at the European parliament and his February 3 statement in Moscow after the Modrow visit. Shevardnadze's messages to Baker came on January 1 and 10; President Bush also spoke with Gorbachev by telephone on January 31.

68. Interview with the *Wall Street Journal*, January 26, 1990, p. A12. This was shortly after the two Thatcher-Mitterrand meetings in Paris, discussed above, in which the two leaders agreed on an "Anglo-French axis" to slow unification.

69. Thatcher, *Downing Street Years*, pp. 792–98, hints at just such a meeting of the minds among Mitterrand, Gorbachev, and herself.

70. Genscher's reference to the "cat table" came during his November 21, 1989, meeting with President Bush in the Oval Office.

71. To illustrate the problems of reliable "insider" accounts, it is worth mentioning that my role at Shannon was to wander around the duty-free store while Baker and his advisers made history with Dumas. I was usually included in Baker's meetings with European leaders (though not with the Soviets), but the secretary wanted maximum secrecy during this round of negotiation.

72. Reflecting on his meetings with Gorbachev and Shevardnadze, Baker (*Politics of Diplomacy*, p. 205) made the trenchant observation that "Gorbachev seemed to believe that the Soviet Union would always be a preeminent power in Europe. I began to think that possibly Shevardnadze saw the future more clearly, and was wary of codifying Soviet decline." The Ottawa meeting was called to discuss the "Open Skies" proposal that President Bush issued in his Texas A&M speech in May 1989. The other important stops on Baker's trip—Prague, Sofia, and Bucharest—will be discussed in Chapter 5.

73. Shevardnadze, *The Future Belongs to Freedom*, pp. 136–37.

74. There were actually two such "One Plus Three" groups—one of political directors, the other of legal advisers.

75. The NSC staff was opposed to moving so quickly—not because of any difference over the Two Plus Four formula (which was a joint State/NSC initiative) but for fear that Moscow would seize the mechanism to intrude prematurely in the unification process. Indeed, it was the final line of the Ottawa statement that caused the most concern: "Preliminary discussions at the official level will begin shortly." State's view, which turned out to more sound, was that the risk of Soviet mischief-making would be reduced if they were brought into an appropriate multilateral framework. There was also some concern at the NSC that Kohl might object to this early invocation of Four Power prerogatives—the deal

at Ottawa was struck by foreign ministers, after all, and the poisonous relationship between Kohl and Genscher was hardly a state secret. As it turned out, a quick call from the president to the chancellor showed these concerns to be groundless. (See Baker's account in *Politics of Diplomacy*, pp. 198–99.)

76. For background, see Garton Ash, *In Europe's Name*, pp. 216–31, esp. pp. 222–31.

77. It is harder to extend this generous assessment of Kohl's motivations to his linking the border issue to the status of the German minority in Poland and Poland's renunciation of reparations claims against the GDR—points that Germany pressed through rough bilateral negotiations.

78. President Mitterrand hosted Polish prime minister Mazowiecki and Foreign Minister Skubiszewski in early March and spoke of a Four Power role in guaranteeing the boundary. Prime Minister Thatcher, in a March 26 interview with *Der Spiegel*, termed resolution of the border issue a "precondition" for German unification. (Pond, *Beyond the Wall*, p. 196.) Even after Kohl had moved substantially to resolve the issue to Poland's satisfaction, the French continued to obstruct, arguing at a "One Plus Three" legal advisers' meeting at the end of May that France would not sign an agreement on German unity until after a border treaty had been signed and ratified by a united German parliament. All this suggests that while the French may have supported the Polish cause out of principle as well, their main interest was in complicating the unification process.

79. There was a certain division between the NSC staff and the State Department on this point, owing partly to somewhat different judgments on Genscher's reliability on security issues and partly to institutional biases in favor of our chief counterparts in Bonn (the chancellery and the foreign ministry, respectively).

80. Zelikow and Rice, *Germany Unified*, pp. 219–22. Bush, as I recall, went beyond the talking points I had prepared on the subject (constrained as I was by the general NSC inclination to go easy on Kohl), so Baker must have gotten to the president directly to recommend a more active mediating role. It was a good thing if he did (though Baker says nothing about it in his memoirs).

81. The resolutions were passed by the two German parliaments on June 21, and Polish foreign minister Skubiszewski attended the third Two Plus Four meeting in Paris on July 17. Shortly after German unification, Chancellor Kohl and Polish prime minister Mazowiecki agreed to negotiate a border treaty, which was signed on June 17, 1991, following difficult negotiations over the status of Poland's German minority.

82. Michael R. Beschloss and Strobe Talbott, *At the Highest Levels: The Inside Story of the End of the Cold War* (Boston: Little, Brown and Company, 1993), p. 188.

83. Zelikow and Rice, *Germany Unified*, pp. 186–87.

84. TASS (Moscow), February 11, 1990, as cited in Günter Müchler and Klaus Hofmann, *Helmut Kohl: Chancellor of German Unity* (Bonn: Press and Information Office of the Federal Government, 1992), pp. 185–86. It is worth noting that the Genscher-Shevardnadze joint statement issued at the same time was much less forthcoming than the Kohl-Gorbachev agreement. Both texts are translated in Freedman, ed., *Europe Transformed*, pp. 472–73 and 474–75.

85. These included the East German sister parties of Kohl's CDU (Christian Democratic Union) and its Bavarian coalition partner CSU (Christian Social Union), as well as the East German "Democratic Awakening."

86. Interviews by Dan Hamilton with Sergei Tarasenko and Nikolai Portugalov, cited with permission of the interviewer.

87. For Prime Minister Thatcher's reaction to the "Franco-German juggernaut," see *Downing Street Years*, pp. 761–63.

88. Remarks by SPD (Social Democratic party) adviser Egon Bahr at the Wehrkunde Conference, Munich, February 1990. See also Szabo, *Diplomacy*, p. 44, and Pond, *Beyond the Wall*, pp. 174 and 317.

89. Some of these proposals by Western analysts are cited in Pond, *Beyond the Wall*, pp. 188–89.

90. McGeorge Bundy, "From Cold War to Trusting Peace," *Foreign Affairs*, Vol. 69, No. 1 (Winter 1989–90), p. 205.

91. Zelikow and Rice, *Germany Unified*, p. 422–58.

92. A fuller version of his August 1990 *Atlantic* article is John J. Mearsheimer, "Back to the Future: Instability in Europe After the Cold War," *International Security* Vol. 15, No. 1 (Summer 1990): 5–56.

93. "German Unity within the European Framework," Speech by Foreign Minister Hans-Dietrich Genscher at a conference at the Tutzing Protestant Academy, January 31, 1990, *Statements and Speeches* Vol. XIII, No. 2, February 6, 1990, German Information Center.

94. Speech by Foreign Minister Hans-Dietrich Genscher at the meeting of the Western European Union, Luxembourg, March 23, 1990, *Statements and Speeches* Vol. XIII, No. 8, March 30, 1990, German Information Center, New York.

95. "The Future of a European Germany," speech by Foreign Minister Hans-Dietrich Genscher at the Conference of the American Society of Newspaper Editors, Washington, April 6, 1990, *Statements and Speeches* Vol. XIII, No. 9, April 10, 1990, German Information Center, New York. (Emphasis added.)

96. Kiessler and Elbe, *Ein runder Tisch mit scharfen Ecken*, p. 80.

97. Pond, *Beyond the Wall*, p. 319 n.19.

98. Both texts are carried in full in *Public Papers of the Presidents: George Bush, 1990* (Washington, D.C.: U.S. Government Printing Office, 1991), pp. 264–66.

99. Teltschik, *329 Tage*, p. 162. The president's remark is cited in his memoirs (forthcoming from Alfred A. Knopf, Inc.).

100. "News Conference of President Bush and President François Mitterrand of France in Key Largo, Florida, April 19, 1990," in *Public Papers of the Presidents: George Bush, 1990*, p. 523.

101. Pond, *Beyond the Wall*, p. 212.

102. Havel's February 1990 visit to Washington is discussed in Chapter 5.

103. On the Bush-Havel relationship, see Chapter 6.

104. "Statement by the Press Secretary on the President's Meeting with Prime Minister Lothar de Maizière of the German Democratic Republic, June 11, 1990," in *Public Papers, 1990*, p. 810.

105. Shevardnadze's remarks during a meeting with Secretary Baker in Windhoek, Namibia (where both were attending that country's independence celebrations), March 20, 1990, as cited in Beschloss and Talbott, *Highest Levels*, p. 198.

106. Shevardnadze, *Future Belongs to Freedom*, pp. 132, 136.

107. *Ibid.*, p. 133. In fact, Shevardnadze acknowledges that even he is not satisfied with his explanation: "I must admit that I reread these statements now with mixed feelings. It seems that not even three months went by and we turned our attitude around 180 degrees. (*Ibid.*, p. 138.)

108. ARD television, March 6, 1990, as cited in Teltschik, *329 Tage*, p. 168.

109. *Izvestia*, April 7, 1990, as translated in *Current Digest of the Soviet Press*, Vol. XLII, No. 14 (1990), p. 9.

110. *Izvestia*, May 6, 1990, as translated and condensed in *Current Digest of the Soviet Press*, Vol. XLII, No. 18 (1990), pp. 10–12.

111. Edward Hallett Carr, *The Twenty Years' Crisis, 1919–1939* (New York: Harper and Row Publishers, 1964).

112. Pond, *Beyond the Wall*, p. 214; Szabo, *Diplomacy*, p. 83; and Serge Schmemann, "German Coalition Leaders Split on Soviet Proposal for Unification," *New York Times*, May 9, 1990.

113. Shevardnadze, *The Future Belongs to Freedom*, p. 139.

114. Beschloss and Talbott, *At the Highest Levels*, pp. 207–9.

115. In press coverage of the visit, much was made of the fact that Prunskiene's entry into the White House grounds was delayed for several minutes, which reporters insisted on interpreting as a deliberate snub. For the record: the gate was really stuck.

116. Interview with the *Wall Street Journal*, January 26, 1990, p. A12; and Thatcher, *Downing Street Years*, p. 797.

117. Oberdorfer, *The Turn*, p. 404.

118. Soviet defense minister Dimitri Yazov, one of the leaders of the August 1991 coup attempt, later complained that "Gorbachev often traveled abroad in recent years, and frequently we had no idea what important issues he discussed. . . . Take Gorbachev's report to the [July 1991] G-7 meeting in London—none of us knew what was said there." (*New York Times*, October 7, 1991, p. A7.)

119. See, e.g., Shevardnadze's remarkable interview with *Literaturnaya Gazeta*, April 19, 1990, in which he warned of the "death of perestroika" and the advent of dictatorship and chronicled the growing internal attacks against himself and Gorbachev. (*Foreign Broadcast Information Service*, FBIS-SOV-90-181, 26 April 1990, pp. 5–11.)

120. "NATO and the U.S. Commitment to Europe," Address by President Bush at the Oklahoma State University commencement, Stillwater, Oklahoma, May 4, 1990, in *Public Papers (1990)*, pp. 625–29.

121. See, e.g., Thomas Friedman, "U.S. Will Press the Soviets to Accept Plan on Germany," *New York Times*, June 5, 1990, p. A17.

122. Remarks during a question-and-answer session following Teltschik's presentation at the American Institute for Contemporary German Studies, Washington, November 26, 1991.

123. For a wonderfully detailed examination of the Washington Summit, see Joseph G. Whelan, *Soviet Diplomacy and Negotiating Behavior—1988–90*, Committee on Foreign Affairs Special Studies Series, Vol. III (Washington, D.C.: U.S. Government Printing Office, 1991), pp. 291–418.

124. For a blow-by-blow account, see Beschloss and Talbott, *At the Highest Levels*, pp. 215–24, and Bush's account in his memoirs (forthcoming from Alfred A. Knopf, Inc.).

125. A few days earlier, in a meeting with Mitterrand in Moscow, Gorbachev had explored the idea of a "French solution" whereby Germany would be politically but not militarily integrated into NATO. (Teltschik, *329 Tage*, pp. 243–48.)

126. "Press Conference by the President and President Mikhail Gorbachev," June 3, 1990, Office of the Press Secretary, The White House. Baker, *Politics of Diplomacy*, notes that Gorbachev was leaning in this direction during the secretary's visit to Moscow in

mid-May (p. 252) and that as far back as February Kohl had predicted that "Gorbachev will make that concession [on Germany's NATO membership] to the President of the United States" (p. 231).

127. Beschloss and Talbott, *At the Highest Levels*, p. 230; Pond, *Beyond the Wall*, p. 216. This was another of those historic events at which I was there but not there. I was invited to sit in on most of Baker's meetings at Copenhagen but not the Shevardnadze "bilat" (bilateral meeting with a foreign leader).

128. "The NATO Alliance and the Future of Europe," intervention by Secretary Baker before the North Atlantic Council meeting, June, 7, 1990, Turnberry, Scotland, United States Department of State, Current Policy Document No. 1284 (June 1990).

129. "Ministerial Meeting of the North Atlantic Council at Turnberry, United Kingdom, 7th–8th June 1990," NATO Press Service, Communiqué M-1 (90) 29, June 8, 1990.

130. Szabo, *Diplomacy*, p. 88; Beschloss and Talbott, *At the Highest Levels*, pp. 232–33.

131. The NSC draft of the declaration was done by Philip Zelikow. For his detailed account, see Zelikow and Rice, *Germany Unified*, pp. 303–24. See also Szabo, *Diplomacy*, pp. 95–97, 106 and Shevardnadze, *The Future Belongs to Freedom*, pp. 140–42.

132. "London Declaration on a Transformed North Atlantic Alliance, Issued by the Heads of State and Government participating in the meeting of the North Atlantic Council in London on 5th–6th July 1990," NATO Press Service, Communiqué S-1 (90) 36, July 6, 1990.

133. Thatcher, *Downing Street Years*, pp. 811–12. As she put it (p. 811), "I found myself at odds with the Americans and indeed with the NATO Secretary-General [Manfred Wörner] about how we should approach the NATO Summit." (Wörner, a former West German defense minister, played a critically important role in encouraging NATO's transformation and building consensus around a new vision for the alliance.)

134. I recall being asked by academic specialists and think-tankers just before the London Summit what initiatives we had in mind. Since I was not at liberty to say, I challenged them to offer some ideas. They had plenty with regard to CSCE, many of which were in fact already in our draft declaration, but almost none with respect to the alliance itself.

135. I later learned from senior German officials that similar discussions were going on in Bonn. On the European security debate after German unification, see Chapters 4 and 7.

136. It is an open question whether even this concession, made preemptively by Genscher at the beginning of the process, could have been averted.

137. This language was tabled by the FRG representative to the August 23 One Plus Three political directors' meeting in London and prompted me to write a memorandum for Scowcroft ("German Unification: New Problems at End-Game") warning that differences over this issue "cast serious doubt on the agreement we thought was at hand for the united Germany's remaining a full member of NATO." From the way the Germans broached the subject, it seemed to me and others on the American delegation that a prior arrangement to that effect had already been worked out between Bonn and Moscow.

138. British foreign secretary Hurd's insistence on clarifying this point at Moscow was not, as some have interpreted it, a last-ditch British effort to derail the Two Plus Four agreement. We were as adamant as the British that all of united Germany, including the territory of the former GDR, be fully within NATO's sphere of competence. We were sat

isfied that this was already assured under the draft treaty, and the Agreed Minute provided further clarification.

139. The text is reprinted in Szabo, *Diplomacy*, pp. 131–34.

140. After the December 1990 all-German elections, with no state (*Land*) elections scheduled for nearly two years, we felt that this was the ideal time to build U.S.-German cooperation and coleadership on key issues like GATT. For all their protestations to the contrary, there was scant evidence that the Germans lifted a finger to try to broker an EC compromise.

141. Office of the Press Secretary, The White House, April 29, 1992. These nuances, ignored in the media coverage of the visit, were immediately picked up by the von Weizsäcker entourage and cabled back to Bonn.

Chapter 4

1. As will be seen as Chapter 8, however, Yazov performed a last malevolent act in helping lead the anti-Gorbachev coup attempt in August 1991.

2. John Lewis Gaddis, *The Long Peace: Inquiries into the History of the Cold War* (New York: Oxford University Press, 1987).

3. Lord [Thomas] Macauley, "The Earl of Chatham," in *Critical and Historical Essays* Vol. IV (London: Longmans, Green, and Co., 1895), p. 274.

4. The "Eastern question" traditionally refers to the protracted decline of the Ottoman empire in the nineteenth and early twentieth centuries. Yet it is related as well to the Polish question, Czech question, and others that arose in Central and Eastern Europe in the context of the collapse of the Habsburg, Russian, and Ottoman empires. In short, the term connotes the dilemmas, past and present, posed by the break up of multiethnic empires in the entire region from the Baltic Sea to the Balkans.

5. James Goodby, "Commonwealth and Concert: Organizing Principles of Post-Containment Order in Europe," *The Washington Quarterly*, Summer 1991, p. 78. See also Stanley Hoffmann, "Balance, Concert, Anarchy, or None of the Above," in Gregory F. Treverton, ed., *The Shape of the New Europe* (New York: Council on Foreign Relations Press, 1992), pp. 194–220; and Philip Zelikow, "The New Concert of Europe," *Survival*, Summer 1992, pp. 12–30.

6. See Chapter 1.

7. The Helsinki Final Act was issued at the 1975 summit meeting of the Conference on Security and Cooperation in Europe.

8. Joseph S. Nye, Jr. ("What New World Order?" *Foreign Affairs* Vol. 71, No. 2 [Spring 1992], pp. 83–96) was not quite right in arguing that the Bush administration "thought and acted like Nixon, but borrowed the rhetoric of Wilson and Carter." In fact, the two strands were more nearly balanced in both action and rhetoric, albeit with a realistic tilt, until public discomfort with this dual explanation for American action in the Persian Gulf (as if a country could not have interests in principles of international conduct as well as in secure oil supplies) pushed the rhetoric toward moralism and universalism.

9. See Goodby, "Commonwealth and Concert," as well as Richard Rosecrance, "A New Concert of Powers," *Foreign Affairs* Vol. 71, No. 2 (Spring 1992), pp. 64–82.

10. "Toward a New World Order," Address by President Bush before a Joint Session of the Congress, September 11, 1990, Current Policy No. 1298, Bureau of Public Affairs, U.S. Department of State.

11. See Chapter 8.

12. "Remarks by the President to the Czechoslovak Federal Assembly," November 17, 1990, White House press release of that day.

13. This frame of mind was much like that of the peacemakers at Versailles in 1919. There were other parallels to which we should have been more alert, such as Baker's discerning genuine democrats among some of the warmed over despots from Kazakhstan or other points east, just as Wilson had done three generations before. "Why, they are just like us!" was the wishful thought that crowded out hard reason.

14. Margaret Thatcher, *The Downing Street Years* (New York: HarperCollins Publishers, 1993), p. 815.

15. Ever the gentleman, President Bush sat through each one, though heads of other delegations absented themselves from time to time for the many "bilats" (bilateral meetings with other leaders) held on the margins of the summit. When it came time to prepare for the next CSCE summit, held in Helsinki in July 1992, our first requirement at staff level was that the session be orchestrated so that presidents and prime ministers were not obliged to be present for interventions by each of the countries represented (by then totalling 52).

16. Ole Waever, "Three Competing Europes: German, French, Russian," *International Affairs*, Vol. 66, No. 3 (1990): 481. Waever's breakdown of the competing European visions differs from mine, but it captures the same contradictions and incompatibilities.

17. *Ibid.*, 480.

18. These visions were spelled out, e.g., in the 1967 Harmel Report, which affirmed NATO's ultimate goal as the achievement of "a just and lasting peaceful order in Europe," and the Treaty of Rome, which called on the European Community to "eliminate the barriers which divide Europe" and "lay the foundations for an ever closer union among the peoples of Europe."

19. Bush was born in 1924; Scowcroft, in 1925; and Baker, Brady, and Eagleburger, in 1930.

20. On this point, see Hoffmann, "Balance, Concert, Anarchy, or None of the Above," p. 212.

21. In truth, the advice coming from outside was rarely helpful. The inside-the-Washington-Beltway think tanks tried to replicate what we were doing inside government but could not do it as well, and scholars and thinkers farther removed from Washington usually offered insights too abstract and detached from the exigencies of policy making. The difference was that early in the administration we made the effort to tap the best and most relevant thinking, but by mid-term—whether from weariness, overwork, or sheer hubris—we rarely did so.

Another point that needs making—without naming names—is that the mid-term turnover at State produced a marked deterioration in policy making, especially from the European bureau. From both the conceptual and operational perspectives, the falloff was dramatic.

22. See the Introduction.

23. Jiří Dienstbier, "Central and Eastern Europe and a New European Order, Address at Harvard University, May 15, 1990, reprinted in Tim Whipple, ed., *After the Velvet Revolution: Václav Havel and the New Leaders of Czechoslovakia Speak Out* (New York: Freedom House, 1992), p. 120. (The citation here is from the as-delivered copy I got from the Czechoslovak embassy. The wording differs slightly from Whipple's version.)

Dienstbier's speech echoed the 1985 "Prague Appeal," which he and other Charter 77 signatories sent to the fourth Amsterdam conference on disarmament.

24. "The Common European Interest: America and the New Politics Among Nations," address by Secretary Baker upon receiving the Hans J. Morgenthau Award, New York City, May 14, 1990, Current Policy No. 1278, Bureau of Public Affairs, U.S. Department of State.

25. I heard Bush ask Kohl at least a dozen times whether Germans would still want an American military presence after unification and the departure of Soviet troops. Though equally worried about American public attitudes, he felt he could make the case so long as European developments did not conspire to push U.S. forces out.

26. "Remarks by the President at the Aspen Institute Symposium," The Aspen Institute, Aspen, Colorado, August 2, 1990, Office of the Press Secretary, The White House. Emphasis added.

27. "Remarks by the President at Luncheon Hosted by Prime Minister [Ruud] Lubbers," Binnenhof, The Hague, The Netherlands, November 9, 1991, Office of the Press Secretary, The White House.

28. Negotiating positions taken by the USTR had to be approved by the president and so were not always as authoritative as the Europeans might have wished, but our decision-making system was simplicity itself compared to the EC's cumbersome process.

29. "Declaration on US-EC Relations," Rome, Brussels, and Washington, November 23, 1990. The French fought against any commitments at all, ultimately agreeing only to stipulations for biannual consultations at head-of-state level, additional biannual consultations at foreign-minister level, and somewhat strengthened contacts between the United States and the EC Commission.

30. Robert B. Zoellick, "The New Europe in a New Age: Insular, Itinerant, or International? Prospects for an Alliance of Values," address before a conference on U.S.-EC relations, Annapolis, Maryland, September 21, 1990, *Current Policy* No. 1300, Bureau of Public Affairs, U.S. Department of State.

31. Zoellick, in *ibid.*, put it this way: "The United States, the European Community, and Japan are colleagues in pursuit of common ends. The three of us together could, however, accomplish a great deal more. We can be the catalysts and major contributors toward addressing the post–Cold War problems. We can draw other nations into existing or new international structures that support our common interests and objectives."

32. "Remarks by President Bush and President von Weizsäcker of Germany in Exchange of Toasts," The State Dining Room, The White House, Office of the Press Secretary, April 29, 1992. As was noted in the chapter on German unification, these remarks, though offered at a social occasion, did not pass unnoticed by the German delegation, which immediately faxed the texts back to Bonn.

33. "A New Europe, A New Atlanticism: Architecture for a New Era," Address by Secretary of State James A. Baker, III, to the Berlin Press Club, Steigenberger Hotel, December 12, 1989, U.S. Department of State, Office of Public Affairs; and "The Euro-Atlantic Architecture: From West to East," Address to the Aspen Institute, Berlin, Germany, June 18, 1991, U.S. Department of State *Dispatch,* June 24, 1991, pp. 439–43.

34. "Partnership with the Countries of Central and Eastern Europe," Statement issued by the North Atlantic Council meeting in ministerial session in Copenhagen on 6th and 7th June 1991, NATO Press Service, Brussels, June 6, 1991.

35. Comecon, the Council for Mutual Economic Assistance, was the Soviet-directed trading bloc with Eastern Europe.

36. "From Revolution to Democracy: Central and Eastern Europe in the New Europe," Charles University, Prague, Czechoslovakia, February 7, 1990, U.S. Department of State, Bureau of Public Affairs, Current Policy No. 1248. (Baker's visit to Prague is discussed in Chapter 5.)

37. Cited in Bernard Wheaton and Zdeněk Kavan, *The Velvet Revolution: Czechoslovakia, 1988–1991* (Boulder, Co.: Westview Press, 1992), p 149.

38. The "Pentagonale" originally included Hungary, Czechoslovakia, and the northern republics of Yugoslavia (Slovenia and Croatia) and was later expanded to include Poland and renamed the Central European Initiative. The less ambitious "Alpe-Adria" involved regional cooperation among sub-national units (republics, Länder, autonomous regions) of Italy, Austria, Yugoslavia, Hungary, and, as an observer, the German Free State of Bavaria. (See Paolo Perulli, "The Political Economy of a 'Mid-European Region,'" in Colin Crouch and David Marquand, eds., *Towards Greater Europe* [Cambridge, Ma.: Blackwell Publishers, 1992], pp. 154–69.)

39. The security aspects of Western integration strategies will be explored in Chapter 7.

40. EFTA at this time consisted of Austria, Norway, Sweden, Switzerland, Finland, and Iceland.

41. Kalypso Nicolaidis, "East European Trade in the Aftermath of 1989: Did International Institutions Matter?" in Robert O. Keohane, Joseph S. Nye, and Stanley Hoffmann, eds., *After the Cold War: International Institutions and State Strategies in Europe, 1989–1991* (Cambridge, Ma.: Harvard University Press, 1993), pp. 207–10 and 220–27. For more on the "Europe agreements," more commonly known as the "association agreements," see Chapter 5.

42. For the text of the rambling, emotional resignation speech, see Eduard Shevardnadze, *The Future Belongs to Freedom* (New York: The Free Press, 1991), pp. 223–26.

43. Michael R. Beschloss and Strobe Talbott, *At the Highest Levels: The Inside Story of the End of the Cold War* (Boston, Ma.: Little, Brown and Company, 1993), p. 302.

44. Quoted by Charles Gati in the *New York Times*, February 14, 1991.

45. On Mitterrand's proposal, see *Le Monde*, December 31, 1989; Delors's was carried in the *Financial Times*, October 16, 1989. Mitterrand held out the prospect of a confederation that would "associate all the states of our continent in a common organization," but this was to be the second of two stages, followed by a protracted period in which the priority would be for the European Community to "reinforce its structures."

46. On this point, see Keohane and Nye in their introduction to Keohane, Nye, and Hoffmann, eds., *After the Cold War*, p. 16.

Chapter 5

1. Comment made to Chancellor Helmut Kohl in Bonn, November 10, 1989, as cited in Horst Teltschik, *329 Tage: Innenansichten der Einigung* (Berlin: Siedler Verlag, 1991), p. 16.

2. Although Kafka wrote the book literally in the shadow of Hradčany, the castle on which his was modeled was another one, situated some miles from Prague.

3. See Chapter 3, as well as Baker's account of his meeting with Havel, in James A. Baker, III, with Thomas M. DeFrank, *The Politics of Diplomacy: Revolution, War and Peace, 1989–92* (New York: G. P. Putnam's Sons, 1995), pp. 200–1.

4. "From Revolution to Democracy: Central and Eastern Europe in the New Europe," Charles University, Prague, Czechoslovakia, February 7, 1990, United States Department of State, Bureau of Public Affairs, Current Policy No. 1248.

5. See Baker's account, in *Politics of Diplomacy*. He argues that security concerns were the reason for the delayed decision to visit, but at least some among his staff believed there was a policy debate involved as well.

6. Slovak wariness was evident in a question-and-answer session following a lecture I gave at the institute of my host, Dr. Jozef Kučerák. While polite and curious, the questions nonetheless betrayed a reserve about the United States that differed sharply from my encounters with others from Central and Eastern Europe.

7. My tour guide was my other cohost in Bratislava, Public Against Violence official Andrej Bartosiewicz.

8. This was later confirmed. When Havel called Boris Yeltsin in early 1992, shortly after the collapse of the Soviet Union, Yeltsin told him that he had found in his—until recently, Gorbachev's—office in the Kremlin a sealed letter marked "Never to be opened." (Kafka in Moscow?) Yeltsin of course had opened it promptly and told Havel what he had found inside: the notorious "letter from the Czechoslovak comrades" which Soviet leader Leonid Brezhnev had invoked in justifying the Soviet-led Warsaw Pact invasion of 1968. Most of us in the West doubted that such a letter actually existed, but here it was—signed by five senior Czechoslovak communist officials, including Vasil Bil'ak.

9. In addition to Zhelev, the group included UDF Spokesman Rumen Vodenicharov, Petŭr Beron of the environmental movement Ecoglasnost, Yanko Yankov of the Social Democratic party, and Father Christopher Subev, chairman of the Committee for Human Rights—joined, we presumed, by an unseen, uninvited functionary at the other end of a listening device installed in the room.

10. See Chapter 3.

11. This official went on to note that their successors evoked no such feelings of awe.

12. The strategy of forming a united front against communist rule was probably justified for these first elections, when it was essential to break the ruling parties' monopolistic grip on power, but it may have arrested the natural development of a stable party system by forcing such diverse political bedfellows into largely artificial coalitions like the UDF.

13. David Stark, "Path Dependence and Privatization Strategies in East Central Europe," *East European Politics and Societies* Vol. 6, No. 1 (Winter 1992), pp. 17–54.

14. Tony Judt, "*Ex Oriente Lux?* Post-Celebratory Speculations on the 'Lessons' of '89," in Colin Crouch and David Marquand, eds., *Towards Greater Europe?: A Continent without an Iron Curtain* (Oxford and Cambridge, MA: Blackwell Publishers, 1992), p. 94.

15. Alexis de Tocqueville, *The Old Regime and the French Revolution*, trans. Stuart Gilbert (Garden City, NY: Doubleday and Doubleday, Inc., 1955), p. 161.

16. Jadwiga Staniszkis, *The Dynamics of the Breakthrough in Eastern Europe: The Polish Experience* (Berkeley: University of California Press, 1991), xii.

17. Bronisław Geremek, "Postcommunism and Democracy in Poland," *The Washington Quarterly*, Summer 1990, p. 129, set this task—what he called "building local democracy from the bottom up"—among the highest priorities for Poland's postcommunist transformation.

18. Giuseppe Di Palma, "Why Democracy Can Work in Eastern Europe," *Journal of Democracy*, Vol. 2, No. 1 (Winter 1991), p. 28.

19. Among the many excellent analyses of the challenges of the postcommunist economic reforms, see especially the country and sectoral surveys in Paul Marer and Salvatore Zecchini, eds., *The Transition to a Market Economy* (Paris: Organization for Eco-

nomic Cooperation and Development, 1991); Vittorio Corbo, Fabrizio Coricelli, and Jan Bossak, eds., *Reforming Central and Eastern European Economies* (Washington, D.C.: The World Bank, 1991); U.S. Congress, Joint Economic Committee, *East-Central European Economies in Transition* (Washington, D.C.: U.S. Government Printing Office, 1994); and many excellent articles in the journal *East European Politics and Societies*.

20. Edmund Burke, "Reflections on the Revolution in France," in *Edmund Burke*, The Harvard Classics, ed. Charles W. Eliot (New York: P. F. Collier and Son, 1909, 1937), p. 179.

21. *Ibid.*, p. 375.

22. Adam Michnik, "The Two Faces of Eastern Europe," *The New Republic*, November 12, 1990, p. 23.

23. Samuel P. Huntington, *The Third Wave: Democratization in the Late Twentieth Century* (Norman and London: University of Oklahoma Press, 1991), p. 258.

24. *Ibid.*, p. 263.

25. Ralf Dahrendorf, *Reflections on the Revolution in Europe* (New York: Times Books, Random House, 1990) p. 78.

26. *Ibid.*, p. 84.

27. "Address by Václav Havel, President of the Czech Republic, at the George Washington University, Washington, April 22, 1993," press release of that day by the embassy of the Czech Republic.

28. For background, see "The Bonn CSCE Conference on Economic Cooperation in Europe," in *From Vienna to Helsinki: Reports of the Inter-Sessional Meetings of the CSCE Process* (Washington, D.C.: Commission on Security and Cooperation in Europe, 1992), pp. 53–66; and Vojtech Mastny, *The Helsinki Process and the Reintegration of Europe, 1986–91: Analysis and Documentation* (New York: New York University Press, 1992), pp. 215–22.

29. *Document of the Bonn Conference on Economic Cooperation in Europe of the CSCE* (Washington, D.C.: Commission on Security and Cooperation in Europe, 1990). The text is excerpted in Mastny, *The Helsinki Process*, pp. 222–28.

30. Mastny, *The Helsinki Process*, p. 222.

31. "CSCE: The Conscience of the Continent," Remarks by Secretary of States James A. Baker, III, at the CSCE Conference on the Human Dimension, Copenhagen, Denmark, June 6, 1990, Department of State, Office of the Assistant Secretary/Spokesman. The full text is also carried in Samuel F. Wells, Jr., ed., *The Helsinki Process and the Future of Europe* (Washington, D.C.: The Woodrow Wilson Center Press, 1990), pp. 185–94.

At Copenhagen, Baker also met with Soviet foreign minister Shevardnadze to build on the progress made in the Bush-Gorbachev Washington Summit of the previous week and to further move Soviet thinking toward acceptance of united Germany's remaining in NATO. From there, Baker's party went directly to Turnberry, Scotland, for a NATO foreign ministers meeting, where we advanced a radical agenda for transforming the Atlantic alliance.

32. *Document of the Copenhagen Meeting of the Conference on the Human Dimension of the CSCE, June 1990* (Washington D.C.: Commission on Security and Cooperation in Europe, 1990).

33. Thomas Buergenthal, "The Copenhagen CSCE Meeting: A New Public Order in Europe," *Human Rights Law Journal* 11 (1990), as excerpted in Mastny, *The Helsinki Process*, pp. 246 and 252.

34. "State of the Union Address," The U.S. Capitol, Washington, D.C., January 31, 1990, Office of the Press Secretary, The White House. Earlier the same day, the White House had announced that President Havel would pay an official visit in late February, followed by Polish prime minister Mazowiecki in March.

35. "U.S. Foreign Policy Priorities and FY 1991 Budget Request," February 1, 1990, United States Department of State, Bureau of Public Affairs, Current Policy Bulletin No. 1245. Baker's remarks included a reminder of the limits of U.S. influence: "Ultimately, we believe that the staggering task of transforming the Soviet Union and the East European countries into democratic, prosperous societies depends on the decisions freely made by the people themselves and the extent to which [their leaders] have the consent and confidence of the governed."

36. In fact, we at the NSC staff—principally my colleague Adrian Basora—had been managing the assistance programs since the president's July 1989 trip to Poland and Hungary, but the job was getting much too large for this arrangement to continue.

37. I succeeded Ambassador Robert Barry, who ably directed the assistance program from 1990 to 1992.

38. The State/A.I.D. relationship, although difficult at times, developed into an effective partnership, with State providing the strategic vision and political direction, and A.I.D. bringing the developmental perspective and sectoral knowledge that State lacked.

39. "America's Opportunities in Eastern Europe," Remarks by Deputy Secretary Lawrence S. Eagleburger before American Chamber of Commerce's International Forum, Washington, D.C., February 16, 1990, United States Department of State, Bureau of Public Affairs, Current Policy No. 1250.

40. "Citizens Democracy Corps Proposed for Eastern Europe," Commencement Address by President Bush at the University of South Carolina, May 12, 1990, U.S. Department of State, Bureau of Public Affairs, Current Policy No. 1277. The president's speech, one of his best on Eastern Europe, addressed "the landscape of moral destruction . . . , the tragic consequence of four decades of communist rule. . . . Fortunately, the moral destruction . . . was not complete. Individuals somehow managed to maintain an inner strength. . . . They did so, as Václav Havel put it, by the simple act of 'living in truth.' They created 'flying universities' where lecturers taught in private homes. They formed underground publishing houses and groups to monitor human rights—an authentic 'civil society' beyond the reach of the ruling establishment. . . ."

41. Romanian, Baltic, and Albanian Funds were created in 1993–94.

42. These programs spanned virtually every sphere of political, economic, and social activity, from health care partnerships linking American and East European medical centers to local agrobusiness ventures relying on American volunteers.

43. Robert L. Hutchings, "US Aid to Central and Eastern Europe: A Call for Imagination," U.S. Department of State *Dispatch*, Vol. 4, No. 17, April 26, 1993, pp. 292–94. The testimony also noted that "G. K. Chesterton once said that anything worth doing is worth doing badly, by which he meant that there are some things so important, some tasks so urgent, that we should be prepared to take risks and be prepared to make mistakes."

44. See Chapter 6.

45. "Fact Sheet: Trade Enhancement Initiative for Central and Eastern Europe," Office of the Press Secretary, The White House, March 20, 1991.

46. "Fact Sheet: American Business and Private Sector Development Initiative for Central and Eastern Europe," Office of the Press Secretary, The White House, March 20, 1991.

47. Statement by the Press Secretary and Fact Sheets, Office of the Press Secretary, The White House, September 11, 1991.

48. Welcoming Havel to Washington two weeks after Baker's speech in Prague, President Bush repeated the point: "We know there is no room for illusions. Difficult work lies ahead. The damage of four decades of fear and repression cannot be repaired in a day." ("Remarks by the President and President Havel of Czechoslovakia Upon Departure," February 20, 1990, Office of the Press Secretary, The White House.)

49. Having heard the charge so often from my academic friends that U.S. officials led East Europeans to believe that prosperity would come quickly if only they would embrace "the market," I scoured the record of public and private statements in 1989–91 and could find not a single statement, public or private, implying that prosperity was just around the corner. What we *did* say was that prosperity could only follow some essential, and inevitably painful, steps toward economic restructuring and that the sooner these steps were taken, the sooner this painful period would be over.

50. Commission of the European Communities, "Operation PHARE: A Legal Basis for the Community's 'Action Plan,'" Information Memo P–63, Brussels, 26 October 1989, and "EC-Eastern Europe Relations," ICC Background Brief, Brussels, 19 January 1990.

51. Corbo, Coricelli, and Bossak, eds., *Reforming Central and Eastern European Economies.*

52. See, e.g, Marer and Zecchini, *The Transition to a Market Economy,* as well as the OECD's series of detailed country surveys.

53. See, e.g., "Cooperation and Assistance Programmes with Central and Eastern European Countries," Annual Report for 1991, Council of Europe, Directorate of Political Affairs, Strasbourg, 6 January 1992.

54. Stephan Haggard and Andrew Moravcsik, "The Political Economy of Financial Assistance," in Robert O. Keohane, Joseph S. Nye, and Stanley Hoffmann, eds., *After the Cold War: International Institutions and State Strategies in Europe, 1989–91* (Cambridge, Ma.: Harvard University Press, 1993), pp. 265–72.

55. Our reservations about Attali's qualifications were muted by the prospect of his removal from Paris and away from Mitterrand's ear, where we worried that his influence would make it harder to forge a Franco-American understanding on the basic elements of a new European and transatlantic order.

56. For the first three years, Soviet borrowing was limited to the level of its paid-in capital (roughly $216 million). After the dissolution of the USSR, the rule was eliminated, but with the understanding that the main focus of the bank would remain on Central and Eastern Europe.

57. All figures are from the "Scoreboard of G-24 Assistance" published by the Commission of the European Communities, Brussels, 8 April 1992.

58. The attentive reader may recall from Chapter 2 that 20 percent had become our informal benchmark dating from our assembling of the Polish Stabilization Fund in the early fall of 1989. We in fact exceeded that percentage in 1990–91 but then began to fall behind.

59. For a survey of the stabilization funds mounted for Poland, Czechoslovakia, Hungary, Bulgaria, and Romania, see "Progress Report on the G-24 Medium-Term Financial Assistance Initiative for Central and Eastern European Countries," Commission of the European Communities, Brussels, 6 April 1992.

60. *Ibid.*; and Organization for Economic Cooperation and Development, *Reforming the Economies of Central and Eastern Europe,* p. 23

61. See Chapter 6.

62. George F. Kennan, *Memoirs 1925–50* (Boston: Little, Brown and Company, 1967), pp. 352–53.

63. I advanced several such plans in 1991 and 1992—my target being a round $1 billion—but was singularly unsuccessful in winning support at the cabinet level.

64. In his memoirs (written with President Bush), Scowcroft found the Treasury Department resolutely "tone deaf" to any agreement in favor of increased aid to Eastern Europe. (Forthcoming from Alfred A. Knopf; draft manuscript shared with author in July 1996.)

65. Baker (*Politics of Diplomacy*, pp. 45–46) does, however, refer to a "tacit division of labor with our Western allies, whereby Germany and others would focus on economic assistance to the East Europeans and Soviets, while we would focus more . . . working to demilitarize Soviet foreign policy and push Gorbachev on political reform." This does not explain why we were unable to come up with an aid level for this entire region that was no more than what we once offered Costa Rica alone.

Chapter 6

1. The best of the books so far on this early period are J. F. Brown, *Hopes and Shadows: Eastern Europe after Communism* (Durham, N.C.: Duke University Press, 1994), and Gale Stokes, *The Walls Came Tumbling Down: The Collapse of Communism in Eastern Europe* (New York and Oxford: Oxford University Press, 1993), but even these admirable volumes seem almost telegraphic to those who followed the postcommunist transitions in all their detail and complexity.

2. The Cabinet Room meetings normally included, on our side, the president, vice president, secretary of state, national security adviser, chief of staff, and one or two senior staff members each from the State Department and NSC. In photographs of these sessions, the NSC staff note-taker can be identified as the one with head down concentrating on the note pad.

3. Skubiszewski had made essentially the same points to Baker in their bilateral meeting at Ottawa the month before. See James A. Baker, III, with Thomas M. DeFrank, *The Politics of Diplomacy: Revolution, War and Peace, 1989–92* (New York: G. P. Putnam's Sons, 1995), pp. 210–11.

4. "Remarks by the President and Prime Minister Tadeusz Mazowiecki of Poland Upon Arrival," The White House, Office of the Press Secretary, March 21, 1990. The reference to secure borders referred in particular to Polish concerns over the disposition of Germany's borders after unification, as did the president's assurance earlier in his remarks that "in any decisions affecting the fate of Poland, Poland must have a voice."

5. In preparing the president's talking points for a telephone call to Chancellor Kohl the next day, I emphasized Mazowiecki's concern over the Polish border issue, his commitment to radical economic reform, and then, having to surmise the president's personal view of Mazowiecki, ventured that "I liked the man." Bush, who followed his scripts only when he believed them, used the line, so it must have been so.

6. Press Conference by the President, The White House, Office of the Press Secretary, March 22, 1990.

7. In a gracious message to Jaruzelski, President Bush renewed the invitation for Jaruzelski to visit in a private capacity.

8. Lech Wałęsa, *The Struggle and the Triumph: An Autobiography* (New York: Arcade Publisher, 1992), pp. 278–9.

9. Wałęsa used almost precisely those words as late as October 1991, speaking to an investment mission to Poland led by Commerce Secretary Robert Mosbacher.

10. A self-confessed "zombie," Tymiński claimed to have had several out-of-body experiences while living in Peru. He had also amassed a small fortune and was able to project himself to Polish voters as a self-made man (or zombie) capable of leading his country to a capitalist promised land.

11. The NSC staff and the State Department's European bureau compared notes and strategy regularly with the Polish American Congress, particularly its Washington-based vice president, the indefatigable Jan Nowak.

12. See, e.g., Jan Krzysztof Bielecki, "Problems of the Polish Transformation," *Communist Economies and Economic Transformation*, Vol. 4, No. 3 (1990). I later came to know and respect Bielecki as my Polish point of contact when I directed the U.S. assistance program for Eastern Europe in 1992–93.

13. General Scowcroft was reluctant to accede even to an informal document, on grounds that virtually every country around the world was eager to codify a bilateral security relationship with the United States—security being what we provided and others accepted—and that Poland could set a precedent. We at staff level ultimately won his agreement to an informal political declaration that did not contain language implying a security commitment, forewarning him that we could expect a similar request from Czechoslovakia when Havel arrived six months later on an already scheduled state visit.

14. I hammered out the final text at the Polish embassy in Washington shortly before Wałęsa's arrival, but only after Polish ambassador Kazimierz Dziewanowski and Professor Tadeusz Ziółkowski, a genial former academic seconded to service in the Belevedere (Poland's presidential palace), overruled Deputy Foreign Minister Jan Majewski, whose negotiating style was a product of his long and mindless service to the communist regime.

15. "Declaration of Principles Between the United States of America and the Republic of Poland," signed by President George Bush and President Lech Wałęsa, March 20, 1991, and released that day by the Office of the Press Secretary, The White House.

16. The precise formulae applied were complex in the extreme. The details are explained in "Fact Sheet: The Reduction of Poland's Debt," Office of the Press Secretary, The White House, March 20, 1991.

17. "Remarks by the President and President Wałęsa of Poland During Arrival Ceremony," The South Lawn, Office of the Press Secretary, The White House, March 20, 1991. In an interview with the Polish press agency just before Wałęsa's visit, President Bush had put it this way: "We are full of admiration for the courage and tenacity with which Poland has pursued [its] unprecedented economic transformation. We believe it is the right course and have supported it wholeheartedly, and we expect it to succeed. Its success is crucial, not only to Poland but to the other new democracies in the region. Because Poland was the first to take this bold step and because of Poland's important role in Europe, others are watching the reform closely."

18. Office of the Press Secretary, The White House, March 20, 1991. (Pope John Paul II was of course the most popular public figure, but Bush was the most popular politician.)

19. I had discussed precisely this issue with Jan Nowak, vice chairman of the Polish American Congress, who had briefed Wałęsa personally on the appropriate line to take. Wałęsa got it right with Bush but reverted to type later on.

20. During the Bush-Olszewski meeting in the Oval Office, I was seated across from Zdzisław Najder, a noted biographer of Joseph Conrad who had become adviser to the prime minister. Just eight years before, we had been together at Radio Free Europe in Munich. Najder was director of the Polish service while I was RFE's acting director. Little could we have imagined. . . .

21. For those who have lost count, they were: Mieczysław Rakowski during Bush's July 1989 visit, Mazowiecki in March 1990 at the White House (as well as at the UN General Assembly in September 1990 and in Paris for the November 1990 CSCE Summit), Bielecki at the White House in September 1991, and now Olszewski. Bush's meeting with Prime Minister Hanna Suchocka in Warsaw during his July 1992 visit made five in three years. (In November 1995, Wałęsa was defeated in his bid for reelection. He was succeeded by Alexander Kwasniewski of the Left Democratic Alliance, an offshoot of the communist party.)

22. "Statement by the Press Secretary," April 13, 1992, Office of the Press Secretary, The White House.

23. Such also was the judgment of veteran Solidarity adviser (and speaker of the Sejm) Bronisław Geremek, with whom I stood just below the dais from which the two presidents spoke.

24. "Address by the President at Castle Square," Warsaw, Poland, July 5, 1992, Office of the Press Secretary, The White House.

25. *Nowa Europa* (Warsaw), July 6, 1992. The commentary began by noting, "George Bush has no new money, because this is an election year. The mood in America is bad because of the lingering recession, record unemployment, the trade deficit and the budget deficit. The world's expectations exceed America's ability to meet them. . . ."

26. Juraj Mihalík, *Velvet Failures* (Bratislava, 1993), pp. 11–12.

27. *New York Times*, February 22, 1990. The text is also carried in Tim D. Whipple, ed., *After the Velvet Revolution: Václav Havel and the New Leaders of Czechoslovakia Speak Out* (New York: Freedom House, 1992), pp. 69–80.

28. By 1992, when I was directing the East European assistance program from the Department of State, Václav Klaus, by then prime minister, and Economic Minister Karel Dyba would visit Washington to tell members of Congress that they sought no assistance and indeed thought it worthless, repeating the same line for media consumption, and then repaired to the Department of State where they would unveil a long list of assistance requests.

29. The protocol for an "official working visit" by a head of state called for the following sequence: one-on-one meeting in the Oval Office, expanded meeting in the Cabinet Room, small working lunch in the Old Family Dining Room of the White House, and departure ceremony.

30. "Remarks by the President and President Havel of Czechoslovakia Upon Departure," February 20, 1990. The White House, Office of the Press Secretary.

31. In addition to the two presidents and their interpreters, there were just six of us: Secretary Baker, Chief of Staff John Sununu, and myself on our side and Havel advisers Alexander (Saša) Vondra, Michael Žantovsky, and Milan Kňažko (a key Slovak leader during the Velvet Revolution—invited to the meeting at my insistence) on theirs. For me, it was the beginning of a close friendship with Vondra, later the number two in the Czech foreign ministry, and Žantovsky, who succeeded Rita Klimova as Czech ambassador in Washington. Vondra, a delightfully disheveled man then in his late twenties, was an activist in the younger generation of Czech dissidents. A signer of Charter 77 and by 1989 its spokesman, he was one of the cofounders of the Civic Forum movement during the

Velvet Revolution. Žantovsky's career took him by a different route to a similar destination. Trained in clinical and social psychology, he migrated to literature, translating into Czech such writers as James Baldwin, Norman Mailer, and Joseph Heller. A founding member of the Czech chapter of the international writers organization P.E.N., he was another cofounder of Civic Forum and, by December, its spokesman. Possessed of a wonderful Puckish sense of humor, Žantovsky was at that time forty but looked years younger. One could not ask for better or more congenial colleagues—for that is what we were—than these two men at the elbow of Václav Havel. Kňažko, a popular movie actor who resembled the young Glenn Ford, later became my chief interlocutor in Bratislava when he was Slovak foreign minister and I directed the U.S. assistance program for Eastern Europe.

32. The president later described how Havel was moved to tears in thinking about freedom's return to Czechoslovakia while standing in the room where Lincoln signed the Emancipation Proclamation. ("Remarks by the President in University of Texas Commencement Address," The White House, Office of the Press Secretary, Austin, Texas, May 19, 1990.)

33. When the president delivered the line to the hushed assembly hall, someone in the audience gasped audibly. It was the appropriate punctuation mark.

34. "Remarks by the President at Wenceslas Square," Prague, November 17, 1990, The White House, Office of the Press Secretary. I recall that on an early draft of the speech, General Scowcroft had written "Too much?" in the margin next to the "we shall not fail you" line. With memories of the Western failures (betrayals?) of 1938, 1948, and 1968, I left the line in—more out of ardent hope than sound judgment.

35. Citing Alexander Hamilton but having Slovak premier Vladimír Mečiar in mind, Havel warned against "the perverted ambition of another group of people determined to profiteer from the confusion prevailing in the country."

36. As the president's tight schedule did not permit a visit to Bratislava, we arranged for his radio address to serve as a kind of surrogate. The president also used this venue to announce the reopening of the American consulate in Bratislava.

37. Valtr Komárek was dropped from the Council of Ministers in June 1990.

38. Brown, *Hopes and Shadows*, pp. 133–34.

39. Václav Havel, *Summer Meditations*, trans. Paul Wilson (New York: Alfred A. Knopf, 1992), pp. 26–7.

40. The plan, elaborated on at Harvard a month later, is explained in Jiří Dienstbier, "Central and Eastern Europe and a New European Order," Address at Harvard University, May 15, 1990, reprinted in Whipple, ed., *After the Velvet Revolution*, pp. 115–25.

41. For more on the period, see Wheaton and Kavan, *The Velvet Revolution*, pp. 175–86.

42. The "Visegrád Four" initiative was one that we had developed at staff level, and the senior levels of the administration were too preoccupied with more pressing business in the Persian Gulf either to endorse or overrule it. In Warsaw, the foreign ministry was also thinking along these lines and welcomed an American initiative in Bratislava and Prague.

43. See Chapter 8.

44. Interestingly, some who had accused the United States of clinging too long to the Yugoslav federation now urged us to pull out all the stops to keep Czechoslovakia intact. We in the administration made mistakes, but we didn't usually make the same one twice.

45. These included dinner with František Mikloško, chairman of the Slovak parliament (the Slovak National Council), and four members of the foreign relations committee representing the Slovak National party (SNS), the Movement for a Democratic Slovakia (HZDS), and the Christian Democratic party (KDH); breakfast with Minister of International Relations Pavol Demeš; and separate meetings with the deputy prime minister and deputy chairman of parliament.

46. Reminiscent of Franz-Josef Strauss, the late minister-president of Bavaria (whom I used to see occasionally in Munich's Tivoli restaurant), Mečiar had the same rude populist appeal, bluff manner, and personal magnetism—a kind of Franz-Josef Strauss without the brains.

47. In March 1993, traveling from Prague, where I was deputy head of the U.S. delegation to a CSCE economic forum, I arrived in Bratislava during a political crisis. Mečiar had fired his foreign minister and political rival, Milan Kňažko, and the case had been referred to the president, Michal Kováč. Indeed, it was in the middle of my meeting with Kováč in Bratislava Castle that he was interrupted to sign the order finalizing Kňažko's dismissal.

48. My other purpose in Prague was to join up with a U.S. Defense Department delegation for two days of meetings with Czechoslovak counterparts, headed by Defense Minister Luboš Dobrovský.

49. The NACC will be discussed in the next chapter.

50. "Joint Declaration of the United States of America and the Czech and Slovak Federal Republic," October 22, 1991, Office of the Press Secretary, The White House.

51. The main purpose of the Cheney visit, which also took him to Budapest, was an extended bilateral discussion with Czechoslovak defense minister Luboš Dobrovský on general security issues and U.S.-Czechoslovak military-to-military exchanges and programs.

52. The essay, a speech read in Havel's absence to the October 1989 German Booksellers Association in acceptance of its Peace Prize, was carried in *The New York Review of Books*, January 18, 1990.

53. *New York Times*, February 22, 1990. Havel was elected president of the Czech Republic in January 1993. In June 1996, Václav Klaus was reelected Czech prime minister. In Slovakia, Prime Minister Mečiar and his cabinet were ousted after a no confidence vote in March 1994, only to be reelected the following fall.

54. See, e.g., László Bruszt, "1989: The Negotiated Revolution in Hungary," *Social Research*, Vol. 57, No. 2 (Summer 1990), pp. 365–87; and Rudolf Tökés, "Hungary's New Political Elites: Adaptation and Change, 1989–90," *Problems of Communism*, November–December 1990, pp. 44–65, esp. pp. 56–8.

55. Technically, Göncz was "Acting President" at this time, pending the formality of parliamentary enactment of the new election laws.

56. Office of the Press Secretary, The White House, Austin, Texas, May 19, 1990.

57. A statement and brief transcript of remarks to the press were issued by the Office of the Press Secretary, The White House, May 23, 1991.

58. Bennett Kovrig, *Of Walls and Bridges: The United States and Eastern Europe* (New York: New York University Press, 1991), p. 326. This was the same Warsaw Pact meeting that sent a message of friendship to the NATO foreign ministers meeting in Turnberry, as described in Chapter 3.

59. *Ibid.*, p. 358.

60. "Remarks by the President and Prime Minister Antall of Hungary Upon Arrival," The South Lawn, October 18, 1990, Office of the Press Secretary, The White House.

61. Judith Pataki, "Hungary: New Government Prefers Cautious Changes," *Report on Eastern Europe*, Vol. 1, No. 28, Radio Free Europe Research, July 13, 1990, p. 24.

62. *Hungary in Transformation to Freedom and Prosperity: Economic Program Proposals of the Joint Hungarian-International Blue Ribbon Commission* (Indianapolis, Ind.: Hudson Institute, 1990), p. 14.

63. We maintained regular contact with the opposition parties as well. During this period, for example, I met with FIDESz chairman Viktor Orbán on December 6, 1990, and SDS leader and Budapest mayor Gabor Demszky on April 15, 1991.

64. For a rundown on U.S. policy at the time, see "U.S. Efforts to Promote a Peaceful Settlement in Yugoslavia," Statement before the Senate Foreign Relations Committee by Ralph Johnson, principal deputy assistant secretary of state for European and Canadian affairs, October 17, 1991, U.S. Department of State *Dispatch*, October 21, 1991.

65. Gyula Kodolanyi, Antall's able foreign policy adviser and a trusted friend throughout the period, expanded on these issues in meetings at the NSC and State Department in early November.

66. FBIS-EEU-90-107, June 4, 1990, 42, as cited in Stokes, *The Walls Came Tumbling Down*, p. 209.

67. *Magyar Forum*, August 20, 1992. For the sordid details of the article and its political spillover, see Judith Pataki, "Istvan Csurka's Tract: Summary and Reactions," *RFE/RL Research Report*, No. 40, October 9, 1992.

68. Brown, *Hopes and Shadows*, p. 139.

69. These issues were high on the agenda of an interagency assistance delegation I led to Budapest in the fall of 1992. We explained that we had substantial privatization assistance funds notionally allocated for Hungary's use, but disbursement hinged on Hungary's implementing a serious program.

70. The Hungarian Socialist party, in coalition with the Free Democratic party, took power following the elections of May 1994, and Gyula Horn, former foreign minister in the communist regime, became the new prime minister.

71. For two brief accounts of U.S.-Romanian relations during the period, see Roger Kirk, "The U.S. and Romania: Facing a Difficult Future," The Atlantic Council of the United States *Policy Paper*, April 1991; and Sergiu Verona, "Romanian Political Developments and U.S.-Romanian Relations," *CRS Issue Brief*, Congressional Research Service, The Library of Congress, April 14, 1993.

72. Roger Kirk and Mircea Raceanu, *Romania Versus the United States: Diplomacy of the Absurd, 1985–1989* (New York: St. Martin's Press, 1994).

73. In a visit to Bucharest in April 1993, Belgian prime minister Wilfried Martens made precisely this point, focusing particularly on Romania's policies toward national minorities. (Reuters, April 13, 1993.)

74. The Presidential Mission, headed by a Republican governor, spent only a few days in Romania and somehow failed to gain an understanding of the context in which these elections were held. Such are the risks in dispatching a high level mission: the assets of senior political leadership weigh against the lack of control over its findings.

75. See, e.g., the report by Thomas Carothers, a member of the election monitoring team organized by the National Democratic Institute, in Larry Garber and Eric Bjornlund, eds., *The New Democratic Frontier* (Washington, D.C.: National Democratic Institute for

International Affairs, 1992), pp. 75–94. See also *The May 1990 Elections in Romania* (Washington, D.C.: National Republican Institute for International Affairs and National Democratic Institute for International Affairs, 1991).

76. For some of these events, see Nestor Ratesh, *Romania: The Entangled Revolution* (New York: Praeger Publishers, 1991), pp. 131–36; and Martyn Rady, *Romania in Turmoil* (London, IB Tauris & Co., Ltd., 1992), pp. 186–89.

77. "Remarks by Secretary of State Baker at the G-24 Ministerial Meeting, Palais D'Egmont, Brussels, Belgium, July 4, 1990," Current Policy No. 1289, Bureau of Public Affairs, U.S. Department of State, July 1990.

78. This calls to mind an earlier "benchmark" message to the Romanians, in the form of a 1988 letter from Deputy Secretary of State John Whitehead to Ceaușescu, explaining what the United States expected of Romania before it was prepared to restore most favored nation status.

79. In December 1990, Român himself booed Hungarian participants in a ceremony held in Alba Iuliu. See Brown, *Hopes and Shadows*, pp. 196–97.

80. David Binder, "Slight Thaw is Detected in U.S.-Romania Ties, *New York Times*, April 18, 1991.

81. My appointment book during the period is peppered with references to office calls by Romanian ambassador Constantinescu, a decent man given a bad hand to play. He understood that Romania's isolation was of its own making but was obliged to push the line that Washington was pursuing a discriminatory policy.

82. Manolescu visited Washington in late September 1991, for meetings with Eagleburger and others, during which I had two extended conversations with him.

83. There was still a holdout or two in the Department of State's policy planning staff, but the rest of the department and all of us on the NSC staff were ready to move forward with MFN.

84. This was the same John Davis who had been ambassador in Warsaw during the revolutionary year of 1989. If he now succeeded in bringing democracy to Romania, I warned him, the president would probably send him to Pyongyang next.

85. One of the Romanians was Ioan Mircea Pascu, whom I had met (together with Professor Dan Nelson, who sent a wide variety of visiting Romanians my way) in my office a month before.

86. One of the legacies of the Ceaușescu era, especially for Romanian politicians like Iliescu, was a belief that U.S. policies were entirely cynical. To the end, Ceaușescu and his coterie never believed that we were serious about human rights. That we would reward him for upsetting Warsaw Pact unity was something he could understand, but when we raised human rights issues, he always felt this was a smoke screen for some hidden agenda.

87. The Eagleburger entourage, including also Deputy Treasury Secretary John Robson and senior officials from several other agencies, traveled the same route as Baker had taken in February 1990—Prague-Moscow-Sofia-Bucharest—and continued on to Tirana, which Baker had visited in June 1991.

88. Verona, "Romanian Political Developments and U.S.-Romanian Relations," pp. 13–16. The next month (October 1992), Iliescu won reelection as president, naming Nicolae Vacaroiu, a nonpartisan economist, the new prime minister.

89. Vermont governor Madeleine Kunin, for example, participated in a sixty-member international delegation led by Iceland's prime minister Steingrimur Hermannsson. The

U.S. Presidential Mission was ably led by Oklahoma governor Henry Bellmon. For a detailed examination of the June 1990 elections, see Larry Garber, "Bulgaria," in Garber and Bjornlund, eds., *The New Democratic Frontier*, pp. 135–60.

90. "Focus on Central and Eastern Europe," No. 19, July 18, 1990, Bureau of Public Affairs, U.S. Department of State.

91. *Ibid.*

92. Stokes, *The Walls Came Tumbling Down*, pp. 177–78.

93. The agreement, formally initialed on October 5, is detailed in "Focus on Central and Eastern Europe," No. 27, October 31, 1990, Bureau of Public Affairs, U.S. Department of State.

94. When we were leaving the Oval Office after his meeting with Bush, I reminded Zhelev that I was the author of the "island of stability" line—which I used in an August 8 meeting with our ambassador to Bulgaria, Ken Hill, who in turn had conveyed it to Zhelev. I added that I would gladly cede all rights to the phrase, so long as I could be a footnote to history. This is it.

95. The series of bilats was a one-ring circus, with presidents and prime ministers ushered in and out in assembly-line fashion, allowing just enough time to change flags. Although they managed to get some diplomatic business done, Bush, Baker, and Scowcroft were punch-drunk by the time they had received a couple of dozen assorted world leaders. (In a similar marathon on a different occasion, Secretary Baker, ten minutes into an animated discussion with a foreign minister counterpart, handed a note to his nearest aide: "Who is this guy?")

96. Duncan M. Perry, "Bulgaria: A New Constitution and Free Elections," *RFE/RL Research Report*, Vol. 1, No. 1, January 3, 1992, esp. p. 79; and Marvin Zonis and Dwight Semler, *The East European Opportunity* (New York: John Wiley & Sons, Inc., 1992), pp. 307–10.

97. "New U.S.-Bulgarian Agricultural Fund Established," Statement by the Press Secretary, The White House, July 22, 1991.

98. See Brown, *Hopes and Shadows*, pp. 111–12, for a discussion of Dimitrov's "dark blue" faction in the UDF.

99. I was accompanied by Deputy Secretary Eagleburger's senior adviser Kenneth Juster, who had also been on the Eagleburger delegation for a G-24 ministerial in Brussels and a gathering of European ambassadors in Berlin.

100. These main lines of policy were of course worked out in advance in interagency discussions back in Washington, approved in outline form by Scowcroft and Eagleburger, and coordinated via cable with Embassy Sofia.

101. Its fiery leader, Konstantin Trenchev, was out of the country, so the meeting was with Podkrepa deputies Radoslav Nenev and Boyko Proichev.

102. MRF spokesman Yunal Lyufti was particularly determined that MRF be a mainstream democratic party. He opposed seeking local autonomy, for example, on grounds that this would only result in MRF's marginalization from the larger issues of economic and political reform.

103. Our other interlocutor was Filip Bokov, who was at that time the Socialist party's shadow foreign minister.

104. They were National Assembly chairman Stefan Savov, UDF leaders Alexander Yordanov and Mikhail Nedelchev, and MRF spokesman Yunal Lyufti.

105. "Remarks by Deputy Secretary of State Lawrence S. Eagleburger to the Bulgar-

ian-U.S. Trade and Economic Council Conference on 'The Future of Democracy and Economic Transition in Bulgaria,' March 4, 1992," Bureau of Public Affairs, U.S. Department of State.

106. Eagleburger's huge delegation, with three deputy secretaries and numerous other senior officials, had broken up into different parties with separate schedules.

107. The Bulgarian Socialist Party won the December 1994 elections, naming Zhan Vlednov prime minister.

108. Louis Zanga, "Albania: Between Democracy and Chaos," *RFE/RL Research Report* Vol. 1, No. 1, January 3, 1992, pp. 74–7.

109. "Address by Secretary of State James A. Baker, III, to Members of the Assembly, Tirana, Albania, Saturday, June 22, 1991," U.S. Department of State, Office of the Assistant Secretary/Spokesman.

110. In June 22 dispatches from Tirana, Reuters estimated four hundred thousand; AP, "hundreds of thousands." AP also noted that the crowd chanted "Bush, Bush" in addition to "Baker, Baker"—a point I was at pains to stress back at the White House.

111. "Remarks by Secretary of State James A. Baker, III, at Skanderbeg Square, Tirana, Albania, June 22, 1991," U.S. Department of State, Office of the Assistant Secretary/Spokesman.

112. A deeply moved Baker used exactly those words with Prime Minister Buffi just afterwards (State Department press release, June 22, 1991).

113. Elez Biberaj, head of VOA's Albanian broadcast service, was known to virtually every Albanian and regarded as a national hero.

114. These issues, as well as the circumstances surrounding Albania's admission into the CSCE, are discussed in Chapter 7.

115. Berisha was returned to the presidency in June 1996 in elections marred by widespread fraud and intimidation.

116. Skanderbeg—sometimes spelled Skenderbeg or Scanderbeg—took the name after converting to Islam, with the "beg" denoting the military rank to which he rose. (His victory at Kruje gave way to full Ottoman domination in the next century, but our historical analogy need not be carried all the way to that sad end.)

117. Robert L. Hutchings, "Five Years After: Reflections on the Post-Communist Transitions and Western Assistance Strategies," in *East-Central European Economies in Transition*, Joint Economic Committee, Congress of the United States (Washington, D.C.: U.S. Government Printing Office, 1994), pp. 176–90.

118. Stokes, *The Walls Came Tumbling Down*, p. 259.

Chapter 7

1. United States Information Service, January 18, 1990, as cited in Bennett Kovrig, *Of Walls and Bridges: The United States and Eastern Europe* (New York: New York University Press, 1991), p. 361.

2. EC Commission president Jacques Delors made a similar point in 1990: "The Community once again faces the same choices as it did in the 1950s and 1980s: rapid progress or gradual disintegration." (Jacques Delors, "Europe's Ambitions," *Foreign Policy* No. 80 [Fall 1990]: 27.)

3. "A New Europe, A New Atlanticism: Architecture for a New Era," Address by Sec-

retary of State James A. Baker, III, to the Berlin Press Club, Steigenberger Hotel, Berlin, December 12, 1989, U.S. Department of State press release of that date.

4. President Bush, "A Time of Decision for the NATO Alliance," Intervention at the NATO Summit, Rome, Italy, November 7, 1991, U.S. Department of State *Dispatch*, November 11, 1991, p. 823.

5. The Elysée was also dropping hints in the press of a possible rapprochement between Paris and Washington. See, e.g., "French-U.S. Relations Blossom Amid Desert Storm," *Washington Post*, February 26, 1991.

6. The plan, premature in 1990 and 1991, came to fruition in December 1995, when Jacques Chirac, Mitterrand's successor as French president, announced France's rapproachement with NATO's military institutions. For a good analysis, see Ronald Tiersky, "A Likely Story: Chirac, France-NATO, European Security, and American Hegemony," in *French Politics and Society*, Vol. 14, No. 2 (Spring 1996): 1–8.

7. U.S.-French discussions on NATO had been kept so well hidden from the media that not a single question during the extensive press conference touched on the issue but rather focused almost entirely on the Gulf War. (Office of the Press Secretary, The White House, March 14, 1991.)

8. For background on these disputes, see Peter Ludlow, "Europe's Institutions: Europe's Politics," in Gregory F. Treverton, ed., *The Shape of the New Europe* (New York: Council on Foreign Relations Press, 1992), pp. 77–79; and Hans Binnendijk, "The Emerging European Security Order," in Brad Roberts, ed., *U.S. Foreign Policy After the Cold War* (Cambridge, MA: MIT Press, 1992), pp. 41–44.

9. Cited in Binnendijk, "European Security Order," p. 42.

10. Jacques Delors, "European Integration and Security," Alastair Buchan Memorial Lecture, International Institute for Strategic Studies, London, March 7, 1991.

11. A keen political analyst, Josef Joffe is senior editor with Munich's *Süddeutsche Zeitung*.

12. Unpublished UK paper on foreign policy and security issues, February 1991, as cited in Ludlow, "Europe's Institutions," p. 79.

13. "European Defense and Security in the 1990s," Transcript of the Speech given by the Foreign Secretary, Mr. Douglas Hurd, to the Berlin Press Conference in Berlin on Monday, 10 December 1990, copy provided that date by the British Embassy, Washington.

14. Teltschik's successor was Peter Hartmann, later German ambassador to London. As a career diplomat, he lacked Teltschik's independence from the foreign ministry, which meant that relations between the chancellery and the ministry were not as hostile, but also that the latter's views predominated unless Kohl weighed in personally. To make matters worse, the chancellery adviser (under Hartmann) responsible for these issues was an ardent Europeanist whose views were much closer to the French than to ours.

15. Vattani and I discussed these issues over a private dinner on May 7, and I recall being gratified at how close our perspectives were.

16. "Policy Statement by Herr Helmut Kohl, Chancellor of the Federal Republic of Germany, in the German Bundestag on 30 January 1991," facsimile copy transmitted that day to the White House by the Federal chancellery in Bonn.

17. Some weeks before the Genscher visit, we at the NSC staff had come up with the idea of a joint statement and had sketched out what it might include—only to find, when we broached the idea, that Secretary Baker's senior staff had been thinking along the same

lines and indeed had developed an almost identical working draft for negotiation with the Germans.

18. "U.S.-German Views on the New European and Trans-Atlantic Architecture," Joint Statement by Secretary Baker and German Foreign Minister Genscher, May 10, 1991, U.S. Department of State *Dispatch*, May 13, 1991, p. 346.

19. The full texts were reprinted in U.S. Department of State *Dispatch*, June 10, 1991. Both documents likewise reaffirmed NATO's integrated command, reflecting our decision not to accede to French overtures.

20. *Washington Post*, May 28, 1991, p. A15.

21. "The Agenda of German Politics for the Nineties," Speech by Dr. Helmut Kohl, Chancellor of the Federal Republic of Germany, in Washington, D.C., on May 20, 1991. Text provided by the German embassy, Washington, D.C.

22. This was the 95-page draft, or "non-paper," assembled in April 1991 by Luxembourg, as EC presidency country.

23. *Washington Post*, June 26, 1991, p. A13.

24. Indeed, the following January, when I traveled to Bonn mainly to mend fences over the issue of recognition of breakaway Yugoslav republics, I was misled by Kohl's security advisers. No decisions had been taken, I was assured, but the United States would be fully informed. Yet a few weeks later, another Franco-German proposal called for creation of a "Eurocorps," again with the preferred French formulation.

25. President Bush, "A Time of Decision for the NATO Alliance," Intervention at the NATO Summit, Rome, Italy, November 7, 1991, U.S. State Department *Dispatch*, November 11, 1991, p. 824.

26. "Rome Declaration on Peace and Cooperation Issued by the Heads of State and Government participating in the meeting of the North Atlantic Council in Rome on 7th–8th November 1991," NATO Press Service, November 8, 1991.

27. "Opening Address by Mr. François Mitterrand, President of the Republic, At the Conference on Security and Co-operation in Europe," Paris, Kleber Conference Center, November 19, 1990. Text distributed at the Paris Summit.

28. "Address by Mr. Tadeusz Mazowiecki, Prime Minister of the Republic of Poland, to the CSCE Summit of the Heads of State and Government," Paris, November 20, 1990. Text distributed at the summit.

29. Speech to the Sejm, January 1, 1990.

30. "Remarks by Mikhail S. Gorbachev before the Paris CSCE Summit Meeting, November 19, 1990," unofficial Soviet translation distributed at the summit.

31. "Memorandum on the European Security Commission" by the government of Czechoslovakia, Prague, April 6, 1990. Text provided by Mr. Dienstbier.

32. See Chapter 4.

33. *Pravda* (Moscow), January 25, 1991.

34. Gorbachev had signaled his willingness to disband the pact's military organization on the eve of the Visegrád Summit, and the measure was formally agreed on at a contentious February 25 meeting of Warsaw Pact foreign and defense ministers in Budapest. (*Washington Post*, February 26, 1991, p. A16.)

35. Unclassified reporting cable from American Embassy Brussels, dated March 21, 1991. During his meetings with Havel in Prague in November 1990, President Bush had used almost precisely the same image in saying that the United States did not want to see a security vacuum or "no man's land" in the region—an answer, in part, to Henry

Kissinger's proposal, in a June 1990 lecture in Prague, for a "neutral belt" in Central Europe.

36. "Statement by Minister for Foreign Affairs Prof. Krzysztof Skubiszewski to the Polish Sejm, 14 February 1991." English draft provided by the Polish embassy. Skubiszewski also threatened to revoke the 1956 treaty legitimizing the stationing of Soviet forces unless troop withdrawal negotiations were concluded promptly.

37. The "Europe Agreements" were summarized in press releases of the EC Commission in Brussels on November 22, 1991, and March 26, 1992, and printed in full by the Delegation of the Commission of the European Communities, Washington, D.C., on April 16, 1992.

38. *Time*, February 25, 1991, as cited in Vladimir V. Kusin, "Security Concerns in Central Europe," *Radio Free Europe Research*, February 26, 1991, p. 20.

39. William Drozdiak, "France Clouds EC Prospects; Mitterrand Urges Confederation Plan," *Washington Post*, June 13, 1991, p. A31.

40. "US-German Views on the New European and Trans-Atlantic Architecture."

41. "Partnership with the Countries of Central and Eastern Europe," statement issued by the North Atlantic Council meeting in ministerial session in Copenhagen, NATO Press Service, June 6, 1991.

42. "New Initiatives to Reduce Nuclear Forces," Address to the Nation, Washington, D.C., September 27, 1991, U.S. Department of State *Dispatch*, September 30, 1991, pp. 715–18.

43. "Press Conference by the President, The Rose Garden, August 20, 1991," Office of the Press Secretary, The White House.

44. Secretary Baker, "Conflict in the Soviet Union," excerpts from remarks during a meeting of the North Atlantic Council, Brussels, Belgium, August 21, 1991, U.S. Department of State *Dispatch*, August 26, 1991, pp. 632–33.

45. The president had taken the latest, shortest draft from his pocket at the joint press conference in the Rose Garden but, gauging his audience, put it back in his pocket unread. As he must have anticipated, the questions put to him and Kohl by the media did not touch at all on European issues, so the statement would have gotten no media play anyway. ("Press Conference by the President and Chancellor Helmut Kohl," The Rose Garden, September 16, 1991, Office of the Press Secretary, The White House.")

46. "U.S.-German Joint Statement on the Transatlantic Community," Joint Statement by Secretary Baker and German Foreign Minister Hans-Dietrich Genscher, Washington, D.C., October 2, 1991, U.S. Department of State *Dispatch*, October 7, 1991, pp. 736–37.

47. On a trip to Warsaw, Bratislava, and Prague a few days later, I learned from Zbigniew Lewicki, the amiable and able former professor who headed the Americas department in the Polish foreign ministry, how the Visegrád group managed to reply so quickly. As soon as the Poles read the Baker-Genscher statement, Polish foreign minister Skubiszewski instructed Lewicki to draft a reply and coordinate by facsimile with Prague and Budapest. The sequence took but a few hours and enabled the three countries to set a positive tone before Moscow or others had a chance to react to the contrary.

48. Bush, "New Initiatives," p. 16.

49. Secretary Baker, "Intervention at the North Atlantic Cooperation Council (NACC) ministerial meeting," Brussels, March 10, 1992, U.S. Department of State *Dispatch*, March 16, 1992, p. 201.

50. It was the NACC's second meeting overall but the first in which new members from the East participated.

51. "Rome Declaration," November 8, 1991.

52. Colin Powell, "The American Commitment to European Security" (text of the Alastair Buchan memorial lecture, delivered April 7, 1992 in London), *Survival*, Summer 1992, p. 5.

53. "Proposal on National Minorities submitted by the delegations of Austria, Czechoslovakia, Hungary, Italy and Yugoslavia," as reprinted in "International Protection of National Minorities: Memorandum for the Copenhagen Meeting on the Human Dimension," Hungarian Human Rights Foundation, June 1990. [Emphasis added.]

54. "Statement delivered by Mr. Géza Entz, Head of the Hungarian Delegation, at the opening session of the CSCE Expert Meeting on National Minorities," July 2, 1991. (Text provided by Mr. Entz.)

55. "Report of the CSCE Meeting of Experts on National Minorities," Geneva, July 1991. For excerpts and analyses, see Vojtech Mastny, *The Helsinki Process and the Reintegration of Europe, 1986–91* (New York: New York University Press, 1992), pp. 42–43 and 298–306; and the Commission on Security and Cooperation in Europe, *From Vienna to Helsinki: Reports on the Inter-Sessional Meetings of the CSCE Process* (Washington, D.C.: U.S. Congress, Commission on Security and Cooperation in Europe, April 1992), pp. 133–49. Focusing on principles, Mastny (p. 42) termed the conference "heartening"; looking for specific commitments, the Commission (pp. 133 and 144) found its achievements "modest."

56. "Report of the CSCE Meeting of Experts on Peaceful Settlement of Disputes," Valletta 1991, issued in Valletta, Malta, February 8, 1991. See also Commission on Security and Cooperation in Europe, *From Vienna to Helsinki*, pp. 111–23.

57. "Berlin Meeting of the CSCE Council, 19–20 June 1991: Summary of Conclusions." (The issuance of a matter-of-fact summary rather than a tortuous declaration was another innovation designed to move CSCE from the hortatory to the operational.) See also Mastny, *The Helsinki Process*, pp. 41–42 and 311–13.

58. Commission on Security and Cooperation in Europe, *From Vienna to Helsinki*, pp. 151–75; Mastny, *The Helsinki Process*, pp. 320–28.

59. The 68-page declaration was issued as "CSCE Helsinki Document 1992: The Challenges of Change," Helsinki, July 1992. For excerpts and a summary of the negotiations, see "The Helsinki Follow-Up Meeting of the Conference on Security and Co-operation in Europe, March 24–July 8, 1992," report prepared by the staff of the Commission on Security and Cooperation in Europe, United States Congress. (A ministerial meeting in Prague, January 30–31, 1992, prepared the way for the Helsinki Summit, as did another foreign ministers' meeting in Helsinki at the opening of the review conference. Baker attended the former, and Eagleburger the latter, in a memorable forty-hour over-and-back trip to Helsinki.)

60. Ray Stannard Baker and William E. Dodds, eds., *The Public Papers of Woodrow Wilson: The New Democracy*, 2 vols. (New York: Harper, 1926), 2:351.

Chapter 8

1. David Reynolds, "Thawing History: Europe in the 1990s and Pre–Cold War Patterns," in Colin Crouch and David Marquand, eds., *Towards Greater Europe* (Oxford and Cambridge, Ma.: Blackwell Publishers, 1992), p. 28.

2. E.g., the second paragraph of the introduction to Paul Kennedy's *The Rise and Fall of the Great Powers* (New York: Random House, 1987), p. xv: "The triumph of any one Great Power . . . or the collapse of another, has usually been the consequence of lengthy fighting by its armed forces."

3. It is perhaps emblematic of this "paradigm shift" that in 1990 I brought from home my undergraduate historical atlas and kept it close at hand in my office in the Old Executive Office Building.

4. Francis Fukuyama, "The End of History?" *The National Interest*, No. 16 (Summer 1989): 3–18. The article by Fukuyama, deputy director of the State Department's policy planning staff at the beginning of the Bush administration, was more sophisticated than his critics credited, but the debate took on a life of its own. For an elaboration of his thesis, see Francis Fukuyama, *The End of History and the Last Man* (New York: Avon Books, 1992).

5. Reynolds, "Thawing History," p. 9.

6. Mark Brandenburg [pseudonym], "Under the Ice," *New Republic* 190 (April 23, 1984): 13–15.

7. Warren Zimmermann, "The Last Ambassador: Memoirs of the Collapse of Yugoslavia," *Foreign Affairs*, Vol. 74, No. 2, March/April 1995, p. 2.

8. For two authoritative accounts of the Bush administration's approaches toward Yugoslavia, see Zimmermann, "The Last Ambassador," and David Gompert, "How to Defeat Serbia," *Foreign Affairs*, Vol. 73, No. 4, July/August 1994, pp. 30–47.

9. In an article written in 1988 and published in early 1989, I described a Yugoslavia in deep crisis: "Before 1980, central authority was provided by the Communist party and Tito himself. Now there is no Tito, and hardly any party, to hold the country together." (Robert L. Hutchings, "'Leadership Drift' in Communist Systems," *Studies in Comparative Communism*, Vol. XXII, No. 1 (Spring 1989): 7–8.)

10. Zimmermann, *Last Ambassador*, p. 5.

11. For discussion, see J. F. Brown, *Hopes and Shadows: Eastern Europe After Communism* (Durham, N.C.: Duke University Press, 1994), pp. 238–52; and Gale Stokes, *The Walls Came Tumbling Down* (New York and Oxford: Oxford University Press, 1993), pp. 232–41.

12. Stokes, *The Walls Came Tumbling Down*, pp. 241–49.

13. David Binder, "Yugoslavia Seen Breaking Up Soon," *New York Times*, November 28, 1990, p. A7.

14. There is obviously a danger that an overly cozy relationship with the policy community would compromise the intelligence community's critical distance and analytic integrity, but the much more common failing was a hands off approach that rendered intelligence analysis abstract and often unusable. Besides, the "politicization" of intelligence sprang less often from policy advocacy than from a kind of corporate mind-set that foreclosed lines of analysis that went against the grain. This latter problem was more likely to be ameliorated by involvement in the give-and-take with the policy community than in cloistered seclusion.

15. London *Times*, March 19, 1991, p. 7; and *The Independent* (London), March 19, p. 11. On May 19, Croatia overwhelmingly endorsed independence in a referendum widely boycotted by Serbs.

16. *Politika*, June 2, 1991, in *Foreign Broadcast Information Service* Daily Report, Eastern Europe, June 3, 1991, p. 43.

17. *New York Times*, June 29, 1991. The "troika" consisted of past, present, and future EC presidency countries in their six month rotational system.

18. London *Times*, June 20, 1991. See also Richard Weitz, "The CSCE and the Yugoslav Conflict," *Radio Free Europe/Radio Liberty Research Report*, Vol. 1, No. 5, January 31, 1992, p. 24.

19. A member of Rugova's small delegation, having studied Baker's speech in Berlin the day before, discoursed knowledgeably about the secretary's view of the principle of "subsidiarity"—making for an oddly academic discussion under the circumstances.

20. Mercifully, the State Department's reporting cables required only that we summarize the discussions rather than record them verbatim as was required for presidential "memcons" (memoranda of conversation). The sessions were nonetheless grueling. Baker may have been the only one of the exhausted American delegation to stay awake throughout.

21. My recollection of the meetings tracks precisely with Zimmermann's, in *The Last Ambassador*, pp. 11–12. Secretary Baker's account in his memoirs, because it accentuates his warnings against the use of force in his several conversations, may tilt the overall message toward greater toughness than was perceived by his interlocutors. (James A. Baker, III, with Thomas M. DeFrank, *The Politics of Diplomacy: Revolution, War and Peace, 1989–92* [New York: G. P. Putnam's Sons, 1995], pp. 478–83.)

22. Zimmermann, *The Last Ambassador*, p. 12.

23. Baker said as much in his message to President Bush that night: "Frankly, I'm dubious about the effect." (Baker, *Politics of Diplomacy*, p. 483.)

24. Secretary Baker, "U.S. Concerns about the Future of Yugoslavia," Excerpts from Remarks at the Federation Palace, Belgrade, Yugoslavia, June 21, 1991, U.S. Department of State *Dispatch*, Vol. 2, No. 26, July 1, 1991, p. 468.

25. For a blow-by-blow account, see Marc Weller, "The International Response to the Dissolution of the Socialist Federal Republic of Yugoslavia," *American Journal of International Law*, Vol. 86, No. 3 (July 1992): 569–607.

26. Zimmermann, *The Last Ambassador*, pp. 12–13.

27. Weller, "International Response," pp. 575–77.

28. "Violent Crisis in Yugoslavia," Address by Secretary Baker before the UN Security Council, New York City, September 25, 1991, in U.S. Department of State *Dispatch*, Vol. 2, No. 39, September 30, 1991, p. 723.

29. In his memoirs, Secretary Baker explained that "there was never any thought at that time of using U.S. ground troops" with reference to the two world wars and the Cold War (Baker, *Politics of Diplomacy*, pp. 635–36), yet there were many military options that stopped far short of open-ended commitment. Indeed, Baker also notes his endorsement, a year later, of a "game plan" (which was never implemented) for Bosnia-Herzegovina that involved a naval blockade and limited air strikes (pp. 648–50).

30. In a March 5 letter sent to the European allies, as well as Carrington and Vance, Secretary Baker posed but did not resolve the problem: "We have wrestled with the question of whether recognition of Bosnia-Herzegovina's independence would contribute to stability in that delicately balanced republic or encourage efforts by the large Serbian minority to destabilize the situation." (Baker, *Politics of Diplomacy*, p. 641.)

31. These were reported in a series of articles by Roy Gutman in *Newsday*, August 2, 3, 5, 6, and 9, 1992.

32. The State Department initially confirmed the reports through its spokesman, then retracted the statement in congressional testimony the next day, stressing that we had no

independent confirmation. Critics within the State Department—including the acting Yugoslav desk officer, who resigned in protest over U.S. passivity in the face of genocide—felt that the administration was deliberately suppressing what it knew so as to avoid being pushed to take stronger action.

I was not directly involved in this issue, having moved from the NSC the month before to direct the U.S. assistance program for Eastern Europe, but my sense was and is that there was no conspiracy of silence. It was, rather, a difference of judgment as to whether we had at that time sufficient corroborated evidence to confirm the press reports. The department may have been overcautious in its public statements and less than zealous in trying to draw out of the intelligence community the evidence it needed, but there was not, to my knowledge, a deliberate effort to suppress or conceal.

33. Secretary Baker had moved to the White House to help direct the president's reelection campaign, and Eagleburger served as acting secretary and then secretary.

34. Eagleburger issued these charges in a December 16 speech before the Geneva conference. (*New York Times*, December 17, 1992.)

35. *New York Times*, August 27, 1992, p. 22.

36. *New York Times*, August 27, 1992; and "Material Relating to the London Conference (August 26–27, 1992) and the Crisis in the Former Yugoslavia," U.S. Department of State *Dispatch* Vol. 3, Supplement No. 7, September 1992.

37. Foreign policy officials are accustomed to hearing from their academic and journalistic counterparts that when something good happens in the world, the United States was not a factor, but when something bad happens, we were responsible for it.

38. This is about the time that we sent our urgent cables to all European capitals. Our instincts were right, but our follow-through was weak.

39. By the time of the London conference, I took it as my main mission—given my conspicuously ineffectual role hitherto—to ensure that policy papers destined for NSC principals were scrupulously honest about the likely effect of a given policy option. Although I disagreed with the policies we were pursuing, I fully respected the fact that the president and other NSC principals had life and death responsibilities that I could only dimly imagine. Yet it was no service to mislead them into believing they could have their cake and eat it too—that they could avoid risky policies yet still achieve our stated objectives. If half-measures were likely to fail, we owed it to them to say so.

40. Long after leaving office, Baker addressed this point directly: "Does the United States have an interest in stopping the humanitarian nightmare . . . [and] supporting the territorial integrity of Bosnia? Of course. But are our interests in either sufficiently vital to warrant the introduction of ground forces into a potential military quagmire? The answer is clearly no—as it has been from the beginning." (*Los Angeles Times*, June 25, 1995.) Baker went on to argue that U.S. interests lay in containing the conflict and averting a broader Balkan war.

In his memoirs, Secretary Baker asserted again that "our vital interests were not at stake." (Baker, *Politics of Diplomacy*, p. 636.) But this begged the question of whether there were *any* important interests involved. Thus, his explanation of U.S. policy toward Yugoslavia (pp. 634–51) tends to frame the issues so starkly as to obscure the wide range of policy choices between passivity and Armageddon in a conflict that impinged on important, though arguably not "vital," American interests.

41. Gompert, "How to Defeat Serbia," p. 42.

42. Meeting between Wilson and Frank P. Walsh and Edward F. Dunne, Paris, June 11, 1919, as cited in Daniel Patrick Moynihan, *Pandaemonium* (Oxford: Oxford University Press, 1993), p. 85.

43. Lansing's Confidential Diaries, as cited in *ibid.*, p. 81.

44. For detailed discussion of the concept, see *ibid.*, pp. 63–106, esp. pp. 66–71, and Kamal S. Shehadi, *Ethnic Self-Determination and the Break-up of States*, Adelphi Paper 283 (London: International Institute of Strategic Studies, December 1993), pp. 4–10.

45. "Political Declaration: Strengthening the International Order," London Economic Summit 1991, July 16, 1991. Text distributed at the summit.

46. James Crawford, *The Creation of States in International Law* (Oxford: Clarendon Press, 1979), pp. 31–128, esp. pp. 36–48.

47. "U.S. Approach to Changes in the Soviet Union," Statement by Secretary of State James A. Baker, III, in U.S. Department of State *Dispatch*, Vol. 2, 1991, p. 667.

48. "Guidelines on the Recognition of New States in Eastern Europe and in the Soviet Union," Declaration of the European Community, Brussels and the Hague, December 16, 1991. The EC also stipulated that "The Community and its Member States will not recognize entities which are the result of aggression."

49. Shehadi, *Ethnic Self-Determination*, p. 21.

50. Cited in Michael R. Beschloss and Strobe Talbott, *At the Highest Levels: The Inside Story of the End of the Cold War* (Boston: Little, Brown and Company, 1993), p. 317.

51. *Figaro*, February 11, 1991.

52. Beschloss and Talbott, *At the Highest Levels*, p. 323; Baker, *Politics of Diplomacy*, p. 391. See also Anatoly Chernyaev's first-hand account of Ambassador Jack Matlock's meeting with Gorbachev on January 24, 1991, in A. S. Chernyaev, *Shest' let s Gorbachevym* [Six Years with Gorbachev] (Moscow: Progress Publishers, 1993), pp. 416–19. Gorbachev said that he had told Baltic leaders that "if you've decided to leave, then leave, but legally, constitutionally" and also asked Matlock to assure President Bush that "I will act as we agreed. . . . I will do everything."

53. "Address by the President on the State of the Union," The U.S. Capitol, Washington, D.C., January 29, 1991, Office of the Press Secretary, The White House.

54. Yeltsin was elected Russian president on June 12, 1991, with 57 percent of the vote against just 17 percent for Gorbachev's preferred candidate, former Soviet prime minister Nikolai Ryzhkov.

55. "The Soviet Cauldron," Report of the Office of Soviet Analysis, Central Intelligence Agency, April 25, 1991, declassified and approved for release, November 1994, from "Briefing Book for Cold War Endgame," documents compiled by the National Security Archive for a conference at Princeton University, March 29–30, 1996.

56. See Chernyaev's account of Matlock's meeting with Gorbachev to deliver the letter, as well as verbatim excerpts of Bush's subsequent telephone conversation with Gorbachev, in Chernyaev, *Shest' let*, pp. 451–55.

57. For Baker's account, see *Politics of Diplomacy*, pp. 470–71.

58. Graham Allison and Robert Blackwill, "America's Stake in the Soviet Future," *Foreign Affairs* Vol. 70, No. 3 (Summer 1991): 77–97.

59. Such were the conclusions of my NSC colleague Condoleezza Rice in her valedictory memo before returning to the Stanford faculty. (Beschloss and Talbott, *At the Highest Levels*, pp. 345–46.)

60. On the G-7 decisions, see U.S. Department of State *Dispatch*, Vol. 2, No. 29, July 22, 1991, pp. 519–27.

61. For background on the START and CFE negotiations in the spring and early summer of 1991, see Beschloss and Talbott, *At the Highest Levels*, pp. 362–73 and 402–6.

62. On the summit documents and agreements, see U.S. Department of State *Dispatch*, Vol. 2, No. 32, August 12, 1991, pp. 591–98; and various fact sheets distributed by the White House's Office of the Press Secretary, July 30 and 31, 1991.

63. The text was reprinted in *ibid.*, pp. 597–99. It was indelibly dubbed the "Chicken Kiev" speech by William Safire in the *New York Times*, August 29, 1991.

64. In addition to Yanayev, the leaders of the coup were Defense Minister Dmitri Yazov, KGB chairman Vladimir Kryuchkov, Interior Minister Boris Pugo, Prime Minister Valentin Pavlov, and three others.

65. See Baker's detailed account, in *Politics of Diplomacy*, pp. 514–23.

66. In principle, our line was quite similar to that we had taken in Romania in the midst of the December 1989 revolution.

67. Bush's various statements are carried in U.S. Department of State *Dispatch*, Vol. 2, No. 33, August 19, 1991, pp. 615–17. See also Secretary Baker's press briefing en route to Brussels, issued by the Office of the Assistant Secretary/Spokesman, U.S. Department of State, August 20, 1991.

68. For Gorbachev's account, see Mikhail Gorbachev, *The August Coup: The Truth and the Lessons* (New York: HarperCollins, 1991).

69. See, e.g., Beschloss and Talbott, *At the Highest Levels*, p. 444. (The point, which administration critics ignored, was that recognition by a small European country was one thing, recognition by the United States quite another.)

70. Cited in Baker, *Politics of Diplomacy*, pp. 524–25.

71. *Ibid.*, p. 558.

72. In his memoirs, General Powell, chairman of the Joint Chiefs, described his strong support for the nuclear reductions package that Bush announced in late September and criticized the opposition from the "Reagan-era hard-liners" on the civilian side of the Pentagon. But he failed to disclose his thinking on the prospect of the dissolution of the Soviet Union. See Colin Powell, *My American Journey* (New York: Random House, 1995), pp. 540–41.

73. "US Approach to Changes in the Soviet Union," opening statement at a news conference, Washington, D.C., September 4, 1991, U.S. Department of State *Dispatch*, September 9, 1991, p. 667.

74. See Chapter 7. See also Bush's address to the nation, Washington, D.C., September 27, 1991, U.S. Department of State *Dispatch*, Vol. 2, No. 39, September 30, 1991, pp. 715–18.

75. For background to the Moscow CSCE conference, see Chapter 7. On the margins of the conference, Baker met with the Russian leadership and then traveled to Kazakhstan and the three Baltic states.

76. Baker, *Politics of Diplomacy*, pp. 659–65 and 668–71.

77. *Ibid.*, pp. 564–83.

78. President Bush, "US Welcomes New Commonwealth of Independent States," Address to the nation, Washington, D.C., December 25, 1991, U.S. Department of State *Dispatch*, December 30, 1991, pp. 911–12.

79. Baker, *Politics of Diplomacy*, pp. 614–33.

80. *Ibid.*, pp. 665–68. The establishment of diplomatic relations actually came on April 23, just before Baker's visit.

81. "America and the Collapse of the Soviet Empire: What Has to Be Done," Address

by Secretary of State James A. Baker, III, at Princeton University, December 12, 1991, U.S. Department of State, Office of the Assistant Secretary/Spokesman.

82. "Remarks by the President in Address to International Conference on Humanitarian Assistance to the Former USSR," U.S. Department of State, Washington, D.C., January 22, 1992, Office of the Press Secretary, The White House.

83. "Multilateral Financial Assistance Package for Russia," Office of the Press Secretary, The White House, April 1, 1992. It was inadvertent but perhaps appropriate that the document was released on the American "April Fool's Day."

84. "Declaration on U.S.-Ukrainian Relations and the Building of a Democratic Partnership, by President Bush and President Kravchuk," May 6, 1992, Office of the Press Secretary, The White House, May 6, 1992; and "Declaration by President Bush and President Nazarbayev on Relations between the United States and Kazakhstan," Office of the Press Secretary, The White House, May 19, 1992.

85. Press releases and fact sheets issued by the Office of the Press Secretary, The White House, June 17, 1992.

86. "Camp David Declaration on New Relations, by President Bush and President Yeltsin," Camp David, Maryland, Office of the Press Secretary, The White House, February 1, 1992.

87. This personal relationship also redounded to our benefit. See, e.g., Bush's vivid account, in his memoirs, of the very close relationship with Gorbachev that was cemented in their June 1990 meeting at Camp David. (Forthcoming from Alfred A. Knopf, Inc.; draft manuscript shared with the author in July 1996.)

88. Quoted in Don Oberdorfer, *The Turn: From the Cold War to a New Era* (New York, Simon and Schuster, 1991), p. 404.

Conclusion

1. Harold Nicolson, *Peacemaking 1919* (London: Constable and Peter Smith, 1943), pp. ix–x.

2. David Reynolds, "Thawing History: Europe in the 1990s and Pre–Cold War Patterns," in Colin Crouch and David Marquand, eds., *Towards Greater Europe?* (Oxford and Cambridge, Ma.: Blackwell Publishers, 1992), pp. 16–17.

3. Robert Hutchings, "The 'Eastern Question' Revisited," *Problems of Post-Communism* (Fall 1994), pp. 45–49.

4. "Waiting for the Barbarians," in *C. P. Cavafy: Collected Poems*, ed. George Savidis, trans. Edmund Keeley and Philip Sharrard (Princeton: Princeton University Press, 1975; rev. ed. 1992), p. 18.

5. John Lewis Gaddis, *The United States and the End of the Cold War* (New York and Oxford: Oxford University Press, 1992), p. vii.

6. William L. Neumann, *After Victory: Churchill, Roosevelt, Stalin and the Making of the Peace* (New York: Harper and Row, 1967), pp. 33–38.

7. *Ibid.*, pp. 38–44; and Lynn Etheridge Davis, *The Cold War Begins: Soviet-American Conflict over Eastern Europe* (Princeton, N.J.: Princeton University Press, 1974), pp. 70–74. The organization and charter of the advisory committee are described in Harley Notter, *Postwar Foreign Policy Preparation, 1939–45* (Washington, D.C.: U.S. Government Printing Office, 1949).

8. See, e.g., Richard N. Gardner, "The Comeback of Liberal Internationalism," *The Washington Quarterly*, Summer 1990, pp. 23–39; Richard H. Ullman, "Enlarging the Zone of Peace," *Foreign Policy* No. 80 (Fall 1990), pp. 102–20; and Francis Fukuyama's often misrepresented "The End of History," *The National Interest*, Summer 1989, pp. 3–18.

9. In the European context, see, e.g., Stephen Van Evera, "Primed for Peace: Europe After the Cold War," *International Security*, Vol. 15, No. 3 (Winter 1990/91), pp. 7–57; and W. R. Smyser, "Vienna, Versailles, and Now Paris: Third Time Lucky?" *The Washington Quarterly*, Summer 1991, pp. 61–70.

10. Mearsheimer, "Back to the Future"; Charles Krauthammer, "The Unipolar Moment," *Foreign Affairs*, Vol. 70, No. 1 (Winter 1990/91), pp. 23–33; and John Lukacs, *The End of the Twentieth Century and the End of the Modern Age* (New York: Ticknor and Fields, 1993). See also Stanley Kober, "Revolutions Gone Bad," *Foreign Policy* No. 91 (Summer 1993), pp. 102–20, which, as he acknowledges, contrasts sharply with his earlier "Idealpolitik," *Foreign Policy* No. 79 (Summer 1990).

11. In Moscow in May 1992, Secretary Eagleburger delivered a speech—meant to show empathy, presumably—whose message was basically that: "We both sacrificed dearly and suffered greatly. . . . [We] squandered [our] energies and wasted precious resources in the colossal folly which was the Cold War." ("A Democratic Partnership for the Post-Cold War Era," address before the Trade and Economic Council's annual meeting, the Kremlin, Moscow, Russia, May 27, 1992, U.S. Department of State *Dispatch*, Vol. 3, No. 23, June 8, 1992, p. 441.) The speechwriters had distributed the draft too late for those of us on the delegation to suggest a different tone than that of "colossal folly," but the speech, mercifully, was ignored by the traveling press.

12. President Bush, State of the Union Address, January 28, 1992, excerpted in U.S. Department of State *Dispatch*, February 3, 1992, p. 73.

13. Council on Foreign Relations, Conference on "US National Interests After the Cold War," Wye Center, Queenstown, Maryland, December 14–16, 1995, summarized in a Council Memorandum on "Vital US Interests," dated January 8, 1996.

14. Robert L. Hutchings, "Rediscovering 'The National Interest' in American Foreign Policy," Occasional Paper, Woodrow Wilson International Center for Scholars, Washington, D.C., March 1996.

15. Kissinger puts it well in Henry Kissinger, *Diplomacy* (New York: Simon & Schuster, 1994), pp. 19–25.

16. "The North Atlantic Treaty," in *NATO Handbook* (Brussels: NATO Office of Information and Press, 1992), pp. 143–46.

17. See Chapter 1.

18. Michael Mandelbaum, "Our Outdated Russia Policy," *Time*, February 5, 1996, p. 39.

19. Gaddis, *United States and the End of the Cold War*, p. 211.

Bibliography

Books

Allison, Graham, and Gregory F. Treverton, eds. *Rethinking America's Security: Beyond Cold War to New World Order.* New York: W. W. Norton and Co., Inc., 1992.

Asmus, Ronald D., J. F. Brown, and Keith Crane. *Soviet Foreign Policy and the Revolutions of 1989 in Eastern Europe.* Durham, N.C.: Duke University Press, 1991.

Baker, James A., III, with Thomas M. DeFrank. *The Politics of Diplomacy: Revolution, War and Peace, 1989–92.* New York: G. P. Putnam's Sons, 1995.

Baranczak, Stanisław. *Breathing Underwater and Other East European Essays.* Cambridge, Ma.: Harvard University Press, 1990.

Batt, Judy. *East Central Europe: From Reform to Transformation.* New York: Council on Foreign Relations Press, 1991.

Behr, Edward. *Kiss the Hand You Cannot Bite: The Rise and Fall of the Ceauşescus.* New York: Villard Books, 1991.

Beres, Witold, and Jerzy Skoczyslas. *General Kiszczaks Mowi . . . Prawie Wszystko* [General Kiszczak tells us . . . almost everything]. Warsaw: Polska Oficya Wydawnicza "BGW," 1991.

Bertram, Christoph. *Europe in the Balance: Securing the Peace Won in the Cold War.* Washington, D.C.: Carnegie Endowment for International Peace, 1995.

Beschloss, Michael R., and Strobe Talbott. *At the Highest Levels: The Inside Story of the End of the Cold War.* Boston: Little, Brown and Company, 1993.

Boldin, Valery. *Ten Years That Shook the World: The Gorbachev Era as Witnessed by his Chief of Staff.* New York: Basic Books, 1994.

Brandon, Henry, ed. *In Search of a New World Order: The Future of U.S.-European Relations.* Washington, D.C.: The Brookings Institution, 1992.

Brown, J. F. *Surge to Freedom: The End of Communist Rule in Eastern Europe.* Durham, N.C.: Duke University Press, 1991.

———. *Hopes and Shadows: Eastern Europe after Communism.* Durham, N.C.: Duke University Press, 1994.

Brown, J. F., Robert D. Hormats, and William H. Luers. *Western Approaches to Eastern Europe.* New York: Council on Foreign Relations Press, 1992.

Brzezinski, Zbigniew K. *The Grand Failure: The Birth and Death of Communism in the Twentieth Century.* New York: Collier Books, 1990.

Bush, George, and Victor Gold. *Looking Forward.* New York: Doubleday and Co., 1987.

Carrere d'Encausse, Helene. *The End of the Soviet Empire: The Triumph of the Nations.* New York: Basic Books, 1993.

Chase, James. *The Consequences of Peace: The New Internationalism and American Foreign Policy.* New York: Oxford University Press, 1992.

Chernyaev, A. S. *Shest' let s Gorbachevym* [Six years with Gorbachev]. Moscow: Progress Publishers, 1993.

Chirot, Daniel. *The Crisis of Leninism and the Decline of the Left: The Revolutions of 1989.* Seattle: University of Washington Press, 1991.

Codrescu, Andrei. *The Hole in the Flag.* New York: William Morrow and Co., 1991.

Corbo, Vittorio, Fabrizio Coricelli, and Jan Bossak. *Reforming Central and Eastern European Economies: Initial Results and Challenges.* Washington, D.C.: World Bank, 1991.

Crawford, James. *The Creation of States in International Law.* New York: Oxford University Press, 1979.

Crouch, Colin, and David Marquand, eds. *Towards Greater Europe? A Continent without an Iron Curtain.* Cambridge, Ma.: Blackwell Publishers, 1992.

Dahrendorf, Ralf. *Reflections on the Revolution in Europe.* New York: Random House, 1990.

Dawisha, Karen. *Eastern Europe, Gorbachev, and Reform.* Cambridge: Cambridge University Press, 1988.

Echikson, William. *Lighting the Night: Revolution in Eastern Europe.* New York: William Morrow and Co., 1990.

Elbe, Frank, and Richard Kiessler. *Ein Runder Tisch mit Scharfen Ecken* [A round table with sharp corners]. Baden-Baden: Nomos Verlags Gesellschaft, 1993.

Fischer, Stanley, and Alan Gelb. *Issues in Socialist Economy Reforms.* Washington, D.C.: The World Bank, Country Economics Department, 1990.

Frankland, Mark. *The Patriot's Revolution: How Eastern Europe Toppled Communism and Won its Freedom.* Chicago: I. R. Dee Publishers, 1992.

Freedman, Lawrence, ed. *Europe Transformed: Documents on the End of the Cold War.* New York: St. Martin's Press, 1990.

Gaddis, John L. *The Long Peace: Inquiries into the History of the Cold War.* New York: Oxford University Press, 1987.

———. *The United States and the End of the Cold War.* New York: Oxford University Press, 1992.

Garton Ash, Timothy. *The Uses of Adversity; Essays on the Fate of Central Europe.* New York: Random House, 1989.

———. *The Magic Lantern: The Revolutions of '89 Witnessed in Warsaw, Budapest, Berlin, and Prague.* New York: Random House, 1990.

———. *In Europe's Name: Germany and the Divided Continent.* New York: Random House, 1993.

Gates, Robert M. *From the Shadows: The Ultimate Insider's Story of Five Presidents and How They Won the Cold War.* New York: Simon and Schuster, 1996.

Gedmin, Jeffrey. *The Hidden Hand; Gorbachev and the Collapse of East Germany.* Washington, D.C.: AEI Press, 1992.

Gelb, Alan H., and Cheryl W. Gray. *The Transformation of Economies in Central and Eastern Europe: Issues, Progress and Prospects.* Washington, D.C.: The World Bank, 1991.

Glenny, Misha. *The Rebirth of History: Eastern Europe in the Age of Democracy.* London: Penguin Books, 1990.

———. *The Fall of Yugoslavia: The Third Balkan War.* New York: Penguin Books, 1992.

Golden, Nancy L., and Sherrill Brown Wells, eds. *American Foreign Policy: Current Documents*. Washington, D.C.: Department of State, 1990.

Goldfarb, Jeffrey C. *After the Fall: The Pursuit of Democracy in Central Europe*. New York: Basic Books, 1992.

Gomułka, Stanisław, and Anthony Polonsky. *Polish Paradoxes*. New York: Routledge, 1991.

Gorbachev, Mikhail. *Perestroika: New Thinking for Our Country and the World*. New York: Harper and Row Publishers, 1987.

———. *The August Coup: The Truth and the Lessons*. New York: HarperCollins Publishers, Inc., 1991.

Gordon, Lincoln, et al. *Eroding Empire: Western Relations with Eastern Europe*. Washington, D.C.: The Brookings Institution, 1987.

Griffith, William E., ed. *Central and Eastern Europe: The Opening Curtain?* Boulder, Co.: Westview Press, 1989.

Gwertzman, Bernard, and Michael T. Kaufman, eds. *The Collapse of Communism*. New York: Times Books, 1990.

Haftendorn, Helga, and Christian Tuschhoff. *America and Europe in an Era of Change*. Boulder, Co.: Westview Press, 1993.

Hankiss, Elemer. *East European Alternatives*. New York: Oxford University Press, 1990.

Havel, Václav. *The Power of the Powerless: Citizens Against the State in Central-Eastern Europe*. New York: M. E. Sharpe, Inc., 1985.

———. *Disturbing the Peace: A Conversation with Karel Hvizdala*. First American ed. New York: Alfred A. Knopf, 1990.

———. *Summer Meditations*. New York: Alfred A. Knopf, 1992.

Heisenberg, Wolfgang. *German Unification in European Perspective*. Washington, D.C.: Brassey's, Inc., 1991.

Heller, Agnes, and Ferenc Feher. *From Yalta to Glasnost: The Dismantling of Stalin's Empire*. Cambridge, Ma.: Blackwell Publishers, 1991.

Hewett, Ed A., and Victor H. Winston, eds. *Milestones in Glasnost and Perestroyka: Politics and People*. Washington, D.C.: The Brookings Institution, 1991.

Hill, Ronald, and Jan Zielonka. *Restructuring Eastern Europe: Towards a New European Order*. Brookfield, Vt.: Edward Elgar Publishers, 1990.

Hobsbawm, E. J. *Nations and Nationalism since 1780: Programme, Myth, Reality*. New York: Cambridge University Press, 1992.

Huntington, Samuel. *The Third Wave: Democratization in the Late Twentieth Century.* Norman, Ok.: University of Oklahoma Press, 1991.

Hutchings, Robert L. *Soviet–East European Relations: Consolidation and Conflict.* Madison: University of Wisconsin Press, 1983; rev. paperback ed., 1987.

James, Harold, and Marla Stone. *When the Wall Came Down: Reactions to German Unification.* New York: Routledge, 1992.

Jarausch, Konrad H. *The Rush to German Unity.* New York: Oxford University Press, 1994.

Jarausch, Konrad H., and Volker Gransow. *Uniting Germany: Documents and Debates, 1993–1994.* Translated by Allison Brown and Belinda Cooper. Providence, R.I.: Berg Publishers, 1994.

Kaiser, Robert. *Why Gorbachev Happened: His Triumphs and His Failures.* New York: Simon and Schuster, 1991.

Kennedy, Paul. *The Rise and Fall of the Great Powers: Economic Change and Military Conflict from 1500 to 2000.* New York: Random House, 1987.

Keohane, Robert O., Joseph S. Nye, Jr., and Stanley Hoffman, eds. *After the Cold War: International Institutions and State Strategies in Europe, 1989–91.* Cambridge, Ma.: Harvard University Press, 1993.

Kirk, Roger, and Mircea Raceanu. *Romania versus the United States: Diplomacy of the Absurd, 1985–1989.* New York: St. Martin's Press, 1994.

Kornai, János. *The Road to a Free Economy.* New York: W. W. Norton and Co., 1990.

Kovrig, Bennett. *Of Walls and Bridges: The United States and Eastern Europe.* New York: New York University Press, 1991.

Kraljic, Matthew A., ed. *The Breakup of Communism: The Soviet Union and Eastern Europe.* New York: H. W. Wilson, 1993.

Krause, Axel. *Inside the New Europe.* New York: HarperCollins, 1991.

Kwizinskij, Julij A. *Vor dem Sturm: Erinnerungen eines Diplomaten* [Before the storm: A diplomat's memoirs]. Translated by Hilde and Helmut Ettinger. Berlin: Siedler Verlag, 1993.

Lederer, Ivo. *Western Approaches to Eastern Europe.* New York: Council on Foreign Relations Press, 1992.

Legters, Lyman H., ed. *Eastern Europe: Transformation and Revolution, 1945–1991.* Lexington, Ma.: D. C. Heath and Company, 1992.

Lesourne, Jacques, and Bernard Lecomte. *After Communism: From the*

Atlantic to the Urals. Chur, Switzerland: Harwood Academic Publishers, 1991.

Levine, Robert A. *Toward a Stable Transition in Europe: A Conservative/Activist Strategy for the United States*. Santa Monica, Ca.: The RAND Corporation, 1990.

Ligachev, E. K. *Inside Gorbachev's Kremlin: The Memoirs of Yegor Ligachev*. New York: Pantheon Books, 1993.

Lukacs, John. *The End of the Twentieth Century and the End of the Modern Age*. New York: Ticknor and Fields Books, 1993.

Lundestad, Geir. *The American "Empire" and Other Studies of US Foreign Policy in a Comparative Perspective*. New York: Oxford University Press, 1990.

Lynn-Jones, Sean M., ed. *The Cold War and After: Prospects for Peace*. Cambridge, Ma.: The MIT Press, 1991.

Marer, Paul, and Salvatore Zecchini. *The Transition to a Market Economy*. Paris: Organization for Economic Cooperation and Development, 1991.

Mason, David S. *Revolution in East-Central Europe: The Rise and Fall of Communism and the Cold War*. Boulder, Co.: Westview Press, 1992.

Mastny, Vojtech. *The Helsinki Process and the Reintegration of Europe, 1986–1991: Analysis and Documentation*. New York: New York University Press, 1992.

Matlock, Jack F., Jr. *Autopsy on an Empire: The American Ambassador's Account of the Collapse of the Soviet Union*. Cambridge, Ma.: Harvard University Press, 1995.

Menges, Constantine C. *The Future of Germany and the Atlantic Alliance*. Washington, D.C.: AEI Press, 1991.

Merkl, Peter H. *German Unification in the European Context*. University Park, Pa.: Pennsylvania State University Press, 1993.

Moynihan, Daniel P. *On the Law of Nations*. Cambridge, Ma.: Harvard University Press, 1990.

———. *Pandaemonium*. Oxford: Oxford University Press, 1993.

Müchler, Günter and Klaus Hofmann. *Helmut Kohl, Chancellor of German Unity: A Biography*. Bonn: Press and Information Office of the Federal Government, 1992.

Murrell, Peter. *The Nature of Socialist Economies: Lessons from Eastern European Foreign Trade*. Princeton, N.J.: Princeton University Press, 1990.

Nye, Joseph S., Jr. *Bound to Lead: The Changing Nature of American Power.* New York: Basic Books, 1990.

Oberdorfer, Don. *The Turn: From the Cold War to a New Era.* New York: Simon and Schuster, 1991.

O'Donnell, Guillermo, Phillippe C. Schmitter, and Laurence Whitehead, eds. *Transitions from Authoritarian Rule: Tentative Conclusions about Uncertain Democracies.* Baltimore: John Hopkins University Press, 1986.

Organization for Economic Cooperation and Development. *Transition to a Market Economy in Central and Eastern Europe.* Paris: OECD, 1991.

———. *Reforming the Economies of Central and Eastern Europe.* Paris: OECD, 1992.

Pinder, John. *The European Community and Eastern Europe.* London: The Royal Institute of International Affairs, 1991.

Pond, Elizabeth. *Beyond the Wall: Germany's Road to Unification.* Washington, D.C.: The Brookings Institution, 1993.

Powell, Colin. *My American Journey.* New York: Random House, 1995.

Przeworski, Adam. *Democracy and the Market: Political and Economic Reforms in Eastern Europe and Latin America.* New York: Cambridge University Press, 1991.

Rady, Martyn C. *Romania in Turmoil: A Contemporary History.* New York: IB Tauris, 1992.

Rakowski, Mieczysław F. *Jak to sie stało?* [How did it happen?] Warsaw: Polska Oficyna Wydawnicza "BGW," 1991.

Ratesh, Nestor. *Romania: The Entangled Revolution.* Washington, D.C.: Center for Strategic and International Studies, 1991.

Roberts, Brad, ed. *U.S. Foreign Policy After the Cold War.* Cambridge, Ma.: MIT Press, 1992.

———. *U.S. Security in an Uncertain Era.* Cambridge, Ma.: MIT Press, 1993.

Rostow, Eugene. *Toward Managed Peace: The National Security Interests of the United States, 1759 to the Present.* New Haven: Yale University Press, 1993.

Rupnik, Jacques. *The Other Europe: The Rise and Fall of Communism in East Central Europe.* New York: Schocken Books, 1989.

Schäuble, Wolfgang. *Der Vertrag: Wie Ich Über die Deutsche Einheit*

Verhandelte [The Treaty: How I Negotiated German Unity].
Stuttgart: Deutsche Verlag-Anstalt, 1991.

Schöpflin, George, and Nancy Wood, eds. *In Search of Central Europe.*
Cambridge: Cambridge University Press, 1989.

Shehadi, Kamal S. *Ethnic Self-Determination and the Break-up of
States.* Adelphi Paper 283. London: International Institute of Strategic Studies, 1993.

Shevardnadze, Eduard A. *The Future Belongs to Freedom.* New York:
Free Press, 1991.

Simons, Thomas F., Jr. *The End of the Cold War?* New York: St. Martin's Press, 1990.

———. *Eastern Europe in the Postwar World.* New York: St. Martin's
Press, 1991.

Sodaro, Michael J. *Moscow, Germany, and the West from Khrushchev
to Gorbachev.* Ithaca, N.Y.: Cornell University Press, 1990.

Staar, Richard F. *U.S.–East European Relations in the 1990s.* New
York: Crane Russak, 1989.

Staniszkis, Jadwiga. *The Dynamics of the Breakthrough in Eastern Europe: The Polish Experience.* Berkeley: University of California Press,
1991.

Stokes, Gale. *From Stalinism to Pluralism: A Documentary History of
Eastern Europe since 1945.* New York: Oxford University Press, 1991.

———. *The Walls Came Tumbling Down: The Collapse of Communism in Eastern Europe.* New York: Oxford University Press, 1993.

Szabo, Stephen F. *The Diplomacy of German Unification.* New York:
St. Martin's Press, 1992.

Teltschik, Horst. *329 Tage: Innenansichten der Einigung* [329 Days: An
Insider's View of Unification]. Berlin: Siedler Verlag, 1991.

Thatcher, Margaret. *The Downing Street Years.* New York: HarperCollins Publishers, 1993.

Tismaneanu, Vladimir. *In Search of Civil Society: Independent Peace
Movements in the Soviet Bloc.* New York: Routledge, 1990.

Treverton, Gregory F. *America, Germany and the Future of Europe.*
Princeton, N.J.: Princeton University Press, 1992.

Treverton, Gregory F., ed. *The Shape of the New Europe.* New York:
Council on Foreign Relations Press, 1991.

van Brabant, Josef M. *The New Eastern Europe and the World Economy.* Boulder, Co.: Westview Press, 1993.

Verdery, Catherine. *National Ideology under Socialism: Identity and Cultural Politics in Ceauşescu's Romania.* Berkeley: University of California Press, 1991.

Volten, Peter M. E. *Bound to Change: Consolidating Democracy in East Central Europe.* New York: Institute for East-West Studies, 1992.

von Weizsäcker, Richard. "Speeches for Our Time, May 8, 1985–December 13, 1991." *German Issues 1992.*

Wałęsa, Lech. *The Struggle and the Triumph: An Autobiography.* New York: Arcade Publishers, 1992.

Wheaton, Bernard, and Zdeněk Kavan. *The Velvet Revolution: Czechoslovakia, 1988–1991.* Boulder, Co.: Westview Press, 1992.

Whelan, Joseph G. *Soviet Diplomacy and Negotiating Behavior, 1988–1990: Gorbachev-Reagan-Bush Meetings at the Summit,* vol. 3. Washington, D.C.: Committee on Foreign Affairs, U.S. Congress, 1991.

Whipple, Tim D., ed. *After the Velvet Revolution: Václav Havel and the New Leaders of Czechoslovakia Speak Out.* New York: Freedom House, 1991.

Wolchik, Sharon. *Czechoslovakia in Transition: Politics, Economics, and Society.* New York: Pinter Publishers, 1991.

Yakovlev, A. N. *The Fate of Marxism in Russia.* New Haven: Yale University Press, 1993.

Zelikow, Philip, and Condoleezza Rice. *Germany Unified and Europe Transformed: A Study in Statecraft.* Cambridge, Ma.: Harvard University Press, 1995.

Articles

Adelman, Irma. "Should There be a Marshall Plan for Eastern Europe?" *Review of Black Political Economy* 19 (Fall 1990): 17–42.

Adomeit, Hannes. "Gorbachev and German Unification: Revision of Thinking, Realignment of Power." *Problems of Communism* 39 (July–August 1990): 1–23.

Allison, Graham. "Testing Gorbachev." *Foreign Affairs* 67, no. 4 (Fall 1988): 19–32.

Allison, Graham, and Robert Blackwill. "America's Stake in the Soviet Future." *Foreign Affairs* 70, no. 3 (Summer 1991): 77–97.

Ardito-Barletta, Nicolas. "Democracy and Development." *The Washington Quarterly* 13, no. 3 (Summer 1990): 165–75.

Asmus, Ronald. "Evolution of Soviet–East European Relations under Mikhail Gorbachev." *Radio Free Europe Research,* RAD Background Report 153 (August 22, 1989): 1–25.

Banac, Ivo. "Yugoslavia: The Fearful Asymmetry of War." *Daedalus* 121, no. 2 (Spring 1992): 150.

Bialer, Seweryn. "Interview: Aleksandr Yakovlev—Redefining Socialism at Home and Abroad." *Journal of International Affairs* 42, no. 2 (Winter 1988/89): 333–55.

Bielecki, Jan Krzysztof. "Problems of the Polish Transformation." *Communist Economies and Economic Transformation* 4, no. 3 (1990).

Breslow, Aimee. "Monitoring Eastern Europe's Transition." *The Washington Quarterly* 14, no. 4 (Autumn 1991): 205–18.

Brumberg, Abraham. "Poland: The Demise of Communism." *Foreign Affairs* 69, no. 1 (America and the World: 1989/90): 70–88.

Brus, Włodzimierz. "From Revisionism to Pragmatism: Sketches Towards a Self-Portrait of a 'Reform Economist.'" *Acta Oeconomica* 40, no. 3 (1989): 204–10.

Bruszt, László. "Hungary's Negotiated Revolution." *Social Research* 57, no. 2 (Summer 1990): 365–87.

Brzezinski, Zbigniew. "Post-Communist Nationalism." *Foreign Affairs* 68, no. 5 (Winter 1989/90): 1–25.

———. "Selective Global Commitment." *Foreign Affairs* 70, no. 4 (Fall 1991): 1–20.

Bunce, Valerie. "Rising above the Past." *World Policy Journal* 7, no. 3 (Summer 1990): 395–430.

Bundy, McGeorge. "Chronology 1989: From Cold War Toward Trusting Peace." *Foreign Affairs* 69, no. 1 (America and the World: 1989/90): 197–212.

Burley, Anne-Marie. "The Once and Future German Question." *Foreign Affairs* 68, no. 5 (Winter 1989/90): 65–83.

Butler, William E. "International Law, Foreign Policy and the Gorbachev Style." *Journal of International Affairs* 42, no. 2 (1988/89): 363–75.

Chernoff, Fred. "Ending the Cold War: The Soviet Retreat and the U.S. Military Buildup." *International Affairs* 67 (January 1991): 111–26.

Connor, W. R. "Why Were We Surprised?" *The American Scholar* 60, no. 2 (Spring 1991): 175.

Dahrendorf, Ralf. "Roads to Freedom: Democratization and its Problems in East and Central Europe." *Institute for East-West Security Studies Occasional Paper* no. 16 (1990).

Dashichev, Vyacheslav. "The Soviet Perspective." *Problems of Communism* 37 (May–August 1988): 60–7.

de Montbrial, Thierry. "Die Aussenpolitik Frankreichs." *Europa Archiv* 44 (May 25, 1989): 283–90.

Deak, Istvan. "Uncovering Eastern Europe's Dark History." *Orbis* 34 (Winter 1990): 51–65.

Delors, Jacques. "The Meaning of 1992." *Harvard International Review* 11 (Summer 1989): 23–7.

———. "The Two Europes, East and West." *International Affairs* (London) 65 (Autumn 1989): 653–58.

———. "Europe's Ambitions." *Foreign Policy* (Fall 1990): 14–27.

Di Palma, Giuseppe. "Why Democracy Can Work in Eastern Europe." *Journal of Democracy* 2 (Winter 1991): 21–31.

Diamond, Larry. "Beyond Authoritarianism and Totalitarianism: Strategies for Democratization." *The Washington Quarterly* 12 (Winter 1989): 141–63.

Frank, Andre G. "Europe from Helsinki to Finlandization." *Review of International Affairs* 41 (February 20, 1990): 16–18.

Fukuyama, Francis. "The End of History." *The National Interest* no. 16 (Summer 1989): 3–18.

———. "The Beginning of Foreign Policy: America Confronts the Post–Cold War World." *The New Republic* (August 17, 1992): 24–25.

Gardner, Richard. "The Comeback of Liberal Internationalism." *The Washington Quarterly* (Summer 1990): 23–39.

Garton Ash, Timothy. "The Empire in Decay." *New York Review of Books* (September 29, 1988): 52–60.

———. "The German Revolution." *New York Review of Books* (December 21, 1989): 14–19.

Gati, Charles. "East-Central Europe: The Morning After." *Foreign Affairs* (Winter 1990–91): 129–45.

———. "From Sarajevo to Sarajevo." *Foreign Affairs* 71, no. 4 (Fall 1992): 64–78.

Genscher, Hans-Dietrich. "Let's Put Mr. Gorbachev's 'New Policy' to the Test." Ministry of Foreign Affairs, Federal Republic of Germany. *Reihe: Berichte und Dokumentationen* (February 1, 1987).

Geremek, Bronisław. "Postcommunism and Democracy in Poland." *The Washington Quarterly* 13, no. 3 (Summer 1990): 125–31.

Giscard d'Estaing, Valéry, Yasuhiro Nakasone, and Henry A. Kissinger. "East-West Relations." *Foreign Affairs* 68, no. 3 (Summer 1989): 1–21.

Gligorov, Vladimir. "Balkanization: A Theory of Constitution Failure." *East European Politics and Societies* 6, no. 3 (Fall 1992): 283–302.

Gompert, David. "How to Defeat Serbia." *Foreign Affairs* 73, no. 4 (July/August 1994): 30–47.

Goodby, James. "Commonwealth and Concert: Organizing Principles of Post-Containment Order in Europe." *The Washington Quarterly* (Summer 1991): 71–90.

Hacker, Jens. "The Berlin Policy of the USSR under Gorbachev." *Aussenpolitik* 3 (1989): 232–50.

Hartley, Anthony. "After the Thatcher Decade." *Foreign Affairs* 68, no. 5 (Winter 1989/90): 102–18.

Hassner, Pierre. "Europe Beyond Partition and Unity: Disintegration or Reconstruction?" *International Affairs* 66 (July 1990): 461–75.

Hendrickson, David C. "The Renovation of American Foreign Policy." *Foreign Affairs* 71, no. 2 (Spring 1992): 48–63.

Hoagland, Jim. "Europe's Destiny." *Foreign Affairs* 69, no. 1 (America and the World: 1989/90): 35–50.

Hoffman, Stanley. "The European Community and 1992." *Foreign Affairs* 68, no. 4 (Fall 1989): 27–47.

———. "A New World and Its Troubles." *Foreign Affairs* 69, no. 4 (Fall 1990): 115–22.

Horelick, Arnold P. "U.S.-Soviet Relations: The Threshold of a New Era." *Foreign Affairs* 69, no. 1 (America and the World: 1989/90): 51–69.

Hormats, Robert D. "Redefining Europe and the Atlantic Link." *Foreign Affairs* 68, no. 4 (Fall 1989): 71–91.

Howard, Michael. "The Springtime of Nations." *Foreign Affairs* 69, no. 1 (America and the World: 1989/90): 17–32.

Hutchings, Robert L. "The 'Eastern Question' Revisited." *Problems of Post-Communism* (Fall 1994): 45–9.

———. "Five Years After: Reflections on the Post-Communist Transitions and Western Assistance Strategies." In *East Central Europe in Transition,* 176–90. Joint Economic Committee, U.S. Congress. Washington, D.C.: Government Printing Office, 1994.

———. "Rediscovering the 'National Interest' in American Foreign Policy." Occasional Paper. Woodrow Wilson International Center for Scholars (March 1996).

Janos, Andrew C. "Social Science, Communism, and the Dynamics of Political Change." *World Politics* 44 (October 1991): 81–112.

Kaiser, Karl. "German Unification." *Foreign Affairs* 70, no. 1 (America and the World: 1990/91): 179–205.

Kirk, Roger. "The U.S. and Romania, Facing a Difficult Future: Policy Recommendations." The Atlantic Council of the United States *Policy Paper* (April 1991).

Klaus, Václav. "Transition—An Insider's View." *Problems of Communism* 41 (January–April 1992): 73.

Kligman, Gail. "Reclaiming the Public: A Reflection on Creating Civil Society in Romania." *East European Politics and Societies* 4, no. 3 (Fall 1990): 393–439.

Kober, Stanley. "Idealpolitik." *Foreign Policy* 79 (Summer 1990): 3–24.

Kohl, Helmut. "East-West Relations and Arms Control: Challenges for the Future." *Harvard International Review* (Summer 1989): 46–52.

Kovács, János M. "From Reformation to Transformation: Limits to Liberalism in Hungarian Economic Thought." *East European Politics and Societies* 5, no. 1 (Winter 1991): 41–72.

Kramer, Mark. "Beyond the Brezhnev Doctrine." *International Security* 14, no. 3 (Winter 1989/90): 25–67.

Kramer, Steven P. "The French Question." *The Washington Quarterly* 14, no. 4 (Autumn 1991): 83–96.

Krauthammer, Charles. "The Unipolar Moment." *Foreign Affairs* 70, no. 1 (Winter 1990/91): 23–33.

Kusin, Vladimir. "Mikhail Gorbachev's Evolving Attitude to Eastern Europe." *Radio Free Europe Research*, RAD Background Report 128 (July 20, 1989): 1–12.

Kux, Ernst. "Revolution in Eastern Europe—Revolution in the West?" *Problems of Communism* 40 (May–June 1991): 1–13.

Larrabee, Stephen F. "Long Memories and Short Fuses: Change and Instability in the Balkans." *International Security* 15, no. 3 (Winter 1990/91): 58–91.

Legvold, Robert. "The Revolution in Soviet Foreign Policy." *Foreign Affairs* 68, no. 1 (America and the World 1988/89): 82–98.

Levy, Jack S. "Preferences, Constraints, and Choices in July 1914." *International Security* 15, no. 3 (Winter 1990/91): 151–86.

Lewis, Flora. "Bringing in the East." *Foreign Affairs* 69, no. 4 (Fall 1990): 15–26.

Linz, Juan J. "Transitions to Democracy." *The Washington Quarterly* 13, no. 3 (Summer 1990): 143–64.

Lynch, Allen. "Changing Contours of Soviet–East European Relations." *Journal of International Affairs* 42, no. 2 (1988/89): 423–34.

Mandelbaum, Michael. "Ending the Cold War." *Foreign Affairs* 68, no. 2 (Spring 1989): 16–36.

McNeil, William H. "Winds of Change." *Foreign Affairs* 69, no. 4 (Fall 1990): 152–75.

Mearsheimer, John. "Back to the Future: Instability in Europe after the Cold War." *International Security* 15 (Summer 1990): 5–56.

Millar, James R. "The Conversion of the Communists: Gorbachev's Legacy." *Soviet Union/Union Sovietique* 16, nos. 2–3 (1989): 201–10.

Moens, Alexander. "American Diplomacy and German Unification." *Survival* 33, no. 6 (November–December 1990): 531–45.

Moïsi, Dominique. "Mitterrand's Foreign Policy: The Limits on Continuity." *Foreign Affairs* 60, no. 2 (Winter 1981/82): 347–57.

———. "French Foreign Policy: The Challenge of Adaptation." *Foreign Affairs* 67, no. 1 (Fall 1988): 151–64.

Newhouse, John. "The Diplomatic Round: Sweeping Change." *The New Yorker* (August 27, 1990): 78–89.

Nitze, Paul H. "America: Honest Broker." *Foreign Affairs* 69, no. 4 (Fall 1990): 1–14.

Nixon, Richard. "American Foreign Policy: The Bush Agenda." *Foreign Affairs* 68, no. 1 (America and the World 1988/89): 199–219.

Nye, Joseph S., Jr. "What New World Order?" *Foreign Affairs* 71, no. 2 (Spring 1992): 83–96.

Pond, Elizabeth. "A Wall Destroyed: The Dynamics of German Unification in the GDR." *International Security* 15, no. 2 (Fall 1990): 35–66.

———. "Germany in the New Europe." *Foreign Affairs* 71, no. 2 (Spring 1992): 114–30.

Powell, Colin. "The American Commitment to European Security." *Survival* (Summer 1992): 3–11.

Prybyla, Jan S. "The Road from Socialism: Why, Where, What, and How." *Problems of Communism* 40 (January–April 1991): 1–17.

Rosecrance, Richard. "A New Concert of Powers." *Foreign Affairs* 71, no. 2 (Spring 1992): 64–82.

Rubinstein, Alvin Z. "The USSR in Turmoil: Views from the Right, Center, and Left." *Orbis* (Spring 1991): 267–84.

———. "Soviet Client-States: From Empire to Commonwealth." *Orbis* (Winter 1991): 69–78.

Sachs, Jeffrey, and David Lipton. "Poland's Economic Reform." *Foreign Affairs* 69, no. 3 (Summer 1993): 47–66.

Schwartz, Herman. "Constitutional Developments in East Central Europe." *Journal of International Affairs* 45, no. 1 (1991/92): 71–89.

Shipler, David K. "Letter from Budapest." *The New Yorker* (November 20, 1989): 74–99.

Smith, Geoffrey. "Britain in the New Europe." *Foreign Affairs* 71, no. 4 (Fall 1992): 155–70.

Smyser, W. R. "Vienna, Versailles, and Now Paris: Third Time Lucky?" *The Washington Quarterly* 14, no. 3 (Summer 1991): 61–90.

Snyder, Jack. "Averting Anarchy in the New Europe." *International Security* 14 (Spring 1990): 5–41.

Sorensen, Theodore C. "America's First Post–Cold War President." *Foreign Affairs* 71, no. 4 (Fall 1992): 13–30.

Stark, David. "Path Dependence and Privatization Strategies in East Central Europe." *East European Politics and Societies* 6, no. 1 (Winter 1992): 17–54.

Stent, Angela. "The One Germany." *Foreign Policy* 81 (Winter 1990/91): 53–70.

Surovell, Jeffrey. "Ligachev and Soviet Politics." *Soviet Studies* 43, no. 2 (1991): 355–74.

Tarrow, Sidney. "Aiming at a Moving Target: Social Science and the Recent Rebellions in Eastern Europe." *Political Science* (March 1991): 12–20.

Teltschik, Horst. "Gorbachev's Reform Policy and the Outlook for East-West Relations." *Aussenpolitik* 3 (1989): 201–14.

———. "The Federal Republic and Poland: A Difficult Partnership in the Heart of Europe." *Aussenpolitik* (January 1990): 3–15.

Tiersky, Ronald. "France in the New Europe." *Foreign Affairs* 71, no. 2 (Spring 1992): 131–46.

Tismaneanu, Vladimir. "The Quasi-Revolution and Its Discontent." *East European Politics and Societies* 7, no. 2 (Summer 1993): 309–48.

Tismaneanu, Vladimir, and Matei Calinescu. "The 1989 Revolution and Romania's Future." *Problems of Communism* 40 (January–April 1990): 42–59.

Tökés, Rudolf L. "The Science of Politics in Hungary in the 1980s." *Südosteuropa* 37 (January 1988): 8–32.

Treadgold, Donald W. "Mikhail Sergeevich and the World of 1990." *Soviet Union/Union Sovietique* 16, nos. 2–3 (1989): 211–20.

Tucker, Robert W. "1989 and All That." *Foreign Affairs* 69, no. 4 (Fall 1990): 93–114.

Ullman, Richard H. "Enlarging the Zone of Peace." *Foreign Policy* 80 (Fall 1990): 102–20.

"U.S.-Soviet Relations: An Agenda for the Future," a report to the 41st president of the United States, Foreign Policy Institute, School of Advanced International Studies, the Johns Hopkins University, Washington, D.C., (December 1988).

Van Evera, Stephen. "Primed for Peace: Europe After the Cold War." *International Security* 15, no. 3 (Winter 1990/91): 7–57.

Vardary, Tibor. "Collective Minority Rights and Problems in Their Legal Protection: The Example of Yugoslavia." *East European Politics and Societies* 6, no. 3 (Fall 1992): 260–82.

Waever, Ole. "Three Competing Europes: German, French, Russian." *International Affairs* 66 (July 1990): 477–93.

Wandycz, Piotr S. "Poland's Place in Europe in the Concepts of Pilsudski and Dmowski." *East European Politics and Societies* 4, no. 3 (Fall 1990): 451–68.

Weller, Marc. "The International Response to the Dissolution of the Socialist Federal Republic of Yugoslavia." *American Journal of International Law* 86, no. 3 (July 1992): 569–607.

Wells, Samuel F., Jr. "Mitterrand's International Policies." *The Washington Quarterly* 11, no. 3 (Summer 1988): 59–75.

Weschler, Lawrence. "A Grand Experiment." *The New Yorker* (November 13, 1989): 65.

Winik, Jay. "The Quest for Bipartisanship: A New Beginning for a New World Order." *The Washington Quarterly* 14, no. 4 (Autumn 1991): 115–30.

Yankelovich, Daniel. "Foreign Policy after the Election." *Foreign Affairs* 71, no. 4 (Fall 1992): 1–12.

Zelikow, Philip. "The New Concert of Europe." *Survival* (Summer 1992): 12–30.

Zielonka, Jan. "East Central Europe: Democracy in Retreat?" *The Washington Quarterly* 14, no. 3 (Summer 1991): 107–20.

Zimmerman, Warren. "The Last Ambassador: Memoirs of the Collapse of Yugoslavia." *Foreign Affairs* 74, no. 2 (March/April 1995): 2–20.

Index